Industrial Locomotives of Buckinghamshire,

Bedfordshire & Northamptonshire

INDUSTRIAL

LOCOMOTIVES

of

BUCKINGHAMSHIRE,

BEDFORDSHIRE &

NORTHAMPTONSHIRE

Compiled by Robin Waywell

Series Editor R K Hateley

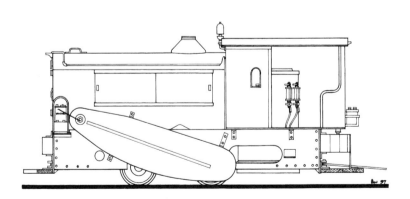

Sentinel 7243/1928 – one of the special Sentinel steam locomotives built for the London Brick
Co & Forders Ltd for use at its Pillinge Brickworks (later renamed Stewartby Brickworks) near
Bedford.   Drawing by Roger West

INDUSTRIAL RAILWAY SOCIETY

Published by the INDUSTRIAL RAILWAY SOCIETY

at 47 Waverley Gardens, LONDON, NW10 7EE

© **INDUSTRIAL RAILWAY SOCIETY 2001**

ISBN 1 901556 23 9 (hardbound)

ISBN 1 901556 24 7 (softbound)

British Library Cataloguing-in-Publication Data
A catalogue record for this book is available from the The British Library.

Handbook BN

Printed by AB Printers, 27 Nether End, Great Dalby, Leicestershire LE14 2EY

CONTENTS

Dedication
In loving memory of my dear parents
Cecil (1921 — 2001) and Phyllis (1923 – 1983).
Sadly missed.

Bucks, Beds & Northants Handbook – Page 6

INTRODUCTION

This book is a further volume in the series covering the industrial locomotives and railways of Great Britain and deals with the counties of Buckinghamshire, Bedfordshire and Northamptonshire. The first of these counties was last covered in a section of Pocket Book 'C', 'Industrial Locomotives of South Eastern England', published in 1958, while the remaining two were included in Pocket Book 'D' 'Industrial Locomotives of Eastern England', which was published in 1960. Neither of these Pocket Books has been available for many years. In this new volume the information has been greatly amplified, containing many more sites than were known about in the previous editions. It incorporates and describes not only the locomotives and their locations, but includes non-locomotive, contractors' and preservation sites within the three counties. Appropriate maps, and site diagrams, have also been included.

The three counties form a coherent geographical area although each has a distinctive character. None is greatly industrialised and most of the railway activity has been associated with extractive industry. Buckinghamshire was predominantly rural, at least until the extension of the London suburban development, in the area often known as Metroland, in the early 20th century. This has affected the part of the county south east of Aylesbury whilst the remainder of the county has retained its agricultural nature. Mineral extraction which employed rail transport has included gravel, often with associated narrow gauge lines, and chalk for cement.

Of the three counties, Bedfordshire is the most urbanised. Industry with associated railways has included gravel and chalk workings similar to those in Buckinghamshire. Additionally there have been very extensive clay workings to supply brickworks. These have been supported by industrial railway systems which used a wide variety of track gauges and motive power. Finally some of the larger towns, such as Luton and Dunstable, have supported factories large enough to need extensive railway sidings with privately owned locomotives.

Moving north to Northamptonshire the nature of the landscape changes. The extraction now changes to that of ironstone and this also resulted in the development of iron and steel works for its processing. The Corby area in its heyday provided work for a large fleet of standard gauge steam locomotives. We are fortunate that the late Eric Tonks, for many years President of the Industrial Railway Society, made a lifetime study of these quarries, railways and locomotives. His researches have been published and make fascinating reading, but the entries in this Handbook for 'ironstone' locations can be taken as a precis of his work on the subject.

Some relevant information for the 19th century can be quoted from the official goverment "Mineral Statistics".

Iron ore was far and away the most important mineral mined in the region. In 1883, Northamptonshire produced 1,290,087 tons of ore, this being 7.4% of the UK total. However, only 217,183 tons of pig iron were produced in the county, which accounted for just under half the ore mined. The remainder was sent elsewhere, notably to iron- and steelworks in South Wales, the West Midlands and Derbyshire, for smelting there. Although the iron ore output for Nothamptonshire in 1896 was marginally down on the 1883 figure, at 1,263,650 tons, this actually reprresented an increase in percentage of the UK output as a whole - almost 10% - due to significant decline in ore production elsewhere.

Other mineral deposits in the region were also exploited. One mineral almost unique to this area, and quarried mainly in Bedfordshire, was phosphate of lime, or coprolite. Some 18,000 tons were quarried in 1883, but by 1894 the output for the whole of the UK was down at 700 tons, and it was noted that competition from abroad was bringing about a "lingering death" for this particular extractive industry.

The building trades were responsible for stimulating the mining of chalk, sand and clay. In 1896 the region produced some 50,000 tons of sand, mostly from the Leighton Buzzard area, though Buckinghamshire's contribution at 8,700 tons was significant. Northamptonshire and Bedfordshire were also by this time producing large quantities of clay for brickmaking - 241,607 and 96,938 tons respectively. Finally, chalk and limestone were being quarried in ever-increasing amounts for agriculture and the relatively young cement industry: the Northamptonshire output of limestone in 1896 was 155,000 tons; that of chalk in Bedfordshire for the same year was 69,293 tons.

The information relating to each county is set out in four sections as follows:-

1. Industrial locations where privately owned locomotives were used.
2. Known details of locomotives used on civil engineering contracts, including contracts involving the construction of many sections of public railway.
3. Preservation and Pleasure Railway locations where the gauge exceeds 1ft 3in.
4. Known details of non-locomotive worked systems which were of sufficient length to be of interest.

Indexes are included for the ease of referring to locomotives and locations listed within the volume.

I have over the years received help from enthusiasts and correspondents too numerous to mention who have answered questions or brought items to my attention and gladly given freely of their time and information, for which I will always be grateful. Thanks are also due to the members of the Industrial Railway Society, whose observations over the years form the basis of the Society's records. The journals and newsletters of like-minded societies such as the Industrial Locomotive Society and the Narrow Gauge Railway Society have also formed a reliable source of research. In particular the advertisement extracts published by the ILS have given many leads to follow. Likewise the county record offices and reference libraries have proved their worth and I thank their attendants for their patience. I am indebted to a book called 'Clay That Burns' written by Richard Hillier for the London Brick Company Ltd for its invaluable help on the history of the Fletton brick industry. Another invaluable source of reference has been 'A survey of Bedfordshire Brickmaking', a history and gazetteer produced for Bedfordshire County Council by Alan Cox.

My especial thanks to: Vic Bradley, Michael Cook, Bob Darvill, Adrian Foster, Brian Gent, Gordon Green, Eric Hackett, Bruce Henderson; Dave Holroyde, John Hutchings, Ken Plant, Richard Sherwood, John Scholes, Geoffrey Starmer, the late Eric Tonks, D.H. Townsley, Clive Walters, A.J. Warrington, Russell Wear, Rodney Weaver and the late W.K. Williams for their assistance over many years, also to Christopher Perks for his considerable help in locating Ordnance Survey maps and to Maj. J.A. Robins of the Museum of Army Transport, Beverley, Humberside for his assitance in locating plans of MoD sites, and lastly to Roger Hateley for his encouragement in finally getting this volume into print.

Comments on and corrections to any information given in this book will be most welcome, as will any additional information that may have been omitted, this should be sent to :

Robin Waywell
August 2001.

29 Readshill,
CLOPHILL,
Bedfordshire MK45 4AG.

EXPLANATORY NOTES

GAUGE
The gauge of the railway is given at the head of the list. If the gauge is uncertain, then this is stated. Metric measurements are used where the equipment was designed to these units.

GRID REFERENCE
An indexed six-figure grid reference is given in the text, where known, to indicate the location of salient features of the site.

NUMBER, NAME
A number or name formerly carried is shown in brackets (   ), if it is an unofficial name or number then inverted commas are used "   "

TYPE
The Whyte system of wheel classification is used wherever possible, but when the driving wheels are not connected by outside rods but by chains or motors they are shown as 4w, 6w, 8w etc. For ex-BR diesel locomotives the usual development of the Continental system is used. The following abbreviations are employed:-

T	Side tank or similar. The tanks are invariably fastened to the frame.
CT	Crane Tank, a side tank locomotive equipped with load lifting apparatus.
CST	Crane saddle tank, a saddle tank locomotive equipped with load lifting apparatus.
PT	Pannier Tank, a special type of side tank where the tanks are not fastened to the frame.
ST	Saddle Tank, a round tank which covers the boiler top. This type includes the 'Box' and 'Ogee' versions popular amongst certain manufacturers during the nineteenth century.
IST	Inverted Saddle Tank, a design where the tank passed under the boiler.
WT	Well Tank, a tank located between the frames below the level of the boiler.
VB	Vertical boilered locomotive.
Tram	Tram locomotive with wheels and motion protected.
DM	Diesel locomotive; mechanical transmission.
DE	Diesel locomotive; electric transmission.
DH	Diesel locomotive; hydraulic transmission.
PM	Petrol or Paraffin locomotive; mechanical transmission.
PE	Petrol or Paraffin locomotive; electric transmission.
R	Railcar, a vehicle primarily designed to carry passengers.
BE	Battery powered electric locomotive.
RE	Third rail powered electric locomotive.
WE	Overhead wire powered electric locomotive.
F	Fireless steam locomotive.
+T	Steam tank locomotive with additional tender.

CYLINDER POSITION

IC	Inside cylinders
OC	Outside cylinders
3C/4C	Three or four cylinders
VC	Vertical cylinders
G	Geared transmission (used with IC, OC or VC)
HC	Horizontal cylinders (where not apparent)

FLAMEPROOF
Diesel or battery-electric locomotives that are flameproofed are shown with the suffix F to the type (e.g. 4wDMF).

STEAM OUTLINE
Diesel or petrol locomotives with a steam locomotive appearance added are shown as S/O.

MAKERS
Abbreviations used to denote makers are listed on a later page.

MAKERS NUMBER AND DATE
The first column shows the works number, the second shows the date which appeared on the plate, or the date the loco was built if none appears on the plate.

It should be noted that the ex-works date given in the locomotive index may be in a later year than that recorded as the building date.

Rebuilding details are denoted by the abbreviation 'reb', usually recording significant alterations to the locomotive.

SOURCE OF LOCOMOTIVE
'New' indicates that a locomotive was delivered from the makers to a location. A bracketed letter indicates that a locomotive was transferred to this location or subject to temporary transfer away. Full details, including the date of arrival, where known, appear in the footnotes below.

DISPOSAL OF LOCOMOTIVE
A locomotive transferred to another location is shown by a bracketed number and footnote, the date of departure being given in the footnote if it is known. In other cases the following abbreviations are used :-

OOU	Loco noted to be permanently out of use on the date shown.
Dere	Loco noted to be derelict and no longer capable of being used.
Dsm	Loco both OOU and incomplete on the date shown.
Scr	Loco broken up for scrap on the date shown.
s/s	Loco sold or scrapped; disposal unknown.
Wdn	Withdrawn from traffic.

Many sales of locomotives have been effected through dealers and contractors and details are given where known. If the dealers name is followed by a location, e.g. Abelson, Sheldon, it is understood that the loco went to Sheldon depot before resale. If no location is given, the loco either went direct to its new owner or else definite information on this point is lacking. If a direct transfer is known to have been effected by a dealer, the word 'per' is used.

GENERAL ABBREVIATIONS

c	circa; i.e. about the time of the date quoted
f or form	formerly
orig	originally
prev	previously
reb	rebuilt

FOOTNOTE ABBREVIATIONS

In addition to the abbreviations listed below, the abbreviations used to denote the various locomotive builders are also used in footnotes where appropriate.

APCM	- Associated Portland Cement Manufacturers Ltd
BAOR	- British Army of the Rhine
BEA	- British Electricity Authority
BOCM	- British Oil & Cake Mills Ltd
BPCM	- British Portland Cement Manufacturers Ltd
CAD	- Central Ammunition Depot
CEA	- Central Electricity Authority
CEGB	- Central Electricity Generating Board
COD	- Central Ordnance Depot
contr	- Contractor
CVD	- Central Vehicle Depot
DoE	- Department of the Environment
GK&B	- Guest, Keen Baldwins Iron & Steel Co Ltd
GWS	- Great Western Society
ICI	- Imperial Chemical Industries Ltd
LBC	- London Brick Co Ltd
LBLR	- Leighton Buzzard Light Railway
LPTB	- London Passenger Transport Board
LTB	- London Transport Board
LTE	- London Transport Executive
LUL	- London Underground Limited
MoD	- Ministry of Defence
MoDAD	- Ministry of Defence, Army Department
MoDAFD	- Ministry of Defence, Air Force Department
MoDND	- Ministry of Defence, Navy Department
MoM	- Ministry of Munitions
MoS	- Ministry of Supply
NATO	- North Atlantic Treaty Organisation
NCB	- National Coal Board
NCBOE	- National Coal Board, Opencast Executive
PEE	- Proof & Experimental Establishment
PLA	- Port of London Authority
RAF	- Royal Air Force
RNAD	- Royal Naval Armament Depot
ROF	- Royal Ordnance Factory
RPC	- Rugby Portland Cement Co Ltd
RPCM	- Rugby Portland Cement Manufacturers Ltd
RTB	- Richard Thomas & Baldwins Ltd
S&L	- Stewarts & Lloyds Ltd
SDSI	- South Durham Steel & Iron Co Ltd
SPA	- Specialist Plant Associates Ltd
WD	- War Department
WDLR	- War Department Light Railways

MAIN LINE RAILWAY COMPANIES

B&NCR	- Belfast & Northern Counties Railway
BR	- British Rail
BR(ER)	- British Railways (Eastern Region)
BR(SR)	- British Railways (Southern Region)
BREL	- British Rail Engineering Ltd
CLC	- Cheshire Lines Committee
E&WJR	- East & West Junction Railway
GCR	- Great Central Railway
GN&GE Joint	- Great Northern & Great Eastern Joint Railway
GNR	- Great Northern Railway
GWR	- Great Western Railway
LBSCR	- London Brighton & South Coast Railway
LMR	- London Midland Region (of British Railways)
LMSR	- London Midland & Scottish Railway
LNER	- London & North Eastern Railway
LNWR	- London & North Western Railway
LSWR	- London & South Western Railway
Met	- Metropolitan Railway
MS&LR	- Manchester, Sheffield & Lincolnshire Railway
NBR	- North British Railway
NER	- North Eastern Railway
S&MJR	- Stratford & Midland Junction Railway
SER	- South Eastern Railway
SR	- Southern Railway

DOUBTFUL INFORMATION

Information which is known to be of a doubtful nature is denoted as such by the wording chosen, or else printed in brackets with a question mark, e.g. (1910?).

ABBREVIATIONS USED FOR LOCOMOTIVE BUILDERS

AB	Andrew Barclay, Sons & Co Ltd, Caledonia Works, Kilmarnock, Strathclyde.
Adams	A.R. Adams & Son, Pill Bank Ironworks, Newport, Gwent.
AE	Avonside Engine Co Ltd, Avonside Engine Works, Fishponds, Bristol.
AK	Alan Keef Ltd, orig Bampton, Oxon; then Lea Line, Hereford & Worcs.
AP	Aveling & Porter Ltd, Invicta Works, Canterbury, Kent.
ARC	A.R.C.Ltd, Stanton Harcourt Depot, near Witney, Oxon.
AtW	Atkinson Walker Wagons Ltd, Frenchwood Works, Preston.
AW	Sir W.G. Armstrong, Whitworth & Co (Engineers) Ltd, Scotswood Works, Newcastle-upon-Tyne.
B	Barclays & Co, Riverbank Works, Kilmarnock, Ayrshire.
Bartholemew	
	C.W.Bartholemew, Blakesley Hall, Northants.
BBT	Brush Bagnall Traction Ltd, Loughborough, Leics and Stafford.
BD	Baguley-Drewry Ltd, Burton-on-Trent.
BE	Brush Electrical Engineering Co Ltd, Loughborough, Leics.
BEV	British Electric Vehicles Ltd, Southport, Lancs.
Bg	E.E.Baguley Ltd, Burton-on-Trent.
BgE	Baguley (Engineers) Ltd, Burton-on-Trent.
BgC	Baguley Cars Ltd, Burton-on-Trent.
BH	Black, Hawthorn & Co Ltd, Gateshead, Co. Durham.
BL	W.J. Bassett Lowke Ltd, Northampton.

Blackwell	Blackwell & Son, Cotton End Works, Northampton.
BLW	Baldwin Locomotive Works, Philadelphia, Pennsylvania, USA.
BP	Beyer, Peacock & Co Ltd, Gorton, Manchester.
BRCW	Birmingham Railway Carriage & Wagon Co Ltd, Smethwick, Staffs.
R.Bro	Rowland Brotherhood, Chippenham, Wilts.
Bton	Brighton Works (LBSCR/SR/BR).
Bury	Edward Bury & Co, Clarence Foundry, Liverpool.
CE	NEI Mining Equipment Ltd, Clayton Equipment, Hatton near Derby.
CF	Chapman & Furneaux Ltd, Gateshead.
Chaplin	Alexander Chaplin & Co Ltd, Cranstonhill Works, Glasgow.
Chr	Fabryka Lokomotyw im F Dzierzynskiego, Chrzanow, Poland.
Clay Cross	Clay Cross Co Ltd, Clay Cross Iron Works, Derbyshire.
Cockerill	Societe pour L'Exploitation Des Etablissements John Cockerill, Seraing, Belgium.
Corpet	Corpet Louvet & Cie, La Courneuve, Seine, France.
CP	Crompton, Parkinson Co Ltd, Chelmsford, Essex.
Crewe	Crewe Works (LNWR/LMSR/BR).
Dar	Darlington Works (NER/LNER/BR).
DC	Drewry Car Co Ltd, London (suppliers only).
Decauville	Society Nouvelle des Establissements Decauville Aine, Corbeil, France
Derby	Derby Works (Midland Railway/LMSR/BR).
Derby C&W	Derby Carriage & Wagon Works (Midland Railway/LMSR/BR).
Desborough	Desborough Co-operative Society Ltd.
DeW	DeWinton & Co, Union Foundry, Caernarvon.
Diema	Diepholzer Maschinenfabrik (Fr Schottler Gmbh), Diepholz, Germany.
DK	Dick, Kerr & Co Ltd, Preston, Lancs.
Don	Doncaster Works (GNR/LNER/BR).
Dtz	Motorenfabrik Deutz AG, Köln, Germany
Easton Gibb	Easton Gibb & Sons, contractors
Edge Hill	Liverpool & Manchester Railway
EE	English Electric Co Ltd, Preston, Lancs.
EES	English Electric Co Ltd, Stephenson Works, Darlington (Successors to RSHD).
EEV	English Electric Co Ltd, Vulcan Works, Newton-le-Willows, Lancs (Successors to VF).
Elh	Eastleigh Works (LSWR/SR/BR).
EV	Ebbw Vale Steel, Iron & Coal Co Ltd, Ebbw Vale, Monmouthshire.
FE	Falcon Engine & Car Works Ltd, Loughborough, Leics.
FH	F.C. Hibberd & Co Ltd, Park Royal, London.
FJ	Fletcher, Jennings & Co, Lowca Engine Works, Whitehaven, Cumberland.
Forder	B.J.Forder & Sons, Stewartby, Beds.
Freud	Stahlbahnwerke Freudenstein & Co, Berlin, Germany.
FW	Fox, Walker & Co, Atlas Engine Works, Bristol.
Garrett	Richard Garrett Engineering Works Ltd, Leiston, Suffolk.
GB	Greenwood & Batley Ltd, Albion Ironworks, Leeds.
GE	George England & Co Ltd, Hatcham Ironworks, London.
GECT	GEC Traction Ltd, Newton-le-Willows, Lancs.
GEU	General Electric Co, Erie, Pennsylvania, USA.
Glas Rly Eng	
	Glasgow Railway Engineering Co Ltd, Govan, Glasgow.

Glengarnock
Glengarnock Iron & Steel Works, Ayrshire.
GRC   Gloucester Railway Carriage & Wagon Co Ltd, Gloucester.
Groom & Tattershall
Groom & Tattershall Ltd, Towcester, Northants.
Gulliver   Gulliver's Land Theme Park, Milton Keynes, Bucks.

H   James & Fredk Howard Ltd, Britannia Ironworks, Bedford.
Hardy   Hardy Railmotor Co Ltd, Slough, Bucks (later Berks).
Harrison & Clayton, Engineers, Northampton.
HCR   Hudswell, Clarke & Rodgers, Railway Foundry, Leeds.
HC   Hudswell, Clarke & Co Ltd, Railway Foundry, Leeds.
HE   Hunslet Engine Co Ltd, Hunslet, Leeds.
HF   Haigh Foundry Co Ltd, Wigan.
HIW   Holwell Iron Works Co Ltd, near Melton mowbray, Leics.
HL   R & W. Hawthorn, Leslie & Co Ltd, Forth Banks Works, Newcastle-Upon-Tyne.
Hor   Horwich Works, Lancs (L&YR/LMSR/BR).
HU   Robert Hudson Ltd, Gildersome Foundry, near Leeds.

Irchester   Irchester Ironstone Co Ltd, Irchester, Northants.
Iso   Iso Speedic Co Ltd, Charles Street, Warwick.

Jacot   P.M.M Jacot, Handsworth, Birmingham
JF   John Fowler & Co (Leeds) Ltd, Hunslet, Leeds.
JTE   Jones, Turner & Evans, Viaduct Foundry, Newton-le-Willows, Lancs.
Jung   Arn Jung Lokomotivfabrik GmbH, Jungenthal, Germany.

K   Kitson & Co Ltd, Airedale Foundry, Leeds.
KC   Kent Construction & Engineering Co Ltd, Ashford, Kent.
KE   Kilmarnock Engineering Co Ltd, Britannia Works, Kilmarnock.
Krauss   Lokomotivfabrik Krauss & Co, Munich, Germany & Linz, Austria.
KS   Kerr, Stuart & Co Ltd, California Works, Stoke-on-Trent, Staffs.

L   R.A. Lister & Co Ltd, Dursley, Glos.
LB   Lister Blackstone Traction Ltd, Dursley, Glos.
LBC   London Brick Co Ltd, Stewartby, Beds.
LBNGRS   Leighton Buzzard Narrow Gauge Railway Society, Beds.
Lenwade   Lenwade Hydraulic Services.
Lewin   Stephen Lewin, Dorset Foundry, Poole, Dorset.
LG   Lingford Gardiner Co Ltd, Bishop Aukland, Co.Durham.
Loco Ent   Locomotion Enterprises (1975) Ltd, Bowes Railway, Gateshead, Tyne & Wear.
Longridge   R.B.Longridge & Co, Bedlington, Northumberland.

McGarigle   McGarigle, Niagara Falls, near Buffalo, New York State, USA.
Mercury   The Mercury Truck & Tractor Co, Gloucester.
MF   Mercia Fabrication Ltd, Dudley, West Midlands.
MH   Muir-Hill (Engineers) Ltd, Trafford Park, Manchester.
Mkm   Markham & Co ltd, Chesterfield, Derbys.
R.P.Morris   R.P.Morris, 193 Main Road, Longfield, Kent.
MR   Motor Rail Ltd, Simplex Works, Bedford, (formerly Motor Rail & Tramcar Co Ltd).
MW   Manning, Wardle & Co Ltd, Boyne Engine Works, Hunslet, Leeds.

N   Neilson & Co, Hyde Park Works, Springburn, Glasgow.
NB   North British Locomotive Co Ltd, Glasgow.

NBH	North British Locomotive Co Ltd, Hyde Park Works, Glasgow.
NBQ	North British Locomotive Co Ltd, Queen's Park Works, Glasgow.
Neasden	Neasden Works, London (Metropolitan Railway)
NELP	Northampton Electric Light & Power Co.
Nohab	Nydqvist & Holm AB, Trollhattan, Sweden.
OK	Orenstein & Koppel AG, Drewitz Works, Potsdam, near Berlin, Germany.
Oliver	Oliver & Co Ltd, Broad Oak Works, Chesterfield, Derbys.
P	Peckett & Sons Ltd, Atlas Locomotive Works, Bristol.
PS	Pressed Steel Ltd, Linwood Works, Paisley, Strathclyde.
PWR	Pickrose & Co Ltd, Wingrove & Rogers Division, Audenshaw, Greater Manchester.
R&R	Ransomes & Rapier Ltd, Riverside Works, Ipswich, Suffolk.
Resco	Resco (Railways) Ltd, Erith, Greater London.
RH	Ruston & Hornsby Ltd, Lincoln.
Ridley Shaw	
	Ridley, Shaw & Co Ltd, Middlesbrough, Yorks (NR).
Robel	Robel & Co, Maschinenfabrik, München, Germany
RR	Rolls-Royce Ltd, Sentinel Works, Shrewsbury (Successors to S).
RS	Robert Stephenson & Co Ltd, Newcastle and Darlington.
RSHD	Robert Stephenson & Hawthorns Ltd, Darlington.
RSHN	Robert Stephenson & Hawthorns Ltd, Forth Banks Works, Newcastle-upon-Tyne.
RTB	Richard Thomas & Baldwins Ltd, Irthingborough, Northants.
S	Sentinel (Shrewsbury) Ltd, Battlefield, Shrewsbury
	(previously Sentinel Waggon Works Ltd).
Sb	Sheepbridge Coal & Iron Co Ltd, Sheepbridge, Derbys.
Sch	Berliner Maschinenbau AG, vormals L Schwartzkopff, Berlin, Germany.
Sdn	Swindon Works, Wilts (GWR/BR).
SG	Slaughter, Gruning & Co, Bristol.
SIW	Stanton Ironworks Co Ltd, near Ilkeston, Derbys.
SMH	Simplex Mechanical Handling Ltd, Elstow Rd, Bedford (successors to MR).
SPA	Specialist Plant Associates Ltd, near Wellingborough, Beds.
SR	Sharp Roberts & Co, Atlas Works, Manchester.
SS	Sharp, Stewart & Co Ltd, Atlas Works, Manchester and Glasgow.
St Rollox	St Rollox Works, Glasgow (Caledonian Railway).
TG	T Green & Son Ltd, Leeds.
TH	Thomas Hill (Rotherham) Ltd, Vanguard Works, Kilnhurst, S. Yorks.
TH/S	built by TH utilising frame of Sentinel steam loco.
Track Supplies	
	Track Supplies & Services Ltd, Wolverton, Bucks.
VF	Vulcan Foundry Ltd, Newton-le-Willows, Lancs.
Wake	J.F. Wake, dealer, Geneva Works, Darlington, Co.Durham.
WB	W.G. Bagnall Ltd, Castle Engine Works, Stafford.
Wkm	D. Wickham & Co Ltd, Ware, Herts.
Woodward	Woodwards Ltd, Birdingbury, near Marton, Warwicks.
WR	Wingrove & Rogers Ltd, Kirkby, Liverpool.
WSO	Wellman, Smith, Owen Engineering Corporation Ltd, Darlaston, Staffs.
YE	Yorkshire Engine Co Ltd, Meadow Hall Works, Sheffield.
J&T Young	John & Thomas Young, Vulcan Foundry, Ayr.

There are numerous references in footnotes to **Petrol Loco Hirers (Ltd)** and **Diesel Loco Hirers Ltd**. These companies specialised in the hire of Motor Rail locomotives and further details can be found in the entry for Simplex Mechanical Handling Ltd, Bedfordshire.

LOCATION CODES

In the Industrial section within each county each location entry is numbered in numerical sequence from 1. This number is prefixed by a letter indicating the key map on which the site appears. Similarly the locations in the other sections are each numbered from 1 and are prefixed by first the map letter and then also by C, D, P or H (for Contractor, Dealer, Preserved or Non-loco systems (where H = 'Hand, Horse or Haulage') respectively. For example, EC25 denotes map E, and location 25 in the Contractors section. The letter X as a prefix indicates an entry which, for whatever reason, is not indicated on any key map.

MAPS

KEY MAPS

A	Buckinghamshire
B	South-East Buckinghamshire
C	High Wycombe & Marlow
D	Aylesbury
E	Bletchley & Wolverton
F	Bedfordshire
G	Bedford
H	Dunstable & Luton
G1	Bedford – Industrial Area (also Britannia Ironworks, 1932)
J	Elstow & Stewartby
K	Leighton Buzzard
L	Northamptonshire
M	Northampton & Blisworth
N	Northampton Town
P	Weedon
Q	Wellingborough & Irthlingborough
R	Kettering
S	Thrapston
T	Corby Area

SYSTEM MAPS

Halton Camp Railway [1917] Buckinghamshire
Pitstone Cement Works
Calvert Brickworks
Westhorpe Gravel Pits / Iver Court Brickworks
Hedsor Mills / Soho Mills, Wooburn
Air Ministry, Cardington, Bedfordshire
Air Ministry, Henlow
ROF Elstow
Coronation Brickworks
Goldington Power Station / Little Barford Power Station
Arlesey [1922]
Northampton Gas Works [1925] / Northampton Power Station [1938]
Corby Steelworks
Wellingborough Ironworks
Yardley Chase Depot
WD Barby / WD Weedon

LEGEND FOR MAPS :

—————— Public railway (standard gauge)

—————— Industrial railway (standard gauge)

—————— Narrow gauge railway or tramway

▬▬▬▬ Canal or waterway

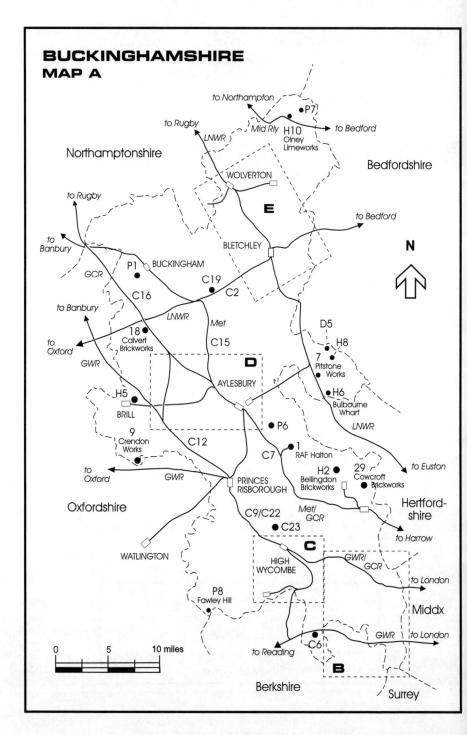

BUCKINGHAMSHIRE
MAP A

to Northampton

● P7

to Bedford

Mid Rly   H10
Olney
Limeworks

LNWR

to Rugby

Northamptonshire

Bedfordshire

WOLVERTON

E

to Rugby

to Bedford

BLETCHLEY

N

to Banbury

GCR

● P1   BUCKINGHAM

C16

C19

C2

to Banbury

LNWR   Met

to Oxford

GWR

18 ●
Calvert
Brickworks

C15

D5

H8
7 ●
Pitstone
Works

D

AYLESBURY

H5
BRILL

9
Crendon
Works

C12

● P6

H6
Bulbourne
Wharf

LNWR

to Oxford

GWR

PRINCES
RISBOROUGH

C7

1 ●
RAF Halton

H2 ●
Bellingdon
Brickworks

29
Cowcroft
● Brickworks

to Euston

Hertford-
shire

Oxfordshire

C9/C22

Met/
GCR

● C23

C

HIGH
WYCOMBE

GWR/
GCR

to Harrow

to London

WATLINGTON

Middx

P8 ●
Fawley Hill

to Reading

● C6

GWR

to London

B

0   5   10 miles

Berkshire

Surrey

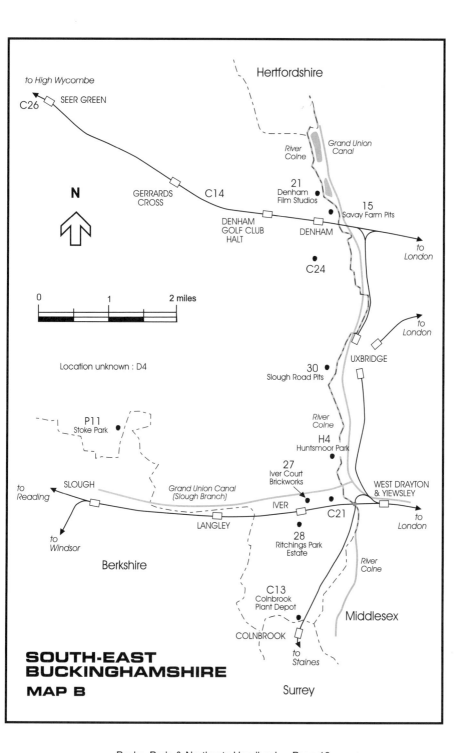

to High Wycombe

C26 SEER GREEN

Hertfordshire

N

GERRARDS
CROSS

C14

River
Colne

Grand Union
Canal

21
Denham
Film Studios

15
Savay Farm Pits

DENHAM
GOLF CLUB
HALT

DENHAM

to
London

C24

0   1   2 miles

Location unknown : D4

30
Slough Road Pits

to
London

UXBRIDGE

P11
Stoke Park

River
Colne

H4
Huntsmoor Park

27
Iver Court
Brickworks

WEST DRAYTON
& YIEWSLEY

to
Reading

SLOUGH

Grand Union Canal
(Slough Branch)

IVER

C21

to
London

LANGLEY

28
Ritchings Park
Estate

to
Windsor

Berkshire

River
Colne

C13
Colnbrook
Plant Depot

Middlesex

COLNBROOK

to
Staines

SOUTH-EAST
BUCKINGHAMSHIRE
MAP B

Surrey

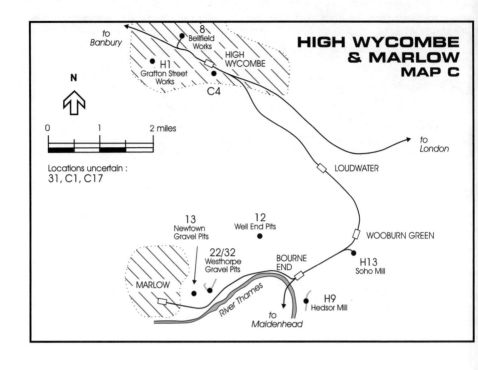

HIGH WYCOMBE & MARLOW MAP C

N

0   1   2 miles

Locations uncertain :
31, C1, C17

to Banbury

8 Bellfield Works

H1 Grafton Street Works

HIGH WYCOMBE

C4

to London

LOUDWATER

13 Newtown Gravel Pits

12 Well End Pits

22/32 Westhorpe Gravel Pits

BOURNE END

WOOBURN GREEN

H13 Soho Mill

MARLOW

River Thames

to Maidenhead

H9 Hedsor Mill

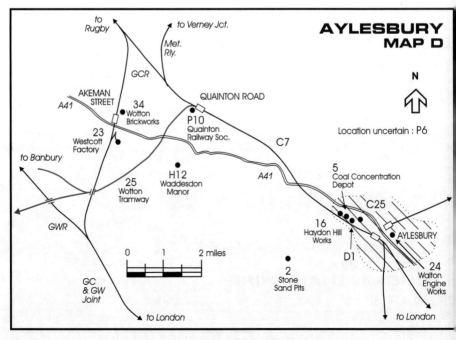

AYLESBURY MAP D

N

to Rugby

to Verney Jct.

Met. Rly.

GCR

AKEMAN STREET

A41

QUAINTON ROAD

Location uncertain : P6

34 Wotton Brickworks

P10 Quainton Railway Soc.

C7

23 Westcott Factory

to Banbury

25 Wotton Tramway

H12 Waddesdon Manor

A41

5 Coal Concentration Depot

C25

GWR

16 Haydon Hill Works

AYLESBURY

D1

GC & GW Joint

0   1   2 miles

2 Stone Sand Pits

24 Walton Engine Works

to London

to London

BLETCHLEY & WOLVERTON

MAP E

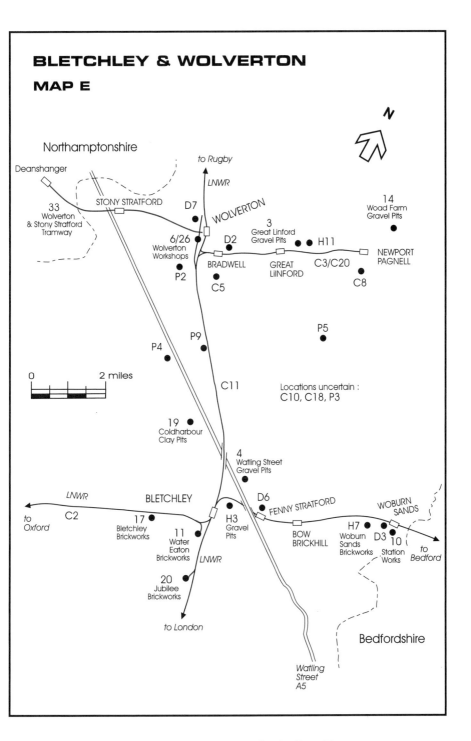

N

Northamptonshire

Deanshanger

to Rugby

LNWR

33
Wolverton
& Stony Stratford
Tramway

STONY STRATFORD

D7

WOLVERTON

14
Woad Farm
Gravel Pits

6/26
Wolverton
Workshops

D2

3
Great Linford
Gravel Pits

H11

NEWPORT
PAGNELL

P2

BRADWELL

GREAT
LilNFORD

C3/C20

C5

C8

P5

0   2 miles

P4

P9

C11

Locations uncertain :
C10, C18, P3

19
Coldharbour
Clay Pits

4
Watling Street
Gravel Pits

LNWR

BLETCHLEY

D6

FENNY STRATFORD

WOBURN
SANDS

to
Oxford

C2

17
Bletchley
Brickworks

11
Water
Eaton
Brickworks

H3
Gravel
Pits

BOW
BRICKHILL

H7
Woburn
Sands
Brickworks

D3

10
Station
Works

to
Bedford

LNWR

20
Jubilee
Brickworks

to London

Bedfordshire

Watling
Street
A5

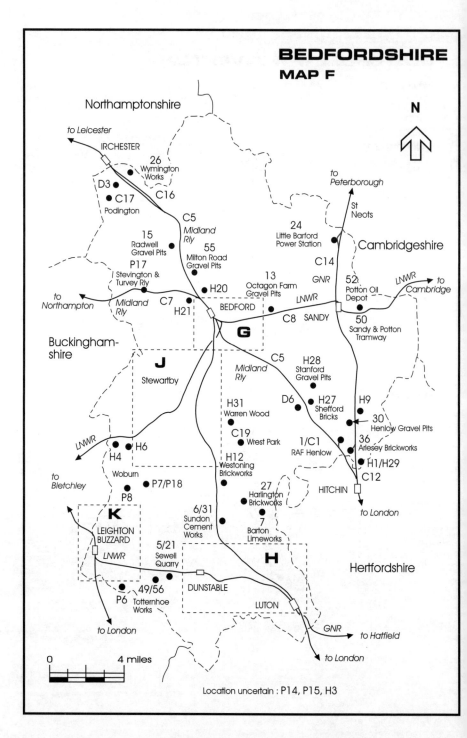

BEDFORDSHIRE
MAP F

N

Northamptonshire

to Leicester

IRCHESTER

26 Wymington Works

D3
C17
Podington

C16

C5
Midland Rly

15 Radwell Gravel Pits

55 Milton Road Gravel Pits

P17 Stevington & Turvey Rly

Midland Rly

to Northampton

C7
H21

H20

BEDFORD

G

13 Octagon Farm Gravel Pits

LNWR

C8   SANDY

to Peterborough

St Neots

24 Little Barford Power Station

Cambridgeshire

C14

GNR

52 Potton Oil Depot

LNWR   to Cambridge

50 Sandy & Potton Tramway

Buckingham-
shire

J

Stewartby

LNWR

H6
H4

Woburn

P7/P18
P8

to Bletchley

C5

Midland Rly

H31 Warren Wood

C19   Wrest Park

H12 Westoning Brickworks

H28 Stanford Gravel Pits

D6
H27 Shefford Bricks

1/C1 RAF Henlow

H9

30 Henlow Gravel Pits

36 Arlesey Brickworks

H1/H29

C12

HITCHIN

27 Harlington Brickworks

to London

K

LEIGHTON BUZZARD

LNWR

5/21 Sewell Quarry

6/31 Sundon Cement Works

7 Barton Limeworks

H

Hertfordshire

49/56 Totternhoe Works

P6

DUNSTABLE

LUTON

to London

GNR   to Hatfield

to London

0   4 miles

Location uncertain : P14, P15, H3

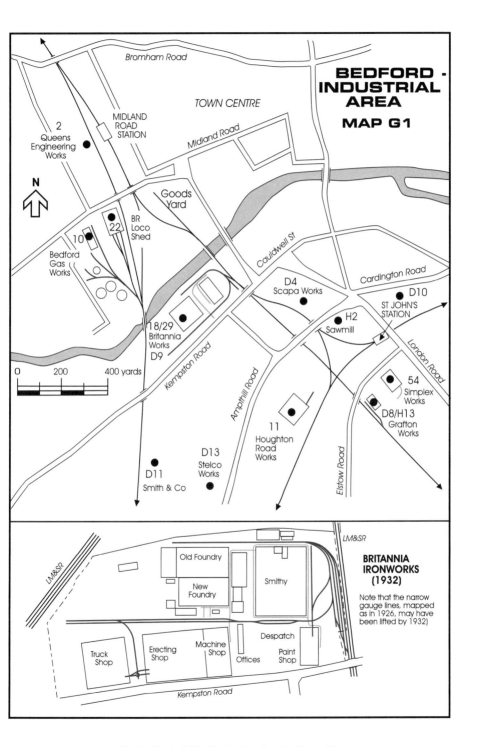

BEDFORD - INDUSTRIAL AREA
MAP G1

TOWN CENTRE

Bromham Road

MIDLAND ROAD STATION

Midland Road

2 Queens Engineering Works

N

Goods Yard

22

10

BR Loco Shed

Bedford Gas Works

Cauldwell St

Cardington Road

D4 Scapa Works

D10

ST JOHN'S STATION

H2 Sawmill

18/29 Britannia Works **D9**

Kempston Road

London Road

54 Simplex Works

D8/H13 Grafton Works

Ampthill Road

0   200   400 yards

11 Houghton Road Works

D13 Stelco Works

Elstow Road

D11 Smith & Co

BRITANNIA IRONWORKS (1932)

LM&SR

Old Foundry

Smithy

New Foundry

LM&SR

Truck Shop

Erecting Shop

Machine Shop

Offices

Despatch

Paint Shop

Kempston Road

Note that the narrow gauge lines, mapped as in 1926, may have been lifted by 1932)

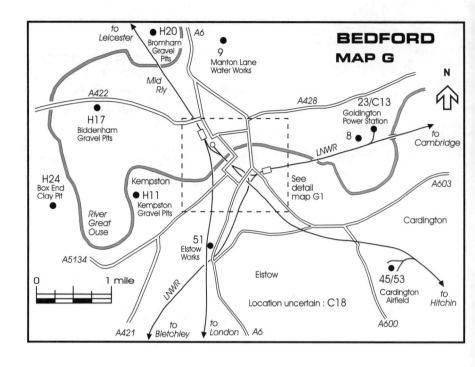

BEDFORD MAP G

N

● H20
Bromham Gravel Pits

to Leicester

A6

9
Manton Lane Water Works

Mid Rly

A422

A428

23/C13
Goldington Power Station

8 ●

LNWR

to Cambridge

H17
Biddenham Gravel Pits

A603

H24
Box End Clay Pit

Kempston

See detail map G1

Cardington

● H11
Kempston Gravel Pits

River Great Ouse

A5134

51
Elstow Works

Elstow

45/53
Cardington Airfield

to Hitchin

0   1 mile

Location uncertain : C18

LNWR

A600

A421

to Bletchley

to London

A6

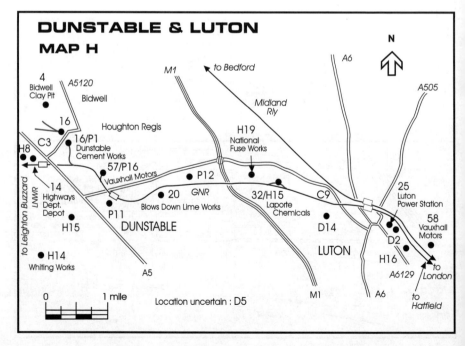

DUNSTABLE & LUTON
MAP H

N

M1

to Bedford

A6

A505

4
Bidwell Clay Pit

A5120

Bidwell

Midland Rly

16

Houghton Regis

H19
National Fuse Works

C3

16/P1
Dunstable Cement Works

H8

57/P16
Vauxhall Motors

P12

25
Luton Power Station

to Leighton Buzzard

LNWR

14
Highways Dept. Depot

P11

20

GNR

32/H15
Laporte Chemicals

C9

58
Vauxhall Motors

H15

DUNSTABLE

Blows Down Lime Works

D14

D2

● H14
Whiting Works

A5

LUTON

H16

A6129

to London

0   1 mile

Location uncertain : D5

M1

A6

to Hatfield

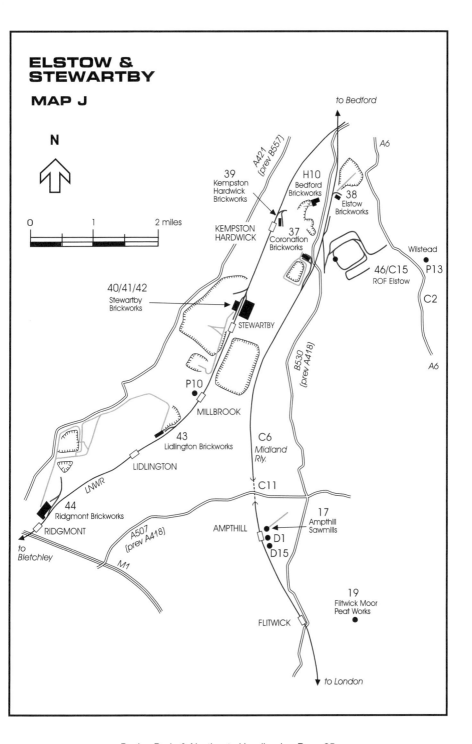

ELSTOW & STEWARTBY

MAP J

N

0   1   2 miles

to Bedford

A6

A421
(prev B557)

39
Kempston
Hardwick
Brickworks

H10
Bedford
Brickworks

38
Elstow
Brickworks

KEMPSTON
HARDWICK

37
Coronation
Brickworks

Wilstead

P13

46/C15
ROF Elstow

C2

A6

40/41/42
Stewartby
Brickworks

STEWARTBY

B530
(prev A418)

P10

MILLBROOK

43
Lidlington Brickworks

C6
Midland
Rly.

LIDLINGTON

LNWR

C11

44
Ridgmont Brickworks

17
Ampthill
Sawmills

RIDGMONT

A507
(prev A418)

AMPTHILL

D1

to
Bletchley

D15

M1

19
Flitwick Moor
Peat Works

FLITWICK

to London

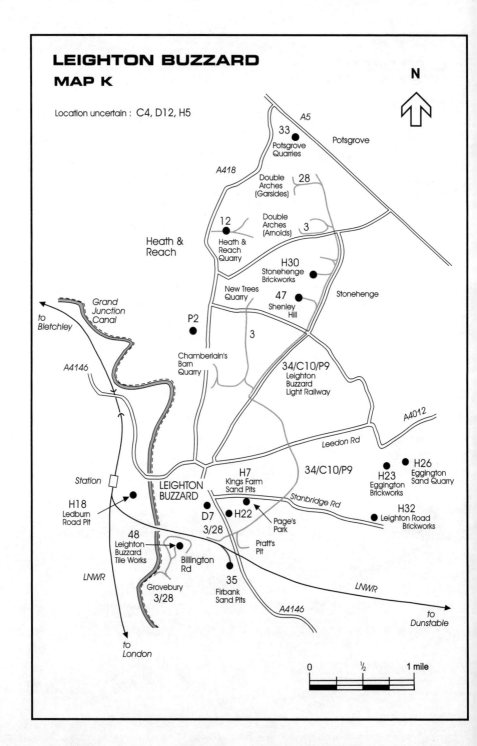

LEIGHTON BUZZARD
MAP K

N

Location uncertain : C4, D12, H5

A5

33
Potsgrove
Quarries

Potsgrove

A418

Double
Arches
(Garsides)

28

12
Heath &
Reach
Quarry

Double
Arches
(Arnolds)

3

Heath &
Reach

H30
Stonehenge
Brickworks

47
Shenley
Hill

Stonehenge

New Trees
Quarry

Grand
Junction
Canal

P2

to
Bletchley

Chamberlain's
Barn
Quarry

3

34/C10/P9
Leighton
Buzzard
Light Railway

A4146

A4012

Leedon Rd

Station

LEIGHTON
BUZZARD

H7
Kings Farm
Sand Pits

34/C10/P9

H26
Eggington
Sand Quarry

H23
Eggington
Brickworks

H18
Ledburn
Road Pit

Stanbridge Rd

H32
Leighton Road
Brickworks

D7
3/28

H22

Page's
Park

48
Leighton
Buzzard
Tile Works

Pratt's
Pit

Billington
Rd

LNWR

LNWR

to
Dunstable

Grovebury
3/28

35
Firbank
Sand Pits

A4146

to
London

0   ½   1 mile

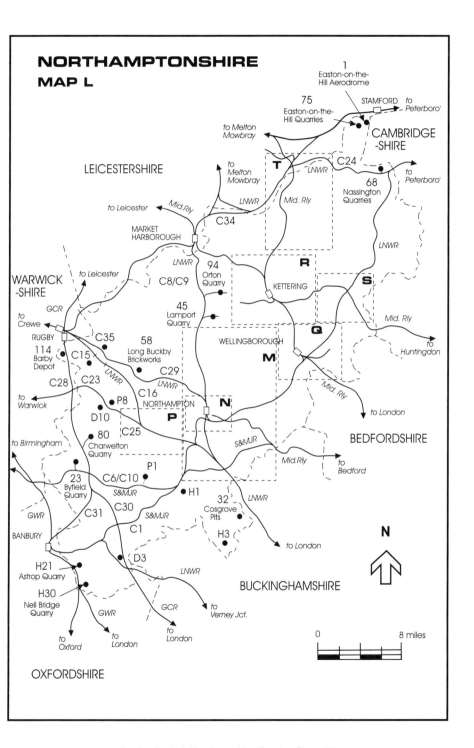

NORTHAMPTONSHIRE
MAP L

1
Easton-on-the-Hill Aerodrome

75
Easton-on-the-Hill Quarries

STAMFORD

to Peterboro'

CAMBRIDGE-SHIRE

to Melton Mowbray

to Melton Mowbray

LEICESTERSHIRE

LNWR

T

LNWR

Mid. Rly

C24

68
Nassington Quarries

to Peterboro'

to Leicester

Mid.Rly

C34

LNWR

LNWR

MARKET HARBOROUGH

LNWR

94
Orton Quarry

R

S

to Leicester

C8/C9

KETTERING

Mid. Rly

WARWICK-SHIRE

GCR

45
Lamport Quarry

Q

to Huntingdon

to Crewe

RUGBY

C35

58
Long Buckby Brickworks

WELLINGBOROUGH

M

114
Barby Depot

C15

C29

LNWR

Mid. Rly

C28

C23

LNWR

C16
NORTHAMPTON

N

to Warwick

P8

to London

D10

P

C25

BEDFORDSHIRE

to Birmingham

80
Charwelton Quarry

S&MJR

Mid.Rly

P1

to Bedford

23
Byfield Quarry

C6/C10

H1

32
Cosgrove Pits

LNWR

GWR

C31

C30

S&MJR

H3

BANBURY

C1

to London

D3

H21
Astrop Quarry

LNWR

N

H30
Nell Bridge Quarry

BUCKINGHAMSHIRE

to Oxford

GWR

GCR

to London

to Verney Jct.

to London

0   8 miles

OXFORDSHIRE

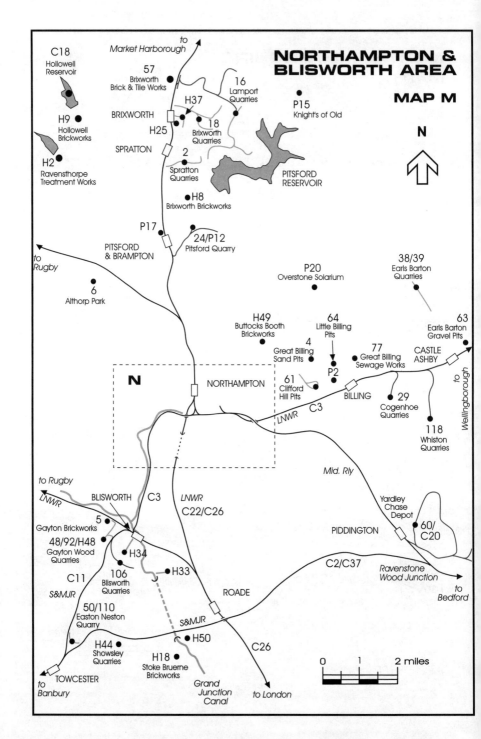

NORTHAMPTON & BLISWORTH AREA

MAP M

N

C18
Hollowell
Reservoir

to
Market Harborough

57
Brixworth
Brick & Tile Works

16
Lamport
Quarries

P15
Knight's of Old

H37

BRIXWORTH

H25

18
Brixworth
Quarries

H9
Hollowell
Brickworks

SPRATTON

2
Spratton
Quarries

H2
Ravensthorpe
Treatment Works

PITSFORD
RESERVOIR

H8
Brixworth Brickworks

P17

24/P12
Pitsford Quarry

PITSFORD
& BRAMPTON

to
Rugby

38/39
Earls Barton
Quarries

P20
Overstone Solarium

6
Althorp Park

H49
Buttocks Booth
Brickworks

64
Little Billing
Pits

63
Earls Barton
Gravel Pits

4
Great Billing
Sand Pits

77
Great Billing
Sewage Works

CASTLE
ASHBY

to
Wellingborough

N

NORTHAMPTON

61
Clifford
Hill Pits

P2

BILLING

29
Cogenhoe
Quarries

LNWR

C3

118
Whiston
Quarries

Mid. Rly

to Rugby

LNWR

BLISWORTH

C3

LNWR
C22/C26

Yardley
Chase
Depot

60/
C20

5
Gayton Brickworks

PIDDINGTON

48/92/H48
Gayton Wood
Quarries

H34

C2/C37

Ravenstone
Wood Junction

C11

106
Blisworth
Quarries

H33

ROADE

to
Bedford

S&MJR

50/110
Easton Neston
Quarry

S&MJR

C26

0   1   2 miles

H44
Showsley
Quarries

H50

TOWCESTER

H18
Stoke Bruerne
Brickworks

Grand
Junction
Canal

to London

to
Banbury

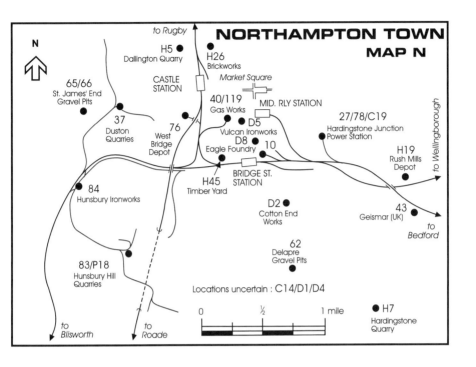

NORTHAMPTON TOWN
MAP N

N

to Rugby

65/66
St. James' End
Gravel Pits

H5 ●
Dallington Quarry

H26 ●
Brickworks

CASTLE
STATION

Market Square

37
Duston
Quarries

76

West
Bridge
Depot

40/119 ●
Gas Works

MID. RLY STATION

D5 ●
Vulcan Ironworks

27/78/C19
Hardingstone Junction
Power Station ●

D8
Eagle Foundry ●

10 ●

H19
Rush Mills
Depot ●

to Wellingborough

84 ●
Hunsbury Ironworks

H45
Timber Yard

BRIDGE ST.
STATION

D2 ●
Cotton End
Works

43
Geismar (UK) ●

to
Bedford

83/P18
Hunsbury Hill
Quarries

62
Delapre
Gravel Pits

Locations uncertain : C14/D1/D4

to
Blisworth

to
Roade

0   ½   1 mile

● H7
Hardingstone
Quarry

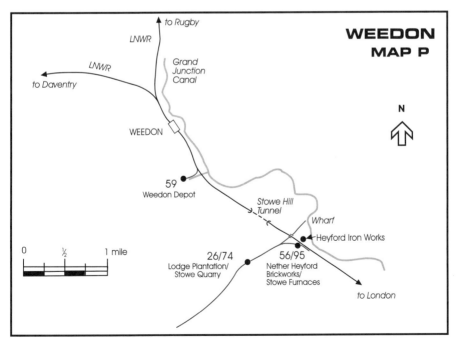

WEEDON
MAP P

to Rugby

LNWR

LNWR

to Daventry

Grand
Junction
Canal

N

WEEDON

59
Weedon Depot

Stowe Hill
Tunnel

Wharf

Heyford Iron Works ●

0   ½   1 mile

26/74
Lodge Plantation/
Stowe Quarry

56/95
Nether Heyford
Brickworks/
Stowe Furnaces

to London

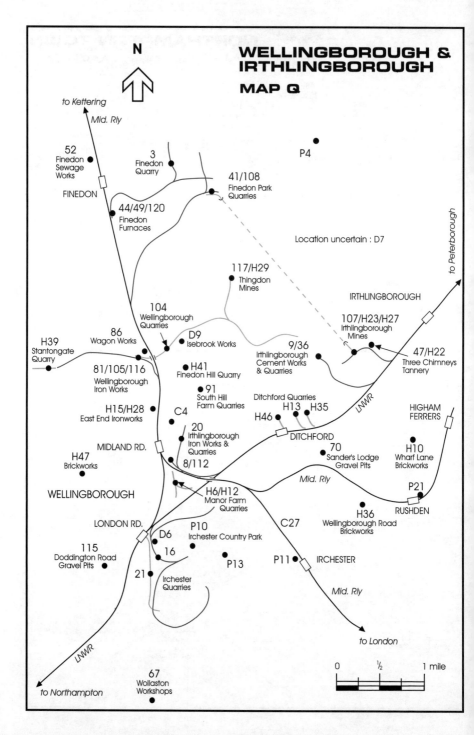

N

WELLINGBOROUGH &
IRTHLINGBOROUGH

MAP Q

to Kettering

Mid. Rly

52
Finedon
Sewage
Works

3
Finedon
Quarry

P4

FINEDON

41/108
Finedon Park
Quarries

44/49/120
Finedon
Furnaces

Location uncertain : D7

117/H29
Thingdon
Mines

to Peterborough

IRTHLINGBOROUGH

104
Wellingborough
Quarries

107/H23/H27
Irthlingborough
Mines

H39
Stantongate
Quarry

86
Wagon Works

D9
Isebrook Works

9/36
Irthlingborough
Cement Works
& Quarries

47/H22
Three Chimneys
Tannery

81/105/116
Wellingborough
Iron Works

H41
Finedon Hill Quarry

H15/H28
East End Ironworks

91
South Hill
Farm Quarries

C4

Ditchford Quarries
H13 H35

LNWR

HIGHAM
FERRERS

H46

20
Irthlingborough
Iron Works &
Quarries

DITCHFORD

H10
Wharf Lane
Brickworks

MIDLAND RD.

8/112

70
Sander's Lodge
Gravel Pits

P21

H47
Brickworks

H6/H12
Manor Farm
Quarries

Mid. Rly

RUSHDEN

WELLINGBOROUGH

H36
Wellingborough Road
Brickworks

LONDON RD.

D6

P10
Irchester Country Park

C27

115
Doddington Road
Gravel Pits

16

P13

P11

IRCHESTER

21

Irchester
Quarries

Mid. Rly

LNWR

to London

0   ½   1 mile

to Northampton

67
Wollaston
Workshops

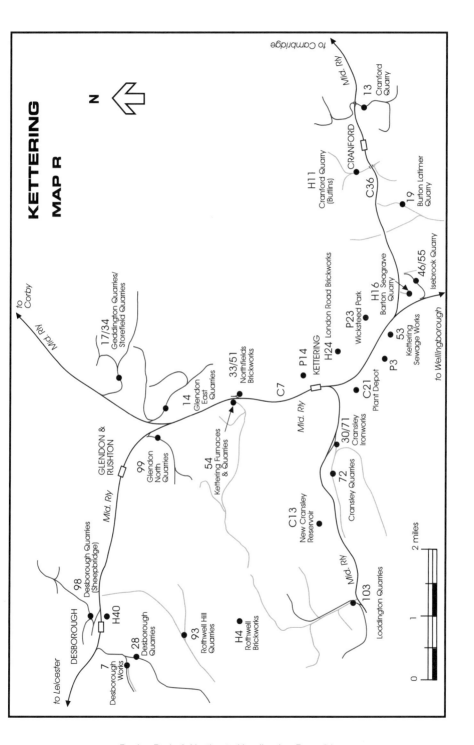

KETTERING

MAP R

N

to Leicester

to Corby

to Cambridge

to Wellingborough

DESBOROUGH

GLENDON & RUSHTON

KETTERING

CRANFORD

Mid. Rly

Mid. Rly

Mid. Rly

Mid. Rly

Mid. Rly

98 Desborough Quarries (Sheepbridge)

H40

7 Desborough Works

28 Desborough Quarries

93 Rothwell Hill Quarries

H4 Rothwell Brickworks

99 Glendon North Quarries

14 Glendon East Quarries

17/34 Geddington Quarries/ Storefield Quarries

54 Kettering Furnaces & Quarries

33/51 Northfields Brickworks

C7

C13 New Cransley Reservoir

72 Cransley Quarries

30/71 Cransley Ironworks

C21 Plant Depot

P14

H24 London Road Brickworks

P23 Wicksteed Park

P3

53 Kettering Sewage Works

H16 Barton Seagrave Quarry

46/55 Isebrook Quarry

19 Burton Latimer Quarry

C36

H11 Cranford Quarry (Butlins)

13 Cranford Quarry

103 Loddington Quarries

0   1   2 miles

Bucks, Beds & Northants Handbook – Page 31

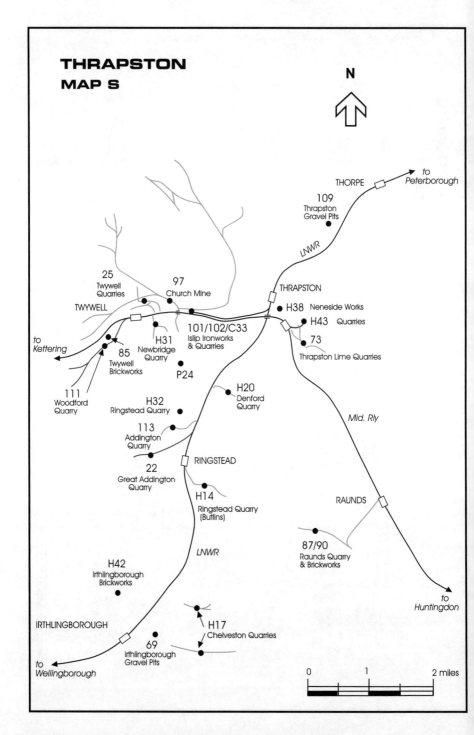

THRAPSTON
MAP S

N

THORPE — to Peterborough

109
Thrapston
Gravel Pits

LNWR

25
Twywell
Quarries

97
Church Mine

THRAPSTON

H38 Neneside Works

H43 Quarries

TWYWELL

101/102/C33
Islip Ironworks
& Quarries

73
Thrapston Lime Quarries

to Kettering

H31
Newbridge
Quarry

85
Twywell
Brickworks

P24

Mid. Rly

111
Woodford
Quarry

H32
Ringstead Quarry

H20
Denford
Quarry

113
Addington
Quarry

22
Great Addington
Quarry

RINGSTEAD

H14
Ringstead Quarry
(Butlins)

RAUNDS

87/90
Raunds Quarry
& Brickworks

to Huntingdon

LNWR

H42
Irthlingborough
Brickworks

IRTHLINGBOROUGH

H17
Chelveston Quarries

69
Irthlingborough
Gravel Pits

to Wellingborough

0   1   2 miles

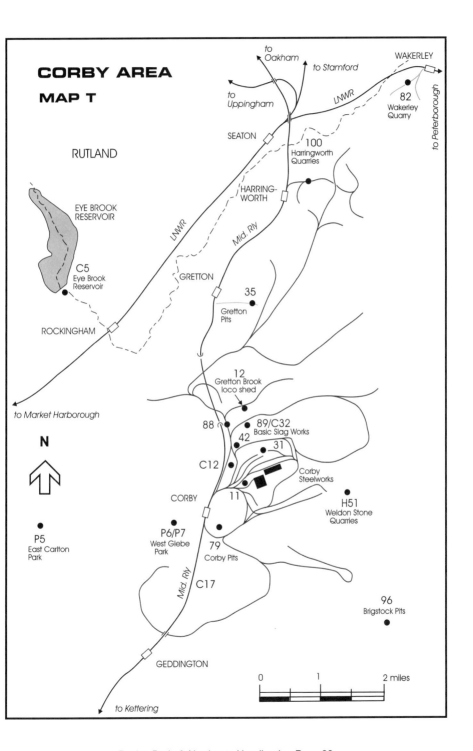

CORBY AREA
MAP T

to Oakham

to Stamford

WAKERLEY

to Uppingham

LNWR

82
Wakerley
Quarry

to Peterborough

SEATON

100
Harringworth
Quarries

RUTLAND

HARRING-
WORTH

LNWR

Mid. Rly

EYE BROOK
RESERVOIR

GRETTON

35
Gretton
Pits

C5
Eye Brook
Reservoir

ROCKINGHAM

to Market Harborough

12
Gretton Brook
loco shed

N

88

89/C32
Basic Slag Works

42

31

C12

Corby
Steelworks

11

CORBY

H51
Weldon Stone
Quarries

P5
East Carlton
Park

P6/P7
West Glebe
Park

79
Corby Pits

Mid. Rly

C17

96
Brigstock Pits

0   1   2 miles

GEDDINGTON

to Kettering

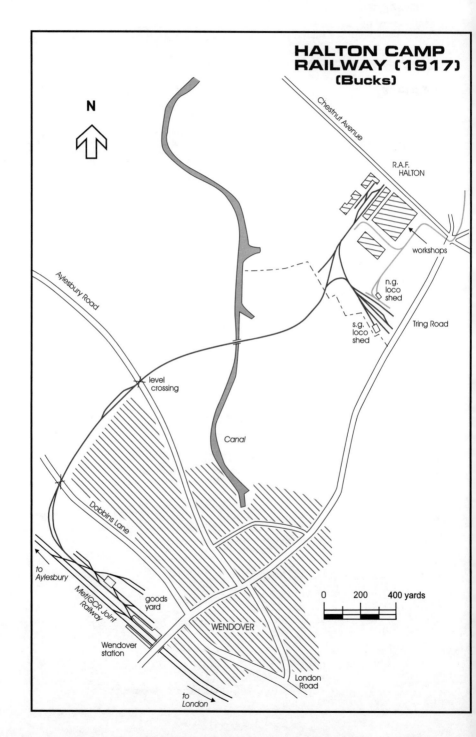

HALTON CAMP RAILWAY (1917)
(Bucks)

Chestnut Avenue

N

R.A.F. HALTON

workshops

n.g. loco shed

Aylesbury Road

s.g. loco shed

Tring Road

level crossing

Canal

Dobbins Lane

to Aylesbury

Met/GCR Joint Railway

goods yard

Wendover station

WENDOVER

London Road

0   200   400 yards

to London

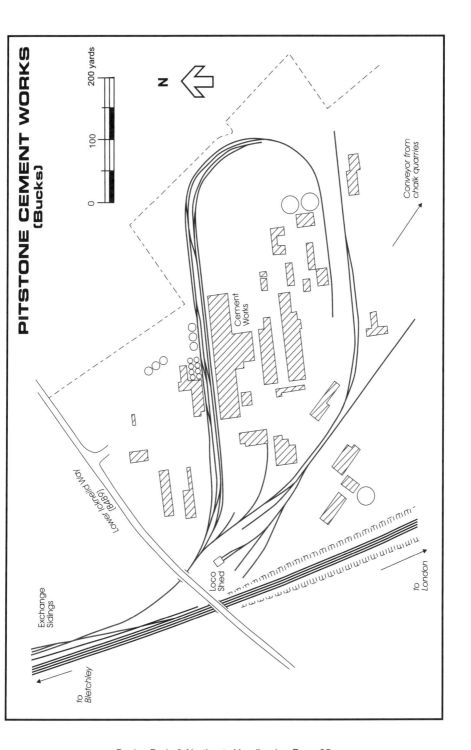

PITSTONE CEMENT WORKS (Bucks)

0 100 200 yards

N

Conveyor from chalk quarries

Cement Works

Lower Icknield Way (B489)

Exchange Sidings

Loco Shed

to Bletchley

to London

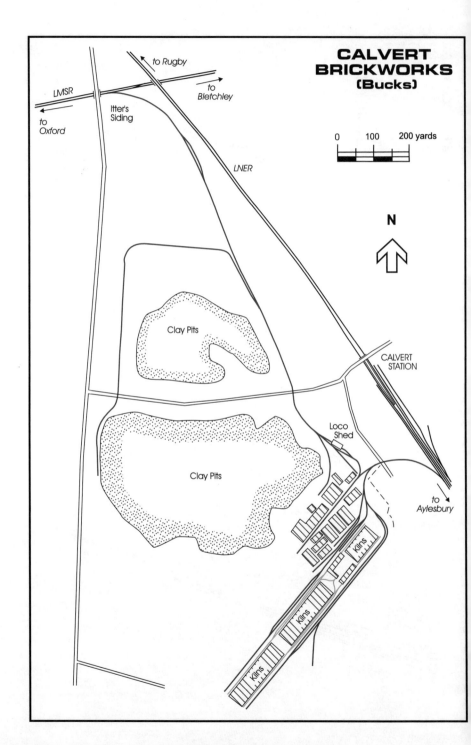

CALVERT BRICKWORKS (Bucks)

to Rugby
LMSR
to Bletchley
Itter's Siding
to Oxford
LNER

0   100   200 yards

N

Clay Pits

CALVERT STATION

Clay Pits

Loco Shed

to Aylesbury

Kilns

Kilns

Kilns

Kilns

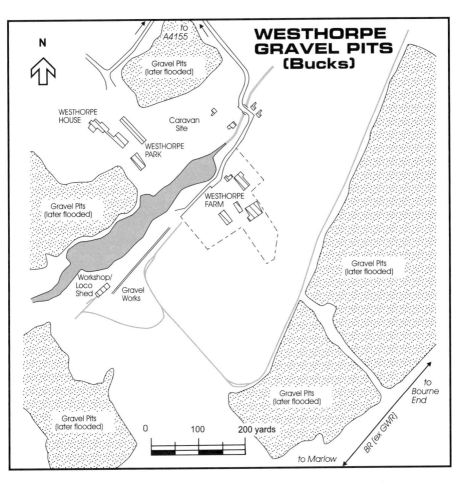

WESTHORPE GRAVEL PITS (Bucks)

N

to A4155

Gravel Pits (later flooded)

WESTHORPE HOUSE

Caravan Site

WESTHORPE PARK

WESTHORPE FARM

Gravel Pits (later flooded)

Gravel Pits (later flooded)

Workshop/ Loco Shed

Gravel Works

Gravel Pits (later flooded)

Gravel Pits (later flooded)

Gravel Pits (later flooded)

0   100   200 yards

to Bourne End

BR (ex GWR)

to Marlow

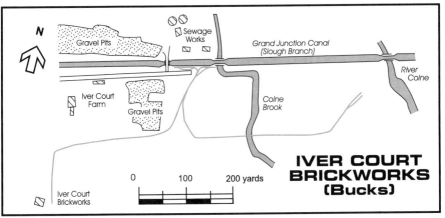

N

Gravel Pits

Sewage Works

Grand Junction Canal (Slough Branch)

River Colne

Iver Court Farm

Gravel Pits

Colne Brook

Iver Court Brickworks

0   100   200 yards

IVER COURT BRICKWORKS (Bucks)

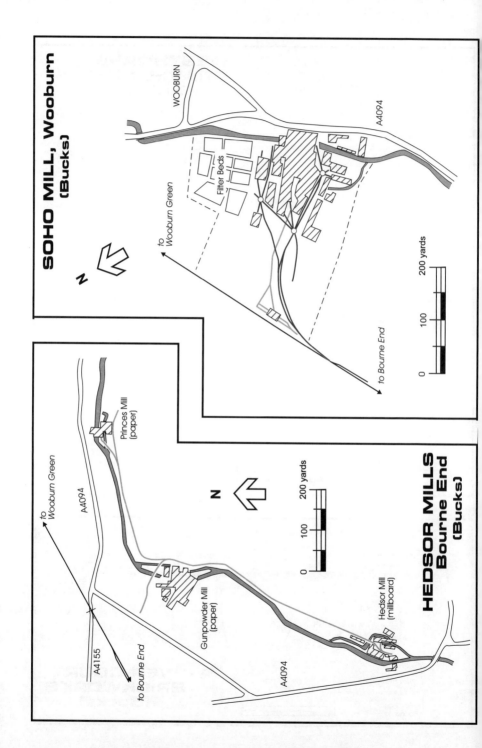

SOHO MILL, Wooburn (Bucks)

WOOBURN

A4094

to Wooburn Green

Filter Beds

to Bourne End

N

0 100 200 yards

HEDSOR MILLS Bourne End (Bucks)

to Wooburn Green

A4094

Princes Mill (paper)

A4155

to Bourne End

Gunpowder Mill (paper)

N

0 100 200 yards

Hedsor Mill (millboard)

A4094

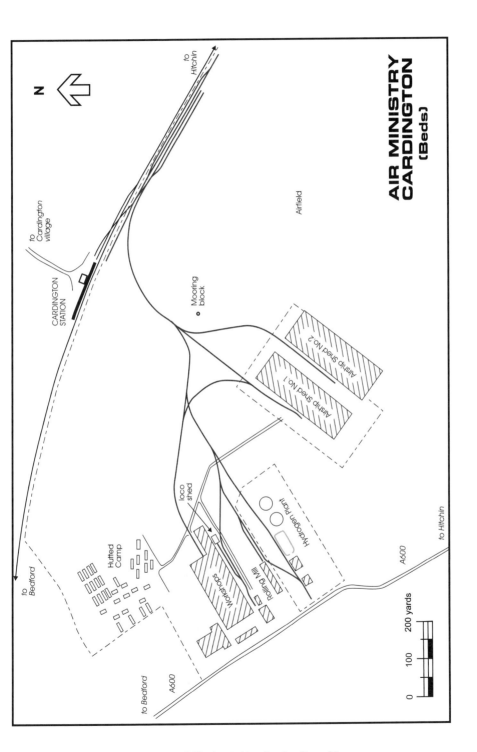

AIR MINISTRY
CARDINGTON
(Beds)

N

to Hitchin

to Cardington village

CARDINGTON STATION

to Bedford

Mooring block

Airfield

Airship shed No.1

Airship shed No.2

loco shed

Hutted Camp

Workshops

Rolling Mill

Hydrogen plant

to Bedford

A600

A600

to Hitchin

0   100   200 yards

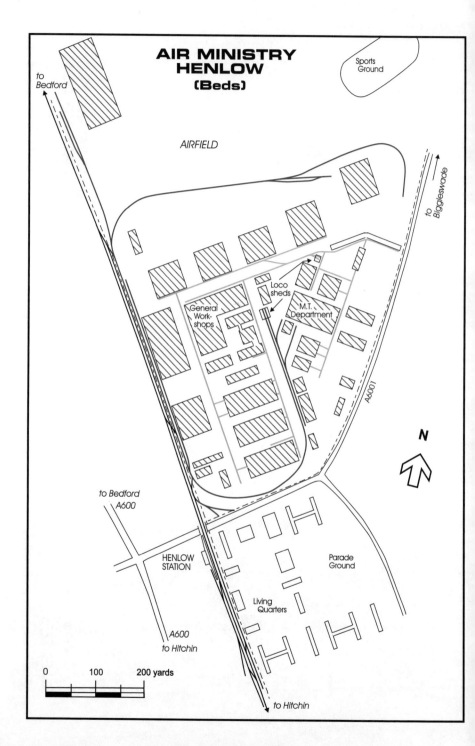

AIR MINISTRY HENLOW
(Beds)

to Bedford

Sports Ground

AIRFIELD

to Biggleswade

Loco sheds

General Work-shops

M.T. Department

A6001

N

to Bedford
A600

HENLOW STATION

Parade Ground

Living Quarters

A600
to Hitchin

0   100   200 yards

to Hitchin

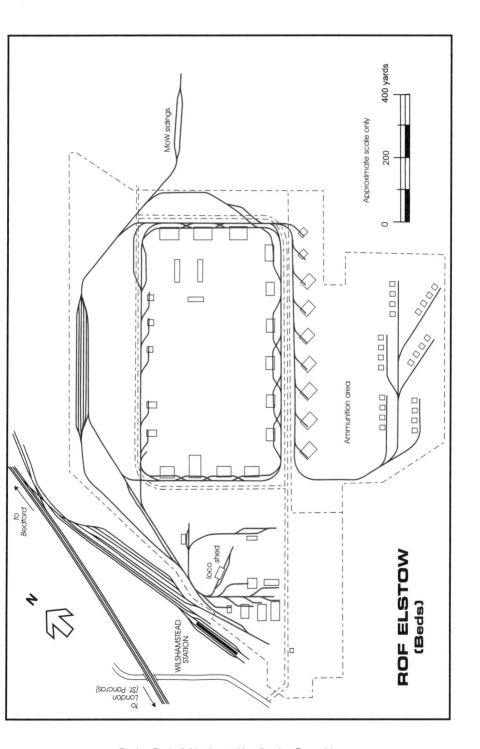

ROF ELSTOW
(Beds)

N

to Bedford

to London (St. Pancras)

WILSHAMSTEAD STATION

loco shed

Ammunition area

MoW sidings

Approximate scale only

0   200   400 yards

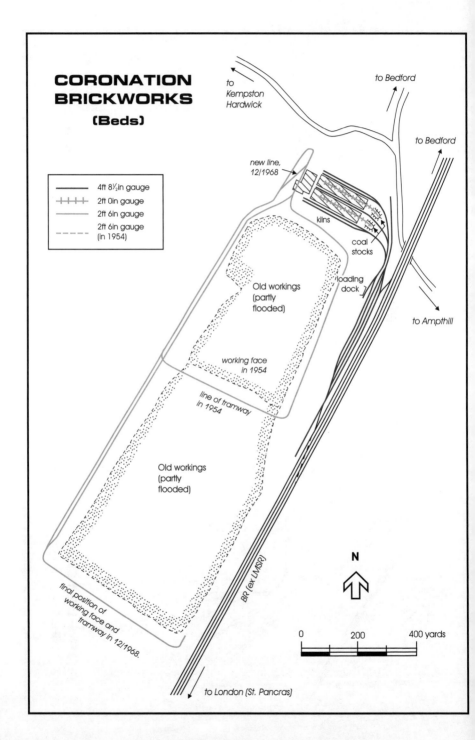

CORONATION BRICKWORKS (Beds)

to Kempston Hardwick

to Bedford

to Bedford

to Ampthill

to London (St. Pancras)

new line, 12/1968

kilns

coal stocks

loading dock

Old workings (partly flooded)

Old workings (partly flooded)

working face in 1954

line of tramway in 1954

final position of working face and tramway in 12/1968.

BR (ex LMSR)

N

——	4ft 8½in gauge
+++	2ft 0in gauge
——	2ft 6in gauge
- - -	2ft 6in gauge (in 1954)

0   200   400 yards

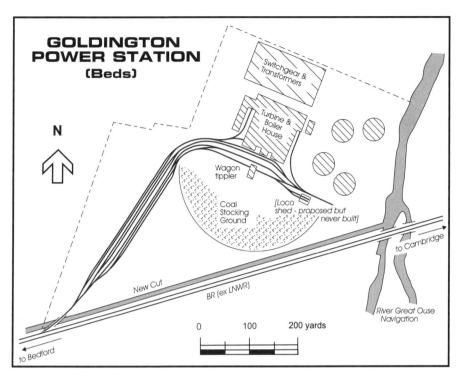

GOLDINGTON POWER STATION (Beds)

Switchgear & Transformers

Turbine & Boiler House

N

Wagon tippler

Coal Stocking Ground

[Loco shed - proposed but never built]

to Cambridge

New Cut

BR (ex LNWR)

River Great Ouse Navigation

to Bedford

0   100   200 yards

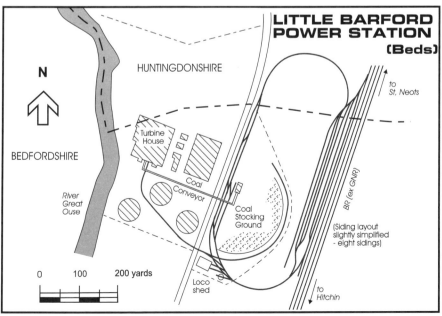

LITTLE BARFORD POWER STATION (Beds)

HUNTINGDONSHIRE

N

BEDFORDSHIRE

Turbine House

Coal Conveyor

River Great Ouse

Coal Stocking Ground

to St, Neots

BR (ex GNR)

(Siding layout slightly simplified - eight sidings)

Loco shed

to Hitchin

0   100   200 yards

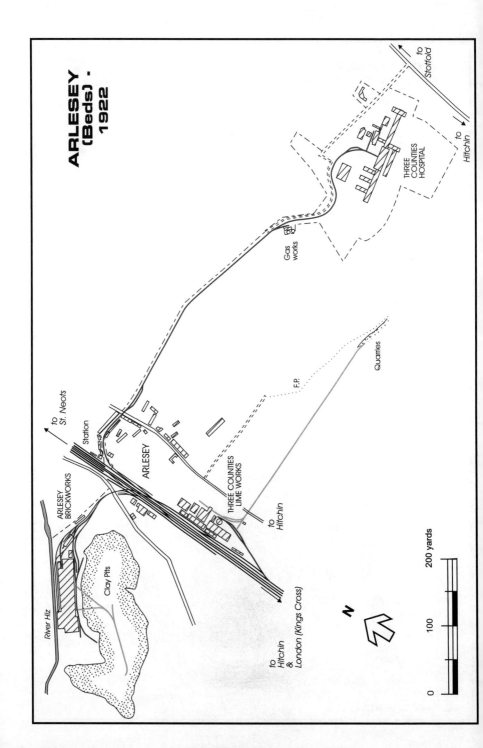

ARLESEY (Beds) - 1922

to Stotfold

to Hitchin

THREE COUNTIES HOSPITAL

Gas works

Quarries

F.P.

to St. Neots

Station

ARLESEY

ARLESEY BRICKWORKS

River Hiz

Clay Pits

THREE COUNTIES LIME WORKS

to Hitchin

to Hitchin & London (Kings Cross)

N

0   100   200 yards

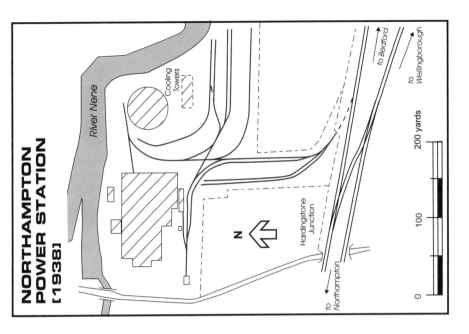

NORTHAMPTON POWER STATION [1938]

River Nene

Cooling Towers

N

Hardingstone Junction

to Northampton

to Bedford

to Wellingborough

0   100   200 yards

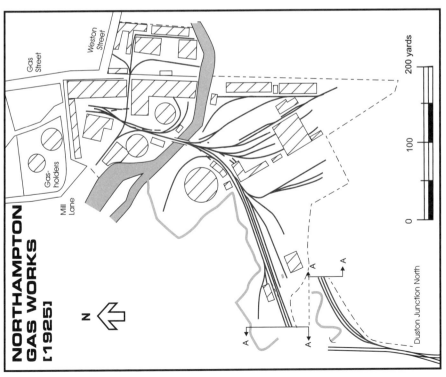

NORTHAMPTON GAS WORKS [1925]

Gas Street

Weston Street

Gasholders

Mill Lane

N

A

Duston Junction North

0   100   200 yards

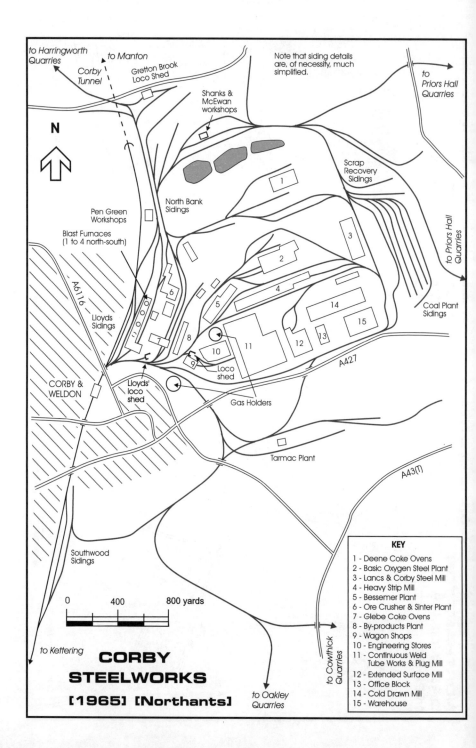

to Harringworth Quarries

to Manton

Corby Tunnel

Gretton Brook Loco Shed

Shanks & McEwan workshops

Note that siding details are, of necessity, much simplified.

to Priors Hall Quarries

N

Scrap Recovery Sidings

North Bank Sidings

Pen Green Workshops

Blast Furnaces (1 to 4 north-south)

A6116

Lloyds Sidings

CORBY & WELDON

Lloyds' loco shed

Loco shed

Gas Holders

to Priors Hall Quarries

Coal Plant Sidings

A427

Tarmac Plant

A43(T)

Southwood Sidings

0   400   800 yards

to Kettering

to Cowthick Quarries

to Oakley Quarries

CORBY STEELWORKS
[1965] [Northants]

KEY

1 - Deene Coke Ovens
2 - Basic Oxygen Steel Plant
3 - Lancs & Corby Steel Mill
4 - Heavy Strip Mill
5 - Bessemer Plant
6 - Ore Crusher & Sinter Plant
7 - Glebe Coke Ovens
8 - By-products Plant
9 - Wagon Shops
10 - Engineering Stores
11 - Continuous Weld Tube Works & Plug Mill
12 - Extended Surface Mill
13 - Office Block
14 - Cold Drawn Mill
15 - Warehouse

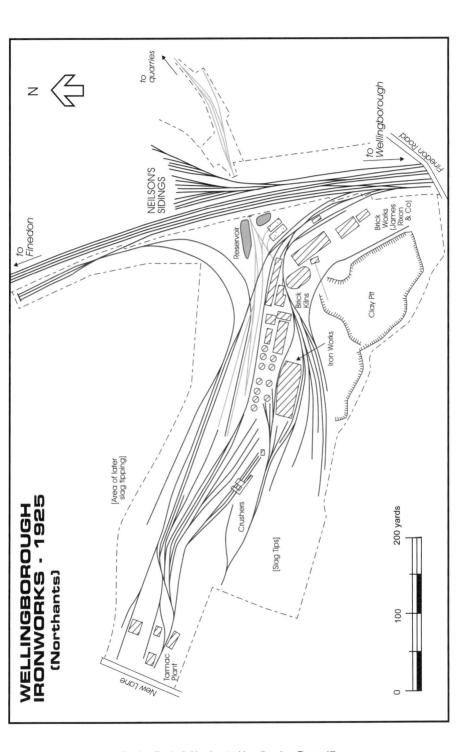

WELLINGBOROUGH
IRONWORKS · 1925
(Northants)

N

to Finedon

to quarries

NEILSON'S
SIDINGS

to Wellingborough

Finedon Road

Reservoir

Brick Works (James Rixon & Co)

Brick Kilns

Clay Pit

Iron Works

[Area of later slag tipping]

Crushers

[Slag Tips]

Tarmac Plant

New Lane

0   100   200 yards

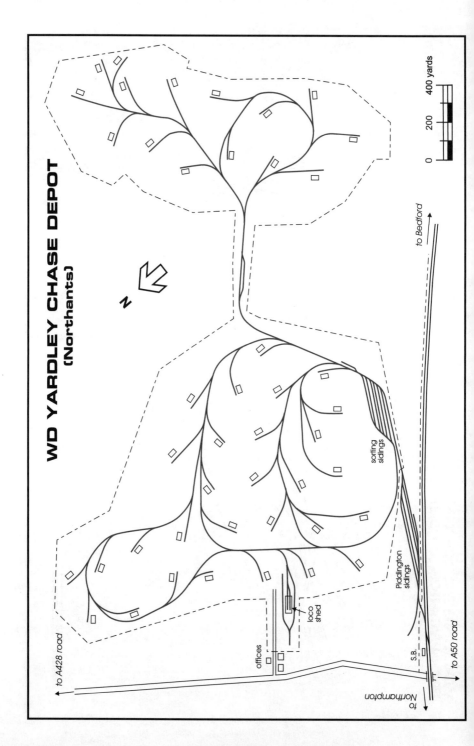

WD YARDLEY CHASE DEPOT
(Northants)

N

to A428 road

offices

loco shed

to Northampton

Piddington sidings

sorting sidings

S.B.

to A50 road

to Bedford

0 200 400 yards

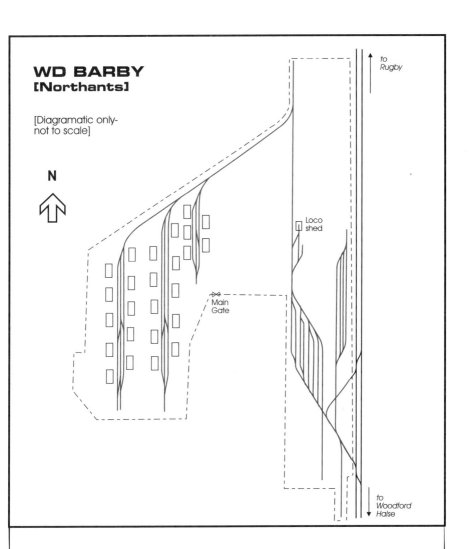

WD BARBY
[Northants]

[Diagramatic only-
not to scale]

N

to
Rugby

Loco
shed

Main
Gate

to
Woodford
Halse

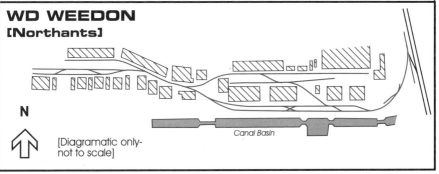

WD WEEDON
[Northants]

N

[Diagramatic only-
not to scale]

Canal Basin

BUCKINGHAMSHIRE

INDUSTRIAL LOCATIONS

AIR MINISTRY, ROYAL AIR FORCE
HALTON CAMP   A1
Royal Flying Corps until 1/4/1918

Standard gauge loco shed SU 877090
Narrow gauge loco shed SU 877091

This camp, built by **Sir Robert McAlpine & Sons** 10/1914-1915 (no known locos), was opened as an Royal Flying Corps Training Camp by 20/6/1917 and was located on the west side of Wendover Woods. A standard gauge railway (the Halton Light Railway) was constructed by German prisoners-of-war and was opened in 1917. This line ran from a point north of Wendover station yard on the east side of the Met / GCR line and then curved eastwards for about a mile to Halton Camp where it terminated near the workshops. A narrow gauge railway was also built during the First World War to carry timber from the nearby Halton Estate for use by the military. The narrow gauge line crossed the Tring road and terminated near to the standard gauge sidings in the camp; it remained until it was lifted early in World War Two. The standard gauge Halton Light Railway finally closed 4/1963.

Reference : "The Halton Light Railway", Tony Coldwell (private circulation), 1992.

Gauge : 4ft 8½in

	BENTON	0-4-0ST	OC	BH	1099	1896	(a)	(1)
	INCE	0-4-0ST	OC	HE	425	1887		
		reb		HE		1901	(b)	(3)
	SOUTHPORT	0-6-0ST	IC	HE	392	1886	(c)	(5)
No.112	HALTON	0-6-0T	IC	MW	1100	1888	(d)	s/s after 6/1938
	-	0-4-0ST	OC	WB	#		(e)	(2)
	-	0-4-0ST	OC	HL			(f)	(4)
AMWB 103		0-6-0ST	IC	MW	212	1866		
		reb		HC		1907	(g)	(8)
AMW No.188		0-6-0DM		JF	22885	1940	New	(9)
AMW No.219		0-4-0DM		JF	22966	1941	New	(6)
AMW No.223		0-4-0DM		JF	22970	1942	(h)	(7)
AMW No.240		0-4-0DM		JF	22994	1942	(i)	(7)

\# "Surplus" 1/4/1922 and "Machinery Market" 14/4/1922 stated that Humbert & Flint were to auction on 3-5/5/1922, re RAF Halton, plant including two locos by MW and WB; the WB loco has not yet been identified. However "Engineer" 2/1/1920 and "Machinery Market" 9/1/1920 stated that Humbert & Flint were to auction on 21/1/1920 re Ministry of Munitions No.1 Anti Gas Factory, Watford, plant including WB loco NOGI, four-wheel coupled, 10 x 15in cyls. This was WB 1493/1896 and since MW 212 came here from Watford, it is possible that WB 1493 came here also.

(a)   ex H.M. Nowell, East India Dock Improvements (1912-c1915) contract, London.
(b)   earlier G. Trollope & Sons and Colls & Sons Ltd, Oldham Aircraft Factory contract, Lancs, until 7/1919 at least; here by 4/1920.
(c)   ex Ministry of Munitions, Gretna, Dumfriesshire, SOUTHPORT, after 15/12/1920, by 4/1921. (Advertised for sale at Gretna in "Surplus" of 15/11/1920). Possibly to Air Ministry, Watford, Herts (for repairs?), by 2/1924; returned after 3/1924, by 9/1932.
(d)   arrived here after 17/7/1911, by 11/1929; earlier Logan & Hemingway, contrs. Possibly ex Ministry of Munitions, Gretna, /1920 (a MW 0-6-0tank, 13in cyls, 'No.4 DES 123' was advertised for sale at Ministry of Munitions, Gretna, Dumfriesshire, in "Surplus" of 15/11/1920; this loco may be HALTON).
(e)   origin and identity uncertain, but see note above.
(f)   ex HL, loan, /1925
(g)   ex Air Ministry, Watford, Herts.

| (h) | ex JF, Leeds, after rebuilding, 10/1954; earlier Air Ministry, Heywood, Lancs. |
| (i) | ex JF, Leeds, after rebuilding, 3/1955; earlier Air Ministry, Henlow, Beds. |

(1) later Ministry of Munitions, Woolston Rolling Mills, Southampton, Hampshire, by
     6/1919; for sale there 4/1923.
(2) for sale, 5/5/1922; s/s
(3) here until 11/1920 at least; spares ordered by RAF Stores Dept, Watford, Herts,
     8/1921 (loco may still have been here, or possibly at Watford).
     Later at "Ammunition Depot, Altrincham, Cheshire", by 11/1924
(4) returned to HL off loan, /1925 (too heavy for the track here)
(5) s/s after 9/1932, by 6/1938.
(6) to Air Ministry, Henlow, Beds, 1/1955.
(7) later Ministry of Public Building & Works, Burtonwood, Lancs, 4/1963.
(8) to Thos.W. Ward Ltd, Columbia Wharf, Grays, Essex, by 23/6/1949; scrapped c/1949.
(9) to Thos.W. Ward Ltd, Columbia Wharf, Grays, Essex, c/1956 (after 5/1955, by
     17/10/1960); resold to Eagre Construction Co Ltd, Scunthorpe, Lincs, by 7/2/1961.

Gauge : 2ft 0in

| - | 0-4-0ST | OC | KS | 1252 | 1914 | (a) | (1) |
| - | 4wDM | | RH | 191661 | 1938 | (b) | (2) |

(a) New to MacDonald, Gibbs & Co, WD Fovant Camp construction contract, Wilts; here
     by 8/1922.
(b) earlier Ministry of War Transport, Poppylot Farm, Southery, Norfolk; here after
     20/7/1943, by 26/7/1944, possibly for storage only, although it was repaired here in
     1944. Spares were ordered on 26/7/1944 for 'Divisional Road Engineer, Ministry of
     War Transport, Bedford' for delivery to "M.W.T., Halton Camp, Bucks", so the loco
     appears to have remained the property of M.W.T.

(1) advertised for sale at Halton Park Camp in "Surplus" 1/8/1922, 1/9/1922-1/3/1923,
     1/6/1923. If unsold then to Cohen & Armstrong Disposal Corporation- no further trace.
(2) to George W. Bungey Ltd, dealers, Hayes, Middlesex, c/1950 (by 31/10/1950); resold
     to Dinorwic Slate Quarries Co Ltd, Llanberis, Caerns, 16/11/1950.

JOSEPH ARNOLD & SONS LTD
STONE SAND PITS, Stone, near Aylesbury   D2
Joseph Arnold & Sons until 9/1937   SP 779127
earlier Aylesbury Sand Co, established c1911.

Sand pits, served by a narrow gauge tramway, in Eyethorpe Road, to the north of Stone
village, about two miles west of Aylesbury. Arnold's were trading here as the **Aylesbury
Sand Co** by 1928. Pits closed c1971, but much of the rail system remained intact for several
years after that.

Gauge : 2ft 0in

No.8	4wDM(ex PM)	MR	4599	1932	(a)	s/s
8	4wDM	MR	9409	1948	(b)	(1)
8	4wDM	MR	7215	1938	(c)	(1)

(a) ex Leighton Buzzard Quarries, Beds, after 11/1953, by /1957
(b) ex Leighton Buzzard Quarries, Beds, 29/11/1966.
(c) ex Leighton Buzzard Quarries, Beds, 29/11/1969.

(1) returned to Leighton Buzzard Quarries, Beds, 6/1973.

BLETCHLEY CONCRETE AGGREGATES CO

subsidiary of **Thos Roberts (Westminster) Ltd**

GREAT LINFORD GRAVEL PIT, Newport Pagnell

E3
SP 848427

Gravel workings, served by a narrow gauge tramway, to the north of Great Linford village and between the BR (ex LNWR) Newport Pagnell branch and the River Great Ouse. In 1943 the site was being worked by C.A.E.C. Howard (of Bedford). Tramway out of use by 10/1952 and locos stored under cover. Track lifted c1955. The company also operated gravel pits at Hyde Lane, Buckingham (SP 725352), which were in existence by 1943.

Gauge : 2ft 0in

| | 4wPM | MR | 5018 | 1929 | (a) | (1) |
| | 4wPM | MR | 5055 | 1930 | (b) | (1) |

(a)   new to Andrew Gray, Kirkcaldy, Fife; here by 10/1952.
(b)   earlier at Watling Street Pits; here by 10/1953.

(1)   to Goodman Bros Ltd, New Bradwell, near Wolverton, Bucks, for scrap, c/1955

WATLING STREET GRAVEL PITS, Fenny Stratford

E4
SP 875349

Company in existence by 1931; these gravel pits on the north of the A5 road appear to have been opened after 1943. Pits later closed and flooded. Locomotive information taken from makers' records.

Gauge : 2ft 0in

| - | 4wPM | MR | 5055 | 1930 | (a) | (1) |

(a)   ex Thrapston Washed Sand & Ballast Co, Thrapston, Northants.

(1)   to Great Linford Gravel Pit by 10/1953.

BRITISH FUEL CO

COAL CONCENTRATION DEPOT, Aylesbury

D5

Cawoods Ltd until 1989.
SP 804143
Southern Depot Co Ltd (subsidiary of NCB) until 5/10/1986.
earlier **G.W. Talbot & Son (Aylesbury) Ltd**

Coal Concentration Depot, established by the NCB but operated by the contractors as listed. Located at Griffin Lane, on the east of the BR (ex-Met Rly) Aylesbury - Quainton Road line, about half a mile north of Aylesbury station and served by standard gauge sidings from this line. Set up about 1967; rail traffic had ceased by 1990.

Gauge : 4ft 8½in

	-	0-4-0DM	RSHN	6990	1940	(a)	(1)
(D2324)		0-6-0DM	RSHD	8183	1961		
			DC	2705	1961	(b)	(2)

(a)   ex Coal Mechanisation (Tolworth) Ltd, Tolworth, London, /1967.
(b)   ex BR, York, D2324, 1/1969.

(1)   to Ben Reeves, Engineers, Chapel Lane Depot, Northall, near Leighton Buzzard, Beds, for scrap, /1972; scrapped c/1974.
(2)   to Redland Aggregates Ltd, Barrow-upon-Soar Rail Loading Terminal, Leics, c10/1989.

BRITISH RAIL MAINTENANCE LTD
WOLVERTON WORKSHOPS

earlier **British Rail Engineering Ltd**
earlier **British Railways Board**
London Midland & Scottish Railway until 1/1/1948
London & North Western Railway until 1/1/1923
London & Birmingham Railway until 16/7/1846

Major engineering workshops established by the London & Birmingham Railway in 1838. Steam locomotives were built here new up to 1863 and repaired until 1877. From 1864 it became the main carriage works of the LNWR and since then has been involved in the construction and repair of these, including electrical multiple unit stock in more recent years. For many years departmental steam locomotives were kept here for shunting work and until about 1930 they also hauled workmans' passenger services to and from Northampton.

A handworked system, of 1ft 6in gauge, was constructed within the works in three phases during 1980. It comprised three lines with several passing loops and a crossover to connect with the opposite side of the works. Disused by 10/1988.

On 6th June 1995 the works was transferred to the ownership of Railcare Ltd (which see) as part of the privatisation of British Rail.

Reference : The Trainmakers - The story of Wolverton Works, 1838 -1981, Bill West, Barracuda Books, 1982.

Gauge : 4ft 8½in

1118	ACTON	0-4-0tank IC	SB		663	1850	(a)	(1)
	Carr Dept 1	2-4-0CT OC	Crewe		228	1852		
		reb from 2-4-0 in 8/1868					(b)	Wdn 6/1896
	Carr Dept 2	2-4-0T OC	Crewe			1851		
		reb from 2-4-0 in 10/1868					(c)	s/s
	Carr Dept 3	2-4-0T OC	Crewe		204	1851		
		reb from 2-4-0 in 8/1867					(d)	Wdn 2/1897
	Carr Dept 4	2-4-0T OC	Crewe		186	1851		
		reb from 2-4-0 in 7/1864					(e)	Wdn 8/1895
	Carr Dept 5	2-4-0T OC	Crewe		217	1852		
		reb from 2-4-0 in 9/1864					(f)	Wdn 2/1895
	Carr Dept 1	0-6-0ST IC	Crewe	2107		1877	(g)	Scr 6/1937
	Carr Dept 2	0-4-2CST IC	Crewe	3437		1894	(h)	Wdn 3/1929
	Carr Dept 3	0-6-0ST IC	Crewe	2342		1880	(i)	Wdn 8/1959
	Carr Dept 5	0-4-2CST IC	Crewe	3438		1894	(j)	Wdn /1929
	Carr Dept 6	0-6-0ST IC	Crewe	1944		1875	(k)	Wdn 5/1959
	Carr Dept 7	0-6-0ST IC	Crewe	2200		1878	(l)	Wdn 11/1959
	Carr Dept 8							
	EARLESTOWN	0-6-0ST IC	Crewe	2308		1879	(m)	Wdn /1957
	1311-G	4wPM	Mercury	5337		1927	New	(2)
(9125)	TITCHIE	4wDM	SMH	103GA078		1978	New	(3)

Note that the locomotives listed as withdrawn were all later scrapped, at Crewe or elsewhere. It is likely that there were other early locomotives here, and latterly many locomotives still in capital stock (particularly of LMS Class 3F 0-6-0T and BR Class 08 0-6-0DE were used as works shunters).

(a)   ex traffic stock, 9/1865.
(b)   ex traffic department, 951, 7/1877.
(c)   ex traffic department, 70, 12/1877.
(d)   ex traffic department, 3076, 3/1890.
(e)   ex traffic department, 1974, 5/1886.

(f)   ex traffic department, 1866, 9/1885.
(g)   earlier Earlestown Wagon Works, Lancs, in /1932; ex LNWR 3260, 6/1896 (new as
      LNWR 2261, then 3260, 4/1895)
(h)   ex LNWR 144, 2/1895
(i)   earlier Earlestown Wagon Works, Lancs, in /1932; ex LNWR 1860, 2/1897 (new as
      LNWR 317; then 1860, 11/1896)
(j)   ex LNWR 3310, /1898 (new as LNWR 195, then CD 4, 8/1895; 1842, 2/1896 and
      3310, 4/1897)
(k)   earlier Earlestown Wagon Works, Lancs, in /1932; ex LNWR 3155, 5/1901 (new as
      LNWR 186, then 3155, 8/1892)
(l)   earlier Earlestown Wagon Works, Lancs, in /1932; ex LNWR 3416, 12/1911 (new as
      LNWR 2329; then 1946, 3/1896; 3317, 1/1901; 1548, 3/1909 and 3416, 11/1911)
(m)   ex Earlestown Wagon Works, Lancs; LNWR 2359 until 5/1881.

(1)   to Shropshire Union Railways & Canal Co, Pontcysyllte, Denbighs, 12/1870.
(2)   to Midland Railway Trust, Butterley, Derbys, 23/1/1980, via J.A.Corbard (Contractors)
      Midlands Ltd, Aspley, Notts, 19/1/1980
(3)   to Railcare Ltd, with site, 6/6/1995.

Gauge : 1ft 10¼ in

		4wBE			(a)	s/s

(a)   origin and details unknown

CASTLE CEMENT (PITSTONE) LTD
PITSTONE CEMENT WORKS, near Ivinghoe   A7
Tunnel Portland Cement Co Ltd until 1/11/1986   SP 932153
Tunnel Cement (Pitstone) Ltd (subsidiary of **Tunnel Portland Cement Ltd**) until 10/1950
Cement works opened in 1937 and located to the east of the ex-LNWR West Coast main line
railway and south of the Icknield Way road (B 489) about a mile east of Ivinghoe village.
Chalk was supplied from extensive quarries to the south east of the works whilst incoming
coal and outgoing cement traffic used a rail line which ran under the Icknield Way road to
exchange sidings with the main line just north of the works. Rail traffic ceased c1990; works
closed 20/12/1991.   Demolition of the buildings commenced in 9/1998 by Redhead
Demolition Co Ltd in order to clear the site for housing development.

Gauge : 4ft 8½ in

	NORSEMAN	0-4-0ST	OC	AB	1711	1921	(a)	(3)
	MONARCH	0-6-0ST	OC	P	1923	1937	New (b)	(4)
	ANGLO-DANE	0-4-0ST	OC	P	1318	1913	(c)	(1)
	SENTINEL 1	4wVBT	VCG	S	9547	1952	New	(4)
	BRAMLEY No.6	0-6-0ST	OC	HE	1644	1929		
			reb	HE		1938	(d)	(2)
	-	0-4-0DM		RH	310081	1951	New	(5)
2		4wDH		S	10159	1963	New	(9)
3	(SENTINEL No.3)	4wDH		RR	10264	1966	New	(10)
	T.P.C. No.5	4wDH		RR	10230	1965	(e)	(6)
211		0-4-0DE		YE	2854	1961	(f)	(7)
	-	0-6-0DM		WB	3160	1959		
			reb	Resco	L112	1980	(g)	(8)

(a) ex West Thurrock Works, Essex, c4/1937.
(b) to MoS, Farnley Opencast Site, Leeds, c/1942; ex West Thurrock Works, Essex, after 7/1945, by 10/1946.
(c) ex West Thurrock Works, Essex, after 10/1937.
(d) ex Thos.W. Ward Ltd, Grays, Essex, hire, c/1953 (by 10/1953); earlier WD Bramley, Hampshire and WD Tidworth, Hampshire.
(e) ex West Thurrock Works, Essex, c9/1976 (by 9/1/1977).
(f) ex West Thurrock Works, Essex, c5/1977.
(g) ex Resco Railways, 19/12/1980; formerly Mobil Oil Co Ltd, Coryton Refinery, Stanford-le-Hope, Essex.

(1) to West Thurrock Works, Essex, after 4/1946, by 8/1952.
(2) returned to Thos.W. Ward Ltd, off hire, /1954 (by 30/7/1954).
(3) to George Cohen, Sons & Co Ltd, Cransley, Northants, for scrap, 4/1964.
(4) scrapped on site by R. Fenwick & Co Ltd, Brackley, Northants, c7/1967.
(5) to West Thurrock Works, Essex, /1973 (by 9/1973).
(6) to Gartsherrie Works, Lanarks, c7/1977.
(7) to Padeswood Hall Works, Buckley, Clwyd [North Wales], 10/10/1980.
(8) to Ketton Works, Rutland, 2/1992.
(9) to Rushden Historical Transport Society, Rushden, Northants, 15/5/1998.
(10) to Staffordshire Locomotives, private location, 19/6/1998.

COMPAIR BROOMWADE LTD
BELLFIELD WORKS, High Wycombe C8
Compair Industrial Ltd until /1978 SU 863936
Broom & Wade Ltd until 1/10/1973

Works, located in Hughenden Avenue, to the north of High Wycombe town centre, on the west of the A4128 (Great Missenden) road, served by standard gauge sidings which ran north from the GWR/GCR Joint line about half a mile north-west of the station. Rail traffic ceased and track lifted.

Gauge : 4ft 8½in

1	4wPM	MH	30	1928	(a)	(2)
	4wDM	FH	3264	1948	(b)	(1)
T1	4wDM	FH	2102	1937	(c)	(3)

One or more locomotives of LNER Class Y3 (Sentinel built 4wVBT) were used on hire/loan at various times during World War II to assist the MH with heavy wagon loads, including military (fighting) tanks brought to the works for repair.

(a) ex George Cohen, Sons & Co Ltd, Stanningley, Leeds, /1935; earlier Leeds De-Tinning Ltd, Beeston, Yorkshire (WR), 11/1934 (for sale by George Cohen, Sons & Co Ltd, "Contract Journal" 3/4/1935)
(b) ex M.E. Engineering Ltd, Cricklewood, London, /1957; earlier Phoenix Timber Co Ltd, Rainham, Essex.
(c) ex Shell-Mex & BP Ltd, Trafford Park, Manchester, /1957.

(1) returned to M.E. Engineering Ltd, London, /1957.
(2) withdrawn c/1957; engine removed to repair a MH dumper and remains scrapped c/1959 (after 4/1958).
(3) to Quainton Railway Society Ltd, Quainton Road, 19/8/1978.

CRENDON GRAVEL & CONCRETE CO LTD
THAME ROAD WORKS, Long Crendon, near Thame   A9
SP 705080

Works, in production by 1940 and until at least 1953, to the east of the B4011 road about a mile north of Thame. Served by a narrow gauge tramway for internal traffic. Rail traffic ceased and track lifted. The works was later closed.

Gauge : 2ft 0in

-	4wPM	L	3834	1931	(a)	(1)
-	4wPM	MR	5265	1931	(b)	(2)

(a)   ex South Essex Waterworks Co, Langham Valley Works, Essex.
(b)   ex R.R. Paton Ltd, dealers, Cardiff, after 5/1931, by 1/1936; orig a Petrol Loco Hirers loco.

(1)   to George Ward (Moxley) Ltd, Baggott's Bridge Clayworks, Darlaston, Staffs [West Midlands], per Thos.W. Ward Ltd, Sheffield, 11/1935.
(2)   to Ribble Sand & Gravel Co, Samlesbury, Lancs, by 2/1940.

DUDLEY (WOBURN) TILE CO LTD
STATION WORKS, Woburn Sands   E10
earlier **Dudley & Sons** (by 1914 until after 1943 but before 1953)   SP 925362
Chas Dudley (by 1898)
James Dudley c1890.

Brick and tile works, sited immediately to the south of the LMSR station, served by an internal narrow gauge tramway. Rail traffic ceased and track lifted. Site taken over by Plysu Products Ltd for construction of a new factory.

Gauge : 2ft 0in

	4wDM	MH	22	1927	(a)	(1)
	4wPM	L	4460	1932	(b)	(2)

(a)   ex M.E. Engineering Ltd, dealers, Cricklewood, London, /1947; earlier M.J. Gleeson Ltd, contrs.
(b)   ex M.E. Engineering Ltd, dealers, Cricklewood, London, /1947; earlier O.L. Davies, Briton Ferry, dealers (Lister records state New to: "Mr Maberley Parker, Glamorgan").

(1)   to Perkins, dealer, Isleworth, Middlesex, c/1948.
(2)   to Stanley's Haulage Ltd, contrs, Watling Street, Hockliffe, Leighton Buzzard, Beds, but not used; resold to M.E. Engineering Ltd, 2/1960; and to Smith & Sons (Oil Distillers) Ltd, Rye Harbour, Sussex, 10/1960.

FLETTONS LTD
WATER EATON BRICKWORKS, near Bletchley   E11
Works SP 869326
Clay Pits SP 868325 and SP 868328

The company was registered 10/10/1924 and in the 1930s was controlled by **Henry Boot & Sons Ltd** (building and public works contractor). The brickworks, dating from 1929, was built on the site of Home Farm, on the west side of the ex-LNWR West Coast main line south of Bletchley station. Standard gauge sidings (built before 1938) connected with the ex-

LNWR Bletchley - Oxford line and are thought to have been shunted by main line locos. Narrow gauge system connected the works with clay pits. Rail traffic ceased and track lifted. The works was purchased by the Milton Keynes Development Corporation in 11/1969, and after demolition of the buildings the site was developed as a public park and nature reserve. Flettons Ltd, having disposed of its brick manufacturing assets, changed its name to Northborough Investment Trust Ltd on 24/5/1971 and continued to trade.

Gauge : 2ft 0in

	4wDM	MR	5634	1933	(a)	(1)
-	4wDM	MR	5635	1933	(a)	(1)
-	4wDM	MR	5636	1933	(a)	s/s c/1965
-	4wDM	MR	5637	1933	(a)	s/s c/1965
-	4wDM	MR	5873	1935	(b)	(2)
-	4wPM	MR	1933	1919	(c)	(1)
-	4wPM	FH			(d)	s/s
-	4wDM	MR	8588	1941	(e)	(3)
-	4wDM	MR	8592	1940	(e)	(3)

(a)   ex MR, 8/12/1933; earlier Petrol Loco Hirers.
(b)   ex MR, 1/8/1935; earlier Petrol Loco Hirers.
(c)   ex Willesden Urban District Council, London; earlier Wm. Moss & Sons Ltd, contrs.
(d)   ex Howard Farrow Ltd, contrs.
(e)   ex Bedford Silica Sand Mines Ltd, Heath & Reach Works, Beds, 6/1964.

(1)   derelict by 11/1953; to Flettons Ltd, Kings Dyke Works, Cambs.
(2)   to Kings Dyke Works, Cambs, c/1965.
(3)   to Kings Dyke Works, Cambs, 6/1964.

FOLLEY BROS LTD
Folley Bros until c/1943
(listed also as **W.E. Folley & Bros** at Newtown Pits in 1937)

FLACKWELL HEATH   C12
This company of sand and gravel merchants operated from headquarters at Flackwell Heath, near High Wycombe. Many spares orders for locomotives were recorded from this address, but it appears to have been purely an office; delivery was to be to other locations in all known cases. Wm. Folley had been listed in trade directories as a farmer from 1903 until 1928, whilst Folley Bros are listed from 1931 until 1939 as Gravel Merchants with pits at Flackwell Heath, Well End and Sonning. **WELL END PITS**, Little Marlow, (SU 883884) were being worked for gravel and sand by 1928 and closed after 1948. It is not known if a narrow gauge tramway was used at these pits, and no locomotives have been recorded there.

NEWTOWN SAND PIT, Marlow   C13
SU 864867

Sand pits served by an internal narrow gauge system. Workings at this site appear to have commenced after 1948, but before 1953. Rail traffic ceased c4/1957 and tramway dismantled.

Gauge : 2ft 0in

	4wDM	RH	229640	1944	(a)	(3)
-	4wDM	RH	211648	1942	(b)	(1)
-	4wDM	RH	223738	1946	(c)	(2)

(a)   ex MoS, by 4/1953
(b)   ex Sonning Eye Pits, Oxon, c/1954.

(c)   ex Sonning Eye Pits, Oxon, c/1955.

(1)   to Sonning Eye Pits, Oxon, c/1955.
(2)   s/s after 4/1958, by 8/1965
(3)   to Sonning Eye Pits, Oxon, c/1961 (by 9/7/1962).

G.F.X. HARTIGAN LTD
WOAD FARM PITS, Bedford Road, Newport Pagnell   E14
SP 883446

This old-established concern of public works contractors and gravel merchants became a limited company in 1933. Sand and gravel pits to the west of the River Great Ouse about ½ mile north-east of Newport Pagnell. Served by an internal narrow gauge rail system which was replaced by lorries in 1959 and dismantled by 1962. The quarrying operations of this company at this site only date from the 1950s, but it is thought that the company may have worked other quarries in the Rickmansworth area (exact location not known), possibly at an earlier date.

Gauge : 2ft 0in

-	4wDM	R&R	67	1935	(a)	s/s c/1958
-	4wDM	Diema	568	1930	(b)	(1)
-	4wDM	RH	193975	1938	(c)	(3)
-	4wDM	MR	8704	1942	(d)	(2)

(a)   believed new to G.F.X. Hartigan, at unknown location.
(b)   orig new to Richter & Pickis Ltd.
(c)   ex Billing Gravel Co Ltd, Little Billing Sand Pits, Northants, after 14/7/1941, by 17/2/1942.
(d)   ex Richter & Pickis Ltd, by 11/1953.

(1)   to unknown destination, Northampton, for scrap, 2/1957.
(2)   to Ace Sand & Gravel Co Ltd, Oare, Kent, c/1962.
(3)   to Charles Limb & Co Ltd, Saxilby, Lincs, repairs, c1/1951 (by 10/1/1951); returned after 28/3/1951; to Limb, Saxilby, again, by 23/1/1956; returned; to unknown destination, Rickmansworth, (possibly Vales Plant Register Ltd ?), c6/1962.

INNS & CO LTD
SAVAY FARM GRAVEL PITS, Denham   B15
TQ 050880

Gravel pits located to the north of the GWR/GCR Joint railway and to the east of the River Colne. The workings were served by an internal narrow gauge tramway. Tramway replaced by road haulage, c1964.

Gauge : 2ft 0in

-	4wDM	MR	5662	1934	(a)	s/s c/1955
-	4wPM	MR	7016	c1936	(b)	(1)
-	4wDM	MR	7046	1937	(c)	(2)
-	4wDM	MR	4807	1936	(d)	(4)
-	4wDM	MR	4806	1936	(e)	(3)
-	4wDM	MR	8598	1940	(f)	(5)
-	4wDM	MR	7457	1939	(f)	Scr c2/1969

	4wDM	MR	5932 1935	(g)	(7)
-	4wDM	MR	5933 1935	(h)	(6)

(a) ex Wheathampstead Pits, Herts, by 9/1949.
(b) origin uncertain, here by 9/1949.
(c) ex R. Fielding & Sons, Harlington Brickworks, Beds, by 9/1949.
(d) ex Henlow Pits, Beds, after 9/1949, by 6/1952.
(e) ex Waterford Shops, Herts, c/1955.
(f) ex Little Mardyke Pits, Essex, c/1961.
(g) ex Harper Lane Pits, Herts, /1963 (by 7/1963).
(h) ex Upper Sundon Rubbish Tip, Beds, /1963 (by 7/1963).

(1) derelict by 6/1952; s/s after 3/1953
(2) to South Hornchurch Pits, Essex.
(3) to Holwell Hyde Rubbish Tip, Herts, c/1963.
(4) to Nazeing New Road Pits, Herts, c/1963.
(5) to Waterford Depot, Herts, c/1964 (after 7/1963).
(6) to Caversham Pits, Oxon, c/1964.
(7) to Farnborough Pits, Hampshire, 6/1964.

INTERNATIONAL ALLOYS LTD
HAYDON HILL WORKS, Aylesbury

D16

SP 803143

The company was established in 1931 (and re-registered in 12/1938) and was one of the first secondary aluminium companies to be set up for the production of high quality aluminium alloy ingots recycled from scrap. The factory was located to the south of the Bicester Road, A41(T), about a mile north-west of Aylesbury. Served by standard gauge sidings which ran north from the Met / GCR railway. Rail traffic ceased c/1968 and the works closed in September 1982.

Gauge : 4ft 8½in

	4wDM	RH	210482 1942	New	(1)

(1) to Goodman Bros.Ltd, scrap dealers, New Bradwell, /1971; resold to N.V.Sobermai, Maldegem, Belgium, c6/1972.

Locomotives stored here on behalf of the London Railway Preservation Society:

L44		0-4-4T	IC	Neasden	3 1896	(a)	(2)
	(TOM PARRY)	0-4-0ST	OC	AB	2015 1935	(b)	(3)

(a) ex London Railway Preservation Society, Luton Depot, Beds, 5/11/1968, after attending the Midland Railway London Extension Centenary Exhibition at Bedford, 1/10/1968 - 4/11/1968..
(b) ex London Railway Preservation Society, Dunstable Town Station, 28/3/1968.

(2) to Quainton Railway Society, Quainton Road, 23/9/1970.
(3) to Quainton Railway Society, Quainton Road, 19/11/1970.

LONDON BRICK CO LTD

BLETCHLEY BRICKWORKS, Newton Longville, near Bletchley   E17

London Brick Co & Forders Ltd until 22/4/1936   SP 852325
Bletchley Brick Co Ltd until 1929
Read & Lamb until c1925.
Read & Andrews until 1915.
T.G. Read until 1907.
J.T. Read until 1903

Works opened c1890 by John Thornton Read. He was later joined by Richard Andrews and by W.T. Lamb & Son in 1919 and the works first produced Fletton bricks in 1924. Located on the south side of the ex-LNWR Bletchley - Oxford line ½ mile north of Newton Longville village, about one mile west of Bletchley station. Served by standard gauge sidings (installed after 1925, by 1927) connecting with this line and also by internal narrow gauge systems from the clay pits. The overhead wire system (220volts DC) was dismantled by 11/1953. All rail traffic ceased and track lifted. Works closed in 1991 and demolished c1994.

Gauge : 4ft 8½in

L 37	(L 2)	4wVBT	VCG	S	9322	1937	(a)	(2)
L 15	(16)	4wWT	G	AP	5935	1906	(b)	(1)

(a)   ex Calvert Works, by /1947; to Coronation Works, Beds, 4/11/1948; returned 23/6/1949.
(b)   ex Coronation Works, 8/11/1948.

(1)   returned to Coronation Works, 5/8/1949.
(2)   to Steel Supply Co (Eastern) Ltd, Stelco Works, Ampthill Rd, Bedford, for scrap, 7/1959.

Gauge : 2ft 11in (Overhead wire system)

2		4wWE				(a)	(1)
4		4wWE				(a)	(1)
4	(TX1)	4wWE	EE	776	1930	New	(2)
14		4wWE				(a)	(1)
26	3	4wWE				(a)	(1)

(a)   origin and identity not known; here by 6/1950.

(1)   one to Jubilee Works; the rest s/s by 11/1953.
(2)   to Stewartby Central Workshops, Beds, 11/4/1951; returned; noted derelict 11/1953; s/s by /1958.

Gauge : 2ft 11in (clay pits system)

L 34	(L 6)		4wDM	MR	5606	1931	New	(1)
L 26	B/L 2		4wDM	MR	5607	1931	New	(4)
L 94			4wDM	MR	10125	1949	New	Scr /1965
L 95			4wDM	MR	10126	1949	New	s/s c/1965
L 96			4wDM	MR	10127	1949	New	s/s c/1965
L 97			4wDM	MR	10128	1949	New	s/s c/1965
L 108	-		4wDM	MR	10430	1954	New	s/s c/1965
L 27			4wPM	MR	3738	1925	(a)	(2)
L 28	B/L 4	B/L 6	4wPM	MR	5026	1929	(b)	(2)
L 29			4wDM	RH	175828	1935	(c)	(3)
L 8			4wPM	H	937	1930	(d)	(4)
L 102	C/L 11		4wDM	MR	10159	1949	(e)	(5)

(a)   ex Stewartby Brickworks, Beds, by 23/3/1934.
(b)   ex Stewartby Brickworks, Beds.
(c)   ex Stewartby Clay Pits, Beds, after 8/5/1936, by 16/5/1936.
(d)   ex Stewartby Central Workshops, Beds, 6/11/1947.
(e)   ex Calvert Works, 6/9/1960.

(1)   later converted to 2ft 0in gauge (which see)
(2)   to Stewartby Central Workshops, Beds, 30/1/1950.
(3)   to Stewartby Central Workshops, Beds, 3/2/1950.
(4)   to Stewartby Central Workshops, Beds, 14/4/1950.
(5)   to Hick's No.1 Works, Fletton, Hunts, 29/1/1965.

Gauge : 2ft 0in

L 7			4wPM	MR			(a)	(1)
L 33	B/L 8		4wDM	MR	5601	1930	(b)	(7)
L 34	B/L 6		4wDM	MR	5606	1931	(c)	(7)
L 35	B/L 7	(L 9)	4wDM	MR	5667	1934	New	(5)
L 36	B/L 6	(L10)	4wDM	MR	5668	1934	New	(4)
			4wPM	L			(d)	(6)
L 30			4wPM	MR	4073	1927	(e)	(3)
L 31	(L 2)		4wPM	MR	3868	1929	(f)	(3)
L 32			4wPM	H	969	1930	New	(2)

(a)   origin and identity not known.
(b)   ex Arlesey Works, Beds.
(c)   converted from 2ft 11in gauge.
(d)   origin and identity not known.
(e)   ex Petrol Loco Hirers.
(f)   ex Petrol Loco Hirers, 30/6/1929; rebuild of MR 2181 formerly with Cleveland Bridge &
      Engineering Co Ltd, Truro, Cornwall.

(1)   dismantled by 1/1/1946; remains scrapped.
(2)   to Stewartby Central Workshops, Beds, 12/9/1947.
(3)   to Stewartby Central Workshops, Beds, 1/6/1948.
(4)   to Stewartby Central Workshops, Beds, 20/10/1948.
(5)   to Stewartby Central Workshops, Beds, 23/3/1949.
(6)   s/s by 6/1950.
(7)   to Stewartby Central Workshops, Beds, 9/8/1951.

CALVERT BRICKWORKS (ITTER'S BRICKWORKS until 1934)   A18
Itter's Brick Co Ltd until 30/10/1936   SP 687242
   (subsidiary of **London Brick Co and Forders Ltd** from 1928)
Itter Ltd from 1920 until 19/4/1926
A.W. Itter & Co from 1915
Exors of A.W. Itter (by 1911)
A.W. Itter (by 1903, until after 1907)

Itters Brick Co Ltd existed as a company until going into liquidation on 30/10/1936, having
been acquired by **London Brick Co Ltd**. From 1928 it had been 'controlled' by the **London
Brick Co & Forders Ltd**, under whose name it traded until becoming a subsidiary of **London
Brick Co Ltd** on 22/4/1936.

Brickworks established in 1900 by Arthur Werner Itter. Situated near Steeple Claydon on the
west of the ex-GCR main line to the south of Calvert station, served by standard gauge

sidings (in use by 1904) from this line and from the LNWR Bletchley – Oxford line . An internal narrow gauge system was used to transport clay from pits both north and south of the works. The line passed through a tunnel between the two pits. A further OHW 220volts DC, narrow gauge system served the works and kilns area. These systems were closed and dismantled by 1964. Standard gauge rail traffic ceased 6/12/1977 when it was replaced by road transport and track removed. Works closed 1991 and the chimneys demolished 28/6/1995; clay pits used as a landfill site. The clay pit at SP 683250 was flooded and became the Calvert Jubilee Nature Reserve, opening as such on 20/3/1978.

Gauge : 4ft 8½ in

L 15	(16)	4wWT	G	AP	5935	1905	New (f)	(5)
	PRESTON	0-6-0ST	IC	MW	205	1866	(a)	Scr /1928
	MIDDLESBROUGH	0-6-0ST	IC	MW	1598	1903	(b)	Scr /1938
L 85	(PL 7)	4wDM #		MR	3822	1925	New (c)	(1)
L 48		0-6-0VBT	VCG	S	6711CH	1926	New (d)	(3)
L 50	MAINDEE	0-6-0ST	IC	MW	1599	1903		
		reb		Adams		1932	(e)	(4)
L 47	1	4wVBT	VCG	S	9284	1937	New (g)	(7)
L 37	(L 2)	4wVBT	VCG	S	9322	1937	New	(2)
L 46	(L 1) PHORPRES	0-4-0ST	OC	WB	2586	1938	New	(6)
C/L 15		0-4-0DM		JF	22895	1940	(h)	(9)
MH/L 1		4wDM		MR	9922	1959	(i)	(10)
	-	0-4-0DM		JF	22888	1938	(j)	(8)

\#   rebuilt from 4wPM at unknown date

(a)   earlier L.P. Nott, Princes Risborough (GW/GC Joint) (1902-1906) contract; possibly came here c/1906.

(b)   earlier John Scott, Vittoria Dock (1906-1914) contract, Birkenhead, Cheshire; here by 2/1928.

(c)   rebuild using parts of MR 1337.

(d)   earlier Morris & Shaw Ltd, Birch Coppice Colliery, near Tamworth, Warwicks; loco was a rebuild of 0-6-0ST OC FW 383/1878.

(e)   ex A.R. Adams & Son, dealers, Newport, Gwent, /1938; earlier Easton Gibb & Son Ltd, Rosyth Naval Base (1908-c1918) contract, Fife, No.50.

(f)   to Coronation Works, Beds, /1940; returned 5/4/1950.

(g)   to Bearts Works, Beds, 4/1946; returned 13/5/1953.

(h)   ex ICI, Randle's Works, Runcorn, Cheshire, /1958.

(i)   ex Marston Hall Crushing Plant, Warwicks, 20/1/1962; returned 26/1/1962; to Calvert Works, 2/8/1966.

(j)   ex Joseph Pugsley & Sons Ltd, dealers, Stoke Gifford, Bristol, hire, 29/11/1965 (rebuilt by JF with Paxman engine in /1960).

(1)   to Stewartby Works, Beds, by /1945

(2)   to Bletchley Works, by /1947.

(3)   to Stewartby Works, Beds, 3/9/1947, for transfer to Fletton LB2 Engineers Depot, 8/9/1947; returned, /1947; to Stewartby Central Workshops, 17/11/1947.

(4)   scrapped on site by Cox & Danks Ltd, Bedford, 12/7/1948

(5)   to Cox & Danks Ltd, Bedford, for scrap, 10/1953.

(6)   to Furness Shipbuilding Co Ltd, Haverton Hill, Co.Durham [Cleveland], per George W. Bungey Ltd, dealer, (sale date 5/1959; sent away c6/1959)

(7)   to Steel Supply Co (Eastern) Ltd, Stelco Works, Ampthill Rd, Bedford, for scrap, 6/1959.

(8)   returned to Joseph Pugsley & Sons Ltd, Bristol, 15/12/1965.

(9)   to George Cohen, Sons & Co Ltd, Pendleton Depot, Lancs, c2/1980 (by 20/2/1980).

(10)   to George Cohen, Sons & Co Ltd, Cransley Depot, Northants, 4/1980.

Gauge : 3ft 1¼ in

L 11	(L 12)	4wPM	MR	3832	1926	New	(1)
L 43	(L 3)	4wPM	MR	3838	1926	New	(1)

(1) converted to 2ft 11in gauge.

Gauge : 2ft 11in (works and kilns system)

1		4wWE	LBC	New	s/s c/1964
2		4wWE	LBC	New	s/s c/1964
3		4wWE	LBC	New	s/s c/1964
4		4wWE	LBC	New	s/s c/1964
5		4wWE	LBC	New	s/s c/1964
6		4wWE	LBC	New	s/s c/1964
7		4wWE	LBC	New	s/s c/1964
8		4wWE	LBC	New	s/s c/1964
9		4wWE	LBC	New	s/s c/1964
10		4wWE	LBC	New	s/s c/1964
11		4wWE	LBC	New	s/s c/1964
12		4wWE	LBC	New	s/s c/1964
13		4wWE	LBC	New	s/s c/1964
31		4wWE	LBC	(a)	s/s by 12/1953
	TX 10	4wWE	LBC	(b)	s/s
16		4wWE	LBC	(c)	s/s c/1964
17		4wWE	LBC	(d)	(1)
-		4wWE		(e)	s/s
-		4wWE		(e)	s/s

(a)   ex Stewartby Works, Beds, 10/11/1947
(b)   ex Arlesey Works, Beds, 19/3/1956.
(c)   ex Stewartby Works, Beds, 6/2/1960.
(d)   ex Stewartby Works, Beds, 8/2/1960.
(e)   ex Jubilee Works, Skew Bridge, near Bletchley, 17/10/1960.

(1)   to LB2 Engineers Depot, Fletton, Hunts, 9/2/1951.

Gauge : 2ft 11in (tramway from clay pits to works)

L 40	C/L 5 (L 22)		4wDM	MR	5722	1939	New	(6)
L 39	C/L 4 (L 21)		4wDM	MR	5723	1939	New	(6)
L 41	C/L 6 (L 23)		4wDM	MR	5724	1939	New	(6)
L 38	C/L 3 (L 20)		4wDM	MR	5725	1939	New	(6)
L 91	C/L 7		4wDM	MR	7998	1947	New	(8)
L 92			4wDM	MR	7999	1947	New	(14)
L 101	C/L 10		4wDM	MR	10158	1949	New	(11)
L 102	C/L 11		4wDM	MR	10159	1949	New	(9)
L 105	C/L 12		4wDM	MR	10160	1950	New	(12)
L 106	C/L 13		4wDM	MR	10161	1950	New	(10)
	C/L 14		4wDM	MR	10455	1955	New	(13)
L 8			4wPM	H	937	1928	(e)	(1)
L 9	(L 10)	A/L 1	4wDM	FH	1914	1935	(d)	(2)
L 11	(L 12)		4wPM	MR	3832	1926	(a)	(4)
L 12	(L 13)		4wPM	FH	1913	1935	(c)	(3)
L 42	(L 24)		4wPM	MR			(f)	(7)

L 43	(L 3)		4wPM	MR	3838	1926	(b)	(4)
L 44	(L 4)	C/L 9	4wPM	MR			(g)	(5)
L 45	(L 5)		4wPM	MR			(g)	(4)

(a) converted from 3ft 1¼ in gauge;
to Stewartby Central Workshops, Beds, by 1/1/1946; returned 8/8/1946.
(b) converted from 3ft 1¼ in gauge;
to Stewartby Central Workshops, Beds, 11/11/1947; returned.
(c) ex Stewartby Works, Beds, 2/8/1946;
to Stewartby Central Workshops, 9/1947; returned 1/10/1947.
(d) ex Stewartby Central Workshops, Beds, 10/10/1946;
to Stewartby Central Workshops, 17/4/1947; returned 6/8/1947.
(e) ex Stewartby Clay Pits, Beds, 21/2/1947.
(f) origin and identity not known; here by 11/1950
(g) origin and identity not known; here by /1947 (when records were compiled).

(1) to Stewartby Central Workshops, Beds, 4/7/1947.
(2) to Arlesey Works, Beds, 31/12/1947.
(3) to Stewartby Central Workshops, Beds, 18/2/1948.
(4) to Stewartby Central Workshops, Beds, 30/4/1948
(5) to Stewartby Central Workshops, Beds, 12/9/1952.
(6) to Elstow Works, Beds, 30/6/1953.
(7) to Thos.W. Ward Ltd, 3/1954.
(8) to New Peterborough 2 Works, Fletton, Hunts, 15/10/1957.
(9) to Bletchley Works, Newton Longville, 6/9/1960.
(10) to Stewartby Clay Pits, Beds, 10/10/1950; returned to Calvert Works, 12/1951;
to Arlesey Works, Beds, 28/9/1957.
(11) to LB 2 Engineers Depot, Fletton, Hunts, 11/10/1960; then to NP2 Works, 7/3/1961.
(12) to Bearts Works, Beds, 11/10/1960.
(13) to Stewartby Central Workshops, Beds, 12/10/1960.
(14) to LB2 Engineers Depot, Fletton, Hunts, 18/10/1960.

COLDHARBOUR CLAY PIT, Loughton, near Bletchley   E19
Bletchley Flettons Ltd until 6/2/1951   SP 848360

Because of geological difficulties at the Skew Bridge Works, where overburden was 40 feet deep, a new clay pit was opened in 1945 at Coldharbour Farm, to the west of the A5 road and the LMSR main line two miles north of Bletchley. The clay from this pit was transported by road to Skew Bridge Works. The pit was later closed and became flooded. The site, now incorporated into the Borough of Milton Keynes, has been landscaped and redeveloped and is known as Furzton Lake. A second, smaller, clay pit was worked after 1958 on the east of the A5 road (at SP 851364); this was flooded by 1972.

Gauge : 2ft 0in

L112	J/L 1	4wDM	MR	5880	1935	(a)	(1)
	J/L 2	4wPM	MR	3990	1934	(b)	(1)
	J/L 3	4wPM	MR	1013	1918	(c)	(1)

(a) ex Jubilee Works
(b) ex Joseph Pugsley & Sons Ltd, dealers, Bristol; earlier Greenham Plant Hiring Co Ltd,
Isleworth, Middlesex.
(c) to Flettons Ltd, (unknown location) 4/12/1933; here before /1950 when taken over
with site by LBC; orig WDLR 2734.

(1) to Stewartby Central Workshops, 12/1950.

JUBILEE BRICKWORKS, Skew Bridge, near Bletchley

E20

Bletchley Flettons Ltd until 6/2/1951
orig **Bletchley Brick Co Ltd** until 1934
    (registered 1/11/1934 and managed by **Flettons Ltd**)

Works SP 870312
Clay Pits SP 868311

A.E. Lamb of Bletchley Brick Co constructed the **SKEW BRIDGE WORKS** in 1933 on the site of Slad Farm. It became Bletchley Flettons Ltd (registered 1/11/1934: managed by Flettons Ltd) and, after acquisition by London Brick Co Ltd, it was re-named **JUBILEE WORKS**. The works was closed in 12/1939 and not reopened until after 12/1940. The works was located about one mile south of Bletchley on the west side of the ex-LNWR West Coast main line at Skew Bridge. Standard gauge sidings (known as W.T. Lamb & Sons' Siding), shunted by main line locos, connected the works with the main line and a narrow gauge line, using an overhead wire electrified system, served the kilns. The system was replaced by fork-lift trucks and no trace of the narrow gauge remained by 1965. Works closed 17/11/1974.

Gauge : 2ft 11in (220V dc system)

-	4wWE		(a)	(1)
-	4wWE		(b)	(1)

(a)   ex Bletchley Brickworks.
(b)   origin and identity not known

(1)   to Calvert Works, 17/10/1960.

Gauge : 2ft 0in

-	4wPM	MR	3857	c1928	(a)	(2)
-	4wDM	MR	5880	1935	New	(1)

(a)   ex Petrol Loco Hirers (after 2/4/1928).

(1)   to Coldharbour Pit.
(2)   returned to Petrol Loco Hirers; later to Dan & Stone (and to Westbere Ballast Pits Ltd, Ramsgate, Kent, by 12/11/1938).

LONDON FILM PRODUCTIONS
DENHAM STUDIOS, Denham

B21
approx TQ 042883

The following locomotives were purchased for use in the film "Knights without Armour" in which they masqueraded as Russian locomotives.

Reference : "Locomotives of the LNER, Part 5", RCTS, 1966.

Gauge :4ft 8½in

-	0-6-0	IC	Str		1888	(a)	(2)
-	0-6-0	IC	Str		1889	(b)	(1)

(a)   ex LNER 7541, Class J15, 9/1936 (orig GER 541).
(b)   ex LNER 7835, Class J15, 9/1936 (orig GER 835).

(1)   later WD, 212; on Shropshire & Montgomeryshire Railway, 11-12/7/1942
(2)   later WD, 221; on Shropshire & Montgomeryshire Railway, 17-18/7/1942

MARLOW SAND & GRAVEL CO LTD
WESTHORPE PITS, Little Marlow

C22

SU 867870

Extensive gravel workings (adjacent to Folley's Marlow Pit) to the north of the River Thames and the ex-GWR Marlow branch railway about a mile east of Marlow. A narrow gauge system was used to convey gravel from the pits to an elevated tipping dock. Lorries loaded here then ran over a private driveway for about a mile to the main road. Pits closed and rail traffic ceased 1/1983. The railway was subsequently dismantled in 6/1983.

Gauge : 2ft 0in

-		4wDM	MR	4703	1934	(a)	(1)
3		4wDM	MR	7176	1937	(b)	(4)
-		4wDM	MR	9263	1947	(c)	(2)
3	(2)	4wDM	MR	5867	1934	(d)	(3)
4		4wDM	MR	8790	1943	(e)	(3)
5		4wDM	MR	21283	1965	New	(3)

(a)   orig new to Petrol Loco Hirers; reb to 4wDM at unknown date; here by c/1950.
(b)   ex David Way & Son, High Wycombe, 17/8/1948.
(c)   ex Richter & Pickis Ltd, by 6/1952.
(d)   ex George W. Bungey Ltd, dealer, Hayes, Middlesex, by 7/1954; earlier Hughes Bros (Derbyshire Granite) Ltd, Buxton, Derbys.
(e)   ex George W. Bungey Ltd, dealer, Hayes, Middlesex, after 7/1954, by 4/1958.

(1)   derelict by 6/1952; s/s after 4/1953.
(2)   to J. & A. Jackson Ltd, Adswood Brickworks, Cheshire, after 7/1954, by 4/1958.
(3)   to Track Supplies & Services Ltd, Wolverton, 26/3/1983
(4)   dismantled and frames used as buffer stop by /1979; then to Track Supplies & Services Ltd, Wolverton, after 5/4/1983, by 1/7/1983

MINISTRY OF AVIATION, ROYAL AIRCRAFT ESTABLISHMENT
ROCKET PROPULSION DEPARTMENT, Westcott, near Aylesbury

D23

Ministry of Supply until 21/10/1959

SP 708164

A former wartime airfield at Westcott was taken over by the MoS and became the Rocket Propulsion Department of the Royal Aircraft Establishment in 1947. Subsequent work there included the development of propellant for the ill fated Blue Streak missile. In 1958 Westcott became the Rocket Propulsion Establishment whose work has included the development of motors for Sea Wolf and other missiles. The works is situated to the south of the A41(T) road between Westcott village and the ex-GCR Grendon Underwood Jct - Ashendon Jct railway. It was served by sidings off this line and the northern section from the factory to Grendon Underwood was retained for this traffic. Rail traffic ceased in 1975.

Reference: "Action Stations", Vol.6, M.J.F.Bowyer, Patrick Stevens Ltd, 1983.

Gauge : 4ft 8½in

-	4wDM	RH	312433	1951	(a)	(1)

(a)   ex MoS, Eskmeals, Cumbs, after 23/8/1955, by 1/12/1956.

(1)   to Powell Duffryn Wagon Co Ltd, Maindy Works, Cardiff, 20/3/1976.

WILLIAM C. MORRIS
WALTON ENGINE WORKS, Aylesbury

D24

SP 825134

A firm of brass and iron-founders and agricultural and general engineers with premises in Walton Road, Aylesbury. Photographic evidence shows a narrow gauge locomotive and wagons in use (possibly for demonstration purposes) at this site. The works was later operated by Edward F. Morris in 1920 and was closed by 1931.

Reference : "Industrial Railway Record" No.94, Sept. 1982.

Gauge : (about 3ft ?)

	4wTG	IC	?	c1906 ?	(a)	s/s

(a)   origin uncertain; possibly built by Wm Morris.

OXFORD & AYLESBURY TRAMROAD COMPANY
WOTTON TRAMWAY

D25

Wotton Tramway until 1/4/1894

Brill loco shed SP 657153

The Wotton Tramway was built by the Duke of Buckingham using labour from his estate. Work began on the construction of the line from Quainton Road to Brill in 9/1870. Contractors Lawford & Haughton were used to lay the track which was of light construction, being 30lb bridge pattern rail. The line finally reached Brill station, 6½ miles from Quainton, in 3/1872. There was a branch of length about one mile which ran from Church Siding to Kingswood to serve the estate's brick and tile works. Traffic on the line was horse worked until the first locomotive arrived in 1/1872. On 1/4/1894 the line was taken over by the Oxford & Aylesbury Tramroad Co and subsequently the Metropolitan Railway took responsibility for its operation from 12/1899. Baldry & Yerburgh renewed the permanent way, 2-10/1894 (no known locos). The Kingswood branch was used to carry material during the construction of the GWR & GCR Joint Line, but was closed in 12/1915. The remainder of the line closed on 1/12/1935, latterly being worked by the well known Metropolitan 4-4-0T locos.

References : "The Brill Tramway", Bill Simpson, OPC, 1985.
"The Wotton Tramway (Brill Branch), Ken Jones, Oakwood Press, 1974
"From Quainton to Brill – a history of the Wotton Tramway", Ian Melton Undergound No.13 (Journal of the London Undergound Railway Society), 1984
"Metropolitan Steam Locomotives", Frank Goudie, Capital Transport, 1990

Gauge : 4ft 8½in

No.1		4wWT	G	AP	807	1872	New	(1)
No.2		4wWT	G	AP	846	1872	New	(1)
	BUCKINGHAM	0-4-0ST	IC	WB	16	1876	New (a)	(2)
	WOTTON	0-4-0IST	IC	WB	120	1877	New	(3)
WOTTON No.1 (HUDDERSFIELD)		0-6-0ST	IC	MW	616	1876	(b)	(4)
BRILL No.1 (EARL TEMPLE)		0-6-0ST	IC	MW	1249	1894	New	(5)
WOTTON No.2		0-6-0ST	IC	MW	1415	1899	New	(6)

Two further locomotives (not yet identified) were hired from C.D. Phillips, dealer, of Newport, Gwent, one (and possibly both) arriving 7/1893. Ther track proved unfit for these locos and they were returned off hire.
An advert in "Machinery Market" 15/12/1916 for Thos. W. Ward Ltd, Sheffield, included standard gauge six-wheel coupled ic saddletanks 12 x 18in, BRILL and WOTTON, by MW.

(a) ex WB, hire, 12/1876.

(b) ex Perry, Cutbill & De Lungo, Easton & Church Hope Railway contract, Dorset, 2/1894.

(1) to Nether Heyford Brickworks, Northants, (possibly in the ownership of Blisworth & Stowe Brick & Tile Co Ltd), 23/9/1895.

(2) returned to WB, c3/1878 and later resold.

(3) scrapped after /1894.

(4) to C.D. Phillips, dealer, Emlyn Works, Gloucester, "delivered", 18/6/1901 (probably became EMLYN No.87, for sale there 8/1901 to 10/1916).

(5) to Thos W.Ward Ltd, dealers, Sheffield, TW.23859, /1915; later F. Hayes & Isherwood Bros Ltd, Great West road (1922-1924), contract, Brentford, Middx, BRILL No.1.

(6) to Thos W.Ward Ltd, dealers, Sheffield, TW.23860, /1915; later Holland & Hannen and Cubitts Ltd, Downham Housing Estate (London County Council) (1924?-1930) contract, Kent, 3 DOWNHAM, by 8/1928 (prior to or after being with C.J. Wills & Sons Ltd, Becontree Housing Estate (London County Council) (1920-1934) contract, Chadwell Heath, Essex)

RAILCARE LTD
WOLVERTON WORKS, Wolverton

E26

SP 812413

A company (registered 13/12/1994) as a joint venture by Babcock and Siemens to take over the operation, from 6/6/1995, of the former BR Wolverton works as part of the privatisation of British Rail. [As this volume was closed for print, the operator of this site became **Alstom Railcare** (from 25/5/2001)]

Gauge : 4ft 8½in

08 484		0-6-0DE	Hor		1958	(a)
08 629	WOLVERTON	0-6-0DE	Derby		1959	(a)
	TITCHIE	4wDM	SMH	103GA078	1978	(a)

(a) ex BR, 6/6/1995, with site (08 424 and 08 629 being transferred from capital stock).

E.B. REED & CO LTD
IVER COURT BRICKWORKS, Iver
Edward Baron Reed from 1887 until c1926

B27

TQ 041802

A brickworks located to the east of Iver station on the north side of the GWR main line. Served by a narrow gauge tramway which ran from the works to a wharf on the Slough branch of the Grand Union Canal. By 3/1958 locomotive working had ceased, although the remaining 30 yards of track was still in use, presumably hand worked. The works is believed to have closed shortly afterwards.

Gauge : 2ft 0in

-		4wPM	MH		8	1926	New	s/s by 3/1958

RICHINGS PARK ESTATE (1928) LTD
RICHINGS PARK HOUSING ESTATE, Iver

B28

TQ 035795

Locomotives and narrow gauge tramways thought to have been used during the construction of this residential housing estate in the 1928-1930 period. "Machinery Market" 18/12/1931 notes : "to auction re Receiver of Richings Park Estate Ltd, Richings Park Gravel Pit, Iver - plant including a Simplex petrol loco" (presumably a locomotive additional to those listed below).

Gauge : 2ft 0in:

-	4wPM	MR	1798	1919	(a)	(1)
-	4wPM	FH	1657	1930	New	(2)
-	4wPM	MR	5363	1931	(b)	(3)

(a)   orig MoM, France, WDLR 2519.

(b)   ex Petrol Loco Hirers, 27/5/1934

(1)   to Wm Allbon (? - possibly W. Alban Richards & Co, contrs), by 5/6/1929; to FH; reconditioned and resold as FH 1671 to J.W. Ellingham Ltd, New Coastal Road contract, Herne Bay, Kent, 9/1930..

(2)   to FH; reconditioned and resold as FH 1672 to J.W. Ellingham Ltd, New Coastal Road contract, Herne Bay, Kent, 8/1930.

(3)   to E.J. Pugsley, Harrow Manorway, Abbey Wood, London SE2, 13/6/1935.

STEWART & PARTNERS LTD
COWCROFT BRICKWORKS, Ley Hill, near Chesham   A29
Wm. John Stewart until before 1928   SP 987017

COWCROFT BRICK KILNS & CLAY & SAND PITS, Ley Hill, near Chesham, (on the eastern side of Cowcroft Wood) were operated by **Stewart & Partners Ltd** in 1928 and until at least 1965. The works was served by an internal narrow gauge tramway, which was closed in 1958 and replaced by road transport. Subsequently the works was owned by **Dunton Bros Ltd** and closed in the 1970s.

Gauge : 2ft 0in

-	4wPM	MR	270	1916	(a)	s/s
-	4wPM	MR	1080	1918	(b)	(1)
-	4wPM	MR	1796	1918	(c)	(2)
-	4wDM	HE	1964	1939	(d)	s/s after 9/1959

(a)   here by 23/4/1927; orig MoM, France, WDLR 270

(b)   ex Bolton Waterworks, here by 23/4/1927; orig MoM, France, WDLR 2801.

(c)   ex Leeds Waterworks, here by 23/4/1927; orig MoM, France, WDLR 2517.

(d)   ex Dungannon Brick Co Ltd, Dungannon, Co.Tyrone, Northern Ireland.

(1)   later with South Devon Granite Co Ltd, near Tavistock, Devon.

(2)   later with P.D. Hayes & Son, Stockport, Cheshire, by 20/1/1933.

UXBRIDGE SAND & BALLAST CO LTD
SLOUGH ROAD PITS, Iver Heath   B30
TQ 043836

Company in existence by 1931. Information below taken from maker's records. Official FH locomotive records give FH 1835 as being owned by "A.S. Royle, Sandstone Pits, Iver Heath, Bucks". However, "Machinery Market" 22/9/1933 advertises the sale by tender of the business of Uxbridge Sand & Ballast Co Ltd, Sandstone Estates, Iver Heath, plant including a Montania oil loco. ('Montania' was a trade name for OK locos.)

Gauge : 2ft 0in

-	4wPM	FH	1835	1933	(a)	s/s

(a)   orig new to J.L. Rogers & Son Ltd (contractors of Castleford, Yorkshire (WR)), Sutton contract, Surrey.

WAR DEPARTMENT
HIGH WYCOMBE DEPOT   C31

The location and details of this depot are not known. It was possibly a storage facility holding surplus plant and stores prior to disposal.

Gauge : 2ft 0in

Ten 4wPM locomotives are stated to have been sent from this depot to F.C. Hibberd's works for overhaul, and presumably resale, about 5-6/1949. *Further late information on p.112.*

DAVID WAY & SON
WESTHORPE FARM, Little Marlow   C32

This firm of contractors, with an office address at Picts Lane, Princes Risborough, is listed in trade directories as early as 1928. A possible connection between this firm and the Marlow Sand & Gravel Co Ltd has not been confirmed, but it is possible that it operated gravel pits at Westhorpe Farm either before or on behalf of Marlow Sand & Gravel Co Ltd. Information below is taken from locomotive makers' records.

Gauge :2ft 0in

-	4wDM (ex PM)	MR	5412	1933	New (a)	s/s
-	4wDM	MR	7176	1937	(b)	(1)

(a)   ordered by Richter & Pickis for David Way & Son, Westhorpe Farm, Little Marlow.
(b)   ordered by Richter & Pickis for David Way & Son, at a site near High Wycombe.

(1)   later with Marlow Sand & Gravel Co Ltd, 17/8/1948.

WOLVERTON & STONY STRATFORD & DISTRICT NEW TRAMWAY CO LTD
WOLVERTON & STONY STRATFORD TRAMWAY   E33
Wolverton & Stony Stratford & District Light Railways Co Ltd until 15/9/1893.
Wolverton & Stony Stratford District Tramway Co Ltd until 10/1886.
Wolverton & Stony Stratford Tramways Co Ltd, formed 4/11/1882, until 6/9/1883.

The tramway company was incorporated in 1882 but construction did not begin until 1886. The line ran for 2½ miles from Wolverton station to the Barley Mow Inn in Stony Stratford. opened on 27/5/1887. In 1888 a two mile extension was opened to Deanshanger, where the line terminated at the green by the Fox & Hounds Inn, to serve the ironworks of E & H Roberts. Freight traffic from the foundry did not materialise and the extension closed in 1889. Competing bus services introduced in 1914 caused the decline of the tramway, which was in a near derelict condition when taken over by the LNWR in 1920. It passed to the

LMSR, and was finally closed on 4/5/1926 after the General Strike of 1926. The track was lifted between 10/1933 and 5/1934.

Reference : "The Wolverton & Stony Stratford Steam Trams", Frank D. Simpson,
Omnibus Society, 1981.
Locomotive Magazine, 15/2/1924.

Gauge : 3ft 6in

1	0-4-0Tram	OC	Krauss	1861	1887	New	(1)	
2	0-4-0Tram	OC	Krauss	1862	1887	New	(1)	
3	0-4-0Tram	OC	Krauss	1863	1887	New	(1)	
4	0-4-0Tram	OC	Krauss	1864	1887	New	(1)	
1	0-4-0Tram	OC	TG	43	1887	New	Wdn /1926; s/s	
2	0-4-0Tram	OC	TG	51	1887	New	Wdn /1926; s/s	
-	0-4-0Tram	OC	BE	308	1904	New	Wdn /1926; s/s	
5	0-4-0ST	OC	WB	2153	1921	New	Wdn /1926; s/s	

The Krauss locomotives were found to be underpowered, the first two being replaced in 1887. "The Engineer" 15/5/1891 advertised : "Durham, Gotto & Samuel to auction 11/6/1891, re Wolverton, Stony Stratford & District Light Railways Co Ltd, all plant including two condensing engines by Thomas Green three engines by Krauss, six cars, six trucks and two parcels vans".

(1) One loco s/s after 3/1889, by 6/1891; two more s/s by 31/12/1912, leaving one, apparently numbered 3 (but not necessarily the original 3) in unworkable condition at the takeover by the LNWR.

WOODHAM BRICK CO LTD
WOTTON BRICKWORKS, near Westcott   D34
SP 707188

Company established by 1937. The brickworks was located north of the A41(T) road and on the east side of the ex-GCR Grendon Underwood Jct - Ashenden Jct railway, adjacent to Akeman Street station. The works was served (by 1938) by a standard gauge siding from this line and by an internal narrow gauge system. Narrow gauge tramway closed c/1968. Works closed 1968 and plant sold by auction 2/1969.

Gauge : 2ft 0in

-	4wPM #	OK				(a)	(2)
-	4wDM	OK	6135	1935	(a)	(1)	
-	4wDM	OK	10283	1939	(b)	(3)	
-	4wDM	OK	10253	1939	(c)	(4)	
-	4wDM	OK	8986	1938	(d)	(5)	

- rebuilt from 4wDM at unknown date.

(a) origin not known.
(b) ex Wm. Jones Ltd, dealers, Greenwich, London, by 12/1953.
(c) ex Wm. Jones Ltd, dealers, Greenwich, London, c/1963 (by 8/1964).
(d) ex Wm. Jones Ltd, dealers, Greenwich, London, c10/1965 (by 11/1965).

(1) dismantled for spares by 12/1953; scrapped c/1957 (after 6/1956).
(2) derelict by 12/1953; scrapped c4/1959.
(3) to Wm. Jones Ltd, dealers, Greenwich, London, c/1961.
(4) to Wm. Jones Ltd, dealers, Greenwich, London, c3/1965.
(5) to Goodman Bros Ltd, New Bradwell, Bucks, by 21/4/1969.

CONTRACTORS LOCOMOTIVES

THOS BEIGHTON LTD
HIGH WYCOMBE CONTRACT   CC1

This company of public works contractors, which specialised in the construction of sewag
works, was based at Brimington, Chesterfield, Derbys. Details of this contract are uncertair
possibly construction work at High Wycombe Sewage Works.

Gauge : 2ft 0in

-	4wDM	RH 187102 1937	New	(1)	
-	4wDM	RH 182155 1937	(a)	(2)	

(a)   ex Whittington Sewage Works contract, Chesterfield, Derbys, after 27/8/1937, by
        21/12/1937.

(1)   to another contract ?; later to Chesterfield Corporation, Whittington Sewage Works,
        Derbys, by /1960
(2)   to another contract ? (after 10/2/1938); later to Chesterfield Corporation, Whittington
        Sewage Works, Derbys, by /1960

THOMAS BRASSEY
BLETCHLEY CONTRACT   EC2

Construction of the Bletchley to Oxford railway for the LNWR. First sod cut 20/4/1847 an
work commenced 7/1847.   Sections opened, Bletchley to Banbury on 1/5/1850; Verne
Junction to Islip on 1/10/1850; Islip to Banbury Road on 2/12/1850, and Banbury Road t
Oxford on 20/5/1851.

Gauge : 4ft 8½in

TRIO	0-4-2	IC	JTE 1838	(a)	(1)
KENNEDY	0-4-0	IC	Bury	(b)	s/s

(a)   earlier LSWR maintenance (1839-1853) contracts, Surrey
(b)   ex LNWR, Southern Division, hire (with option to purchase), 12/1849. (Loco was
        possibly one of LNWR 65 or 71 which were transferred from running stock to
        permanent way stock in 1848; these took the names KENNEDY and BURY (in no
        particular order) from two permanent way locos of similar type which, in 1848, were
        transferred to running stock as LNWR 61 and 82. However, the original records are
        unclear and the loco recorded as "KENNEDY" and hired to Brassey could possibly relate
        to either the then-present "KENNEDY" or the former KENNEDY.)

(1)   later Newport, Abergavenny & Hereford Railway working (1854) contract, Gwent

JOHN BRAY
NEWPORT PAGNELL RAILWAY CONTRACT   EC3

Construction of the line for the Newport Pagnell Railway Company from Wolverton t
Newport Pagnell (3¾ miles), authorised by Act of 29/6/1863.   The starting date is no
known, but work was in progress by 8/1864.   A first through train ("navvies special"
traversed the line on 30/9/1865.   There is a reference to the contractors being "Bray &
Wilson" but this is not substantiated.   An extension from Newport Pagnell to join the Midland
Railway at Olney (5¼ miles) was authorised 2/6/1865; work commenced 12/10/1865 bu
ceased on 2/6/1866 with little or no work done thereafter.

The line was opened to goods traffic 23/7/1866, and to passengers on 2/9/1867, being operated by the Company until the line was taken over by the LNWR pursuant to an Act of 29/6/1875 (hence possibly as from 1/7/1875). Initial arrangements for the operation of trains were that they would be operated by "the contractor" who would provide rolling stock, staff, etc. This may, or may not, refer to John Bray; in later years the contractor was John Taylor (which see).

The Company was in constant financial difficulties, and on 17/3/1868 there commenced a six-day auction of a wide range of equipment which included three tank loco engines 'the property of John Bray', presumably indicating his severance from the Company. These locos have been listed elsewhere as being 0-6-0 tanks by HC and MW, but the source of this cannot be traced. A possible candidate for the "HC" loco is listed below.

Gauge : 4ft 8½in

OLNEY	0-6-0ST	IC	MW	56	1862	(a)	(1)
-	0-4-0ST	OC	H&C	26	1864	(b)	(2)
	one other loco, details unknown						(2)

a) earlier James Bray & Co, contrs, at "Holden Clough" (the old name for Howden Clough) presumably for the Adwalton Junction-Batley (Leeds Halifax & Bradford Junction Railway) (1861-1864) contract, Yorks (WR)).

b) identity not confirmed here; H&C 26 was earlier John Wilson & Sons, Brighton-Tunbridge Wells (LBSCR) (-1867) contract, Sussex; for sale there 26-28/11/1867.

1) for sale, 3/1868; then or later to MW; thence ex works 15/9/1870 to E. Clark, Punchard & Co, Bedford & Northampton Railway (1870-1872) contract, Beds.

2) for sale 3/1868; no further trace.

CLEVELAND BRIDGE & ENGINEERING CO LTD
HIGH WYCOMBE CONTRACT   CC4

Construction of High Wycombe Goods Yard for GWR, 1937 - 1938. Chalk from cutting excavations here was transported for use by the **Caffin & Co**, Northolt – Ruislip (LT Central Line Extension) contract, Middlesex and so Caffin & Co may have had an involvement here.

Gauge : 4ft 8½in

NAIROBI	0-6-0ST	OC	WB	2169	1922	(a)	(1)

a) ex Pauling & Co Ltd, Crymlyn Burrows Plant Depot, West Glamorgan, 18, /1938; earlier Kilindini Harbour contract, Kenya.

1) to Darlington Works, Co.Durham, c/1939.

GEORGE DEW & CO LTD
NEW BRADWELL CONTRACT   EC5

Tunnelling work at New Bradwell, 1972, probably associated with that of the T. & A.M. Kilroe Ltd contract.

Gauge : 1ft 6in

-	0-4-0BE		WR	6600	1962	(a)	(1)
-	0-4-0BE		WR	C6711	1963	(a)	(1)

) ex T. & A.M. Kilroe Ltd, contrs, Manchester, by 4/1972.

) to T. & A.M. Kilroe Ltd, Newport Pagnell contract, by 1/1973.

HOWARD FARROW LTD
TAPLOW CONTRACT   AC6

Contract believed to be construction of sidings for GWR, c1940 - c1942

Gauge : 4ft 8½in

TRYM	0-4-0ST	OC	HE	287	1883	(a)	(1)

(a)   earlier Nott, Brodie & Co Ltd, Otterspool Riverside Promenade (1929-1933) contract, Liverpool.

(1)   to Colindeep (Hendon) Plant Depot, Middlesex, c/1941; repaired /1942; thence to Exeter St.David's Station Sidings (GWR) (1943) contract, Devon.

J. T. FIRBANK
METROPOLITAN RAILWAY CONTRACTS   AC7

J.T. Firbank undertook a series of contracts as follows – new lines from Rickmansworth (Hertfordshire) to Chalfont Road and Chesham in 1887-1889, from Chalfont Road to Aylesbury in 1890-1892, and rebuilding from Aylesbury to Quainton Road and Verney Junction in 1894-1897. This latter included conversion to double track of the former Aylesbury & Buckingham Railway, which had been taken over by the Metropolitan Railway on 1/7/1891. [Note that J. Firbank (Joseph) was the father of J.T. Firbank]

Gauge : 4ft 8½in

HENRY APPLEBY	0-6-0ST	IC	HE	45	1870	(a)	(1)
WELLINGTON	0-6-0ST	IC	HE	72	1872	(b)	(2)
RICKMANSWORTH	0-6-0ST	IC	HE	224	1879	(c)	(3)
GROOMBRIDGE	0-4-0ST	OC	HE	386	1885	(d)	(4)
WREXHAM	0-6-0ST	IC	MW	81	1863	(e)	(5)
AMERSHAM	0-6-0ST	IC	MW	129	1864	(f)	(1)
BOURNEMOUTH	0-6-0ST	IC	MW	655	1877	(g)	(6)
HARBORO'	0-4-0ST	OC	MW	901	1885	(h)	(7)

(a)   earlier J. Firbank, Derby - Burton (GNR) (1875-1878) contract, Derbys.

(b)   earlier Smardale - New Biggin (Midland Railway, Settle & Carlisle) (1870-1875) contract, Westmorland.

(c)   earlier Lucas & Aird, Hull, Barnsley & West Riding Junction Railway & Dock (1881-1885) construction, Yorkshire (ER).

(d)   earlier J. Firbank, Oxted & Groombridge Rly (LBSCR)(1885-1888) contract, Surrey/Sussex.

(e)   earlier J. Woolley, Buckley Junction–Shotton (WM&CQJR) (1889-1890) contract, Flint [North Wales].

(f)   earlier Kelk & Lucas, Alexandra Palace and railways (1864-1873) construction, London. ALEXANDRA, and later with Lucas & Aird at unknown location until 1/1883 at least.

(g)   earlier Christchurch–Brockenhurst (LSWR) (1885-1888) contract, Hampshire.

(h)   earlier Christchurch–Brockenhurst (LSWR) (1885-1888) contract, Hampshire; and possibly used at Market Harborough new lines & widening (Midland Railway/LNWR) (1882-1886) contract, Leics.

(1)   later Marylebone–St.John's Wood (MS&LR) (1894-1899) contract, London.

(2)   later Hunslet Railway (GNR) (1896-1899) contract, Yorkshire (WR), by 9/1898.

(3)   later Hunslet Railway (GNR) (1896-1899) contract, Yorkshire (WR), by 9/1897.

(4)   later Hunslet Railway (GNR) (1896-1899) contract, Yorkshire (WR), by 5/1898.

(5)   later Paddock Wood–Hawkhurst (SER) (1891-1893) contract, Kent.

(6) later Acton–Northolt (GWR) (1899-1905) contract, Middlesex, by 5/1900.

(7) later Acton–Northolt (GWR) (1899-1905) contract, Middlesex, by 2/1901.

A loco of name CHESHAM is reputed to have worked on this contract. It has been described as an unidentified 0-6-0ST built by FW, and is said to have been subsequently used on the Hawkhurst–Paddock Wood contract in Kent. Photographs exist of a CHESHAM 0-4-0ST OC, thought to be the unidentified four-coupled loco named CHESHAM that was repaired at Brighton Works (LBSCR), in 12/1893, for J.T.Firbank, who apparently had it in use on Redgate Mill–Eridge (LBSCR) (-1894) alterations contract, Sussex.

T. & A.M. KILROE LTD
NEWPORT PAGNELL CONTRACT   EC8

Construction of sewage outfall and associated works at Newport Pagnell, 1972 -1973.

Gauge : 1ft 6in

-	4wBE	CE	5827	1970	(a)	(4)
MB 433	0-4-0BE	WR	(? 4320)		(b)	(5)
-	4wBE	CE	5858	1971	(c)	(3)
-	0-4-0BE	WR	6600	1962	(d)	(1)
-	0-4-0BE	WR	C6711	1963	(d)	(3)
-	0-4-0BE	WR	N7611	1972	New	(2)
-	0-4-0BE	WR	N7612	1973	New	(3)
-	0-4-0BE	WR	N7612	1973	New	(3)
-	0-4-0BE	WR	N7613	1973	New	(3)
-	0-4-0BE	WR	N7614	1973	New	(3)

(a) ex A. Waddington & Son Ltd, contrs, hire, /1972.

(b) ex Mitchell, Sons & Co Ltd, Peterborough, Cambs, /1972.

(c) ex Anglo-Scottish Plant Ltd, Peterborough, Cambs, /1972.

(d) ex hire to George Dew & Co Ltd, New Bradwell contract, /1972.

(1) to Widnes contract, Lancs, c8/1973.

(2) to Widnes contract, Lancs, c6/1973.

(3) returned to Radcliffe Plant Depot, Lancs, after completion of contract.

(4) returned to A. Waddington & Son Ltd, off hire, on completion of contract.

(5) returned to Mitchell, Sons & Co Ltd, off hire, on completion of contract.

MACKAY & DAVIES
HIGH WYCOMBE CONTRACT   AC9

Reconstruction and doubling of the existing GWR High Wycombe to Princes Risborough railway, and building of 3¾ miles of new railway north of Princes Risborough, to become the GWR/GCR Joint Line. Tenders for the job were required by 6/5/1902; on 3/7/1902 it was reported as "recently let" and on 10/7/1902 it was reported that work had begun. The line was opened to goods traffic on 20/11/1905, and to passengers on 2/4/1906.

There was a series of sales at the end of the contract, conducted by C.D. Phillips Junior, which included locomotives. An initial advert (*Contract Journal* 10/5/1905) listed three 6wc locos 14in, 13in and 12in, plus three 4wc locos 10in, 9in and 8in, but subsequently on 14/6/1905 the advert listed two 6wc and three 4wc, and gave the sale date as 28-29/6/1905. It appears the locos were not then sold, as a later sale held 19-20/10/1905 was listed as including three 6wc 13in and 12in, and two 4wc 9in and 8in locos. Either one c two locos had been sold at different times, or else errors were made in the advertising. It i considered significant that five locomotives, fitting the description of those last sold appeared as new entries in the catalogue of C.D. Phillips, dealer, Gloucester, in 4/1906.

Gauge : 4ft 8½in

DONALD (or DOLLY ?)	0-6-0ST	IC	HE	63	1871	(a)	(1)
HELEN	0-6-0ST	IC	MW	620	1876	(b)	(2)
(HAROLD ?)	0-6-0ST	IC	K	(1829	1872?)	(c)	(3)
MAY	0-4-0ST	OC	(BH ?)				
		reb	C.D. Phillips			(d)	(4)
(MINNIE ?)	0-4-0ST	OC	MW	893	1884	(e)	(5)
JANE (or SAM ?)	0-4-0ST	OC	HC	444	1895	(f)	(6)

(a) earlier S. Pearson & Son Ltd, Wootton Bassett-Patchway (GWR) (1897-1903) contract, Wilts/, CWM TAFF, until 8/1902 at least; with Mackay & Davies by 4/1903 at unknown location, but a photograph taken near Saunderton is apparently of this loco.

(b) earlier Bassaleg-Risca widening (GWR) (1898-1910) contract, Gwent.

(c) possibly this was earlier with C.D. Phillips, dealer, EMLYN No.70 (which was with Phillips until 4/1899 at least, and may have been hired to Mackay & Davies on Bassaleg-Risca widening (GWR) (1898-1910) contract, Gwent). A photograph taken a Saunderton appears to be of this loco.

(d) photographed at West Wycombe. Origin unknown, though obviously earlier in the hands of C.D. Phillips.

(e) not confirmed here, but was with Mackay & Davies at unknown location in early 1900 (per MW records); earlier London & India Docks Joint Committee; thence sold "to a firn in Gloucester in 1900" [which could well be C.D. Phillips, hence may be item 2642g in Phillips Register until 2/1899, if the 1900 date above is not precise].

(f) not confirmed here, but earlier S. Pearson & Son Ltd, Wootton Bassett-Patchway (GWF (1897-1903) contract, Wilts/Glos, 57 SAM, and subsequently owned by Mackay & Davies. The Leicester Collection reputedly includes a photograph of "HC 444 SAM No.75" [sic] taken at Princes Risborough.

(1) believed to C.D. Phillips, dealer, Gloucester, EMLYN No.102, for sale 4-10/1906; s/s.

(2) believed to C.D. Phillips, dealer, Gloucester, EMLYN No.103, for sale 4-11/1906; s/s.

(3) believed to C.D. Phillips, dealer, Gloucester, EMLYN No.104, for sale 4/1906-6/1908; s/s.

(4) believed to C.D. Phillips, dealer, Gloucester, EMLYN No.105, for sale 4-8/1906; s/s.

(5) if here, then believed to C.D. Phillips, dealer, Gloucester, EMLYN No.106, for sale 4/1906-7/1907; s/s

(6) later Mackay & Davies, Craig-yr-Hesg Quarry, Pontypridd, Mid Glamorgan.

MILLER BROTHERS & BUCKLEY LTD
MILTON KEYNES CONTRACT   EC10

Construction of Tongwell Trunk Sewers, Milton Keynes, 2/1973 - ?

Gauge : 1ft 6in

L12	4wBE	CE	5965A	1973	New	(1)
L13	4wBE	CE	5965B	1973	New	(1)
L14	4wBE	CE	5965C	1973	New	(1)

(1) returned to Rugby Plant Depot, Warwicks, on completion of contract.

THOMAS NELSON
BLETCHLEY CONTRACT

EC11

Bletchley - Roade railway widening for LNWR.
See entry in Northamptonshire for details.

L. P. NOTT LTD
PRINCES RISBOROUGH CONTRACT

AC12

Construction of the new railway from a point 3¾ miles north of Princes Risborough to Grendon Underwood for the Great Western & Great Central Railways Joint Committee. The contract had been let by 3/7/1902; work apparently started in 6/1902. The line was opened to goods traffic on 20/11/1905, and to passengers 2/4/1906. During this contract, a materials access depot was established at Wotton station (Wotton Tramway) and a shed for three of the contract locos was erected there.

Gauge : 4ft 8½in

HADDENHAM	0-4-0ST	OC	HC	599	1902	New	(1)
CHEARSLEY	0-4-0ST	OC	HC	637	1903	New †	(2)
LIVERPOOL	0-4-0ST	OC	MW	1518	1901	(a)	(3)
PETERHEAD	0-6-0ST	IC	MW	1378	1898	(b)	(4)
PRESTON	0-6-0ST	IC	MW	205	1866	(b)	(5)
LLANELLY	0-6-0T	IC	MW	1065	1888	(b)	(6)
BIRKENHEAD	0-4-0ST	OC	HC	650	1903	New	(7)
TRANMERE	0-6-0ST	IC	HC	654	1903	New	(8)
LLIEDI	0-4-0ST	OC	HE	199	1878	(c)	(6)
NORMAN	0-6-0ST	IC	HE	454	1888	(d)	(9)
SWANSEA	0-6-0ST	IC	MW	818	1882	(e)	(10)

† Photographed on this contract and may have been new here but this is not confirmed by HC records. Ordered by L.P. Nott at a Bristol address with delivery address not recorded.

In the "Contract Journal", 6/12/1905, G.N.Dixon advertises for sale on 14-16/2/1906 from this contract five 4 & 6-coupled locos, 10, 12 and 13in, built 1902-3 by MW, HE and HC.

a) earlier Canada Branch Dock No.2 (1900-1903) contract, Liverpool.
b) earlier North Dock (1898-1903) contract, Llanelly, Carms [Dyfed]
c) here by 14/5/1904; earlier Lliedi Reservoir (1900-) contract, Carms [Dyfed]
d) photographed on this contract and owned by L.P.Nott (unknown location) 22/5/1903; earlier H.M. Nowell to 12/1902 at least (and was very possibly the 12in 6wc HE for sale on 12/5/1903 at Dunston Coal Staithes (NER) (1898-1903) contract, Co.Durham).
e) photographed at Grendon Underwood on this contract and has been mis-identified as MW 595 in some sources. Earlier with L.P. Nott in Liverpool, hence probably at Canada Branch Dock No.2 (1900-1903) contract, Liverpool.

1) later Topham, Jones & Railton Ltd, Kings Dock (1904-1909) contract, Swansea, West Glamorgan, 32 HADDENHAM, in or by /1907
2) later Topham, Jones & Railton Ltd, by /1913 (and probably in or by /1907 as is thought to be TJR number 31, and possibly also used at Kings Dock, Swansea).
3) later Llwyn-on Reservoir (1910-1915) contract, Mid Glamorgan
4) to H.M. Nowell, Grange Park Jn - Cuffley (GNR) (1906-1910) contract, Herts.
5) to Itters Ltd, Calvert Brickworks, possibly c/1906.
6) later Birkenhead Shipyards (Cammell Laird & Co Ltd) (1902-1909) contracts, Cheshire.
7) later Edmund Nuttall, Sons & Co Ltd, of Trafford Park, Manchester, by /1911.

(8)   later Buchanan's Flour Mills Ltd, Seacombe, Cheshire, SILVER QUEEN, after 10/1904, by 3/1913.

(9)   possibly later Birkenhead Shipyards (Cammell Laird & Co Ltd) (1902-1909) contracts, Cheshire; later Llwyn-on Reservoir (1910-1915) contract, Mid Glamorgan, by 5/1912.

(10) later Ministry of Works, Bramley, Hampshire, by 2/1921

EDMUND NUTTALL, SONS & CO (LONDON) LTD
COLNBROOK PLANT DEPOT   BC13
TQ 035766

Company registered 9/1935. Locomotives kept at this plant depot between use o¤ contracts.

Gauge : 4ft 8½ in

	BARRY	0-6-0ST	IC	HC	440	1896	(a)	(2)
	ASHENDON	0-6-0ST	IC	MW	1733	1908	(b)	(1)
S L 1	NUTTALL	0-6-0ST	OC	HE	1685	1931	(c)	(3)
S L 2	CUNARDER	0-6-0ST	OC	HE	1690	1931	(d)	(4)
(S L 3	WALLASEY) E N 3	0-6-0ST	OC	HE	1686	1931	(e)	(5)
S L 4	SOUTHERN	0-6-0ST	OC	HE	1688	1931	(f)	(5)

(a)   ex Motspur Park - Chessington (SR) contract, Surrey, 3/1939; purchased from George Cohen, Sons & Co Ltd, London, 12/1936; earlier C.J. Wills & Sons Ltd, Becontree housing contract (London County Council), Essex (so possibly also here between 12/1936 and 3/1937.)

(b)   ex Motspur Park - Chessington (SR) contract, Surrey, 3/1939; earlier Walter Scott & Middleton Ltd, contrs (purchased 16/6/1937)

(c)   ex Wallasey contract, Cheshire, 3/1939; to Glascoed ROF contract, Gwent, 8/1939; ex MoFP Temple Newsam Opencast Coal Disposal Point, Waterloo Main, Yorkshire (WR), (where on hire and used by operators Sir Lindsay Parkinson & Co Ltd), 9/1947.

(d)   ex Glascoed ROF contract, Gwent, 9/1940; to Hirwaun ROF contract, Mid Glamorgan, 9/1941; returned 12/1941; to Whitehall Securities Corporation Ltd, Purfleet, Essex, hire, 4/1944; returned 8/1944; to Samuel Williams & Sons Ltd, Dagenham, Essex, hire, 1/1945; returned 9/1945; to Ransomes & Rapier Ltd, Ipswich, Suffolk, hire, 10/1947; returned, 3/1948; to Cliff Quay Power Station contract, Ipswich, 3/1949; returned 2/1952; to Metal Union Ltd, (Plant Dealers ?), unknown location, 12/1952; returned 6/1953; to Samuel Williams & Sons Ltd, Dagenham, Essex, hire, 11/1954; returned 3/1955.

(e)   ex Glascoed ROF contract, Gwent, 3/1941; to Hirwaun ROF contract, Mid Glamorgan, 9/1941; returned 6/1942; to MoFP Temple Newsam Opencast Coal Disposal Point, Waterloo Main, Yorkshire (WR), (where on hire and used by operators Sir Lindsay Parkinson & Co Ltd), 8/1942; returned 9/1946; to HE, Leeds, for overhaul, 9/1947; returned 1/1948; to Samuel Williams & Sons Ltd, Dagenham, Essex, hire, 7/1952; returned 4/1953; to Samuel Williams & Sons Ltd, Dagenham, Essex, hire, 10/1954; returned 4/1956.

(f)   ex Glascoed ROF contract, Gwent, 9/1940; to Hirwaun (ROF) contract, Mid Glamorgan, 9/1941; returned, 3/1942; to Pontrilas ROF contract, Herefordshire, by 12/1942; returned 9/1943; to British Sugar Corporation Ltd, Ipswich, Suffolk, hire, 9/1945; ex Cliff Quay Power Station contract, Ipswich, 2/1950.

(1)   to Joseph Pugsley & Sons Ltd, dealers, Stoke Gifford, 9/1940; re-sold to Keighley Corporation, Keighley Gas Works, Yorkshire (WR), /1941 (after 3/1941).

(2) sold to Demolition & Construction Co Ltd, London, 10/1941; at Lever Bros (Port Sunlight) Ltd, Cheshire, by 12/1941.

(3) sold to MoFP, unknown location, per plant merchants, 7/1948; to NCB, Walsall Wood Colliery, Staffs [West Midlands], 7/1948.

(4) to APCM Ltd, Harbury Cement Works, Warwicks, per R.L. Smith, machinery merchant, 3/1957.

(5) to Purfleet-Dartford Road Tunnel contract, Essex; thence to Tunnel Portland Cement Co Ltd, West Thurrock, Essex, c11/1959 (by 5/1960)

Gauge : 3ft 0in

-	4wBE	GB	420274-1	1970	New	(1)
-	4wBE	GB	420274-2	1970	New	(1)
-	4wDM	MR	60S393	1970	New	(1)

(1) to Foyers Hydro-Electric contract, Inverness-shire, /1970

Gauge : 2ft 0in

-	4wDM	RH	175122	1935	(a)	(1)
-	4wDM	RH	175123	1935	(b)	(2)
-	4wDM	RH	175129	1935	(c)	(3)
-	4wDM	RH	181822	1936	(d)	(4)
-	4wDM	RH	182134	1936	(e)	(5)
-	4wDM	RH	183768	1937	(f)	(6)
-	4wDM	RH	183750	1937	(g)	(7)
-	4wDM	RH	189949	1938	(h)	(8)
-	4wDM	RH	189952	1938	(i)	(9)
	4wDM	RH	189943	1938	(j)	s/s after 1/1954
EN 1	4wBE	GB	1426	1936	(k)	s/s
EN 2	4wBE	GB	1427	1936	(k)	s/s
EN 3	4wBE	GB	1428	1936	(k)	s/s
EN 4	4wBE	GB	1429	1936	(k)	s/s
EN 5	4wBE	GB	1430	1936	(k)	s/s
EN 6	4wBE	LMM	(1001	1949 ?)	(l)	s/s after 1/1954
EN 7	4wBE	LMM	1002	1949	(l)	s/s after 1/1954
EN 8	4wBE	LMM	1003	1949	(m)	(10)
EN 9	4wBE	LMM	1004	1949	(l)	s/s
EN 10	4wBE	LMM	1005	1949	(l)	s/s
EN 1	4wDM	RH	173397	1935	(n)	s/s
EN 2	4wDM	RH	173399	1935	(o)	(11)
L No.2	4wDM	RH			(p)	s/s after 3/1953
EN 31	4wDM	RH	183748	1937	(q)	s/s after 3/1953
EN 33	4wDM	RH	183771	1937	(r)	(12)
EN 33	4wDM	RH	187112	1937	(s)	s/s
EN 36	4wDM	RH	189939	1937	(t)	(13)
EN 39	4wDM	RH	189948	1938	(u)	(14)
EN 43	4wDM	RH	198270	1939	(v)	s/s after 1/1954
EN 44	4wDM	RH	200779	1941	(w)	s/s after 1/1954
EN 45	4wDM	RH	200780	1941	(x)	s/s after 5/1959
EN 46	4wDM	RH	200781	1941	(y)	s/s after 1/1954
EN 47	4wDM	RH	200782	1941	(z)	(15)
EN 50	4wDM	RH	200786	1941	(aa)	(16)
EN 51	4wDM	RH	200785	1941	(ab)	s/s

EN 56	4wDM	RH			(ac)	s/s
EN 59	4wDM	RH	189946	1938	(ad)	(17)
EN 60	4wDM	RH	189980	1938	(ae)	(18)
EN 61	4wDM	RH	187093	1937	(af)	(19)
EN 62	4wDM	RH	187113	1937	(ag)	(20)
EN 64	4wDM	RH	187067	1937	(ah)	s/s
EN 66	4wDM	RH	187110	1937	(ai)	s/s after 1/1954
EN 68	4wDM	RH	187111	1937	(aj)	(21)
EN 69	4wDM	RH	189988	1938	(ak)	(22)
EN 71	4wDM	RH			(al)	s/s
EN 72	4wDM	RH	202033	1941	(am)	(23)
EN 73	4wDM	RH	202034	1941	(an)	(24)
EN 75	4wDM	RH	202035	1941	(ao)	(25)
76	4wDM	RH	202029	1941	(ap)	s/s after 1/1954
EN 77	4wDM	RH	202030	1941	(aq)	s/s after 4/1954
79	4wDM	RH	202032	1941	(ar)	s/s after 3/1952
EN 100	4wDM	RH	189981	1938	(as)	s/s after 1/1954
EN 101	4wDM	RH	189984	1938	(at)	s/s after 1/1954
EN 102	4wDM	RH	189945	1938	(au)	(26)
EN 103	4wDM	HE	4187	1948	(av)	s/s after 4/1966
EN 37	4wBE	GB	2779	1957	(aw)	s/s
EN 38	4wBE	GB	2780	1957	(aw)	s/s
EN 39	4wBE	GB	2781	1957	(aw)	s/s
EN 41	4wBE	GB	2873	1958	(ax)	s/s 3/1970
-	4wDM	RH	462374	1961	New (ay)	(27)
-	4wDM	RH	462375	1961	New (ay)	(27)
EN 45	4wBE	WR	6892	1964	New	(28)
EN 46	4wBE	WR	6893	1964	New	(28)
EN 47	4wBE	WR	6894	1964	New	(28)
EN 48	4wBE	WR	6895	1964	New	(28)
EN 49	4wBE	WR	6896	1964	New	(29)
EN 50	4wBE	WR	6897	1964	New	(28)
-	4wDM	MR	22106	1961	(az)	s/s
-	4wDM	RH	7002/0467/2	1967	(ba)	s/s

* Note that RH 183771 and RH 187112 both carried running number EN 33

The entry in certain footnotes – here at an unknown date (?) – derives from official information (obtained by the late Pete Roberts on a visit in 5/1953) of locomotives which had at some time been at Colnbrook depot.

In 4/1958 the yard contained a pile of four 4-wheeled frames. Two were devoid of identification, the third carried 'NUTTALL 22' and plate LMM 1057/1950; and the fourth plate LMM 1064/1950. Due to various fittings and attachments they could not be confirmed as from locomotives but may well have been so originally. All later s/s.

(a)   ex Port of Spain Harbour contract, Trinidad, West Indies, by 12/9/1939.
(b)   ex Port of Spain Harbour contract, West Indies, after 8/12/1937, by 13/10/1939.
(c)   ex Wallasey contract, Cheshire, after 15/4/1937, by 1/5/1939.
(d)   ex Chessington (SR) contract, Surrey, after 21/4/1938, by 21/4/1939.
(e)   ex Chessington (SR) contract, Surrey by 3/7/1940.
(f)   ex Ilford contract, Essex, after 3/1/1940, by 4/12/1940.
(g)   ex Trecwn (Admiralty) contract, Pembs, after 5/8/1937, by 13/2/1939.
(h)   ex Chessington (SR) contract, Surrey, after 1/3/1938, by 16/12/1938.
(i)   ex Chessington (SR) contract, Surrey, by 23/2/1939.
(j)   here by 6/1952; earlier at Glascoed (ROF) contract, Gwent, until after 8/3/1940.

(k)	earlier Crombie (RNAD) contract, Fife.

(k)   earlier Crombie (RNAD) contract, Fife.

(l)   here by 4/1950; orig new to Nuttall (location not known).

(m) here by 5/1953; orig new to Nuttall (location not known).

(n)   here by 3/1953; earlier Dodworth contract, Yorkshire (WR), until after13/9/1945.

(o)   ex Port of Spain Harbour contract, West Indies, after 16/2/1939, by 18/9/1939.

(p)   here by 5/1949; origin and identity unknown.

(q)   here by 3/1953; at Glascoed (ROF) contract, Gwent, until after 20/11/1939.

(r)   spares ordered by Colnbrook (was loco here ?), 18/2/1948; earlier at Elstow (ROF) contract, Beds, until after 31/3/1942.

(s)   spares ordered by Colnbrook (was loco here?), 5/12/1951; earlier at Inveruglas contract, Dunbartonshire, until after 26/10/1950.

(t)   ex Chessington (SR) contract, Surrey, by 17/3/1939; to Glascoed (ROF) contract, Gwent, by 12/7/1939; ex Inveruglas contract, Dunbartonshire, after 4/3/1950, by 3/1953.

(u)   here in 5/1949; RH spares orders show it as on the Inveruglas contract, Dunbartonshire, on 10/11/1947 and 12/9/1949, with spares ordered by Colnbrook (was loco here?) on 22/9/1949.

(v)   here by 3/1953; earlier at Elstow (ROF) contract, Beds, until after 6/10/1941.

(w) here by 1/1954; earlier at Cliff Quay Power Station contract, Ipswich, Suffolk, until after 15/8/1947.

(x)   here by 5/1949; earlier at Cliff Quay Power Station contract, Ipswich, Suffolk, until after 9/8/1946.

(y)   here by 4/1950; spares ordered by Colnbrook (was loco here?) on 10/10/1952; orig new to Hirwaun ROF contract, Mid Glamorgan.

(z)   ex Royal Victoria Dock contract, London, after 3/4/1944, by 5/1949. Spares ordered by Colnbrook (was loco here?) on 17/5/1946, 28/9/1949 and 10/10/1952.

(aa) here by 1/1954; earlier at Inveruglas contract, Dunbartonshire, until after 21/4/1949. Spares ordered by Colnbrook (was loco here?) on 10/10/1952.

(ab) earlier at Inveruglas contract, Dunbartonshire, until after 31/8/1948. Spares ordered by Colnbrook (was loco here?) on 10/10/1952.

(ac) here by 3/1953; origin and identity unknown.

(ad) here by 1/1954; earlier at Chessington (SR) contract, Surrey, until after 1/3/1938.

(ae) spares ordered by Colnbrook (was loco here?) on 5/12/1951; earlier Inveruglas contract, Dunbartonshire, until after 9/6/1949.

(af) here by 3/1953; earlier at Inveruglas contract, Dunbartonshire, until after 28/8/1951.

(ag) spares ordered by Colnbrook (was loco here?) on 21/7/1947 and 28/4/1949; here by 10/1949. Earlier at Chessington (SR) contract, Surrey, until after 10/2/1938.

(ah) here by 3/1953; orig new to Trecwn (Admiralty) contract, Pembs.

(ai) here by 1/1954; earlier at Inveruglas contract, Dunbartonshire, until after 5/6/1951.

(aj) here by 10/1949; earlier at Warminster contract, Wiltshire, until after 6/7/1943.

(ak) here at unknown date (?); orig new to Trecwn (Admiralty) contract, Pembs.

(al) origins and identity unknown.

(am) spares ordered by Colnbrook (was loco here?) on 13/9/1948; here by 10/1949; earlier at Pontrilas (ROF) contract, Herefordshire, until after 26/2/1943.

(an) here by 3/1953; earlier at Inveruglas contract, Dunbartonshire, until after 13/8/1951.

(ao) here by 3/1953; earlier at Inveruglas contract, Dunbartonshire, until after 10/10/1950. Spares ordered by Colnbrook (was loco here?) on 26/4/1955.

(ap) here by 10/1949; earlier at Trecwn (Admiralty) contract, Pembs, until after 8/9/1941. Spares ordered by Colnbrook (was loco here) on 20/4/1949.

(aq) here by 5/1949; earlier at Trecwn (Admiralty) contract, Pembs, until after 29/1/1942. Spares ordered by Colnbrook (was loco here?) on 24/10/1949. to Standard Brick & Sand Co Ltd, Redhill, Surrey, hire, c/1950 and returned. Spares ordered by Colnbrook (was loco here?) on 22/4/1954.

(ar) Spares ordered by Colnbrook (was loco here?) on 4/10/1948 and 15/6/1949. Here by 10/1949; earlier at Cliff Quay Power Station contract, Ipswich, until after 30/8/1946;

(as) at Trecwn (Admiralty) contract, Pembs, until after 25/2/1941; here at unknown date(?).

(at) here by 3/1953; earlier at Inveruglas contract, Dunbartonshire, until after 3/10/1950.

(au) at Trecwn (Admiralty) contract, Pembs, until at least 8/12/1939; here at unknown date(?).

(av) here by 3/1952; orig new to unknown contract.

(aw) here by /1966; orig new to Dartford Tunnel contract, Kent;

(ax) here by /1966; orig new to unknown contract.

(ay) to Leith Harbour contract, Edinburgh; here again by 4/1966.

(az) here by /1966; origins unknown; orig new to Railway Mine & Plantation Equipment Ltd.

(ba) here in 6/1970; orig new to Leith Harbour contract, Edinburgh

(1) to Elstow ROF contract, Beds, after 22/7/1940, by 26/3/1941.

(2) to Elstow ROF contract, Beds, after 12/6/1940, by 25/2/1941.

(3) to MoS, Home Grown Timber Production Department, Dunoon, Ayrshire, by 13/3/1943.

(4) to Elstow ROF contract, Beds, after 4/12/1940, by 3/7/1941.

(5) to Elstow ROF contract, Beds, after 3/7/1940, by 7/6/1941.

(6) to LMSR, Engineers Dept, Bridge St, Northampton, after 12/3/1942, by 18/5/1946; thence to BR, Engineers Dept, Newton Heath, Manchester, by 16/2/1948.

(7) to Glascoed (ROF) contract, Gwent, after 17/2/1939, by 20/3/1939.

(8) to Glascoed (ROF) contract, Gwent, after 9/5/1939, by 12/7/1939.

(9) to Glascoed (ROF) contract, Gwent, after 13/3/1939, by 12/7/1939.

(10) to Ballingarry Collieries (Production) Ltd, Gurteen, Co.Tipperary, after 5/1953.

(11) last recorded at Board of Trade, Home Grown Timber Dept, Tillicoultry, Clackmannanshire, on 3/12/1946.

(12) last recorded at Inveruglas contract, Dunbartonshire, on 8/3/1949.

(13) to George W. Bungey Ltd, dealers, Hayes, Middlesex, after 1/1954; resold to W.J. Keen & Sons, Bishops Stortford Sandpits, Herts, by 1/1955.

(14) later Jenkins Lane Contract, Barking, Essex, by 27/11/1951 (and subsequently to Standard Brick & Sand Co Ltd, Redhill, Surrey, by 6/1958).

(15) s/s after 10/10/1952.

(16) later at Upton Brickworks Ltd, Upton, Poole, Dorset, by c/1960.

(17) to Aberthaw Power Station (CEGB) contract, South Glamorgan, by 6/10/1958.

(18) s/s after 5/1953.

(19) to George W. Bungey Ltd, dealers, Hayes, Middlesex, after 1/1954, by 7/1955; resold to W.J. Keen & Sons, Bishops Stortford Sandpits, Herts, /1955.

(20) later Jenkins Lane contract, Barking, Essex, by 11/9/1951 (and subsequently to Standard Brick & Sand Co Ltd, Redhill, Surrey, by 6/1958).

(21) later Jenkins Lane contract, Barking, Essex, by 5/9/1951

(22) later to Joseph Place & Sons Ltd, Hoddlesden, Lancs, by 13/2/1943.

(23) later at Glen Lochay contract, Killin, Perthshire, by 13/6/1955.

(24) later at Glen Lochay contract, Killin, Perthshire, by 5/12/1955.

(25) later at Glen Lochay contract, Killin, Perthshire, by 22/3/1955.

(26) later at Cliff Quay Power Station contract, Ipswich, until after 23/10/1947.

(27) s/s after 21/9/1966

(28) to Aberthaw Power Station (CEGB) contract, South Glamorgan.

(29) to Aberthaw Power Station (CEGB) contract, South Glamorgan.

PAULING & CO LTD
HIGH WYCOMBE and UXBRIDGE CONTRACTS BC14

Construction of the GW & GC Joint Railway from Northolt (Middlesex) to High Wycombe, and concurrently the GWR branch line from Denham Junction to Uxbridge. Tenders for the main line were required by 3/5/1901 and work started soon thereafter. Work on the branch was in hand by 11/1903. The main line opened to freight on 20/11/1905, and to passengers 2/4/1906; the branch opened 1/5/1907. The contractor's office and principal plant depot were at Gerrards Cross (with a shed for 22 locos) and there were smaller loco sheds at Northolt, Ickenham, and Uxbridge. There was later a depot at Greenford, which would actually be upon the Acton to Northolt section constructed by Firbank. Some of the locos were registered by the GWR for use between High Wycombe and Greenford from 11/1905.

An early disposal sale of "several locomotives" at Gerrards Cross ("The Engineer" 4/12/1903) is difficult to understand. A later sale held 8-10/12/1908 mentioned only one locomotive, DENMARK. It is noteworthy that many of Pauling's locos are not heard of for ten years or more after this contract. Perhaps many remained in store at Greenford until the depot there was sold after 1918.

Reference : "Great Central, Vol.3", George Dow, Ian Allan, 1965.

Gauge : 4ft 8½in

No.	Name	Type		Builder	Works No.	Date		Notes
No.7		0-6-0ST	IC	MW	890	1883	(a)	(1)
No.9	STANLEY	0-4-0ST	OC	MW	334	1871	(a)	(2)
No.10	CEFN	0-6-0ST	IC	HE	256	1881	(b)	(3)
No.12	WESTMINSTER	0-6-0ST	IC	MW	1071	1888	(a)	(4)
No.13	ROCA	0-6-0T	IC	MW	1005	1887	(a)	(5)
No.14	PALACIOS	0-6-0ST	IC	HE	464	1888	(c)	(6)
No.15	PELLON	0-6-0ST	IC	MW	1112	1889	(a)	(7)
No.17	PARANA	0-4-0ST	OC	MW	1141	1889	(a)	(8)
No.19		0-4-0ST	OC	MW	722	1879	(d)	(9)
No.26	TYERSALL	0-6-0ST	IC	MW	1068	1888	(a)	(10)
No.27	ELY	0-4-0ST	OC	MW	932	1885	(e)	(11)
No.29	GROSVENOR	0-6-0ST	IC	HE	288	1884	(f)	(12)
No.50	(or No.30)	0-6-0ST	IC	MW	1146	1890	(g)	(13)
No.55	DUDLEY HILL	0-6-0ST	IC	MW	683	1878	(h)	(14)
No.56	NORTHOLT	0-6-0ST	IC	MW	1555	1902	New	(10)
No.57	WYCOMBE	0-6-0ST	IC	MW	1556	1902	New	s/s
No.58	BEACONSFIELD	0-6-0ST	IC	MW	1535	1902	New	(15)
No.59	GERRARDS CROSS	0-6-0ST	IC	MW	1541	1902	New	(16)
No.60	PENN	0-6-0ST	IC	MW	1539	1902	New	(17)
No.61	DENHAM	0-6-0ST	IC	MW	1542	1902	New	s/s
No.63	PUNCH	0-4-0ST	OC	MW	713	1879	(i)	(18)
No.64	DUNRAGIT	0-6-0ST	IC	MW	1232	1891	(j)	(19)
No.66		0-6-0ST	IC	MW	1070	1888	(k)	(20)
No.69	ABER	0-6-0ST	IC	MW	1214	1891	(l)	(21)
No.71	RIVER	0-4-0ST	OC	MW	692	1878	(m)	(22)
No.75	HORNBY	0-6-0ST	IC	MW	1211	1891	(n)	(23)
No.80	No.4 BARROW DOCKS	0-6-0ST	IC	MW	174	1865	(o)	(24)
No.82	CARRINGTON	0-4-0ST	OC	MW	1081	1888	(p)	s/s
No.64	THAMES	0-6-0T	IC	Bton		1876	(q)	(25)
No.79	BISHOPSGATE	0-6-0T	IC	Bton		1876	(r)	Scr 10/1909
No.87	DENMARK	0-6-0T	IC	Bton		1878	(s)	Scr 10/1909
No.88	BRAMLEY	0-6-0T	IC	Bton		1878	(t)	Scr 10/1909
No.90	SURREY	0-6-0T	IC	Bton		1876	(u)	(25)

(a) ex Hungerford - Westbury (GWR) (1897-1900) contract, Wilts.

(b) ex another contract (possibly Hungerford-Westbury (GWR)); loco purchased by Pauling, after 5/1898, by 4/1899, ex Tom N. Brown, dealer, Leeds; earlier Cardiff Corporation, Beacons & Cantreff Reservoirs (1884-1897) construction, Brecknocks [Powys].

(c) ex Andoversford-Cheltenham widening (GWR) (1901-1902) contract, Glos, c/1902.

(d) probably ex Wm. Jones, dealer, London, c/1902. Earlier Mumbles Railway & Pier Co, Swansea, West Glamorgan – for sale there, 23/9/1898

(e) ex a previous contract; earlier Joseph Phillips, Forfar & Brechin Railway (1891-1895) contract, Angus.

(f) ex Hungerford-Westbury (GWR) (1897-1900) contract, Wilts; to HE, Leeds, for repairs, 4/1902, and returned to Pauling (not necessarily to this contract).

(g) earlier Thomas Oliver & Son, Earlswood (LBSCR Quarry Line) (1896-1900) contract, Surrey.

(h) earlier Charles Baker & Sons, Low Moor (GNR) (1891-1895) contract, Yorkshire (WR).

(i) earlier Cheadle Railway Co Ltd, Cheadle Railway (1888-1900) construction, North Staffs.

(j) orig S.W. Pilling & Co, St Helens, (Liverpool, St. Helens & South Lancs Rly) (1888-1900) contract, Lancs.

(k) ex A. Braithwaite & Co, Penkridge (Littleton Colliery railway) contract, South Staffs, PENKRIDGE, after 26/3/1902.

(l) orig T.W. Davies, Aber branch (Caerphilly to Senghenydd) (Rhymney Railway) (1891-1894) contract, Mid Glamorgan.

(m) ex Topham, Jones & Railton, Queen Alexandra Dock (1899-1907) contract, Cardiff, 13, /1902.

(n) ex Herbert Weldon, Aberbeeg (1899-1902) contract, Gwent, c/1902.

(o) earlier R.T.Relf & Son, contractors (probably used on Westleigh Quarry railway (1898) contract, Burlescombe, Devon).

(p) earlier S.Pearson & Son Ltd, Port Talbot (Port Talbot Railway) (1895-1900) contract, West Glamorgan.

(q) ex LBSCR, 657 THAMES, 5/1902.

(r) ex LBSCR, 649 BISHOPSGATE, 6/1902.

(s) ex LBSCR, 39 DENMARK, 7/1902.

(t) ex LBSCR, 36 BRAMLEY, 9/1902.

(u) ex LBSCR, 652 SURREY, 9/1902.

(1) later Skipton Magazine contract, Salterforth, Lancs, possibly by 15/10/1917 when MW supplied a spark arrester for this loco. Loco for sale by Ministry of Munitions Disposals Board at Skipton Magazine, 4/1921; later West Sussex Railway, Sussex, RINGING ROCK, by 5/10/1925.

(2) later Welsh Navigation Steam Coal Co Ltd, Coedely Colliery, Tonyrefail, Mid Glamorgan, by c/1918.

(3) later Slimbridge Explosives Depot (MoM) (1916-1917) contract, Glos, by 7/1916.

(4) later used on other contracts, including probably Skipton Magazine contract, Salterforth, Lancs, possibly by 15/10/1917 when MW supplied a spark arrester for this loco. Loco recorded in MW records as with Disposal & Liquidation Commission at Skipton in early 1920s

(5) later Furness Shipbuilding Co, Haverton Hill, Co.Durham [Cleveland], probably via Holloway Bros (London) Ltd, Haverton Hill (1917-1918) contract;
then Exors of L.P. Nott, Avonmouth Portway road contract, Bristol, by /1918.

(6) later Austin Motor Co Ltd, Longbridge Works, Birmingham, by 10/1917.

(7) MW records indicate later owner as J.& J.Charlesworth, Rothwell Haigh, Yorkshire (WR), but this is believed to be an error of identity – see MW 1211 disposal. No other trace.

(8)   later E.J.& W. Goldsmith Ltd, Grays, Essex, possibly c/1910 (and possibly via Charles Wall Ltd, Chingford Reservoir (1908-1913) contract, Essex).

(9)   later Brentford Gas Co, Southall Gas Works, Middlesex (possibly via W. Jones, dealer, London), by c/1918.

(10) to Dunkerton (GWR) (1908-1910) contract, Somerset, by 8/11/1909 (MW 1068) and 31/3/1910 (MW 1555).

(11) later David Caird Ltd, Furness Foundry, Barrow-in-Furness, possibly by /1923.

(12) later Ministry of Munitions, Slimbridge, Glos, by 7/1917, possibly via Pauling's Slimbridge contract.

(13) to Holloway Bros (London) Ltd, Haverton Hill (1917-1918) contract, Co.Durham [Cleveland]; thence to Furness Shipbuilding Co Ltd, Haverton Hill, /1918.

(14) ex "Pauling's Yard" (Greenford ?) to Sir Robert McAlpine & Sons Ltd, No.36, 26/2/1919; at McAlpines' Slough Motor Transport Repair Depot (WD) contract, Bucks [Berkshire], by 10/1919.

(15) later Davies, Middleton & Davies Ltd, Cherry Orchard (Rhymney Railway) (1912-1915) contract, Cardiff.

(16) later Sir Robert McAlpine & Sons, Cuffley (GNR) (1912-1918) contract, Herts, No.20.

(17) later Ebbw Vale Steel Iron & Coal Co Ltd, Ebbw Vale, Gwent, by /1921.

(18) later J.F.Wake Ltd, dealer, Darlington, Co.Durham, (c/1916 ?); rebuilt Wake 2257 thence to Port of Par Ltd, Par Harbour, Cornwall, (c/1916-/1917 ?), by /1921.

(19) later Austin Motor Co Ltd, Longbridge Works, Birmingham, by /1919.

(20) later Ministry of Munitions, Salterforth Magazine, Skipton, Lancs, c/1917.

(21) later Oxted Greystone Lime Co Ltd, Oxted Limeworks, Surrey, possibly by 6/1908.

(22) later Hugh Symington & Sons Ltd, Gretna Factory (MoM) (1915-1917) construction, Dumfriesshire

(23) later J.F. Wake, dealer, Darlington, Co.Durham, by /1915; then to J. & J. Charlesworth Ltd, Rothwell Haigh, Yorkshire (WR), No.12, /1916.

(24) later Brentford Gas Co, Brentford, Middlesex, (by 6/1918 ?)

(25) reputedly to F.C. La Plata, Argentina.

Gauge : 3ft 6in

BRANCKER	0-4-0ST	OC	WB	1116	1889	(a) (1)

(a)   ex Pauling & Co Ltd, Burtonport & Cardonagh (Londonderry &Lough Swilly Railway) (1899-1903) contracts, Co.Donegal (for sale at Letterkenny 1/4/1903).

(1)   later Sir John Jackson Ltd, Blackwater Reservoir contract, (1904-1910) Kinlochleven, Argyll, by 8/1907 and at Grays Plant Depot, Essex, by 8/1921.

FRANCIS RUMMENS
AYLESBURY CONTRACT   AC15

The contract for construction of the Aylesbury & Buckingham Railway, authorised 6/8/1860, was let to Rummens. Work started at the Claydon end in 2/1861 and the line, from Aylesbury to Verney Jct, opened 23/9/1868, being worked by the GWR. It is unclear if construction actually took so long, or if Rummens was also working on the Wycombe Railway, Princes Risborough to Aylesbury, 1861-1863, as stated in Popplewell Gazetteer.

Gauge : 4ft 8½in

Per a minute of 20/6/1861, the LNWR Southern Division agreed to hire "an engine" to "Rummens, the contractor for the Winslow to Aylesbury line". This loco has not been identified.

WALTER SCOTT & CO
QUAINTON ROAD CONTRACT AC16

Construction of the Woodford Halse - Quainton Road railway (25 miles) for the MS&LR (later GCR), 1894 - 1898. Contracts let 10/1894 and the line was opened on 15/3/1899. The line ran for approximately equal distances through Buckinghamshire and Northamptonshire plus a short distance in Oxfordshire near Finmere. See the entry in Northants for further details.

Reference : "Great Central, Vol.2", George Dow, Locomotive Publishing Co, 1962.

J. SMITH & SONS (WALTER'S ASH) LTD
Great Marlow CC17

This company was listed in Kelly's Trade Directories in 1931 (but not in 1928), and until 1939, as Public Works Contractors & Pavers with an address at Walter's Ash, Naphill, near High Wycombe. Use of the locomotive is not known; information taken from builders records.

Gauge : 2ft 0in

-	4wDM	RH	242903	1946	New	(1)

(1)   (? sold by 24/3/1948 when spares were ordered by Thos W. Ward Ltd for delivery to an unstated destination)

A. STREETER & CO LTD
MILTON KEYNES CONTRACT EC18

Construction of the Ouzel Valley Trunk Sewer, Bow Brickhill Sewage Disposal Works to Cotton Valley Sewage Works, for Milton Keynes Development Corporation., 1972 - ?

Gauge : 2ft 0in

-	0-4-0BE	WR			(a)	(1)
2	0-4-0BE	WR			(a)	s/s
5 -	0-4-0BE	WR	F7026	1966	(b)	s/s
-	0-4-0BE	WR	E6946	1965	(c)	(2)
-	4wBE	CE	5961A	1972	New	(3)
-	4wBE	CE	5961B	1972	New	(3)
-	4wBE	CE	5961C	1972	New	(3)
-	4wBE	CE	5961D	1972	New	(3)
-	4wBE	CE	B0107A	1973	New	(3)
-	4wBE	CE	B0107B	1973	New	(3)
-	4wBE	CE	B0107C	1973	New	(3)
-	4wBE	CE	B0113A	1973	New	(3)
-	4wBE	CE	B0113B	1973	New	(3)

(a)   ex Godalming Plant Depot, Surrey, c10/1972.
(b)   orig new to Waterlooville cotract, Portsmouth, Hampshire, 31/3/1966.
(c)   orig new to Tolworth contract, Surrey, 13/9/1965.

(1)   returned to Godalming Plant Depot, c1/1973 (by 21/1/1973).
(2)   to Tickhill Plant Ltd, Doncaster, South Yorkshire, by /1978.
(3)   transferred to Costain Ltd, Wetherby, North Yorkshire, 10/1984.

TARSLAG LTD
Winslow

Location uncertain. Information from makers records gives "c/o RAF Winslow, near Bletchley". The company originated in Stockton-on-Tees and their operations at this site are unknown. "Machinery Market" 14/12/1945 gives : "For sale by Tarslag Ltd, Wolverhampton; two 25hp Hudson-Hunslet locos, purchased 1942 and only done four weeks work"

Gauge : 2ft 0in

-	4wDM	HE	2665	1942	New	(1)
-	4wDM	HE	2666	1942	New	(1)

(1)   to Penlee Quarries Ltd, Newlyn, Cornwall, 1/1947

JAMES TAYLOR
NEWPORT PAGNELL RAILWAY OPERATION CONTRACT
EC20

Contract for (or hire of locomotives for) the operation of freight and passenger trains on this line, which had been constructed, and possibly operated, by John Bray, contractor (which see). Taylor became involved c1870 (by 12/1870) and continued until 2/1872 at least. At other times it appears that the Newport Pagnell Railway Company operated their own trains using assorted locos hired from, for example, the LNWR. The company was taken over by the LNWR (Act of 29/6/1875).

Gauge : 4ft 8½in

-	0-6-0ST	IC	IWB	c1869	(a)	(1)
WHITMORE	0-6-0ST	IC	MW	45 1862	(b)	(2)

(a)   ex I.W.Boulton, dealers, Ashton-under-Lyne, Lancs, hire, c/1870
(b)   not confirmed here, but spares were purchased by the LNWR c12/1870, hence possibly indicating repairs (at Wolverton ?) for Taylor. Loco previously with Taylor at Aldershot (possibly on Pirbright Junction-Farnham (LSWR) (1868-1870) contract, Hampshire).

(1)   returned off hire, either to I.W.Boulton or direct to next hire at Cowbridge Railway, South Glamorgan. Some time later, this loco was named CYCLOPS.
(2)   later Barnstaple-Ilfracombe railway (LSWR) (1871-1874) contract, Devon, by 6/1874

THYSSEN (GB) LTD
IVER CONTRACT
BC21

Construction of a 6km tunnel, 2.54m diameter, from Wraysbury Reservoir (Middlesex) to Three Valleys Water Treatment Works, Iver (TQ 046801). Work ran from 6/1983 to 7/1985.

Gauge : 2ft 0in

-	4wBE	CE	B3070A	1983	New	s/s
-	4wBE	CE	B3070B	1983	New (a)	s/s
-	4wBE	CE	B3070C	1983	New	s/s
-	4wBE	CE	B3070D	1983	New	s/s
-	4wBE	CE	B3214A	1985	(b)	(1)
-	4wBE	CE	B3214B	1985	(b)	(1)

(a)   to Heathrow Terminal 4 contract, London, c4/1984; returned c11/1984.
(b)   supplied new by Track Supplies & Services Ltd, Wolverton, 4/1985.

(1)   returned to Track Supplies & Services Ltd, Wolverton, 19/7/1985.

THOMAS TREDWELL
WYCOMBE RAILWAY CONTRACT   AC22

Contract for the construction of the line from High Wycombe to Princes Risborough and Thame awarded to Tredwell, of Gloucester. First sod cut 9/1859, line opened 1/8/1862 and worked by GWR.

Gauge : 7ft 0¼in

Tredwell advertised 29/12/1860 (from his Gloucester address) that he wished to obtain 40 broad gauge ballast trucks and a broad gauge engine suitable for ballasting. Subsequently a Mr Slade, of High Wycombe, advertised in The Builder 30/8/1862 for sale, 30 broad gauge trucks used in working ballast between Wycombe and Thame, and also a broad gauge loco with 16½ x 26 in cylinders and 4ft 8in driving wheel "has not been in use for 13 months". A similar advert appeared in Railway Times 6/12/1862 stating that the driving wheels were coupled and the loco had "only been in use 13 months", for sale "in consequence of Messrs Tredwell having finished their contract".

This loco has not been identified, though a possible candidate is the 0-6-0tank with 16½/17x24 IC and 4ft 8in wheels built by Brotherhood 1857/58, possibly used on Brotherhood contracts, and advertised for sale by Brotherhood continuously from 9/1863 to 1871/72. This loco is referred to in Industrial Railway Record No.24, page 45

AUBREY WATSON LTD

DASHWOOD HILL CONTRACT   AC23

Construction of a new two mile section of the A40 road from Myze Farm (near West Wycombe) to the top of Dashwood Hill. Work started 7/1925 for completion in 8/1926.

Gauge : 2ft 0in

No.1	0-4-0ST	OC	KS	2420	1915	(a)	(1)
No.4	0-4-0ST	OC	KS	4262	1922	(b)	(1)

There were probably other locos in use on this contract.

(a) orig new to Secretary of State for War, per Harper Bros & Co (agents for WD) Catterick Camp, Yorkshire (NR).

(b) earlier R.H.Neal & Co, dealers, Barkingside, Essex, (probably for Muirhead, McDonald Wilson & Co Ltd, Southend Road (1921-1925) contract, Essex).

(1) later Denham (1928-1930) contract, by 1/9/1929.

DENHAM CONTRACT   BC24

Construction of the Denham to West Hyde (Hertfordshire) (A412) road for Buckinghamshire County Council, 1928-1930.

Gauge : 2ft 0in

No.1	0-4-0ST	OC	KS	2420	1915	(a)	(1)
No.4	0-4-0ST	OC	KS	4262	1922	(a)	(2)
No.5	0-4-0ST	OC	KS	4267	1922	(b)	(3)
No.7	0-4-0ST	OC	KS	4023	1919	(c)	(1)
No.8	0-4-0ST	OC	KS	2473	1916	(d)	(4)
No.9	0-4-0ST	OC	KS	2474	1916	(d)	(1)
No.10	0-4-0ST	OC	KS	2477	1916	(d)	(1)

(a) here by 1/9/1929; earlier Dashwood Hill (1925-1926) contract.

(b) here by 1/9/1929; earlier R.H.Neal & Co, dealers, Barkingside, Essex, (probably for Muirhead, McDonald Wilson & Co, Southend Road (1921-1925) contract, Essex).

(c) orig new to Furness Shipbuilding Co Ltd, Haverton Hill, Co.Durham [Cleveland].

(d) here by 1/9/1929; earlier John Mowlem & Co Ltd, Rotherwas (National Filling Factory) (1916-1917) contract, Hereford.

(1) later Twickenham to Richmond Thames Bridge (1931-1933) contract, Middlesex/Surrey, by 7/1932.

(2) to Cochran & Sons, Sproughton Road Underpass (1930) contract, Ipswich, Suffolk, loan, 4/4/1930; returned to Aubrey Watson (possibly Plant Depot elsewhere), 10/9/1930; and later to Billing Gravel Co Ltd, Great Billing, Northants, c/1931 by 12/1933.

(3) to Cochran & Sons, Sproughton Road Underpass contract Ipswich, Suffolk, hire, c6/1930 (by 9/1930); returned to Watson and to Benson By-pass road contract, Oxon.

(4) to Benson By-pass road (1931-1932) contract, Oxon.

T. WILKINSON (Trading as B COOKE & CO)
AYLESBURY CONTRACT   DC25

Alterations to existing sewage works, and construction of new beds and filters at Aylesbury (SP 806141) for Aylesbury Corporation, 1903 - 1904. This works was located about a mile north west of Aylesbury on the east side of the Met & GC Joint line. A narrow gauge tramway around the filter beds is indicated on the 1925 OS map.

Gauge : 2ft 3in

-	0-4-0WT	OC	OK	686	1901	(a) (1)

(a) presumably ex another contract. Loco was New to "L. Cook, London" (error for B.Cooke ?), 1/1901.

(1) A 20hp OK loco of 2ft 3in gauge was advertised for sale by auction re T Wilkinson in "Engineer", 12/1904 and again in June 1905 as lying at Sewage Works, Aylesbury; probably was later the loco of this description for sale at R. Blackett & Son (brickmakers and/or contractors), Darlington, Co.Durham, in 10-11/1912; later J.F. Wake, dealer, Darlington (loco of this description for sale 12/1913 to 4/1915); later used (by H. Boot & Sons ?) on Catterick Military Railway construction (1915-1916) contract, Yorkshire (NR);; later advertised for sale by MoM in "Surplus", 2/8/1920 as lying at R.E. Yard, Catterick Bridge, Yorkshire (NR); still for sale 1/4/1922 and scrapped /1924.

GEORGE WIMPEY & CO LTD
BEACONSFIELD CONTRACT   BC26

Widening of the GWR & LNER Joint Railway at Beaconsfield, 1938 -1939.

Gauge : 4ft 8½in

MOMBASA	0-6-0ST	OC	WB	2167	1921	(a) (1)

(a) ex Pauling & Co Ltd, Crymlyn Burrows Plant Depot, Swansea, 15, hire, 19/6/1938.

(1) to North Acton-Northolt widening (GWR) (1938-1940) contract, London/Middlesex, /1938.

DEALERS

AYLESBURY SCRAP METALS LTD
Griffin Lane, Aylesbury   **DD1**

One locomotive is known to have been broken up at this scrap yard (at SP 804141).

Gauge : 4ft 8½in

(DOM)	4wVBT	VCG S	6994 1927	(a)	Scr 4/1973

(a)   ex Kent & East Sussex Railway, Rolvenden, Kent, 31/3/1973.

E. GOODMAN & BROS
NEW BRADWELL DEPOT, near Wolverton   **ED2**
Edward Goodman from c1920 until after 1931   SP 832413

This firm of scrap merchants was operating at a scrapyard in Bradwell Road by 1951 and locomotives were stored there for a number of years prior to their resale. An associated firm was W. Goodman Bros, of Newport Road, New Bradwell.

Gauge : 4ft 8½in

No.81	(No.14)	0-6-0ST	OC	HL	3138 1915	(a)	(1)
No.84	(SWORDFISH)	0-6-0ST	OC	AB	2138 1941	(b)	(2)
-		4wDM		RH	210482 1942	(c)	(3)

(a)   ex S&L (Minerals) Ltd, Glendon East Quarries, Northants, 17/8/1962.
(b)   ex S&L (Minerals) Ltd, Glendon East Quarries, Northants, 16/8/1962.
(c)   ex International Alloys Ltd, Aylesbury, /1971.

(1)   to T. Buck, Deep Meadows, Ledger Lane, Fifield, near Windsor, Berkshire, c6/1985.
(2)   to Quainton Railway Society, Quainton Road, 15/8/1980.
(3)   exported to Sobermai NV, Maldegem, Belgium, c6/1972.

Gauge : 2ft 0in

	4wPM	MR	5018 1929	(a)	(1)
	4wPM	MR	5055 1930	(a)	(1)
-	4wDM	OK	8986 1938	(b)	(2)

(a)   ex Bletchley Concrete Aggregates Co, Great Linford Gravel Pit, c/1955
(b)   ex Woodham Brick Co Ltd, near Westcott, by 21/4/1969.

(1)   to E.L. Pitt & Co Ltd, dealers, Finmere Station, Oxon, by 7/1959; resold to M.E. Engineering Co Ltd, Cricklewood, London, c/1964.
(2)   to Leighton Buzzard Narrow Gauge Railway Society, Leighton Buzzard, Beds, c1/1970.

ENGLAND HOPKINS LTD
Railway Goods Yard, Woburn Sands   **ED3**

A company of scrap metal merchants and dealers, registered 5/1957. Two batches of narrow gauge locomotives are known to have been handled at this yard.

Gauge : 2ft 0in

12		4wDM	MR	7932	1941	(a)	(1)
10		4wDM	MR	10272	1951	(a)	(1)
No.13	RETRIAL	4wDM	MR	5870	1935	(b)	Scr
No.36	RELKO	4wDM	MR	7145	1936	(b)	Scr
No.13	ARKLE	4wDM	MR	7152	1936	(b)	Scr
No.28	FLUSH ROYAL	4wDM	MR	8917	1944	(b)	Scr
No.30	LARKSPUR	4wDM	MR	7195	1937	(b)	Scr
-		4wDM	MR	7115	1936	(b)	Scr
-		4wDM	MR	7414	1939	(b)	Scr
No.14	DEVON LOCH	4wDM	MR	7492	1940	(b)	Scr
-		4wDM	MR	8725	1941	(b)	Scr
No.35	DOUTELLE	4wDM	MR	8713	1941	(b)	Scr
-		4wDM	MR	7154	1937	(b)	Scr

(a)   ex George Garside (Sand) Ltd, Leighton Buzzard, Beds, /1965.
(b)   ex George Garside (Sand) Ltd, Leighton Buzzard, Beds, for scrap, 29/3/1976.

(1)   exported to Jonallen, Singapore, 31/8/1966.

H. PARKER
Machinery Merchant, Iver
BD4

Advertised a number of locomotives as follows:

Gauge : 4ft 8½in
Three 6-wheel tender locos by BP ("Contract Journal" 11/1/1893)
Ten contractors locos 0-4-0 and 0-6-0 ("Contract Journal" 11/1/1893)

Gauge : 3ft 0in
Tank locos ("Contract Journal" 11/1/1893)
Tank loco 8¼in x 14in ("The Engineer" 17/2/1893)
Tank loco 8½in by HE ("The Engineer" 25/1/1895)
This could be the same H. Parker who had previously advertised from various addresses in South Wales – see the forthcoming "South and Mid Glamorgan Handbook" for details.

BEN REEVES ENGINEERS
CHAPEL LANE DEPOT, Northall, near Leighton Buzzard
AD5
TL 950202

Locomotive purchased by this dealer but never used or resold.

Gauge : 4ft 8½in

-	0-4-0DM	RSHN	6990	1940	(a)	Scr c/1974

(a)   ex Southern Depot Co Ltd, NCB Coal Concentration Depot, Aylesbury, Bucks, /1972.

ROWLAND BROS
STEAM SAW MILLS & FENCING WORKS, Fenny Stratford   ED6
SP 883343

This company was in business by 1877 until at least 2/1922, as machinery dealers, plan
suppliers, and as contractors erecting fencing along railway lines etc.

Gauge : 4ft 8½in

Advertisements in "Contract Journal" 19/12/1888 – for sale, standard gauge four and si
coupled locos, and in "The Engineer" 4/1/1889 – for sale, one 6 wheels coupled and one
wheels coupled locos.

TRACK SUPPLIES & SERVICES LTD
HAVERSHAM BANK SIDINGS, Old Wolverton Road, Old Wolverton   ED7
SP 818416

This company was active from about 1971 to 1988 in the purchase and resale of railwa
locomotives and equipment, both standard and narrow gauge. Yard located on the west sid
of the ex-LNWR West Coast main line and north of the Grand Union Canal, north o
Wolverton Carriage Works.

Gauge : 4ft 8½in

	YARD No.6953	0-4-0DM	HE	4263	1952	(a)	(1)
	YARD No.6954	0-4-0DM	HE	4264	1952	(a)	(2)
	(YARD No.124)	4wDM	RH	221644	1943	(b)	(7)
	YARD No.764	0-4-0DM	RH	319286	1953	(c)	(5)
	ARMY 101	4wDM	RH	224341	1944	(d)	(8)
No.1		4wDM	RH	200796	1941	(e)	(8)
No.2		4wDM	RH	263000	1949	(e)	(3)
No.1		4wDM	RH	275886	1949	(f)	(4)
	ARMY 401	0-4-0DH	NBQ	27422	1955	(g)	(10)
	ARMY 403	0-4-0DH	NBQ	27424	1955	(h)	(9)
	ELY	4wDH	FH	3967	1961	(i)	(6)
	THE BUGGY	2-2wBER	Track Supplies				
			NP/LO23	1985	New	(11)	

(a)   ex MoDND, Portsmouth Dockyard, Hampshire, c6/1971.
(b)   ex MoDND, RNAD Llangennech, Carms, after 8/1971, by 11/1972.
(c)   ex MoDND, RNAD Bedenham, Hampshire, 12/1975.
(d)   ex MoDAD, Hessay, North Yorkshire, 26/4/1976.
(e)   ex Central Electricity Generating Board, St Swithin's Power Station, Lincoln, after
       13/7/1977, by 1/10/1978.
(f)   ex Central Electricity Generating Board, Nechells Power Station, Birmingham,
       24/6/1981.
(g)   ex MoDAD, Ruddington, Notts, 23/9/1981.
(h)   ex MoDAD, Bramley, Hampshire, 1/10/1981.
(I)   ex Wiggins, Teape Ltd, Ely Paper Works, Cardiff, South Glamorgan, 30/6/1982.

(1)   to Thos.E. Gray Ltd, Isebrook Quarry, Burton Latimer, Northants, 4/1972.
(2)   to Tyne & Wear PTE, Middle Engine Lane Test Centre, North Shields, Northumberland,
       c2/1974 (after 2/2/1974).
(3)   to Raynesway Plant Ltd, Raynesway, Derby, after 15/4/1979, by 4/7/1979.
(4)   to Thos.E. Gray Ltd, Isebrook Quarry, Burton Latimer, Northants, 20/2/1982; returned
       here 24/6/1982; then to Northampton Steam Railway Preservation Society, Pitsford
       Station, Northants, 6/9/1984.

(5)	to Northampton Steam Railway Preservation Society, Pitsford Station, Northants, 8/10/1983.
(6)	to Northamptonshire Ironstone Railway Trust Ltd, Hunsbury Hill Railway & Museum, Northampton, 3/12/1983.
(7)	scrapped on site, after 25/2/1984, by 13/4/1984.
(8)	to Grant Lyon Eagre Ltd, Civil Engineers, Scunthorpe Plant Depot, Humberside, after 4/3/1986, by 24/5/1986.
(9)	scrapped on site c8/1986, (by 27/9/1986).
(10)	s/s c11/1987 (after 26/9/1987, by 2/1988).
(11)	to Bovis Construction Ltd, Aldwych Station (LUL) contract, London.

Gauge : 3ft 0in

L1		4wDM	RH	170200	1934	(a)	(1)
L3		4wDM	RH	182146	1936	(a)	(2)
L5		4wDM	RH	187058	1937	(a)	(3)
-		4wDM	RH	244574	1947	(a)	(2)
L7	(20)	4wDM	RH	244575	1947	(a)	(3)
L2	(21)	4wDM	RH	252798	1947	(a)	(2)
-		4wDM	RH	186304	1937	(b)	(2)
-		4wDM	MR	10160	1950	(c)	(4)

a)	ex London Brick Co Ltd, Central No.2 Works, Whittlesey, Cambs, 9/4/1980.
b)	ex London Brick Co Ltd, Central No.2 Works, Whittlesey, Cambs, after 2/2/1982, by 13/4/1982.
c)	ex Fisons Ltd, Horticulture Division, British Moss Peat Works, Swinefleet, near Goole, Humberside, c9/1984 (after 14/8/1984, by 27/12/1984).

1)	to J. Craven, Walesby, Notts, 7/1985 (after 25/3/1985, by 18/10/1985).
2)	scrapped on site by Ampthill Scrap Metal Processing Co Ltd, Ampthill, Beds, c5/1986 (after 4/3/1986, by 24/7/1986)
3)	scrapped on site by Ampthill Scrap Metal Processing Co Ltd, Ampthill, Beds, c5/1986 (after 29/3/1986, by 24/7/1986)
4)	to May, Gurney & Co Ltd, Southend Pier contract, Southend, Essex, after re-gauging to 3ft 6in, by 27/12/1984.

Gauge : 2ft 6in

YARD No.B22	ND 3063	0-4-0DM	HE	2401	1941	(a)	(1)
YARD No.B24	ND 3065	0-4-0DM	HE	2403	1941	(b)	(1)
YARD No.B8	ND 3057	0-4-0DM	HE	2268	1940	(c)	(1)
YARD No.B9	ND 3058	0-4-0DM	HE	2269	1940	(c)	(1)

a)	ex MoDND, RNAD, Trecwn, Dyfed, 4/1982.
b)	ex MoDND, RNAD, Trecwn, Dyfed, c19/6/1982.
c)	ex MoDND, RNAD, Trecwn, Dyfed, after 6/1982.

1)	Scrapped on site by Ampthill Scrap Metal Processing Co Ltd, Ampthill, Beds, after 29/3/1986, by 24/7/1986.

Gauge : 2ft 0in

23	(758115)	4wDM	RH	226278	1944	(a)	(4)
26	(758106)	4wDM	RH	229631	1944	(a)	(5)
29	(758195)	4wDM	HE	2477	1941	(b)	(2)
24	(758120)	4wDM	RH	223749	1944	(c)	(1)

	M.P.18	4wDM	RH	202969	1940	(d)	(6)
	M.P.17	4wDM	RH	217967	1941	(d)	(3)
	-	4wDM	RH	183773	1937	(e)	(17)
8		4wDM	RH	354043	1953	(f)	(9)
	-	4wDM	RH	174139	1935	(g)	(10)
5		4wDM	RH	239381	1946	(h)	(14)
	-	4wDM	RH	432652	1959	(i)	(7)
	-	4wDM	RH	182137	1936	(i)	(8)
1	175	4wBE	GB	1611	1939	(j)	(15)
2	176	4wBE	GB	1612	1939	(j)	(16)
3	177	4wBE	GB	1613	1939	(j)	(15)
	(A.M.W. No.160?)	4wDM	RH	194771	1939	(j)	(11)
	A.M.W. 166	4wDM	RH	193987	1939	(j)	(18)
	A.M.W. No.204	4wDM	RH	200802	1941	(j)	(18)
	A.M.W. No.224	4wDM	RH	203020	1941	(j)	(18)
15/26		4wDM	MR	9869	1953	(k)	(13)
15/27		4wDM	MR	9978	1954	(k)	(13)
	-	4wDM	MR	22119	1961	(l)	(12)
	-	4wBE	WR	M7556	1972	(m)	(20)
3		4wDM	MR	5867	1934	(n)	(19)
4		4wDM	MR	8790	1943	(n)	(19)
5		4wDM	MR	21283	1965	(n)	(19)
	-	4wDM	MR	7176	1937	(o)	(23)
	-	4wBE	CE	B0182A	1974	(p)	(21)
	T/E 319	4wBE	CE	B0182B	1974	(p)	(21)
	-	4wBE	CE	B3214A	1985		
		Rebuild of	CE	B1559	1977	(q)	(22)
	-	4wBE	CE	B3214B	1985		
		Rebuild of	CE	B1808	1978	(q)	(22)

(a) ex MoDAD, Branston, Burton-on-Trent, Staffs, 2/8/1972.

(b) ex MoDAD, Barlow, North Yorkshire, 7/8/1972.

(c) ex MoD, Royal Ordnance Factory, East Riggs, Dumfries, 14/8/1972.

(d) ex Ministry of Public Building & Works, Shoeburyness, Essex, by 11/2/1973.

(e) ex Bressingham Steam Museum, Bressingham, near Diss, Norfolk, 12/1974.

(f) ex M.E. Engineering Ltd, Cricklewood, London, c5/1975 (after 4/2/1975, by 1/3/1976)

(g) ex Alan Keef Ltd, Cote Farm, Bampton, Oxon, 2/1976, by 1/3/1976).

(h) ex M.E. Engineering Ltd, Cricklewood, London, c/1976.

(i) ex Bala Lake Railway Ltd, Llanuwchllyn, Gwynedd [North Wales], 23/11/1976.

(j) ex William Pike Ltd, scrap merchants, Westbury, Wilts, 11/1976 (after 22/9/1976, by 11/1976); earlier MoDAFD, Chilmark, Wilts.

(k) ex Anglian Water Authority, Great Ouse River Division, Ely, Cambs, c4/1977 (by 7/1977).

(l) ex Anglian Water Authority, Great Ouse River Division, Ely, Cambs, 4/1977

(m) ex MBZ Consortium Joint Venture, Dinorwic Power Station contract, Dinorwic, Gwynedd (North Wales), c7/1980 (by 1/8/1980).

(n) ex Marlow Sand & Gravel Co Ltd, Westhorpe Pits, Little Marlow, 26/3/1983.

(o) ex Marlow Sand & Gravel Co Ltd, Westhorpe Pits, Little Marlow, c5/1983 (after 5/4/1983, by 1/7/1983).

(p) ex J.F. Donelon & Co Ltd, Plant dealers, Bredbury, Gtr Manchester, 21/3/1985 (? on hire for a contract ?).

(q) ex CE, 4/1985, new to use on Thyssen (GB) Ltd contract, Iver; returned here by 19/7/1985; earlier Laporte Industries Ltd, Sallet Hole Mine, Stoney Middleton, Derbys.

(1) to Woburn Abbey Railway, Woburn Park, c/1973 (after 19/11/1972, when being altered to S/O, by 11/2/1973).

(2) to Alan Keef Ltd, Cote Farm, Bampton, Oxon, c5/1973 (by 10/6/1973).

(3) to Leisuretrack Ltd, Warwick Castle railway, Warwick, c/1973.

(4) to Leisuretrack Ltd, Cotswold Wildlife Park, Burford, Oxon, 7/1974 (after 23/6/1974).

(5) to Leisuretrack Ltd, Cotswold Wildlife Park, Burford, Oxon, /1975 (after 2/2/1974, by 22/4/1975).

(6) to Leisuretrack Ltd, Cotswold Wildlife Park, Burford, Oxon, c/1975 (after 2/2/1974); ex Leisuretrack Ltd, Stratford-upon-Avon, Warwicks, 3/1981 (by 11/4/1981); to Yaxham Light Railways, Yaxham, near Dereham, Norfolk, 25/2/1984.

(7) to Leisuretrack Ltd, Cotswold Wildlife Park, Burford, Oxon, 11/1976 (? directly from Bala Lake Railway ?); ex Leisuretrack Ltd, Stratford-upon-Avon, Warwicks, 3/1981 (after 5/10/1979, by 11/4/1981); regauged to 2ft 6in and sold to Centriline Ltd, Bamber Bridge, Preston, Lancs; exported to India 8/1983.

(8) to K. Fenwick, Shipston-on-Stour, Warwicks, c/1976 (? direct from Bala Lake Railway); s/s from there c/1980.

(9) to GEC Traction Ltd, Vulcan Works, Newton-le-Willows, Merseyside, c/1976 (after 1/3/1976) for rebuilding; to Nobel's Explosives Co Ltd, Ardeer Works, Strathclyde, c3/1977.

(10) to GEC Traction Ltd, Vulcan Works, Newton-le-Willows, Merseyside, c/1976 (after 1/3/1976) for rebuilding; to Nobel's Explosives Co Ltd, Ardeer Works, Strathclyde, 4/1978.

(11) to Bala Lake Railway Ltd, Llanuwchllyn, Gwynedd (North Wales), 23/11/1976.

(12) to Festiniog Railway Co, Portmadoc, Gwynedd (North Wales), 24/6/1977.

(13) to Leisuretrack Ltd, Cotswold Wildlife Park, Burford, Oxon, after 20/8/1977, by 30/5/1978.

(14) to Woburn Abbey (Narrow Gauge) Railway, Woburn Park, Beds, c/1976 (by 15/7/1978).

(15) to Leisuretrack Ltd, Stratford-upon-Avon, Warwicks, after 3/8/1979, by 5/10/1979.

(16) to contract, Hong Kong, per Sheridan Contractors Ltd, Nechells Green, West Midlands, c2/1981 (after 3/10/1980, by 25/4/1981).

(17) to Woburn Abbey (Narrow Gauge) Railway, /1974

(18) to contract, Bangkok, per Sheridan Contractors Ltd, Nechells Green, West Midlands, 16/12/1981.

(19) regauged to 2ft 6in; and sold to Centriline Ltd, Bamber Bridge, Preston, Lancs; exported to India 8/1983.

(20) to WR for renovation, 21/1/1982; returned here, 19/2/1982; sold to WR, after 11/2/1984, by 31/3/1984; rebuilt as WR 10114/1984 and sold to Carnarvon Mining Co Ltd, Clogau St Davids Mine, Bontddu, Gwynedd (North Wales), c9/1984.

(21) returned to J.F. Donelon & Co Ltd, Plant dealers, Bredbury, Gtr Manchester, c4/1985 (after 25/3/1985, by 26/7/1985).

(22) to Lilley Plant Ltd, for use on Cairo Wastewater Project, Egypt, after 23/8/1985, ? by 18/10/1985.

(23) scrapped on site c5/1986 (after 4/3/1986), (? by Ampthill Scrap Metal Processing Co Ltd).

Gauge : 1ft 6in

-		4wBE	CE	5370	1967	(a)	(1)
-		4wBE	Track Supplies		1984	New	(2)

(a) ex Laporte Industries Ltd, Ladywash Mine, near Eyam, Derbys, 3/1985 (after 30/1/1985, by 25/3/1985).

(1) to Gwynfynydd & Beddcoedwr Gold Mines Ltd, Gwynfynydd Gold Mine, Mawddach Falls, near Ganllwyd, Gwynedd [North Wales], c4/1985 (? via South Western Mining & Tunnelling Co).
(2) nearly complete on 2/5/1984; being built for McNicholas Construction, Elstree, Herts; believed scrapped (never completed), /1985.

UNCORRELATED DATA :

"Contract Journal" 14/2/1912 - Hodson's, Wendover to sell a 13in cyls 6-coupled MW, 10in cyls 4-coupled HC, 3ft gauge and a 7½in cyls 4-coupled KS, 2ft gauge.

J. Hodson & Son Ltd were contractors, based in Nottingham, who were mainly involved in waterworks jobs. They built Carno Reservoir (1905-1911) for Ebbw Vale UDC (see the Gwent Handbook, page 214), and this Wendover advertisement doubtless refers to locos MW 1006 and KS 1057 which were used at Carno, and to 3ft 0in gauge HC 495 which was owned by Hodsons and was possibly used at Carno. The KS loco was also offered for sale by Hodsons at "MR Goods Depot, Cricklewood", North London ("Contract Journal" 31/7/1912), but was included in the sale at Carno on 22-23/10/1913 ("Contract Journal" 1/10/1913). It was later at the WD depot, Newbury, Berkshire.

"Machinery Market", 12/1/1951 - For sale, eight Ruston & Hornsby 20DL 2ft 0in gauge locos - Lipton Products Ltd, Lower Glory Mill, Wooburn Green, Bucks (also advertised on 22/8/1952 and 6/8/1954 (three locos only)).

"Machinery Market", 1/10/1954 - For sale, lying Bucks, 1940 Hudson-Hunslet diesel loco - John Cullum (Contractors) Ltd, London SW1.

PRESERVATION LOCATIONS

MIKE BROWN
Gawcott, near Buckingham   AP1

Locomotive preserved at a private location.

Gauge : 2ft 0in

-	4wPM	L	26288	1944	(a)	(1)
-	4wDM	HE	6013	1961	(b)	

(a)   ex M. Brown, North Harrow, Middlesex, c/1996.
(b)   ex F.M.B. Engineering, Oakhanger, Hampshire, 6/10/1999; earlier National Power plc, Uskmouth Power Station, Gwent.

(1)   to R.P. Morris, Blaenau Ffestiniog, Gwynedd [North Wales], 7/10/1999.

M. CAPRON
8 Moon Street, Wolverton   EP2
SP 818409

Locomotive kept for preservation for some time at this private location.

Gauge : 1ft 11in

-	4wDM	RH	183773	1937	(a)	(1)

(a)   ex Woburn Abbey (Narrow Gauge) Railway, Beds, 10/10/1981.

(1)   to M.Capron, Hartley, Plymouth, Devon, 31/12/1986; then to Plym Valley Railway Association, Plympton, Devon, 22/4/1987.

A.COCKLIN & J.THOMAS
Bletchley   EP3

These locomotives were bought for preservation and stored at two sites in the Bletchley area:
         A : exact location unknown. (Shenley Brook Road ?)
         B : J.Thomas, 40 Wye Close, Bletchley (SP 852345)

Gauge : 2ft 0in

-	4wDM	OK	4805	1933	(a)	(1)	A
1	4wDM	OK	6705	1936	(b)	(1)	B
	4wDM	OK	7371	1937	(b)	(1)	A
2	4wDM	OK	7600	1937	(b)	(2)	B
-	4wPM	L	4228	1931	(c)	(3)	B

(a)   ex Redland Bricks Ltd, Warnham, Sussex, 6/1972.
(b)   ex Oxted Greystone Lime Co Ltd, Oxted, Surrey, 2/6/1972.
(c)   ex R.P.Morris, Longfield, Kent, 5/1972.

(1)   believed sold for scrap, c/1977 (after 10/8/1976).
(2)   to P.Wilson, Benfleet, Essex, c/1986 (after 4/8/1984, by 9/1986).
(3)   to Leighton Buzzard Narrow Gauge Railway Society, Leighton Buzzard, Beds, c8/1989.

P. ELMS
Bletchley

EP4

SP 831373

Locomotive stored awaiting preservation for some time at the premises of London Road Garage (Loughton) Ltd, Loughton, near Bletchley.

Gauge : 4ft 8½in

ROBERT	0-6-0ST	OC	AE	2068 1933	(a)	(1)

(a)   ex Stewarts & Lloyds Minerals Ltd, Lamport Ironstone Quarries, Northants, 9/1969.

(1)   to London Railway Preservation Society Ltd, Quainton Road, near Aylesbury, c3/1970.

GULLIVER'S LAND THEME PARK
Milton Keynes

EP5

SP 870400

Narrow gauge pleasure line, opened 31/3/1999.

Gauge : 1ft 3in

-	2-4-0 + 6wDE	S/O	Gulliver	New

ALAN KEEF
THE RED HOUSE, Aston Clinton, near Aylesbury

DP6

Locomotives kept in private preservation for some time by this well known narrow gauge locomotive engineer.

Gauge : 2ft 0in

-	0-4-0PM	BgC	760 1918	(a)	(1)

(a)   ex The Old Vicarage, Woburn, Beds, /1964

(1)   to R.P.Morris, 193, Main Rd, Longfield, Kent, 3/1968.

Gauge : 1ft 10¾in

(KATHLEEN)	0-4-0VBT	VC	DeW	1877	(a)	(1)

(a)   ex R.P.Morris, 193, Main Rd, Longfield, Kent, 6/1965.

(1)   to Walcroft Bros, Pershore, Worcs, by 8/1968.

LAVENDON NARROW GAUGE RAILWAY
Lavendon, near Olney

AP7

SP 920535

A private 7¼in gauge railway opened in 1991, open to the public on advertised dates. The locomotive listed below is preserved in working order on a short section of track.

Gauge : 3ft 0in

-	4wBE	GB	(a)

(a)   ex W.T. Sheppard & Sons Ltd, Wellingborough, c12/1999.

Sir WILLIAM H.McALPINE
FAWLEY HILL, Fawley Green, near Henley-on-Thames

A private location, not open to the public. Preserved locomotives and stock are operated on the Fawley Hill Railway, about ½ mile long, which includes a steep incline and a reversal.

Gauge : 4ft 8½in

No.31		0-6-0ST	IC	HC	1026	1913	(a)	
	PITSFORD	0-6-0ST	OC	AE	1917	1923	(b)	(1)
No.11	SIRAPITE	4wWT	G	AP	6158	1906	(c)	(3)
29	ELIZABETH	0-4-0ST	OC	AE	1865	1922	(d)	(5)
No.5		0-4-0DM		Bg	3027	1939	(e)	(6)
	EYU 338 C	4wPM		Austin Champ				
			reb	McAlpine		1965	(f)	(2)
	JOYCE	4wVBT	VCG	S	7109	1927	(g)	(4)
	FIREFLY	0-6-0T	OC	HC	1864	1952	(h)	(7)
D2120	(03 120)	0-6-0DM		Sdn		1959	(i)	
(No.5	FLYING FLEA)							
	SIR WILLIAM	4wDM		RH	294266	1951	(j)	
9112		4wDMR		Bg	3538	1959	(k)	
	-	4wDM		FH	3894	1958		
			reb	AB	6930	1988	(l)	

(a)   ex Sir Robert McAlpine & Sons Ltd, Hayes, Middlesex, 9/1965; to Market Overton Industrial Association, c1/3/1977; returned 29/5/1979; to Steamtown Railway Museum, Carnforth, Lancs, c3/1985; returned, 29/7/1985.

(b)   ex Byfield Ironstone Co Ltd, Pitsford Quarries, Northants, 7/1966, via E.E.Kimbell & Co, Engineers, Northampton.

(c)   ex Richard Garrett Engineering Works Ltd, Leiston, Suffolk, left there 16/5/1966 for restoration at a private site in Dunston-on-Tyne; moved to Fawley in /1970.

(d)   ex South Eastern Gas Board, Waddon Marsh Works, Croydon, Surrey, 22/7/1969.

(e)   ex Flying Scotsman Enterprises, Market Overton, Rutland, after rebuild at BD, c3/1975 (by 27/4/1975). Originally Bass, Mitchells & Butlers Ltd, Burton-on-Trent, Staffs.

(f)   converted from road vehicle (here?); to here by 27/4/1975.

(g)   ex Alan Bloom, Bressingham Hall, Norfolk, c/1975 (after 24/8/1975).

(h)   ex Steamtown Railway Museum, Carnforth, Lancs, c29/4/1983.

(i)   ex BR, Landore Depot, Swansea, West Glamorgan, 18/12/1986.

(j)   ex Steamtown Railway Museum, Carnforth, Lancs, 6/6/1990.

(k)   ex MoDAD, CAD, Bramley, Hampshire, 18/6/1996.

(l)   ex South Yorkshire Railway Preservation Society, Meadowhall, Rotherham, South Yorkshire, 24/9/1997 (via MoDAD, CAD, Bramley, Hampshire, arriving here c1/1998); earlier Royal Ordnance plc, Bishopton, Strathclyde.

(1)   to Peterborough Railway Society, Wansford, Cambs, 2/1973.

(2)   to Flying Scotsman Enterprises, Market Overton, Rutland, 11/1975.

(3)   to Steamtown Railway Museum, Carnforth, Lancs, 3/1978.

(4)   to B. Turner, Ripley, Surrey, for restoration, by 9/1/1983.

(5)   to Steamtown Railway Museum, Carnforth, Lancs, after 15/7/1984, by 7/9/1985.

(6)   to Steamtown Railway Museum, Carnforth, Lancs, after 15/7/1984, by 31/1/1987.

(7)   returned to Steamtown Railway Museum, Carnforth, Lancs, by 3/1987.

Gauge : 2ft 6in

CHEVALLIER	0-6-2T	OC	MW	1877	1915	(a)	(1)
CONQUEROR	0-6-2T	OC	WB	2192	1922	(b)	(2)
SUPERIOR	0-6-2T	OC	KS	4034	1922	(b)	(2)

(a)   ex Sir Robert McAlpine & Sons Ltd, Hayes Plant Depot, Middlesex, after 8/1969.
(b)   ex Bowater United Kingdon Paper Co Ltd, Sittingbourne, Kent, /1970.

(1)   to Pleasure Rail Ltd, Whipsnade Zoo, Beds, /1970
(2)   to Pleasure Rail Ltd, Whipsnade Zoo, Beds, c10/1970

Gauge : 2ft 0in

A 4365	4wDM	MR	8998	1946	(a)	(1)

(a)   ex Sir Robert McAlpine & Sons Ltd, Lowdham, Notts, 4/1970.

(1)   to Pleasurerail Ltd, Knebworth, Herts, by 8/1971.

MILTON KEYNES DEVELOPMENT CORPORATION
MILTON KEYNES CENTRAL STATION, Milton Keynes   EP9
SP 842381

A non-working replica has been on static display here since 3/10/1991. It is not a locomotive, but the information is included here for interest.

Gauge : 4ft 8½in

1009	WOLVERTON	2-2-2	IC	MF	1991	New

QUAINTON RAILWAY SOCIETY LTD
BUCKINGHAMSHIRE RAILWAY CENTRE   DP10
Quainton Road Station, near Aylesbury   SP 739190 and SP 736189
London Railway Preservation Society Ltd until 24/4/1971

Preservation centre established in 1969 around the site of Quainton Road station on the Met/GCR line north of Aylesbury. Museum buildings, workshops and stock storage sheds have been developed, together with demonstration running lines, on both sides of the BR line. During major weekend events chartered passenger services have operated over the BR line to and from Aylesbury. The LNWR station buildings from Rewley Road, Oxford, have been reconstructed here as an exhibition and visitor centre.

Gauge : 4ft 8½in

(30585)	E 0314		2-4-0WT	OC	BP	1414	1874	(ma)
L 44	1		0-4-4T	IC	Neasden	3	1896	(mb)
L 99	(7715)		0-6-0PT	IC	KS	4450	1930	(mc)
6024	KING EDWARD I		4-6-0	4C	Sdn		1930	(md)	(14)
6989	WIGHTWICK HALL		4-6-0	OC	Sdn		1948	(me)
7200			2-8-2T	OC	Sdn		1934	(mf)
9466			0-6-0PT	IC	RSHN	7617	1952	(mg)
34016	BODMIN		4-6-2	3C	Bton		1945	(mh)	(5)
41298			2-6-2T	OC	Crewe		1951	(mj)
41313			2-6-2T	OC	Crewe		1952	(mk)
46447			2-6-0	OC	Crewe		1950	(ml)

76017		2-6-0	OC	Hor		1953	(mm)	(6)
D2298	(LORD WENLOCK)	0-6-0DM		RSHD	8157	1960		
	(No.1)			DC	2679	1960	(mn)	
25057	(D5207)	Bo-Bo.DE		Derby		1963	(mo)	(17)
	SYDENHAM	4wWT	G	AP	3567	1895	(a)	(21)
	(PUNCH HULL)	0-4-0ST	OC	AB	776	1896	(b)	(9)
		0-4-0ST	OC	AB	1865	1926	(c)	(8)
(V 75)		0-4-0ST	OC	WB	2469	1932	(d)	
	TRYM	0-4-0ST	OC	HE	287	1883	(e)	(15)
	CUNARDER	0-6-0ST	OC	HE	1690	1931	(f)	(4)
	SWANSCOMBE	0-4-0ST	OC	AB	699	1891	(g)	
	JUNO	0-6-0ST	IC	HE	3850	1958	(h)	
No.1	SIR THOMAS	0-6-0T	OC	HC	1334	1918	(j)	
No.14	BRILL	0-4-0ST	OC	MW	1795	1912	(k)	
		0-6-0ST	OC	YE	2498	1951	(l)	
No.2		0-4-0F	OC	AB	1493	1916	(m)	(1)
		0-4-0ST	OC	HC	1742	1946	(n)	
	ROBERT	0-6-0ST	OC	AE	2068	1933	(o)	(2)
11		4wVBT	VCG	S	9366	1945	(p)	
	(TOM PARRY)	0-4-0ST	OC	AB	2015	1935	(q)	(20)
No.1	COVENTRY No.1	0-6-0T	IC	NBH	24564	1939	(r)	
377	KING HAAKON VII	2-6-0	OC	Nohab	1164	1919	(s)	(3)
(No.3)		0-4-0ST	OC	HL	3717	1928	(t)	
	(GF No.3)	0-4-0F	OC	AB	1477	1916	(u)	
7		4wVBT	VCG	S	9376	1947		
		Reb	TH			1960	(v)	(19)
		0-4-0T	OC	P		1900	1935	(w)	
LNER 49	(No.2 ISEBROOK)	4wVBT	VCG	S	6515	1926	(x)	(23)
	HORNPIPE	0-4-0ST	OC	P	1756	1928	(y)	(10)
	LAPORTE	0-4-0F	OC	AB	2243	1948	(z)	
		0-4-0ST	OC	P	2104	1950	(aa)	(12)
		0-4-0ST	OC	P	2105	1950	(ab)	
		0-4-0ST	OC	P	2129	1952	(ac)	(7)
(66)		0-6-0ST	IC	HE	3890	1964	(ad)	
	ARTHUR	0-6-0ST	IC	HE	3782	1953	(ae)	
	(SWORDFISH)	0-6-0ST	OC	AB	2138	1941	(af)	(13)
65		0-6-0ST	IC	HE	3889	1964	(ag)	(11)
No.2	GIBRALTAR (2087)	0-4-0ST	OC	P	2087	1948	(ah)	
(7)	SUSAN	4wVBT	VCG	S	9537	1952	(aj)	
(5208)		2w-2-2-2w-4-4R	12CG	S	9418	1950	(ak)	
	THE BLUE CIRCLE	2-2-0WT	G	AP	9449	1926	(al)	
	SIR VINCENT	4wWT	G	AP	8800	1917	(am)	
	REDLAND	4wDM		KS	4428	1930	(da)	
	(OSRAM)	0-4-0DM		JF	20067	1933	(db)	
		4wDM		FH	3765	1955	(dc)	
T1		4wDM		FH	2102	1937	(dd)	
		0-4-0DM		HE	2067	1940	(de)	
		0-4-0DM		EE/DK	1192	1941		
				DC	2161	1941	(df)	(22)
HILSEA	(FLEET NO.1139)	4wDM		RH	463153	1961	(dg)	
	(WALRUS)	0-4-0DM		FH	3271	1949	(dh)	

12D	NCB 63/000/342	0-6-0DH	HE	7016	1971	(dj)	(16)
No.24		4wDH	TH/S	188C	1967		
		Reb of S		9597	1955	(dk)	(18)
9037		2w-2PMR	Wkm	8197	1958	(ra)	
9040		2w-2PMR	Wkm	6963	1955	(rb)	
		2w-2PMR	Wkm	8263	1959	(rc)	
53028		2w-2-2-2wRER	BRCW		1938	(rd)	
54233		2w-2-2-2wRER	GRC		1940	(re)	
51899	AYLESBURY COLLEGE						
		2-2w-2w-2DMR	DerbyC&W		1960	(rf)	
51886		2-2w-2w-2DMR	DerbyC&W		1960	(rg)	

Note that locos P 2104 and 2105 were built in 1948 but carried plates dated 1950.

(ma) ex BR (SR), 19/3/1964; stored at Bishops Stortford, Herts, until 9/5/1969.

(mb) ex London Transport Board, 20/3/1964; stored at Skimpot Lane, Luton, Beds; to Midland Railway London Extension Centenary Exhibition, Bedford, 1/10/1968; to International Alloys Ltd, Aylesbury, for storage, 4/11/1968; to Quainton Road, 23/9/1970.

(mc) ex London Transport Executive, Neasden Depot, London, 1/1970; to Llangollen Railway, Denbighs [North Wales], 12/3/1987; returned, /1987.

(md) ex Woodham Bros, Barry Dock, South Glamorgan, 31/3/1973.

(me) ex Woodham Bros, Barry Dock, South Glamorgan, 10/1/1978.

(mf) ex Woodham Bros, Barry Dock, South Glamorgan, 24/9/1981.

(mg) ex Woodham Bros, Barry Dock, South Glamorgan, 25/9/1975.

(mh) ex Woodham Bros, Barry Dock, South Glamorgan, 29/7/1972.

(mj) ex MoDAD, Longmoor, Hampshire, 12/12/1970.

(mk) ex Woodham Bros, Barry Dock, South Glamorgan, 2/7/1975.

(ml) ex Woodham Bros, Barry Dock, South Glamorgan, 7/6/1972.

(mm) ex Woodham Bros, Barry Dock, South Glamorgan, 1/1/1974.

(mn) ex Derwent Valley Light Railway, East Yorkshire, 22/10/1982.

(mo) ex BR, via Vic Berry, Leicester, 5/8/1988.

(a) ex Skimpot Lane, Luton, Beds, 16/4/1969; earlier Enfield & District Veteran Vehicle Society until 5/9/1965.

(b) ex Skimpot Lane, Luton, Beds, 16/4/1969; earlier APCM, Dunstable Works until 1/3/1967.

(c) ex Skimpot Lane, Luton, Beds, 17/4/1969; earlier North Thames Gas Board, Southall, Middlesex until 20/4/1966.

(d) ex Skimpot Lane, Luton, Beds, 17/4/1969; earlier C.A.Parsons Ltd, Erith, Kent until 28/10/1966.

(e) ex Skimpot Lane, Luton, Beds, 18/4/1969; earlier Howard Farrow & Co Ltd, contrs, Hendon, Middlesex, until 13/5/1964.

(f) ex APCM, Harbury Works, Warwicks, 24/4/1969.

(g) ex Skimpot Lane, Luton, Beds, 10/5/1969; earlier Thurrock Chalk & Whiting Co Ltd, West Thurrock, Essex until 6/2/1966.

(h) ex Stewarts & Lloyds Minerals Ltd, Buckminster Ironstone Quarries, Lincs, 31/5/1969.

(j) ex Oxfordshire Ironstone Co Ltd, Banbury, Oxon, 1/6/1969.

(k) ex South Durham Steel & Iron Co Ltd, Irchester Ironstone Quarries, Northants, 27/8/1969; to Northamptonshire Ironstone Railway Trust, Hunsbury Hill, Northants, 26/9/1977; returned here 19/10/1998.

(l) ex NCB, Chislet Colliery, Kent, 6/1/1970.

(m) ex Laporte Industries Ltd, Luton, Beds, 2/3/1970.

(n) ex storage at BR, Millom, 3/1970; earlier Millom Hematite Ore & Iron Co Ltd, Millom Ironworks, Cumbs, until 3/1969.

(o)   ex P. Elms, store at London Road Garage (Loughton) Ltd, Bletchley, Bucks, until c3/1970.

(p)   ex Eastern Gas Board, Tottenham Gas Works, London, 4/8/1970.

(q)   ex store at International Alloys Ltd, Aylesbury, 19/11/1970; stored at Dunstable Town Station, Beds, until 28/3/1968; earlier APCM, Dunstable Works, Beds until 1/3/1967.

(r)   ex NCB, South Midlands Area, Newdigate Colliery, Warwicks, 18/1/1971.

(s)   ex Alan Bloom, Bressingham, Norfolk, 6/5/1971.

(t)   ex APCM, Swanscombe Works, Kent, 2/6/1971.

(u)   ex Laporte Industries Ltd, Luton, Beds, 7/1971.

(v)   ex GR-Stein Refractories Ltd, Deepcar, Yorkshire (WR), 16/7/1971.

(w)   ex Courtaulds Ltd, Grimsby, Lincs, 9/1971; to Lakeside & Haverthwaite Railway, Cumbria, 15/6/1983 and then to Steamtown Railway Museum, Carnforth, Lancs, 3/9/1983; returned here 22/11/1983; to North Downs Steam Railway, Kent, by 31/3/1986; returned by 8/1986.

(x)   ex Thos.E.Gray Ltd, Burton Latimer, Northants, 31/5/1972; to Birmingham Railway Museum, Tyseley, Birmingham, 6/9/1988; returned, 6/10/1988; to Chinnor & Princes Risborough Railway, Oxon, 30/7/1991; returned 23/3/1994.

(y)   ex APCM, Holborough Works, Kent, 8/8/1972.

(z)   ex Laporte Industries Ltd, Luton, Beds, 27/11/1972.

(aa)   ex CEGB, Croydon "B" Generating Station, Croydon, Surrey, 12/12/1972.

(ab)   ex CEGB, Croydon "B" Generating Station, Croydon, Surrey, 14/12/1972.

(ac)   ex Michael Croft, Theberton, Suffolk, 12/7/1974.

(ad)   ex NCB, South Yorkshire Area, Cadeby Colliery, 4/11/1975.

(ae)   ex J.M.Walker, Lindsey Farm, High Cogges, Oxon, 1/12/1979.

(af)   ex Goodman Bros, New Bradwell, Wolverton, 15/8/1980.

(ag)   ex NCB, Cadley Hill Colliery, Derbys, 14/1/1983.

(ah)   ex Lakeside & Haverthwaite Railway, Cumbria, 9/12/1983.

(aj)   ex J.Morris, Lytham Creek Motive Power Museum, Lancashire, 29/6/1984; to Nene Valley Railway, Cambs, 5/8/1997; returned 22/9/1997.

(ak)   ex Egyptian State Railways, 18/1/1985.

(al)   ex Northamptonshire Ironstone Railway Trust, Hunsbury Hill, Northants, 24/10/1997.

(am)   ex Nene Valley Railway, Wansford, Cambs, 5/8/1998.

(da)   ex Redland Flettons Ltd, Kempston Hardwick, Beds, 15/4/1969.

(db)   ex General Electric Co Ltd, North Wembley, Middlesex, 10/1971.

(dc)   ex Tarmac Roadstone Ltd, Hayes, Middlesex, 21/4/1974.

(dd)   ex Compair Broomwade Ltd, High Wycombe, 19/8/1978.

(de)   ex Esso Petroleum Ltd, Purfleet, Essex, 29/4/1983.

(df)   ex Esso Petroleum Ltd, Purfleet, Essex, 10/10/1983; orig WD 34, later WD 70035.

(dg)   ex British Gas Corporation, Hilsea Works, Portsmouth, Hampshire, 25/7/1986.

(dh)   ex Arthur Guinness Ltd, Park Royal, London, 9/11/1986.

(dj)   ex C.F.Booth Ltd, Rotherham, 31/10/1986; earlier NCB Bold Colliery, Merseyside.

(dk)   ex C.F.Booth Ltd, Rotherham, 28/12/1987; earlier CEGB, Stella North Power Station, Tyne & Wear.

(ra)   ex MoDAD, Bicester, Oxon, 15/8/1972.

(rb)   ex scrap dealer, Abingdon, Oxon, 25/6/1969; earlier MoDAD., Bicester, Oxon,.

(rc)   ex BR, Northampton, 9/3/1968; stored at Skimpot Lane, Luton, Beds, until 4/4/1969.

(rd)   ex London Transport Executive, Ruislip Depot, London, 30/6/1984.

(re)   ex London Transport Executive, Neasden, London, 10/10/1981.

(rf)   ex BR, Old Oak Common Depot, London, 15/2/1994.

(rg)   ex BR, Old Oak Common Depot, London, 22/2/1994

(1) to Ayris & Jeacock, Bicester, Oxon, for scrap, 22/5/1970.
(2) to Foxfield Light Railway, Staffs, 3/10/1971.
(3) to South Eastern Steam Centre, Ashford, Kent, 1/1972.
(4) to APCM, Dunstable Works, Beds, for storage, 7/3/1976.
(5) to Winchester & Alton Railway Co Ltd, Hampshire, 31/10/1976.
(6) to Winchester & Alton Railway Co Ltd, Hampshire, 2/1978.
(7) to B.Roberts, Hill Farm, Tollerton, Notts, 27/3/1982.
(8) to West Lancs Black 5 Fund, Thornton, near Fleetwood, Lancs, 21/11/1986.
(9) to Rutland Railway Museum, Cottesmore, Leics, 18/7/1987.
(10) to T.Buck, Deep Meadows, Fifield, Berks, 30/5/1987.
(11) to Rutland Railway Museum, Cottesmore, Leics, 28/12/1987.
(12) to Northamptonshire Steam Railway, Pitsford, Northants, 23/3/1989.
(13) to Rutland Railway Museum, Cottesmore, Leics, 8/7/1989.
(14) to Birmingham Railway Museum, Tyseley, West Midlands, 9/10/1989.
(15) to Northamptonshire Ironstone Railway Trust, Hunsbury Hill, Northants, 4/11/1989.
(16) to Yorkshire Engine Co Ltd, Rotherham, moved directly to BREL, Crewe Works for rebuild, 30/8/1990; resold to Balfour Beatty Railway Engineering Ltd, Cheriton, Kent.
(17) to North Norfolk Railway, Sheringham, Norfolk, 2/4/1991.
(18) to Rutland Railway Museum, Cottesmore, Leics, 19/3/1992.
(19) to Rutland Railway Museum, Cottesmore, Leics, 13/5/1994.
(20) to Pontypool & Blaenavon Railway, Gwent, 3/6/1997
(21) to Chatham Dockyard Historic Trust, Chatham, Kent, on long term loan, 5/9/1997.
(22) to STIBANS, Watergraafsmeer, Amsterdam, Holland, 9/3/2001
(23) to The Rosemary Vineyard, Ryde, Isle of Wight, 31/5/2001.

Gauge : 4ft 8½in - Visiting Locomotives:

The following locomotives have visited the Quainton Railway Society for short periods in connection with special events:

5080	DEFIANT	4-6-0	4C	Sdn		1939	(a)	(1)
6106		2-6-2T	OC	Sdn		1931	(b)	(2)
	ROCKET	0-2-2	OC	Loco Ent. 2		1979	(c)	(3)
32	GOTHENBURG	0-6-0T	IC	HC	680	1903	(d)	(4)
L 44		4w-4w.BE/RE	Don		L44	1973	(e)	(5)
	SIR VINCENT	4wWT	G	AP	8800	1917	(f)	(6)
69523		0-6-2T	IC	NBH	22600	1921	(g)	(7)
76017		2-6-0	OC	Hor		1953	(h)	(8)
73080	(73096) MERLIN	4-6-0	OC	Derby		1955	(j)	(9)
	LOCOMOTION	0-4-0	VC	Loco Ent 1		1975	(k)	(10)
DS238	WAINWRIGHT	0-6-0T	OC	VIW	4433	1943	(l)	(11)
56		0-6-0ST	IC	RSHN	7667	1950	(m)	(12)
7760		0-6-0PT	IC	NBQ	24048	1930	(n)	(13)
41708		0-6-0T	IC	Derby		1880	(o)	(14)
41312		2-6-2T	OC	Crewe		1952	(p)	(15)
7754		0-6-0PT	IC	NBQ	24042	1930	(q)	(16)
68153	59	4wVBT	VCG	S	8837	1933	(r)	(17)
5541		2-6-2T	OC	Sdn		1928	(s)	(18)

(a) ex Birmingham Railway Museum, Tyseley, W. Midlands, 5/1990.
(b) ex Great Western Society, Didcot Railway Centre, Oxon, 10/1991.
(c) ex National Railway Museum, York, after 18/5/1991;.
(d) ex East Lancashire Railway, Bury, Gtr Manchester, 9/1992; to Main Line Steam Trust, Loughborough, Leics, by 23/10/1992; ex East Lancashire Railway, Bury, Gtr Manchester, 5/10/1993.
(e) ex London Underground Ltd, Ruislip Depot, London, 1/7/1993.

(f)	ex Northamptonshire Ironstone Railway Trust, Northants, 23/9/1993.
(g)	ex Great Central Railway, Loughborough, Leics, 26/4/1994.
(h)	ex East Somerset Railway, Cranmore, Somerset, 23/5/1994.
(j)	ex Mid-Hampshire Railway, Ropley, Hampshire, 18/8/1994.
(k)	ex South Devon Railway, Buckfastleigh, Devon, 16/8/1995.
(l)	ex Kent & East Sussex Railway, Rolvenden, Kent, 24/9/1998.
(m)	ex Great Central Railway (Northern), Ruddington, Notts, 19/8/1998.
(n)	ex Standard Gauge Steam Trust, Tyseley, Birmingham, 26/3/1999.
(o)	ex Swanage Railway, Dorset, 9/1999.
(p)	ex Mid Hampshire Railway, Ropley, Hampshire, 19 or 20/4/2000.
(q)	ex Llangollen Railway, Denbighs, [North Wales], 28/4/2000.
(r)	ex Middleton Railway, Leeds, 22/10/1998.
(s)	ex Dean Forest Railway, Lydney, Glos, c5/2000.

(1)	returned to Birmingham Railway Museum, Tyseley.
(2)	returned to Great Western Society, Didcot Railway Centre, 16/10/1991.
(3)	returned to National Railway Museum, York, after 25/5/1991, by 2/6/1991.
(4)	returned to East Lancashire Railway, Bury, 20/10/1993.
(5)	returned to London Underground Ltd, Ruislip Depot, 7/7/1993.
(6)	returned to Northamptonshire Ironstone Railway Trust, 22/10/1993.
(7)	to London Underground Ltd, Ruislip Depot, Middlesex, 10/5/1994.
(8)	to Mid-Hants Railway, Ropley, Hampshire, 7/6/1994.
(9)	returned to Mid-Hants Railway, Ropley, after 28/8/1994.
(10)	to Weardale Railway Society, Co.Durham, 25/9/1995.
(11)	returned to Kent & East Sussex Railway, Rolvenden, Kent, c21/10/1998.
(12)	returned to Great Central Railway (Northern), Ruddington, Notts, 7/9/1998.
(13)	returned to Birmingham Railway Museum, Tyseley, c7/1999 (by 4/9/1999).
(14)	to North Norfolk Railway, Norfolk, after 31/10/1999.
(15)	returned to Mid Hampshire Railway, 27/4/2000.
(16)	to Adtranz Crewe open day, 20-21/5/2000; thence to Llangollen Railway, Denbighshire.
(17)	returned to Middleton Railway, Leeds, 30/11/2000.
(18)	returned to Dean Forest Railway, Lydney, Glos, c6/2000 (by 18/8/2000).

Gauge : 3ft 6in:

| 3405 | JANICE | | 4-8-4 | OC | NBH | 27291 | 1953 | (a) | |

| (a) | ex South African Railways, 28/10/1991. |

Gauge : 2ft 0in

LO 23		4wDM	RH	277273	1949	(a)	(1)
-		4wDM	FH	2586	1941	(b)	(2)
803		2w-2-2-2wRE	EE	803	1931	(c)	

a)	ex A.M. Keef, Bampton, Oxon, 18/4/1973; earlier. A. Waddington & Son Ltd, Darent Valley Pipeline contract, Farningham, Kent.
b)	ex M.E. Engineering Ltd, Cricklewood, Middlesex, 23/8/1973.
c)	ex Post Office Railway, Mount Pleasant, London, 22/3/1983.

| 1) | to A.M.Keef, 11/1974; then to Boothby Peat Co Ltd, Bolton Fell Mill, Cumbria, 11/1974. |
| 2) | to Island Narrow Gauge Group, Isle of Wight, 22/4/1974. |

Gauge : 1ft 10¾in

HOLY WAR	0-4-0ST	OC	HE	779	1902	(a)	(1)

(a)   ex Dinorwic Slate Quarries Co Ltd, Llanberis, Caerns [North Wales], 20/3/1970.

(1)   to Bala Lake Railway Ltd, Bala, Gwynedd [North Wales], 13/12/1975.

SLOUGH & WINDSOR RAILWAY SOCIETY
STOKE PLACE RESIDENTIAL HOME, Stoke Green, Stoke Poges.   BP11
SU 984822

A 2ft gauge line, replacing an earlier 7¼in gauge minature railway, was built from about 1990 with a circular route about 400 yards in length. This ran beside a lake in the grounds of Stoke Place. The standad gauge locos were static exhibits. The railway closed 31/7/1998 and the stock has been dispersed.

Gauge : 4ft 8½in

SLOUGH ESTATES No.3	0-6-0ST	OC	HC	1544	1924	(a)	(2)
-	0-4-0DH		JF 4220031		1964	(b)	(1)

(a)   ex Mid-Hampshire Railway, Alresford, Hampshire, 2/1992.
(b)   ex Kent & East Sussex Railway, Tenterden, Kent, c/1987 (after 19/7/1987).

(1)   to Swindon & Cricklade Railway, Wilts, 2/7/1999.
(2)   to Swindon & Cricklade Railway, Wilts, 5/7/1999.

Gauge : 2ft 6in

(YARD No.54) (T0235)	4wDMR	FH	2196	1940	(a)	(1)

(a)   ex MoDND, RNAD, Trecwn, Dyfed, c2/1990 (after 24/2/1989, by 30/10/1990).

(1)   to Moseley Railway Trust, Whaley Bridge, Derbys, for storage, 15/5/1999.

Gauge : 2ft 0in

-	4wDM		MR	8717	1941	(a)	(1)
-	4wDM		MR	8995	1946	(a)	(1)
649 SIR TOM	4wDM		MR	40S273	1966	(b)	(3)
-	4wDM		RH	211609	1941	(c)	(2)
HORATIO	4wDM	S/O	RH	217967	1941	(d)	(3)

(a)   ex Knebworth West Park & Wintergreen Railway, Knebworth, Herts, c10/1989; converted to brake vans and dismantled.
(b)   ex Knebworth West Park & Wintergreen Railway, Knebworth, Herts, c10/1990; converted to brake van and dismantled.
(c)   ex Department of the Environment, Lydd Gun Ranges, Kent, c/1989 (after 2/1989).
(d)   ex Knebworth West Park & Wintergreen Railway, Knebworth, Herts, c11/1990; converted to brake van and dismantled.

(1)   to Moseley Railway Trust, Whaley Bridge, Derbys, for storage, 15/5/1999.
(2)   to FMB Engineering, Oakhanger, Hampshire, 9/4/1999.
(3)   to Tony Guy, private location, Hazlemere, Surrey, 5/2001.

NON-LOCOMOTIVE SYSTEMS

WILLIAM BARTLETT & SONS LTD
GRAFTON STREET WORKS, High Wycombe

CH1
SU 849936

A firm of chair makers, established c1895, which had a narrow gauge tramway within the works.

BELLINGDON BRICK CO
BELLINGDON BRICKWORKS, near Chesham

AH2
SP 946050

Brickworks established in 1891 by J. Mead and taken over in 1923 by H.G. Matthews. The works is believed to have had a narrow gauge tramway - "Contract Journal" 13/7/1904 advertises W. Brown & Co to sell 22/7/1904 re Bellingdon Brick Co, near Chesham, plant including about ½ mile of portable track and tip wagons. The works is still in production in 2000.

BLETCHLEY SAND & GRAVEL CO
Western Road, Bletchley
Faulkner & Son (proprietor) by c1931
H.G. Brown (proprietor) from c1924

EH3
SP 874341

Gravel pit located on the south side of the ex-LNWR Bedford - Bletchley railway, to the west of the A5 road, which utilised a narrow gauge tramway within the pits. Workings closed by 1939.

WM. BOYER & SONS LTD
HUNTSMOOR PARK SAND PIT

BH4
TQ 045809

The company was established by 1935. A sand and ballast works was located in Ford Lane, on the edge of Huntsmoor Park. This works had a narrow gauge tramway shown on the 25in OS map of 1925. The company is known to have had two diesel locos (FH 2288 and FH 2291) at pits in West Drayton and it is possible that these may have earlier worked at this location. Additionally Wm Boyer & Sons advertised for sale, in "Contract Journal" 22/10/1952 and again 11/11/1953, two 2ft 0in gauge Simplex 20hp 2½ton locos at nearby pits in Trout Lane, Yiewsley.

BRILL BRICK & TILE CO LTD
The Grove, Brill

AH5
SP 682176

A narrow gauge tramway was used within this works, which was opened c1895 and closed in 1911.

BRITISH WATERWAYS BOARD
BULBOURNE WHARF, near Tring

AH6

SP 934137

A handworked line of 3ft 6in gauge which connects a workshops producing lock gates with wharf alongside the Grand Union Canal. The track is embedded in concrete and stoc comprises two flat wagons.

FLETTON BRICK CO
WOBURN SANDS BRICKWORKS

EH7

Fletton Brick Co by c1940

SP 921342

Eastwoods & Co from c1906 - c1924

Fletton & Co c1903

A brickworks which was located on the south side of the ex-LNWR Bedford - Bletchle railway about ¼ mile west of Woburn Sands station. Served by standard gauge siding which connected with this line and also by a narrow gauge tramway (shown on the 1925 O map) from the clay pit to the works.

IVINGHOE LIME CO LTD
Ivinghoe Aston, near Dunstable

AH8

SP 960175

A limeworks and quarry which may have had a narrow gauge tramway (an order was place with Motor Rail on 14/4/1930 for the purchase of two side-tipping wagons). Proprietc Thomas Ashby is listed in trade directories as a farmer in 1920 and a lime merchant in 193 – the quarry came into use after 1924, but by 1928.

JACKSON'S MILLBOARD & FIBRE CO LTD
HEDSOR MILL, Bourne End

CH9

Jackson's Millboard & Paper Co Ltd (established 1891) until c1899

SU 896867

The 1925 OS map shows a narrow gauge tramway which ran between the company's thre mills. These were Hedsor Mill, Gunpowder Mill (SU 897871) and Princes Mill (SU 901872) The latter two were known as Lower and Upper Mills respectively.

OLNEY LIMESTONE CO
OLNEY LIMEWORKS

AH10

SP 900517

A limeworks and associated quarry was established here by Emmanuel Gould at the turn o the century. It was served by a standard gauge siding, known as Goulds Siding, off the LMS Bedford - Northampton railway. The works closed c1938. A 2ft 6in gauge tramway wa used to connect the quarry and works and its remains were still in existence in 1961.

ROCLA PIPES LTD
Wolverton Road, Newport Pagnell

EH11

SP 857430

Manufacturers of concrete pipes, in production in 1978 (and probably much earlier). The factory contained ten bays, each with a broad gauge track of 6ft 0in gauge. Three of these racks were each about 160ft in length, extending through the rear of the building to a traverser about 200 yards long and built of light rail to 6ft 6in gauge. This was used to move pipes from the factory to an open air storage area at the rear of the works. Factory closed by 1991 and remains derelict at the time of writing (2001).

BARON FERDINAND DE ROTHSCHILD
WADDESDON MANOR, near Aylesbury

DH12

SP 732165

Construction of this manor, the home of Baron Ferdinand de Rothschild, began in 1876. In conjunction with the extensive works a standard gauge branch railway was laid from the Brill Tramway. This branch, which was horse worked, commenced at a junction between Waddesdon and Westcott stations on the Brill Tramway and ran uphill towards the site of the manor. From the end of this branch a narrow gauge tramway continued uphill to the Manor. The tubs on the narrow gauge were moved by cable haulage powered by a steam winch and were used to convey bricks, stone and timber for the construction work. The manor was completed in 1889 and the railways subsequently dismantled.

Reference : "The Brill Tramway", Bill Simpson, OPC, 1985.

THOMAS & GREEN LTD
SOHO MILL, Wooburn

CH13

SU 906877

Company established in 1890. The Mill was purchased in 1892 and was served by extensive standard gauge sidings, with several wagon turntables, and also a narrow gauge tramway. The standard gauge wagons were moved by horses until these were replaced by a road tractor in 1942. The Mill closed in July 1984.

WAR DEPARTMENT
HIGH WYCOMBE DEPOT   C31

It was reported to the IRS Records Officer in a letter dated 6/6/1949 that :
"Ten 2ft gauge 4wPetrol locos recently arrived at F.C. Hibberd for overhaul ex WD Hig
Wycombe. The works numbers are hard to decypher but appear to fall in the 2510 to 252
range". Study of existing F.C. Hibberd builders records leads to the following list, which
must be stressed is only circumstantial –

Gauge : 2ft 0in

-	4wPM	FH	2515	1941	(a)	(1)
-	4wPM	FH	2516	1941	(a)	(2)
-	4wPM	FH	2517	1941	(a)	(3)
-	4wPM	FH	2518	1941	(a)	(4)
-	4wPM	FH	2519	1941	(a)	(5)
-	4wPM	FH	2520	1941	(a)	(6)
-	4wPM	FH	2521	1941	(a)	(4)
-	4wPM	FH	2522	1941	(a)	(5)
-	4wPM	FH	2523	1941	(a)	(7)
-	4wPM	FH	2524	1941	(a)	(8)

(a)   new to War Office; delivery location not known.

(1)   repurchased by FH and reconditioned; to Kwong Borneo Development Co, Sandakan,
       Borneo (despatched 12/5/1950).
(2)   repurchased by FH and reconditioned; to C.O. Ytterburg, Stockholm, Sweden
       (despatched 2/2/1950).
(3)   repurchased by FH and reconditioned; resold to Wm Jacks & Co Ltd, Winchester House
       Old Broad St, London EC2, and despatched to Penang, 29/4/1949.
(4)   repurchased by FH and reconditioned; resold to New Consolidated Goldfields Ltd, 49
       Moorgate, London EC2, and despatched to West Africa, 8/9/1949.
(5)   repurchased by FH and reconditioned; resold to Francis Theakston (1933) Ltd, 53
       Victoria St, Westminster, London SW1, and despatched to Sandakan via Singapore,
       29/12/1949.
(6)   repurchased by FH and reconditioned; resold to Wm Jacks & Co Ltd, Winchester House
       Old Broad St, London EC2, and despatched to Penang, 29/3/1949.
(7)   repurchased by FH and reconditioned; resold to Christiani & Nielson Ltd, 54 Victoria St,
       London, and despatched to Lourenco Marques, 19/12/1949.
(8)   repurchased by FH and reconditioned; to Westbere Ballast Pits, Sturry, Kent, 31/5/194

BEDFORDSHIRE

LOCOMOTIVE WORKED SYSTEMS

AIR MINISTRY
HENLOW

Standard gauge TL 167362: Narrow gauge TL 168363

Construction at this site started in April 1918 to establish the No.5 Eastern Area Aircraft Depot. It became operational within a few months for the overhaul of aircraft such as the Bristol Fighter, but repair work was halted after the Armistice at the end of World War I. In February 1920 a further area of 161 acres of land was purchased for the construction of a flight testing airfield. By March of that year the station had become the Inland Area Aircraft Depot, which by the end of 1921 was repairing about ten aircraft per month.

The station was served by a standard gauge railway system which opened in 1917 and connected to the Midland Railway (later LMSR and BR) Bedford - Hitchin line north of Henlow station. Standard gauge rail traffic ceased, c1/1964. There was also an extensive narrow gauge railway, including a two road engine shed, which was used to transfer materials between the sheds for the repair of aircraft. This closed some time earlier than the standard gauge operation.

Reference: "Action Stations", Vol.6, M.J.F. Bowyer, Patrick Stevens Ltd, 1983.

Gauge : 4ft 8½in

	TALBOT	0-6-0ST OC	HE	573	1893	(a)	(1)
AMW No.114		0-4-0ST OC	HE	588	1893	(b)	(2)
No.125	LORD FISHER	0-4-0ST OC	AB	1398	1915	(c)	(5)
No.134		4wPM	Hardy		1930	(New?)	(3)
AMW No.154		0-4-0DM	JF	22604	1939	New	(4)
AMW No.157		0-4-0DM	RSHN	6979	1940	New	(7)
AMW No.173	(AMW No.174)	0-4-0DM	RSHN	6991	1940	New	(8)
AMW No.213		0-4-0DM	JF	22960	1941	(d)	(6)
AMW No.174	HARDWICKE						
	(AMW No.173)	0-4-0DM	RSHN	6990	1940	(e)	(10)
AMW No.219		0-4-0DM	JF	22966	1941	(f)	(11)
AMW No.240		0-4-0DM	JF	22994	1942	New (g)	(9)

(a) ex P.& W. Anderson Ltd, Henlow (Air Ministry) contract, after 23/11/1917, by 10/1918.
(b) ex Groby Granite Co Ltd, Leics, after 29/7/1918, by 27/8/1920.
(c) possibly earlier Air Ministry, Cardington; earlier Royal Naval Airship Station, Kingsnorth, Kent; here by 15/2/1939.
(d) ex Air Ministry, Cardington, 1/1942.
(e) ex Air Ministry, Stafford, by 3/1950.
(f) ex Air Ministry, Halton, Bucks, 1/1955.
(g) to Air Ministry, Cardington; returned after 3/1950, by 5/1950.

(1) for sale at Henlow, 6/1920, per MoM "Surplus" lists; s/s.
(2) for sale at Henlow (by Allan Smethurst & Co, dealers, London SE19), 10/1934; s/s.
(3) later with Richard Thomas & Co Ltd, Blisworth Quarry, Northants, after /1939, by /1943.
(4) to Air Ministry, Quedgeley, Glos, 26/6/1940.
(5) to Yorktown & Camberley Gas Co, Blackwater Gas Works, Camberley, Surrey, 1/1942.
(6) to Air Ministry, Pembroke Dock, Pembs, 3/1942.
(7) to Air Ministry, Quedgeley, Glos.
(8) to Thos.W. Ward Ltd, Grays, Essex, TW2919, /1950 (by 3/1950); resold to Darwen Paper Mill Co Ltd, Lancs, c/1955.
(9) to JF, Leeds for rebuilding; then to Air Ministry, Halton, Bucks, 3/1955.

(10) to George Cohen, Sons & Co Ltd, Stanningley, Yorkshire (WR), c/1962 (by 9/1963);
used as plant hire loco until resold to Coal Mechanisation (Tolworth) Ltd, Greater
London, 8/1966..

(11) to JF, 1/1964; rebuilt to 203hp 0-4-0DH; resold to Eastern Gas Board, St.Albans,
Herts, after 6/1965.

Gauge: 2ft 0in

HENLOW	0-4-0ST	OC	WB	2042	1917	New (a)	(1)
-	0-4-0ST	OC	KS	4002	1918	New	(2)
-	0-4-0ST	OC	KS	4003	1918	New	(3)
-	0-4-0ST	OC	KS	4004	1918	New	(3)
-	0-4-0ST	OC	KS	4005	1918	New	(2)

(a) New to Ministry of Munitions, Aeronautical Dept, location unspecified; the name
suggests that it was here, but this is unconfirmed

(1) (possibly to RAF Uxbridge, Middlesex); later to Alfred Hickman Ltd, Bilston Works,
Staffs, by 3/1920.

(2) to Muirhead, McDonald, Wilson & Co Ltd, Southend Arterial Road etc (1921-1925)
contracts, Essex.

(3) for sale by unspecified seller, London, 4-5/1925; possibly E.T. Pugsley, Abbey Wood,
who advertised two 2ft gauge KS for sale in "Machinery Market", 27/2/1925. Later
with South Shields Corporation, Coast Road contract (1925-1927), Co.Durham, per/via
Watts, Hardy & Co, Newcastle-upon-Tyne.

W.H. ALLEN, SONS & CO LTD
QUEENS ENGINEERING WORKS, Ford End Rd, Bedford   G2
W.H. Allen, Sons & Co until 6/1900   TL 041497

The company was founded in 1880 by William Henry Allen, with premises at York Street,
Lambeth, and later moved from London to establish a new works, opened in 1894, in
Bedford. The company is well known for the design and construction of large diesel engines
and pumps for marine purposes; in 1909 the company supplied generating sets for the ocean
liners "Olympic" and "Titanic". In the 1930s they supplied diesel engines for the series of
Bo-Bo diesel locomotives built by BTH for the Ford Motor Co of Dagenham. Other railway
work, in 1935, was the reconstruction for the War Department of **4wBE EE 687/1925** as an
0-4-0DE locomotive, used at Shoeburyness and eventually WD 813. This is the only
locomotive known to have been rebuilt in the works. Allen's biggest customer was the Royal
Navy and much equipment was supplied for installation in many famous warships, including
the aircraft carrier "Ark Royal".

In 1968 W.H.Allen merged with **Bellis & Morcom** to become **Amalgamated Power Engineering
Ltd** and in 1989 this company became part of Rolls Royce Ltd.

The works was served by a standard gauge rail connection to the Midland Railway, by 1904.
This was shunted by rail cranes as well as the motive power listed below. Rail traffic ceased
in 1971.

Reference : "The Story of Queens Engineering Works, Bedford, a History of W.H. Allen, Sons
& Co Ltd", Michael R. Lane, Unicorn Press, 1995.

Gauge : 4ft 8½in

-	4wDH	(a)	(1)

(a) rebuilt by Allen from Jones Crane; fitted with RH engine No.247970.

(1) scrapped on site by W.Heselwood, Sheffield, w/e 27/3/1971.

Joseph Arnold & Sons until /1937.

High quality silica sand has been extracted in the Leighton Buzzard area since the 19th century, but output was greatly increased after the outbreak of the First World War. This was due to the cessation of imports from Belgium and the increased requirements for munitions manufacture. Road transport was used from the pits to the main line sidings at Grovebury until the Leighton Buzzard Light Railway (which see) was built by the sand companies and opened in 11/1919.

Joseph Arnold was operating quarries by 1880 (Spinney Pool, off Billington Rd) and later sites included Pratt's; Rackley Hill, Grovebury; Nine Acres, Shenley Hill; Chamberlain's Barn (from c/1912); Double Arches (from 1915); Twenty One Acres (1920s to 1930s); New Trees, Shenley Hill (from 1963). All except Spinney Pool were served by narrow gauge lines connected to the LBLR. This transported the sand to Arnold's washery and screens at Billington Rd, where the main locomotive shed and workshops were situated (SP 927241), and to the main line exchange sidings.

Arnold's Billington Siding connected with the LNWR at Grovebury Crossing and was in use by 1904. The nearby Arnold's Harris Siding (latterly Washer Siding) was in use by 1925; both remained in use until after 1956.

Latterly locomotives were also stabled at Chamberlain's Barn (SP 926265), Double Arches (SP 942287), Nine Acre (Chances) (SP 939274) and Double Arches (SP 943285).

In 1958 the Leighton Buzzard Light Railway ceased to be the operator of the "main line". Arnold's took over the LBLR loco shed and workshops and both Arnold's and Garside's ran their own trains over the LBLR line.

During the 1970s the use of narrow gauge railways decreased and finally ceased c17/11/1978. Quarrying continued with road transport of the sand produced.

Reference : "The Leighton Buzzard Light Railway", S. A. Leleux, Oakwood Press, 1969 & 1996.

Arnold's original fleet of petrol locos appears to have been numbered from 1 to approximately 30. A visit by G.P. Roberts in 1952 reported a total of 32 locos, of which 11 could be identified, either by works plate or WDLR number plate. Some of these petrol locos were converted to diesel engines and re-numbered, presumably to fill-in blanks in the list to replace locos disposed of. Additionally, the switching of bonnet covers has added to the confusion.

Gauge: 2ft 0in

12 (1 WINNIE)		4wDM (ex PM)	MR	1757	1918	(a)	(2)
2		4wPM	MR	1169	1918	(b)	(2)
-		4wPM	MR	5073	1930	New	s/s by /1968
3		4wPM	MR			(c)	Scr 19/9/1959
4		4wPM	MR			(c)	(5)
5		4wPM	MR			(c)	(5)
6		4wPM	MR	(? 4578)	1930	(h)	(4)
7		4wDM (ex PM)	MR	3862	1928	(i)	Scr c5/1961
20		4wDM (ex PM)	MR	3982	1928	(c)	s/s after 6/1959
8		4wDM (ex PM)	MR	4599	1932	(d)	(3)
9		4wPM	MR	3996	1933	New	(6)
10	BERTHA	4wPM	MR			(c)	s/s after 11/1953
(11 ?)		4wPM	FH	1851	1934	(e)	s/s after 5/1962
(12 ?)		4wDM	FH	1893	1934	(f)	s/s after 11/1953
(13 ?)		4wPM	FH	1960	1935	(g)	s/s after 11/1953
-		4wDM	MR	5854	1934	(j)	(1)
14		4wPM	MR	1704	1918	(k)	Scr c/1960

26	(19 15)	4wDM (ex PM)	MR	4701	1934	(l)	(35)
16		4wDM (ex PM)	MR	4709	1936	(m)	(17)
14	(2 17)	4wDM (ex PM)	MR	4707	1936	(n)	(35)
-		4wPM	MR	4705	1935	(o)	Scr c5/1983
24	(18)	4wDM (ex PM)	MR	4805	1934	(p)	(34)
15	(19)	4wDM (ex PM)	MR	4803	1934	(q)	(21)
20		4wPM	MR	999	1918	(r)	Scr c/1960
-		4wPM	MR	916	1918	(s)	s/s by /1960
-		4wPM	MR	341	1917	(t)	Scr /1963
27		4wDM	MR	5863	1934	New	(26)
26	(13 4)	4wDM	FH	1917	1935	New	s/s c/1963
33		4wDM (ex PM)	MR	4708	1936	(u)	s/s
12		4wDM	FH	2288	1940	(v)	s/s after 10/1952
30		4wPM	FH	1922	1935	(w)	s/s after 11/1953
36		4wDM	MR	8756	1942	(x)	(18)
23	(6)	4wDM	MR	7128	1936	(y)	(32)
36	(25 24)	4wDM	MR	7214	1938	(y)	(31)
6		4wDM	MR	7403	1939	(y)	(29)
1	(33 13)	4wDM	MR	8683	1941	(z)	(24)
35		4wDM	MR	7126	1936	(aa)	(24)
40		4wDM	MR	7153	1937	(ab)	(19)
38	(39)	4wDM	MR	8540	1940	(ac)	(15)
14	(32)	4wDM	FH	2161	1938	(ad)	s/s c/1965
42		4wDM	MR	7710	1939	(ae)	(23)
44		4wDM	MR	7933	1941	(ae)	(13)
34	(41)	4wDM	MR	9547	1950	(ae)	(16)
43		4wDM	MR	10409	1954	(ae)	(10)
4	(3)	4wDM	MR	7201	1937	(af)	(20)
30		4wDM	MR	8695	1942	(ag)	(11)
2		4wDM	MR	8700	1941	(ag)	(8)
22		4wDM	MR	8727	1941	(ag)	(9)
20		4wDM	MR	8748	1942	(ag)	(22)
33	(4)	4wDM	MR	7037	1936	(ah)	(27)
26	(18)	4wDM	MR	8720	1941	(ai)	(20)
14	(7)	4wDM	MR	8723	1941	(ai)	(25)
-		4wDM	MR	8732	1941	(aj)	Scr by /1968
17	(13)	4wDM	MR	8994	1946	(ak)	(19)
8		4wDM	MR	9409	1948	(al)	(30)
34		4wDM	MR	9415	1949	(am)	Scr /1965
-		4wDM	MR	9418	1949	(am)	(12)
41		4wDM	MR	5859	1934	(an)	(28)
3		4wDM	MR	5881	1935	(an)	(7)
18	(1)	4wDM	MR	7188	1937	(an)	(27)
21	(8)	4wDM	MR	7215	1938	(ao)	(33)
-		4wDM	MR	8724	1941	(ap)	Scr /1966
-		4wDM	MR	8597	1940	(aq)	Scr c/1978
-		4wDM	MR	20558	1955	(ar)	(14)

ex Leighton Buzzard Light Railway, c/1923; orig. WDLR 2478.
orig WDLR 2890; to here by /1945 (possibly c/1928).
origin unknown; here by /1951 (probably much earlier)
earlier with Sir Robert McAlpine & Sons Ltd, Hayes Plant Depot, Middlesex, PN 3646,
31/10/1941; here by /1951 (probably much earlier).
ex FH, 2/1934 (a reconditioned "Simplex" loco)

(f)   ex FH, 10/1934 (a reconditioned "Simplex" loco previously with J. Wardell & Co)

(g)   ex FH, 11/1935 (utilising a new frame and parts, including the engine, from MR 1211)

(h)   (works number may have been 4579.) Earlier Sir Robert McAlpine & Sons Ltd, Ebbw Vale contract, Gwent (in /1938), PN 3094; here by /1951.

(i)   ex Amalgamated Roadstone Corporation Ltd, Allington Quarry, Maidstone, Kent, (early 1930s ?)

(j)   ex Petrol Loco Hirers, 31/5/1934

(k)   orig WDLR 2425; to here by 11/1945 (possibly c/1936).

(l)   ex Petrol Loco Hirers Ltd, 19/2/1936

(m)   ex Petrol Loco Hirers Ltd, 10/9/1936

(n)   ex Petrol Loco Hirers Ltd, 19/10/1936

(o)   earlier J.C. Oliver Ltd, dealers, Leeds

(p)   ex Petrol Loco Hirers Ltd, 11/10/1937

(q)   ex Petrol Loco Hirers Ltd, c11/10/1937

(r)   orig WDLR 2720; to here by 11/1945 (possibly c/1938).

(s)   orig WDLR 2637; to here by 4/1952 (possibly earlier).

(t)   orig WDLR 1742; ex J. Summerville, Dunfermline, after 11/1940, by 11/1945.

(u)   ex Diesel Loco Hirers Ltd, late 1940s (after 11/1946)

(v)   earlier Holloway Bros. (London) Ltd, ROF No.7 Contract, Kirkby, Liverpool; possibly here c/1941.

(w)   ex Holloway Bros. (London) Ltd, contractors, 1950s (loco was a rebuild of MR 3651 including its original frame).

(x)   ex George W. Bungey Ltd, dealers, Hayes, Middlesex, c/1955; earlier Cromhall Quarries Ltd, Charfield, Glos.

(y)   ex Land Reclamation Co Ltd, contrs, London N1, 2/1956.

(z)   ex George W. Bungey Ltd, dealers, Hayes, Middlesex, c9/1956; earlier Slindon Gravel Co Ltd, Slindon Common, near Arundel, Sussex.

(aa)   ex Richard Briggs & Sons Ltd, Clitheroe, Lancs, by 5/1958.

(ab)   ex River Ouse (Yorks) Catchment Board, Riccal, Yorkshire (ER), by 5/1958.

(ac)   ex British Waterways, Southall, Middlesex, /1958.

(ad)   ex Admiralty, RNAD Ernesettle, Devon, c/1958.

(ae)   ex Leighton Buzzard Light Railway, 3/12/1958

(af)   ex Kennel, Hayes, Middlesex, 8/1959; earlier Cementation Co Ltd, contrs.

(ag)   ex River Ouse (Yorks) Catchment Board, Riccal, Yorkshire (ER), 1/1960.

(ah)   ex Sir Robert McAlpine & Sons Ltd, contrs, PN 4365, c/1960.

(ai)   ex Sir Robert McAlpine & Sons Ltd, contrs, PN 5032 and PN 5035 respectively, c/1960.

(aj)   ex M. MacLean Ltd, contrs, Cromer, Norfolk, c/1966 (after 5/1965)

(ak)   ex Diesel Loco Hirers Ltd, c/1963; orig Sir Robert McAlpine & Sons Ltd, contrs, Hayes Plant Depot, Middlesex; PN A4461, rebuilt from MR 8618.

(al)   ex Holloway Bros. (London) Ltd, contrs, Battersea, London, c/1964 (after 6/1962); to Stone Pits, Aylesbury, Bucks, 29/11/1966; returned by 6/1973.

(am)   ex Holloway Bros. (London) Ltd, contrs, Battersea, London, c/1964 (after 6/1962).

(an)   ex Ham River Grit Co Ltd, Bletchingley, Surrey, via Washington Depot, Surrey, c1/1965.

(ao)   ex Ham River Grit Co Ltd, Bletchingley, Surrey, 111, via Washington Depot, Surrey, c1/1965; to Stone Pits, Aylesbury, Bucks, 29/11/1969; returned by 3/1973.

(ap)   ex Diesel Loco Hirers Ltd, after 11/8/1965, for spares.

(aq)   ex Diesel Loco Hirers Ltd, c/1966, for spares.

(ar)   ex Hall & Ham River Ltd, Woodside Brickworks, Croydon, c/1967.

(1)   returned to MR (defective engine; replaced by MR 5863), 28/8/1934.

(2)   s/s after 11/1953.

(3)   to Stone Sandpits, Bucks, after 11/1953, by /1957.
(4)   scrapped c/1960 (after 6/1959)
(5)   stored 5/1962; s/s
(6)   scrapped c/1963 (after 5/1962)
(7)   to Thos.E. Gray Ltd, Burton Latimer, Northants, 13/8/1969.
(8)   to Sir William Lithgow, Duchal Grouse Moor, Kilmalcolm, Renfrewshire, 9/1969.
(9)   to Overstone Solarium Light Railway, Sywell, Northants, 7/1970.
(10) to Leighton Buzzard Narrow Gauge Railway Society, 22/4/1972.
(11) to Bedfordshire County Council, Dovery Down County Primary School, Leighton Buzzard, for preservation, c/1972; later to Light Railway Association, Turvey, after 1/1987.
(12) frame only by /1968; remains scrapped, c/1973.
(13) to Leighton Buzzard Narrow Gauge Railway Society, for preservation, 22/2/1975.
(14) to I.B. Jolly, Mold, Clwyd (North Wales), for preservation, 8/12/1978.
(15) to J.L. Butler, Ripley, Surrey, for preservation, 13/1/1979.
(16) to I.B. Jolly, Mold, Clwyd (North Wales), for preservation, 15/1/1979.
(17) to J.L. Butler, Ripley, Surrey, for preservation, 27/1/1979.
(18) to Northamptonshire Ironstone Railway Trust, Hunsbury Hill, Northants, for preservation, 10/2/1979.
(19) to J.L. Butler, Ripley, Surrey, for preservation, 17/2/1979.
(20) to Runcorn Transport Collection Ltd, Runcorn, Cheshire, for preservation, 10/3/1979.
(21) to Runcorn Transport Collection, Runcorn, Cheshire, for preservation, 20/3/1979.
(22) to Rev.E.R. Boston, Cadeby Light Railway, Leics, for preservation, 4/5/1979.
(23) to Rev.E.R. Boston, Cadeby Light Railway, Leics, for preservation, 12/5/1979.
(24) to Vale of Teifi Narrow Gauge Railway, Henllan, near Llandyssul, Dyfed, for preservation, 2/6/1979.
(25) to I.B. Jolly, Mold, Clwyd (North Wales), for preservation, 2/6/1979.
(26) to R. Marner, Horley, Surrey, for preservation, 18/8/1979; then to Chalk Pits Museum, Amberley, Sussex.
(27) to Scottish Agricultural Industries Ltd, Bolton Fell Peat Works, Cumbria, 18/10/1979.
(28) to I.B. Jolly, Mold, Clwyd (North Wales), for preservation, 1/12/1979.
(29) to D. Billmore, Barnsley, Yorkshire (WR), for preservation, 18/1/1980.
(30) to Drusilla's Zoo Park, Bewick, East Sussex, BILL, 2/1981.
(31) to Leighton Buzzard Narrow Gauge Railway Society, for preservation, 5/1981.
(32) to Surrey & Hampshire Industrial Tramway, Surrey, for preservation (frame only), 25/7/1981.
(33) to Vale of Teifi Narrow Gauge Railway, Henllan, Dyfed, for preservation, 20/3/1982.
(34) to Leighton Buzzard Narrow Gauge Railway Society, for preservation, 2/5/1983.
(35) frame only at Billington Road, by 1/1979; remains scrapped there, c5/1983.

ASSOCIATED PORTLAND CEMENT MANUFACTURERS LTD

BIDWELL CLAY PIT, near Dunstable   H4
TL 009241

Clay pits located west of the A5120 road, about ½ mile north of the Houghton Regis cement works. Pit closed by 1950.

Gauge: 2ft 0in

-	0-4-0PM	BgC	760	1918	(a)	(1)
-	4wPM	MR	2113	1921	(b)	s/s by 8/1950

(a)   orig Board of Trade, Timber Supply Department.
(b)   ex Petrol Loco Hirers, 28/4/1928.

(1) locomotive derelict by 8/1950 on the floor of an abandoned pit which gradually flooded; loco under water by /1961; to A.M. Keef, Woburn, for restoration, 6/1962.

SEWELL LIMESTONE QUARRY, Dunstable F5
SP 996224

Quarry located to the south of the ex-LNWR Leighton Buzzard - Dunstable line and to the north-east of the Totternhoe Quarry of RPCM Ltd. Workings commenced 1890 to serve the Sewell Limeworks of Forders Ltd (later BPCM (which see)) until the closure of the latter in 1940. The workings then supplied limestone to the Dunstable cement works and locomotives were used by APCM from 1966 until the closure of the quarry c2/1971. The standard gauge system was isolated and was not connected to the BR (ex LNWR) line.

Reference : "Totternhoe Quarries", Chris Down & Doug Semmens, Industrial Railway Record 145, IRS, 6/1996.

Gauge : 4ft 8½ in

-	0-4-0DH	JF 4220037 1966	New	(1)
1	0-4-0DE	RH 421437 1958	(a)	(1)

(a)   ex Dunstable Works, after 3/1967, by 26/8/1967.

(1)   to Dunstable Works, c2/1971.

SUNDON CEMENT WORKS F6
form. **British Portland Cement Manufacturers Ltd** TL 037275
B.J.Forder & Son Ltd until 4/1912.
B.J.Forder & Son from c1885 until 25/5/1900.

This cement works was located on the east side of the BR (ex-Midland Railway) Bedford - London main line about one mile west of Sundon village and was served by standard gauge sidings (in use by 1895) connected to this line and shunted by main line locomotives. A narrow gauge system was used within the works and the adjacent quarry. The narrow gauge operations ceased c1975; the works closed in 1976 and was demolished by 1978. The quarry, together with the workings of the nearby Sundon Lime Works, was being reclaimed by landfill in 2000.

Gauge: 3ft 0in

-	4wPM	* MR	1901	1919	New	(1)
-	4wPM	MR	2004	1920	New	s/s by 6/1950
-	4wPM	MR	2020	1920	(a)	(1)
No.2	4wDM	MR	3965	1939	New	(7)
5	4wPM	# MR	3797	1926		
	reb of	MR	1363	1918	(b)	(2)
3	4wDM	MR			(c)	(6)
1	4wDM	MR			(c)	(8)
3	4wDM	MR	10118	1949	New	(4)
4	4wDM	JF	3930044	1950	New	(3)
1	4wDM	MR	11206	1962	(d)	(4)
2	4wDM	MR	10159	1949	(d)	(5)

* Converted to burn paraffin, /1922.
\# Rebuilt from 4wPM to 4wDM by 5/1965.

(a) ex Blows Down Lime Works, Dunstable, by /1948.
(b) ex Lower Penarth Works, South Glamorgan, c/1950 (by 6/1950).
(c) ex APCM, Ufton Works, Warwickshire.
(d) ex London Brick Co Ltd, Hicks Works, Hunts, 15/7/1971, via A.M. Keef, Bampton, Oxon.

(1) derelict by 6/1950; s/s after 5/1958.
(2) to MR, Bedford, for preservation, 2/11/1974.
(3) to Brockham Museum Association, Surrey, 18/11/1974.
(4) to A.M. Keef, Bampton, Oxon, 5/1975.
(5) to A.M. Keef, Bampton, Oxon, 5/1975; re-sold to British Moss Litter Co Ltd, Swinefleet, Yorkshire (WR), 5/1975.
(6) scrapped on site, by F.D. O'Dell & Sons, Shefford, Beds, 11/1975.
(7) to MR, Bedford, for preservation, 7/6/1976.
(8) scrapped on site by F.D. O'Dell & Sons, Shefford, Beds, c/1970.

BARTON LIME CO (1957) LTD
BARTON LIME WORKS, Barton-in-the-Clay
F7

Barton (Beds) Lime Co Ltd (established by c1931),until /1957   TL 078296

The works, in production by 1928, was at a location known as Barton Cutting about one mile south of Barton village on the east side of the A6 trunk road, about 5 miles north of Luton. Works closed. Track removed by 1965.

Gauge : 1ft 8in

-	4wDM	OK	6703	1936	(a)	(1)

(a) origin unknown; here by 6/1954.

(1) to P.J. Mackinnon, Wilstead, for preservation, c/1967.

BEDFORD CORPORATION, PUBLIC WORKS DEPARTMENT
GOLDINGTON DEPOT
G8

TL 066495

Public works depot served by sidings off the ex-LNWR Bedford - Cambridge railway at a point which later became the western end of the Goldington loop. Depot closed and the site subsequently re-developed as a leisure complex. The former railway bridge over the new cut of the River Great Ouse was still in use in 2000 as a public footpath and cycleway.

Gauge : 4ft 8½in

-	0-4-0ST	OC	MW	1381	1899	(a)	s/s c/1943

(a) ex J. & F. Howard Ltd, Bedford, /1933 (after 22/7/1932).

BEDFORD CORPORATION WATER BOARD
MANTON LANE WATER WORKS, Bedford
G9

TL 043514

A 2ft gauge tramway was constructed in 1945-6 to carry sand between the filter beds and the washing plant. This line was about 320 yards long and remained in operation until 1960, when a new works was built to the west near the River Ouse. Rolling stock consisted of side tipping skip wagons built by Robert Hudson & Co Ltd of Leeds. The remains of the tramway were dismantled and sold for scrap in 1963.

Reference : "Industrial Railway Record" No.20, p290.

Gauge: 2ft 0in

	4wDM	MR	8969	1945	New	(3)
-	4wDM	MR	21286	1958	(a)	(1)
-	4wDM	MR	4813	1937	(b)	(2)

(a) ex Diesel Loco Hirers Ltd, 4/1960.

(b) ex Diesel Loco Hirers Ltd.

(1) returned to Diesel Loco Hirers Ltd, 11/1960; reconditioned by MR and resold to Cumberland Moss Litter Industries Ltd, Wigton, Cumberland, 7/3/1966.

(2) to W.J. Redden & Sons Ltd, Wellingborough, Northants, c/1962.

(3) to Edward Redden, Little Irchester scrapyard, Northants, by 12/1967.

BEDFORD DISTRICT GAS CO

BEDFORD GAS WORKS, Ford End Rd, Bedford G10
Bedford Gas Light & Coke Co Ltd until before 1924
Bedford Gas Light Co from 1832 until before c1894.

TL 041493

The original gas works was opened in Priory Street in 1832 and closed c1864. With the arrival of the railways in Bedford a larger site was purchased in 1863 for a new gas works built adjacent to the railway in Ford End Road. This was situated on the north of the River Great Ouse and west of the Midland Railway line south of Bedford station. The works was served by standard gauge sidings (in use by 1895 and probably much earlier) and shunted by steam cranes as well as the locomotive detailed below. On 1/5/1949 the works passed to the Eastern Gas Board (without locomotives) and later, with the advent of North Sea gas, the works was closed c1970 and demolished in 1971.

Gauge : 4ft 8½in

MARY	0-4-0ST	OC	HC	309	1888	(a)	(1)

(a) ex L.J. Speight, Dagenham Dock Works (Ford Motor Co Ltd) (1929-1932) contract, Essex, /1932.

(1) to A.R. Adams & Son, dealers, Newport, Gwent, c/1940; later Robert Gilchrist & Co, Newport, Gwent, /1941.

BEDFORD ENGINEERING CO

HOUGHTON ROAD WORKS, Bedford G11

TL 049487

A general engineering firm and crane manufacturers established in 1893 by George Fiegehen. The company built many steam railway cranes which were sold world-wide. During the First World War petrol locomotives were assembled for the Motor Rail & Tramcar Co, most being 2ft gauge machines for the WDLR. Later, locomotives were also built for FH, the last built at Bedford being FH 1795, ordered by Thos W. Ward for Rochdale Corporation Waterworks, Water Grove Reservoir, Lancs and delivered on 19/5/1932. The company may also have built some early standard gauge locomotives. Works closed in 1932; the business was auctioned on 16/11/1932, the factory having by then already been sold..

BEDFORD SILICA SAND MINES LTD
HEATH & REACH QUARRIES, near Leighton Buzzard   K12
Earlier operated by Waste Recovery Syndicate Ltd by 1925   SP 926284

Sand pits about two miles north of Leighton Buzzard on the east of the A418 road were in production from about 1900, The Bedford Silica Sand Mines Ltd, registered in 8/1928, took over the operations and introduced an internal narrow gauge railway system. This system (which had no connection to the Leighton Buzzard Light Railway) was horse worked until the Motor Rail locomotives were purchased from 1946. A conveyor belt system came into use in 5/1963, and the railway was then dismantled. The company ceased operations after 1977, by 1980, and the pits were taken over by the Buckland Silica Sand Co, part of the ARC group, without rail traffic.

Reference : "The Leighton Buzzard Light Railway", S A Leleux, Oakwood Press, 1969 & 1996.

Gauge: 2ft 0in

-	4wDM	MR	8592	1940	(a)	(1)
-	4wDM	MR	8588	1941	(b)	(1)

(a)   ex Diesel Loco Hirers Ltd, 13/6/1946; earlier Admiralty.

(b)   ex MR, 25/3/1948; earlier. Chas.T. Olley & Sons, South Ockendon, Essex; orig War Office, Donnington, Shropshire.

(1)   to Fletton's Ltd, Kings Dyke Works, Cambs, via Water Eaton Works, Bucks, 6/1964.

BEDFORD WASHED GRAVEL CO LTD
OCTAGON FARM GRAVEL PITS, Cople, near Bedford   F13
    TL 095494

Gravel pits, in existence by 1942, located north of the A603 Bedford – Sandy road and south of the River Great Ouse, four miles east of Bedford. The company supplied aggregates for the construction of the nearby Goldington Power Station but the pits were worked out by 1954. Two other gravel pits were worked in the Cople area (at TL 100498 and TL 097488) but there is no confirmation of the use of railways at these sites.

Gauge : 2ft 0in

-	4wDM	MR	8677	1942	(a)	(1)
-	4wDM	MR	8596	1941	(b)	(2)

(a)   ex Diesel Loco Hirers Ltd, by 25/1/1945 (when repaired on site by MR).

(b)   ex Diesel Loco Hirers Ltd, by 12/4/1946 (when repaired on site by MR).

(1)   returned to Diesel Loco Hirers Ltd; then to W.R. Wallace Industries Ltd, (location unknown), 22/1/1952; later with Inns & Co Ltd, Harpur Lane Pits, Radlett, Herts.

(2)   returned to Diesel Loco Hirers Ltd; then to Landbeach Sand & Gravel Co Ltd, Ely Road Sand Pits, Landbeach, Cambs, by 6/3/1952.

BEDFORDSHIRE COUNTY COUNCIL
HIGHWAYS & BRIDGES DEPARTMENT, Dunstable   H14
    TL 009226

Plant depot located south of the LMSR Dunstable - Leighton Buzzard railway and west of the A5 Watling Street road. The locos were possibly kept here between use on road building and/or housing contracts.

-	4wPM	MR	3854	1927	(a)	(2)
-	4wPM	MR	5006	1929	(b)	(1)
-	4wDM	MR	4813	1937	(c)	(3)

(a)   ex Petrol Loco Hirers, 15/3/1930; rebuild of MR 1808, earlier with Manchester Corporation Waterworks.

(b)   ex Petrol Loco Hirers, by 10/1/1931.

(c)   ex Diesel Loco Hirers Ltd, on hire, by 27/8/1948 (rebuilt from 4wPM, 27/2/1945).

(1)   to Surrey County Council, Green Lane Depot, Leatherhead, Surrey, 1/9/1931.

(2)   s/s after 2/1/1948 (when the loco was examined on site by a MR fitter)

(3)   returned to Diesel Loco Hirers Ltd, off hire.

BISHOPS STORTFORD BRICK & TILE CO LTD
RADWELL GRAVEL PITS, near Milton Earnest   F15
TL 002567

These pits were excavated, on land owned by C.V. Ibbett, during the winter of 1940 - 1941 to supply gravel for the construction of the nearby Thurleigh Airfield. A 2ft gauge tramway ran from a cart track off the Radwell - Milton Earnest road for about 250 yards to the pits, with a passing loop about half way along the length. Two diesel locos were hired to work the line. Some remains of the tramway were still extant in 1961.

Reference : "Industrial Railway Record" No.22, 1968, A.J.Warrington

Gauge : 2ft 0in

-	4wDM	MR	(a)	(1)
-	4wDM	MR	(a)	(1)

(a)   ex Diesel Loco Hirers Ltd, hire, c/1940

(1)   returned to Diesel Loco Hirers Ltd, off hire, by c/1942.

BLUE CIRCLE INDUSTRIES plc
DUNSTABLE CEMENT WORKS, Houghton Regis   H16
Blue Circle Industries Ltd until 8/10/1981   TL 015233, 016232
Associated Portland Cement Manufacturers Ltd until 31/5/1978
Dunstable Portland Cement Co Ltd (registered 1925) until 30/10/1931

The works, built 1925 - 1926, had two kilns and a production capacity of 110,000 tons per year. A third kiln was added in 1936 and capacity had trebled by the early 1950s. Sited to the north of the BR (ex-GNR) Dunstable branch east of Dunstable North station, it was served by extensive standard gauge sidings with a triangular connection to the BR line. The works was supplied from a large chalk quarry to the west of both the works and the A5120 road. This had its own standard gauge railway system, isolated from the main works. Cement production ceased 31/3/1971 and subsequently the works was used as a distribution depot for cement brought in from Northfleet Works, Kent. This rail traffic ceased on 3/6/1988 and the depot closed in July 1988. The works has subsequently been demolished and the site redeveloped as an industrial estate and business park.

Reference : "History of Blue Circle", Peter Pugh, Cambridge Business Press, 1988.

Gauge : 4ft 8½in

No.	Name	Type	Cyl	Builder	Works No	Year	Origin	Disposal
	-	4wDM (ex PM)		MR	3786	1925	New (a)	Scr c/1969
	-	4wVBT	VCG	S	6020	1925	New (b)	s/s c2/1950
	WESTMINSTER	0-6-0ST	OC	P	1378	1914	(c)	(4)
	ECCLES	0-6-0ST	IC	MW	1245	1894	(d)	(2)
	EDITH	0-6-0ST	OC	P	1391	1915	(e)	s/s by 12/1949
	TAY	0-4-0ST	OC	AB	1828	1924	(f)	(1)
	TOM PARRY	0-4-0ST	OC	AB	2015	1935	(g)	(7)
	PUNCH HULL	0-4-0ST	OC	AB	776	1896		
		reb		Baker		1928	(h)	(7)
	-	4wDM		MR	5752	1939	New	(3)
	SEWELL	0-4-0DM		JF	21322	1936	New	(6)
	GRAHAMS (7)	0-4-0DM		JF	21455	1936	(i)	(6)
7144	HOUGHTON	0-4-0DM		JF	21941	1937	(j)	(6)
	-	0-4-0DH		JF	4230001	1957	(k)	(5)
1		0-4-0DE		RH	421437	1958	New (p)	(12)
2		0-4-0DE		RH	425477	1959	New (t)	
		reb		Resco		1979		(13)
	(PATRICIA)	0-6-0DH		JF	4240017	1966	New(r)	(15)
	-	0-4-0DH		JF	22887	1939	(l)	(8)
	-	4wDM		FH	3990	1962	(m)	(9)
	(D9526)	0-6-0DH		Sdn		1965	(n)	(10)
	-	0-4-0DH		JF	4220037	1966	(o)	(11)
	-	0-4-0DM		JF	4110008	1950	(q)	s/s c/1972
	-	0-4-0DH		EEV	D1122	1966	(s)	(14)

Note - "Baker" = P. Baker & Co Ltd, Engineers & Machinery Merchants, East Moors, Cardiff.

(a)   ex MR, new, /1925; ordered by GWR, 4/1923, as MR 2215, but not delivered.
(b)   ex S, /1926, after exhibition at Centenary of Railways Exhibition, Wembley, Middlesex.
(c)   ex George Cohen, Sons & Co Ltd, Larkhill Camp Railway demolition (War Office) (1929) contract, Amesbury, Wiltshire, after 2/1929, by 5/1929.
(d)   ex Burham Works, Kent, (after 10/1931 ?), by 10/1933.
(e)   ex G. & T. Earle Ltd, Hessle Quarry, Hull, Yorkshire (ER), /1935.
(f)   ex Johnson's Branch Works, Greenhithe, Kent, c/1942 (by 7/1945).
(g)   ex Alpha Cement Ltd, Kirton Lindsey, Lincs, /1949 (by 8/1949).
(h)   ex Alpha Cement Ltd, Shipton-on-Cherwell, Oxon, after 6/1952, by 12/1952.
(i)   ex Alpha Cement Ltd, West Thurrock, Essex, after 5/6/1949, by 8/1950.
(j)   ex Hadfields Ltd, East Hecla Works, Tinsley, Sheffield, c8/1948 (by 12/8/1948).
(k)   ex JF, Leeds, on demonstration, 2/1958 (by 9/2/1958).
(l)   ex Thos.W. Ward Ltd, Templeborough Works, Sheffield, loan, c/1968; form. ROF, Crossgates Factory, Leeds (rebuilt by JF from 0-4-0DM, /1963).
(m)   transferred from Dunbar Works, East Lothian, but first sent to TH, 10/4/1969 for conversion from 3ft 6in to 4ft 8½in gauge, and sent here, 28/8/1969.
(n)   ex Westbury Works, Wilts, 5/1971.
(o)   ex Sewell Quarry, c2/1971.
(p)   to Sewell Quarry, /1967; returned c2/1971.
(q)   ex Lower Penarth Works, South Glamorgan., c/1969.
(r)   to Westbury Works, Wilts, c5/1971; returned c/1971.
(s)   ex British Nuclear Fuels Ltd, Sellafield, Cumbria, on hire from TH, 27/11/1987
(t)   to Resco Railways, Erith, Kent, for rebuilding, /1979; returned 22/1/1980.

(1)   to Johnson's Branch Works, Greenhithe, Kent, c/1946 (by 6/1947).
(2)   scrapped, after 9/1948, by 4/1949.

(3) to Thos. W. Ward Ltd, Grays, Essex, TW3098, after 8/1951, by 16/3/1952; later Effra Sales & Service Ltd, Apedale, Newcastle-under-Lyne, North Staffs, possibly by 15/10/1953.
(4) to Alpha Cement Ltd, Shipton-on-Cherwell, Oxon, after 4/1952, by 6/1952.
(5) returned to JF, Leeds, after trials.
(6) withdrawn /1959; one good loco made from the components of all three. This loco to BPCM, Lower Penarth Works, South Glamorgan, after 9/1962 and the remains of the others scrapped on site c/1962 (after 9/1962).
(7) to British Railways, Dunstable Town Station (which see) for storage, 1/3/1967.
(8) returned to Thos.W. Ward Ltd, /1969.
(9) to Norman Works, Cherry Hinton, Cambs, c10/1970.
(10) to Westbury Works, Wilts, 26/11/1971.
(11) to Oxford Works, Shipton-on-Cherwell, Oxon, c5/1971.
(12) scrapped on site, c/1978, by 22/2/1979.
(13) to Ampthill Scrap Metal Processing Co Ltd, Ampthill, Beds, c10/1988.
(14) returned to TH off hire, 6/6/1988
(15) to Croxton & Garry Ltd, Melton Depot, near Hull, 3/1989.

BOARD OF TRADE, TIMBER SUPPLY DEPARTMENT
AMPTHILL SAWMILL

J17

TL024371

In 8/1917 a sawmill was established alongside the Midland Railway station, with a standard gauge siding from the Midland Railway line. This was to deal with timber being felled by the **Canadian Forestry Corps** in plantations owned by the **Duke of Bedford**. Much of this timber was transported to the mill by road, but a 3ft gauge line was laid from the mill to woods at Cooper's Hill (TL 028377). Work ceased at the sawmills on 16/11/1918 and buildings were auctioned on 4/5/1920 although railway equipment appears to have been removed before then.

Reference: "The Kerry Tramway and other timber light railways", Cox & Krupa,
Plateway Press, 1992

Gauge: 3ft 0in

CTS 5	0-6-0T	OC	KS	3084	1917	New	(1)

(1) later Leeds Corporation, Leighton Reservoir (1921-1926) construction, Masham, Yorkshire (NR), by /1922

BRITANNIA IRON & STEEL WORKS LTD
BRITANNIA IRON WORKS, Bedford

G18

TL 045490

After the demise of J. & F. Howard Ltd (which see) in 1932, this works in Kempston Road lay idle until acquired by Britannia Iron & Steel Works Ltd, a private company (registered in 3/1933) under Swiss control and a member of the George Fischer group of companies. As ironfounders the company established a reputation for high quality "Whiteheart" malleable iron tube fittings and castings. Located on the south bank of the River Great Ouse, to the east of the BR (ex-Midland Railway) Bedford - London main line, the foundry was connected by standard gauge sidings to the BR (ex-Midland Railway) Bedford - Hitchin line. Rail traffic ceased and track removed, 1970.

Gauge : 4ft 8½in

B 84	4wPM	H	957	1926	(a)	(1)
-	4wDM	RH	207103	1941	(b)	(2)

(a) ex James & Fredk Howard Ltd, with site, /1932.
(b) ex George Cohen, Sons & Co Ltd, 22/5/1964; earlier Admiralty, Wrabness, Essex.

(1) withdrawn 5/1964; to Bluebell Railway Preservation Society, Sheffield Park, Sussex, 8/3/1965.
(2) to British Benzole By-Products Ltd, Bedwas, Mid Glamorgan, c10/1970.

BRITISH GAS PURIFYING MATERIALS CO LTD

FLITWICK MOOR PEAT WORKS, Flitwick, near Bedford   J19
TL 047354

A narrow gauge line ran from a tipping dock on the western edge of Flitwick Moor, through woods, to reach the peat workings. There was formerly a branch which curved in a southerly direction to old workings which were flooded by 1960. Wagons used were side tipping skips built by Robert Hudson.

Gauge: 2ft 0in

1	4wPM	MR	4027	1926	(a)	s/s after 5/1965

(a) orig Welwyn Transport Ltd, Welwyn Garden City, Herts; purchased by British Gas Purifying Materials Co Ltd, Leicester, by 3/6/1949.

BRITISH PORTLAND CEMENT MANUFACTURERS LTD

BLOWS DOWN LIME WORKS, Caddington, near Dunstable   H20
B.J. Forder & Son Ltd until 4/1912
earlier B.J. & H. Forder from 31/12/1895
TL 039220

The works and chalk quarry (in production by 1928 and closed c1934) was located on the south side of the GNR (later LNER & BR) Luton - Dunstable branch line, east of Dunstable Town station and at the foot of the chalk hill known as Blows Down. Served by standard gauge sidings (in situ by 1895 and closed after 1944, by 1949) from this line and also by a narrow gauge tramway from the quarry into the works.

Gauge: 3ft 0in

-	4wPM	MR	2020	1921	New	(1)

(1) to Sundon Cement Works, by /1948.

SEWELL LIMEWORKS, Dunstable   F21
B.J. Forder & Son Ltd until 4/1912
B.J. Forder & Son until 25/5/1900
SP 995226

The limeworks, opened c1890, was located on the south side of the LNWR (later LMSR & BR) Leighton Buzzard - Dunstable line near Sewell village with standard gauge sidings (in use by 1895) connecting with this branch at Forder's Sidings signal box. A narrow gauge tramway ran from the kilns east to the quarry at the base of the chalk hill known as Maiden

Bower. The limeworks closed c1940. The quarry was then re-utilized as APCM, Sewell Limestone Quarry (which see) with standard gauge sidings.

Reference : "Industrial Railway Record" No.145, "Totternhoe Quarries", Chris Down & Doug Semmens, IRS, 6/1996.

Gauge: 3ft 0in

-	4wPM	MR	2003	1920	New	s/s

BRITISH RAILWAYS
BEDFORD LOCOMOTIVE DEPOT
G22
TL 042494

In 1964, a LMR Departmental locomotive was transferred to Bedford to work engineers trains and shunt at the engineering sidings at Kempston Road Junction. However the locomotive was not a success on these duties and spent almost all its time out of use at Bedford locomotive shed. ED3 was hired to CEGB Goldington Power Station on one occasion during 1965 for one day only, presumably to cover for a failed steam loco, and was replaced there by a 350hp 0-6-0DE locomotive hired from BR.

Gauge : 4ft 8½in

ED3	0-4-0DM	JF	4200042	1949	(a)	(1)

(a)   ex Beeston Sleeper Depot, Nottingham, 2/1964 (by 12/2/1964).

(1)   withdrawn 9/1967; to George Cohen, Sons & Co Ltd, Coborn Works, Cransley, near Kettering, Northants, for scrap, by c26/11/1967; scrapped there, 6/1968.

CENTRAL ELECTRICITY GENERATING BOARD
Central Electricity Authority until 1/1/1958
British Electricty Authority until 1/4/1955

GOLDINGTON POWER STATION, Bedford
G23
TL 075498

This power station, about two miles east of Bedford, was built by **Mitchell Construction Co Ltd**, of Peterborough (which see). Preliminary site work began in 1951 and construction proper in 5/1952. The first 30Mw generating set was commissioned in 6/1955 and others at intervals up to 5/1957 when capacity reached 150Mw. The station was officially opened on 16/8/1957 when it was anticipated that the final 30Mw set would be commissioned in 1/1/1958. A standard gauge line was laid from the BR (ex-LNWR) Bedford - Cambridge line parallel to the single track Cambridge line to connect with that which entered Bedford Corporation Depot, thus creating a loop line later known as the Goldington loop. It ran north over the New Cut of the River Great Ouse, to the power station reception sidings, and from the north end of these the line curved round to the coal tippler, with other sidings to the main generating hall and workshops. Rail traffic ceased 1980. Station closed 10/1983 and demolished from 3/1987; the site has been redeveloped for housing.

Gauge : 4ft 8½in

ED 3	BIRKENHEAD	0-4-0ST	OC	RSHN	7386	1948	(a)	(1)
ED 9		0-4-0ST	OC	AB	2352	1954	New	(3)
ED 10	RICHARD .TREVITHICK	0-4-0ST	OC	AB	2354	1954	New	(4)
ED 5	LITTLE BARFORD	0-4-0ST	OC	AB	2069	1939	(b)	(2)

ED 8		0-4-0ST	OC	AB	2353	1954	(c)	Scr c5/1972
BLISWORTH No.1		0-4-0ST	OC	AB	2365	1955	(d)	Scr c2/1972
HORSA		0-4-0DH		RSHD	8368	1962		
				WB	3213	1962	(e)	(5)

BR Departmental Locomotive ED3 (0-4-0DM JF 4200042/1949) was here on hire from BR for one day in 1965.
ED9 and ED10 (AB 2352/2354) were overhauled and converted to oil burning by AB; 2354 to Kilmarnock, 10/1955, returned 4/1956; 2352 to Kilmarnock 7/1958, returned c/1958.

(a)   ex BEA, Brimsdown Power Station, Middlesex, loan, c6/1953.
(b)   ex Little Barford Power Station, 11/1963.
(c)   ex Bow Power Station, Essex, c/1967.
(d)   ex RTB, Blisworth Ironstone Quarries, Northants, 29/5/1970.
(e)   ex Richborough Power Station, Kent, 7/1972.

(1)   to CEA, Brimsdown Power Station, Middlesex, off loan, c10/1954.
(2)   to Acton Lane Power Station, Middlesex., 31/7/1965.
(3)   to J.W.Hardwick, Sons & Co Ltd, West Ewell, Surrey, 28/4/1973; resold to "Titanic Steamship Co", Rocester, Staffs, for preservation, 4/1973.
(4)   to Swanage Railway Society, Swanage Station, Dorset, 2/3/1979.
(5)   to Peterborough Railway Society, Nene Valley Railway, Wansford, Cambs, c6/1980.

LITTLE BARFORD POWER STATION, near St.Neots   F24
Bedfordshire, Cambridgeshire & Huntingdonshire Electricity Company until 1/4/1948,
operated by : **Edmundsons Electricity Corporation Ltd** until 1/4/1948   TL 183576

A power station, later known as the "A" Station, was built between 1939 and 1941 by **Sir Robert McAlpine & Sons Ltd**. Located on the west side of the ex-GNR East Coast main line about two miles south of St Neots, it was served by standard gauge sidings from this line. A second unit, the "B" Station, was under construction in 1958. At this time a second loco shed was built, alongside the older one, to stable the diesel locomotive, and a turntable had been installed to turn the locomotives periodically to even out tyre wear. Rail traffic ceased 1980 and the station was closed and demolished. The site has been re-used for a new gas-fired power station completed in 1995.

Gauge : 4ft 8½in

No.56	0-6-0ST	IC	HC	1494	1923	(a)	(1)
ED 5 LITTLE BARFORD	0-4-0ST	OC	AB	2069	1939	New	(4)
SIR THOMAS ROYDEN	0-4-0ST	OC	AB	2088	1940	New	(2)
GENERAL WADE HAYES	0-4-0ST	OC	WB	2665	1942	New	(3)
ED 4 EDMUNDSONS	0-4-0ST	OC	AB	2168	1943	New	(5)
No.11	0-4-0DM		AB	413	1957	New	(6)

BR 68512 (0-6-0T IC Str /1890, Class J69) was here on hire, c10/1952.

(a)   hire from Sir Robert McAlpine & Sons Ltd, contrs, to Bedfordshire, Cambridgeshire & Huntingdonshire Electricity Company during /1942.

(1)   to Sir Robert McAlpine & Sons Ltd, Yardley Chase (ROF) (1942-1943) contract, Northants, 10/6/1942.
(2)   to Stourport Power Station, Worcs, by 3/1943.
(3)   to Stourport Power Station, Worcs.
(4)   to Goldington Power Station, 11/1963.
(5)   to North Norfolk Railway Co Ltd, Sheringham, Norfolk, 29/8/1982.
(6)   to Ampthill Scrap Metal Processing Ltd, Ampthill, 2/9/1982.

LUTON POWER STATION

Luton Corporation Electricity Works until 1/4/1948

H25

TL 096212

Power station, established by c1903, sited to the south of the BR (ex-GNR) Hertford - Dunstable line east of Luton station, and served by standard gauge sidings from this line. The power station was converted to oil-fired in 1963 and the rail system then dispensed with. Station ceased generating in 1969 and since demolished.

Gauge : 4ft 8½in

-	4wBE	GB	1210	1930	New	(1)

(1)   to Taylors Lane Power Station, Middlesex, c6/1963.

CHETTLES FEATHER HAIR PRODUCTS LTD
GOOSEY LODGE, Wymington, near Rushden

F26

TL 964636

Locos used as stationary power generators, with cabs and wheels removed.   No rail operations at the site.

Gauge : 4ft 8½in

-	0-4-0DM	HE	2068	1940	(a)	(1)
-	0-4-0DM	JF	4210143	1958	(b)	(2)
-	4wDH	NBQ	27544	1959	(c)	(3)

(a)   ex George Cohen, Sons & Co Ltd, Coborn Works, Cransley, Northants, by 6/1/1974.
(b)   ex George Cohen, Sons & Co Ltd, Coborn Works, Cransley, Northants, by 19/1/1974.
(c)   ex George Cohen, Sons & Co Ltd, Coborn Works, Cransley, Northants, 11/1974.

(1)   to Mays By-Products, Bourne, Lincs, as a generator, c12/1974 (after 10/3/1974).
(2)   to E.M. Wilcox Ltd, Royce Road, Peterborough, Cambs, as a generator, c/1975 (after 10/3/1974).
(3)   to Chettle & Son, Podington scrapyard, near Wymington, c/1975 (after 19/4/1975); dismantled.

R. FIELDING & SON
HARLINGTON BRICKWORKS, Westoning

F27

TL 050313

Brickworks, located on the road between Harlington and Sharpenhoe, started by Edward Kitchener c1922-1924 and operated by R. Fielding & Son between at least 1931 and c1934-1937 after which it passed into the ownership of R. Lancaster & Son (Cleveleys) Ltd. The brick kilns were subsequently demolished and the site was taken over by the Production Tool Alloy Co Ltd for the construction of a factory by 1941.

Gauge: 2ft 0in

-	4wPM	MR	7046	1937	New	(1)

(1)   later with Inns & Co Ltd, Denham Pits, Bucks, by 9/1949.

GEORGE GARSIDE (SAND) LTD
LEIGHTON BUZZARD SILICA SAND QUARRIES   K28

George Garside until 1960

George Garside commenced trading about 1890 initially with a sand pit in Billington Road which employed a horse worked 500mm gauge line to a standard gauge exchange siding. This pit was worked out by about 1916 and later, from 1920 to 1964, was the site of the washery for sand from other workings (SP 928241). From 1964 a new drying plant was operated in Eastern Way (**Double Arches**) (SP 942283). **Grovebury Pit** was commenced about 1916 on the south of the LNWR Dunstable branch and from 1926 workings were at SP 918234 about half a mile south of the initial site. Extensive 2ft gauge tramways were used at these workings. Also about 1916 **Rackley Hill** Quarry (SP 920241) was purchased from Joseph Arnold & Sons and was extended and worked until the late 1920s.

During World War I workings were commenced on the west side of the Watling Street some three miles north-west of Leighton Buzzard at **Double Arches** (SP 941292 and SP 943284). These workings were served by the Leighton Buzzard Light Railway (which see) from its opening in 1919, as were the quarries at **Munday's Hill** (SP 940280) which opened in 1926.

Later quarries included **Churchways** at Heath & Reach (1931-1937), **Shenley Hill** (in 1928), and **Brickyard Pit and Rackley Hill Quarry** at Grovebury (1928)

Locomotive sheds and workshops were at **Grovebury** (not connected with the LBLR) and at **Billington Road** and **Double Arches** (both connected with the Leighton Buzzard Light Rly). A separate shed at Double Arches was used to house the Engineer's loco (No.21).

As with Arnold's, after closure of the Leighton Buzzard Light Railway company the traffic over the "main line" was worked by the company's own locomotives.

Rail traffic ceased 2/6/1981 and track lifted in the quarries by 9/1981.

Reference : "The Leighton Buzzard Light Railway", S A Leleux, Oakwood Press,
                                1969 & 1996.

Locomotives :

As with Arnold's, it has been difficult to establish the identity of many of the locomotives here, because the running numbers carried by these locos were frequently changed; the racehorse names carried were amended with even greater frequency dependent on the competitive success of the namesakes. IRS records contain many observations which cannot be reconciled with known works numbers.

As examples, in 1952 G.P.Roberts recorded 31 locos identified either by running number and/or works number plus approximately 20 further unidentifiable derelicts. In 1958 A.D.Semmens recorded a total of approximately 50 locos with this company, but by 1965 this total had reduced to about 25.

The first list below consists of identified locomotives with works number (where known), and final known running number and/or name. Following the footnotes is a supplementary list attempting to set out known details of renumbering and re-naming.

Gauge: 2ft 0in

	-	4wPM	MR	1856	1919	(a)	s/s
	-	4wPM	MR	974	1918	(b)	s/s
No.1	BENGHAZI	4wPM	MR	374	1917	(c)	Scr c/1961
No.2	STEADY AIM	4wPM	MR	1044	1918	(d)	Scr c/1960
No.9		4wPM	MR	1107	1918	(e)	Scr c/1959
No.2		4wPM	MR	3789	1926	New (f)	Scr c/1960
No.5	MY LOVE	4wDM (ex PM)	MR	3795	1926	New (g)	Scr c/1961
No.10	MIGOLI	4wDM (ex PM)	MR	3828	1926	New (h)	Scr c/1961

No.6		4wPM	MR	3841	1926	New (i)	s/s by /1959
50		4wPM	MR	3850	1927	(j)	Scr by 6/1959
No.7	M'SIEUR L'ADMIRAL	4wPM	MR	4019	1926	(k)	Scr by 6/1959
No.9	CIDER APPLE	4wPM	MR	4568	1929	(l)	Scr /1965
No.21	FESTOON	4wPM	MR	4570	1929	(m)	(7)
No.11	EL ALAMEIN	4wDM (ex PM)	MR	5002	1929	(m)	(2)
No.12		4wPM	MR	5008	1929	(n)	Scr by /1958
No.13	RETRIAL	4wDM	MR	5870	1935	(o)	(5)
No.36	RELKO	4wDM	MR	7145	1936	New	(5)
No.15	BROWN JACK	4wDM	MR	7148	1936	New	Scr /1976
No.16	ANGLO	4wDM	MR	7149	1936	New	Scr 8/1980
No.13	ARKLE	4wDM	MR	7152	1936	New	(5)
No.27		4wDM	MR	5852	1933	(p)	(6)
		4wDM	Jung	(?4465	1929)	(q)	(1)
No.69		4wDM	Jung	5215	1931	(q)	(1)
No.28	FLUSH ROYAL	4wDM	MR	8917	1944	(r)	(5)
No.26	SCRATCH II	4wPM	MR	5011	1929	(s)	Scr /1960
No.30	LARKSPUR	4wDM	MR	7195	1937	(t)	(5)
No.31	MILL REEF	4wDM	MR	7371	1939	(t)	(10)
No.32	HARD RIDDEN	4wDM	MR	7372	1939	(t)	(4)
No.29	AYALA	4wDM	MR	7374	1939	(t)	(9)
-		4wDM (ex PM)	MR	4808	1936	(u)	Scr c/1965
-		4wDM (ex PM)	MR	4809	1936	(u)	Scr c/1965
-		4wDM	MR	5864	1934	(u)	s/s c/1968
No.13	ARKLE	4wDM	MR	7036	1936	(v)	(8)
No.34	RED RUM	4wDM	MR	7105	1936	(w)	(10)
No.13	ARKLE	4wDM	MR	7108	1936	(x)	(10)
-		4wDM	MR	7115	1936	(y)	(5)
-		4wDM	MR	7414	1939	(y)	(5)
No.33		4wDM	MR	7140	1936	(z)	Scr by 1/1979
12		4wDM	MR	7932	1941	(aa)	(3)
10		4wDM	MR	10272	1951	(aa)	(3)
No.14	DEVON LOCH	4wDM	MR	7492	1940	(ab)	(5)
-		4wDM	MR	8725	1941	(ac)	(5)
No.35	DOUTELLE	4wDM	MR	8713	1941	(ad)	(5)
-		4wDM	MR	7154	1937	(ae)	(5)
No.33	UTRILLO	4wDM	MR	8587	1941	(af)	Scr 7/1/1980

(a)   ex Lamb & Phillips, LBLR construction contract, after 12/6/1920.
(b)   orig MoM, France, WDLR 2695.
(c)   ex WDLR 1775; purchased by Garside by 15/11/1921.
(d)   ex WDLR 2765; (purchased by Garside, c/1926 ?)
(e)   ex Wilson, Kinmond & Marr Ltd, contrs, Glasgow, by /1946; orig WDLR 2828.
(f)   rebuilt from MR 369/1917, orig WDLR 1770.
(g)   rebuilt from MR 219/1916, orig WDLR 219.
(h)   rebuilt from earlier loco (possibly MR 1821/1919); converted to diesel, 9/12/1935; later reverted to petrol.
(i)   rebuilt from MR 3684 (formerly Dolberg Jones Railways, Durban, South Africa).
(j)   ex Petrol Loco Hirers, 2/6/1927; rebuild of unidentified older loco formerly Heaton Park Reservoir, Manchester, No.14.
(k)   ex MR, 7/5/1928; orig Petrol Loco Hirers.
(l)   ex Petrol Loco Hirers, 13/7/1929; converted to diesel, 12/11/1935
(m)   ex Petrol Loco Hirers, 16/2/1931
(n)   ex Petrol Loco Hirers, 22/7/1931

(o) ex Petrol Loco Hirers Ltd, 19/7/1936

(p) orig A.H. Worth & Co, Fleet, Lincs; to here after 2/1952, by 5/1958.

(q) Jung 4465/1929 was new to "Baxter Fell, London", 24/4/1929 – identity assumed; Jung 5215/1931 was new to Standard Steel Co, London, 28/5/1931.

(r) ex George W. Bungey Ltd, dealers, Hayes, Middlesex, by /1951, after 4/1950.

(s) ex George Cohen, Sons & Co Ltd, by /1951; earlier Peter Lind & Co Ltd, contrs.

(t) ex George W. Bungey Ltd, dealers, Hayes, Middlesex, by 4/1952; earlier James N. Connell Ltd, Coatbridge.

(u) ex Sir Robert McAlpine & Sons Ltd, contrs, (MR 4808, 4809 and 5864 were ?PN 4361, PN 4362 and ?PN 4115 respectively), by /1958.

(v) ex Sir Robert McAlpine & Sons Ltd, contrs, for spares, 5/1958.

(w) ex George W. Bungey Ltd, dealer, Hayes, Middlesex, by 5/1958; earlier English Clays, Lovering Pochin & Co Ltd, Drinnick Mill, Cornwall.

(x) ex A. Grubb & Son Ltd, Water Hall Farm Gravel Pits, near Hertford, by 5/1958.

(y) ex James N. Connell Ltd, Coatbridge, Lanarks, (possibly via George W. Bungey Ltd, dealers, Hayes, Middlesex), for spares, by 5/1958.

(z) ex Sir Lindsey Parkinson & Co Ltd, contrs, by 5/1958.

(aa) ex Leighton Buzzard Light Railway, 3/12/1958.

(ab) ex George W. Bungey Ltd, dealer, Hayes, Middlesex, by /1968; earlier Shelton Iron, Steel & Coal Co Ltd, Staffs.

(ac) ex Sir Robert McAlpine & Sons Ltd, contrs, PN 5037, for spares, 8/1968.

(ad) ex Sir Robert McAlpine & Sons Ltd, contrs, PN 5025, by 8/1968.

(ae) ex Sir Robert McAlpine & Sons Ltd, PN 4274, for spares, after 1/1970, by 1/1973.

(af) orig War Office; earlier Merer Ltd, Falkirk, Stirlingshire, until at least 9/1952; here by /1977.

(1) to George W. Bungey Ltd, dealers, Hayes, Middlesex, 5/1951; later with Lancashire Moss Litter, Horwich, Lancs.

(2) scrapped, after 8/1954, by /1958.

(3) to England Hopkins, scrap metal merchant, Woburn Sands, /1965; then to Jonallen, Singapore, 31/8/1966.

(4) dismantled by 1/1970; scrapped by /1973.

(5) to England Hopkins, scrap metal merchant, Woburn Sands, for scrap, 29/3/1976.

(6) to I.B. Jolly, Mold, Clwyd (North Wales), for preservation, 24/11/1979.

(7) to Leighton Buzzard Narrow Gauge Railway Society, for preservation, 21/6/1981.

(8) to Leighton Buzzard Narrow Gauge Railway Society, for preservation, 9/11/1981.

(9) to G.A. & R.J. Feldwick, Wickford, Essex, for preservation, 10/11/1981.

(10) to West Lancashire Light Railway, Hesketh Bank, Lancs, 14/11/1981.

Identities :

(MR 374)	4wPM	No.1 BENGHAZI
(MR 1044)	4wPM	No.2 FLYON STEADY AIM by 4/1952
(unidentified)	4wPM	No.2 NICKEL COIN (noted 4/1952 - 6/1959)
(unidentified)	4wPM	No.3 (not named) (derelict 4/1952; s/s after 11/1953)
(MR 3828)	4wPM	No.3 MIGOLI (derelict 4/1952 - 6/1959)
		No.4 (not recorded at any time)
(MR 3795)	4wPM	No.5 COLORADO KID (MY LOVE, derelict 4/1952 - 6/1959)
(unidentified)	4wPM	No.5 AIRBORNE (derelict 4/1952; s/s after 11/1953)
(unidentified)	4wPM	No.6 BRENDANE COTTAGE (un-named, derelict 4/1952 - 6/1953)
(MR 4019)	4wPM	No.7 HELLENI QUA (M'SIEUR L'AMIRAL, derelict 4/1952 - 4/1958)
(unidentified)	4wPM	No.8 (not named) (derelict 4/1952 - 6/1953)
(unidentified)	4wPM	No.8 GOLDEN MILLER (derelict 4/1952 - 5/1958)
(unidentified)	4wPM	No.9 SUPERTELLO (un-named, derelict 6/1959)
(MR 4568)	4wPM	No.10 FOXTROT; CIDER APPLE (4/1952); No.19(un-named) 5/1962

(MR 5002)	4wPM	No.11 EL ALAMEIN (4/1952 - 8/1954)
(MR 4570)	4wPM	No.12 BLACK SPECK (4/1952); FESTOON (6/1959); No.21(5/1965)
(MR 5870)	4wDM	No.13 RE-TRIAL (6/1953 - 5/1965)
(MR 7145)	4wDM	No.14 SUN CHARIOT (4/1952); HALLOWEEN (11/1953); DEVON LOCH (6/1959 - 5/1965); No.36 RELKO (1970s)
(MR 7148)	4wDM	No.15 HYPERBOLE (4/1952); TULYAR (11/1953); MUCH OBLIGED (10/1959); BROWN JACK (1970s)
(MR 7149)	4wDM	No.16 PATCH; THREE CHEERS (4/1952 - 11/1953); AURIOLE (8/1954); RIBOT (/1959 - 5/1965); ANGLO
(MR 7152)	4wDM	No.17 ALEXANDER;(un-named 10/1952);FRENCH DESIGN (5/1962) DAMREDUB (8/1963); No.13 ARKLE (after 1965)
(unidentified)	4wDM	No.18 LANGTON ABBOT (6/1953); HONEYLIGHT (10/1957-5/65)
(unidentified)	4wDM	No.19 LOVELY COTTAGE (6/1953)
(unidentified)	4wDM	No.20 (un-named 6/1952)
(unidentified)	4wDM	No.21 (un-named 11/1953 - 6/1958)
(unidentified)	4wDM	No.21 TOSCA (8/1958 - 5/1962, Engineers loco) (earlier No.5)
(unidentified)	4wPM	No.22 (un-named 11/1953 - 4/1955)
(unidentified)	4wPM	No.23 MONTY (derelict 6/1953 - 9/1959)
(unidentified)	4wPM	No.24 SHEILA'S COTTAGE (derelict 4/1952 - 9/1959)
(unidentified)	4wPM	No.25 ALICYDON (4/1952 - 6/1959)
(unidentified)	4wPM	25 (un-named, derelict 4/1952 - 6/53 - possibly ex Mowlem 25)
(unidentified)	4wPM	26 (un-named, derelict 4/1952 - possibly ex Mowlem 26)
(MR 5011)	4wPM	No.26 SCRATCH II (/1951 - 9/1959)
(unidentified)	4wDM	No.27 ARCTIC PRINCE; TORCH SINGER (6/1959); un-named (5/1962)
(MR 8917)	4wDM	No.28 FLUSH ROYAL
(MR 7374)	4wDM	No.29 SUPREME COURT; QUARE TIMES (6/1959 - 5/1962); AYALA (5/1965)
(unidentified)	4wDM	No.30 FLEETING MOMENT (4/1952 - 5/1962); No.10 TEARAWAY (5/1965)
(MR 7195)	4wDM	No.10 TEARAWAY (6/1953 - 5/1962); No.30 LARKSPUR (5/1965)
(MR 7371)	4wDM	No.31 GOOD TASTE (4/1952 - 6/1959); OXO (5/1962 - 8/1963); TEAM SPIRIT (5/1965); MILLREEF (1970s)
(MR 7372)	4wDM	No.32 TEAL (11/1953);GAY DONALD (6/1959); un-named (5/1962); HARD RIDDEN (5/1965);
(MR 7140)	4wDM	No.33 WILWYN (6/1953); ROYAL TAN; CREPELLO (6/1959 - 5/62); UTRILLO (5/1965 - 8/1967)
(MR 7108)	4wDM	No.34 DARIUS; SUNDEW (6/1959 - 5/1962); KILMORE (5/1965); No.13 ARKLE
(MR 7105)	4wDM	No.35 DOVETELLE (5/1958 - 5/1965); KILMORE; RED RUM
(MR 5852)	4wDM	No.36 (un-named 3/1957 - 5/1962); RELKO (5/1965); No.27 (unnamed)
(MR 7036)	4wDM	(un-numbered & un-named, 5/1958); No.37 HARD RIDDEN (5/1959) GAY DONALD (5/1962 - 5/1965); No.13 ARKLE

4wPM locos with running numbers 100, 109 and 110 were here derelict in 4/1952; assumed scrapped c/1959. These running numbers suggest that they were from the Ham River Grit Co fleet.

JAMES & FREDK. HOWARD LTD
BRITANNIA IRONWORKS, Bedford

G29

TL 045490

This company had its origins in 1851 when James Howard took over his father's business and in 1855 commenced the manufacture of steam cultivating machinery. By 1856 he had purchased 15 acres of land in Kempston Road for the construction of a new works to replace the original Britannia Foundry in Castle Meadow which had become too small. The new Britannia Iron Works was built betwen 1857 and 1859 and at that time was the largest factory in Bedford. (An advert in "The Engineer" 14/8/1857 stated 'wanted, light flat bottom rails for tramway - J. & F. Howard, Bedford'.) The works was served by an extensive 2ft gauge hand-worked tramway with wagon turntables. This connected the various workshops with the storage areas. Production included tram wagons, portable railway equipment and, from about 1923 to 1931, internal combustion locomotives. By 1931 the firm was a subsidiary of **Agricultural & General Engineers Ltd** and the financial problems of this company caused the works to close on 15/2/1932 and the company to go into receivership in 3/1932. Following closure the locomotive drawings and patents were purchased about 8/1932 by F.C.Hibberd & Co Ltd, of Park Royal , London, who continued to build locomotives to Howard designs. The plant and site were auctioned on 19-22/7/1932 by Leopold Farmer & Sons - this auction included nine items of narrow gauge rolling stock. The works was acquired in 1933 by Britannia Iron & Steel Works Ltd, which see.

Reference : "Railway Magazine", Vol XLV, August 1919.

Gauge : 4ft 8½in

-	2-2-0WT	IC	H		1895	(a)	s/s after /1904
FARMERS FRIEND	0-6-0ST	OC	HCR	173	1875	(b)	s/s
-	0-4-0ST	OC	MW	1381	1899	(c)	(3)
-	4wPM		MR	?	1919	(d)	s/s
-	4wPM		MR	2132	1922	(e)	(1)
-	4wPM		H	957	1926	New	(2)

(a) converted from traction engine, 12/1895.
(b) if here, then earlier Thomas Mitchell & Sons Ltd, dealers, Bolton, Lancs, until /1907 (possibly /1908) at least; orig Garstang & Knott End Railway, Lancs.
(c) ex Axholme Joint Railway, Lincs, after 5/10/1904, by 28/1/1909.
(d) unknown origins (? possibly on trial from MR), /1919.
(e) ex Petrol Loco Hirers, hire, 1/8/1922.

(1) returned to Petrol Loco Hirers, off hire, 7/10/1922; later with Joseph Boam Ltd, Gayton Road, Norfolk.
(2) to Britannia Iron & Steel Works Ltd, with site, /1933 (after 22/7/1932).
(3) to Bedford Corporation, Goldington Depot, /1933 (after 22/7/1932).

Gauge: 2ft 6in

-	0-4-0ST	OC	FE		c1882	(a)	(1)

(a) origin and identity unknown.

(1) to G.J. Rollox & Sons, contractors, Elveden Hall Estate, near Thetford, Suffolk, c1/1898.

INNS & CO LTD

HENLOW PITS
F30

earlier J. Inns & Co

TL 184380/TL 184375

Gravel pits located on land in the Henlow Grange estate, also in Arlesey Road, to the north and south of the A507 road, and east of Henlow village, and later in Langford Road, Henlow (TL 181392). Pits opened in 3/1936; closed after 1964 and railway lifted.

Gauge: 2ft 0in

-	4wPM	MR	4807	1936	New	(1)

(1)   to Denham Pits, Bucks, after 9/1949, by 6/1952.

UPPER SUNDON RUBBISH TIP
F31

TL 040280 approx

Works established on the site of the former Sundon Limeworks and its associated quarries. Tramway replaced by dumpers c1962; track partially lifted 1963 and all removed by 5/1965.

Gauge: 2ft 0in

-	4wDM	MR	5913	1935	New	(2)
-	4wDM	MR	5931	1935	New	(1)
-	4wDM	MR	10031	1948	New	(4)
-	4wDM	MR	5933	1935	(a)	(3)
-	4wDM	MR	5716	1937	(b)	(5)

(a)   ex Willoughby Lane Pits, Tottenham, London, by 6/1950.
(b)   ex Nazeing New Road Pits, Broxbourne, Herts, by 5/1958.

(1)   to Holwell Hyde Rubbish Tip, Cole Green, Herts, by 6/1950.
(2)   to Wheathamstead Rubbish Tip, Herts, by 5/1953.
(3)   to Savay Farm Pits, Denham, Bucks, /1963 (by 7/1963).
(4)   to Nazeing New Road Pits, Herts, c/1963.
(5)   to Caversham Pits, Oxon.

NOTE that Inns & Co Ltd also operated the following quarries in Bedfordshire. It is likely that narrow gauge systems were used at some or all of them, but confirmation is lacking :
WARREN HILL PITS, Tingrith, near Dunstable (1937 -1964; latterly as sand pits) (TL009380)
SANDY SAND PITS, near Biggleswade (1959 -1964)
HEATH & REACH SAND PITS, Leighton Buzzard (1952 - at least 1964)   (SP926286)
All these sites had closed by 1968.

LAPORTE INDUSTRIES LTD

LUTON CHEMICALS WORKS
H32

Laporte Chemicals Ltd until 31/7/1968

TL 069221

B. Laporte (1948) Ltd until 3/1953;
B. Laporte Ltd until 10/3/1948
B. Laporte until 7/1/1908

Bernard Laporte started the manufacture of hydrogen peroxide at Shipley, Yorkshire (WR), in 1888 to meet the needs of woollen bleachers. By 1898 a branch works had been started in Luton to supply hydrogen peroxide as a bleaching agent to the straw plait industry. The Luton works soon proved to be too small and a new, larger, plant was built in Park Street.

By the outbreak of the First World War the British hydrogen peroxide industry was dependent on imported raw materials and an extensive new factory, covering 17 acres, was set up in Kingsway to remedy this. Construction commenced in 1915 and production had started by 1916. After the end of World War I, new offices, laboratories and and an improved hydrogen peroxide plant were added, in production by 1920. Expansion continued until by 1950 the site covered 60 acres.

The works, located on the north side of the BR (ex-GNR) Hertford - Dunstable branch about a mile west of Luton station, was served by standard gauge sidings (into use by 1916) to this line. Rail traffic ceased about 1970 and the rail connection was removed in 1972.

The works has subsequently been closed and demolished and the site re-developed.

Gauge : 4ft 8½in

(No.1)	GF No.3	0-4-0F	OC	AB	1477	1916	(a)	(3)
(No.2)		0-4-0F	OC	AB	2243	1948	New(b)	(4)

Gauge : 4ft 8½in (locomotives stored here awaiting preservation)

No.1	0-4-0F	OC	AB	1492	1916	(c)	(2)
No.2	0-4-0F	OC	AB	1493	1916	(c)	(1)

Additionally at least five LNER Class Y1/Y3 4wVBT Sentinel locos (LNER 55/61/62/65/86; S 8320/8322/8323/8326 of 1930 and 8609/1931 respectively) were used here on loan and returned to LNER during the period 1941-8

(a)   ex MoM, Gretna, Dumfriesshire, by 8/1923 (possibly in /1920).
(b)   to Baronet Works, Warrington, Lancs, c18/1/1958; returned, /1960 (by 4/1960).
(c)   ex Van den Berghs & Jurgens Ltd, Purfleet, Essex, 9/1968.

(1)   to London Railway Preservation Society Ltd, Quainton Road, Bucks, 2/3/1970; sold for scrap to Ayris & Jeacock, Bicester, Oxon, 22/5/1970.
(2)   to London Railway Preservation Society Ltd, Quainton Road, Bucks, 3/3/1970 (not accepted and awaited scrapping at the premises of Peterborough Heavy Haulage Co, 6/3/1970; sold for scrap to George Cohen, Sons & Co Ltd, Coborn Works, Cransley, Northants, 5/5/1970).
(3)   to London Railway Preservation Society Ltd, Quainton Road Station, Bucks, 7/1971.
(4)   to London Railway Preservation Society Ltd, Quainton Road Station, Bucks, 27/11/1972.

LEIGHTON BUZZARD BRICK CO LTD
POTSGROVE QUARRIES, Leighton Buzzard

K33
SP 939298

Sand quarries, opened 9/1944, on the south of the Watling Street near to the Double Arches workings of George Garside. A 2ft gauge system was installed in 1945 but was short and steeply graded and only operated for about a year. Track was lifted and stored until remaining equipment was sold in 1952.

Reference : "The Leighton Buzzard Light Railway", S.A. Leleux, Oakwood Press, 1969 & 1996.

Gauge: 2ft 0in

HAIG	0-4-0ST	OC	KS	3105	1918	(a)	(1)
-	4wPM	MR				(b)	s/s /1949
-	4wDM	RH	172902	1935		(c)	(2)
-	4wDM	RH	174545	1935		(b)	(2)

(a) earlier Air Ministry, Kidbrooke, London; here by 31/3/1945.
(b) origin and identity not known.
(c) ex John Heaver Ltd, Chichester, Sussex, c9/1944.

(1) derelict by /1945; scrapped on site after 2/1952, by 5/1952.
(2) derelict by /1949; to Frank Isaacson Ltd, West Drayton, Middlesex, after 2/1952, by 5/1952.

LEIGHTON BUZZARD LIGHT RAILWAY LTD
LEIGHTON BUZZARD LIGHT RAILWAY   K34

Light railway about four miles in length which connected the sand workings at Double Arches, north east of Leighton Buzzard, and other quarries, to the washing plant and standard gauge exchange sidings at Billington Road, Leighton Buzzard. The line was opened on 20/11/1919 using equipment acquired from WDLR. The stock was maintained at workshops at Billington Road (SP 928241).

Shunting in the silica quarries, screening plant, etc., connected with the LBLR system was performed by locomotives belonging to the quarry owners, Joseph Arnold & Sons Ltd, and George Garside, and which worked over the LBLR to some extent. From 12/1958, operation of the LBLR was taken over completely by Arnolds and Garsides, who purchased certain locos as shown in the list; Arnolds also took over the LBLR loco shed and works.

Rail haulage of sand traffic ceased in 1981 and the majority of the line was then taken over by the Leighton Buzzard Narrow Gauge Railway Society (which see in the Preservation section) as a passenger carrying line

References : "Industrial Railway Record" No.9, March 1966.
          "The Leighton Buzzard Light Railway", S A Leleux, Oakwood Press,
               1969 & 1996.

Gauge: 2ft 0in

-	0-6-0WT	OC	HC	1377	1918	(a)	(1)
-	0-6-0WT	OC	HC	1378	1918	(a)	(1)
-	4wPM		MR	1856	1919	(b)	(2)
-	4wPM		MR	1757	1918	(c)	(4)
(11 ?) -	4wPM		MR	849	1919	(d)	(5)
4	4wPM		MR	468	1918	(e)	(3)
3	4wPM		MR	478	1918	(e)	(3)
3	4wPM		MR	574	1918	(f)	s/s after 11/1953
2	4wPM		MR	1383	1918	(g)	(6)
6	4wPM		MR	1299	1918	(h)	Scr 10/1957
-	4wPM		MR	2213	1924	(i)	s/s by /1950
1	4wPM		MR	3674	1924	(j)	(6)
5	4wPM		MR	3848	1934	(k)	(3)
7	4wPM		MR			(l)	(6)
8	4wPM		MR			(l)	(6)
9	4wPM		MR			(l)	Scr /1950
10	4wPM		MR			(m)	(6)
(4 ?)	4wPM		MR	3675	1924	(n)	Scr
(6 ?)	4wPM		MR	1283	1918	(o)	Scr 10/1957
-	4wDM		MR	8682	1942	(p)	(7)
9	4wDM		MR	9547	1950	New	(8)
10	4wDM		MR	10272	1951	New	(9)

11	4wDM	MR	10409	1954	New	(8)
12	4wDM	MR	7932	1941	(q)	(8)
13	4wDM	MR	7933	1941	(r)	(8)
14	4wDM	MR	7710	1939	(s)	(8)

(a) ordered 6/1918 by WDLR (3207/8 respectively) and built to 600mm gauge but not delivered. Regauged to 2ft 0in and delivered here 31/5/1919, per/via Robert Hudson & Co Ltd, dealers, Leeds..

(b) ex Lamb & Phillips, contractors for LBLR construction, on hire, /1919.

(c) ex WDLR, 2478, (1/1920?)

(d) ex WDLR, 2570, 1/1920

(e) ex WDLR (2189/2199 respectively), (c/1921 ?).

(f) orig WDLR, 2295; here by c/1950 (presumably actually much earlier)

(g) ex WDLR, 3104, by /1921

(h) ex WDLR, 3020, c/1921

(i) ex MR, 12/3/1924, rebuild of MR 1775/1918 (WDLR 2496),.

(j) ex MR, 3/5/1924; rebuild of MR 595/1918 (WDLR 2316).

(k) ex MR, 5/1934; earlier Manchester Waterworks; reb of MR 507/1917 (WDLR 2228).

(l) origin unknown; here by /1930s

(m) origin unknown; here by 12/1952

(n) ex John Mowlem & Co Ltd, contractors, 26, for spares, /1946; rebuild of MR 1284/1918 (WDLR 3005).

(o) ex John Mowlem & Co Ltd, contractors, 27, for spares, /1946; orig. WDLR 3004.

(p) ex MR, hire, probably c/1948

(q) ex George W. Bungey Ltd, dealers, Hayes, Middlesex, 10/1956; orig Sir Alfred McAlpine & Sons Ltd, Pant Farm Gravel Pits, Gresford, Denbighs [North Wales].

(r) ex George W. Bungey Ltd, dealers, Hayes, Middlesex, 10/1956; earlier Sir Alfred McAlpine & Sons Ltd, Hartington Quarries, Derbys.

(s) ex George W. Bungey Ltd, dealers, Hayes, Middlesex, 10/1956; earlier Derbyshire Stone Quarries Ltd, Hopton Quarry, Derbys.

(1) to R.H. Neal & Co, Ealing, London, dealers, 16/8/1921; possibly then to Bryant & Langford Quarries Ltd, Portishead, Somerset, c/1922.

(2) returned to Lamb & Phillips Ltd, off hire, c/1920; probably then to George Garside, after 12/6/1920.

(3) scrapped c1/1959, by Smith & Co (Bedford) Ltd, Bedford.

(4) to Joseph Arnold & Sons Ltd, c/1923, following collision.

(5) scrapped after 10/1957.

(6) scrapped at Billington Road, c2/1959, by Smith & Co (Bedford) Ltd, Bedford.

(7) returned to MR, off hire, 11/1950; later hired to Inns & Co Ltd, Sawbridgeworth Pits, Herts, and purchased by them, 12/1954.

(8) to Joseph Arnold & Sons Ltd, 3/12/1958.

(9) to George Garside, 3/12/1958.

LEIGHTON BUZZARD SAND CO LTD
FIRBANK SAND PITS, Leighton Buzzard

K35

SP 924240

Sand pits on the south of the LNWR Leighton Buzzard - Dunstable line to the east of the various Grovebury workings. The quarry was served by a long standard gauge siding (agreement dated 4th March 1897) from the LNWR. This siding was worked by horse or main line loco for most of its existence, until after 1944 (but closed by 1949). However for about a year in the 1920s, when the pit was being operated by **Dagnalls Ltd**, a steam locomotive was hired and worked the traffic. The company also worked sand pits at Springwell Lane, Rickmansworth, Herts. **Bott and Stennett** were directors of this company – see also the contractors' section.

Reference : "The Leighton Buzzard Light Railway", S.A. Leleux, Oakwood Press, 1969 &1996.

Gauge: 4ft 8½in

| No.19 | AVON | | 0-6-0ST | IC | MW | 738 | 1881 | (a) | (1) |

(a)   ex Wm. Muirhead, MacDonald, Wilson & Co Ltd, contrs, Fulham, London, hire, after 14/5/1920

(1)   returned to Wm. Muirhead, MacDonald, Wilson & Co Ltd, c/1921; later (hire ?) to Charles Brand & Son Ltd, Hendon (London Electric Railway Co) (1922-1923) contract, Middlesex.

LONDON BRICK CO LTD

The **London Brick Company** was formed in 1889 with works at Fletton, Peterborough. As part of its continual expansion, on 15/9/1923 it merged with **B.J.Forder & Son Ltd** to become **London Brick Company & Forders Ltd.** The first chairman of this new company was Halley Stewart; hence the naming of the major new Stewartby Works. In 1936 it became the **London Brick Co Ltd.** Later the London Brick Co Ltd and Butterley Brick Co Ltd merged on 1/10/1995 to become **Hanson Brick Ltd.**

ARLESEY BRICKWORKS, Arlesey   F36
London Brick Company & Forders Ltd until 22/4/1936   TL 186352
The Arlesey Brick Co (Beart's) Ltd from 7/5/1898 until 1928
Beart's Patent Brick Co (in association with **Arlesey Brick Co**) by 1885.
Beart's Patent Brick Co from 1853.
Robert Beart from 1852.

Brickworks established in 1852 by Robert Beart of Godmanchester. Situated on the west side of the BR (ex-GNR) Hitchin - Peterborough main line south west of the former Three Counties station. The original Bearts kiln with ten chambers was demolished in 1937 and a new, 32 chamber, kiln built on the site with production commencing in 6/1938. Brick production ceased about 1932 but the works continued to produce drainage pipes until 10/1981. Standard gauge sidings connected the works with the main line but were disused from c1948. The works was served by several distinct narrow gauge tramways. One of 2ft 11in gauge was used within the works to move drainage pipes and later building blocks from the kilns to the stock yard, using electric locomotives (known as Hoffman Trams) hauling transfer trailers A/TX/8 - 21. This system was replaced by fork lift trucks about 1965. A hand/cable worked line of this gauge was used for coaling on the east kilns (which were demolished in 1979). A third line of 2ft 11in gauge brought clay from the pits to the works; locomotives were used in the pits until 11/11/1975 and a cable worked incline up to the works was replaced in 1970, both by conveyors. The locomotives used remained on site for some time after this until their disposal. Also a 2ft 0in gauge line (closed 12/1977) worked on the top of the western kilns (TL 184353).

Both original sets of kilns were demolished and replaced by new kilns for specialised brick production about 1983. The original claypits have been used for landfill. After the elimination of rail traction the works passed to Butterley Brick Co Ltd and subsequently to the Hanson Brick group. It had closed by 2001.

Gauge : 4ft 8½in

	MOLTKE	0-6-0ST	IC	MW	848	1882	(a)	(1)
	ANCOATS	4wVBT	HCG	Blackwell		1922		
		reb of 0-4-0ST	OC	MW	1091	1888	(b)	(2)
L49	SENTINEL	0-6-0VBT	HCG	S	5667	1924	(c)	(3)
L47	1 A/L/5	4wVBT	VCG	S	9284	1937	(d)	(4)

(a)   ex Leonard Foster, Southgate - New Barnet (GNR) (c1890-1893) widening contract, Herts; 4/1894.

(b)   ex Blackwell & Son, engineers, Northampton, on trial, c/1922-/1924, (prior to the rebuild of MW 848 as S 5667); MW 1091 was earlier with Stanley Bros Ltd, Stockingford, Warwicks.

(c)   ex Blackwell & Son, engineers, Northampton, after rebuilding from MW 848, /1924

(d)   ex Calvert Works, Bucks, 4/1946.

(1)   to Blackwell & Son, engineers, Northampton, for conversion to VB locomotive of Sentinel design (Blackwell's second such conversion), c/1924.

(2)   returned to Blackwell & Son, engineers, Northampton, c/1924

(3)   to Fletton's LB 4 Works, Peterborough, Hunts, for overhaul, 6-7/1946.

(4)   returned to Calvert Works, 13/5/1953.

Gauge: 2ft 11in (internal 220v DC works system)

A/TX/1	4wWE	LBC		New	Scr /1966
A/TX/2	4wWE	LBC		New	Scr /1966
A/TX/3	4wWE	LBC		New	Scr /1966
A/TX/3	4wWE	LBC		New	Scr /1966
A/TX/5	4wWE	LBC		New	Scr /1966
A/TX/6	4wWE	LBC		New	Scr /1966
A/TX/7	4wWE	LBC		New	Scr /1966
S/TX/18	4wWE	LBC		(a)	Scr /1966

(a)   ex Stewartby Works, 16/10/1952

Gauge: 2ft 11in (clay pits system)

	BEARTS ARLESEY	0-4-0ST	OC	HE	808	1903	New	s/s after 4/1928
L5	S5	4wVBT	HCG	S	6754CH	1927	New	(1)
L2	S2	4wVBT	HCG	S	7699	1929	New	(2)
L 9	A/L 1 (10)	4wDM		FH	1914	1935	(a)	(5)
L12	(13)	4wPM (ex DM)		FH	1913	1935	(b)	(3)
L 93	A/L 2	4wPM		MR			(c)	Scr /1966
L10	(11)	4wPM		MR			(d)	(6)
L 55		4wPM		MR			(e)	(4)
L 56	A/L 3	4wPM		MR			(e)	s/s after /1960
L 106	C/L13 2	4wDM		MR	10161	1950	(f)	(8)
L 105	C/L12 1	4wDM		MR	10160	1950	(g)	(7)
	C/L14 3	4wDM		MR	10455	1955	(h)	(7)

(a)   ex Calvert Works, Bucks, 31/12/1947

(b)   ex Stewartby Central Workshops, 10/3/1948

(c)   ex Stewartby Central Workshops, 17/3/1948

(d)   ex Stewartby Central Workshops, 11/11/1949; to Stewartby Central Workshops, 27/9/1950; returned 8/1/1952

(e)   identity and origins unknown.

(f)   ex Calvert Works, Bucks, 28/9/1957.
(g)   ex Calvert Works, Bucks, 11/10/1960.
(h)   ex Stewartby Central Workshops, 15/10/1960.

(1)   to Stewartby Clay Pit, /1936.
(2)   to Stewartby Clay Pit, by /1947
(3)   to Stewartby Central Workshops, 7/4/1948
(4)   to Stewartby Central Workshops, 14/4/1948
(5)   to Stewartby Central Workshops, 3/1952
(6)   s/s after 4/1958.
(7)   to Fisons Ltd, Swinefleet Works, Yorkshire (WR), c6/1977 (by 10/1977).
(8)   to Robin Pearman, Church St., Langford, for preservation, 9/12/1977.

Gauge: 2ft 6in (locos for spares only)

L 8	DS/L8	L74	4wPM	MR	1670	1918	(a)	s/s after 4/1958
L 9	DS/L9		4wDM	MR	20080	1953	(b)	Scr 10/1964

(a)   ex Dogsthorpe Works, near Peterborough, /1957; orig WDLR 2391.
(b)   ex Dogsthorpe Works, Peterborough, 12/1/1961.

Gauge: 2ft 0in.

L 57	A/L 4		4wPM	MR			(a)	s/s c/1968
L 33	B/L 8		4wDM	MR	5601	1930	New	(1)
L 51			4wDM	OK	5480	1934	(b)	(3)
L 52			4wDM	OK	5125	1933	(b)	(4)
L 53			4wDM	OK	5123	1933	(b)	(5)
L 31	L 2		4wPM	MR	3868	1929	(c)	(2)
L 84	L 1	(PL 9)	4wPM	MR			(d)	(6)
L 107	CH/L 6		4wDM	MR	8927	1944	(e)	(11)
	CH/L 7		4wDM	MR	7474	1940	(f)	(9)
L 131	OR/L 2		4wDM	MR	11001	1956	(g)	(8)
L 135	OR/L 6		4wDM	MR	11312	1966	(h)	(10)
L 104	CH/L 5		4wDM	MR	8936	1944	(j)	(7)

(a)   origin and identity unknown; here by 4/1958.
(b)   origins unknown; possibly new to here.
(c)   ex Stewartby Central Workshops, 20/12/1948
(d)   ex Stewartby Central Workshops, 4/4/1949
(e)   ex Stewartby Central Workshops, 29/5/1963.
(f)   ex Warboys Works, Hunts, 14/11/1968; to Warboys Works, Hunts, 27/10/1969; ex Warboys Works, c/1970; to Warboys Works again, 14/6/1971; returned here again, 1/5/1974.
(g)   ex Orton Works, Hunts, 25/11/1971.
(h)   ex Orton Works, 23/12/1971
(j)   ex Warboys Works, Hunts, 29/3/1974

(1)   to Bletchley Works, Bucks, by 6/1950.
(2)   to Stewartby Central Workshops, 15/1/1949.
(3)   to Stewartby Central Workshops.
(4)   to Dennis Ruabon Ltd, Ruabon, Denbighs [North Wales], 3/3/1949.
(5)   to Cox & Danks Ltd, Bedford, 3/1949
(6)   to Stewartby Central Workshops, 13/7/1949
(7)   returned to Warboys Works, Hunts.
(8)   to Robin Pearman, Church St., Langford, for preservation, 9/12/1977.
(9)   to Warboys Works, Hunts, 25/8/1978.

10) dismantled and parts used to rebuild MR 10161; frame removed for scrap by Smith & Co (Bedford) Ltd, Bedford, /1978.

11) dismantled c/1976 and remains removed for scrap by Smith & Co (Bedford) Ltd, Bedford, after 1/1982.

CORONATION BRICKWORKS, Kempston Hardwick, near Bedford   J37

Bedford Brick Co Ltd until 12/1936   TL 034440

A brickworks opened in 1935 (as **BEDFORD BRICKWORKS**) and re-named **CORONATION WORKS** in 1936 after acquisition by London Brick Co Ltd in 12/1936. Situated adjacent to the A418 road and west of the BR (ex Midland Railway) Bedford - London railway line at Kempston Hardwick. Served by standard gauge sidings which connected with the main line and were electrified using an unusual 'trolleybus' style twin wire overhead system. A 2ft 0in gauge system was originally used to move clay from the pits to the works but was replaced after World War II by a 2ft 6in gauge system. LBC upgraded many clay haulage systems at this time - the cable hauled systems were known as 'ground' (as opposed to aerial ropeway) haulage. The 2ft 6in line was originally continuous cable but had been converted to end to end operation, retaining two tracks, before final closure. These tracks were still in situ in 1980. Production ceased and the works closed on 24/4/1970. It was reopened in 1972 to meet a heavy demand for bricks but closed again on 3/5/1974; later demolished (all eighteen chimneys being felled by explosives on Sunday, 30/11/1980) and the clay pits flooded.

Reference : "Industrial Railway Record No.35", 2/1971.

Gauge : 4ft 8½in

L 16	(17)	RUTH	4wWE		EE	899	1935	New	Scr 1/1971
		AVON	0-6-0ST	OC	FW	328	1877	(a)	(1)
L 15	(16)		4wWT	G	AP	5935	1906	(b)	(2)
L 37	K/L 2		4wVBT	VCG	S	9322	1937	(c)	(3)

a) ex Wm. Jones Ltd, dealer, Greenwich, London, hire, /1935; earlier Salt Union Ltd, Stoke Works, Droitwich, Worcs.

b) ex Calvert Works, Bucks, /1940; to Fletton's LB3 Works, Peterborough, Hunts, for repair, 4/3/1947; returned 5/7/1948; to Bletchley Works, Bucks, 8/11/1948; and returned 5/8/1949.

c) ex Bletchley Works, Bucks, 4/11/1948.

1) returned to Wm. Jones Ltd, dealer, Greenwich, London, /1936 (after 4/1936).

2) to Calvert Works, Bucks, 5/4/1950.

3) returned to Bletchley Works, Bucks, 23/6/1949.

Gauge : 6ft 6in (Brick transfer cars to carry flat trucks loaded with green bricks)

-	6wWE	EE	904	1935	New	s/s after 5/1958
-	6wWE	EE	1086	1937	New	s/s after 5/1958

Gauge: 2ft 0in

L25		4wDM	RH	172904	1935	New (a)	(1)
L 17		4wDM	OK	5484	1934	(b)	(2)
L 36	B/L 6 (L 10)	4wDM	MR	5668	1934	(c)	(3)

a) originally supplied here by RH to Marston Moretain Flettons Ltd on one months trials (but acquired by Bedford Brick Co Ltd, after 19/2/1935, by 29/3/1935).

b) ex Wm. Jones Ltd, dealer, Greenwich, London,

c) ex Stewartby Central Workshops, 4/10/1949

(1)   to Elstow Works, after 3/12/1937, by21/1/1938.
(2)   to Stewartby Central Workshops, 4/10/1949
(3)   to Stewartby Central Workshops, 15/11/1950

ELSTOW BRICKWORKS   J38
London Brick Company & Forders Ltd until 22/4/1936   TL 042455
B.J. Forder & Son Ltd until 9/1923
B.J. Forder & Son until 25/5/1900

A brickworks established in 1897. Situated south west of Elstow village on the east side of the BR (ex Midland Railway) Bedford - London main line. Served by standard gauge sidings connecting to this line which were shunted by main line locomotives. There was also an internal narrow gauge system which commenced operation in 1920, being initially of 2ft 0in gauge, but later relaid to 2ft 11in gauge. The wagons, each of 1½ cu yd capacity, were loco hauled from the pit face to the foot of an incline. This incline, from the clay pit to the works, was chain operated by electric motor; the chain passing over the steel side-tipping wagons and engaging in clips on them. In 1962 this system was replaced by a conveyer belt and fork-lift trucks. Production ceased and the works closed on 24/4/1970; it reopened in 1972 to meet a heavy demand for bricks; finally closed again, 1/10/1973. Two of the five chimneys were dropped in 5/1974; demolition of the rest of the works began in 9/1978 and was completed in 1979.

Gauge: 2ft 11in

		Type					
-		4wPM	MR			(a)	s/s after 10/1952
-		4wPM	MR			(a)	s/s after 10/1952
-		4wDM	OK			(a)	s/s after 10/1952
L 38	C/L 3 (L 20)	4wDM	MR	5725	1939	(b)	(1)
L 39	C/L 4 (L 21)	4wDM	MR	5723	1939	(b)	s/s
L 40	C/L 5 (L 22)	4wDM	MR	5722	1939	(b)	(1)
L 41	C/L 6 (L 23)	4wDM	MR	5724	1939	(b)	(1)

(a)   origins and identities unknown; here by 9/1950.
(b)   ex Calvert Works, Bucks, 30/6/1953.
(1)   to Stewartby Central Workshops for store, after 5/1958.

Gauge: 2ft 6in

		Type					
L 99	4wDM	MR	20054	1949	(a)	(1)
L 100	4wDM	MR	20055	1949	(a)	(1)
L 10	4wDM	MR	20081	1953	(b)	s/s

(a)   ex Dogsthorpe Works, Cambs, 7/11/1960.
(b)   ex Dogsthorpe Works, Cambs, 12/1/1961.

(1)   returned to Dogsthorpe Works, Cambs.

Gauge: 2ft 0in

		Type					
L 21		4wDM	OK	3040	1928	(a)	(5)
L 22		4wDM	OK	4112	1930	(a)	(4)
L 23		4wDM	OK	5124	1933	(a)	(3)
L 24		4wDM	OK	5668	1934	(a)	(2)
L 25		4wDM	RH	172904	1935	(b)	(1)
L 19	E/L 2	4wPM	MR			(c)	(6)
L 20	E/L 3	4wPM	MR			(c)	(6)

L 18	E/L 1		4wPM	MR			(d)	(6)
L 84	(PL 9)	(L 1)	4wPM	MR			(e)	(6)
L 35	B/L 7	(L 9)	4wDM	MR	5667	1934	(f)	s/s
L 36	B/L 6	(L 10)	4wDM	MR	5668	1934	(f)	s/s

(a) ex Wm. Jones Ltd, dealer, Greenwich, London.
(b) ex Coronation Works, after 3/12/1937, by 21/1/1938.
(c) origins not known; here by 1/1/1946.
(d) origins not known; here before /1947.
(e) ex Stewartby Central Workshops, 30/9/1949.
(f) ex Warboys Works, Hunts, for spares, 11/2/1960.

(1) to Stewartby Brickworks, after 25/2/1941, by 17/7/1946.
(2) to Stewartby Central Workshops, 2/3/1948.
(3) to Stewartby Central Workshops, 11/3/1948.
(4) to Stewartby Central Workshops, 19/3/1948.
(5) to Wm. Jones Ltd, dealer, Greenwich, London, 22/2/1951.
(6) to Steel Supply Co (Eastern) Ltd, Bedford, 7/1955.

KEMPSTON HARDWICK BRICKWORKS

J39

TL 027448

Redland (Flettons) Ltd until 1971
Rugby Portland Cement Co Ltd in 1962
Eastwoods Flettons Ltd (registered 30/6/1927) until 1962

This brickworks was built in 1927 and commenced production in 1928. Situated on the east side of the BR (ex LNWR) Bedford -Bletchley railway near to Kempston Hardwick station and served by standard gauge sidings connecting with this line. Standard gauge rail traffic ceased by 4/1966 although the loco remained here out of use until later disposal.

Latterly two narrow gauge tramways were in use. One connected a working face to an aerial ropeway which supplied clay to the works. On this line trains comprised six flat wagons, each carrying one ropeway bucket. This line is said to have been replaced by a conveyor in 4/1969. The second line, finally operated by the larger 60hp locomotives hauling conventional "V" skips, fed a conveyor to the works and appears to have been retained as a back-up to the main conveyor until 9/1972.

The works closed about 1978 and was replaced by a new works, without rail transport, on the same site. This later works passed to the Hanson Brick group and was due for closure in 1999.

Gauge : 4ft 8½in

LIGHTMOOR	0-4-0ST	OC	P	906	1902	(a)	Scr /1944
-	0-4-0ST	OC	AB	919	1902		
		reb	Wake			(b)	(1)
-	4wDM		KS #	4428	1930	(c)	(2)

LMSR 7122 (0-6-0T) was on hire here for the week ending 2/6/1934 and LMSR 7160 (4wVBT, Sentinel 8209/1930) for the following week.

  # Carried plate HE K4428.

(a) ex Eastwoods Cement Ltd, Barrington Works, Cambs c/1930.
(b) ex Eastwoods Lewes Cement Ltd, Lewes, Sussex.
(c) ex HE, 4/1932 (actually built /1929).

(1) to Eastwoods Cement Ltd, Barrington Works, Cambs, /1933; returned here, 8/1943; to Barrington Works again, c/1946 (by 5/1947).
(2) to London Railway Preservation Society, Quainton Road Station, Bucks, 15/4/1969.

Gauge: 2ft 0in

-		4wPM	H	978	1930	New	s/s
-		4wDM	MR	5603	1931	New	(3)
-		4wDM	FH	1823	1933	(a)	(1)
-		4wDM	FH	2051	1937	New	(5)
-		4wDM	MR	7129	1936	(b)	(3)
-		4wDM	MR	9235	1946	(c)	(5)
L130	OR/L 1	4wDM	MR	11002	1957	New	(2)
-		4wDM	MR	11264	1964	New	(6)
-		4wDM	MR	22070	1960	New	(7)
-		4wDM	MR	21282	1959	(d)	(9)
L134	OR/L 5	4wDM	MR	11311	1966	(e)	(4)
-		4wDH	MR	121U117	1971	(f)	(8)

(a) new 30/6/1933 on trial from FH.
(b) ex Diesel Loco Hirers Ltd, 5/1938.
(c) ex Eastwoods Humber Cement Ltd, South Ferriby, Lincs; to Orton Works, Hunts, loan, 4/1958; returned here, 4/1958.
(d) ex MR, 28/4/1965.
(e) ex Orton Works, Hunts, after 5/1966; to Orton Works, Hunts, /1967 (by 8/1967); returned here 17/11/1971.
(f) ex MR, for trials, 5/6/1971

(1) returned to FH, 11/1933; then to W.H. Benstead & Son, Coombe Quarries, Maidstone, Kent, 22/2/1934
(2) to Orton Works, Hunts, c4/1966.
(3) to Leighton Buzzard Narrow Gauge Railway Society, 24/7/1970.
(4) s/s after 17/11/1971.
(5) to A.M. Keef, Bampton, Oxon, c5/1972.
(6) to Warboys Works, Hunts, 17/10/1972.
(7) to A.M. Keef, Bampton, Oxon, c8/1972.
(8) returned to MR, after trials, c8/1972.
(9) to A.M. Keef, Bampton, Oxon, 2/1973.

STEWARTBY BRICKWORKS   J40
London Brick Co & Forders Ltd from 9/1923 until 22/4/1936   TL 016426

A brickworks which evolved during the 1920s (and was known as the **PILLINGE BRICKWORKS** until c1930), incorporating several older works.   These included those of : **B.J. Forder & Son** (from 1897) (TL 016427), the **Wootton Pillinge Brick Co Ltd** (incorporated 10/4/1900, until 1922) (TL 014423) and the site of the works of **James Randall** (from c1879 until closed c1900 and demolished by 6/1901) (TL 018431). Production at Wootton Pillinge in 1926 had reached 118 million bricks. In that year work commenced on a new Garden Village, to be called Stewartby, for employees and by 1928 fifty houses had been built. By 1936 the new works had been named **STEWARTBY WORKS**; it became the largest brickworks in the world, with thirty-two chimneys, employing 2000 people to make 500 million bricks per year. It was situated on both sides of the BR (ex LNWR) Bedford - Bletchley railway and served by a network of standard gauge sidings shunted by main line locomotives. There was also an extensive narrow gauge tramway system within the works and serving the nearby clay pits. These lines were later replaced by conveyor belts and fork-lift trucks. Works still in operation, without rail traffic, in 2001.

A 2ft 11in gauge tramway with 220v DC overhead wire electric locomotives known as "Hoffman Trams" was used to move "Green Bricks" (unfired bricks) from the brick press sheds to the kilns, and brick transfer cars built by English Electric also worked on this system within the press sheds.

A separate 2ft 11in gauge tramway, in existence by 1929 and probably earlier, operated between the works and the **MARSTON CAULCOTT CLAYPIT** (TL 005425). This tramway was locomotive worked from the pit face to a loading station. From here it was worked by an electrically powered endless chain which passed over the wagons (of 5 tons capacity), engaging in a fork both fore and aft, allowing the wagons to be hauled up the incline to the works tippler. This system was abandoned in 1953 and replaced by conveyor belts.

A third narrow gauge tramway was used on the lip of the Marston Caulcott pits to remove callow (brown clay covering the Oxford clay) for tipping into the old worked out pit at TL 010430.

Gauge : 4ft 8½in

L 85	(PL 7)	4wDM (ex PM)	MR	3822	1925	(a)	(1)

(a)   ex Calvert Works, Bucks, by /1945

(1)   to Kings Dike Works, Cambs, 27/9/1945

Gauge: 2ft 11in

["English Electric Journal" mentions six sets of electrical equipment supplied here in 1935 (and two further sets subsequently) for transfer cars (not trams) in the kiln areas]

1		4wWE	EE	751	1929	New	Scr /1951
2		4wWE	EE	750	1929	New	Scr /1951
3		4wWE	EE	792	1930	New	Scr /1951
4		4wWE	EE	791	1930	New	Scr /1951
1		4wWE	LBC			New	s/s by 8/1965
2		4wWE	LBC			New	s/s by 8/1965
3		4wWE	LBC			New	s/s by 8/1965
4		4wWE	LBC			New	s/s by 8/1965
5		4wWE	LBC			New	s/s by 8/1965
6		4wWE	LBC			New	s/s by 8/1965
7		4wWE	LBC			New	s/s by 8/1965
8		4wWE	LBC			New	s/s by 8/1965
9		4wWE	LBC			New	s/s by 8/1965
10		4wWE	LBC			New	s/s by 8/1965
11		4wWE	LBC			New	s/s by 8/1965
12		4wWE	LBC			New	s/s by 8/1965
13		4wWE	LBC			New	s/s by 8/1965
14		4wWE	LBC			New	s/s by 8/1965
15		4wWE	LBC			New	s/s by 8/1965
16		4wWE	LBC			New	(7)
17		4wWE	LBC			(c)	(8)
18		4wWE	LBC			(d)	(6)
31		4wWE	LBC			(d)	(4)
-		6wWE	LBC			(d)	s/s by 8/1965
2		4wPM	MR			(a)	s/s
(10)	L 9	4wDM	FH	1914	1935	New	(1)
(11)	L 10	4wPM	MR			(b)	(2)
(13)	L 12	4wPM (ex DM)	FH	1913	1935	New	(3)
(14)	L 13	4wPM	(FH?)			(b)	(5)

(a)   origins and identity unknown

(b)   origins and identity unknown; here by 1/1/1946.
(c)   ex Northam Works, Eye Green, Peterborough, Hunts, c1/1960.
(d)   origins unknown.

(1)   to Stewartby Clay Pit by 1/1/1946.
(2)   to Stewartby Clay Pit
(3)   to Calvert Works, Bucks, 2/8/1946
(4)   to Calvert Works, Bucks, 10/11/1947
(5)   to Stewartby Central Workshops, 25/2/1948
(6)   to Bearts Works, Arlesey, 16/10/1952
(7)   to Calvert Works, Bucks, 6/2/1960
(8)   to Calvert Works, Bucks, 8/2/1960

STEWARTBY CLAY PITS   J41

Marston Caulcott TL 005425
Wooton Pillinge TL 014426
Millbrook TL 007414

Rail system from the clay pits to the brick works abandoned and track removed.
Reference : "The British Clayworker Magazine", May 1922
Gauge: 2ft 11in

-		6wWT	VCG	Forder	c1920	New	s/s
-		6wWT	VCG	Forder	c1920	New	s/s
-		6wWT	VCG	Forder	c1920	New	s/s
L 66		4wVBT	HCG S	7243	1928	New	(8)
L 1	S 1	4wVBT	HCG S	7700	1929	New	(11)
L 2	S 2	4wVBT	HCG S	7699	1929	(b)	(9)
L 3	S 3	4wVBT	HCG S	9221	1935	New (j)	(11)
L 4	S 4	4wVBT	HCG S	9259	1936	New	(11)
L 5	S 5	4wVBT	HCG S	6754CH	1927	(a)	(10)
L 6	1	4wPM	MR	4155	1926	New	(12)
L 27	B/L 7	4wPM	MR	3738	1925	New	(1)
L 28	B/L 4 B/L 6	4wPM	MR	5026	1929	New (h)	(7)
L29	-	4wDM	RH	175828	1935	New	(2)
-		4wPM	MR	2075	1922	(c)	s/s
L 7	(8) 3	4wPM	MR	2079	1922	(c)	(12)
L 8		4wPM	H	937	1928	(d)	(3)
L 9	(10)	4wDM	FH	1914	1935	(e)	(4)
L 10	(11)	4wPM	MR			(f)	(5)
L 103	S/L 9	4wDM	MR	9010	1949	New	(13)
L 106	C/L 13	4wDM	MR	10161	1950	(g)	(6)

(a)   ex Arlesey Works, /1936; to Stewartby Central Workshops for repair and returned, 4/12/1951; to Stewartby Central Workshops for repair again 1/11/1952; returned, 5/12/1952; to Workshops again, 12/12/1952; returned again 16/12/1952.
(b)   ex Arlesey Works, by 28/3/1942; to Stewartby Central Workshops for repair and returned, 1/11/1952.
(c)   earlier Hughes & Lancaster Ltd, Thirlmere Aqueduct Fourth Pipeline (c1920-1923) contract, Longridge, near Preston, Lancs; here by 1/1/1946.
(d)   orig Beeby's Brickworks, Yaxley, Peterborough; here by 1/1/1946; converted from 2ft 6in gauge.
(e)   ex Stewartby Works; here by 1/1/1946.
(f)   ex Stewartby Brickworks.
(g)   ex Calvert Works, Bucks, 10/10/1950

(h) to Bletchley Brickworks, Bucks; ex Stewartby Central Workshops, 6/4/1950; to Stewartby Central Workshops, 15/8/1951; returned 26/11/1951.

(j) to Stewartby Central Workshops, and returned, 12/1/1954.

(1) to Bletchley Works, Bucks, by 23/3/1934.
(2) to Bletchley Works, Bucks, after 8/5/1936, by 16/5/1936.
(3) to Calvert Works, Bucks, 21/2/1947.
(4) to Stewartby Central Workshops.
(5) to Stewartby Central Workshops, 29/10/1949.
(6) to Calvert Works, Bucks, 12/1951
(7) to Stewartby Central Workshops, 20/1/1954.
(8) to NP1 Works, Hunts,
(9) to Stewartby Central Workshops, 11/7/1953
(10) to Stewartby Central Workshops, 12/1/1954
(11) to Steel Supply Co (Eastern) Ltd, Bedford, for scrap, 3/1955
(12) to Steel Supply Co (Eastern) Ltd, Bedford, for scrap, 7/1955
(13) to NP2 Works, Hunts, 29/2/1956

STEWARTBY CENTRAL WORKSHOPS   J42

Central workshops within Stewartby Works (which see) providing engineering services for the LBC works in Bedfordshire and Buckinghamshire. Locos came here for repair and also for storage

Gauge: 4ft 8½in

L 48		0-6-0VBT	VCG	S	6711CH	1926	
		reb of 0-6-0ST	OC	FW	383	1878	(a)	(1)

(a) ex Calvert Works, Bucks, 3/9/1947, for transfer to Fletton LB2 Engineers Depot, Hunts, 8/9/1947; ex Calvert Works again, 17/11/1947.

(1) to Cox & Danks Ltd, Bedford, 7/7/1948

Gauge: 2ft 11in

S 2	L 2		4wVBT	HCG	S	7699	1929	(a)	(1)
S 3	L 3		4wVBT	HCG	S	9221	1935	(b)	(2)
S 5	L 5		4wVBT	HCG	S	6754CH	1927	(c)	(3)
L 8			4wPM	H		937	1928	(g)	(6)
L 29	L 11		4wDM	RH	175828	1935	(f)	(4)
L 26	B/L 2		4wDM	MR	5607	1931	(d)	s/s /1952
L 34	B/L 6		4wDM	MR	5606	1931	(e)	(5)
L 27	B/L 7		4wPM	MR	3738	1925	(h)	(7)
L 44	C/L 9 (4)		4wPM	MR			(j)	(7)
L 28	B/L 4	B/L 6	4wPM	MR	5026	1929	(h)	(8)
L 43	(3)		4wPM	MR	3838	1926	(k)	(9)
L 45	(5)		4wPM	MR			(l)	(10)
L 55			4wPM	MR			(m)	(10)
L 82			4wPM	MR			(n)	s/s
L 93	L 2		4wPM	MR			(o)	(11)
L 9	A/L 1 (10)		4wDM	FH	1914	1935	(p)	(12)
L 10	(11)		4wPM	MR			(q)	(13)
L 11	(12)		4wPM	MR	3832	1926	(r)	(14)
L 12	(13)		4wPM (ex DM)	FH	1913	1935	(s)	(15)

L 13	(14)	4wPM	(FH?)			(t)	(16)
	TX1	4wWE	EE	776	1930	(u)	(17)
	C/L 14	4wDM	MR	10455	1955	(v)	(18)
L 38	C/L 3	4wDM	MR	5725	1939	(w)	s/s
L 40	C/L 5	4wDM	MR	5722	1939	(w)	s/s
L 41	C/L 6	4wDM	MR	5724	1939	(w)	s/s

(a)   ex Stewartby Clay Pits, for repair; returned there, 1/11/1952; ex Stewartby Clay Pits again, 11/7/1953.

(b)   ex Stewartby Clay Pits, for repair.

(c)   ex Stewartby Clay Pits, for repair; returned there, 4/12/1951; ex Stewartby Clay Pits, for repair again, 1/11/1952; to Clay Pits, 5/12/1952; back here, 12/12/1952; to Clay Pits, 16/12/1952; ex Clay Pits for overhaul again, 12/1/1954.

(d)   ex Bletchley Works, Bucks, 14/4/1950.

(e)   ex Bletchley Works, Bucks, 9/8/1951; converted from 2ft 0in gauge.

(f)   ex Bletchley Works, Bucks, 3/2/1950

(g)   ex Calvert Works, Bucks, 4/7/1947; to Bletchley Works, Bucks, 6/11/1947; returned here, 14/4/1950

(h)   ex Bletchley Works, Bucks, 30/1/1950

(j)   ex Calvert Works, Bucks, 12/9/1952

(k)   ex Calvert Works, Bucks, 11/11/1947

(l)   ex Calvert Works, Bucks, 30/4/1948

(m)   ex Arlesey Works, 14/4/1948

(n)   ex Kings Dike Works, Cambs, 22/9/1949

(o)   origin unknown, here by /1947

(p)   ex Stewartby Clay Pit; to Calvert Works, Bucks, 10/10/1946; returned 17/4/1947; to Calvert Works, 6/8/1947; returned from Arlesey Works, 3/1952

(q)   ex Stewartby Clay Pit, 29/10/1949; to Arlesey Works, 11/11/1949; returned 27/9/1950

(r)   ex Calvert Works, Bucks, here by 1/1/1946; to Calvert Works, 8/8/1946; returned here 30/4/1948

(s)   ex Calvert Works, Bucks, 9/1947; to Calvert Works, 1/10/1947; returned 18/2/1948; to Arlesey Works, 10/3/1948; returned 7/4/1948.

(t)   ex Stewartby Works, 25/2/1948.

(u)   ex Bletchley Works, Bucks, 11/4/1951

(v)   ex Calvert Works, Bucks, 12/10/1960.

(w)   ex Elstow Works, after 5/1958

(1)   to Steel Supply Co (Eastern) Ltd, Bedford, 3/1955.

(2)   returned to Stewartby Clay Pit, 12/1/1954.

(3)   to Steel Supply Co (Eastern) Ltd, Bedford, 3/1955.

(4)   to George W. Bungey Ltd, dealers, Hayes, Middlesex, for scrap, 18/5/1951.

(5)   to Fletton LB2 Engineers Depot, Peterborough, Hunts, 4/7/1955, for onward transfer to Kings Dike Works, Cambs.

(6)   to George Cohen, Sons & Co Ltd, 12/1951

(7)   to Steel Supply Co (Eastern) Ltd, Bedford, 3/1954

(8)   to Stewartby Clay Pit, 6/4/1950; returned 15/8/1951;
to Stewartby Clay Pit, 26/11/1951; returned here 20/1/1954;
later sold to Steel Supply Co (Eastern) Ltd, Bedford, 7/1955.

(9)   to Calvert Works, Bucks; returned 30/4/1948; to Cox & Danks Ltd, Bedford, 3/1949

(10) to Cox & Danks Ltd, Bedford, 3/1949

(11) to Arlesey Works, 17/3/1948

(12) to Thomas Mitchell & Sons Ltd, dealer, Bolton, Lancs, 28/10/1953; thence to
W.L. Hobbs (Dyserth) Ltd, Dyserth Limeworks, Flints [North Wales], 3/1954.

(13) to Arlesey Works, 8/1/1952.
(14) to Fletton LB3 Works, Cambs, 14/7/1948.
(15) to Fletton LB3 Works, Cambs, 28/2/1949; later sold to Cementation Co Ltd, Doncaster, Yorkshire (WR), 10/1955.
(16) to Cox & Danks Ltd, Bedford, 3/1949.
(17) returned to Bletchley Works, Bucks.
(18) to Arlesey Works, 15/10/1960.

Gauge: 2ft 6in

L 69		4wPM	H		968	1930	(a)	(2)
L 70	(PL 2)	4wPM	H		966	1930	(a)	(3)
L 75	(PL 14)	4wPM	MR				(b)	(1)
L 99		4wDM	MR	20054		1949	(c)	(4)

(a)   ex Dogsthorpe Works, Cambs, 14/11/1950.
(b)   ex Warboys Works, Hunts, 28/10/1947.
(c)   possibly ex Dogsthorpe Works, Cambs, for repair, by 6/1953.

(1)   to Dogsthorpe Works, Cambs, 12/12/1947.
(2)   to George Cohen, Sons & Co Ltd,   /1951.
(3)   to George Cohen, Sons & Co Ltd, 12/1951.
(4)   returned to Dogsthorpe Works, Cambs.

Gauge: 2ft 0in

L 35	B/L 7	(L 9)	4wDM	MR	5667	1934	(a)	(1)
J/L 1	L 112		4wDM	MR	5880	1935	(b)	(2)
J/L 2			4wPM	MR	3990	1934	(b)	(2)
J/L 3			4wPM	MR	1013	1918	(c)	(4)
L 90			4wDM	OK	4626	1931	(d)	(3)
L 89	L 1		4wDM	OK	5122	1933	(e)	(3)
	CH/L 7		4wDM	MR	7474	1940	(k)	(10)
L 107	CH/L 6		4wDM	MR	8927	1944	(k)	(8)
L 14			4wDM	OK	7055	1936	(aa)	(6)
L 22			4wDM	OK	4112	1930	(f)	(7)
L 23			4wDM	OK	5124	1933	(g)	(7)
L 24			4wDM	OK	5668	1934	(h)	(7)
L 51			4wDM	OK	5480	1934	(j)	(7)
L 25			4wDM	RH	172904	1935	(m)	(15)
L 30			4wPM	MR	4073	1927	(n)	s/s
L 31			4wPM	MR	3868	1929	(o)	(9)
L 33	B/L 8		4wDM	MR	5601	1930	(p)	s/s
L 36	L 10	(B/L 6)	4wDM	MR	5668	1934	(q)	(11)
L 83	(PL 21)		4wPM	MR	3660	1924	(r)	(7)
L 84	(PL 9)	(L 1)	4wPM	MR			(r)	(12)
L 54			4wDM	(FH	1911?)		(s)	(13)
L 78		(PL 13)	4wPM	MR			(t)	s/s
L 79	W/L 2	(PL 5)	4wPM	MR			(v)	s/s
L 62	(DL 1)		4wDM	H	982	1931	(w)	(7)
L 63	(DL 2)		4wDM	H	981	1931	(x)	(7)
L 64			4wDM	H	967	1930	(ab)	(16)
L 17			4wDM	OK	5484	1934	(y)	(14)
L 32			4wPM	H	969	1928	(z)	(7)

(a) ex Bletchley Works, Bucks, 23/3/1949.

(b) ex Coldharbour Pit, Loughton, Bucks, 12/1950.

(c) ex Coldharbour Pit, Loughton, Bucks, 12/1950; orig WDLR 2734.

(d) ex Warboys Works, Hunts, 6/2/1952.

(e) ex Clockhouse Works, Surrey, 27/12/1951.

(f) ex Elstow Works, 19/3/1948

(g) ex Elstow Works, 11/3/1948

(h) ex Elstow Works, 2/3/1948

(j) ex Arlesey Works

(k) ex Clockhouse Works, Surrey, for store, c/1963

(m) ex Elstow Works, 10/6/1950

(n) ex Bletchley Works, Bucks, 1/6/1948

(o) ex Bletchley Works, Bucks, 1/6/1948

(p) ex Bletchley Works, Bucks, 9/8/1951; to Warboys Works, Hunts, 6/2/1952; returned here, 15/3/1966.

(q) ex Bletchley Works, 20/10/1948

(r) ex Kings Dike Works, Cambs, 26/5/1948

(s) ex Clockhouse Works, Surrey, 27/4/1948; to Warboys Works, Hunts, 10/5/1948; returned 3/1951.

(t) ex Saxon Works, Cambs, 3/1949

(v) ex Warboys Works, Hunts, 3/3/1953

(w) ex Fletton's LB4 Works, Hunts, 13/9/1948

(x) ex Fletton's LB4 Works, Hunts, 17/9/1948

(y) ex Coronation Works, 4/10/1949

(z) ex Bletchley Works, Bucks, 12/9/1947; to Fletton's Engineers Depot, Peterborough, Hunts; returned 14/7/1948.

(aa) ex Wm. Jones Ltd, dealers, Greenwich, London.

(ab) ex Fletton's LB4 Works, Peterborough, Hunts, 16/11/1950

(1) to Warboys Works, Hunts, 26/2/1951.

(2) to Fletton's LB4 Works, Peterborough, Hunts, 3/1952.

(3) to Wm. Jones Ltd, dealer, Greenwich, London, 15/5/1952.

(4) to Steel Supply Co (Eastern) Ltd, Bedford, 3/1954

(6) to Clockhouse Works, Surrey, 25/5/1948; returned 7/12/1949; to Wm. Jones Ltd, dealers, Greenwich, London, 20/2/1951

(7) to Cox & Danks Ltd, Bedford, 3/1949; later to Wheeler & Mansell Ltd, Springhill, Glos.

(8) to Arlesey Works, 29/5/1963.

(9) to Arlesey Works, 20/12/1948; returned 15/1/1949; to Cox & Danks Ltd, Bedford, 3/1949

(10) to Warboys Works, Hunts, by 1/1966.

(11) to Coronation Works, 4/10/1949; returned 15/11/1950; to Warboys Works, Hunts, 27/4/1951

(12) to Arlesey Works, 4/4/1949; returned 13/7/1949; to Elstow Works, 30/9/1949

(13) to Steel Supply Co (Eastern) Ltd, Bedford, 3/1954

(14) to Wm. Jones Ltd, dealer, Greenwich, London, 20/2/1951.

(15) to George W. Bungey Ltd, dealer, Hayes, Middlesex, 18/5/1951.

(16) to George Cohen, Sons & Co Ltd, 12/1951.

MARSTON VALLEY BRICK CO LTD

(Registered 12/6/1929)

LIDLINGTON BRICKWORKS

J43

SP 996396

A brickworks, opened 1929, situated to the north-east of Lidlington village and on the west side of the BR (ex-LNWR) Bedford - Bletchley railway, built on the site of Allen's (Marston) Ltd tile works (which closed after 1927, by 1/1929). It had standard gauge sidings which were connected to this line and were shunted by main-line locomotives. The works was served both by adjacent clay pits and also by pits to the west of Lidlington, near to the B557 road. These pits were connected to the works by a narrow gauge tramway, originally locomotive worked but later cable operated.

The brickworks were taken over by the London Brick Company in 1971, after locomotive use ceased, and were closed on 6/3/1977. The works has since been demolished with the exception of the original office building, which was still extant and in use by Hanson Brick in 2001.

Gauge : 2ft 6in

-	4wVBT	HCG S	9149	1934	New		(1)
-	4wPM	MR	3664	1925	(a)		(1)
-	4wPM	MR	3856	1934	New (b)		(1)
-	4wPM	MR	3861	1928	(c)		(1)
-	4wPM	MR	5252	1930	(c)		(1)
-	4wPM	MR	5345	1931	(d)		(1)
-	4wDM	MR	7141	1936	New		(1)
-	4wDM	MR	7142	1936	New		(1)

(a) ex MR, 19/1/1935; rebuilt from MR 436 and converted from 2ft 0in gauge. Prev Wilson, Kinmond & Marr, Glenafton Reservoir contract, New Cumnock, Ayrshire.

(b) rebuilt from MR 432 and converted from 2ft 0in gauge; earlier Manchester Corporation Waterworks.

(c) converted from 2ft 0in gauge.

(d) ex E.C. Jordan & Son, contractor, Filton Junction, Bristol, via MR, by 15/3/1934; converted from 2ft 0in gauge.

(1) to Ridgmont Works.

Gauge : 2ft 0in

-	4wPM	MR	3861	1928	(a)	(1)
-	4wPM	H	975	1932	New	s/s
-	4wDM	H	987	1932	New	s/s
-	4wPM	MR	5252	1930	(b)	(1)
-	4wPM	MR	5346	1931	(c)	(2)
-	4wPM	MR	5368	1932	(d)	(2)
-	4wPM	MR	5410	1933	New	s/s
-	4wDM	MR	7302	1938	New	(2)
-	4wDM	MR	7303	1938	New	(2)

(a) ex MR, 6/2/1930; rebuilt from MR 371; earlier Wm Moss & Sons, Leicester

(b) ex Petrol Loco Hirers, 20/2/1934.

(c) ex Petrol Loco Hirers, by 3/4/1934.

(d) ex A.M.Carmichael, contractor, New Galloway Station, Kirkudbright.

(1) converted to 2ft 6in gauge.

(2) to Ridgmont Works, date unknown.

Ridgmont Fletton Brick Co (incorporated 7/2/1935) until 6/8/1936   SP 967378
   (Subsidiary of **Marston Valley Brick Co**), merged 1936

A brickworks established in 1935 (production commenced 30/7/1935); thought to be the second largest brickworks in the world, with 25 chimneys. Situated on the west side of the BR (ex-LNWR) Bedford - Bletchley railway just north of Ridgmont station and served by standard gauge sidings connecting with this line. Locomotive worked narrow gauge railways served the clay pits and were later converted to a cable worked line which also served the Marston Valley Works at Lidlington (which see). After locomotive working had ceased, the works was acquired by London Brick Co Ltd in 1971. The 2ft 6in gauge cable worked line from Brogborough pits to the works was replaced by conveyors in 11/1978. Production ceased and the works closed on 29/5/1981; it remained derelict until demolished in September- October 1995. The site has been redeveloped as a distribution centre and business park known as Marston Gate.

Gauge: 2ft 6in

-	4wVBT	HCG	S	9149	1934	(a)	(2)
-	4wPM		MR	3664	1925	(b)	s/s
-	4wPM		MR	3856	1934	(b)	s/s
-	4wPM		MR	3861	1928	(b)	(1)
-	4wPM		MR	5252	1930	(b)	s/s
-	4wPM		MR	5345	1931	(b)	(3)
-	4wDM		MR	5945	1937	New (c)	(4)
-	4wDM		MR	5947	1937	New	(7)
-	4wDM		MR	7141	1936	(b)	(5)
-	4wDM		MR	7142	1936	(b)	(6)

(a)   ex Lidlington Works, by 6/8/1942.
(b)   ex Lidlington Works, date unknown.
(c)   converted from 2ft 0in gauge, 23/3/1937.

(1)   to Thos.W. Ward Ltd, by 20/4/1939.
(2)   to Electricity Supply Board, Ballyshannon, Co.Donegal, Ireland, per Lumley, Stratford-on-Avon, Warwicks, /1946.
(3)   to St.Albans Sand & Gravel Co Ltd, Nazeing, Essex, by 4/1953.
(4)   to Eastwoods Cement Ltd, Barrington Works, Cambs, /1952; regauged to 2ft 0in.
(5)   to Richard Thomas & Co, Ebbw Vale, Gwent, by 11/3/1941; regauged to 2ft 0in.
(6)   to St.Ives Sand and Gravel Co Ltd, Fenstanton, Hunts; regauged to 2ft 0in.
(7)   to Joseph Boam Ltd, Middleton Towers, Norfolk, 21/1/1943; regauged to 2ft 0in.

Gauge: 2ft 0in

-	4wPM	MR	5346	1931	(a)	s/s
-	4wPM	MR	5368	1932	(a)	(3)
-	4wDM	MR	5946	1937	New	(1)
-	4wDM	MR	7302	1938	(a)	(2)
-	4wDM	MR	7303	1938	(a)	s/s

(a)   ex Lidlington Works.

(1)   to Chas. Brand & Son Ltd, contractor, 23/2/1940.
(2)   to George W. Bungey Ltd, dealer, Hayes, Middlesex, 27/2/1940.
(3)   at MR works, by 6/1950; s/s

MINISTRY OF DEFENCE - AIR FORCE DEPARTMENT
CARDINGTON
Air Ministry, Royal Air Force until 1/4/1964

TL 077471

These premises were taken over in 1919 from Short Bros Ltd (which see for earlier history) and established as the Royal Airship Works, which became famous for the construction of the giant airship R101. The disastrous loss of this at Beauvais on October 5th 1930 spelt the end of the British airship industry and subsequently Cardington became involved with the development and construction of Barrage Balloons. The Balloon Development Unit was formed in 1938 and the hydrogen used was supplied by a gas factory served by a standard gauge railway. By 1948 this plant was producing compressed gases for use throughout the RAF. In recent years Cardington has had responsibility for launching balloons for meteorological research purposes. From the late 1940s Cardington was a Royal Air Force reception and initial training centre for new recruits, and thousands of National Servicemen passed through the camp.

The station was located on the south-west of the BR (ex-Midland Railway) Bedford - Hitchin line and was served by sidings, opened in 1917, which connected to this line near to Cardington station. Rail traffic ceased 4/2/1969 although the locomotives remained on site for some further time. Track subsequently lifted. Site closed 3/2000.

Reference : "Action Stations", Vol.6, M J F Bowyer, Patrick Stevens Ltd, 1983.

Gauge : 4ft 8½in

AMW No.127		0-4-0ST	OC	P	1521	1918	(a)	(5)
AMW No.128		0-4-0ST	OC	MW	1523	1901	(b)	(1)
AMW No.125	LORD FISHER	0-4-0ST	OC	AB	1398	1915	(c)	(2)
AMW No.213		0-4-0DM		JF	22960	1941	New	(3)
AMW No.172		0-4-0DM		RSHN	6989	1940	(d)	(7)
AMW No.245		0-4-0DM		JF	23002	1943	(e)	(4)
AMW No.116		0-4-0ST	OC	P	1509	1919	(f)	(8)
AMW No.240		0-4-0DM		JF	22994	1943	(g)	(6)
AMW No.244		0-4-0DM		JF	23001	1943	(h)	(9)
AMW No.214		0-4-0DM		JF	22961	1941	(j)	(9)

(a)   ex Short Bros.Ltd, Cardington, with site, /1919.
(b)   ex Prees Heath Camp, near Whitchurch, Shropshire.
(c)   possibly ex Royal Naval Airship Station, Kingsnorth, Kent, after /1919.
(d)   ex Air Ministry, Stafford, after /1943.
(e)   ex Air Ministry, Heywood, Lancs, 2/1944.
(f)   ex Air Ministry, Ruislip, Middlesex, 9/1946.
(g)   ex Air Ministry, Henlow.
(h)   ex Pembroke Dock, Pembs, after 4/1954, by 12/1955, via JF, Leeds for rebuild.
(j)   ex Air Ministry, Stafford, 6/2/1956, via JF, Leeds for rebuild.

(1)   to White Moss Coal Co Ltd, Skelmersdale, Lancs, via W. Reynolds & Sons (Bedford) Ltd, agricultural engineers, /1933
(2)   if here, then to Air Ministry, Henlow, by 15/2/1939.
(3)   to Air Ministry, Henlow, 1/1942.
(4)   returned to Air Ministry, Heywood, Lancs.
(5)   to Air Ministry, Cranwell, Lincs, after 12/2/1944, by 8/1951.
(6)   returned to Air Ministry, Henlow, after 3/1950, by 5/1950.
(7)   to Birmingham Railway Carriage & Wagon Co Ltd, Smethwick, Staffs, /1950.
(8)   to Air Ministry, Pemroke Dock, c2/1955.
(9)   to Ministry of Public Buildings & Works, Burtonwood, Lancs, by 6/1970.

Page 155 – Bedfordshire

MINISTRY OF DEFENCE - ARMY DEPARTMENT

ELSTOW STORAGE DEPOT

J46

War Department until 1/4/1964

TL 040438

Ministry of Supply, Royal Ordnance Factory No.16 until 1960.

The Royal Ordnance Factory at Kempston Hardwick was built in 1941-2 by **Edmund Nuttall, Sons & Co (London) Ltd** (which see in contractors section). It covered an extensive area on the east of the BR (ex-Midland Railway) Bedford - London main line about 3 miles south of Bedford and was served by a standard gauge system; this was connected to the main line by the LMSR Wilhamstead branch. The latter ran from a junction near Wilhamstead Signal Box on the main line to reception sidings and Wilhamstead Station platform adjacent to the ROF. It opened on 3/8/1941; workmen's trains commenced 18/8/1941 (from Bedford) and 6/10/1941 (from Luton) and ceased by 5/1946.

In 1960 the site became a WD Storage Depot, after which some WD diesel locomotives were stored here pending their disposal. It is thought that there was no regular rail traffic under WD or MOD-AD administration. During 1961-2 the exchange sidings on the north side of the factory were lifted using prison labour from Bedford Jail. The depot closed on 31/3/1964 and the track was subsequently lifted; the BR reception sidings were lifted in 10/1968 and the depot was deleted from railway group facilities on 31/3/1969.

Gauge : 4ft 8½in

R.O.F. 16 No.1	0-4-0ST	OC	HC	1727	1941	New	(4)
R.O.F. 16 No.2	0-4-0DM		JF	22950	1941	New	(1)
R.O.F. 16 No.3	0-4-0ST	OC	WB	2649	1941	New	(2)
R.O.F. 16 No.4	0-4-0DM		JF	22977	1942	New	(6)
R.O.F. 16 No.5	0-4-0DM		JF	22981	1942	New	(8)
R.O.F. 16 No.6	0-4-0ST	OC	WB	2677	1942	New	(5)
No.2	0-4-0DM		JF	22000	1937	(a)	(7)
R.O.F. 14 No.1	0-4-0ST	OC	WB	2650	1941	(b)	(3)
WD 843	0-4-0DM		AB	370	1945	(c)	(9)
WD 842	0-4-0DM		AB	369	1945	(d)	(11)
WD 846	0-4-0DM		DC	2047	1933		
			EE	874	1933	(e)	(10)

(a)   ex Paradise Factory, Coven, Staffs, 12/1949.
(b)   ex ROF Ruddington, Notts, after 2/1954, by 5/1956.
(c)   ex WD, Wem Depot, Shropshire, 8/2/1961.
(d)   ex WD, Swindon, Wilts, 10/8/1961.
(e)   ex WD, Bicester, Oxon, 15/11/1961.

(1)   to Bridgend Factory, Mid Glamorgan (10/1943 ?).
(2)   to Chorley Factory, Lancs, 8/1946.
(3)   returned to ROF Ruddington, Notts, by 2/1960.
(4)   to Cox & Danks Ltd, dealers, Bedford, by 8/1960; resold to Wm. Pepper Ltd, for NCBOE, Wath & Elsecar Screens, Yorkshire (WR), 6/1961.
(5)   to Cox & Danks Ltd, dealers, Bedford, by 8/1960;
         resold to The Carron Company, Falkirk, 16/8/1961.
(6)   to WD, Bicester, Oxon, 8300, c8/1961.
(7)   to WD, Bicester, Oxon, 8/1961.
(8)   to WD, Bicester, Oxon, 8305, c/1961.
(9)   to WD, Bicester, Oxon, 16/11/1961.
(10) to WD, West Moors, Dorset, 3/4/1964.
(11) to ROF Ruddington, Notts, 22/10/1964.

PARROTT & JANES LTD
SHENLEY HILL SAND PITS, Leighton Buzzard

K47

SP 938274

This firm of haulage contractors, of 63 North St, Leighton Buzzard, was in existence by 1920 (not listed in 1914). It was associated with **Gregory Harris & Son**, sand and gravel merchants of Leighton Buzzard (in existence by 1914 and until at least 1948), who traded from the same address as Parrott & Janes, at 63 North Street, by 1928. Harris owned several sand pits in the Leighton Buzzard area - at Vandyke Road (SP 929255), Grovebury (SP 925241) and Low Mead, and also at Heath & Reach. One of these pits at Shenley Hill, jointly operated with **Frederick, Scott, Parrott** in 1927, was served by a narrow gauge system connected by a 300 yard branch to the Leighton Buzzard Light Railway.. This quarry was working by 1926 and was derelict by 1937. Two locomotives are identified in makers records as being delivered to this firm and they are assumed to have been used here. It is thought that Mr Parrott also operated other sand & gravel pits at Willington in 1936 and, as **Parrott & Read**, at Clapham in 1937.
Reference : "The Leighton Buzzard Light Railway", S.A. Leleux, Oakwood Press, 1969 & 1996.

Gauge : 2ft 0in

-	4wPM	FH	1668	1930	New	(1)
-	4wPM	FH	1676	1930	New	s/s

(1) returned to FH, 5/1933; then to East Sussex County Council, Willingdon, Sussex.

REDLAND TILES LTD
LEIGHTON BUZZARD TILE WORKS

K48

SP 921240

(Subsidiary of **Eastwoods Ltd**)
Leighton Buzzard Tiles Ltd until 1/4/1963

Works opened about 1930 on the south of the BR (ex LNWR) Leighton Buzzard - Dunstable branch. Connected to, and served by, the 2ft gauge system of George Garside's Grovebury Quarries (which see). A locomotive was purchased in 1957 to handle traffic when insufficient of Garside's locomotives were serviceable, but was rarely used. Railway replaced by lorries and closed from 5/1964. Track lifted by 1965.

Gauge: 2ft 0in

	4wDM	OK	4105	1930	(a)	s/s c/1964

An unidentified 4wDM, possibly ex Eastwoods Barrington, may have been here by 10/1952.

(a) ex Eastwoods Ltd, Bobbing Clay Pits, Kent, c/1957.

RUGBY PORTLAND CEMENT CO LTD
TOTTERNHOE QUARRIES, near Dunstable

F49

SP 979224

The Rugby Portland Cement Co was established in 1825 and incorporated as a limited company on 30/6/1925. In the 1930s it took over most of the chalk quarrying activities at Totternhoe from Totternhoe Lime & Stone Co Ltd (which see) in order to supply much increased quantities of chalk to Rugby and Southam Works, Warwicks. As part of this agreement the Rugby Co took over the use of quarry equipment and standard and narrow gauge locomotives. The narrow gauge system was abandoned before 1952. Extensive new

quarries were worked to the east of the original Totternhoe one. These activities terminate
in 1965 with the opening of a chalk slurry pipeline to provide an alternative supply from
Kensworth Quarry (TL 017197) (never rail connected), near Whipsnade, to Rugby and
Southam. Rugby Portland Cement ceased production at Totternhoe on 17th April 1965 and
the track was removed from the RPC quarry in 1965. Totternhoe Lime & Stone Co Ltd then
continued a more limited production from their original quarry and their works remains in
operation in 2001.

The standard gauge locomotives worked both at the exchange sidings and in the quarries
(which were at a higher level). The two systems were linked by a cable-worked incline
620ft long with a gradient of 1 in 7.95, on which wagons of chalk from the quarry were
lowered to the exchange sidings and empties hauled up on a one up, one down, principle. A
locomotive shed and workshops were sited in the quarry, with another shed, for the loco
working the exchange sidings, located at the foot of the incline.

Reference : "Industrial Railway Record" No.145, "Totternhoe Quarries", Chris Down & Doug
Semmens, IRS, June 1996.

Gauge : 4ft 8½in

-	4wWT	G	AP	11087	1924	(a)	(1)
5	0-4-0ST	OC	P	947	1903	(b)	(2)
No.2 (form. ISOBEL)	0-4-0ST	OC	AE	1875	1921	(c)	(7)
No.3 (form. 2)	0-6-0ST	IC	MW	1995	1920	(d)	(4)
No.4	0-6-0ST	OC	RSHN	7413	1948	New	(5)
No.5	0-6-0ST	IC	MW	1972	1919	(e)	(3)
No.1	4wVBT	VCG	S	9559	1953	New	(6)
No.6	4wVBT	VCG	S	9564	1954	New	(8)
No.7 (COURTYBELLA)	4wVBT	VCG	S	9627	1957	(f)	(10)
No.8	4wVBT	VCG	S	9565	1954	(g)	(8)
No.9 CRAVEN	4wVBT	VCG	S	9556	1953	(h)	(9)

(a)   taken over from Totternhoe Lime & Stone Co Ltd, Stanbridgeford, with site.

(b)   ex Rugby Works, Warwicks, /1937.

(c)   ex Thos.W. Ward Ltd, Charlton Works, Sheffield, 12/1/1938; orig Bombay Harbour
      Improvement Trust No.10; to unknown location, after 7/5/1948, by 7/1949; returned
      by 8/1950.

(d)   ex Rugby Works, Warwicks, 2/1940; to Rugby, after 7/1949, by 27/8/1949;
      returned here after 8/1951, by 5/1952.

(e)   ex Rugby Works, Warwicks, /1949 (by 7/1949).

(f)   ex Whitehead Iron & Steel Co Ltd, Courtybella Works, Newport, Gwent,
      per TH, after 2/1/1961, by 26/1/1961.

(g)   ex CEGB, Willington, Derbys, per TH, c10/1961 (after 29/9/1961).

(h)   ex Craven Bros. (Manchester) Ltd, Reddish, Manchester, per TH, c12/1962 (after
      6/12/1962).

(1)   withdrawn by 10/11/1940; scrapped on site c/1943-44.

(2)   scrapped on site, after 5/1952, by 3/1953.

(3)   withdrawn /1952; derelict by 3/1958 and scrapped on site /1960.

(4)   withdrawn 10/1960; dismantled by 4/1962 and scrapped on site after 3/3/1965, by
      30/5/1965.

(5)   to NCB, East Midlands Division, No.7 Area, Cadley Hill Colliery, South Derbys, 9/1961.

(6)   to New Bilton Works, Rugby, Warwicks, 9/1964.

(7)   to Eastwoods Cement Ltd, Barrington Works, Cambs, 2/1965.

(8)   to Eastwoods Cement Ltd, Barrington Works, Cambs, 4/1965.

(9)   to Eastwoods Cement Ltd, Barrington Works, Cambs, after 7/1965, by 12/1965.

(10) to Rochester Works, Kent, after 7/1965, by 9/1965.

Gauge: 2ft 6in

-	4wPM	OK	4621	1931	(a)	(3)	
-	4wPM	OK	4547	c1931	(a)	(3)	
-	4wDM	RH	172334	1935	(a)	(1)	
-	4wDM	RH	172336	1935	(a)	(4)	
-	4wDM	RH	172337	1935	(a)	(4)	
-	4wDM	RH	172342	1935	(a)	(2)	
-	4wDM	RH	183427	1937	New (b)	s/s after 3/1953	

(a) taken over from Totternhoe Lime & Stone Co Ltd, with site.

(b) to RPC, Totternhoe; possibly to Southam Works, Warwicks, by 7/1938; and returned /1938 (after 12/8/1938).

(1) to Rochester Works, Halling, Kent, after 24/3/1941, by 21/11/1941.

(2) to RH, Lincoln, for overhaul, 29/12/1937; returned 1/1938; to Rochester Works, Halling, Kent, by 7/1950.

(3) to Rochester Works, Halling, Kent, by 7/1950; one or possibly both to Paddlesworth Clay Pit, Kent, after re-gauging to 2ft 0in..

(4) to Draper Bros, scrap merchants, Leighton Buzzard, /1957; then to F.D. O'Dell & Son Ltd, Shefford, until at least 6/1959; s/s.

SANDY & POTTON RAILWAY

Sandy   F50

Sir William Peel began the construction of this railway in May 1856. The line, laid with light contractors rails, was three and a half mile long and the route ran from the village of Potton to the GNR at Sandy. The railway opened on 23/6/1857 for goods traffic, which consisted mainly of fruit and vegetables. Later passengers were carried, using coaching stock hired from the GNR. The railway closed in 12/1861 after which much of the route was relaid as part of the Bedford & Cambridge Railway (incorporated 6/8/1860, and worked by the LNWR from its opening on 7/7/1862). The brick built engine shed of the original tramway remains at TL 219490 in 2000.

Gauge : 4ft 8½in

SHANNON	0-4-0WT	OC	GE	1857	New	(1)
LITTLE ENGLAND	2-2-2WT	IC	GE	1850	(a)	(2)

(a) ex GE, London, /1857; possibly orig London & Blackwall Railway 'PIGMY GIANT' of 1/1850

(1) to Bedford & Cambridge Railway, and resold to Joseph Firbank, contractor, 3/1862; currently survives in preservation at the Great Western Society, Didcot, Oxon.

(2) to Bedford & Cambridge Railway, for use in construction of that line, /1862; later LNWR DWARF, /1863.

SAUNDERSON TRACTOR & IMPLEMENT CO LTD

ELSTOW WORKS, Bedford   G51

trading as **Saunderson & Mills Ltd** from 1912   TL 042473 & TL 042475
formerly **Saunderson & Gifkins Ltd** by c1910.
H.P. Saunderson & Co Ltd from 1900

This firm of agricultural engineers built a few paraffin engined narrow gauge rail tractors for sale to local brickfields and quarries. These were advertised as being fitted with single or twin cylinder engines of 6hp to 16hp and weights of 1¼ - 1¾ tons. Otherwise little is known about these machines, or how many were sold. The company was still offering its locomotives, some of which are known to have been built after 1920, when it was taken over in 1925 by **Crossley Brothers Ltd**. At this time three petrol locomotives were under construction for Beswick's Limeworks, Hindlow, Derbyshire; two were 2ft 0in gauge machines of 5 tons, fitted with 25hp Crossley engines and the third a standard gauge locomotive about which little is known.

References : "Industrial Railway Record" No.153 (June 1998)
"Locomotive Magazine", 15/3/1912

SHELL-MEX & B.P. LTD
POTTON DEPOT
F52
TL 201482

Petroleum products storage depot (originally a Government Petroleum Board Depot) on the north of the BR (ex-LNWR) line between Sandy and Potton stations, and served by standard gauge sidings from this line. The site was used to store aviation fuel for RAF and USAAF airfields in East Anglia during World War II. Rail traffic ceased and track lifted.

Gauge : 4ft 8½in

A.M.W. No.246	0-4-0DM	JF	23003	1943	New	(1)	
No.9	4wDM	FH	1853	1934	(a)	s/s after 6/1959	
No.10	4wDM	FH	1977	1936	(b)	(2)	

(a)   ex Purfleet Depot, Essex, by 4/1950.
(b)   ex Purfleet Depot, Essex, c/1955.

(1)   to Anglo-American Oil Co Ltd, Purfleet, Essex, by 3/1953.
(2)   purchased by H. Hooker, of Rye, Sussex, 12/1969 (but probably never moved); resold to Cox & Danks Ltd, Park Royal, London, /1971.

SHORT BROS. LTD
CARDINGTON AIRCRAFT WORKS
G53
Short Bros (established 1908) until 28/5/1919
TL 077471

Short Bros were involved in airship construction and in 1915 selected Cardington as the site to construct a 700ft long hangar. In this were built two rigid airships (R31 and R32) for the Admiralty, which were launched in 1918 and 1919 respectively. A further order for R38 and R39 was cancelled when the Admiralty informed Short's that Cardington was to be nationalised. By April 1919 Short's were vacating the factory, which was then taken over as the Royal Airship Works (which see under Ministry of Defence).

Reference : "Action Stations", Vol. 6, M J F Bowyer, Patrick Stephens Ltd, 1990.

Gauge : 4ft 8½in

-	0-4-0ST	OC	P	1521	1918	New	(1)

(1)   to Air Ministry, Cardington, with site, /1919.

SIMPLEX MECHANICAL HANDLING LTD

SIMPLEX WORKS, Elstow Road, Bedford

G54

Motor Rail Ltd until 1972.

TL 053488

Motor Rail & Tram Car Co Ltd (incorporated 20/3/1911) until 16/41931

Motor Rail & Tram Car Co Ltd was incorporated 20/3/1911 with an office at 79, Lombard St, London and commenced production from a factory at Lewes in Sussex. The initial order came in 1912 from agents John Birch & Co for a railcar and trailer to be exported to Siam. This order was subsequently cancelled but further orders were received for exports to India. In December 1915 the company opened negotiations with the Bedford Engineering Company (which see) to move production to Bedford. The following year the company received enquiries from the War Office for the supply of petrol engined Trench Tractors of 600mm gauge. Large contracts were then placed for the supply of these machines, primarily to the War Department Light Railways front line systems in Northern France (hence the name "Trench Tractors"). Early in 1918 the company purchased a new factory, which became known as the Simplex Works, in Elstow Road, Bedford. The first locomotives to be built at Simplex works were for the War Office, works numbers 1642 - 1841.

Between July 1953 and April 1954 the board of directors of Motor Rail Ltd was in negotiations with George W. Bungay Ltd to purchase a majority shareholding in that company with proposals that Mr G.W. Bungay would then remain as managing director of that company but in the employ of Motor Rail Ltd. Consideration of the financial state of George W. Bungay Ltd resulted in the termination of negotiations and the merger plans were dropped in April 1954.

Motor Rail formed a subsidiary company in South Africa, **Motor Rail (Simplex) Pty Ltd**, registered 8/6/1954, to look after its interests there.

A takeover bid for Motor Rail Ltd was made in April 1965 by **Loco Holdings Ltd** of 4-5, Westmorland St, Dublin. This bid was accepted by four of the Motor Rail directors, with a majority shareholding in the company, and Loco Holdings Ltd took over the company on 4/5/1965. It installed its own directors and on the same date Messrs T.D. Abbott, J.R. Abbott and R.F. Williams resigned from the Motor Rail board.

The works was closed and locomotive building rights passed to Alan Keef Ltd, c7/1987. An auction sale took place on 15/9/1987 and the site was subsequently cleared and redeveloped for housing.

PETROL LOCO HIRERS (LTD) / DIESEL LOCO HIRERS LTD

At a board meeting on 20/6/1921, the directors of the Motor Rail & Tram Car Co Ltd took the decision not to go into the locomotive hiring business. This resulted in the formation of **Petrol Loco Hirers** in or before 1924 as a private venture. The four partners, J.D. Abbott (chair), T.D. Abbott, A.H. Brown and George Gale were also directors of M.R. & T. C. Co Ltd and the purpose of the enterprise was to hire out petrol locos purchased from M.R. & T. C. Co Ltd.

The first meeting of the partners took place on 23/5/1924 when it was recorded that the total locomotive stock held by PLH at that time was sixteen 20hp 2½ton locos, of which eleven were out on hire at £5 per week, with five more locos on order. By June 1930 the stock had risen to 103 locos purchased, of which 64 were sold, 33 were on hire and six out of service.

By June 1930 the partners had decided to sell the business to the M.R. & T. C. Co Ltd for £12,400 and as a result M.R. & T. C. Co Ltd took over the assets of PLH on 1/7/1930. PLH continued to trade under M.R. & T. C. Co Ltd ownership until 1935. **Petrol Loco Hirers Ltd** and **Diesel Loco Hirers Ltd** were incorporated on 19/2/1935 and registered on 24/4/1935 as wholly owned subsidiaries.

Subsequently Petrol Loco Hirers Ltd became **Dumpahirers Ltd**, registered on 11/1/1960.

Gauge: 2ft 0in : Shunting in the works was performed as required by hire locos or new locos.

F.M. SPARROW

MILTON ROAD GRAVEL PITS, Clapham, near Bedford   F55
Clapham Folley Sand & Gravel Co Ltd until 1943   TL 025530
T.C Ginn & Co by 6/1927

Gravel pits on the eastern side of Milton Road, operated by T.C. Ginn & Co after 1924; worked by **Parrott & Read** by 6/1927 but had reverted to T.C. Ginn by 7/1940.

F.M. Sparrow was a sand and gravel merchant, and also, by 1947, an engineer, contractor and plant hirer with premises at 87, High St, Clapham. In 7/1952 Sparrow offered for sale ("Machinery Market") the locomotive listed below which is thought to have worked at these pits.

Gauge : 2ft 0in

-	4wDM	RH	183430 1937	(a)	s/s

(a)   ex George W. Bungey Ltd, dealers, Hayes, Middlesex, after 2/1950; earlier East Acton Brickworks & Estates Co Ltd (until after 7/8/1949, gone by 12/1949); originally Sir Lindsay Parkinson & Co Ltd, contractors.

TOTTERNHOE LIME & STONE CO LTD
registered 9/7/1915
TOTTERNHOE LIMEWORKS   F56
Totternhoe Lime Stone & Cement Co Ltd until 1914   SP 979224
De Berenger & Gower until 1890
De Berenger until c1840

Long established quarries (rail connected by 1895) which produced Totternhoe building stone and chalk, and later chalk for lime burning. Totternhoe Lime Stone & Cement Co Ltd went into liquidation in 1914 and the works was subsequently put up for sale in 1916 by the proprietor, Rt Hon Earl Brownlow, owner of the Totternhoe Estate. Quarries partly taken over in 1936 by Rugby Portland Cement Co Ltd, which also assumed responsibility for the locos. On closure of the RPC operation in 1965, working of the original quarry area and works was continued by the Totternhoe company.

Reference : "Industrial Railway Record" No.145, "Totternhoe Quarries", Chris Down & Doug Semmens, , IRS, June 1996.

Gauge : 4ft 8½in

-	2-2-0WT	G	AP	?	?	(a)	(1)
-	0-4-0ST	OC	?			(a)	s/s
-	4wWT	G	AP	3730	1896	(b)	Scr /1937-40
-	4wWT	G	AP	11087	1924	New	(2)

At least two other locomotives were here prior to AP 3730 (which may have been here considerably before 1924) and a 'new' loco was said to have been acquired in 1912. An advert was placed in "Contract Journal", 29/11/1911 which stated 'Wanted immediately; standard gauge, two speed geared loco, 10/12hp, Totternhoe Lime Co Ltd.'

Photographic evidence suggests that one of the two unidentified locos may be an Aveling & Porter similar to a single cylinder 'Steam Sapper' which had been converted and fitted with buffer beams.

The unidentified 0-4-0ST bears all the characteristics in design of one of a batch of locos known to have been built by Thomas Spittle, Cambrian Iron Foundry, Newport, Gwent, between 1877 and 1879. An advert appeared in "Machinery Market" 15/11/1912, which stated 'for sale four-wheeled saddle tanks standard gauge, HE 9x10in, AP 9x16in, and

'Spittle' 10½x15in - King, engineer, Maidstone. A later advert on 10/7/1914 for an AP 9x18 refers to T. King of Maidstone. The three locos mentioned in the first advert may include the two unidentified locos here, which may have come from the cement industry in Kent.

(a)   origin and details unknown.
(b)   ex Fraser & Chalmers Ltd, Erith, Kent, by /1924.

(1)   scrapped on site by Drapers, of Leighton Buzzard, /1935.
(2)   taken over by Rugby Portland Cement Co Ltd, Stanbridgeford, /1936.

Gauge: 2ft 6in:

-	4wPM	Crewe			(a)	Scr c/1930
-	4wPM	Crewe			(a)	Scr c/1930
-	4wPM	OK	4621	1931	(b)	(1)
-	4wPM	OK	4547	c1931	(c)	(1)
-	4wDM	RH	172334	1935	New	(1)
-	4wDM	RH	172336	1935	New	(1)
-	4wDM	RH	172337	1935	New	(1)
-	4wDM	RH	172342	1935	New	(1)

(a)   origin uncertain; here by /1919. Ford engined units believed to have been examples of the well known 'Crewe Tractors' built from Model 'T' Ford motors.
(b)   possibly ex Wm. Jones Ltd, dealer, Greenwich, London.
(c)   possibly ex J.C. Oliver & Co, dealers, Leeds.

(1)   taken over by Rugby Portland Cement Co Ltd, with site, /1936.

VAUXHALL MOTORS LTD

BEDFORD TRUCK PLANT, Dunstable

H57
TL 024224

The Bedford Truck Plant originated in 1939, when land was purchased, and the first stage of the works was completed in 1941 to produce components for use at the Luton factory. 1954 saw the start of expansion for the production of light commercial vehicles, under the 'Bedford' trade name, for the Vauxhall company. No.6 Bay was completed in April 1955 and in 1956 further bays were added to form part of the DA Block. These contained the engine assembly and test facilities together with the production line, from which the first Dunstable built Bedford truck was rolled off on 2/8/1955. DE Block was added as a Parts and Accessories Warehouse in 1958 and expansion continued up to the completion of the DJ Block, at the northern end of the site, in 1968.

Bedford extended into the heavy truck business in 1974 with the new TM range and in 1983 the Bedford Commercial Vehicle Division was separated from Vauxhall Motors Ltd as a part of the General Motors Overseas Commercial Vehicle Corporation, of the USA.

The works, sited on the north-east of the BR Luton - Dunstable line east of Dunstable station (and the connection to Dunstable Cement Works) was served by standard gauge sidings from the BR line. Rail traffic commenced in 1955 and ceased in 1981. The works was taken over by David Brown and renamed AWD Ltd in 1987; production was later transferred to Marshall's of Cambridge. Part of the works was later demolished and the site redeveloped.

Gauge : 4ft 8½in

30722		4wDM	RH	394012	1956	New	(1)

(1)   to Smith & Co (Bedford) Ltd, dealers, Bedford, 4/5/1984; scrapped 8/1984.

The company was founded in 1857 by Alexander Wilson, a Scottish engineer who established the Vauxhall Ironworks in Wandsworth Road, South London, for the production of marine engines. This company initially traded as Alexander Wilson & Co but in 1897 changed its name to the Vauxhall Ironworks Company Ltd. The company produced its first single cylinder petrol engine in the late 1890s and its first complete car in 1903, and by 1904 seventy-six cars had been sold. In 1905 the company moved to Luton and in 1906 amalgamated with West Hydraulic Engineering Co Ltd, makers of hydraulic machinery. The new company was known as Vauxhall & West Hydraulic Engineering Co Ltd.

In 1907 it was decided to separate the different activities and Vauxhall Motors Ltd was formed. A new works was opened, located on the east side of the Midland Railway (later LMSR & BR) Bedford - London main line, about 1½ miles south of Luton station, and with standard gauge sidings (built by 1912) connecting to that line.

The company became part of the General Motors Corporation (of the USA) in 1925 and entered the commercial vehicle market in 1931 with the introduction of the Bedford 2ton truck and chassis for 14 and 20 seat buses. During the Second World War the factory concentrated on building Bedford trucks and Churchill tanks for the war effort, with civilian production resuming in 1946.

Rail traffic ceased 10/1982 and the sidings were later lifted.

Reference : "The Story of Vauxhall, 1857 - 1946", L.C. Darbyshire, Vauxhall Motors Ltd,
c1946

Gauge : 4ft 8½in

-		0-4-0ST	OC	P		1874	1935	New	(1)
	C.J.WILLS	0-6-0ST	IC	HC		671	1904	(a)	Scr c/1950
-		0-4-0DM		JF	4200022	1948	New	(3)
-		0-4-0DM		JF	4210012	1950	New	(3)
	KITCHENER	0-4-0ST	OC	MW	1843	1915	(b)	(2)
29368		4wDM		RH	338419	1954	New	(4)

At least one LNER Class Y1/Y3 Sentinel 4wTG locomotive (No.62) (S 8323/1930) was hired in 1943 and later returned to the LNER.

(a)   earlier John Mowlem & Co Ltd, Swynnerton (ROF No.5) contract, Staffs,
        per/via Geo W. King Ltd, Hartford Works, Hitchin, Herts (engineers); here by /1941.

(b)   ex Thos.W. Ward Ltd Templeborough Works, Sheffield, hire, c/1953 (after 29/5/1953).

(1)   to Joseph Boam Ltd, Middleton Towers, Norfolk, /1954, per Three Star (Luton) Ltd.

(2)   to Thos.W. Ward Ltd, Templeborough Works, Sheffield, c/1954 (after 29/12/1953).

(3)   to George Cohen, Sons & Co Ltd, Coborn Works, Cransley, Northants, 12/1972.

(4)   to Smith & Co (Bedford) Ltd, dealers, Bedford, 4/5/1984; scrapped 8/1984.

CONTRACTORS LOCOMOTIVES

P. & W. ANDERSON LTD
HENLOW CONTRACT   FC1

Contract for the construction, and possibly subsequent repair, of the Air Ministry Eastern Aircraft Repair Depot at Henlow, c1916 to c1919.

Gauge : 4ft 8½in

TALBOT	0-6-0ST	OC	HE	573	1893	(a)	(1)

(a)   ex W. Alban Richards & Co, NFF Holbrook Lane (MoM) contract, Coventry, Warwicks, after 30/4/1917, by 7/9/1917.

(1)   to Air Ministry, Henlow, c/1919.

BEDFORDSHIRE COUNTY COUNCIL,
HIGHWAYS & BRIDGES DEPARTMENT

WILSTEAD CONTRACT   JC2

The A6 trunk road was reconstructed between Bedford and Luton during the period from 1934 to about 1937. Locomotives and a narrow gauge system are known to have been used during the construction between Wilstead and Haynes, c1934.

Gauge : 2ft 0in
At least three 4wPM, MR locos, possibly supplied by Petrol Loco Hirers, Bedford.

HOUGHTON REGIS CONTRACT   HC3

Reconstruction of the A5 trunk road through Bedfordshire took place from 1930 to about 1935. As part of this work a narrow gauge tramway is known to have been used on the section through Chalk Hill, near Houghton Regis.

NOTE - See also the Bedfordshire County Council entry in the Industrial section.

BOTT & STENNETT
LEIGHTON BUZZARD   KC4

Details unknown; this entry may relate to either a Plant Yard or a Contract. Mr Bott and Mr Stennett were directors of Leighton Buzzard Sand Co Ltd, and Rickmansworth Gravel Co Ltd. Bott & Stennett Ltd apparently gave up contracting c1909 and their plant was auctioned at a number of locations. Per "Contract Journal" of 22/3/1911, the following locos were to be auctioned on 4/4/1911 at "the yard, close to Leighton Buzzard Station (LNWR)".

Gauge: 4ft 8½in

GREENWICH	0-4-0ST	OC	MW	887	1884	(a)	(1)
CANADA	0-4-0ST	OC	HE	525	1890	(b)	(2)

(a)   earlier Harrow & Uxbridge Railway (Metropolitan Rly) (1901-1904) contract, Middlesex.
(b)   earlier Cleobury Mortimer & Ditton Priors Light Railway construction (1906-1908) contract, Shropshire.

(1)   for sale at Leighton Buzzard, 4/1911; probably thence to John Forster & Sons Ltd, St Helens, Lancs.

(2)   to Thos.W.Ward Ltd, dealers, Sheffield, after 4/4/1911 by 4/8/1911; there until 9/4/1915 at least. Later at Blainscough Colliery Co Ltd, Coppull, Lancs, after 10/1915, possibly by 5/1916 and certainly by 5/1918.

THOMAS BRASSEY
HITCHIN CONTRACT   FC5

Construction of the Leicester and Hitchin Extension for the Midland Railway. The line ran for 62 miles from Wigston (Leics) through Northants with the southernmost 25 miles to Hitchin being in Bedfordshire. Work commenced 4/1854 near Cardington; the line was opened to minerals on 15/4/1857, to goods on 4/5/1857, and to passengers on 8/5/1857.

Gauge: 4ft 8½in

TRIO	0-4-2	IC	JTE		1838	(a)	(1)
GIPSY LASS	2-4-0	OC	HF	42	1840	(b)	(2)

(a)   here by 23/1/1856; earlier with Brassey on Newport, Abergavenny & Hereford Railway working (1854) contract, Gwent, until 12/1854 at least.

(b)   here by 16/2/1856. May be the loco GIPSY used by Brassey on Newport, Abergavenny & Hereford Railway working (1854) contract, Gwent, until 12/1854 at least.

(1)   to Salisbury - Yeovil (LSWR) (1857-1860) contract, Wilts/Dorset.

(2)   to Worcester & Hereford Railway (1858-1861) contract, Worcs.

BRASSEY & BALLARD
BEDFORD CONTRACT   JC6

Construction of the Bedford to Radlett (Herts) railway as London Extension Contracts Nos. 5, 6, 7 for the Midland Railway. The line ran for 35 miles with the final 8 miles being in Herts. The construction of Ampthill tunnel was let separately to John Knowles, but no locomotives have been traced to this work. Work commenced in 4/1865; the line was used by goods trains from 9/9/1867 with a formal opening to all traffic on 13/7/1868 .

Gauge: 4ft 8½in

FREDERICK	0-4-0WT	OC	FJ	48	1865	New	s/s
LINDEN	0-6-0ST	IC	HE	1	1865	New	(1)
BRIGHT	0-6-0ST	IC	HE	5	1866	New	s/s
STONEYWAY	0-6-0ST	IC	MW	155	1865	New	(2)
YAXLEY	0-6-0ST	IC	MW	165	1865	New	(3)
COBDEN	0-6-0ST	IC	MW	174	1865	New	(4)
SHAKESPEARE	0-6-0ST	IC	MW	177	1865	(a)	s/s
LINK	0-6-0ST	IC	MW	180	1866	New	(5)
-	0-6-0ST	IC	MW	196	1866	(b)	(6)
LINCOLN	0-6-0ST	IC	MW	204	1866	New	(7)
MAIDSTONE	0-6-0ST	IC	MW	205	1866	New	(8)

(a)   ex T.R. Crampton, Towcester (Northants) - Stratford-on-Avon (Warwicks) (East & West Junction Railway) (1864-1873) contract.

(b)   hired new from MW, (ex MW, 16/11/1866)

(1) possibly to Joseph Firbank, Dewsbury-Ossett-Wakefield (GNR) (1872-1874) railway contract, Yorkshire (WR); and/or possibly with Baker & Firbank, Dewsbury-Batley (GNR) (1877-1880) railway contract.   Re-boilered by HE, Leeds, in 1878 and re-named PATRICROFT; thence possibly to Baker & Firbank, Barton Moss-Patricroft-Cross Lane (LNWR) (1878-1883) widening contract, Lancs.

(2) possibly to T.Brassey and/or Brassey & Field, Ruabon-Dolgelley (GWR) (1859-1868) railway contracts, Merioneth [North Wales]; otherwise s/s.

(3) later Thomas Brassey & Co, Callao Docks (1870-1875) contract, Peru, by /1872.

(4) later Furness Railway, Barrow Docks (1872-1879) construction, Barrow in Furness.

(5) later J. & G. Wells Ltd, Renishaw Park Colliery, Derbys, c/1875.

(6) returned to MW, 12/9/1867; thence to Eckersley & Bayliss, Chesterfield, Derbys, (probably for use on Dronfield-Chesterfield Tapton Junction (Midland Railway) (1866-1870) contract. Loco later named BRETTBY per MW records (hence possibly used on Bretby branch (Midland Railway) (-1868) contract, Staffs).

(7) to Brassey, Ogilvie & Harrison, Wolverhampton & Walsall (1867-1872) contract, Staffs [West Midlands].

(8) later Thomas Oliver, Mansfield-Worksop (Midland Railway) (1869-1875) contract, Notts, FRANK, by 11/1870.

E. CLARK, PUNCHARD & CO
BEDFORD CONTRACT   FC7

Construction of the Bedford & Northampton Railway (later Midland Railway). The contract was initially placed with **Waring Bros**, who commenced work on 29/11/1865 but apparently did little in fact, withdrawing in 1870. E. Clark Punchard & Co took over in 1870 and completed the line, which was opened to traffic on 10 or 11/6/1872.

Gauge: 4ft 8½in

No.1	NORTHAMPTON	0-6-0ST	IC	MW	315	1870	New	(3)
	HESKETH	0-6-0ST	IC	MW	56	1862	(a)	(2)
No.3	TURVEY	0-6-0ST	IC	MW	325	1870	New	(1)
No.4	BEDFORD	0-6-0ST	IC	MW	368	1871	New	s/s

(a) ex MW, Leeds, 15/9/1870; earlier John Bray, Newport Pagnell Railway contract, Bucks.

(1) later Nassjo - Oskarshamn Railway contract, Sweden.

(2) renamed HESKETH, late 1873/early 1874; which suggests possible transfer to Southport-Hesketh Bank (West Lancashire Rly) (1873-c1875) contract, Lancs; otherwise s/s.

(3) renamed SANTA ROSA, probably in /1872; which suggests possible transfer to Salto-Santa Rosa (North Western Rly of Monte Video) (1872-1875) contract Uraguay; otherwise s/s.

JOSEPH FIRBANK
BEDFORD CONTRACT   FC8

Construction of the Bedford & Cambridge Railway (later LNWR). The line was 30 miles in length, of which 12 miles were in Cambridgeshire, and incorporated the Sandy & Potton Railway, which had itself been opened on 23/6/1847. Contract let c8/1860; lines opened to passengers 7/7/1862 and to freight 1/8/1862, Firbank remaining here with a permanent way maintenance contract until 7/7/1863.

Gauge: 4ft 8½in

SHANNON	0-4-0WT	OC	GE	1857	(a)	(1)

Also one unidentified loco here by 14/11/1861 – s/s
and 2-2-0 tender loco of Bury type, built Wolverton /1845 – ex LNWR, 1156, 1/1863 – s/s

(a)   ex Bedford & Cambridge Railway, after 8/1/1862, by 19/3/1862.

(1)   to LNWR, 1104, 10/1862.

JACKSON & BEAN
LUTON CONTRACT   HC9

The contract for construction of the Luton, Dunstable & Welwyn Junction Rly, authorised 16/7/1855, was awarded to Jackson & Bean and the first sod was cut at Luton on 16/10/1855. Work was at first concentrated on the Luton-Dunstable section; this line was opened to freight 5/4/1858 and to passengers 3/5/1858, using "trains" hired from the LNWR. Other construction had begun at Welwyn in 4/1856 but by 2/1858 little had been done.

Under Act of 28/6/1858, the LD&WJR amalgamated with the Hertford & Welwyn Junction Rly to become the Hertford & Luton & Dunstable Rly. After another first sod ceremony on 28/1/1859 construction continued, with inspection trains on 12/6/1860 and 17/6/1860, and the line from Luton to Welwyn Junction opened 1/9/1860.

Reference : "Hatfield, Luton & Dunstable Railway", G.& S. Woodward, Oakwood, 1977

Gauge : 4ft 8½in

An engine was used to haul wagons from a ballast pit "beside the Bedford Road" (the later A6 ?) on the Luton-Dunstable section - a crowd gathered - it was the first loco they had seen (etc). Later, on 6/8/1857, shareholders had a trip (presumably from Luton) "to Dunstable and back" in goods wagons fitted with seats (presumably implies a loco, possibly a contractor's loco). The identity of loco/s used is yet unknown.

It is probable that the later inspection trains of 6-7/1860 would also involve contractor's locomotives.

Jackson earlier had several ex-main line locos, but positive information as to their locations of use is lacking.

LAMB & PHILLIPS LTD
LEIGHTON BUZZARD CONTRACT   KC10

Company based at 107, Clerkenwell Rd, London, EC1. This contract was for the construction of the 2ft 0in gauge Leighton Buzzard Light Railway, from Billington Road to Double Arches, for the Leighton Buzzard Light Railway Co Ltd. Work is thought to have started in 8/1919 with a formal opening on 20/11/1919. The petrol locomotive was ordered on 1/8/1919 and delivered by road to Lamb & Phillips at Billington Road, Leighton Buzzard.

Gauge : 2ft 0in

-	4wPM	MR	1856	1919	New	(1)

(1)   hired to Leighton Buzzard Light Railway, /1919; then sold to George Garside after 12/6/1920.

HENRY LOVATT

AMPTHILL CONTRACT   JC11

Construction of the Ampthill second tunnel for the Midland Railway, 1893.

Gauge : 4ft 8½in

H. LOVATT No.1	0-6-0ST	IC	HE	57	1871	(a)	(1)
JUBILEE	0-4-0ST	OC	MW	990	1887	(b)	(1)
DEVONSHIRE	0-6-0ST	IC	MW	996	1886	(b)	(1)

(a) earlier Robinson & Adams, Coleford (Severn & Wye Railway) (1872-1875) contract, Glos, BERKELEY.

(b) earlier Wm Mousley & Co, Skipton-Ilkley (Midland Railway) (1885-1888) contract, Yorkshire (WR).

(1) to East Leake - Aylestone (MS&LR) (1894-1898) contract, Notts/Leics.

ARLESEY CONTRACT   FC12

Widening of the up side of the main line from Arlesey to Hitchin for the GNR, 1898.

Gauge : 4ft 8½in

H. LOVATT No.1	0-6-0ST	IC	HE	57	1871	(a)	(1)

(a) ex East Leake - Aylestone (MS&LR) (1894-1898) contract, Notts / Leics, by 7/1898.

(1) spares ordered by Henry Lovatt, St.Albans, Herts, 16/8/1898, but no contract known there; later at New Mills-Heaton Mersey No.2 (Midland Rly) (1899-1902) contract, Cheshire, by 9/1899.

MITCHELL CONSTRUCTION CO LTD
BEDFORD CONTRACT   GC13

This company of civil engineering contractors, based at Wharf Works, Peterborough, was the main contractor for the construction of Goldington Power Station, Bedford, for the British Electricity Authority, 1951 -1957.

Photographic evidence exists of four narrow gauge Ruston locomotives being used on this contract. Thus it seems possible that at least four of the locomotives listed below, known to have been delivered new to Mitchell, may have been used on this contract

Gauge: 2ft 0in

-	4wDM	RH	327931	1952	(a)	s/s
-	4wDM	RH	331251	1952	(a)	s/s
-	4wDM	RH	331267	1952	(a)	s/s
MCC 308	4wDM	RH	339209	1952	(a)	(2)
-	4wDM	RH	339210	1952	(a)	s/s
-	4wDM	RH	346001	1952	(a)	s/s
-	4wDM	RH	346007	1952	(a)	s/s
MCC 309	4wDM	RH	347731	1953	(a)	(1)

(a) New to Mitchell Construction Co Ltd, Moriston contracts 48 & 49 (North of Scotland Hydro-Electric Board), Inverness-shire.

(1) later at Manshead Tunnel contract, Ripponden, Yorkshire (WR), by 4/1962.

(2) later with Bell Rock Gypsum Industries Ltd, Staunton-in-the-Vale, Notts, c/1965.

WILLIAM MOUSLEY
SANDY CONTRACT   FC14

Widening of the up side of the main line from Sandy to Huntingdon for the GNR, 1896 -1898.

Gauge : 4ft 8½in

VICTORIA	0-4-0ST	OC	P	634	1897	New	(1)

(1)   to Bingley-Thwaites widening (Midland Railway) (1899-1901) contract, Yorkshire (WR).

EDMUND NUTTALL, SONS & CO (LONDON) LTD
ELSTOW CONTRACT   JC15

Construction of **ROF Elstow** for the **Ministry of Supply**. Work commenced 25/11/1940, with anticipated completion 8/1941.

Gauge : 4ft 8½in

SL1 NUTTALL	0-6-0ST	OC	HE	1685	1931	(a)	(1)

(a)   ex Glascoed (ROF) contract, Gwent, 3/1941.

(1)   to MoFP Temple Newsam Opencast Coal Disposal Point, Waterloo Main, Yorkshire
       (WR), 9/1942 (on hire and used by operators Sir Lindsay Parkinson & Co Ltd).

Gauge : 2ft 0in

-	4wDM	RH	172900	1934	(a)	(1)
-	4wDM	RH	172906	1934	(b)	(2)
-	4wDM	RH	173401	1935	(c)	(3)
-	4wDM	RH	173402	1935	(d)	(4)
-	4wDM	RH	174538	1935	(e)	(5)
-	4wDM	RH	174546	1935	(f)	(6)
-	4wDM	RH	175122	1935	(g)	(7)
-	4wDM	RH	175123	1935	(h)	(8)
-	4wDM	RH	175128	1935	(i)	(9)
-	4wDM	RH	181822	1936	(j)	(10)
-	4wDM	RH	182134	1936	(k)	(11)
-	4wDM	RH	183759	1937	(l)	(12)
-	4wDM	RH	183761	1937	(m)	(13)
-	4wDM	RH	183769	1937	(n)	(14)
-	4wDM	RH	183771	1937	(o)	(15)
-	4wDM	RH	187117	1937	(p)	(16)
-	4wDM	RH	189938	1937	(q)	(17)
-	4wDM	RH	189939	1937	(r)	(18)
-	4wDM	RH	189949	1938	(s)	(19)
-	4wDM	RH	198270	1939	(t)	(20)

(a)   ex Glascoed (ROF) contract, Gwent, after 19/1/1940, by 20/5/1941.
(b)   ex Glascoed (ROF) contract, Gwent, after 31/8/1939, by 6/3/1941.
(c)   ex Glascoed (ROF) contract, Gwent, after 25/6/1940, by 31/1/1941.
(d)   ex Glascoed (ROF) contract, Gwent, after 6/12/1939, by 3/11/1941.
(e)   ex Glascoed (ROF) contract, Gwent, after 2/10/1939, by 6/8/1941.
(f)   ex Glascoed (ROF) contract, Gwent, after 16/4/1940, by 14/2/1941.
(g)   ex Colnbrook Plant Depot, Bucks, after 22/7/1940, by 26/3/1941.

(h)　ex Colnbrook Plant Depot, Bucks, after 12/6/1940, by 25/2/1941.
(i)　ex Glascoed (ROF) contract, Gwent, after 12/12/1939, by 12/8/1941.
(j)　ex Colnbrook Plant Depot, Bucks, after 4/12/1940, by 3/7/1941.
(k)　ex Colnbrook Plant Depot, Bucks, after 3/7/1940, by 7/6/1941.
(l)　ex Glascoed (ROF) contract, Gwent, after 19/2/1940, by 7/2/1941.
(m)　ex Glascoed (ROF) contract, Gwent, after 3/6/1940, by 22/8/1941.
(n)　ex Wallasey contract, Cheshire, after 9/8/1937, by 23/8/1941.
(o)　ex Glascoed (ROF) contract, Gwent, after 13/1/1940, by 16/12/1941.
(p)　ex Glascoed (ROF) contract, Gwent, after 17/1/1940, by 29/5/1941.
(q)　ex Glascoed (ROF) contract, Gwent, after 12/7/1939, by 22/2/1941.
(r)　ex Glascoed (ROF) contract, Gwent, after 4/9/1940, by 31/1/1941.
(s)　ex Glascoed (ROF) contract, Gwent, after 29/11/1939, by 15/4/1942.
(t)　ex Trecwn (RNAD) contract, Pembs, by 15/3/1941.

(1)　to MoS, Home Grown Timber Production Department, Dunoon, Ayrshire, after 26/3/1942, by 8/8/1944 (possibly by 6/4/1944).
(2)　to MoS, Home Grown Timber Production Department, Ardbrecknish, Argyllshire, after 6/3/1941, by 28/8/1943.
(3)　to MoS, Home Grown Timber Production Department, c/o Canadian Forestry Corps, Forres, Morayshire, after 31/1/1941, by 8/1/1943.
(4)　s/s after 10/2/1942.
(5)　to MoS, Home Grown Timber Production Department, c/o Canadian Forestry Corps, Blair Atholl, Perthshire, after 24/2/1942, by 19/5/1943.
(6)　spares ordered by James Bowen & Sons Ltd, 57-59, Pitt St, Edinburgh on 4/9/1945 [agents/repairers for MoS, Home Grown Timber Production Department ?]
(7)　to MoS, Home Grown Timber Production Department, c/o Canadian Forestry Corps, Blair Atholl, Perthshire, after 31/7/1941, by 8/3/1945.
(8)　to Glascoed (ROF) contract, Gwent, after 25/2/1941, by 13/2/1942.
(9)　to MoS, Home Grown Timber Production Department, c/o Canadian Forestry Corps, Blair Atholl, Perthshire, after 13/5/1942, by 23/3/1943.
(10)　to Burtonwood (RAF) contract, Lancs, after 3/7/1941, by 16/7/1943.
(11)　to Dept of Agriculture for Scotland, Whiteless Store, Lanark, after 24/6/1942, by 2/12/1946.
(12)　to MoS, Home Grown Timber Production Department, unknown location, Scotland, by 8/2/1943 (spares supplied through James Bowen & Sons Ltd, 57, Pitt St, Edinburgh, also on 4/3/1943 and 2/7/1943).
(13)　to MoS, Home Grown Timber Production Department, Archiestown, Craigellachie, Morayshire, after 19/5/1942, by 17/11/1942.
(14)　to MoS, Home Grown Timber Production Department, c/o Canadian Forestry Corps, Blair Atholl, Perthshire, after 23/8/1941, by 23/2/1943.
(15)　to Inveruglas contract, Tarbet, Dunbartonshire, after 31/3/1942, by 8/3/1949 (possibly at Colnbrook Plant Depot, Bucks, on 18/2/1948).
(16)　later to Monteiro Gomes Limitada, dealers, Rua Cascais, 47 (Alcantara), Lisbon, after 12/7/1941, by 10/8/1948.
(17)　to Joseph Pugsley & Sons Ltd, Cattybrook Ironworks, Lawrence Hill, Bristol, after 3/11/1941, by 23/5/1945.
(18)　to Inveruglas contract, Tarbet, Dunbartonshire, after 15/10/1941, by 4/3/1950.
(19)　to unknown location, after 10/7/1942; later at Colnbrook Plant Depot, Bucks; s/s by 5/1953.
(20)　s/s after 6/10/1941.

THOMAS OLIVER
SHARNBROOK CONTRACT   FC16

Widening of the Midland Railway's main line from Sharnbrook to Wellingborough (Northants), 1880 -1884.

Detailed under Northamptonshire.

SPECIALIST PLANT ASSOCIATES LTD.
WELLINGBOROUGH PLANT DEPOT   FC17
SP 948608

A plant depot at Podington Airfield, Hinwick (located about two miles south of the county boundary with Northamptonshire). The depot was moved to this site from a location at St Neots, Cambs, in 12/1988. Locos present in the yard between contracts.

Gauge: 2ft 6in

153	49079		4wDH	CE			(a)	
154	4907x		4wDH	CE			(a)	
155	49080		4wDH	CE			(a)	
156	49000		4wDH	CE	B1563Q	1978	(a)	dsm
SP 03	426		4wBE	CE	3135B	1984		
			reb	CE	B4066	1994	(b)	
No.1			4wBE	CE	B4056A	1995	(b)	(1)
No.2			4wBE	CE	B4056C	1995	(b)	(1)
No.3			4wBE	CE	B4056D	1995	(b)	(1)
No.4			4wBE	CE	B4056E	1995	(b)	(1)
No.5			4wBE	CE	B4056F	1995	(b)	(1)
SP 03	425	CLAYTON No.9	4wBE	CE	B3204A		(c)	

(a)   ex R.A. Warren Equipment Ltd, North Bay, Ontario, Canada, c7/1997 (by 9/10/1997).
(b)   ex Aoki/Soletanche J.V., Jubilee Line Extension (London Underground Ltd) Contract 105, c5/1999 (by 15/5/1999).
(c)   origin uncertain; to here after 14/5/1999, by 21/9/1999.

(1)   to CE, c11/2000

Gauge: 2ft 0in

SP 204	4wBE	CE	B1808	1978	
	reb	CE	B3214B	1985	
	reb	CE	B3825	1992	(a)
-	4wBE	CE	B0943	1976	(b)

(a)   ex Balfour Beatty (Raynesway Plant Ltd), c8/1995 (by 9/12/1995).
(b)   ex receivers of HE Loco Hire Ltd, Tickhill, South Yorkshire, 8/2001.

Gauge: 1ft 10in

4wBE	CE	(a)	Scr /1995
4wBE	CE	(a)	Scr /1995

(a)   ex Moorside Mining Co Ltd, Eckington, Derbys, c/1993 (by 20/1/1994) (two of CE B2930A, B2944P and B3077C)

Gauge: 1ft 6in/2ft 0in

SP 82	(JM 82)	4wBE	CE	5806	1970	(a)	
SP 83	(JM 83)	4wBE	CE	5942A	1972	(a)	
SP 84	(JM 84)	4wBE	CE	5942B	1972	(a)	
SP 85	(JM 85)	4wBE	CE	5942C	1972	(a)	
SP 88	(JM 88)	4wBE	CE	B0402A	1974	(a)	
SP 90	(JM 90)	4wBE	CE	B0402C	1974	(a)	
JM 94		4wBE	CE	B1534A	1977	(a)	(1)
SP 80		4wBE	CE	5940B	1972	(b)	
SP 03	364	4wBE	CE			(c)	
SP 36		4wBE	CE			(d)	
03	418	4wBE	CE			(e)	
JM 10		4wBE	CE	B3329B	1986		
		reb	CE	B3804	1991	(f)	
		4wBE	CE	B3686B	1990	(g)	

(a) ex SPA Plant Depot, Barford Rd, St Neots, Cambs, 12/12/1988.
(b) ex Westminster Plant Co Ltd, Wetherby, North Yorkshire, c1/1991 (by 26/7/1991).
(c) origin and identity uncertain; to here c/1998 (by 6/1998).
(d) origin and identity uncertain; to here c/1999 (by 15/5/1999).
(e) origin and identity uncertain; to here by 21/9/1999.
(f) ex J Murphy & Sons Ltd, Kentish Town, London, c5/1999 (by 15/5/1999).
(g) ex Westminster Plant, North Yorkshire, c/1999 (by 21/9/1999).

(1) to J Murphy & Sons Ltd, Kentish Town, London, 5/1989.

Gauge: 1ft 6in

-		2w-2BE	Iso	T15	1972	(a)	(1)
-		2w-2BE	Iso	T40	1973	(a)	(1)
-		2w-2BE	Iso	T41	1973	(a)	(2)
-		2w-2BE	Iso	T46	1974	(a)	(2)
-		2w-2BE	Iso	T49	1974	(a)	(2)
-		2w-2BE	Iso	T57	1974	(a)	(2)
-		2w-2BE	Iso	T66	1974	(a)	(2)
-		2w-2BE	Iso		New?		
SP 100	35	2w-2BE	WR	L800	1983	(a)	
SP 101	35T005	2w-2BE	WR	L801	1983	(a)	
SP 102	JM 102	2w-2BE	WR	544901	1986	(a)	
SP 103		2w-2BE	WR	546002	1987	(a)	
SP 104	(JM 103)	2w-2BE	WR	546001	1987	(a)	
SP 201	(428001)	4wBE	CE	B0156	1973	(b)	
SP 202	(428002)	4wBE	CE	B0176A	1974	(b)	
SP 203	(428005)	4wBE	CE	B0182C	1974	(b)	
SP 86		4wBE	CE				
		reb	SPA		1995	(c)	
SP 87		4wBE	CE				
		reb	SPA		1995	(c)	

(a) ex SPA Plant Depot, Barford Rd, St Neots, Cambs, 12/12/1988.
(b) ex Tarmac Construction Ltd, Wolverhampton, West Midlands, 7/1990.
(c) rebuilt by SPA utilising parts from the two CE locos purchased from Moorside Mining Co, 1/1994.

(1) to Brian Lawson, Tring, Herts, for preservation, 16/8/1994.
(2) exported to Germany, c/1995 (by 21/2/1996).

Unknown Contractor
BEDFORD CONTRACT   GC18

Details unknown.   The contractor may have been E. Clarke, Punchard, but this is not confirmed.

Gauge: 4ft 8½in

PEVERIL	2-4-0ST	IC				
	reb from 2-4-0 by IWB			1871		
	reb of 2-2-2	IC	Edge Hill	c1845	(a)	(1)

(a)   hired from I.W. Boulton, Ashton under Lyne, Lancs, 9/1871; earlier LNWR until c/1870 and believed originally Liverpool & Manchester Railway.

(1)   returned to I.W. Boulton off hire.

Unknown Contractor
WREST PARK CONTRACT, Silsoe   FC19
TL 094348 approx

A contract to dredge the lake in the grounds of Wrest Park, Silsoe, believed in the 1950s. A Priestman Cub dragline excavator was used to dredge the lake and the resulting mud was removed using a locomotive worked narrow gauge railway with "V" skip wagons.

Reference : "Industrial Railway Record" No.147, p.256

Gauge : 2ft 0in

-	4wDM	MR	75xx	?	(a)	s/s

(a)   origins and complete identity unknown.

DEALERS

AMPTHILL SCRAP METAL PROCESSING CO LTD
STATION ROAD YARD, Ampthill

JD1
TL 022372

A yard, operating from 1967, with locos for scrap or resale occasionally present. No rail connection. Site still active in 2000.

Gauge : 4ft 8½in

No.11	0-4-0DM		AB	413	1957	(a)	Scr 9/1983
	0-4-0DM		AB	363	1942	(b)	(1)
	0-4-0DE		RH	425477	1959		
	reb	Resco			1979	(c)	(2)

(a) ex CEGB, Little Barford Power Station, 2/9/1982
(b) ex Farthingstone Silos Ltd, Far Cotton, Northampton, 22/3/1985.
(c) ex Blue Circle Industries Ltd, Dunstable Cement Works, c10/1988.

(1) to Rushden Historical Transport Society, The Old Station, Rushden, Northants, 12/12/1987.
(2) to M.R. Clarkson, private location, Beds, for preservation, c/1995.

BALMFORTH (BOILERS) LTD
RIVER LEA BOILER WORKS, Luton

HD2
TL 097212

earlier T. Balmforth & Co Ltd (registered 7/1904)

A firm of boiler makers, engineers, steel founders, etc., with a works in Pondwicks Road served by a private siding from the GNR by 1904. The company appears later to have been combined with **Three Star (Luton) Ltd** (which see).

"Machinery Market", 12/3/1954 - For sale 4-wheels coupled Peckett outside cylinder tank loco 10 x 15in cyls, 2ft 9in driving wheels, 15 tons - Balmforth (Boilers) Ltd, Waller Avenue, Luton.
(P 1874 ex Vauxhall Motors Ltd)

CHETTLE & SONS LTD
PODINGTON SCRAPYARD, near Wymington

FD3

Gauge : 4ft 8½in

-		4wDH	NBQ	27544	1959	(a)	Scr c/1979

(a) ex Chettles Feather Hair Products Ltd, Goosey Lodge, Wymington, c/1975 (after 19/4/1975).

COX & DANKS LTD
SCAPA WORKS, Melbourne Street, Bedford

Melbourne St. Yard TL 049491

Scrapyard, opened about 1947 served by a siding off the Britannia Iron & Steel Co's private siding. By 1951 the company had re-located to Melbourne St on a small site with one siding at the rear of the ex-LNWR goods yard. This yard closed in 1968. A number of locomotives have been stored and cut up over the years at these sites; however some of those listed below may in fact have been scrapped on site at the vendors premises.

Gauge: 4ft 8½in

L49	SENTINEL	0-6-0VBT	HCG	S	5667	1924		
	reb of 0-6-0ST	IC	MW	848	1882	(a)		Scr
L48		0-6-0VBT	VCG	S	6711CH	1926		
	reb of 0-6-0ST	OC	FW	383	1878	(b)		Scr
	4wWT	G	AP	5935	1906	(c)		Scr
4	4wPE		##		1933			
	reb of 4wT	G	Garrett	32792	1915	(d)		Scr
ROF 16 No.1	0-4-0ST	OC	HC	1727	1941	(e)		(1)
ROF 16 No.6	0-4-0ST	OC	WB	2677	1942	(e)		(2)
WD 8315	0-4-0DM	JF	22974	1942	(f)		Scr 2/1968	
WD 8316	0-4-0DM	JF	22984	1942	(f)		Scr 2/1968	

Built by Tottenham & District Gas Co, London.

(a) ex London Brick Co Ltd, Fletton's LB4 Works, Peterborough, Hunts, 3/1948
(b) ex London Brick Co Ltd, Stewartby Works, 7/7/1948
(c) ex London Brick Co Ltd, Calvert Works, 10/1953.
(d) ex Tottenham & District Gas Co, London, 4/1963.
(e) ex ROF Elstow, c12/1960
(f) ex MODAD, Bicester Depot, Oxon, 1/1965

(1) to Wm Pepper Ltd, Wath & Elsecar NCBOE Screens, Yorkshire (WR), 6/1961.
(2) to The Carron Company, Falkirk, Stirlingshire, 16/8/1961.

Gauge : 2ft 11in

L 43	(3)	4wPM	MR	3838	1926	(a)	Scr
L 45	(5)	4wPM	MR			(a)	Scr
L 55		4wPM	MR			(a)	Scr
L 13	(14)	4wPM	(FH?)			(a)	Scr

(a) ex London Brick Co Ltd, Stewartby Central Workshops, 3/1949

Gauge : 2ft 0in

L 53		4wDM	OK	5123	1933	(a)	Scr
L 22		4wDM	OK	4112	1930	(b)	Scr
L 23		4wDM	OK	5124	1933	(b)	Scr
L 24		4wDM	OK	5668	1934	(b)	Scr
L 31		4wPM	MR	3868	1929	(b)	Scr
L 51		4wDM	OK	5480	1934	(b)	Scr
L 83	(PL 21)	4wPM	MR	3660	1924	(b)	(1)
L 62	(DL 1)	4wDM	H	982	1931	(b)	Scr
L 63	(DL 2)	4wDM	H	981	1931	(b)	Scr
L 32		4wPM	H	969	1928	(b)	Scr

(a)   ex London Brick Co Ltd, Bearts Works, Arlesey, 3/1949.

(b)   ex London Brick Co Ltd, Stewartby Central Workshops, 3/1949

(1)   to Neath Plant Depot, West Glamorgan, 3/1949.

W.A. DAWSON LTD
SUNDON PARK, Luton   **HD5**

A firm of civil engineers and contractors with premises in Whitefield Road, in operation by 1951. In 9/1955 the company offered for sale ("Contract Journal") a 2ft 0in gauge 20hp RH loco and in 8/1960 a similar 16/20hp loco was for sale. These relate to **RH 202984/1940.**

F.D. O'DELL & SONS LTD
Shefford   **FD6**

                                      TL 142389

This firm of dealers and iron and steel merchants (registered 3/1954), with premises in High St, Shefford, has broken up and sold locomotives over the years and was still trading in 2000.
In 5/1957 two Lister engined 10/12hp 2ft 6in gauge diesel locomotives were offered for sale ("Machinery Market"). These are thought to have been **RH 172336** and **RH 172337** from RPC Totternhoe Quarries; they were still for sale 12/1958 but final disposal is unknown.

DRAPER BROS
Leighton Buzzard   **KD7**

                                      SP 925247

A firm of scrap metal merchants and dealers, located in Grovebury Road, Leighton Buzzard. It is thought that this firm sold **RH 172336** and **RH 172337** to F.D. O'Dell & Sons before 1957, as well as other unidentified locos at an earlier date.

C.A.E.C. HOWARD LTD
ENGINEERING DIVISION, GRAFTON WORKS, Bedford   **GD8**

                                      TL 052486

This company was listed as sand and gravel merchants, with pits at Willington, near Bedford, in 1937. By 1951, and until 1963, it was recorded as contractors, at St. Johns, Bedford. By 1964 additional premises were being used in the old Grafton crane works in Elstow Road. These were then known as the Vulcan Works, but the title changed to Grafton Works in 1965. Locomotives were stored at these works in Elstow Road pending further disposal. Company still in existence in 2000; works demolished and the site redeveloped for housing in 2001.

Gauge : 4ft 8½in

PM22	0-4-0DM	RSHN	6967	1939	(a)	(1)
PM23	0-4-0DM	RSHN	6968	1939	(a)	(1)
-	4wDM	MR	9921	1959	(b)	(2)

(a)   ex J.W. Hardwick, Sons & Co Ltd, West Ewell, Surrey, c/1965
(b)   ex private store at Haynes, c/2000; earlier Rotamax Engineering Ltd.

(1)   to George Cohen, Sons & Co Ltd, Cransley Works, Northants, for scrap, c12/1972.
(2)   to Howard Bridge & Engineering Ltd, Britannia Works, Bedford, 5/5/2001.

Gauge : 2ft 0in

No.2   4wDM   MR   9778 1953   (a)   (1)

(a)   ex Yorkshire Handmade Brick Co, Alne, nr Easingwold, North Yorkshire, 2/1987.

(1)   to J. Craven, Main Road, Walesby, Notts, 14/4/1987.

HOWARD BRIDGE & ENGINEERING LTD
BRITANNIA WORKS, Bedford   GD9
TL 045490

This company (registered 14/8/2000) is a successor to C.A.E.C Howard Ltd (which see) and moved to this site in Kempston Road during 4-5/2001, to a works previously occupied by George Fischer Castings Ltd.   The company has family connections with James & Fredk Howard Ltd, makers of steam cultivating machinery and former owners of Britannia Ironworks. Locomotive stored here pending disposal.

Gauge : 4ft 8½in

-                4wDM   MR   9921 1959   (a)

(a)   ex C.A.E.C. Howard Ltd, Grafton Works, Bedford, 5/5/2001.

(1)   to The Battlefield Line, Shackerstone Station, Market Bosworth, Leics, 24/8/2001.

ROTAMAX ENGINEERING LTD
(A member of the **Howard Group**)
ST.JOHNS CENTRE, Rope Walk, Bedford   GD10
C.A.E.C. Howard (Holdings) Ltd until 12/1994   TL 054491
earlier **C.A.E.C. Howard Ltd**

Locomotive stored here pending disposal. Works demolished, 2/1995.

Gauge : 4ft 8½in

4wDM   MR   9921 1959   (a)   (1)

(a)   ex Hemel Hempstead Lightweight Concrete Ltd, Cupid Green, Hemel Hempstead, Herts, 2/1983.

(1)   to private store near Haynes, after 28/3/1994, by 12/1994.

SMITH & CO (BEDFORD) LTD
Cauldwell Walk, Bedford   GD11
(registered 6/1951)   TL 044484

A scrapyard, opened about 1951, located on the east side of the BR (ex-Midland Railway) Bedford - London main line to the south of Bedford station and adjacent to Kempston Rd

Junction. The yard had standard gauge sidings which connected to the main line and some BR rolling stock was broken up here in the 1980s. Site still in operation in 2001.

Gauge : 4ft 8½ in

29368	4wDM	RH 338419 1954	(a)	(1)
30722	4wDM	RH 394012 1956	(b)	(1)

(a) ex Vauxhall Motors Ltd, Luton Works, 4/5/1984.
(b) ex Vauxhall Motors Ltd, Dunstable Works, 4/5/1984.

(1) scrapped on site, 13-15/8/1984

STANLEY'S HAULAGE LTD
HOCKLIFFE DEPOT, Leighton Buzzard   KD12

A firm of contractors with a plant yard at Watling Street, Hockliffe. Locomotive stored at this location but not used.

Gauge: 2ft 0in

-	4wPM	L 4460 1932	(a)	(1)

(a) ex Dudley (Woburn) Tile Co Ltd, Station Works, Woburn Sands, Bucks.

(1) to M.E. Engineering Ltd, dealers, Cricklewood, London, 2/1960.

STEEL SUPPLY CO (EASTERN) LTD
STELCO WORKS, Ampthill Rd, Bedford   GD13
TL 045483

A company of iron & steel merchants (registered 10/1950) with a works where several locomotives have been broken up over the years. In 4/1970 the company offered for sale ("Machinery Market" 16/4/1970) a standard gauge 7½ ton RH loco built in 1946 - possibly RH 207103 of Britannia Ironworks, Bedford, which had been sold c10/1970. Some of the locomotives listed below may in fact have been broken up on site at the vendor's premises. This works was closed after 1971 (by 1972).

Gauge : 2ft 0in

L 27	B/L 7		4wPM		MR	3738 1925	(a)	Scr
L 44	C/L 9	(4)	4wPM		MR		(a)	Scr
L 54			4wDM		(FH	1911?)	(a)	Scr
	J/L 3		4wPM		MR	1013 1918	(a)	Scr
L 2	S 2		4wVBT	HCG	S	7699 1929	(b)	Scr
L 5	S 5		4wVBT	HCG	S	6754CH 1927	(b)	Scr
L 1	S 1		4wVBT	HCG	S	7700 1929	(c)	Scr
L 3	S 3		4wVBT	HCG	S	9221 1935	(c)	Scr
L 4	S 4		4wVBT	HCG	S	9259 1936	(c)	Scr
L 6	1		4wPM		MR	4155 1926	(d)	Scr
L 7	(8) 3		4wPM		MR	2079 1922	(d)	Scr
L 84			4wPM		MR		(e)	Scr
L 18	E/L 1		4wPM		MR		(e)	Scr
L 19	E/L 2		4wPM		MR		(e)	Scr
L 20	E/L 3		4wPM		MR		(e)	Scr
L 80			4wPM		MR	1896 1919	(f)	Scr
L 81			4wPM		MR	3792 1926	(f)	Scr

(a)	ex London Brick Co Ltd, Stewartby Workshops, 3/1954.			
(b)	ex London Brick Co Ltd, Stewartby Workshops, 3/1955.			
(c)	ex London Brick Co Ltd, Stewartby Clay Pits, 3/1955.			
(d)	ex London Brick Co Ltd, Stewartby Clay Pits, 7/1955.			
(e)	ex London Brick Co Ltd, Elstow Brickworks, 7/1955.			
(f)	ex London Brick Co Ltd, King's Dike Works, Whittlesey, Cambs, 8/1955			

THREE STAR (LUTON) LTD
ADAMANT WORKS, Luton

HD14
TL 070218

An engineering firm with premises at 187-195 Waller Avenue, Luton in 1950 but in Dallow Road, Luton in 1960. There seems to have been an association between this company and Balmforth Boilers Ltd (which see).

"Machinery Market", 10/12/1959 advertised - 'For sale, standard gauge Paxman Ricardo 16 ton diesel loco - Three Star (Luton) Ltd, dealers, Luton'. (A similar advert on 7/1/1960 states that it was a "Planet" loco.) This may have been **FH 1853** at Shell-Mex, Potton.

L.W. VASS LTD
STATION ROAD YARD, Ampthill

JD15
TL 022370

This company is recorded as being Agricultural Merchants at Conquest Mills, Ampthill in 1951 and as engineers by 1960. It developed the business of purchasing, overhauling and reselling (often overseas) surplus military vehicles and machinery. The large yard at Ampthill station was served by a private siding by 1938 and locomotives have been stored here pending resale or scrap.

Gauge: 4ft 8½in

		0-6-0DH	RH	448158	1963	(a)	(1)
1476	(CHORLEY No.7)	0-4-0DM	FH	2151	1940	(b)	(2)

(a)   ex RH, Lincoln, for scrap, after 5/1966, by 8/1967.
(b)   ex MoDAD, Ruddington Depot, Notts, 2/1968.

(1)   scrapped on site by Sheppard Bros, of Earls Barton, Northants, 11/1973.
(2)   scrapped on site by Sheppard Bros, of Earls Barton, Northants, c4/1976.

Gauge: 2ft 6in

-	4wDM	RH	297066	1950	(a)	(1)

(a)   ex Fight, Hoddeston, Herts, c/1962; earlier Wills & Packham Ltd, Quinton Clay Pits, Milton Regis, Kent.

(1)   to C. & D. Lawson, Tring, Herts, 28/2/1970.

Gauge: 2ft 0in

	4wDM	RH	179880	1936	(a)	(4)
-	4wDM	RH	179880	1936	(a)	(4)
-	4wDM	RH	186318	1937	(b)	(3)
-	4wDM	RH	260744	1949	(b)	(1)
-	4wDM	RH	277273	1949	(b)	(5)
-	4wDM	RH	285297	1949	(b)	(2)
-	4wDM	RH	338433	1953	(b)	(1)

(a) ex Milton Hall (Southend) Brick Co Ltd, Star Lane Works, Essex, /1966
(b) ex Woodside Brick Works (Croydon) Ltd, Woodside Green, South Norwood, Surrey, /1968

(1) sold overseas, /1968
(2) to Mixconcrete Aggregates Ltd, Earls Barton Sandpits, Northants, /1968 (loco may have moved direct from Surrey and not come here).
(3) to Island Bricks Ltd, Rockley, Isle of Wight, 10/1969
(4) to Crockway Light Railway, Dorset, 12/1969
(5) to Alan Keef Ltd, Bampton, Oxon, /1969; resold to J.M. Hutchings and to Quainton Railway Society Ltd, Quainton Road, Bucks, 18/4/1973.

The company offered for sale a number of locomotives in "Machinery Market" :
8/12/1950 an unidentified 2ft 0in gauge Hudson-Hunslet loco;
1/7/1965 seven unidentified 2ft 0in gauge RH locos;
13/11/1969 one 2ft 6in gauge RH and two standard gauge locos (one 440hp 45ton RH and a 30ton FH loco) - these would have been RH 297066, RH 448158 and FH 2151.

UNCORRELATED DATA :

"Machinery Market" 14/11/1924 - For sale, eight locos by Sharp Stewart, Class D & C, standard gauge, 17 x 26in - E. Maxwell, Bedford.
This appears to refer to Metropolitan Railway Class D 2-4-0T locos Nos.71/73-6 and Class C 0-4-4T Nos.68-70, all built by SS. These locos were actually sold by the Metropolitan Railway to C. Williams, Morriston, West Glamorgan and Maxwell's involvement is not clear.

"Contract Journal" 30/4/1942 - For sale lying Northants, one Simplex petrol loco and one HC loco, wagons and track - Powerlines Construction Co Ltd, Bedford. (This may refer to the locos at Amalgamated Stone & Lime Co Ltd, Thrapston Lime Quarries, Northants).

PRESERVED LOCOMOTIVES

1708 LOCOMOTIVE PRESERVATION TRUST
Houghton Regis, Dunstable   **HP1**
(on the premises of **Blue Circle Industries Ltd, Dunstable Works**)   TL 016231

Preserved locomotives kept at this location for restoration for a few years until they were moved to more suitable premises.

Gauge : 4ft 8½in

1708	0-6-0T	IC	Derby		1880	(a)	(1)
CUNARDER	0-6-0ST	OC	HE	1690	1931	(b)	(2)

(a)   ex Midland Railway Trust Ltd, Ripley, Derbys, 6/3/1976.
(b)   ex Quainton Railway Society Ltd, Bucks, 7/3/1976.

(1)   to Midland Railway Trust Ltd, Ripley, Derbys, 10/3/1979.
(2)   to Swanage Railway Society, Swanage, Dorset, c2/1981 (after 14/1/1981).

BEDFORDSHIRE COUNTY COUNCIL
DOVERY DOWN COUNTY PRIMARY SCHOOL   **KP2**
                                                                      SP 923267

Locomotive displayed at this school in Heath Road, Leighton Buzzard.
Gauge: 2ft 0in

30	4wDM	MR	8695	1941	(a)	(1)

(a)   ex Joseph Arnold & Sons Ltd, Leighton Buzzard, after 6/1974, by 3/1975.

(1)   to Leighton Buzzard Narrow Gauge Railway Society, Leighton Buzzard, 4/7/1986.

M.P. BURGOYNE
Bedford   **XP3**

Locomotives kept at a private location in Bedfordshire and also overhauled at SMH works in Bedford before movement elsewhere.
Gauge: 3ft 0in

-	4wDM	MR	3797	1926		
	reb of	MR	1363		(a)	(2)
No.2	4wDM	MR	3965	1939	(b)	(1)

(a)   ex APCM, Sundon Works, 2/11/1974.
(b)   ex APCM, Sundon Works, 7/6/1976.

(1)   s/s by 16/1/1980
(2)   to Irchester Narrow Gauge Railway Trust, Irchester, Northants, 19/8/1989.

M.R. CLARKSON
Private Location   XP4

Loco acquired for preservation and stored on private property.

Gauge : 4ft 8½in

-	0-4-0DE	RH	425477	1959	
	reb	Resco		1979	(a)

(a)   ex Ampthill Scrap Metal Processing Co Ltd, Ampthill, c/1995.

T.C. FENSOM & SON
Colmworth   XP5

Preserved locomotive stored for a time at the premises of this firm of agricultural engineers.

Gauge: 2ft 6in

3	0-4-0T	OC	AB	984	1903	(a)	(1)

(a)   ex T. Stanhope, Arthington, Yorkshire (WR), 5/1965.

(1)   to S.A. Burgess, Haddenham, Cambs, 13/5/1966.

GREAT WHIPSNADE RAILWAY
WHIPSNADE ZOO   FP6
Whipsnade Wild Animal Park Ltd   Station TL 004172
Zoo Operations Ltd, Great Whipsnade Railway until 10/1992.   Loco shed TL 009177
Pleasure-Rail Ltd, Whipsnade & Umfolozi Railway until 11/1990

A 2ft 6in gauge railway was built and opened for traffic 26/8/1970. The route of about 1½ miles is a loop from the station running through several animal enclosures to give passengers good observation. The 3ft and 3ft 6in gauge locomotives were on static display only.

Reference : "The Whipsnade & Umfolozi Railway", C.S. Thomas, Oakwood Press, 1995.

Gauge: 3ft 6in

390 (No.993)	4-8-0	OC	SS	4150	1896	(a)	(2)
-	2w-2PMR		Ford		1938	(b)	(1)

(a)   ex Zambesi Sawmills Railway, Zambia, 25/3/1975; orig Cape Government Railways, South Africa.
(b)   ex Ford Motor Co Ltd, Dagenham, Greater London, /1976

(1)   to East Somerset Railway Co Ltd, West Cranmore, Somerset, by 24/7/1988.
(2)   to East Somerset Railway Co Ltd, West Cranmore, Somerset, 1/11/1990.

Gauge: 3ft 0in

-	0-4-2ST	OC	KS	3024	1916	(a)	(1)

(a)   ex Hampshire Light Railway & Museum Co Ltd, Durley, Hampshire, /1972 (by 24/1/1972).

(1)   to Alan Keef Ltd, Oxon, c9/1973.

Gauge: 2ft 6in

No.1	CHEVALLIER	0-6-2T	OC	MW	1877	1915	(a)	
No.2	EXCELSIOR	0-4-2ST	OC	KS	1049	1908	(c)	
No.3	CONQUEROR	0-6-2T	OC	WB	2192	1922	(d)	(4)
No.4	SUPERIOR	0-6-2T	OC	KS	4034	1920	(d)	
5	NUTTY LBC L1	4wVBT	HCG	S	7701	1929	(k)	(5)
3		0-4-0DM		RH	435403	1961	(b)	(1)
L116		4wDM		MR	5606	1931	(e)	(3)
8	(9) VICTOR	0-6-0DM		JF	4160005	1951	(f)	
(7)		4wBE		WR	1393	1939	(g)	(3)
(8)	HECTOR	0-6-0DM		JF	4160004	1951	(h)	
11		4wBE		WR	1616	1940	(i)	(3)
19		4wBE		WR	1800	1940	(j)	(2)
20		4wBE		WR	1801	1940	(i)	(3)
10	R7 (ND 6455)	4wDM		RH	221625	1942	(m)	
-		0-6-0DH		Aug	24376	1981	(n)	

(a)   ex Sir W.H. McAlpine, Fawley Green, near Henley on Thames, Bucks, /1970; prev Bowaters United Kingdom Paper Co Ltd, Sittingbourne, Kent.

(b)   ex British Steel Corporation, Nettleton Ironstone Mines, Lincs, 7/1970.

(c)   ex J.B. Latham, Woking, Surrey, 15/12/1970.

(d)   ex Sir W.H. McAlpine, Fawley Green, near Henley on Thames, Bucks, c10/1970; prev Bowaters United Kingdom Paper Co Ltd, Sittingbourne, Kent.

(e)   ex Alan Keef Ltd, 17/9/1971, after regauging to 2ft 6in; earlier London Brick Co Ltd, King's Dike Brick Works, Whittlesey, Cambs.

(f)   ex Welshpool & Llanfair Railway, Llanfair, Powys, 18/3/1972.

(g)   ex Sir Robert McAlpine, Sons & Co Ltd, Dunston on Tyne Plant Depot, Tyne & Wear, c5/1974; prev ROF, Bishopton, Renfrews.

(h)   ex Welsh Highland Light Railway (1964) Ltd, Kinnerley, Shropshire, 14/6/1975.

(i)   ex Knebworth Park Railway, Herts, c5/1976.

(j)   ex Sir Robert McAlpine & Sons Ltd, Dunston on Tyne Plant Depot, Tyne & Wear, c/1975; prev ROF, Bishopton, Renfrews.

(k)   ex Narrow Gauge Railway Museum, Wharf Station, Tywyn, Gwynedd, via Ian Howitt, 27/2/1991.

(m)   ex MoD, NATO Ammunition Depot, Broughton Moor, Cumbria, 1/7/1992.

(n)   ex unknown sugar works, Poland, 11/1998.

(1)   to Sittingbourne & Kemsley Light Railway, Kent, 10/1972.

(2)   scrapped on site, c/1980 (after 1/5/1979)

(3)   to Alan Keef Ltd, Bampton, Oxon, 6/1983.

(4)   to P. Rampton, Reigate, Surrey, 15/12/1994

(5)   to Railworld, Peterborough, Cambs, 12/10/1996

Gauge : 1ft 11½in

99 3461		0-8-0	OC	VW	3852	1925	(a)	(1)
SEZELA No.4		0-4-0T	OC	AE	1738	1915	(b)	(2)

(a)   ex Romney Hythe & Dymchurch Railway, New Romney, Kent, 4/1976

(b)   ex Knebworth Park Railway, Herts, after 3/9/1978, by 16/4/1979.

(1)   to Chemin de Fer Froissy - Dompierre, near Amiens, France, 22/5/1978.

(2)   returned to Knebworth Park Railway, c7/1981.

Visiting Locomotives (Gauge 2ft 6in)

DOUGAL	0-4-0T	OC	AB	2207	1946	(a)	(1)
No.14	2-6-2T	OC	HE	3815	1954	(b)	(2)

(a) ex Welshpool & Llanfair Light Railway, Llanfair, Powys, 5/1992.
(b) ex Welshpool & Llanfair Light Railway, Llanfair, Powys, 4/1993.

(1) returned to Welshpool & Llanfair Light Railway.
(2) returned to Welshpool & Llanfair Light Railway, c4/5/1993.

GREAT WOBURN RAILWAY
PETER SCOTT WOBURN SAFARI PARK
FP7
SP 962343

Pleasure line, opened 16/5/1994.

Gauge : 1ft 8in

ROBIN HOOD	4-6-4DM S/O	HC	D570	1932		
	reb 4-6-4DH	AK		1982	(a)	
4472 FLYING SCOTSMAN	4-6-2DM S/O	HC	D582	1933		
	reb 4-6-2DH	Lenwade Hydraulic Services	1991		(a)	

(a) ex Kilverstone Country Park, Kilverstone Hall, near Thetford, Norfolk, 21/1/1994.

ALAN KEEF
THE OLD VICARAGE, Woburn
FP8

Locomotive preserved at this private location.

Gauge: 2ft 0in

-	0-4-0PM	BgC	760	1918	(a)	(1)

(a) ex APCM Ltd, Bidwell Clay Pit, near Dunstable, 6/1962

(1) to Alan Keef, The Red House, Aston Clinton, near Aylesbury, Bucks, /1964

LEIGHTON BUZZARD NARROW GAUGE RAILWAY SOCIETY
Billington Road, Leighton Buzzard
KP9
Iron Horse Preservation Society until 20/9/1969

Preservation society formed in 1967 to operate an American style narrow gauge service over the former LBLR. The American image never developed and the society therefore changed its name in September 1969. The first diesel hauled public trains ran on 3/3/1968 from Pages Park to Double Arches. In 1975 timetabled services commenced on a regular basis to the present terminus of the line at Stonehenge. Locomotives and stock are kept at Pages Park shed (SP 929242) and Stonehenge Workshops (SP 941275).

Gauge: 2ft 0in

"1"	CHALONER	0-4-0VBT	VC	DeW		1877	(sa)	
"2"	PIXIE	0-4-0ST	OC	KS	4260	1922	(sb)	(9)
4	(THE) DOLL	0-6-0T	OC	AB	1641	1919	(sc)	
No.11	P.C.ALLEN	0-4-0WT	OC	OK	5834	1912	(sd)	
No.3	RISHRA	0-4-0T	OC	BgE	2007	1921	(se)	
(6)	PETER PAN	0-4-0ST	OC	KS	4256	1922	(sf)	(6)
5	ELF (No.932)	0-6-0WT	OC	OK	12740	1936	(sg)	
	PENLEE	0-4-0WT	OC	Freud	73	1901		
			reb	ARC		c1983	(sh)	
778	(LION)	4-6-0T	OC	BLW	44656	1916	(sj)	
	ALICE	0-4-0ST	OC	HE	780	1902	(sk)	
740	MATHERAN	0-6-0T	OC	OK	2343	1907	(sl)	
	SEZELA No.4	0-4-0T	OC	AE	1738	1915	(sm)	
		4wDM		MR	5608	1931	(a)	(3)
	MABEL 1	4wDM		MR	5875	1935	(a)	(2)
5612	R8	4wDM		MR	5612	1931	(a)	Dsm
R7	No.131	4wDM		MR	5613	1931	(a)	Dsm
"7"	(8986) FALCON §							
	(f. PAM)	4wDM		OK	8986	1938	(b)	
	"REDLANDS"	4wDM		MR	5603	1931	(c)	Dsm
36	(6) CARAVAN	4wDM		MR	7129	1936	(c)	
"10"	HAYDN TAYLOR	4wDM		MR	7956	1945	(d)	
31	NEW STAR	4wPM		L	4088	1931	(e)	(5)
12	CARBON	4wPM		MR	6012	1930	(f)	
43		4wDM		MR	10409	1954	(g)	
"14"		4wDM		HE	3646	1946	(h)	
"15"	(TOM BOMBADIL)	4wDM		FH	2514	1941	(j)	
		4wDM		HE	2176	1940	(k)	(4)
16	THORIN OAKENSHIELD	4wDM (ex PM)		L	11221	1939	(l)	
No.44	(KESTREL)	4wDM		MR	7933	1941	(m)	
8	"GOLLUM"	4wDM		RH	217999	1942	(n)	
18	FËANOR	4wDM		MR	11003	1956	(o)	
"19"	(orig. 23)	4wDM		MR	11298	1965	(o)	Dsm
"20"		4wDM		MR	60s317	1966	(o)	Dsm
24		4wDM		MR	11297	1965	(p)	
"25"	"HAD-A-CAB"	4wDM		MR	7214	1936	(q)	
No.21	FESTOON	4wDM		MR	4570	1929	(r)	
No.17	DAMREDUB	4wDM		MR	7036	1936	(s)	
"24"		4wDM		MR	4805	1934	(t)	Dsm
LM 39	T.W.LEWIS	4wDM		RH	375316	1954	(u)	
"30"		4wDM		MR	8695	1941	(v)	
No.13	ARKLE	4wDM		MR	7108	1936	(w)	
(No.11)		4wDM		FH			(x)	Dsm
"23"		4wDM		RH	164346	1932	(y)	
"26"	M.S.R. No.1 YIMKIN	4wDM		RH	203026	1942	(z)	
		4wDMF		RH	425798	1958	(aa)	(7)
		4wDM		RH	444207	1961	(aa)	(7)
"29"	CREEPY							
	YARD No.P 19774	4wDM		HE	6008	1963	(ab)	
27	(POPPY)	4wDM		RH	408430	1957	(ac)	
28	R.A.F. STANBRIDGE							
	A.M.W. 194	4wDM		RH ‡200516		1940	(ad)	

		4wDM	RH	218016	1943	(ae)	Dsm
No.9	(49) MADGE	4wDM	OK	7600	1937	(af)	
"22"	"FINGOLFIN"	4wDM *	LBNGRS	1	1989	New	
"33"		4wDM	FH	3582	1954	(ag)	Dsm
"32"		4wDM	RH	172892	1934	(ah)	
41	(No.34) LOD/758054	4wDM	HE	2536	1941	(ah)	
		2w-2DHR#	Bg	3539	1959	(ai)	
31		4wPM	L	4228	1931	(aj)	
"35"	(No.7)						
	(6619) 9303/507	0-4-0DM	HE	6619	1966	(ak)	
"37"		4wDM	RH	172901	1935	(al)	Dsm
2275	3098	4wPM	MR	1377	1918	(am)	
38	(8) HARRY B	4wDM (ex PM)	L	37170	1951	(an)	
No.34	RED RUM	4wDM	MR	7105	1936	(ao)	
"40"	TRENT						
	(U192 T.R.A. No.13)	4wDM	RH	283507	1949	(ao)	
"42"	SARAH	4wDM	RH	223692	1943	(ap)	
45		4wDM	MR	21615	1957	(aq)	Dsm
46		4wDM	RH	209430	1942	(ar)	Dsm
		4wDM	RH	193974	1938	(as)	(8)
47		4wPM	HU	38384	1930	(at)	
		4-2-0PMR	R Morris		1967	(au)	(1)
		4wDM	MR	8731	1941	(av)	Dsm
		4wDM	HE	4351	1952	(aw)	
No.1	BLUEBELL	4wDM	FH	2631	1943	(ax)	
		4wDM	FH	2586	1941	(ax)	Dsm
(No.1568)		4wPM	FH	1568	1927	(ay)	
80	BEAUDESERT	4wDH	AK	59R	1999	New	
		(reb of SMH	101T018 1979)			New	

* built from parts of RH 425798/1958 & RH 444207/1961.
‡ carries plate from RH 200513.
§ the nameplate is in Arabic.
# rebuilt by Alan Keef Ltd from 4ft 8½in 2w-2DHR to passenger bogie coach No.8

(sa) ex A.R. Fisher, Kings Langley, Herts, on loan, 23/6/1968; to National Railway Museum, York, 7/6/1979; returned 25/2/1984.
(sb) ex Industrial Locomotive Society, Harpenden, Herts, 7/12/1968.
(sc) ex A. Bloom, Bressingham, Norfolk, 9/8/1969.
(sd) ex Sir P.C. Allen, Battle, Sussex, 31/10/1970.
(se) ex Hoogly Docking & Engineering Co Ltd, Calcutta, India, 2/11/1971; to National Railway Museum, York, 7/12/1981; ex Science Museum, London, 6/4/1983.
(sf) ex J.H. Hardy, Bromsgrove, Worcs, 9/1972.
(sg) ex F. Jux, Ripley, Surrey, 12/4/1973; prev Cameroons Development Corporation, Tiko Rubber Mill, 932.
(sh) ex A.R.C.(Southern) Ltd, Swindon Plant Depot, Ermine Street, Stratton St Margaret, Wilts, 6/7/1991.
(sj) ex Chalk Pits Museum, Amberley, West Sussex, 23/4/1994.
(sk) ex Festiniog Railway, Boston Lodge Works, Porthmadog, Gwynedd, 15/6/1994.
(sl) ex Railworld, Woodston, Peterborough, Cambs, 20/8/1994
(sm) ex Welsh Highland Railway Co Ltd, Gelert farm, Porthmadog, Gwynedd, 28/10/2000

(a) ex St.Albans Sand & Gravel Co Ltd, Smallford Pits, Herts, /1967.

(b) ex Goodman Bros.Ltd, dealers, New Bradwell, Bucks, c1/1970; prev. Woodham Brick Co Ltd, Wotton, Bucks.

(c) ex Redland Flettons Ltd, Kempston Hardwick, Beds, 24/7/1970.

(d) ex British Industrial Sand Ltd, Middleton Towers, Norfolk, 8/1971.

(e) ex Rev.E. Boston, Cadeby, Leics, 27/12/1971.

(f) ex M.E. Engineering Ltd, Cricklewood, Middlesex, 25/3/1972; prev. Standard Bottle Co Ltd, Southgate, Middlesex.

(g) ex Joseph Arnold & Sons Ltd, Leighton Buzzard, 4/1972.

(h) ex Arnold & Nathan (Plant Hire) Ltd, East Peckham Plant Depot, near Paddock Wood, Kent, 8/1972; prev. Hall & Co Ltd, Crumbles Gravel Pits, Eastbourne, Sussex.

(j) ex Butterley Brick Co Ltd, Blaby, Leics, 9/1972.

(k) ex Burton Constructional Engineering Co Ltd, Burton-on-Trent, 9/1972.

(l) ex Guard Bridge Paper Co Ltd, Guard Bridge, Fife, 18/11/1973.

(m) ex Joseph Arnold & Sons Ltd, Leighton Buzzard, 22/2/1975.

(n) ex J. Cater, North Fambridge, Essex, 26/7/1975, after storage at a private location at Colney Heath Lane, St Albans, Herts from 24/10/1974.

(o) ex British Industrial Sand Ltd, Middleton Towers, Norfolk, 6/6/1980.

(p) ex British Industrial Sand Ltd, Middleton Towers, Norfolk, 6/6/1980; to Alan Keef Ltd, Bampton, Oxon, 3/6/1982; returned from South Tynedale Preservation Society, Alston, Cumbria, 8/5/1990.

(q) ex Joseph Arnold & Sons Ltd, Leighton Buzzard, 5/1981.

(r) ex George Garside (Sand) Ltd, Leighton Buzzard, 21/6/1981.

(s) ex George Garside (Sand) Ltd, Leighton Buzzard, 10/1981.

(t) ex Joseph Arnold & Sons Ltd, Leighton Buzzard, 18/4/1983.

(u) ex Pleasure-Rail Ltd, Knebworth House, Herts, 1/6/1985.

(v) ex Bedfordshire County Council, Dovery Down County Primary School, Heath Road, Leighton Buzzard, 4/7/1986.

(w) ex West Lancashire Light Railway, Hesketh Bank, Lancs, 12/9/1986.

(x) ex Yaxham Light Railways, Yaxham, Norfolk, 13/12/1986.

(y) ex The Narrow Gauge Railway Centre of North Wales, Gloddfa Ganol, Blaenau Ffestiniog, Gwynedd, 17/5/1987.

(z) ex The Royal Air Force Museum, RAF Cosford, Shropshire, 22/5/1987.

(aa) ex Brecon Mountain Railway, Pontsticill, Powys, 27/9/1987.

(ab) ex W.Smith, dealer, Baughurst, Hampshire, 8/9/1987; to Alan Keef Ltd, Ross-on-Wye, for re-gauging to 2ft and returned, 4/10/1987.

(ac) ex West Lancashire Light Railway, Hesketh Bank, Lancs, 13/7/1988.

(ad) ex MoDAFD, Chilmark Depot, Wilts, 22/9/1988.

(ae) ex L.J. Smith, Battlesbridge, Essex, 26/11/1988.

(af) ex P. Wilson, South Benfleet, Essex, 27/11/1988.

(ag) ex Alan Keef Ltd, Lea Line, Ross-on-Wye, Hereford & Worcs, 16/6/1989.

(ah) ex Southern Industrial History Centre, Chalk Pits Museum, Amberley, West Sussex, 15/7/1989.

(ai) ex Alan Keef Ltd, Lea Line, Ross-on-Wye, Hereford & Worcs, 26/8/1989; prev MODAD, Bramley Depot, Hampshire, via J. Hurst & Sons, St Mary Bourne, Hampshire, 3/1987

(aj) ex J.Thomas, Bletchley, Bucks, c8/1989

(ak) ex South Tynedale Railway Preservation Society, Alston Station, Cumbria, 15/10/1989.

(al) ex T. Hall, North Ings Farm, Dorrington, Lincs, 2/2/1990.

(am) ex National Railway Museum, York, on loan, 30/11/1990.

(an) ex Hollands Moss Peat Co., Chat Moss, Irlam, Grt.Manchester, 27/8/1991.

(ao) ex West Lancashire Light Railway, Hesketh Bank, Lancs, 31/8/1991.

(ap) ex William Blyth, Far Ings Tileries, Barton-on-Humber, Humberside, 29/7/1992.

(aq) ex Festiniog Railway, Minffordd, Porthmadog, Gwynedd, 9/12/1992.

(ar) ex FMB Engineering Co Ltd, Oakhanger, Bordon, Hampshire, 30/7/1993.

(as) ex Alan Keef Ltd, Lea Line, Ross-on-Wye, Hereford & Worcs, 10/10/1993.
(at) ex Bala Lake Railway, Llanuwchllyn, Gwynedd, 23/10/1993.
(au) ex ?
(av) ex Northamptonshire Ironstone Railway Trust, Hunsbury Hill, Northampton, 2/1/1994.
(aw) ex John Macnamara & Co Ltd, 19A Bush Rd, London, SE8, 11/3/1994.
(ax) ex Lowthers Railway Society, Leadhills, Strathclyde, 10/9/1994.
(ayz) ex Narrow Gauge Railway Centre, Gloddfa Ganol Slate Mine, Blaenau Ffestiniog, Gwynedd, 20/2/1998.

(1) to ? , Leamington Spa, Warwicks, 2/1969.
(2) converted to coach No.6, /1971.
(3) converted to coach No.5, /1971.
(4) to Brockham Museum Association, Surrey, 13/3/1974.
(5) returned to Rev.E. Boston, Cadeby, Leics, c2/1975.
(6) to Island Narrow Gauge Group, Isle of Wight, 12/8/1975.
(7) RH 425798 scrapped 27/5/1988 and RH 444207 scrapped 17/3/1988 and parts from both locos used to build LBNGRS 1/1989.
(8) dismantled for spares; frames disposed of to P. Westmacott, Studley, Warwicks, 27/2/1994.
(9) to Stoomcentrum, Maldegem, Belgium, 28/4/2000 (on hire).

Visiting Locomotives :
The following locomotives have visited the railway in connection with special events and/or for storage pending movement elsewhere.

	-	4wDH		MR	121U117	1971	(a)	(1)
3	IRISH MAIL	0-4-0ST	OC	HE	823	1903	(b)	(2)
	BRITOMART	0-4-0ST	OC	HE	707	1899	(c)	(3)
	WENDY	0-4-0ST	OC	WB	2091	1919	(d)	(4)
	JUSTINE	0-4-0WT	OC	Jung	939	1906	(e)	(5)
	JURASSIC	0-6-0ST	OC	P	1008	1903	(f)	(6)
	ALAN GEORGE	0-4-0ST	OC	HE	606	1894	(g)	(7)
22	MONTALBAN	0-4-0WT	OC	OK	6641	1913	(h)	(8)
1	ELIDIR	0-4-0ST	OC	HE	493	1899	(i)	(9)
	-	0-4-0T	OC	AK	38	1991	(j)	(10)
	WOTO	0-4-0ST	OC	WB	2133	1924	(k)	(11)
	BRONHILDE	0-4-0WT	OC	Sch	9124	1927	(l)	(12)
	KATIE	0-6-0WT	OC	Jung	3872	1931	(m)	(13)
	SEZELA No.4	0-4-0T	OC	AE	1738	1915	(n)	(14)
	-	0-4-0WT	OC	OK	6335	1913	(o)	(15)
20	(form. 26)	4wDM		MR	60s318	1966	(p)	(16)
20		4wPM		Bg	3002	1937	(q)	(17)
	-	4wDM		AK	28	1989	(r)	(18)
		4wDM		OK	5926	1935	(s)	(19)
	-	0-6-0DMF		HC	DM1117	1958	(t)	(20)
		4wPM		FH	1776	1931	(u)	(21)
	-	4wDM		Dtz	10248	1932	(v)	(22)
	-	4wDM		RH	223700	1943	(w)	(23)
	NAKLO	0-6-0WTT	OC	Chr	3459	1957	(x)	(24)
	BARBOUILLEUR	0-4-0T	OC	Decauville	1126	1950	(y)	(25)
		4wDM		MR	8969	1945	(z)	(26)
	ELOUISE	0-6-0WT	OC	OK	9998	1922	(aa)	(27)
	CLOISTER	0-4-0ST	OC	HE	542	1891	(ab)	(28)

(a)   ex MR, 27/2/1974, for trials (this loco was allocated works number 121U123 for this purpose, but this may not have been carried).

(b)   ex West Lancashire Light Railway, Hesketh Bank, Lancs, 7/6/1985; returned, 6/1985 here again, 6/6/1986.

(c)   ex Festiniog Railway, Boston Lodge Works, Porthmadog, Gwynedd, 8/9/1986.

(d)   ex Hampshire Narrow Gauge Railway, Durley, Hampshire, 13/9/1986.

(e)   ex North Gloucestershire Railway, Toddington, Glos, 16/9/1986; returned to Toddington, 13/10/1986; to here again, 14/4/1995.

(f)   ex Lincolnshire Coast Light Railway, Humberston, Humberside, 18/9/1986.

(g)   ex Vale of Teifi Narrow Gauge Railway, Henllan, Llandyssul, Dyfed, 10/9/1987.

(h)   ex West Lancashire Light Railway, Hesketh Bank, Lancs, 1/9/1990; returned, 26/9/1990; here again, 7/1992; to Lowthers Railway, Leadhills, Strathclyde, 7/1992; ex South Tynedale Railway, Alston, Cumbria, 1/8/1992; to West Lancs Light Railway, 2/10/1992; ex West Lancs Light Railway,19/6/1994.

(i)   ex Llanberis Lake Railway, Gilfach Ddu, Llanberis, Gwynedd, 31/8/1991.

(j)   ex Alan Keef Ltd, Lea Line, Ross-on-Wye, Hereford & Worcs, for trials, 19/12/1991.

(k)   ex Patrick Keef, Lea Line, Ross-on-Wye, Hereford & Worcs, 8/8/1992; to North Gloucestershire Railway, Toddington, Glos, 9/10/1992; returned from Patrick Keef, Lea Line, 3/7/1993; to West Lancashire Light Railway, Hesketh Bank, Lancs, 17/7/1993; ex South Tynedale Railway, Alston, Cumbria, 8/8/1993; to Stoomcentrum Maldegem, Belgium, 12/8/1993; returned here, 16/8/1993.

(l)   ex Bredgar & Wormshill Light Railway, Bredgar, Kent, 5/9/1992.

(m)   ex Bredgar & Wormshill Light Railway, Bredgar, Kent, 6/9/1992.

(n)   ex Burgh Hall Bygone Village, Fleggburgh, Great Yarmouth, Norfolk,17/6/1994.

(o)   ex Sobemai NV, Maldegem, Belgium, 22/8/1994.

(p)   ex British Industrial Sand Ltd, Middleton Towers, Norfolk, 6/6/1980.

(q)   ex West Lancashire Light Railway, Hesketh Bank, Lancs, 7/6/1985; returned there 6/1985; returned here 6/6/1986; returned to West Lancashire Light Railway, 23/6/1986; ex South Tynedale Railway, Alston, Cumbria, 10/9/1987; to West Lancashire Light Railway, 6/11/1987; ex South Tynedale Railway, Alston, Cumbria, 12/9/1992.

(r)   ex Alan Keef Ltd, Lea Line, Ross-on-Wye, Hereford & Worcs, for trials, 16/6/1986.

(s)   ex Chalk Pits Museum, Amberley, West Sussex, 5/7/1987.

(t)   ex Midland Railway Centre, Butterley, Derbys, 21/4/1993.

(u)   ex Leicestershire Museum of Technology, Abbey Meadows, Leicester, 25/9/1993.

(v)   ex Midland Railway Centre, Butterley, Derbys, 3/6/1994.

(w)   ex Leicestershire Museum of Technology, Abbey Meadows, Leicester, 3/6/1994.

(x)   ex South Tynedale Railway, Alston, Cumbria, 15/8/1992.

(y)   ex Chalk Pits Musem, Amberley, West Sussex, 22/8/1992.

(z)   ex Northamptonshire Ironstone Railway Trust, Hunsbury Hill, Northampton, 7/2/1993.

(aa)   ex Welsh Highland Light Railway (1964) Ltd, Porthmadog, Gwynedd, by 7/9/1996; to Old Kiln Light Railway, Tilford, near Farnham, Surrey, 9/1996; returned here again, 6/9/1997.

(ab)   ex Kew Bridge Steam Museum, Brentford, London, by 5/9/1998; returned to Kew Bridge; to here again ex Bala Lake Railway, Gwynedd, 28/8/1999.

(1)   returned to MR, Bedford, off trials.

(2)   returned to West Lancashire Light Railway, Hesketh Bank. Lancs, 23/6/1986,

(3)   returned to Festiniog Railway, Porthmadog, Gwynedd, 5/10/1986

(4)   returned to Hampshire Narrow Gauge Railway, Durley, Hampshire, 5/10/1986

(5)   returned to North Gloucestershire Railway, Toddington, Glos, /1995.

(6)   returned to Lincolnshire Coast Light Railway, Humberston, Humbeside, 28/9/1986.

(7)   returned to Vale of Teifi Narrow Gauge Railway, Henllan, Dyfed, 3/10/1987.

(8)   to South Tynedale Railway, Alston, Cumbria, 16/7/1994.
(9)   returned to Llanberis Lake Railway, Llanberis, Gwynedd, 18/9/1991.
(10) to Alan Keef Ltd, Lea Line, Ross-on-Wye, Hereford & Worcs, 22/12/1991 (for export to De Efterling Park, Netherlands).
(11) to Patrick Keef, Lea Line, Ross-on-Wye, Hereford & Worcs, 10/10/1993.
(12) returned to Bredgar & Wormshill Light Railway, Bredgar, Kent, 14/9/1992.
(13) returned to Bredgar & Wormshill Light Railway, Bredgar, Kent, 13/9/1992.
(14) to Welsh Highland Railway, Porthmadog, Gwynedd, 3/9/1994.
(15) to Lowthers Railway Society, Leadhills, Strathclyde, 31/8/1994.
(16) to Alan Keef Ltd, Lea Line, Ross-on-Wye, Hereford & Worcs, 3/6/1982.
(17) to West Lancashire Light Railway, Hesketh Bank, Lancs, 13/9/1992.
(18) to Butterley Building Materials Ltd, Star Lane Brickworks, Great Wakering, Essex, 19/6/1986
(19) to Abbey Light Railway, Kirkstall, Leeds, 9/7/1987.
(20) returned to Midland Railway Centre, Butterley, Derbys, 2/8/1993.
(21) returned to Leicestershire Museum of Technology, Abbey Meadows, Leicester, 26/9/1993.
(22) to Leicestershire Museum of Technology, Abbey Meadows, Leicester, 6/6/1994.
(23) returned to Leicestershire Museum of Technology, Abbey Meadows, Leicester, 5/6/1994.
(24) returned to South Tynedale Railway, Alston, Cumbria, 24/10/1992.
(25) returned to Chalk Pits Museum, Amberley, West Sussex, 26/9/1992.
(26) to Alan Keef Ltd, Lea Line, Ross-on-Wye, Hereford & Worcs, 10/10/1993.
(27) to Old Kiln Light Railway, Tilford, near Farnham, Surrey, 26/10/1997.
(28) to Kew Bridge Steam Museum, Brentford, London, 8/9/1999.

Gauge: 2ft 6in

3		0-4-0T	OC	AB	984 1903	(a)	(1)

(a)   ex S.A. Burgess, Haddenham, Cambs, 5/8/1972.

(1)   to A.M. Keef, Cote Farm, Bampton, Oxon, 4/1973.

THE LIGHT RAILWAY ASSOCIATION
MILLBROOK STATION YARD, near Bedford   **JP10**
TL 007406

Group established 18/9/1981. Initially stock was stored at this location but was later moved to Turvey. After some time at the Turvey site the group became the **Stevington & Turvey Light Railway** (which see).

Gauge: 2ft 0in

-		4wDM	OK	6504 1936	(a)	(1)
-		4wDM	MR	9655 1951	(b)	(1)

a)   ex Titchfield Light Railway, Carron Row Farm Museum, Titchfield, Hampshire, c8/1987.
b)   ex Tony Joyce (Light Railway Association), Harlesden, Greater London, 6/10/1987.

1)   to Light Rly Association, Turvey, 11/6/1989.

LONDON RAILWAY PRESERVATION SOCIETY

DUNSTABLE TOWN STATION
HP11

TL 026219

Locomotives stored at this British Railways station for a period before transfer elsewhere.

Gauge: 4ft 8½in

PUNCH HULL	0-4-0ST	OC	AB	776	1896	(a)	(1)
TOM PARRY	0-4-0ST	OC	AB	2015	1935	(a)	(2)

(a)   ex Blue Circle Industries, Dunstable Works, for storage, 1/3/1967

(1)   to Skimpot Lane Depot, Luton, 31/10/1967
(2)   to International Alloys Ltd, Aylesbury, Bucks, for storage, 28/3/1968.

LUTON DEPOT
HP12

TL 045223

Locomotives were stored on sidings at this coldstore depot at Skimpot Lane, Luton, for some time until activities were transferred to the Society's Buckinghamshire Railway Centre at Quainton Road, Bucks (which see under Quainton Railway Society Ltd).

Gauge: 4ft 8½in

L44		0-4-4T	IC	Neasden	3	1896	(a)	(2)
	TRYM	0-4-0ST	OC	HE	287	1883	(b)	(6)
	SYDENHAM	4wWT	G	AP	3567	1895	(c)	(3)
	SWANSCOMBE	0-4-0ST	OC	AB	699	1891	(d)	(7)
	-	0-4-0ST	OC	AB	1865	1926	(e)	(5)
	-	0-4-0ST	OC	WB	2469	1932	(f)	(5)
19		0-4-0ST	OC	Hor	1097	1910	(g)	(1)
	PUNCH HULL	0-4-0ST	OC	AB	776	1896	(h)	(3)
	-	2w-2PMR		Wkm	8263	1959	(i)	(4)

(a)   ex London Transport, Neasden Depot, London, 20/3/1964
(b)   ex Howard Farrow Ltd, Hendon, London, 13/5/1964
(c)   ex Enfield Veteran & Vintage Vehicle Society, Herts, 5/9/1965; prev BOCM Ltd, Erith, Kent
(d)   ex Thurrock Chalk & Whiting, Thurrock, Essex, 6/2/1966
(e)   ex North Thames Gas Board, Southall Gas Works, 20/4/1966
(f)   ex C.A. Parsons Ltd, Erith, Kent, 28/10/1966
(g)   ex United Glass Ltd, Charlton, London, 1/1967
(h)   ex Dunstable Town Station, 31/10/1967
(i)   ex BR, Northampton, 9/3/1968

(1)   to Keighley & Worth Valley Railway, Yorkshire (WR), 10/10/1967
(2)   to BR, Bedford, for exhibition, 1/10/1968; then to International Alloys Ltd, Aylesbury, Bucks, for storage, 4/11/1968
(3)   to London Railway Preservation Society, Quainton Road, Bucks, 16/4/1969
(4)   to London Railway Preservation Society, Quainton Road, Bucks, 4/4/1969
(5)   to London Railway Preservation Society, Quainton Road, Bucks, 17/4/1969
(6)   to London Railway Preservation Society, Quainton Road, Bucks, 18/4/1969
(7)   to London Railway Preservation Society, Quainton Road, Bucks, 10/5/1969

P.J. MACKINNON
WILSTEAD SAWMILLS

JP13

TL 063433

Locomotive preserved at this private location at Walnut Lodge, 36 Luton Road, Wilstead.

Gauge : 1ft 8in

-	4wDM	OK	6703	1936	(a)

(a)   ex Barton Lime Co (1957) Ltd, Barton-in-the-Clay, c/1967.

RAY MASLIN & FRIENDS
Arlesey (Private location)

FP14

Narrow gauge locomotives purchased for preservation on this private railway.

Gauge: 2ft 0in

-	4wDM (ex PM)	L	37911	1952	(a)	
CLARABELL	4wDMF	HE	4758	1954	(b)	
-	4wDM	RH	441951	1960	(c)	
RTT 767187	2w-2PM	Wkm	2559	1939	(d)	
RTT 767094	2w-2PM	Wkm	3033	1941	(e)	Dsm

(a)   ex FMB Engineering Co Ltd, Liphook, Hampshire, 11/2/1993; prev Ian Sutcliffe, Surrey
        Light Railway, Surrey.
(b)   ex FMB Engineering Co Ltd, Liphook, Hampshire, 8/5/1994; prev Moseley Industrial
        Tramway & Museum, Stockport, Manchester.
(c)   ex FMB Engineering Co Ltd, Liphook, Hampshire, 4/5/1996; prev Wickford Narrow
        Gauge Railway group, Wickford, Essex.
(d)   ex FMB Engineering Co Ltd, Liphook, Hampshire, 4/5/1996; prev C. Cross, Upwell Fen
        Light Railway, Upwell, near Wisbech, Cambs.
(e)   ex C. Cross, Upwell Fen Light Railway, Upwell, near Wisbech, Cambs, 1/1998.

ROBIN PEARMAN
Church Street, Langford, near Biggleswade

FP15

Locomotives kept for preservation at this private location.

Gauge: 2ft 11in

-	4wDM	MR	10161	1950	(a)	(1)

(a)   ex London Brick Co Ltd, Bearts Works, Arlesey, 12/1977

(1)   to Brockham Museum Trust, Brockham Museum, Dorking, Surrey, 22/3/1980.

Gauge: 2ft 0in

-	4wDM	MR	11001	1956	(a)	(1)

(a)   ex London Brick Co Ltd, Bearts Works, Arlesey, 12/1977

(1)   to Southern Industrial History Centre Trust, Chalk Pits Museum, Amberley, West
        Sussex, 7/3/1983.

SOUTH MIDLAND RAILWAY
DUNSTABLE

HP16

TL 023224

A preservation group occupying the former sidings of the Bedford Truck Plant in Dunstable on the fomer Luton to Dunstable branch line.

Gauge: 4ft 8½in

No.5	0-4-0DM	VF	D293	1955	
		DC	2566	1955	(a)

(a)   ex Great Eastern Traction, Hardingham Station, near Wymondham, Norfolk, 1/2001.

STEVINGTON AND TURVEY LIGHT RAILWAY
TURVEY STATION

FP17

formerly **The Light Railway Association**

SP 967524

Negotiations began in September 1982 to construct a narrow gauge railway on part of the trackbed of the former Bedford to Northampton railway at Turvey. Construction of the new narrow gauge line began in spring 1983. By 1995 the line was about 300 yards in length with further extensions planned.

Gauge: 2ft 0in

No.15 OLDE	4wDM	HE	2176	1940	(a)	
	4wDM	MR	7128	1936	(b)	Dsm
No.7 COLLINGWOOD						
(No.5, form. No.21)	4wDM	RH	373359	1954	(c)	
(MT 1821)	4wPM	FH	1767	1931	(d)	Dsm
	4wDM	OK	3685	1929	(e)	
11 NEEDHAM	4wDM	OK	6504	1936	(f)	
No.1 PAUL COOPER	4wDM	MR	9655	1951	(f)	
CATFISH	4wDM	Diema	1600	1953	(g)	
No.5	4wDM	OK	7728	1937	(h)	Dsm

(a)   ex Bredgar Railway, Bredgar, Kent, 25/11/1983.
(b)   ex I. Sutcliffe, Bourne Valley Grit Narrow Gauge Railway, Surrey, 9/9/1984.
(c)   ex Pleasure-Rail Ltd, Knebworth House, Herts, 1/6/1985.
(d)   ex I. Sutcliffe, Bourne Valley Grit Narrow Gauge Railway, Surrey, 19/9/1985
(e)   ex J. Crosskey, Surrey Light Railway, Surrey, 29/9/1987.
(f)   ex Light Rly Association, Millbrook Station Yard, 11/6/1989.
(g)   ex Alan Keef Ltd, Lea Line, Hereford & Worcs, 3/8/1995.
(h)   ex Midland Railway Centre, Butterley, Derbys, after 18/11/1997.

Gauge : 1ft 6in

1514	0-4-0BE	WR		(a)

(a)   ex John Crosskey, North Cheam, Surrey, c6/1997 (by 29/8/1997).

WOBURN ABBEY (NARROW GAUGE) RAILWAY
WOBURN ABBEY RAILWAY, Woburn Park FP18

later operated by **Leisure Track Ltd.** SP 968328

Pleasure line originally opened on 3/3/1968 and operated for about a year. Later re-opened by Leisure Track Ltd after some years of closure.

Gauge : 1ft 11½in

No.1	0-4-0ST	OC	HE	1429	1922	(a)	(1)
No.2	4wDM		MR	8993	1946	(b)	(1)
FLYING SCOTSMAN (form. JODIE II;							
prev. DUCHESS)	4wDM	S/O	RH	223749	1944	(c)	(3)
-	4wDM		RH	183773	1937	(d)	(4)
-	4wDM	S/O	RH	239381	1946	(e)	(2)
-	4wDM		MR	40S343		(f)	(5)

(a) ex W.J. Gower, Engineers, Elstow Rd, Bedford, after repairs; /1968; earlier Dinorwic Slate Quarries Ltd, Llanberis, Caerns [North Wales].
(b) ex Sir Robert McAlpine & Sons Ltd, Hayes, Middlesex, c2/1968.
(c) ex Track Supplies & Services Ltd, Wolverton, Bucks, after 19/11/1972, by 11/2/1973; prev. MODAD, East Riggs, Dumfries.
(d) ex Track Supplies & Services Ltd, Wolverton, Bucks, /1974.
(e) ex Track Supplies & Services Ltd, Wolverton, Bucks, /1975; orig. Imperial Smelting (Processes) Ltd, Avonmouth, Glos.
(f) ex A.M. Keef, Cote Farm, Bampton, Oxon, 8/1980.

(1) to Overstone Park Railway, Northampton, c1/1969.
(2) s/s c/1983 (by 11/9/1983)
(3) to Moseley Industrial Tramway Museum, Manor School, Cheadle, Stockport, Greater Manchester, c2/1992 (by 26/4/1992).
(4) to M. Capron, Wolverton, Bucks, 10/10/1981.
(5) returned to A.M. Keef, /1987.

ADDITIONAL LATE ENTRY :
J. FORSHAW
Private Location XP19

Gauge : 600mm

-	0-6-0T	OC	Decauville	1735	1919	(a)

(a) ex Mozabique (exact location not known), 11/2000.

NON-LOCOMOTIVE SYSTEMS

ASSOCIATED PORTLAND CEMENT MANUFACTURERS LTD
THREE COUNTIES LIME WORKS, Arlesey   FH1
Arlesey Lime & Portland Cement Co Ltd from c1885 until 10/7/1900   Works TL 189349
Arlesey Brick & Lime Co c1858   Clay Pits TL 197343

A 3ft 0in gauge tramway ran from the quarry, across the main road, to the works adjacent to the ex-GNR main line south of Three Counties station. The works, which was the first one to have a rotary kiln installed (in 1887), was served by a private siding from the GNR, in place by 1895. The Arlesey Brick & Lime Co advertised in "The Engineer" 8/4/1881 for one mile of light contractors track for a light tramway, so the narrow gauge may date from that year. The quarries were closed and flooded in 1932 but stock (including 19 wagons in two rakes) was still present in the flooded workings in 1976.

ASTELL BROS LTD
ST LEONARDS SAW MILL St Leonards Street Bedford.   GH2
TL 050490

A saw mill which is believed to have had a short narrow gauge tramway. It also had (by 1895) standard gauge sidings, shunted by steam crane, which connected to the ex LNWR Cambridge - Bletchley railway on the eastern side of the triangle adjacent to St Johns station. The standard gauge sidings appear to have been closed between 1949 and 1956.

BEDFORD ESTATES
BEDFORD ESTATES TIMBER YARD, Timber Lane, Woburn   FH3

A 2ft 0in gauge railway about 40 yards in length serves a vessel for pressure impregnating timber with preservative. The system is hand worked using flat wagons.

BOARD OF TRADE, TIMBER SUPPLY DEPARTMENT
ASPLEY HEATH   FH4

During the First World War a narrow gauge tramway (exact route uncertain) ran from Aspley Heath to a sawmill near Woburn Sands station. This conveyed timber which was being felled by the **Canadian Forestry Corps** from plantations in the Duke of Bedford's estate in Aspley Wood. ("The Leighton Buzzard Observer", March 19th 1918.)

BOSS TRUCKS LTD
GROVEBURY ROAD WORKS, Leighton Buzzard.   KH5

The works has a production line for small fork lift trucks utilising a narrow gauge line with flat wagons in use in 1994.

BRITISH FULLERS EARTH CO LTD
ASPLEY HEATH WORKS, near Woburn Sands

FH6
SP926349

The works, established by 1898, was located on part of the Duke of Bedford's Estate on Aspley Heath. A narrow gauge tramway, which was probably worked by hand, complete with wagon turntable, existed within the works. The works had closed by 1901.

H.G. BROWN
KINGS FARM SAND PIT, Leighton Buzzard

KH7
SP 929246.

Sand pits in Stanbridge Road, opened about 1920, were initially worked by carts. About 1926 a 2ft 0in gauge tramway, about 350 yards in length, was laid from the pits to a gantry beside the farm road, using Hudson tip wagons hauled by horses. In 1947 the pit was let to Henry Winfield Ltd and the railway replaced by lorry working.

DUNSTABLE LIME CO LTD
DUNSTABLE LIME WORKS
(Company registered 1909)

HH8
TL 002228.

A lime works, established 1902 by John William Rowe of Peterborough, situated on the north side of the ex LNWR Dunstable - Leighton Buzzard line, to the west of Dunstable North station. The works was served by standard gauge sidings (in use by 1902) connecting to this line. A double track narrow gauge tramway ran between the quarry and the lime kilns. Side tipping skip wagons were hauled up the steep incline on a continuous chain system worked by a windlass. The works was taken over by APCM by 1939 and was later closed and demolished.

EASTWOOD & CO
ARLESEY STATION GAULT BRICKWORKS
James McCallum Craig from 1882 until 1890

FH9
TL 193382

A brickworks opened in 1882, located north of the Henlow to Stotfold road and just east of the GNR main line. The works had its own sidings with a loop off the main line. A narrow gauge tramway, assumed hand or horse worked, connected the clay pit to the works. Working had ceased by 1907 but remains of the track, of approx 2ft gauge, were still present in the flooded clay pits in 1974.

EASTWOODS FLETTONS LTD
BEDFORD BRICKWORKS
Andrew & Parrott until 1927
Wm H.L. Laxton, 1920 -1925
Henry Burridge & Co from c1893 -1920

JH10
TL 038454

A brickworks, in existence by 1888, located on the west side of the (later A418) road. Used by Eastwoods to make bricks for the construction of its new works at Manor Road (TL 027448). The 6in OS map of 1927 shows a narrow gauge tramway (possibly cable worked) from the clay pits to the works. The works closed later in 1927 and the workings destroyed by the clay pits of Eastwood's new works.

W. FOLKES
KEMPSTON GRAVEL PITS
GH11

TL 028483

Gravel extraction commenced here about 1898 by these sand and gravel merchants of Bedford Road, Kempston. The business was in the name of **William Folkes** in 1898, **William Folkes & Son** by 1924, **Walter Folkes** by 1928, **E.N. Folkes** by 1931, later **W. Folkes,** and was still trading in 1970, but had ceased by 1971.

A 2ft 0in gauge tramway was in existence here by c1925. The line ran from a tipping bank near Bedford Road to Hill Ground. The line originally had wooden wagons which were later replaced by side tipping steel wagons which were hauled by two horses. The tramway later closed but some track remains were still extant in 1966.

B.J. FORDER & SON LTD
WESTONING BRICKWORKS
FH12

B.J. Forder & Son until 25/5/1900

TL 035315

Construction of this works began in January 1893 and it was opened in 1894. It was located on the east side of the ex-Midland Railway Bedford - London railway line between Westoning and Harlington. The works had (by 1895) a single standard gauge siding connecting with this line. A narrow gauge tramway within the works was in existence in 1901. The works closed in 1906.

GRAFTON CRANES LTD
VULCAN WORKS, Bedford
GH13

Grafton & Co Ltd until 8/1936

TL 053487

London Crane Works was established by Alexander Grafton in 1883 as agents for Joseph Jessop, Leicester. Manufacture of cranes began in Bedford in 1887 and the company built many hundreds of steam cranes which were sold all over the world. Grafton cranes were used for shunting at many locations. Some diesel cranes were built in the late 1950s and many steam cranes were converted to diesel power. The works had sidings connecting to the ex-Midland Railway Bedford - Hitchin railway line. The last crane was completed in 1960 when production ceased. The works closed in March 1963 and was demolished in 6/2001.

T.J. GRAHAM & SONS
WHITING WORKS, Spoondell, Dunstable.
HH14

Formerly **F. & J. Graham & Sons**, c1901

TL 011208

The quarry and whiting works was in existence in 1927 and had been in operation for about thirty years. The quarry ran to a depth of 80ft and was served by a narrow gauge tramway which ran down an incline to the quarry face. The wagons were rope or chain hauled up the incline by a windlass powered by a gas engine.

J. CARTER HARRISON LTD
Bullpond Lane, Dunstable.
HH15

TL 020210

Works of an engineering company manufacturing grinding machinery. The 25in OS map for 1924 shows a narrow gauge line, probably hand-worked, connecting the foundry and pattern shop with the fitting shop and stores.

HAYWARD TYLER & CO LTD
Crawley Green Road, Luton
Hayward Tyler & Co until 3/1905

HH16
TL 100209

The company was established in 1815 in St John Street, London and in 1872 a new works was built adjacent to the GNR Dunstable Branch with sidings connecting to this line. The company is well known for the manufacture of reciprocating steam pumps and also supplied the Royal Navy with pumps for warships. In more recent times circulation pumps were supplied for Nuclear Power stations, the first being Calder Hall. The works sidings are thought to have been shunted by steam crane.

SAMUEL W. JARVIS & SON
G.T. Jarvis from c1894 until c1906

George Thomas Jarvis is listed in trade directories as a gravel merchant from about 1894 until about 1906. Operations were later by **Samuel W. Jarvis & Son** by 1927, with gravel pits at **The Folley** in Clapham (TL 022530) and a limestone pit at **Dungee Farm**, near Harold (SP 938587), together with a limestone quarry at Turvey (SP 939520). No rail systems have yet been identified at these sites. In 1925 the **Oakley Junction Gravel & Sand Co Ltd** (which see) was formed and was later taken over by S.W. Jarvis & Son. The firm ceased trading after 1964, by 1965.

DEEP SPINNEY GRAVEL PIT, Biddenham

GH17
TL 023503

A 2ft 0in gauge tramway ran from a tipping dock in Day's Lane, near to the main Bedford to Northampton road. The line ran for about 100 yards along Day's Lane before crossing the road and turning to the south west where it ran for about 150 yards further to the gravel pit. Steel side tippping wagons were horse worked to the tipping dock. The pit opened in 1906 and the tramway was in existence by 1920. The pit closed and the tramway was lifted during the 1930s.

Reference : "Industrial Railway Record" No.17, p193.

LEIGHTON BUZZARD BRICK & TILE CO LTD
LEDBURN ROAD PIT, Leighton Buzzard

KH18
SP 914236

These pits were opened in 1923, served by carts to carry the sand to the main-line railway at Wing Sidings. In 1927 a 2ft gauge line was built with Hudson tip wagons hauled by a steam winch. Later a more powerful petrol-driven winch was installed to move three wagons at a time from the pits, up a 200-yard incline to a lorry loading gantry, with a horse being used to move wagons in the pits. The line fell into disuse and most of the equipment was moved in 1944 to the company's Potsgrove Pits.

MINISTRY OF MUNITIONS, NATIONAL ORDNANCE FACTORY
FUZE WORKS, Chaul End, Luton

HH19
TL 064224

Location uncertain but possibly on the site later (by 1925) occupied by the Ministry of Labour Instructional Factory. A 2ft gauge tramway ran from the factory to a loading shed alongside the GNR Dunstable branch railway. ("Surplus", 15/5/1920).

OAKLEY JUNCTION GRAVEL & SAND CO

Registered as a Limited Company on 13/11/1925 to acquire the business of G.T. Jarvis, F. Symonds, A. Calladine and T.S. Porter trading as a partnership. However the limited company never traded and the business continued as a partnership until a Receiver was appointed on 22/2/1930. The business continued under receivership as Oakley Junction Gravel & Sand Co (unlimited); the Ltd Co was struck off on 15/11/1932 never having traded. Both Lower Farm Gravel Pits and Oakley Junction Gravel Pits were later taken over by S.W. Jarvis & Son.

LOWER PARK FARM GRAVEL PITS, Bromham   GH20
TL 030517

This company had gravel pits, in use by 1931, at the end of Park Farm road in Bromham and in April 1931 the company was granted permission by Bedfordshire County Council to lay a tramway across this road. It is thought that track and equipment from Biddenham Gravel Pit, which closed about 1930, may have been transferred to this site.

OAKLEY JUNCTION GRAVEL PITS   FH21
TL 020520

Gravel extraction here commenced by 1927 on land purchased c1924 by Edward Skevington, owner of the nearby Park Farm. A 2ft 0in gauge tramway which ran from the gravel pits to a tipping dock adjacent to the standard gauge sidings near Oakley Junction. Steel side tipping wagons were used with horse haulage. The tramway was disused by c1942 and had been lifted by c1949. The site was taken over by Bedford Quarries Ltd and was still being worked (without any rail system) in 1961.

H. PAUL
PAGES PARK WORKS, Leighton Buzzard   KH22
SP 925245

A small breeze-block making plant alongside Pages Park was set up about 1950. A short 2ft gauge line was laid to move blocks to nearby drying areas. This was hand-worked with wooden platformed tip wagon frames. The plant did not have planning permission and thus was closed by the council about 1954.

CHARLES PRIOR
EGGINGTON BRICKWORKS   KH23
SP 952250

A brickworks located behind King's Cottages, Eggington was opened in 1846 and was operated by Charles Prior. It is believed to have had a tramway to move clay from the pits to the kilns. The works closed in 1888.

FREDK. RAY LTD
BOX END CLAY PIT, Kempston   GH24
Fredk. Ray until c1934   TL 007482

The quarry, on land adjacent to Vicarage Farm owned by Fredk Ray, is believed to have opened about 1886 for the production of lime but had closed by 1911. However it reopened some time later for the production of clay and was in operation in May 1927 with one man working the pit and producing about ten loads of clay per day. A 2ft 0in gauge tramway about 250 yards in length ran from the quarry to the nearby road. This was operated with side tipping wagons hauled by horses. The clay was probably taken to a brickworks at Box End (TL 010491), in production by 1904 and also operated by Fredk Ray. Some remains of track were still extant in 1961 but by 1967 the pit had been filled in and the land returned to agricultural use.

Fredk Ray also worked several gravel pits in the Bedford area – **Elstow Road, Kempston** (TL 034476) from 1898 to 1905; **Harrowden, Eastcotts,** (TL 065481) 1928 – c1936 **Willington** (TL 108501 and TL 108497) from c1931 until after 1948 and **Heath & Reach** (SP 926286) c1928. Narrow gauge tramways may have been used at some of these sites, but confirmation is lacking. The company was still in existence as hauliers, with an office address in Leighton Buzzard, until after 1986 (closed by 1988).

HARRY SEAR
MANOR FARM SAND PIT, Eggington

KH26
SP 959255

Harry Sear, farmer, worked a small sand pit, opened about 1930 and still in production in 1936, on his land at Manor Farm. The sand was dug by hand and loaded into 2ft gauge iron side-tipping wagons which were pushed (or hauled by a horse) to a loading stage for loading into lorries. The pits are thought to have closed in 1940; in 1969 about 20 yards of track were uncovered along the western lip of the quarry.

SHEFFORD BRICKS LTD
HOO STEAM BRICK & TILE WORKS

FH27
TL 158372

Ward & Son until 1937
Plowman & Son Ltd 1901 - c1934.

The brickworks was started between 1885 - 1887 and operated by Eli Plowman from 1901. In 1893 a standard gauge tramway was constructed which ran from the brickworks across the A600 road and under the ex-Midland Railway Bedford - Hitchin railway line. The tramway connected to sidings, known as Plowmans Sidings, on the west side of this line. The tramway was probably worked by horses and had closed by 1940. A narrow gauge tramway may also have been used from the clay pit to the works. Production ceased c1940 and Plowmans sidings were removed in December 1940.

STANFORD SAND & GRAVEL CO
STANFORD GRAVEL PITS

FH28
TL 159407

T. Ellis, proprietor

Gravel extraction commenced here on land owned by Samuel Whitbread in order to provide material for use on his estate at Southill Park. Mr T. Ellis operated a small gravel pit in Station Road, Tempsford. When the pits were worked out in 1936 he commenced extracting gravel from this site at Stanford in 3/1936. A narrow gauge line with tip wagons, assumed horse or hand worked, ran from the workings to a screening plant. The workings, taken over by Shefford Sand & Gravel Ltd by 1952, closed after 11/1952, by 1960.

THREE COUNTIES MENTAL HOSPITAL
THREE COUNTIES HOSPITAL, near Arlesey

FH29
TL 203352

Three Counties Asylum until c1920.

The Asylum, one of the first set up after the passing of the Lunatic Asylums Act in 1853, was built from 1857 by contractor William Webster to the design of George Fowler Jones, of

Sar Hill, York, and was completed in March 1860. A standard gauge single track tramway 1½ miles in length connected the Asylum to sidings adjacent to the Great Northern Railway at Three Counties station on the London - Peterborough main line. It was built to carry construction materials for building the Asylum but subsequently traffic consisted of coal for the gas works and for the boilers of the engine house which powered the laundry. Steam from the boilers also heated the Asylum. The tramway had its own railway carriage which was replaced c1863 by a horse drawn omnibus. The loaded coal wagons were hauled by horses up the gradient to the Asylum and the empty wagons were returned by gravity. In 1935 a tractor was purchased to replace the horses but this may not have been a success. By 1950 the track was in need of major repairs and by 9/1951 it had been decided to transfer coal deliveries to road transport. The tramway was dismantled by contractors Stutley Bros in 2-3/1953.

VANDYKE SAND LIME BRICK LTD
STONEHENGE BRICKWORKS, Mile Tree Road, Leighton Buzzard.   KH30

Brickworks was opened c10/1935 and was rail served for the delivery of sand by Joseph Arnold's Nine Acre Quarry branch. There was also a 2ft 6in gauge hand-worked line with a traverser which connected the press room, autoclaves and brick stacking yard. The bricks were moved on flat wagons which are believed to have been built by William Richter Ltd of Hatfield, Herts. The works closed on 1/4/1977 and was demolished in 4/1985.

WAR DEPARTMENT
WARREN WOODS, Clophill   FH31
                        TL 083371

During the second world war a narrow gauge railway was laid within the woods to serve an ammunition dump located there. The railway is thought to have been hand worked with flat trucks, however the use of a locomotive cannot be ruled out. [Makers records show that 4wDM RH 211606 was delivered new to 27ASD (Ammunition Supply Dump), Royal Army Ordnance Corps at Shefford (probably by rail to Shefford station yard). This loco may have worked at this location, which is only a few miles from Shefford]. Some remains, including a derelict wagon, were still extant in the 1960s, and a buffer stop made from 2ft gauge Jubilee track remained in 2000.

THOMAS YIRRELL
LEIGHTON ROAD BRICKWORKS, Stanbridge   KH32
                        SP 950244

A brickworks established c1879 and operated by Henry Pettit in 1883, later Thomas Yirrell by 1888 and Thomas Yirrell Jnr by 1931. The brickworks covered about five acres with a clay pit extending to a further two acres and worked to a depth of 30 feet. A narrow gauge tramway, possibly rope worked, connected the pits and works. Production in 1925 was of 500,000 bricks; the works closed c1940.

NORTHAMPTONSHIRE

LOCOMOTIVE WORKED SYSTEMS

AIR MINISTRY
EASTON-ON-THE-HILL AERODROME, near Stamford

L1
TF 025023

Initially opened as a small flat-field airstrip on 24/9/1917, this site was subsequently expanded during which time the following locomotives were despatched here. It is assumed that a temporary railway system was used at the site for these works. The aerodrome was for sale in "Surplus" from 1/4/1920 to 1/7/1920, the description then making no mention of railways. The location was a satellite to the nearby RAF Stamford, which, later renamed RAF Wittering, was greatly expanded over an area including this site, and remains operational in 2001. It is believed that a narrow gauge line used at RAF Stamford ran from an interchange with the GNR Stamford to Wansford line at Southorpe Bridge and across the Great North Road to Stamford Airfield. The line at Easton on the Hill may have initially been separate from this, but "Surplus" for 15/1/1920 advertised for sale at Stamford Aerodrome a loco shed 60ft x 21ft, large enough for six narrow gauge locomotives. This suggests that the railways at the two sites were in fact connected. Although RAF Stamford was in Cambridgeshire, a full loccomotive list is appended here for completeness.

Gauge: 2ft 0in

-	0-4-0WT	OC	HC	1167	1918	New	(a)	(1)
-	0-4-0WT	OC	HC	1168	1918	New	(a)	s/s
-	0-4-2ST	OC	KS	2397	1918	New	(b)	(2)
-	0-6-0T	OC	KS	3118	1918	New	(b)	(3)
FILTON	0-4-0ST	OC	WB	2044	1917		(c)	(4)
-	0-4-0ST	OC	WB	2077	1918	New	(b)	(5)

(a) supplied new to Easton-on-the-Hill, per Robert Hudson & Co Ltd, agents, Leeds.
(b) delivered to RAF Stamford.
(c) at RAF Stamford by 4/1918 (possibly new there).

(1) possibly later with Tata, India – otherwise s/s.
(2) for sale here ("Surplus" 1/10/1920-15/11/1920); then for sale at National Projectile Factory, Lancaster ("Surplus" 15/9/1921-15/10/1921); s/s
(3) to Kerry Tramway, Montgomeryshire [Powys], 3/1920.
(4) purchased by WB, 8/3/1920 and despatched to Stafford; regauged to 600mm and sold to Schill Bros of Manchester, No.8, (for export ?), 5/6/1920.
(5) purchased by WB, 8/3/1920 and despatched directly from RAF Stamford to Cliffe Hill Granite Co, Markfield, Leics (arrived by 20/3/1920).

ATTENBOROUGH & TIMMS
SPRATTON IRONSTONE QUARRIES, Brixworth
Attenborough & Co until 1899

M2
SP 743701

Quarries south of Brixworth village, worked from 1873. A 4ft 0in gauge line served the workings, with locomotives used. The line ran west and then descended a cable worked incline to a tipping stage and sidings on the LNWR Northampton - Market Harborough line south of Spratton station. Quarries closed c1912 and track lifted.

Reference : "The Ironstone Quarries of the Midlands, Part 3, Northampton"; Eric Tonks, Runpast Publishing, 1989

Gauge: 4ft 0in

SPRATTON No.2	0-4-0ST	OC	HC	227	1881	New	(1)
LOUISA	0-4-0ST	OC	HE	298	1882	(a)	(1)

(a)   ex Henry Flint, dealer, Ince, Lancs, by 5/1900;
earlier Winstanley Colliery Co Ltd, Leyland Green Colliery, Lancs.

(1)   to Brixworth Ironstone Quarries, after /1908, by 12/1916.

HAROLD BARLOW
FINEDON IRONSTONE QUARRIES
Q3

Charles Barlow from 1901 until c1920.   Loco shed SP 906733

Extensive quarries existed on the west of the A6 road between Finedon and Burton Latimer. Extraction was done in three separate phases, of which this operator comprised the second, Glendon Iron Co Ltd (which see) being the preceding one. In 1901 a narrow gauge tramway, about a mile in length, was laid from the quarries to Mill Lane (SP 906725), where ore was transhipped to the standard gauge line of, and worked by, Islip Iron Co Ltd and later Francis T. Wright Ltd (which see). East of Mill Lane the narrow gauge used the abandoned standard gauge trackbed and was extended through a tunnel under the A6 road to reach re-opened limestone quarries. The last ironstone working (Glebe Quarry) closed c9/1930 and the narrow gauge system was dismantled. Removal of stockpiled ore continued until 1935, using Francis T. Wright's loco ISLIP No.2. Ironstone workings re-commenced in 1937 by Richard Thomas & Co Ltd (which see), with a different rail access.

Reference :   "The Ironstone Quarries of the Midlands, Part 4, Wellingborough"; Eric Tonks, Runpast Publishing, 1990

Gauge: 1ft 11½in

C.B. No.1	DEVIL	0-4-0ST	OC	WB	1643	1901	New	(1)
C.B. No.2		0-4-0ST	OC	WB	1662	1902	New	(1)
C.B. No.3		0-4-0ST	OC	WB	1802	1906	New	(2)

(1)   to W.J. Redden & Sons Ltd, Wellingborough, for scrap.

(2)   withdrawn in early 1920s and parts used as spares; remains to W.J. Redden & Sons Ltd, Wellingborough, for scrap.

BILLING GRAVEL CO LTD
GREAT BILLING SAND PITS
M4

SP 818614

Company in operation by 1933 (but after 1931) until 1960. Gravel pits in Station Road, Great Billing, commenced production after 1931. Tramway closed and dismantled, but extensive quarrying continued until the 1970s.

Gauge: 2ft 0in

No.4	0-4-0ST	OC	KS	4262	1922	(a)	Scr after 7/1942
No.1	0-4-0ST	OC	KS	2420	1915	(b)	(1)
-	4wDM		RH	193975	1938	(c)	(2)

"Contract Journal" 29/7/1942, advertised - For sale, plant including two KS "Wren" 2ft gauge locos - Billing Gravel Co Ltd..

(a)   ex Aubrey Watson Ltd, contrs, by /1933; earlier Cochran & Sons, Sproughton Road Underpass contract, Ipswich, Suffolk, hire, until after 9/1930.

(b)   ex Aubrey Watson Ltd, Richmond contract, London, after 7/1932, by /1935.

(c) ex RH, Lincoln, 5/9/1939; earlier on hire from RH to Henry Williamson & Co Ltd, Broomfleet Brickworks, Yorkshire (ER).

(1) for sale, 7/1942; to Wraysbury Sand & Gravel Co Ltd, Berks.
(2) to RH, Lincoln, repairs, c15/5/1941 until after 14/7/1941; returned ?;
     to G.F.X. Hartigan Ltd, Newport Pagnell, Bucks, by 17/2/1942.

BLISWORTH & STOWE BRICK & TILE CO LTD
GAYTON BRICKWORKS, near Blisworth   M5
SP 714549

Brickworks, in existence by 1903, adjacent to the LNWR London – Rugby main line. It is thought to have used the same connection to this line as R.B. Sparrow's Gayton Wood Ironstone Quarries (which see). The works passed to **Henry Martin Ltd** (which see), without locomotive working, by 1924 and had closed by 1940.

Gauge: 4ft 8½in

                     -          0-4-0VBT VCG Chaplin (? 1056   1869) (a)   (1)

(a) possibly ex Henry Mobbs, Vulcan Ironworks, Northampton.

(1) derelict on site in mid-1920s; s/s

BOARD OF TRADE, HOME GROWN TIMBER SUPPLY DEPARTMENT
ALTHORP PARK   M6
SP 685655

Locomotive assumed to have been used on a short lived line for timber extraction at this estate about 4 miles north-west of Northampton.

Gauge: 600mm

                     -          0-4-0PM   BgC   608 1918   New   s/s

BRITISH GAS PURIFYING MATERIALS CO LTD
DESBOROUGH WORKS   R7
SP797829

From 1918 this company (registered 12/1916 with head office at Wood Green, North London) set up operations alongside those of Cochrane & Co Ltd (which see). Ironstone was quarried south of Harrington Road, about ½ mile west of Desborough and conveyed by a narrow gauge tramway, initially horse worked, to a processing plant. This used the closed brickworks premises of **Desborough Co-op** and produced oxide of iron for use in gas purification. It was connected by a standard gauge line about ½ mile long to the Midland Railway Kettering- Leicester line west of Desborough & Rothwell station. The standard gauge line, originally worked by Cochrane & Co, was taken over on closure of the latter's operations about 1926. The narrow gauge line was diesel worked from 7/1952 until most of it was replaced by road transport in 1966. The works closed 8/1969 and plant and railways dismantled by late 1970.

Reference : "The Ironstone Quarries of the Midlands, Part 6, Corby"; Eric Tonks,
                    Runpast Publishing, 1992

Gauge: 4ft 8½in

-	4wPM			Desborough		(a)	Scr c/1940
MARWIN	0-4-0ST	OC					
		reb	AB		1902	(b)	(1)
-	0-4-0ST	OC	P	1649	1924	(c)	(2)
-	4wDM		FH	3477	1950	New	(3)

a) built at Desborough (from wagon frame and boat engine), probably c/1927.
b) origin unknown, said to have come from a docks in Scotland, c/1940.
c) ex Fison, Packard & Prentice Ltd, Burwell, Cambs, loan, after 5/10/1943, by 21/12/1943.

1) to Blackwell & Son (Engineers) Ltd, Northampton, for repairs, 10/1943; returned 16/5/1944; to George Cohen, Sons & Co Ltd, for scrap, 6/1951.
2) returned to Fison, Packard & Prentice Ltd, Cambs, /1943-/1946.
3) to Thames Metal Co Ltd, Greenwich, London, 5/1970.

Gauge: 2ft 0in (nominally owned by **Desborough Clay & Pigment Ltd**)

L4	4wDM		HE	2459	1941	(a)	Scr 8/1969
-	4wDM		HE	1975	1939	(b)	Scr 8/1969

a) orig MoS; at MoS Mobile Labour Force, Park Royal, Middlesex, 5/1950; here by 7/1952.
b) orig War Office; ex George Cohen, Sons & Co Ltd, 7/1953.

BRITISH LEYLAND UK LTD

NUFFIELD FOUNDRY, Wellingborough   Q8
British Leyland Motor Corporation Ltd until 3/9/1972   SP 907676
Morris Motors Ltd, Engines Foundry until 1968

In 1947 Morris Motors Ltd took over the foundry of the former Irthlingborough Ironworks which see under **United Steel Companies Ltd**) and utilised standard gauge rail sidings on the north side of, and connecting with, the BR (ex-Midland Railway) Kettering - London line about ½ mile south of Wellingborough (Midland) station. The foundry closed in 9/1981 and the site passed to the K.G. Laurence Group on 31/8/1982 (with one locomotive still awaiting disposal); the plant was dismantled and the site cleared by 1985.

Reference : "The Ironstone Quarries of the Midlands, Part 4, Wellingborough"; Eric Tonks, Runpast Publishing, 1990

Gauge: 4ft 8½in

624/9	0-4-0ST	OC	HC	428	1894	(a)	Scr 12/1954
624/16	0-4-0ST	OC	HL	3423	1920	(a)	(1)
-	4wDM		RH	386875	1955	New	(3)
G C R No.1 QWAG	4wDM		RH	371971	1954	(b)	(2)

a) ex United Steel Companies Ltd, with site, /1947.
b) ex Great Central Railway (1976) Ltd, Loughborough, Leics, on hire, 21/9/1979.

1) scrapped by W.J. Redden & Sons (of Wellingborough), 12/1958.
2) returned to Great Central Railway (1976) Ltd, Loughborough, Leics, 27/11/1979.
3) to Northamptonshire Ironstone Railway Trust Ltd, Northampton, 26/11/1983.

BRITISH PORTLAND CEMENT MANUFACTURERS LTD
IRTHLINGBOROUGH CEMENT WORKS, Irthlingborough   Q9
Premier Portland Cement Co Ltd until 20/10/1911   SP 938699
(subsidiary of **Associated Portland Cement Manufacturers** until 1/11/1911)

Cement works with associated quarries located north of the Wellingborough road at the west
end of Irthlingborough village. A standard gauge line (which ran to the west of the later RTB
line) connected the works with the LNWR Wellingborough - Peterborough line and a narrow
gauge line was used in the quarries. In 1901 a brick and tile works (at SP 938701) utilised a
short tramway from clay pits to the works. Premises acquired from Dunmore Ltd (which see)
on 24/1/1907. The works closed 1928 and was used only as a storage depot until 1950,
then abandoned and track later lifted. Rail traffic ceased and locos stored with the works
closure in 1928.

Gauge: 4ft 8½in

STATTER	0-4-0ST	OC	K	1841	1876	(a)	(3)
FLORENCE	0-4-0ST	OC	MW	593	1877	(b)	(1)
-	4wPM		MR	2029	1920	New	(2)

(a)   ex J.G. Statter, Wissington Light Railway contract, Norfolk, c/1905.
(b)   earlier J.D. Nowell & Sons, Finsbury Park-Wood Green widening (GNR) (1898-1901)
       contract, London, FLORENCE.

(1)   to Thos W. Ward Ltd, Sheffield, after 10/1914, by 5/1916 (possibly per J.Pendered &
       Sons Ltd, of Wellingborough); thence to Stanley Bros Ltd, Stockingford Colliery, Brick &
       Tile Works, Warwicks, possibly c/1919.
(2)   to Atlas Stone Co Ltd, Meldreth, Cambs, c/1926-1928.
(3)   scrapped on site by W.J. Redden & Sons Ltd, Wellingborough, 6/1943

Gauge: 2ft 0in

LITTLE TICH	0-4-0ST	OC	GRE		1897	(a)	(2)
MINERALS	0-4-0ST	OC	WB	1668	1903	(b)	(1)
WREN	0-4-0ST	OC	KS	2467	1916	New	(3)
MARCHCROFT	0-4-0ST	OC	KS	3103	1918	(c)	(3)

(a)   ex Dunmore Ltd, with site, 24/1/1907.
(b)   earlier Wm Hill & Co, contrs (possibly Garston Dock contract, Liverpool) until 6/9/1907
       at least; here by 18/2/1913.
(c)   ex R.H. Neal & Co, dealers, Park Royal, London.

(1)   to Arenig Granite Co Ltd, Cwm Celyn, Merioneth [North Wales], after 2/1913, by
       5/5/1914.
(2)   to Ebbw Vale Steel, Iron & Coal Co Ltd, Finedon Park Pits, loan; returned;
       scrapped on site by W.J. Redden & Sons Ltd, Wellingborough, c/1941.
(3)   scrapped on site by W.J. Redden & Sons Ltd, Wellingborough, after 5/1941 (possibly
       /1943).

BRITISH RAILWAYS BOARD
NORTHAMPTON SLEEPER DEPOT   N10

Permanent Way and Stores Depot at Bridge Street, Northampton, served by standard gauge
sidings which were shunted by a departmental locomotive for some years.

Gauge : 4ft 8½ in

ED4		0-4-0DM	JF 4200043	1949	New	(1)

(1) to Derby Locomotive Works for repair, 15/6/1963; withdrawn 2/1964; to John Cashmore Ltd, Great Bridge, Staffs, for scrap 1/8/1967.

BRITISH STEEL plc
[Note that vesting day for the British Steel Corporation was 28/7/1967 but that operation of the pre-nationalisation businesses was not taken over until 1/7/1968]

CORBY WORKS   T11

British Steel plc, Tubes & Pipes until 10/1999   Steelworks Loco Shed SP 900893
British Steel plc, General Steels until c/1993   Tubeworks Loco Shed SP 909899
British Steel Corporation, Tubes Division until 5/9/1988
British Steel Corporation, Northern & Tubes Group until 23/3/1970
Stewarts & Lloyds Ltd until 1/7/1968
Lloyds Ironstone Co Ltd until 1/10/1932 (controlled by Stewarts & Lloyds Ltd from 1923)
Lloyds Ironstone Co until 20/3/1893
Cardigan Iron Ore Co until /1885

Quarrying for ironstone commenced in the Corby area in 1880 subsequent to the construction of the Midland Railway Kettering - Manton line. The workings expanded to cover a considerable area and an ironworks was established, on the east of the Midland Railway and to the north of the Rockingham road, to process the ore locally. The first two furnaces were built in 1910 and a third in 1917. In 1932 a scheme was approved for the rebuilding of the three existing furnaces and the construction of new fourth blast furnace and steelworks; this greatly expanded plant commenced production in 1934 with the fourth furnace being put into blast in 1937. By 1950 the quarrying activities extended several miles from Corby in a number of directions and were transferred to a separate company, Stewarts & Lloyds (Minerals) Ltd (which see). Iron and steelmaking activities finished in April 1980 in line with British Steel's rationalisation of its production facilities. The final blast furnace to operate, No.4, tapped its last iron on 22/4/1980. Since then much of the site has been redeveloped as an industrial and retail park.

Production of tubes has continued on a smaller part of the old site, using steel brought in by rail from other British Steel plants. A new loco shed was established at SP 900899 (but was demolished by 1997). Some outgoing rail traffic has also remained, with both incoming and outgoing wagons being shunted by main line locomotives. All rail connections to the old steel works area have been removed but a rail connection exists from Southwood Sidings to the Tube Works via the bridge under Weldon Road.

In 10/1999 British Steel plc (of the UK) merged with Koninklijke Hoogovens (of Holland) to form Corus plc, and the limited rail operations remaining after that date are listed under the Corus heading.

Reference : "The Ironstone Quarries of the Midlands, Part 6, Corby"; Eric Tonks,
                    Runpast Publishing, 1992

Gauge: 4ft 8½ in

	VIGILANT	0-4-0ST	OC	HE	287	1883	New	(1)	
	IRONSTONE	0-4-0ST	OC	P	485	1889	New	(2)	
1	(CLYDESDALE 6)	0-4-0ST	OC	AB	762	1895	(a)	Scr c/1964	
2	(CLYDESDALE 7)	0-4-0ST	OC	AB	811	1897	(b)	Scr c3/1966	
3	PEN GREEN	0-6-0ST	IC	HC	607	1903	New	Scr c/1965	
4	(WILFRED)	0-4-0ST	OC	AB	1034	1904	(c)	Scr 2/1958	

5	IRONWORKS No.1	0-6-0ST	OC	AB	1241	1911	New(d)	Scr by 5/1965
6	(IRONWORKS No.2)	0-6-0ST	OC	AB	1242	1911	New	Scr 5/1967
7	(CLYDESDALE 13)	0-6-0ST	OC	AB	1268	1912	(e)	Scr /1968
8	(CLYDESDALE 11)	0-4-0ST	OC	AB	1318	1913	(f)	(5)
8	MARGÔT	0-6-0ST	OC	P	1456	1918	(g)	(11)
9	(IRONWORKS No.3)	0-6-0ST	OC	HC	1383	1919	New	(11)
10	TREASURER	0-6-0ST	OC	HE	1446	1929	(h)	Scr c9/1965
11	(S & L 6)	0-6-0ST	OC	HL	3824	1934	New	Scr c6/1969
12	(S & L 7)	0-6-0ST	OC	HL	3825	1934	New	Scr 4/1972
13	(S & L 8)	0-6-0ST	OC	HL	3826	1934	New	Scr c5/1972
14	(S & L 9)	0-6-0ST	OC	HL	3827	1934	New	(13)
15	(S & L 10)	0-6-0ST	OC	HL	3836	1934	New	Scr c6/1972
16	(S & L 11)	0-6-0ST	OC	HL	3837	1934	New	(17)
17		0-6-0T	IC	HC	1595	1936	(i)	Scr c7/1966
18		0-6-0ST	OC	HL	3896	1936	New	Scr c9/1972
19		0-6-0ST	OC	HL	3889	1936	New	Scr c6/1972
20		0-6-0ST	OC	HL	3897	1936	New	Scr c5/1972
21		0-6-0ST	OC	HL	3931	1937	New	(14)
22		0-6-0ST	OC	RSHN	6944	1940	New	Scr c9/1972
23		0-6-0ST	OC	RSHN	7025	1941	New	Scr c6/1969
ɔ.24		0-6-0ST	IC	HE	2411	1941	New	(15)
25	(JUMBO)	0-6-0ST	OC	YE	327	1882	(j)	Scr /1965
26		0-4-0ST	OC	AB	678	1890	(k)	Scr c7/1966
27		0-4-0ST	OC	St.Rollox		1902	(l)	Scr 6/1956
28	BEAUMONT	0-6-0ST	OC	HL	2469	1900	(m)	(9)
29		0-6-0ST	OC	AB	1457	1915	(n)	Scr 5/1967
30	MURIEL	0-6-0ST	OC	HL	2081	1888	(o)	Scr c6/1955
31	SOMERS TOWN	0-4-0ST	OC	MW	590	1876		
		reb	HC			1892	(p)	Scr /1949
31	(61A until /1950, (PHOENIX)	0-4-0ST	OC	AB	1479	1917	(q)	(7)
32	(62 until /1950)	0-6-0ST	OC	HL	3888	1936	New	Scr 4/1972
33	JANSON	0-4-0ST	OC	HE	569	1893	New	(6)
34	CALETTWR	0-6-0ST	IC	MW	1316	1895	(r)	(6)
35	(RHIWNANT)	0-6-0ST	IC	MW	1317	1895	(r)	(6)
36	ISHAM	0-4-0ST	OC	HE	791	1902	(s)	(8)
37		0-6-0T	IC	HC	745	1905	(t)	(4)
37	ADMIRALTY	0-6-0ST	IC	P	679	1898	(u)	(3)
37	(32 until /1950, (IRONSTONE)	0-4-0ST	OC	HE	344	1885	New(v)	(6)
38	DOLOBRAN	0-6-0ST	IC	MW	1762	1910	New	(6)
39	RHOS	0-6-0ST	OC	HC	1308	1918	New	(6)
40		0-6-0ST	OC	HL	3375	1919	(w)	Scr c6/1969
41	RHYL	0-6-0ST	IC	MW	2009	1921	New	(6)
42	RHONDDA	0-6-0ST	IC	MW	2010	1921	New	(6)
43	(SENTINEL)	4wVBT	VCG	S	7299	1928	(x)	Scr 9/1953
44	CONWAY	0-6-0ST	IC	K	5469	1933	New(y)	(10)
45	COLWYN	0-6-0ST	IC	K	5470	1933	New	(6)
46	CARDIGAN	0-6-0ST	IC	K	5473	1933	New	(6)
47	CARNARVON	0-6-0ST	IC	K	5474	1933	New	(6)
48	CRIGGION	0-6-0ST	IC	K	5476	1936	New	(6)
49	CAERPHILLY	0-6-0ST	IC	K	5477	1936	New	(6)
50	CARMARTHEN	0-6-0ST	IC	K	5478	1936	New	(6)

51		0-6-0ST	IC	RSHN	7003	1940	New	(6)
52		0-6-0ST	IC	RSHN	7004	1940	New	(6)
53		0-6-0ST	IC	RSHN	7030	1941	New	(6)
54		0-6-0ST	IC	RSHN	7031	1941	New	(6)
55		0-6-0ST	IC	RSHN	7032	1941	New	(6)
33	WELLINGBORO' No.3	0-4-0ST	OC	HL	3813	1935	(z)	(12)
27	(7)	0-4-0ST	OC	AB	2135	1941	(aa)	Scr c8/1966
D1	(90 until /1950)	6wDE		CP	101	1945		
				AB	367	1945	New(ac)	Scr 4/1970
D2		0-4-0DH		NBH	27079	1950	New	(30)
D3		0-6-0DH		NBQ	27407	1954	New	(30)
D4		0-6-0DH		NBQ	27408	1954	New	(30)
D5		0-6-0DH		NBQ	27409	1954	New	(30)
6		0-6-0DE		BBT	3094	1955	New	(18)
7		0-6-0DE		BBT	3095	1956	New	(16)
D8		0-6-0DH		NBQ	27871	1960	New	(30)
D9		0-6-0DH		NBQ	28051	1962	New	(30)
D10		0-6-0DH		NBQ	28052	1962	New	(30)
D11		0-6-0DH		EEV	D913	1964	New	(30)
D12		0-6-0DH		EEV	D914	1964	New	(30)
D13		0-6-0DH		EEV	D915	1964	New	(30)
(D14)	D33	0-6-0DH		EEV	D916	1964	New	(35)
D15		0-6-0DH		EEV	D1048	1965	New	(30)
(D16)	BSC 1	0-6-0DH		EEV	D1049	1965	New(ai)	(37)
D17		0-6-0DH		EEV	D1050	1965	New	(30)
D18		0-6-0DH		EEV	D1051	1965	New	(30)
D19		0-6-0DH		EEV	D1052	1965	New	(34)
D20		0-6-0DH		EEV	D1053	1965	New	(30)
D21	(D25 until 2/1971)	0-6-0DH		EEV	3970	1969	New	(30)
D22	(D26 until 2/1971)	0-6-0DH		EEV	3971	1969	New	(30)
D23		0-6-0DH		EEV	5354	1971	New	(30)
D24		0-6-0DH		EEV	5355	1971	New	(30)
D25		0-6-0DH		EEV	5356	1971	New	(30)
D26		0-6-0DH		EEV	5357	1971	New	(30)
D27		0-6-0DH		EEV	5358	1971	New	(36)
(D28)	BSC 3	0-6-0DH		GECT	5365	1972	New	(38)
(D29)	D16	0-6-0DH		GECT	5366	1972	New	(30)
D30		0-6-0DH		GECT	5367	1972	New	(30)
D31		0-6-0DH		GECT	5387	1974	New	(30)
D32		0-6-0DH		GECT	5388	1974	New	(36)
(D33)	(D29) 33	0-6-0DH		GECT	5394	1975	New(aj)	(36)
(D34)	BSC 2	0-6-0DH		GECT	5395	1975	New	(38)
D35		0-6-0DH		GECT	5407	1976	New	(36)
D36		0-6-0DH		GECT	5408	1976	New	(23)
D37	(D21) (GRACE)	0-4-0DH		S	10090	1961	(ab)	(16)
D38	(D22) (ALEX)	0-4-0DH		RR	10205	1965	(ab)	Scr c/1974
D39	(D23) (JOHN)	0-4-0DH		RR	10206	1965	(ab)	(19)
D40	(D24) (ALLAN)	0-4-0DH		RR	10208	1965	(ab)	(20)
45	8311/24 (D9520)	0-6-0DH		Sdn		1964	(ag)	(21)
50	8311/29 (D9551)	0-6-0DH		Sdn		1965	(ad)	(22)
60	8411/23 (D9510)	0-6-0DH		Sdn		1964	(ae)	(30)
64	8311/33 (D9549)	0-6-0DH		Sdn		1965	(af)	(26)
20	8311/20	6wDH		RR	10273	1968	(ah)	(29)

25	8311/25	(D9523)	0-6-0DH	Sdn		1964	(ah)	(24)
(30)	8311/1		0-8-0DH	YE	2894	1962	(ah)	(30)
37	8311/18		6wDH	RR	10275	1969	(ah)	(32)
47	8311/26	(D9533)	0-6-0DH	Sdn		1965	(ah)	(31)
48	8311/27	(D9542)	0-6-0DH	Sdn		1965	(ah)	(30)
49	8311/28	(D9547)	0-6-0DH	Sdn		1965	(ah)	(30)
51	8311/30	(D9539)	0-6-0DH	Sdn		1965	(ah)	(33)
54	8311/34	(D9553)	0-6-0DH	Sdn		1965	(ah)	(33)
55	8311/35	(D9507)	0-6-0DH	Sdn		1964	(ah)	(31)
56	8311/36	(D9516)	0-6-0DH	Sdn		1964	(ah)	(25)
57	8311/37	(D9532)	0-6-0DH	Sdn		1965	(ah)	Scr 2/1982
58	8311/38	(D9554)	0-6-0DH	Sdn		1965	(ah)	(30)
61	8311/20	(D9529)	0-6-0DH	Sdn		1965	(ah)	(21)
62	8411/22	(D9515)	0-6-0DH	Sdn		1964	(ah)	(28)
63	8411/24	(D9512)	0-6-0DH	Sdn		1964	(ah)	Scr 2/1982
66	(D9541)		0-6-0DH	Sdn		1965	(ah)	(30)
67	8411/27	(D9548)	0-6-0DH	Sdn		1965	(ah)	(27)
160	(D9538)		0-6-0DH	Sdn		1965	(ah)	(31)

(a) ex Clydesdale Steel & Tube Works, Mossend, Lanarks, 10/1933.

(b) ex Clydesdale Steel & Tube Works, Mossend, Lanarks, 9/1935.

(c) ex Alfred Hickman Ltd, Bilston Works, Staffs, 10/1933.

(d) to Wellingborough Iron Co Ltd, Wellingborough Iron Works, c/1953 (by 7/1954); returned c12/1954.

(e) ex Clydesdale Steel & Tube Works, Mossend, Lanarks, 8/1934.

(f) ex Clydesdale Steel & Tube Works, Mossend, Lanarks, 8/1932.

(g) ex Islip Ironworks, 12/5/1950.

(h) ex Oxfordshire Ironstone Co Ltd, Banbury, Oxon, 7/1/1933.

(i) actually built in 1926; ex HC, /1936.

(j) ex Abelson & Co (Engineers) Ltd, Sheldon, Birmingham, /1945; earlier Heys Bros & Sanderson Quarries (Facit) Ltd, Facit Quarries, Whitworth, Lancs, until 22/3/1945.

(k) ex Cadzow Coal Co Ltd, Wester Gartshore Colliery, near Kirkintilloch, Dunbartonshire, 4/1945.

(l) ex Bent Colliery Co Ltd, Cadzow Colliery, Hamilton, Lanarks, 4/1945; earlier LMSR 16037 (orig Caledonian Railway 628).

(m) ex North Walbottle Coal Co Ltd, North Walbottle Colliery, Northumberland, 5/1945.

(n) ex George Cohen, Sons & Co Ltd, 11/1939; earlier Shell-Mex & BP Ltd, Trafford Park, Manchester.

(o) ex Thos.W. Ward Ltd, /1940; earlier B.A. Colls.Ltd, Digby Collieries, Giltbrook, Notts.

(p) earlier J.D. Nowell & Sons, Carr House (NER) (1894-1894) contract, Co.Durham and possibly Somers Town (Midland Railway) (1895-1898) contract, London; here by /1932.

(q) ex Phoenix Tube Works, Glasgow, /1934; to Wellingborough Iron Co Ltd, Wellingborough Ironworks, 5/1947 or 6/1947; returned /1948.

(r) ex Thos.W. Ward Ltd, /1912; earlier Birmingham Corporation Waterworks, Elan Valley Railway, Rhayader, Radnorshire.

(s) ex Isham Mines (?), c/1910.

(t) ex North Lincolnshire Iron Co Ltd, Frodingham, Lincs, /1931.

(u) ex George Cohen, Sons & Co Ltd, Stanningley, Yorkshire (WR), c/1933; earlier S. Pearson & Son Ltd, Silent Valley Reservoir contract, Co.Down, Northern Ireland.

(v) to Oxfordshire Ironstone Co Ltd, Banbury, Oxon, 4/1923; returned 7/1/1933.

(w) ex North Lincolnshire Iron Co Ltd, Frodingham, Lincs, /1931.

(x) ex Phoenix Tube Works, Rutherglen, Lanarks, /1930.

(y) to S & L Minerals Ltd, Corby, 11/1949; returned, on loan, 2/1961.

(z)   ex Wellingborough Iron Co Ltd, Wellingborough Ironworks, c8/1963.
(aa) ex Wellingborough Iron Co Ltd, Wellingborough Ironworks, c2/1964.
(ab) ex Oxfordshire Ironstone Co Ltd, Banbury, Oxon, 23/10/1967.
(ac) mechanical parts built for Crompton Parkinson Ltd by AB.
(ad) ex Corby Quarries, 7/1980.
(ae) ex Corby Quarries, 10/7/1980, for conversion to brake tender.
(af) ex Corby Quarries, 9/1980.
(ag) ex Corby Quarries, 10/1980.
(ah) ex Corby Quarries, for storage in old Bessemer Plant, 12/1980.
(ai) frame of D16 (EEV D1049/1965) and engine, cab and casings etc., including plates, of
      D36 (GECT 5408/1975).
(aj) frame of D33 (GECT 5394/1974) and cab, etc., of D29 (GECT 5366/1972).

(1)   to Whitaker Bros, contrs (of Leeds), No.2, by 6/1898; later at their Crofton Jct-Shafton
      Jct (LYR) (1902-1905) contract, Yorkshire (WR).
(2)   to Shelton Iron, Steel & Coal Co Ltd, Shelton Works, Etruria, Staffs, by /1901.
(3)   scrapped and frame converted to a "reacher wagon", for use between a locomotive and
      hot metal ladles, /1938; later scrapped (after 6/1959).
(4)   to HC, WILLIAM, 10/1936 (and used as a hire/loan loco).
(5)   to Clydesdale Steel & Tube Works, Mossend, Lanarks, c/1947 (by 5/1947).
(6)   to Stewarts & Lloyds Minerals Ltd, Corby, 11/1949.
(7)   to Phoenix Tube Works, Rutherglen, Lanarks, /1950 (after 9/1950).
(8)   to Wellingborough Iron Co Ltd, Wellingborough Ironworks, /1952.
(9)   scrapped on site, c/1960 (after 2/7/1960).
(10) returned to S & L Minerals Ltd, Corby, 6/1962.
(11) scrapped on site, c/1965 (after 28/3/1965).
(12) to Bromford Tube Works, Warwicks, 30/1/1967.
(13) to Corby Town Council, West Glebe Park, Corby, for preservation, 9/1971.
(14) to Shackerstone Railway Society Ltd, Leics, 10/1973.
(15) to Corby and District Model Railway Club, West Glebe, Corby, c19/10/1973.
(16) scrapped on site, 19/2/1974
(17) to Peterborough Locomotive Society, Peterborough, Cambs, 6/1974.
(18) scrapped on site, c/1974 (after 8/11/1974).
(19) to TH, for resale, 4/7/1977.
(20) to TH, for resale, 15/7/1977.
(21) to North Yorkshire Moors Preservation Society, Grosmont, North Yorkshire, 16/3/1981.
(22) to West Somerset Railway Co, Minehead, Somerset, 5/6/1981.
(23) Engine, cab and casings, etc., including plates, to BSC 1, c7/1981; frames scrapped
      c10/1981 (by 9/10/1981).
(24) to Great Central Railway (1976) Ltd, Loughborough, Leics, 16/10/1981.
(25) to Great Central Railway (1976) Ltd, Loughborough, Leics, 19/10/1981.
(26) to HE, 14/11/1981, for conversion to 5ft 6in gauge and resale for use in Spain.
(27) to HE, 19/11/1981, for conversion to 5ft 6in gauge and resale for use in Spain.
(28) to HE, 12/1981, for conversion to 5ft 6in gauge and resale for use in Spain.
(29) to TH, 20/7/1982; resold to Bardon Hill Quarries (Ellis & Everard) Ltd, Coalville, Leics,
      8/9/1982.
(30) scrapped on site by Shanks & McEwan (England) Ltd, 8/1982.
(31) scrapped on site by Shanks & McEwan (England) Ltd, 9/1982.
(32) to TH, 4/8/1982.
(33) to Gloucestershire & Warwickshire Railway Society, Toddington, Gloucs, 23/2/1983.
(34) scrapped on site, /1984 (by 10/10/1984).
(35) scrapped on site by Shanks & McEwan (England) Ltd, c6/1983.
(36) scrapped on site by Hudson's of Dudley, Brierley Hill, West Midlands, 8-11/6/1992.

(37) to Rutland Railway Museum, Leics, 27/6/1992.
(38) to Rutland Recycling Ltd, 3/1995, and thence to Corus, with site, 10/1999.

Gauge : 4ft 8½in (Tube Works locomotives)

(No.1)		4wD(f.4wBE)	GB	1371	1934	New	(1)
(No.2)		4wD(f.4wBE)	GB	1372	1934	New	(2)

(1) derelict 7/1960; s/s c/1968.
(2) derelict 3/1959; s/s c/1968.

Gauge : 4ft 8½in (Coke Ovens locomotives)

1	A	0-4-0WE	HL		3820	1934	New	(1)
2		0-4-0WE	RSHN		7005	1940	New	(1)
-		4wWE	WSO		4622	1947	New	Scr c/1975
-		0-4-0DH	AB		476	1961	New	(1)
No.3		4wWE	GB	420365/1	1974	New	(2)
No.4		4wWE	GB	420365/2	1974	New	(2)

(1) Scrapped on site, after 3/1980, by 5/1981.
(2) Scrapped on site, c8/1981, by 19/9/1981.

BRITISH STEEL CORPORATION, TUBES DIVISION
British Steel Corporation, Northern & Tubes Group until 23/3/1970
CORBY QUARRIES   T12
Stewarts & Lloyds Minerals Ltd until 1/7/1968;   Gretton Brook Loco Shed SP 900913
Stewarts & Lloyds Ltd until 22/11/1949   Pen Green Workshops SP 897902

In 11/1949 the quarrying operations of Stewarts & Lloyds Ltd were divided from the iron and steel manufacturing plants and were administered separately. From 8/1954 the locomotives for quarry traffic at Corby were transferred to the new locomotive shed at Pen Green. Quarries worked from this centre extended for many miles from Corby. Production of domestic ore was run down during the 1970s in favour of imported ore and production ceased at the Corby Quarries in 1/1980. Locomotive usage ceased at Gretton Brook shed 8/1981; and at Pen Green Workshops 11/1982. Gretton Brook loco shed and Pen Green workshops remain in private use in 2000; all other plant has subsequently been dismantled and the site cleared.

Reference : "The Ironstone Quarries of the Midlands, Part 6, Corby"; Eric Tonks,
Runpast Publishing, 1992

Gauge: 4ft 8½in

33	JANSON	0-4-0ST	OC	HE	569	1893	(a)	Scr 9/1953
34	CALETTWR	0-6-0ST	IC	MW	1316	1895	(b)	Scr 8/1966
35		0-6-0ST	IC	MW	1317	1895	(c)	(13)
37		0-4-0ST	OC	HE	344	1885	(a)	(1)
38	DOLOBRAN	0-6-0ST	IC	MW	1762	1910	(a)	(21)
39	RHOS	0-6-0ST	OC	HC	1308	1918	(d)	(9)
41	RHYL	0-6-0ST	IC	MW	2009	1921	(a)	(21)
42	RHONDDA	0-6-0ST	IC	MW	2010	1921	(g)	(5)
44	CONWAY	0-6-0ST	IC	K	5469	1933	(h)	(18)
45	COLWYN	0-6-0ST	IC	K	5470	1933	(a)	(10)
46	CARDIGAN	0-6-0ST	IC	K	5473	1933	(a)	(15)

No.	Fleet No.	Name/No.	Type		Builder	Works No.	Year	Origin	Ref
47	CARNARVON		0-6-0ST	IC	K	5474	1933	(a)	(12)
48	CRIGGION		0-6-0ST	IC	K	5476	1936	(a)	(14)
49	CAERPHILLY		0-6-0ST	IC	K	5477	1936	(a)	(4)
50	CARMARTHEN		0-6-0ST	IC	K	5478	1936	(f)	(3)
51			0-6-0ST	IC	RSHN	7003	1940	(a)	(2)
52			0-6-0ST	IC	RSHN	7004	1940	(a)	(16)
53			0-6-0ST	IC	RSHN	7030	1941	(a)	(14)
54			0-6-0ST	IC	RSHN	7031	1941	(a)	(18)
55			0-6-0ST	IC	RSHN	7032	1941	(e)	(7)
56			0-6-0ST	IC	RSHN	7667	1950	New	(22)
57			0-6-0ST	IC	RSHN	7668	1950	New	(11)
58			0-6-0ST	IC	RSHN	7669	1950	New	(14)
59			0-6-0ST	IC	RSHN	7670	1950	New	(14)
60			0-6-0ST	IC	RSHN	7671	1950	New	(6)
61			0-6-0ST	IC	RSHN	7672	1950	New	(14)
62			0-6-0ST	IC	RSHN	7673	1950	New	(11)
63			0-6-0ST	IC	RSHN	7761	1954	New	(11)
64			0-6-0ST	IC	RSHN	8050	1958	New	(14)
No.3	(No.80)		0-6-0ST	IC	HE	2417	1941	(i)	(8)
30	8311/1	(1)	0-8-0DH		YE	2894	1962	New	(30)
32		(2)	6wDH		RR	10265	1967	New(j)	(31)
37	8311/18	(18)	6wDH		RR	10275	1969	New(s)	(32)
38	8311/19	(19)	6wDH		RR	10274	1968	New	(28)
20	8311/20	(25)	6wDH		RR	10273	1968	New(ab)	(30)
21			0-6-0DH		RR	10270	1967	(k)	(17)
22			0-6-0DH		RR	10271	1967	(l)	(20)
23			0-6-0DH		RR	10272	1967	(m)	(19)
45 (24)	8311/24	(D9520)	0-6-0DH		Sdn		1964	(t)	(29)
47 (26)	8311/26	(D9533)	0-6-0DH		Sdn		1965	(q)	(30)
48 (27)	8311/27	(D9542)	0-6-0DH		Sdn		1965	(q)	(30)
49 (28)	8311/28	(D9547)	0-6-0DH		Sdn		1965	(q)	(30)
50 (29)	8311/29	(D9551)	0-6-0DH		Sdn		1965	(q)	(24)
51 (30)	8311/30	(D9539)	0-6-0DH		Sdn		1965	(n)	(30)
(31)	8311/31	(D9544)	0-6-0DH		Sdn		1965	(o)	(27)
52 (32)	8311/32	(D9537)	0-6-0DH		Sdn		1965	(p)	(33)
64 (33)	8311/33	(D9549)	0-6-0DH		Sdn		1965	(w)	(26)
54 (34)	8311/34	(D9553)	0-6-0DH		Sdn		1965	(p)	(30)
55 (35)	8311/35	(D9507)	0-6-0DH		Sdn		1964	(p)	(30)
56 (36)	8311/36	(D9516)	0-6-0DH		Sdn		1964	(p)	(30)
57 (37)	8311/37	(D9532)	0-6-0DH		Sdn		1965	(p)	(30)
58 (38)	8311/38	(D9554)	0-6-0DH		Sdn		1965	(p)	(30)
59 (21)	8411/21	(D9552)	0-6-0DH		Sdn		1965	(u)	(27)
60 (23)	8411/23	(D9510)	0-6-0DH		Sdn		1964	(u)	(25)
61 (20)	8411/20	(D9529)	0-6-0DH		Sdn		1965	(v)	(30)
62 (22)	8411/22	(D9515)	0-6-0DH		Sdn		1964	(v)	(30)
63	8411/24	(D9512)	0-6-0DH		Sdn		1964	(v)	(30)
65 (25)	8411/25	(D9503)	0-6-0DH		Sdn		1964	(y)	(27)
66 (26)	8411/26	(D9541)	0-6-0DH		Sdn		1965	(z)	(30)
67 (27)	8411/27	(D9548)	0-6-0DH		Sdn		1965	(z)	(30)
33	8311/03	JEAN	0-4-0DH		RR	10204	1965	(x)	(23)
160		(D9538)	0-6-0DH		Sdn		1965	(aa)	(30)
25	8311/25	(D9523)	0-6-0DH		Sdn		1964	(ac)	(30)

(a) ex S & L, Corby, 11/1949.

(b) ex S & L, Corby, 11/1949; to Glendon East Quarries, c/1950 (by 25/3/1951); returned 11/1951.

(c) ex S & L, Corby, 11/1949; to Glendon North Quarries, 8/1956; returned from Glendon East Quarries, c9/1956.

(d) ex S & L, Corby, 11/1949; to Glendon East Quarries, 2/1952; returned 27/1/1957.

(e) ex S & L, Corby, 11/1949; to Glendon East Quarries, 19/11/1956; returned 27/1/1957.

(f) ex S & L, Corby, 11/1949; to Glendon East Quarries, 27/1/1957; returned 5/1/1960.

(g) ex S & L, Corby, 11/1949; to Glendon East Quarries, 6/1959; returned 24/11/1960; to Glendon East Quarries, 12/1961; returned c/1962 (by 2/1962).

(h) ex S & L, Corby, 11/1949; to S & L, Corby Works, on loan, 2/1961; returned 6/1962.

(i) ex Glendon East Quarries, 4/1967.

(j) ex RR, 25/10/1967 after trials on Severn Valley Railway, Shropshire, 12/10/1967.

(k) ex RR, on extended loan (pending delivery of new 'Steelman' locomotive), 26/9/1967.

(l) ex RR, on extended loan (pending delivery of new 'Steelman' locomotive), 12/10/1967.

(m) ex RR, on extended loan (pending delivery of new 'Steelman' locomotive), 28/11/1967.

(n) ex BR, Hull (Dairycoates), 10/1968.

(o) ex BR, Hull (Dairycoates), 2/11/1968.

(p) ex BR, Hull (Dairycoates), 11/1968.

(q) ex BR, Hull (Dairycoates), 12/1968.

(s) New, 20/10/1969, direct from demonstration to British Steel Corporation, Stocksbridge Works, Yorkshire (WR).

(t) ex Glendon East Quarries, 1/1970.

(u) ex Buckminster Quarries, Lincs, 6/1972.

(v) ex Buckminster Quarries, Lincs, 6/9/1972.

(w) ex BR, Hull (Dairycoates), 11/1968; to Glendon East Quarries, 8/10/1973; ex Glendon East Quarries, 26/6/1974.

(x) ex Storefield Quarries, 25/6/1973.

(y) ex Harlaxton Quarries, Leics, 29/7/1974.

(z) ex Harlaxton Quarries, Leics, 4/8/1974.

(aa) ex Ebbw Vale Works, Gwent, 4/1976.

(ab) to Glendon East Quarries, 26/6/1974; returned 28/5/1980.

(ac) ex Glendon East Quarries, 28/5/1980.

(1) to Eaton Quarries, Leics, 1/1951.

(2) to Market Overton Quarries, Rutland, 8/1951.

(3) to Glendon East Quarries, 24/11/1960.

(4) to Glendon East Quarries, 2/1962 (by 18/2/1962).

(5) to Market Overton Quarries, Rutland, 2/8/1962.

(6) to Harlaxton Quarries, Lincs, 21/8/1962.

(7) to Buckminster Quarries, Lincs, 26/7/1963.

(8) to Glendon East Quarries, 11/1967.

(9) to A.B. Mason, Burnham Market, Norfolk, for preservation, c7/1968.

(10) to Storefield Quarries, c18/2/1969.

(11) to Keighley & Worth Valley Railway Preservation Society, Haworth, Yorkshire.(WR), 4/1969.

(12) to Severn Valley Railway, Bridgnorth, Salop, 11/10/1969.

(13) to Foxfield Light Railway, Dilhorne, Staffs, 25/10/1969.

(14) scrapped on site by George Cohen, Sons & Co Ltd, 10/1969.

(15) scrapped on site by George Cohen, Sons & Co Ltd, 11/1969.

(16) to George Cohen, Sons & Co Ltd, Cransley, for scrap, 17/12/1969.

(17) to TH, 14/9/1969.

(18) to South Cambs.Rural & Industrial Steam Museum, Heydon, Royston, Cambs, 6/1969.
(19) to London Transport Board, Neasden, London, 25/5/1971.
(20) to London Transport Board, Neasden, London, 2/6/1971
(21) to Tenterden Railway Co Ltd, Rolvenden, Kent, 19/8/1972.
(22) to Tenterden Railway Co Ltd, Rolvenden, Kent, 9/1972.
(23) to TH, 5/11/1974; resold to Midland Yorkshire Tar Distillers Ltd, Kilnhurst, Yorkshire.(WR), 13/1/1975.
(24) to Corby Works, 7/1980.
(25) to Corby Works, for conversion to brake tender to work with loco 50, 7/1980 (by 10/7/1980) (project later abandoned).
(26) to Corby Works, 9/1980.
(27) scrapped on site, 9/1980 (by 24/9/1980)
(28) to Tarmac Roadstone Holdings Ltd, Wirksworth, Derbyshire, 7/10/1980.
(29) to Corby Works, 10/1980.
(30) to old Bessemer Plant, Corby Works, for storage, 12/1980.
(31) to Pen Green Workshops, 8/1982; to open store on works site, 11/1982; then to TH, 23/3/1983.
(32) to old Bessemer Plant, Corby Works, for storage, c1/1981; then to TH 4/8/1982.
(33) to Pen Green Workshops, by 15/8/1981, where used for shunting wagons for scrapping; to Gloucestershire & Warwickshire Railway Society, Toddington, Gloucs, 23/11/1982.

Demonstration locomotives : Prior to the introduction of permanent diesel traction, several locomotives were operated on demonstration or hire. Known details are given here.

-	0-6-0DH	NBQ	(? 27717 1957)	(da)	(101)
-	0-6-0DE	YE	2595 1956	(db)	(102)
-	0-8-0DH	YE	2875 1961	(dc)	(103)
-	0-6-0DH	S	10055 1961	(dd)	(104)
-	0-6-0DE	RH	448157 1963	(de)	(105)
-	0-6-0DH	TH	124C 1963	(df)	(106)
-	0-6-0DH	RH	468048 1963	(dg)	(107)
-	0-6-0DH	EEV	D911 1964	(dh)	(108)
-	0-6-0DH	RR	10212 1966	(di)	(109)

(da) on trial in 1950s; identity unconfirmed.
(db) ex NCB, Walkden Yard, Lancs, 2/8/1956, as part of YE demonstration programme.
(dc) ex BR, St Philips Marsh, Bristol, 15/8/1961, as part of YE demonstration programme.
(dd) ex RR, on trial, by 10/10/1961.
(de) ex RH, Lincoln, for a stated hire period of a minimum of six months, 21/5/1964.
(df) ex TH, on demonstration, 19-20/3/1963.
(dg) ex RH, Lincoln, for a stated hire period of a minimum of six months, 27/4/1964.
(dh) ex EEV, on trial, c11/1964.
(di) ex RR, on trial, between 17/10/1966 and 9/1/1967.

(101) returned to NB.
(102) returned to YE, Sheffield, off demonstration, 13/8/1956; then sold to Appleby-Frodingham Steel Co, Scunthorpe, Lincs, 30/8/1956.
(103) returned to YE, Sheffield, off demonstration, 25/8/1961.
(104) returned to RR; then to WD, Bicester, Oxon on demonstration, by 22/11/1961.
(105) returned to RH, Lincoln, after 9/12/1964; then to NCB Clipstone Colliery, Notts, on hire, 1/3/1963.
(106) returned to TH and then to English Steel Corporation Ltd, Tinsley Park Works, Sheffield, 30/3/1963

(107) returned to RH, Lincoln, 9/1965 (by 16/9/1965); then sold to Stephenson Clarke Ltd, Gwaun-cae-Gurwen Disposal Point, West Glamorgan, 15/7/1966.
(108) returned to EE and moved under its own power via Nottingham Victoria to Harlaxton Quarries, Leics, for trials, 11/1964
(109) returned to RR; then to RTB, Llanwern Works, Gwent, on hire, 2/3/1967

CRANFORD IRONSTONE QUARRIES   R13

Stewarts & Lloyds Minerals Ltd until 1/7/1968   West SP 917768
Staveley Minerals Ltd until 1/1/1966   East (Metre Gauge Loco Shed) SP 934770
  (subsidiary of **Staveley Iron & Chemical Co Ltd**)
Cranford Ironstone Co Ltd until 7/3/1961
  (subsidiary of **Staveley Iron & Chemical Co Ltd** by 1940)
Cranford Ironstone Co until 10/4/1920

Quarries on both north and south sides of the Kettering - Thrapston road and Midland Railway line, west of Cranford village, were opened from 1875. They were served by a narrow gauge tramway, horse worked at first, to a tipping point to standard gauge sidings with the Midland Rly. In 1897 these workings were closed (although later reopened by the Clay Cross Co, without locomotives) and the railway equipment moved to new workings to the east. This new east site was again both north and south of the Midland Railway line but this time east of Cranford village. The east quarries were initially served by a metre gauge tramway but in 1923 this was closed and replaced by standard gauge equipment. A 2ft gauge line was in use from 1949 to 1958 to convey ganister (silica sand) from the workings to a calcining plant. Quarries closed 8/1969 and track lifted by 1970.

Reference : "The Ironstone Quarries of the Midlands, Part 5, Kettering"; Eric Tonks, Runpast Publishing, 1991

Gauge: Metre

WILLIAM	0-4-0ST	OC	Oliver #	101	1889	New	(1)
THE BARONET	0-4-0ST	OC	Oliver #	102	1889	New	(2)
HANDYMAN	0-4-0ST	OC	HC	573	1900	(a)	(3)

\# Although built by Oliver, these locos were delivered with works plates of the successor company 'Markham'.

(a) ex Burton Ironstone Co Ltd, Burton Latimer Quarries, /1919; altered from 3ft 0in to metre gauge; stored for most of its time here; to Loddington Ironstone Co Ltd, Loddington Quarries, c/1935 and returned.

(1) to Clay Cross Co Ltd, Crich, Derbys, /1924.
(2) to Loddington Ironstone Co Ltd, Loddington Quarries, c/1923.
(3) to Blackwell & Son (Engineers) Ltd, Northampton, for regauging to 3ft 0in, /1936; then to Staveley Coal & Iron Co Ltd, Lamport Quarries, /1936.

Gauge: 4ft 8½in

8310/9 (CRANFORD)	0-6-0ST	OC	AE	1918	1923	New		Scr 3/1967
STAMFORD	0-6-0ST	OC	AE	1972	1927	(a)		(1)
SIR BERKELEY	0-6-0ST	IC	MW	1210	1890			
		reb	MW		1909	(b)		(2)
8310/11 CRANFORD No.2	0-6-0ST	OC	WB	2668	1942	New (c)		(3)
8310/12 24	0-6-0ST	OC	HC	1579	1926	(d)		Scr 5/1968
8310/10 CRANFORD	0-6-0ST	OC	AE	1919	1924	(e)		(5)
LODDINGTON No.2	0-6-0ST	OC	WB	2655	1942	(f)		(4)

(a) ex Pilton Ironstone Co, Pilton Quarries, Rutland, on loan.
(b) ex Logan & Hemingway, Westbury (GWR) contract, Wiltshire, after 7/1934, by 6/1937;
     to Pilton Ironstone Co, Pilton Quarries, Rutland, 3/1943; returned, 17/4/1944.
(c) to Pilton Ironstone Co, Pilton Quarries, Rutland, c/1946(by 21/8/1946); returned /1946.
(d) ex Appleby Frodingham Steel Co Ltd, Scunthorpe, Lincs, 6/11/1957.
(e) ex Byfield Ironstone Co Ltd, Byfield Quarries, 10/9/1965.
(f) ex Loddington Quarries, 28/4/1966.

(1) returned to Pilton Ironstone Co, Pilton Quarries, Rutland.
(2) to Byfield Ironstone Co Ltd, Byfield Quarries, 5/1959.
(3) to T.L. Barber, Overstone Park, Northampton, for preservation, 28/1/1970.
(4) to Hunt & Co (Hinckley) Ltd, London Road, Hinckley, Leics, for preservation, 1/1970.
(5) to Foxfield Light Railway Society, Dilhorne, Staffs, 22/1/1971.

Gauge: 2ft 0in

PIXIE	0-4-0ST	OC	WB	2090	1919	(a)	(1)

(a) ex Pitsford Ironstone Co, /1949.

(1) to Rev.E.R. Boston, Cadeby Rectory, Leics, 18/5/1962.

GLENDON EAST IRONSTONE QUARRIES   R14
Stewarts & Lloyds Minerals Ltd until 1/7/1968   SP 856824
Stanton Ironworks Co Ltd until 1/1/1950
James Pain Ltd until 1928
James Pain until 9/1905
Glendon Iron Co Ltd until 1892
Glendon Iron Co until 23/6/1886

Quarries on the east of the Midland Railway Kettering - Corby railway, north of Glendon
South Junction. Production commenced about 1884 by the Glendon Iron Co (of the Finedon
Ironworks – which see) but the locomotive worked standard gauge system dates from about
1900 It was presumably originally horse worked; no locomotives are known until after James
Pain took over. Quarries closed 12/1979; a proposal to use the site for domestic waste
tipping was not executed and the track was finally lifted in summer 1983.

Reference : "The Ironstone Quarries of the Midlands, Part 6, Corby"; Eric Tonks,
                      Runpast Publishing, 1992

Gauge: 4ft 8½in

	GORDON	0-4-0ST	OC	P		819	1900	New	(1)
	DOUGLAS	0-4-0ST	OC	P		820	1900	New	(2)
	JAMES	0-4-0ST	OC	P		996	1904	New	(4)
	BUCCLEUCH	0-6-0ST	OC	P		1232	1910	New(f)	(6)
	ROTHWELL	0-4-0ST	OC	P		1258	1912	(a)	(3)
	CURZON	0-6-0ST	IC	HE		422	1887	(b)	(7)
	ADDERLEY	0-6-0ST	OC	AE		1694	1915	(c)	(5)
No.81	HOLWELL No.14	0-6-0ST	OC	HL		3138	1915	(d)	(14)
	DARLINGTON	0-6-0ST	IC	HE		421	1887		
		reb	Wake				1915	(e)	
		reb	HIW				1938		Scr c/1954
	GLENDON	0-4-0ST	OC	HC		1285	1917	(g)	(10)
	SIR JOSEPH	0-6-0ST	OC	HC		1196	1916	(h)	(8)

No.80	No.3 (GEDDINGTON until /1951;								
	No.80 from 1/1957)	0-6-0ST	IC	HE	2417	1941	New (q)	(18)
34	CALETTWR	0-6-0ST	IC	MW	1316	1895	(i)	(9)
39	RHOS	0-6-0ST	OC	HC	1308	1918	(j)	(12)
35		0-6-0ST	IC	MW	1317	1895	(k)	(11)
55		0-6-0ST	IC	RSHN	7032	1941	(l)	(12)
No.2 50	CARMARTHEN	0-6-0ST	IC	K	5478	1936	(m)	(15)
No.84	SWORDFISH	0-6-0ST	OC	AB	2138	1941	(n)	(14)
42	RHONDDA	0-6-0ST	IC	MW	2010	1921	(o)	(13)
No.39 49	CAERPHILLY	0-6-0ST	IC	K	5477	1936	(p)	(16)
	JEAN	0-4-0DH		RR	10204	1965	(r)	(17)
24	D9520	0-6-0DH		Sdn		1964	(s)	(19)
25	D9523 8311/25	0-6-0DH		Sdn		1964	(s)	(22)
4	MAUD	0-4-0DH		S	10142	1962	(t)	(20)
33	(D9549)	0-6-0DH		Sdn		1965	(u)	(21)
20	8311/20	6wDH		RR	10273	1968	(v)	(22)

(a)   ex Glendon North Quarries.
(b)   ex P. Baker, dealer, Cardiff, after 1/1907, by 2/1910;
      earlier Swan Lane Brick & Coal Co Ltd, Hindley Green, Lancs.
(c)   ex Market Overton Quarries, Rutland, 7/1928.
(d)   ex Buckminster Quarries, Lincs, 6/1928; to HIW, 2/1932; ex HIW, 10/1932; to Glendon North Quarries, /1955; returned here c3/1956.
(e)   ex SIW, after repairs, 7/1929 (earlier Market Overton Quarries, Rutland); to HIW, for repairs, 7/1937; then to Eaton Quarries, Leics; ex Eaton Quarries, 9/1938.
(f)   to Market Overton Quarries, Rutland, 1/1930; returned 11/1931;
(g)   ex Market Overton Quarries, 10/1936.
(h)   ex Cudworth & Johnson Ltd, dealers, Wrexham, Denbighs [North Wales], 10/1940; earlier Stancliffe Estates Co Ltd, Darley Dale, Derbys.
(i)   ex Corby Quarries, c/1950 (by 25/3/1951).
(j)   ex Corby Quarries, 2/1952.
(k)   ex Glendon North Quarries, 8/1956.
(l)   ex Corby Quarries, 19/11/1956.
(m)   ex Corby Quarries, 27/1/1957; returned 5/1/1960; ex Corby Quarries, 24/11/1960; to Wellingborough Ironworks site, 1/1964; returned 5/10/1964.
(n)   ex Glendon North Quarries, 18/4/1957; to Glendon North Quarries, 11/1957; ex Glendon North Quarries, 12/1961.
(o)   ex Corby Quarries, 6/1959; returned to Corby Quarries, 24/11/1960; to here again 12/1961.
(p)   ex Corby Quarries, 2/1962 (by 18/2/1962).
(q)   to Corby Quarries, 4/1967; returned 11/1967.
(r)   ex Oxfordshire Ironstone Co Ltd, Banbury, Oxon, 16/5/1968.
(s)   ex BR, Hull, 16/12/1968.
(t)   ex Irchester Quarries, 12/1/1970; to Storefield Quarries, 9/1970; returned 10/1970.
(u)   ex Corby Quarries, 8/10/1973.
(v)   ex Corby Quarries, 26/6/1974.

(1)   to Market Overton Quarries, Rutland, /1912.
(2)   later WD, Royal Engineers, Bramley, Hampshire, after 5/1915, by 28/2/1921.
(3)   to Irchester Quarries, c/1913.
(4)   to Northamptonshire Ironstone Co, Byfield Quarries, c/1915 (by 8/1915).
(5)   to Buckminster Quarries, Lincs, 12/1928.
(6)   to Harlaxton Quarries, Lincs, 10/1946.
(7)   to Market Overton Quarries, Rutland, 11/1931.

(8) to Harlaxton Quarries, Lincs, 9/1943.
(9) to Corby Quarries, 11/1951.
(10) to Shanks & McEwan Ltd, Corby, 12/1953.
(11) to Corby Quarries, c9/1956.
(12) to Corby Quarries, 27/1/1957.
(13) to Corby Quarries, c/1962 (by 2/1962).
(14) to Goodman Bros, scrap dealers, New Bradwell, Bucks, 17/8/1962.
(15) to Irchester Quarries, 13/8/1968.
(16) to Storefield Quarries, 6/8/1968.
(17) to Storefield Quarries, 21/1/1969.
(18) to George Cohen, Sons & Co Ltd, Cransley, for scrap, 10/1969.
(19) to Corby Quarries, 1/1970.
(20) to Panteg Works, Gwent, 12/10/1973.
(21) returned to Corby Quarries, 26/6/1974.
(22) to Corby Quarries, 28/5/1980.

IRCHESTER IRONSTONE QUARRIES   Q15

South Durham Steel & Iron Co Ltd until 1/7/1968   Loco shed SP 905661
Irchester Ironstone Co Ltd until 3/10/1953   Workshops SP 909660
  (subsidiary of **Cargo Fleet Iron Co Ltd** by 1928)
James Pain Ltd until 8/6/1922
  for earlier history see **Thos. Butlin & Co Ltd**

The Thomas Butlin operation of these quarries ceased in 1903 but the workings were re-opened by James Pain Ltd from 1912. Workings extended in total for some two square miles to the east of the London Road (A509) south of the ex-LNWR Northampton - Peterborough railway. Lengthy standard gauge lines served the quarries and connected to the main lines at the north-east end of Wellingborough (London Rd) station. Quarries closed 27/6/1969 and most of the track had been lifted by 3/1970.

Reference : "The Ironstone Quarries of the Midlands, Part 4, Wellingborough"; Eric Tonks, Runpast Publishing, 1990

Gauge: 4ft 8½in

	DAISY	0-4-0ST	OC	HC	535	1900	(a)	(1)
	ROTHWELL	0-4-0ST	OC	P	1258	1912	(b)	(8)
11		0-4-0ST	OC	AB	1047	1905		
		reb	Irchester			1949	(c)	(5)
	COCKSPUR	0-4-0ST	OC	P	1289	1912	(d)	(4)
	ANCOATS	4wVBT	HCG	S	5666	1924		
	Reb of 0-4-0ST	OC	MW	1091		1888	(e)	(2)
No.1		0-4-0ST	OC	HL	2412	1899	(f)	(6)
	PROGRESS	0-6-0ST	OC	P	1402	1915	(g)	(8)
15		0-4-0ST	OC	HL	3892	1936	New	(8)
16		0-4-0ST	OC	CF	1195	1900	(h)	Scr after 2/1964
No.17		0-4-0ST	OC	HL	3946	1937	New	(10)
19		0-4-0ST	OC	AB	2101	1940	New	(3)
	ENTERPRISE	0-4-0ST	OC	WB	1739	1907	(i)	(7)
No.9		0-6-0ST	OC	AE	1787	1917	(j)	(11)
No.14		0-4-0ST	OC	MW	1795	1912		
		reb	Ridley Shaw			1936	(k)	(12)
	MAJOR	0-4-0ST	OC	AB	1363	1914	(l)	(8)
No.8	1918	0-4-0ST	OC	AB	1609	1918	(m)	(8)
No.6		0-6-0ST	OC	AB	1497	1916	(n)	(13)

	HOLWELL No.30	0-4-0ST	OC	HL	3780	1932	(o)	(14)
9		0-4-0ST	OC	AB	2323	1952	(p)	(9)
7		0-4-0ST	OC	AB	2324	1952	(q)	(15)
No.2	50 CARMARTHEN	0-6-0ST	IC	K	5478	1936	(r)	(10)
	MAUD	0-4-0DH		S	10142	1962	(s)	(16)

(a)   ex Corby Brickworks Pits, /1912.

(b)   ex Glendon East Quarries, c/1913.

(c)   ex Cargo Fleet Iron Co Ltd, Cargo Fleet Ironworks, South Bank, Yorkshire (NR), /1922; to Cochrane & Co Ltd, Desborough Quarries, c/1925; returned c/1927;

(d)   ex Morris & Shaw Ltd, Birch Coppice Coll., Warwicks, after 2/1926, by 11/1929.

(e)   ex Blackwell & Sons (Engineers) Ltd, Northampton, /1924 (possibly on trial)

(f)   ex Cargo Fleet Iron Co Ltd, Woodland Colliery, Co Durham, c/1926; to Storefield Quarries, 4/1942; ex Storefield Quarries, /1947 (after 15/6/1947).

(g)   ex Blackwell & Son (Engineers) Ltd, Northampton, c/1930; earlier Cochrane & Co Ltd, Desborough Quarries.

(h)   ex W. Whitwell & Co Ltd, Thornaby, Yorkshire (NR), /1937.

(i)   ex Storefield Quarries, 6/1944; to Storefield Quarries, 1/1945; returned /1948; to Storefield Quarries, after 3/1951, by 11/11/1951; returned 16/3/1960.

(j)   ex Malleable Works, Stockton-on-Tees, Co. Durham, 6/1952.

(k)   ex Wensley Lime Co Ltd, Leyburn, Yorkshire (NR), 8/5/1957.

(l)   ex West Hartlepool Works, Co Durham, 11/1957.

(m)   ex West Hartlepool Works, Co Durham, 2/1959.

(n)   ex Storefield Quarries, 4/1962 (by 24/4/1962).

(o)   ex Stanton & Staveley Ltd, Holwell Ironworks, Leics, 8/1963.

(p)   ex Cargo Fleet Ironworks, Yorkshire (NR), 13/4/1964.

(q)   ex Cargo Fleet Ironworks, Yorkshire (NR), 7/1964.

(r)   ex Glendon East Quarries, 13/8/1968.

(s)   ex Market Overton Quarries, Rutland, 2/1969.

(1)   to Thos.W. Ward Ltd, dealers, Sheffield, 8/1919;
      thence to The Ford Paper Works Ltd, Hylton, Sunderland, Co.Durham, 1/1920.

(2)   believed to United Steel Companies Ltd, Irthlingborough Ironworks, on trial, c/1925; later at Thos.E. Gray & Co Ltd, Isebrook Quarry, Burton Latimer.

(3)   to Storefield Quarries, 3/1942

(4)   to Storefield Quarries, c/1940; ex Storefield Quarries for repairs, 4/1942; to Storefield Quarries, 3/1943.

(5)   to Storefield Quarries, /1949 (by 16/10/1949).

(6)   to Wensley Lime Co Ltd, Leyburn, Yorkshire (NR), /1949.

(7)   to Storefield Quarries, 23/11/1965.

(8)   to George Cohen, Sons & Co Ltd, Cransley, for scrap, 12/1966.

(9)   to Irchester Parish Council, Irchester Recreation Ground, 8/1969.

(10)   to George Cohen, Sons & Co Ltd, Cransley, for scrap, 2-3/9/1969.

(11)   withdrawn 4/1959 and later dismantled after 23/7/1960. Frame later used as a carrier for quarry equipment and then scrapped by Sheppard of Wellingborough, 8/1969.

(12)   to London Railway Preservation Society, Quainton Road Station, Bucks, 26/8/1969.

(13)   to George Cohen, Sons & Co Ltd, Cransley, for scrap, 8/1969.

(14)   to George Cohen, Sons & Co Ltd, Cransley, for scrap, 27/8/1969.

(15)   to George Cohen, Sons & Co Ltd, Cransley, for scrap, 9/1969.

(16)   to Glendon East Quarries, 12/1/1970.

LAMPORT IRONSTONE QUARRIES   M16

Stewarts & Lloyds Minerals Ltd until 1/7/1968
Staveley Minerals Ltd until 1/1/1966
   (subsidiary of **Staveley Iron & Chemical Co Ltd**)
Staveley Iron & Chemical Co Ltd until 7/3/1961
Staveley Coal & Iron Co Ltd until 23/9/1948
Lamport Ironstone Co until c/1923

Hanging Houghton SP 752730
Scaldwell SP 767722
Lamport SP 742731

The original system consisted of a 3ft gauge tramway serving quarries at Scaldwell and another 3ft gauge tramway serving quarries ½ mile to the west at Hanging Houghton (on the edge of the escarpment). An aerial ropeway about 2 miles in length conveyed ore from both sets of quarries to standard gauge sidings alongside the LNWR Northampton - Market Harborough line about ½ mile north of Brixworth station. Production at both sets of quarries commenced about 1914. Private locos were not used on the standard gauge section until required by the introduction of calcining in 1933. In 1942 standard gauge was laid from the sidings as far as Hanging Houghton Quarries, replacing the 3ft gauge tramway there. The standard gauge railway was extended to Scaldwell in 1954 and the ropeway dismantled, but the 3ft gauge tramway at Scaldwell remained in use until closure of the quarries on 8/12/1962. Narrow gauge track was lifted from 4/1963 until 12/1963. The standard gauge track was lifted by autumn 1964 apart from that around the calcine clamps alongside the exchange sidings. This rail traffic ceased 3/1969 and track was lifted during 1970.

Reference : "The Ironstone Quarries of the Midlands, Part 3, Northampton"; Eric Tonks,
Runpast Publishing, 1989

Gauge: 3ft 0in

LAMPORT *	0-6-0ST	OC	P		1315	1913	New	Scr 1/1964
SCALDWELL	0-6-0ST	OC	P		1316	1913	New (a)	(2)
BANSHEE	0-6-0ST	OC	MW		1276	1894		
		reb	MW			1910	(b)	(1)
(HANDYMAN until /1953)	0-4-0ST	OC	HC		573	1900	(c)	(3)

*   Kept at Hanging Houghton Quarries until /1944.

a)   to Eastwell Iron Ore Co Ltd, Leics, /1947; returned 8/1950.
b)   ex Eastwell Iron Ore Co Ltd, by /1928.
c)   ex Blackwell & Son (Engineers) Ltd, Northampton, /1936; earlier Cranford Ironstone Co Ltd.

1)   scrapped 7/1945; parts to Loddington Ironstone Co Ltd, c/1951.
2)   to Narrow Gauge Railway Society, Brockham Museum, Surrey, 21/3/1964.
3)   to Welshpool & Llanfair Railway Preservation Society, Llanfair Caerenion, Montgomeryshire [Powys], 16/5/1964.

Gauge: 4ft 8½in

ROBERT	0-6-0ST	OC	AE	2068	1933	New	(2)
LAMPORT No.2	0-6-0ST	OC	WB	2669	1942	New	Scr 6/1970
LAMPORT No.3	0-6-0ST	OC	WB	2670	1942	New	(3)
HARTINGTON	0-6-0ST	OC	AE	1869	1921	(a)	(1)
DOUGLAS	0-4-0DM		JF	21086	1936	(b)	(4)

a)   ex Staveley Works, 2/1961.
b)   ex Mill Hill Ironstone Quarry, Leics, 12/1965.

1)   to Desborough Mines, 5/1965.
2)   to London Road Garage (Loughton) Ltd, Bletchley, Bucks, 9/1969.

(3)   to CEGB, Leicester, 12/1969 (stored on behalf of Leicester Industrial Locomotive Preservation Group).
(4)   to Hunt & Co (Hinckley) Ltd, Leics, 5/1970; later scrapped by them.

STOREFIELD IRONSTONE QUARRIES   R17
South Durham Steel & Iron Co Ltd until 1/7/1968   Loco shed SP 863831

Extensive quarries on the east side of the ex-Midland Railway Kettering - Corby railway, north of Glendon South Junction and the Glendon East Quarries. Originally worked by **E.P. Davis** (which see) using a narrow gauge tramway; closed 1929. Re-opened for production by South Durham Steel & Iron Co Ltd in 5/1940 with a standard gauge rail system connecting with the ex-Midland Railway line. Closed for production 15/9/1971. Track lifted 5-6/1973.

Reference :   "The Ironstone Quarries of the Midlands, Part 6, Corby"; Eric Tonks, Runpast Publishing, 1992

Gauge: 4ft 8½ in

	ENTERPRISE	0-4-0ST	OC	WB	1739	1907	(a)	(4)
	COCKSPUR	0-4-0ST	OC	P	1289	1912	(b)	Scr 4/1967
No.19		0-4-0ST	OC	AB	2101	1940	(c)	(4)
No.1		0-4-0ST	OC	HL	2412	1899	(d)	(1)
11		0-4-0ST	OC	AB	1047	1905		
		reb	Irchester			1949	(e)	(7)
No.20		0-4-0ST	OC	AB	2143	1942	(f)	(3)
No.6		0-6-0ST	OC	AB	1497	1916	(g)	(2)
No.39	49 CAERPHILLY	0-6-0ST	IC	K	5477	1936	(h)	(4)
	8311/03	0-4-0DH		RR	10204	1965	(i)	(8)
45		0-6-0ST	IC	K	5470	1933	(j)	(6)
	MAUD	0-4-0DH		S	10142	1962	(k)	(5)

(a)   ex George Cohen, Sons & Co Ltd, /1940; earlier Hawkesbury & Exhall Collieries Ltd Warwicks; to Irchester Quarries, /1948; returned /1951 (after 30/7/1951, by 11/11/1951); to Irchester Quarries, 16/3/1960; returned 23/11/1965.
(b)   ex Irchester Quarries, c/1940; to Irchester Quarries for repairs, 4/1942; ex Irchester Quarries, 3/1943.
(c)   ex Irchester Quarries, 3/1942; to Irchester Quarries for repairs, after 25/3/1951, by 3/6/1951; ex Irchester Quarries, after 30/7/1951, by 20/10/1952.
(d)   ex Irchester Quarries, 4/1942.
(e)   ex Irchester Quarries, /1949 (by 16/10/1949
(f)   ex RTB, Blisworth Quarries, 9/1944.
(g)   ex Malleable Works, Stockton-on-Tees, Co. Durham, 8/1954.
(h)   ex Glendon East Quarries, 6/8/1968.
(i)   ex Glendon East Quarries, 21/1/1969.
(j)   ex Corby Quarries, c18/2/1969.
(k)   ex Glendon East Quarries, 9/1970.

(1)   to Irchester Quarries, /1947 (after 15/6/1947).
(2)   to Irchester Quarries, 4/1962 (by 24/4/1962).
(3)   to George Cohen, Sons & Co Ltd, Cransley, for scrap, 25/9/1969.
(4)   to George Cohen, Sons & Co Ltd, Cransley, for scrap, 10/1969.
(5)   returned to Glendon East Quarries, 10/1970.
(6)   to Glendon East Quarries, for loading onto road transport to North Norfolk Railway Co Ltd, Sheringham, Norfolk, 6/1971.
(7)   to R.J.Robinson, South Cambs Rural & Industrial Museum, Heydon, Cambs, 28/2/1971.
(8)   to Corby Quarries, 25/6/1973.

BRIXWORTH IRONSTONE CO LTD
BRIXWORTH IRONSTONE QUARRIES
Subsidiary of **Clay Cross Co Ltd** from 25/3/1928
Attenborough & Timms until 11/3/1909
Attenborough & Co until 1899

M18

SP 748719

Quarrying commenced in 1873 in the area to the east and north of Brixworth village, five miles north of Northampton, and work was being done by ironstone contractor **Edward Coles** by 1884. From 3/1909 operation may have been by **Alfred Hamson** trading as **Brixworth Ironstone Co Ltd**. The workings were served by a 4ft 0in gauge tramway which ran west for ½ mile, descending steeply, to a tipping dock and standard gauge sidings alongside the LNWR Northampton - Market Harborough line. Production ceased on 4/10/1947 and the tramway was dismantled in 1/1948.

Reference : "The Ironstone Quarries of the Midlands, Part 3, Northampton";
Eric Tonks, Runpast Publishing, 1989

Gauge: 4ft 0in

BRIXWORTH No.1	0-4-0ST	OC	HCR	212	1879	New	(1)
BRIXWORTH No.1	0-4-0ST	OC	HC	227	1881	(a)	
(BRIXWORTH No.2		reb	Blackwell,				
until /1938)			Northampton		1938		(2)
LOUISA	0-4-0ST	OC	HE	298	1882	(a)	(3)
-	4wPE		Clay Cross		c1927	(b)	(4)

(a)   ex Spratton Quarries, after /1908, by 12/1916.
(b)   ex Bloxham Quarries, Oxon, c3/1942.

(1)   to Blackwell & Son (Engineers) Ltd, Northampton, /1938; parts used in rebuilding No.2.
(2)   to Blackwell & Son (Engineers) Ltd, Northampton, /1938; rebuilt using parts of HC 212 and returned; to Clay Cross Ironworks, Derbys, for scrap, after 10/1947, by c2/1948.
(3)   to Clay Cross Ironworks, Derbys, /1947 (after 24/8/1947); scrapped c/1953.
(4)   to Clay Cross Ironworks, Derbys for scrap, after 10/1947, by c2/1948; scrapped there.

BURTON IRONSTONE CO LTD
BURTON LATIMER IRONSTONE QUARRIES
Burton Ironstone Co until 24/9/1896
  (subsidiary of **Staveley Coal & Iron Co Ltd** from c1910)
Thomas Butlin & Co Ltd until 1891
Butlin, Bevan & Co until 27/6/1889
Glendon Iron Co until 1882

R19

SP 912760

Quarries on the east of Burton Latimer village, three miles south-east of Kettering. The area may have been worked by Glendon Iron Co from 1873 and was served by a narrow gauge tramway from 1882. This line ran north through the quarrying area to a tipping dock and standard gauge siding on the Midland Railway Kettering - Cambridge line. Workings ceased on 4/2/1921 and the railway equipment was offered in several sales up to Aug.1924. Thomas Butlin & Co Ltd also operated three quarries with standard gauge rail connections, presumably horse-worked.

Reference : "The Ironstone Quarries of the Midlands, Part 5, Kettering"; Eric Tonks,
Runpast Publishing, 1991

Gauge: 3ft 0in

WOODCOCK	0-4-0ST	OC	BH	1046	1892	New	(1)
BANSHEE	0-6-0ST	OC	MW	1276	1894		
		reb	MW		1910	New	(2)
HANDYMAN	0-4-0ST	OC	HC	573	1900	New	(3)

(1)   to Staveley Works, Derbys, and rebuilt, /1919; thence Eastwell Iron Ore Co Ltd, Leics.
(2)   to Eastwell Iron Ore Co Ltd, Leics, c/1921
(3)   to Cranford Ironstone Co Ltd, /1919

THOS. BUTLIN & CO LTD

IRTHLINGBOROUGH IRONSTONE QUARRIES   Q20
Butlin, Bevan & Co until 27/6/1889   SP 907676 approx

Quarrying in the area about a mile to the east of Wellingborough commenced in 1863. Work was in association with Butlin's East End Ironworks in Wellingborough and quarrying ceased in 1925, although the locomotive listed below appears to have gone at a much earlier date.

Reference :   "The Ironstone Quarries of the Midlands, Part 4, Wellingborough"; Eric Tonks, Runpast Publishing, 1990

Gauge: 4ft 8½in

-	0-4-0ST	OC	HCR	86	1867	New	s/s

"The Engineer" 22/12/1871 advertised - For sale, tank loco by first class builders, 10 x 16 in, sold as more powerful loco needed, little used. May be seen at work at Thos. Butlin & Co, Irthlingborough Iron Works, Wellingborough. This may refer to HCR 86 here (see also Ironworks entry).

IRCHESTER IRONSTONE QUARRIES   Q21
Butlin, Bevan & Co until 27/6/1889   East Quarries SP 929664
                                                         West Quarries SP 904650

By 1872 a tramway to the west of the Midland Railway line north of its Irchester station served quarries, and the first locomotive listed below appears to have been used on this system. The line may have been horse worked after the return of this loco to its makers, and it had closed by 1884. Standard gauge locos may also have been used here.

In 1875 quarries were being worked about 1½ miles west of Irchester village and these were served by a narrow gauge system which ran to a tipping stage over standard gauge sidings at the north of Wellingborough (London Rd) station on the LNWR railway. Production here ceased in 1903 and the railway was lifted shortly afterwards. Operation was resumed with a new railway installation in 1912 by James Pain (which see under South Durham Steel & Iron Co Ltd).

Reference :   "The Ironstone Quarries of the Midlands, Part 4, Wellingborough"; Eric Tonks, Runpast Publishing, 1990

Gauge: 3ft 8¼in

SAMSON	0-4-0ST	OC	HCR	104	1871	New	(1)
JONATHAN	0-4-0ST	OC	HCR	145	1874	New	s/s
SOLOMON	0-4-0ST	OC	HCR	156	1875	New	Scr /1909
SAMSON	0-4-0ST	OC	HCR	185	1876	New	(2)
DELILAH	0-4-0ST	OC	HCR	186	1876	New	s/s

Note : Some of the above locomotives may have been at Butlin's Cranford quarries.
"Mining Journal", 1871, p.1002 stated that there were three locomotives here in 1871.
"The Engineer" 18/11/1892 advertised - For sale, 7in loco, 3ft 8½in gauge, also rails to match, F. Butlin & Co, Iron Works, Wellingborough (possibly applies to HCR 185 or 186).

(1)   returned to HCR, /1876; rebuilt as HCR 196 and thence to James Walton, Thorncliffe Quarries, Rawtenstall, Lancs, ANNIE.
(2)   to Thos.W. Ward, dealer, Sheffield, by 6/1909 (probably c/1902).

GREAT ADDINGTON IRONSTONE QUARRIES   S22
Butlin, Bevan & Co until 27/6/1889   SP 959747

Quarries about a mile west of Ringstead & Addington station on the LNWR Wellingborough - Peterborough line, served by a standard gauge railway which connected with the LNWR line. Production appears to have been in the period 1884 -1899; line dismantled subsequently.

Reference :   "The Ironstone Quarries of the Midlands, Part 4, Wellingborough"; Eric Tonks, Runpast Publishing, 1990

Gauge: 4ft 8½in

No.1 JOE	0-4-0ST	OC	HC	252	1884	New	(1)

(1)   sold to HC prior to /1910; rebuilt by HC and to Cammell Laird & Co Ltd, Birkenhead, Cheshire, 9/1910.

BYFIELD IRONSTONE CO LTD
Controlled by Staveley Coal & Iron Co Ltd from 1941

BYFIELD QUARRIES   L23
Northamptonshire Ironstone Co Ltd until 30/11/1928   SP 509531
Northamptonshire Ironstone Co until 3/1922

Quarries to the north of Byfield village with a standard gauge railway system that ran south to connect with the S&MJR Fenny Compton - Towcester line about ½ mile west of Byfield station. Production commenced 5/1915 but ceased about 5/1925. Operation recommenced from 9/1928 until 12/2/1965; all equipment was then dismantled in the following six months.

Reference :   "The Ironstone Quarries Of The Midlands, Part 2, Oxfordshire"; Eric Tonks, Runpast Publishing, 1988

Gauge: 4ft 8½in

	JAMES	0-4-0ST	OC	P	996	1904	(a)	Scr c/1941
	NORTHFIELD	0-6-0ST	OC	P	717	1898	(b)	(1)
	JEANNIE WADDELL	0-6-0ST	IC	P	464	1888		
			reb	AE		1898	(c)	Scr c/1923
	-	0-6-0ST	IC	MW	1235	1890	(d)	Scr c3/1962
	(BYFIELD)							
	(f. LANCE B.PAIN)	0-6-0ST	IC	HC	347	1892	(e)	Scr 2/1965
	BYFIELD No.2	0-6-0ST	OC	WB	2655	1942	New	(2)
	CHERWELL	0-6-0ST	OC	WB	2654	1942	(f)	(5)
	SIR BERKELEY	0-6-0ST	IC	MW	1210	1890		
			reb	MW		1909	(g)	(3)
No.3	AVONSIDE	0-6-0ST	OC	AE	1919	1924	(h)	(4)

(a)   ex James Pain Ltd, Glendon East Quarries, c/1915.

(b)   ex John Griffiths & Son Ltd, Glenburn Colliery, Skelmersdale, Lancs.

(c)   ex Great Mountain Collieries Co Ltd, Great Mountain Colliery, Carms, c/1917; earlier
      Llanelly & Mynydd Mawr Railway, JEANNIE WADDELL.

(d)   ex P, 6/1929; earlier Westleigh Stone & Lime Co Ltd, Burlescombe, Devon

(e)   ex Furness Shipbuilding Co Ltd, Haverton Hill, Co Durham [Cleveland], c/1923; to Park
      Gate Iron & Steel Co Ltd, Charwelton Quarries, c2/1951; returned 12/1956.

(f)   ex Park Gate Iron & Steel Co Ltd, Charwelton Quarries, c10/1945; to Charwelton,
      12/1947; returned 1/1948.

(g)   ex Cranford Ironstone Co Ltd, Cranford Quarries, 5/1959.

(h)   ex Staveley Iron & Chemical Co Ltd, Staveley Ironworks, Derbys, 4/1960.

(1)   to Bloxham Quarries, Oxon,/1918.

(2)   to Oxfordshire Ironstone Co Ltd, Banbury, Oxon, /1946 (after 25/8/1946).

(3)   to Keighley & Worth Valley Railway Preservation Society, Haworth, Yorkshire (WR),
      18/1/1965.

(4)   to Staveley Minerals Ltd, Cranford, 10/9/1965.

(5)   to Daventry Borough Council, New Street Recreation Ground, 11/8/1966.

PITSFORD IRONSTONE QUARRIES

M24

Pitsford Ironstone Co until 9/1962.

SP 738661

Quarries were worked on both sides of the Northampton - Market Harborough road (A508)
south-west of Pitsford village. A standard gauge railway served the workings and ran for
about a mile to connect them with the LNWR Northampton - Market Harborough railway
south of Pitsford & Brampton station. A 2ft gauge system was used for the conveyance of
ganister at intervals from 1923 to 1939. Ironstone working started in 1923 and production
ceased on 27/8/1965. The standard gauge railway was dismantled and the site cleared by
6/1966.

Reference :   "The Ironstone Quarries of the Midlands, Part 3, Northampton"; Eric Tonks,
Runpast Publishing, 1989

Gauge: 4ft 8½in

PITSFORD	0-6-0ST	OC	AE	1917	1923	New(a)	(2)
IRENE	0-6-0ST	IC	MW	1359	1897	(b)	(1)
No.2 (HOLMES)	0-4-0ST	OC	MW	345	1871	(c)	Scr 1/1964
65	0-6-0ST	OC	HC	1631	1929	(d)	(3)

(a)   to Midland Ironstone Co Ltd, Scunthorpe, Lincs, on loan, c9/1934; returned c/1934.

(b)   ex Pilton Ironstone Co, Pilton Quarries, Rutland, c/1931

(c)   ex Park Gate Iron & Steel Co Ltd, Charwelton Ironstone Quarries, c/1935.

(d)   ex Appleby Frodingham Steel Co, Scunthorpe, Lincs, 10/1957.

(1)   returned to Pilton Quarries, c/1935

(2)   to E.E. Kimbell & Co, Engineers, Northampton, 7/1966; re-sold to Sir W. McAlpine,
      Dobson's Farm, Fawley, Bucks, for preservation.

(3)   to Midland Quarry, Scunthorpe, Lincs, 7/1966.

Gauge: 2ft 0in (Ganister line)

PIXIE	0-4-0ST	OC	WB	2090	1919	(a)	(1)

(a)   ex Pilton Ironstone Co, Pilton Quarries, Rutland, c6/1923; to Pilton, /1928; ex Park
      Gate Iron & Steel Co Ltd, Eaton (Basic) Quarries, Leics, c/1933.

(1)   to Cranford Ironstone Co Ltd, /1949.

CARGO FLEET IRON CO LTD
TWYWELL IRONSTONE QUARRIES

S25

SP 956783

Quarries to the north-east of Twywell village and north of the Midland Railway Kettering - Cambridge railway. Operated by **John Young** from 1906 on the earlier workings of the Newbridge Iron Ore Co (which see)., A cable worked 2ft 3in gauge tramway served the workings. The quarries were taken over by Cargo Fleet Iron Co Ltd in the 1918-1920 period and a locomotive, possibly owned by **Robinson**, contractor, was used on construction of calcine banks, 1919 -1922. Quarries closed 8/1924 but later re-opened by SDSI in 10/1963 using road transport.

Reference : "The Ironstone Quarries of the Midlands, Part 5, Kettering"; Eric Tonks, Runpast Publishing, 1991

Gauge: 1ft 8in

KIMBERLEY	0-4-0T	OC	OK	3558	1909	(a)	s/s c/1922

(a) ex Basset Mines Ltd, Redruth, Cornwall, c/1919.

CASTLE DYKES IRON ORE CO LTD
LODGE PLANTATION IRONSTONE QUARRY, near Stowe

P26

SP 630565

Quarrying at Lodge Plantation appears to have commenced from about 1855, until 1857, by the **Northamptonshire Ironstone Co**. Work recommenced in 1863 by the **Stowe Iron Ore Co** with a cable and horse worked narrow gauge tramway which passed under the LNWR railway and ran to a wharf on the Grand Junction Canal at Nether Heyford. Castle Dykes Iron Ore Co Ltd took over in 1867 and about 1869 replaced the tramway with a standard gauge line connecting with the LNWR. The Chaplin loco appears to have worked the section of line at the quarries, while a second (unidentified) loco may have been used at the LNWR end. Quarry closed 1872; re-opened by Nine Churches Iron Ore Co, which see, in 1875.

Reference : "The Ironstone Quarries of the Midlands, Part 3, Northampton"; Eric Tonks, Runpast Publishing, 1989

Gauge : 4ft 8½in

"COFFEE POT"	0-4-0VBT	VCG	Chaplin	1056	1869	(a)	(1)

(a) ex D. Murray, Blisworth (contr ?), by 9/1870.

(1) possibly to Nine Churches Iron Ore Co with site, /1875;
to Henry Mobbs, dealer, Vulcan Ironworks, Northampton, 9/1878.

CENTRAL ELECTRICITY GENERATING BOARD
HARDINGSTONE JUNCTION POWER STATION, Northampton

N27

Central Electricity Authority until 1/1/1958
British Electricity Authority until 1/4/1955
Northampton Electric Light & Power Co Ltd until 1/4/1948

SP 763597

Power station to the south-east of Northampton town centre, located between the River Nene and the Midland Railway Northampton - Bedford railway, and served by standard gauge sidings connected to that line. The station was commissioned in 1919 although the siding connection to the main line was made in 8/1916, possibly for construction traffic. Rail traffic ceased 1976 and the station was closed and partly demolished. Some remains were still extant in 2000. The site was later used, with rail traffic, by Farthingstone Silos Ltd (which see) as a storage depot.

Gauge: 4ft 8½in

-	4wBE		NELP		1919	New	Scr by /1956
-	0-4-0F	OC	HL	3829	1934	New	(2)
-	0-4-0ST	OC	WB	2565	1936	New	(1)
(No.1)	0-4-0ST	OC	P	1438	1916	(a)	(2)

(a)   ex Nechells Power Station, West Midlands, 23/3/1972.

(1)   to M. Bamford, Titanic Steamship Co, Ellastone, Staffs, 29/7/1976.
(2)   to M. Bamford, Titanic Steamship Co, Ellastone, Staffs, 2/1977.

COCHRANE & CO LTD
DESBOROUGH IRONSTONE QUARRIES   R28
Desborough Industrial & Provident Co-operative Society Ltd until c1924   SP 798832
Desborough Co-operative Society Ltd until c1906.

Quarrying commenced in 1905 at Manor Farm, about ½ mile south-west of Desborough village, with a standard gauge line connecting the quarries to the Midland Railway Kettering - Market Harborough line west of Desborough station. In 1913 new quarries were commenced at Thorpe Underwood and the railway was extended by about 1½ miles to reach these and further workings at Harrington nearby. The quarries closed in 1926 shortly after the Cochrane & Co takeover. The northern section of railway was retained to serve the workings of British Gas Purifying Materials Co Ltd, which see.

Gauge: 4ft 8½in

PROGRESS	0-4-0ST	OC	P	1043	1905	New	(1)
JUBILEE	0-6-0ST	OC	P	1254	1913	New	(2)
PROGRESS	0-6-0ST	OC	P	1402	1915	New	(3)
11	0-4-0ST	OC	AB	1047	1905	(a)	(4)

(a)   ex Irchester Ironstone Co Ltd, Irchester Quarries, c/1925.

(1)   to Thos.W. Ward Ltd; then to Monks Hall & Co Ltd, Warrington, Lancs, PROGRESS.
(2)   to Blackwell & Son (Engineers) Ltd, Cotton End Works, Northampton, /1926; then to Furnace Hill & Renishaw Park Collieries Ltd, Derbys.
(3)   to Blackwell & Son (Engineers) Ltd, Cotton End Works, Northampton, /1926; then to Irchester Ironstone Co Ltd, Irchester Quarries.
(4)   to Irchester Ironstone Co Ltd, Irchester Quarries, c/1927.

F. COHEN
COGENHOE IRONSTONE MINES   M29
Cogenhoe Iron Ore Co until /1886   SP 838609

Quarries south of Cogenhoe village were being worked by 1858 and were served by a narrow gauge tramway and also a standard gauge line connecting with the LNWR Northampton - Wellingborough line. Locomotives appear to have replaced horses on the standard gauge, possibly about 1880. Workings closed 1888 and equipment auctioned 16/7/1888.

Reference : "The Ironstone Quarries of the Midlands, Part 3, Northampton"; Eric Tonks,
Runpast Publishing, 1989

Gauge: 4ft 8½in

*	0-4-0ST	OC	MW	40	1861	(a)	(1)
*	4-4-0ST	IC	RS	1959	1870	(b)	(2)

*One of these locos was named ALATHEA CHOICE

(a) orig W.H.& G. Dawes, Elsecar & Milton Ironworks, near Rotherham, Yorkshire (WR);
possibly ex W.H.& G. Dawes, Denby Ironworks, Derbys.

(b) ex South Leicestershire Colliery Co Ltd, Snibston Colliery, Leics.

(1) to Charles D. Phillips, dealers, Newport, Gwent, by 1/1889; s/s

(2) to Charles D. Phillips, dealers, Newport, Gwent, by 1/1889; later Micklefield Lime &
Coal Co Ltd, Peckfield Colliery, near Leeds, No.2 EMLYN, after /1898.

GEORGE COHEN, SONS & CO LTD
COBORN WORKS, Cransley

R30
SP 850775

In 1960 this company of machinery merchants and scrap dealers took over the site of
Cransley Ironworks (formerly New Cransley Iron & Steel Co Ltd, which see) and new sidings
were laid in 1962 by **Eagre Construction Co Ltd.** During the subsequent years up to about
1981 the yard was used for the dismantling of plant which included a large number of
locomotives, both main line and industrial, and much rolling stock. British Rail locomotives
which were scrapped here are not listed. Several industrial locomotives were kept here for
shunting use and resale, and these are detailed below. Sidings closed 9/1980. Yard cleared
by 9/1981 and later re-used as a car breakers yard.

Gauge : 4ft 8½in

NEW CRANSLEY	0-4-0ST	OC	CF	1194	1900			
No.3		reb	HIW		1952	(a)	Scr 3/1966
-	0-4-0ST	OC	P	832	1900	(a)	Scr 3/1966
KETT 22 NELLIE	4wPM		KC	1553	1927	(b)	s/s by 9/12/1973
KETT 39	4wDM		RH	386871	1955	(c)	(1)
2	0-4-0DM		JF	19024	1930	(d)	(3)
D2176	0-6-0DM		Sdn		1961	(e)	(4)
814	4wDM		RH	218046	1943	(f)	(2)
-	0-4-0DM		JF	4210143	1958	(g)	(7)
-	4wDM		RH	252841	1948	(h)	(5)
D2241	0-6-0DM		VF	D291	1956			
			DC	2565	1956	(i)	Scr 10-11/1976
2484C	0-4-0DM		JF	4200022	1948	(j)	(12)
26443C	0-4-0DM		JF	4210012	1950	(k)	(11)
850	0-4-0DM		HE	2068	1940	(l)	(6)
-	4wDH		NBQ	27544	1959	(m)	(10)
-	0-4-0DM		JF	23010	1945	(n)	(13)
221	0-4-0DM		JF	22968	1942	(n)	(8)
268	0-4-0DM		JF	23009	1944	(n)	(9)
(03 018) 600 No.2	0-6-0DM		Sdn		1958	(o)	(15)
243	0-4-0DM		JF	22890	1939	(p)	(16)
9038	2w-2PMR		Wkm	8198	1958	(p)	(14)
-	4wDM		MR	9922	1959	(q)	(16)

(a) ex New Cransley Iron & Steel Co Ltd, Cransley Ironworks, with site, /1962.
(b) ex Kettering Borough Council, Northfield Depot, Kettering, 8/10/1963.
(c) ex Cargo Fleet scrapyard, Middlesbrough, Yorkshire (NR), c4/1966.
(d) ex Canning Town Depot, Essex, c1/1968.
(e) ex BR, Crewe Works, Cheshire, D2176, 10/1968.
(f) ex MoDAD, Bicester Depot, Oxon, 2/1969.
(g) ex Ministry of Power, Portishead, Somerset, c9/1969.
(h) ex East Midlands Gas Board, Northampton Gas Works, after 11/11/1964, by 6/12/1970.
(i) ex BR, Colchester Depot, D2241, 9/1971.
(j) ex Vauxhall Motors Ltd, Luton, Beds, 12/1972.
(k) ex Vauxhall Motors Ltd, Luton, Beds, 12/1972; to APCM Ltd, Johnson's Works, Greenhithe, Kent, c12/1973 (after 11/11/1973); returned c12/1974 (by 4/1/1975).
(l) ex MoDAD, Bicester, Oxon, 8/11/1973.
(m) ex West Midlands Gas Board, Windsor Street Works, Birmingham, 8/1974.
(n) ex MoDAFD, Hartlebury, Worcs, 8/1974.
(o) ex BR, Norwich Depot, 03018, 29/4/1976.
(p) ex MoDAD, Bicester Depot, Oxon, 5/7/1977.
(q) ex London Brick Co Ltd, Calvert Works, Bucks, 4/1980.

(1) to Kingsbury Depot, Warwicks, c/1968.
(2) to Morriston Depot, Swansea, West Glamorgan, 25/6/1969.
(3) to Barking Works, Essex, by 20/6/1970.
(4) scrapped by 10/10/1971.
(5) to Kingsbury Works, Warwicks, by 25/12/1971.
(6) to Chettles Feather Hair Products Ltd, Wymington, Beds, by 6/1/1974.
(7) to Chettles Feather Hair Products Ltd, Wymington, Beds, by 19/1/1974.
(8) to Pollock Brown & Co Ltd, Northam, Hampshire, c9/1974 (after 23/8/1974).
(9) to Salford Depot, Lancs, c9/1974 (after 23/8/1974).
(10) to Chettles Feather Hair Products Ltd, Wymington, Beds, 11/1974.
(11) s/s after 6/7/1975, by 8/2/1976
(12) to Weldit Engineering Ltd, Ramsden Dock, Barrow, Cumbria, c2/1977 (by 6/4/1977).
(13) to Motherwell Machinery & Scrap Co Ltd, Inshaw Yard, Motherwell, Lanarks, 8/1977.
(14) to Dart Valley Railway, Buckfastleigh, Devon, c3/1978 (after 5/2/1978).
(15) to 600 Ferrous Fragmentizers Ltd, Willesden, London, 20/10/1980.
(16) s/s c10/1981 (after 19/9/1981).

The following industrial locomotives are known to have been broken up here for scrap.

NORSEMAN		0-4-0ST	OC	AB	1711	1921	(a)	Scr 6/1964
GRACE		0-4-0ST	OC	P	1894	1936	(b)	Scr
MAUD		0-4-0ST	OC	P	1937	1938	(b)	Scr after 9/1965
JOHN		0-6-0ST	OC	P	1981	1940	(b)	Scr
MARY		0-4-0ST	OC	HC	1818	1950	(b)	Scr
BARABEL		0-4-0ST	OC	HC	1868	1953	(b)	Scr
BETTY		0-4-0ST	OC	HC	1869	1953	(b)	Scr
JOAN		0-4-0ST	OC	AE	1822	1919	(b)	Scr
JEAN		0-4-0ST	OC	HC	1696	1939	(b)	Scr
PHYLLIS		4wVBT	VCG	S	9615	1956	(b)	Scr
PROGRESS		0-6-0ST	OC	P	1402	1915	(c)	Scr 5/1/1967
MAJOR		0-4-0ST	OC	AB	1363	1914	(c)	Scr 12/1966
ROTHWELL		0-4-0ST	OC	P	1258	1912	(c)	Scr 5/1/1967
15		0-4-0ST	OC	HL	3892	1936	(c)	Scr 12/1966
No.8	1918	0-4-0ST	OC	AB	1609	1918	(c)	Scr 12/1966
ED3		0-4-0DM		JF	4200042	1949	(d)	Scr by c6/1968

No.6		0-6-0ST	OC	AB	1497	1916	(e)	Scr	
	HOLWELL No.30	0-4-0ST	OC	HL	3780	1932	(f)	Scr	
7		0-4-0ST	OC	AB	2324	1952	(g)	Scr	
No.2	50 CARMARTHEN	0-6-0ST	IC	K	5478	1936	(h)	Scr	
No.17		0-4-0ST	OC	HL	3946	1937	(i)	Scr	
No.20		0-4-0ST	OC	AB	2143	1942	(j)	Scr 11/1969	
19		0-4-0ST	OC	AB	2101	1940	(k)	Scr 12/1969	
	ENTERPRISE	0-4-0ST	OC	WB	1739	1907	(k)	Scr 12/1969	
No.39	49 CAERPHILLY	0-6-0ST	IC	K	5477	1936	(l)	Scr 12/1969	
No.80	No3	0-6-0ST	IC	HE	2417	1941	(m)	Scr	
	PILTON	0-6-0ST	OC	AE	1832	1919	(n)	Scr 11/1969	
52		0-6-0ST	IC	RSHN	7004	1940	(o)	Scr 12/1969	
	-	0-4-0F	OC	AB	1492	1916	(p)	Scr	
PM22		0-4-0DM		RSHN	6967	1939	(q)	Scr	
PM23		0-4-0DM		RSHN	6968	1939	(q)	Scr	
DS1169		4wDM		RH	237923	1946	(r)	Scr c7/1973	
247		0-4-0DM		AB	342	1940	(s)	Scr	
No.11		0-4-0DM		HE	4679	1955	(t)	Scr 11/1977	
	-	0-6-0DH		HE	6691	1968	(u)	Scr	

(a) ex Tunnel Portland Cement Co Ltd, Pitstone, Bucks, 4/1964
(b) ex Oxfordshire Ironstone Co Ltd, Banbury, Oxon, 9/1965.
(c) ex South Durham Steel & Iron Co Ltd, Irchester Quarries, 12/1966.
(d) ex British Railways, Bedford, c26/11/1967.
(e) ex British Steel Corporation, Irchester Quarries, 8/1969
(f) ex British Steel Corporation, Irchester Quarries, 27/8/1969
(g) ex British Steel Corporation, Irchester Quarries, 9/1969
(h) ex British Steel Corporation, Irchester Quarries, 2/9/1969
(i) ex British Steel Corporation, Irchester Quarries, 3/9/1969
(j) ex British Steel Corporation, Storefield Quarries, 25/9/1969
(k) ex British Steel Corporation, Storefield Quarries, 10/1969
(l) ex British Steel Corporation, Storefield Quarries, 10/1969
(m) ex British Steel Corporation, Glendon East Ironstone Quarries, 10/1969
(n) ex British Steel Corporation, Pilton Quarries, Rutland, 11/1969
(o) ex British Steel Corporation, Gretton Brook, Corby, 17/12/1969
(p) ex Laporte Chemicals Ltd, Luton, via Peterborough Heavy Haulage, Yaxley, Cambs, 5/5/1970
(q) ex C.A.E.C. Howard Ltd, Bedford, by 22/10/1972
(r) ex BR, Yeovil Junction, Dorset, DS1169, after c11/1972, by 23/6/1973
(s) ex MoDAD, Bicester, Oxon, 5/7/1977.
(t) ex National Coal Board, Tilmanstone Colliery, Eythorne, Kent, by 4/11/1977
(u) ex National Coal Board, Woolley Colliery, Darton, South Yorkshire. after 22/9/1977, by 27/7/1978

CORUS plc, WELDED TUBES DIVISION
CORBY WORKS   T31
British Steel plc, Tubes & Pipes until 10/1999   SP 909899

Limited rail use has continued at this works, in Weldon Road, Corby, after the company re-structuring that created "Corus". The locomotives are used to shunt internal HEA hopper wagons at the scrap re-cycling plant.

Gauge: 4ft 8½in

BSC 2		0-6-0DH	GECT 5395 1974	(a)
3		0-6-0DH	GECT 5365 1972	(b)

(a) ex British Steel plc, Tubes & Pipes, with site, 10/1999; to Yorkshire Engine Company Ltd, for repair, 18/12/1999; returned 12/4/2001.

(b) ex British Steel plc, Tubes & Pipes, with site, 10/1999; ; to Yorkshire Engine Company Ltd, for repair, 17/9/1999; returned 17/12/1999.

COSGROVE SAND & GRAVEL CO LTD
(Registered 20/4/1950)
COSGROVE GRAVEL PITS, near Stony Stratford   L32
earlier C.R. Whiting   SP 796424

Trade directories list C.R. Whiting, of The Lodge, Cosgrove, as a farmer in 1924, but from 1931 until 1953 (at least) as a washed sand and gravel merchant. The Cosgrove Sand & Gravel Co Ltd was associated with Betts & Faulkner Ltd, builders and contractors, of Stony Stratford, and went into liquidation on 3/10/1960. A narrow gauge tramway ran from Cosgrove Lock on the Grand Union Canal eastwards for about 800 yards to quarries (which were actually located in Buckinghamshire) about a mile north-west of Wolverton. Tramway closed and lifted by 1965.

Gauge: 2ft 0in

-	4wDM	MR		(a)	(1)
-	4wDM	MR	9204 1946	New (b)	(2)

(a) identity unknown; ex Diesel Loco Hirers Ltd, by 13/9/1943 (when spares were ordered from MR).

(b) rebuild of MR 8623, originally War Department.

(1) returned to Diesel Loco Hirers Ltd, after 11/9/1944.
(2) to E.L. Pitt & Co Ltd, dealers, Brackley, by 16/7/1963.

CUNLIFFE'S KETTERING BRICKWORKS LTD
NORTHFIELD BRICKWORKS, Kettering   R33
William Cunliffe, c1894 -1906   SP 862798

Brickworks located on the east side of the Midland Railway Kettering - Leicester railway about a mile north of Kettering Station (and on the opposite side of the line to Kettering Ironworks), served by standard gauge sidings from this line. The works was in production from about 1894. It was resolved to wind up the company on 31/3/1908 and the works and locomotive were advertised for sale in 1910. From 1929 the site was occupied by Kettering Borough Council (which see).

Gauge: 4ft 8½in

FABIAN	0-4-0ST	OC	MW	720 1880	(a)	s/s

(a) ex T.A. Walker, Manchester Ship Canal (1887-1894) contract, Lancs, after 3/1894.

E.P. DAVIS

GEDDINGTON QUARRIES, Geddington

R34
SP 863831

Ironstone quarries extended for about a mile to the east of the Midland Railway Kettering - Corby line north of Glendon South Junction. Workings were in use by 1902 (siding agreement originally dated 7/10/1897) and were served by a narrow gauge tramway to a tipping dock alongside the Midland Railway line. Output mainly went to the furnaces of the Bennerley Ironworks in Notts, also owned by E.P. Davis. Pits closed 1929 and track lifted. Acquired by South Durham Steel & Iron Co Ltd (siding agreement transferred 15/7/1931), but not re-opened until 1940 as their Storefield Pits. See under South Durham Steel & Iron Co Ltd, for later history.

Reference : "The Ironstone Quarries of the Midlands, Part 6, Corby"; Eric Tonks,
Runpast Publishing, 1992

Gauge: 2ft 6in

-	0-4-0T	OC				(a)	s/s
FILEY	0-4-0ST	OC				(a)	s/s
BLUEBELL	0-6-0ST	OC				(b)	(1)
SCOTCHMAN	0-6-0ST	OC	B	255	1878	(c)	(1)
TOGO	0-6-0T	OC	WB	1785	1905	New	(1)
STAFFORD	0-6-0T	OC	WB	1861	1907	New	(1)

(a)   origins and identities unknown
(b)   ex Gretton Quarries
(c)   ex Gretton Quarries, c/1898.

(1)   scrapped on site, c/1933.

GRETTON IRONSTONE PITS

T35
SP895934

Quarries on the outcrop on the top of the escarpment to the east of the Midland Railway Corby - Manton railway, south of Gretton village. Working commenced in 1888 and a narrow gauge tramway ran for about a mile from the quarries to a cable worked incline down to sidings on the Midland Railway south of Gretton station. Production ceased in 6/1902 and the area was soon restored to agricultural use.

Reference: "The Ironstone Quarries of the Midlands, Part 6, Corby"; Eric Tonks,
Runpast Publishing, 1992

Gauge: 2ft 6in

BLUEBELL	0-6-0ST	OC				(a)	(1)
-	0-4-0ST	OC	HE	307	1883	(b)	(3)
ROCKET	0-4-0T	OC				(a)	s/s
SCOTCHMAN	0-6-0ST	OC	B	255	1878	(c)	(2)

The records of Markham & Co Ltd, Chesterfield (order 1410 of 20/2/1889) show "E.P. Davis. Repairs to narrow gauge loco ex Cransley Iron Co". This loco may be one of the unidentified locos shown above.

(a)   origin and identity unknown
(b)   ex Twywell Iron Ore Co Ltd, Woodford Quarries, c/1890.
(c)   origin unknown

(1)   to Geddington Quarries
(2)   to Geddington Quarries, c/1898

(3) later J. Strachan, Welshpool & Llanfair Railway (1901-1903) contract, Montgomery [Powys], after 9/1899, by autumn 1902.

DUNMORE LTD
IRTHLINGBOROUGH (WEST END) QUARRIES, Irthlingborough   Q36
Arthur Dunmore until 7/10/1898   SP 938699

Quarries, mainly on the north of the Wellingborough road, at the west end of Irthlingborough, being worked for clay, lime and ironstone by 1895. Connected by a standard gauge line to the LNWR Wellingborough - Peterborough railway. The operations were taken over for cement production by Premier Portland Cement Co Ltd (see BPCM for later history), on 24/1/1907.

Gauge: 4ft 8½in

DOVER	0-6-0ST	IC	MW	688	1878	(a)	(1)
-	0-4-0ST	OC	MW	952	1886	(b)	s/s
STATTER	0-4-0ST	OC	K	1841	1876	(c)	(2)

(a) ex Manchester Ship Canal Co, Runcorn, Cheshire, c/1898 (after 11/1897), per Thomas W. Ward, dealer.

(b) ex Thomas Mitchell & Sons Ltd, dealers, Bolton, Lancs, 3/4/1901; earlier Cannington, Shaw & Co Ltd, St.Helens, Lancs.

(c) ex HC, 10/5/1905; earlier Horbury Junction Iron Co Ltd, near Wakefield, Yorkshire (WR), until 31/3/1904.

(1) to Thomas Mitchell & Sons Ltd, dealers, Bolton, Lancs, (bought, in part exchange for MW 952, 23/4/1901).

(2) to Premier Portland Cement Co Ltd, with site, 24/1/1907.

Gauge: 2ft 0in

LITTLE TICH	0-4-0ST	OC	GRE	1897	New	(1)

(1) to Premier Portland Cement Co Ltd, with site, 24/1/1907.

DUSTON IRON ORE CO LTD
DUSTON QUARRIES, near Northampton   N37
Henry Higgins until 28/2/1885   SP 738606
George Pell (trading as the **Northamptonshire Iron Ore Co**) until 1880
Duston Iron Ore Co (subsidiary of the **Staveley Coal & Iron Co Ltd**) until 1859

Quarries located to the west of St James' End, west of Northampton. Production commenced in 1855 using a standard gauge tramway which ran south for about ¾ mile to a wharf on the Grand Junction Canal and also exchange sidings with the LNWR Northampton - Blisworth railway. This tramway also served limestone quarries to the north of the ironstone workings, and Stenson's Foundry about ½ mile to the east. Quarrying ceased about 9/1908 and railway was subsequently lifted.

Reference : "The Ironstone Quarries of the Midlands, Part 3, Northampton"; Eric Tonks, Runpast Publishing, 1989

Gauge : 4ft 8½in

-	0-4-0ST	OC	N	601	1861	(a)	Scr
-	0-4-0ST	OC	R.Bro	c1866		(b)	Scr c/1909

						(b)	s/s
-	(tender loco)						
DUSTON	0-4-0ST	OC	Mkm	103	1891	New	(1)
PETERSTONE	0-4-0ST	OC	MW	1023	1887	(c)	(2)

"Northampton Mercury" 6/10/1866 recorded George Pell (under distress for rent) advertising for sale items including "25hp locomotive engine (Nielson); 2(sic – possibly 20)hp ditto (Brotherhood); 30hp locomotive with tender".

"Contract Journal" 6/1/1909 advertised - For sale, owing to closure of mines, plant including 11in 4-wheel tank loco, Duston Iron Ore Co, Northampton. (Possibly the Brotherhood loco, as the cylinder size does not match any of the other locos.)

(a)   formerly Glasgow Iron Co, Glasgow; to Loddington Ironstone Co Ltd, White Hill Lodge Quarry, Loddington, 11/1894; returned 10/1896.
(b)   origin unknown.
(c)   ex Staveley Coal & Iron Co Ltd, Staveley Works, Derbys, c/1905

(1)   to Staveley Coal & Iron Co Ltd, Staveley Works, Derbys, c/1906
(2)   returned to Staveley Works, /1909.

EARLS BARTON IRON ORE CO LTD
EARLS BARTON IRONSTONE QUARRIES   M38
(Registered 6/1913 and dissolved 3/1927)   SP 857640

Quarries, operating from about 1914, to the east and north of Earls Barton village. Served by a narrow gauge tramway about ½ mile long; from the south end of this an aerial ropeway about a mile in length conveyed the ore to Castle Ashby & Earls Barton station on the LNWR Northampton - Wellingborough railway. Production ceased about 3/1921 and the equipment was dismantled and the ground restored in 1924. Site later re-opened by Earls Barton Silica Co Ltd, working upper strata.

Reference :   "The Ironstone Quarries of the Midlands, Part 3, Northampton"; Eric Tonks, Runpast Publishing, 1989

Gauge: 3ft 0in

NANNIE	0-4-2ST	OC	HC	1087	1914	New	
		reb	HIW		1920		(1)
LIZZIE	0-4-0ST	OC	MW	1038	1887	(a)	(2)

(a)   ex Stanton Ironworks Co Ltd, Orton Quarries, near Loddington, c/1920.

(1)   to Bloxham & Whiston Ironstone Co Ltd, Harringworth Quarries, /1924.
(2)   to Stanton Ironworks Co Ltd, Rothwell Hill Quarries, c/1921.

EARLS BARTON SILICA CO LTD
EARLS BARTON SILICA QUARRIES   M39
                                                                    SP 857640

About 1937 this company worked the white silica sand, used for furnace lining, that overlay the ironstone strata in the Doddington quarry, formerly of Earls Barton Iron Ore Co Ltd (which see). Later worked by the **Rushden Brick & Tile Co Ltd** for fireclay from c1928 until after 1934. A diesel worked narrow gauge line conveyed the output to a lorry loading point on the road north from Earls Barton. Production ceased by 1969 and the site has been cleared.

Reference :   "The Ironstone Quarries of the Midlands, Part 3, Northampton"; Eric Tonks, Runpast Publishing, 1989

Gauge: 2ft 0in

-	4wPM	L	10063	1938	New	(1)
-	4wPM	L	4414	1932	(a)	s/s c/1953
BIG TOM (FURY)	4wDM	RH	163997	1931	(a)	(1)
-	4wDM	OK	7595	1937	(b)	(4)
-	4wDM	OK	8650	c1939	(c)	(1)
-	4wDM	MR	8731	1941	(d)	(3)
-	4wDM	MR	4813	1937	(e)	(2)

(a) ex Earls Barton Sand & Gravel Co Ltd, Earls Barton, 2/1943.
(b) ex Wm. Jones Ltd, dealer, Greenwich, London, by 10/1952.
(c) ex M.E. Engineering Ltd, Cricklewood, 7/1958; earlier E.L. Pitt & Co Ltd, Brackley.
(d) ex MR, 9/1963, earlier Westbury Brick & Pipe Co, Shropshire.
(e) ex Conduit Construction Co Ltd, contrs, per W.J. Redden & Sons Ltd, Wellingborough, /1969 (after 6/1969).

(1) to Edward Redden Ltd, Little Irchester, for scrap, c5/1964.
(2) to Mixconcrete Aggregates Ltd, Earls Barton Quarry, /1969.
(3) to Mixconcrete Aggregates Ltd, Charlecote, Warwicks, 7/1969.
(4) to A.M. Keef, Cote Farm, Bampton, Oxon, c12/1971.

EAST MIDLANDS GAS BOARD
NORTHAMPTON GAS WORKS   N40
Northampton Gaslight Co until 1/5/1949   SP 750599

A small municipal gasworks, established in 1824, was enlarged between 1854 and 1887. The site was further expanded by the purchase of seven acres of land on which was built a new gasholder, capacity 1,125,000 cu ft, commissioned in 1889. The works was located north of the River Nene and south of Northampton (Castle) station. Initially and until 1876 coal was carted by road to the works under contract by Thomas Whitehouse (who see). Standard gauge sidings were built (private siding agreement 27/7/1871), which ran west from the works to a connection with the LNWR Northampton (Castle) - Northampton (Bridge St) railway. Prior to nationalisation, the undertaking operated its own fleet of 220 coal wagons, built by F.T. Wright of Finedon. Rail traffic ceased c5/1969 and the works was subsequently dismantled although a large gasholder remains (in 2000).

Reference : "Northampton Gas Undertaking, 1823 -1949", D.E. Roberts & J.H. Frisby,
East Midlands Gas, 1980.

Gauge: 4ft 8½in

CROCODILE	0-4-0WT	G	Lewin		1876	New	s/s by c/1907
-	0-4-0VBT	VCG	Chaplin	2368	1885	New	(3)
DANE	0-4-0ST	OC	HE	183	1877	New	Scr after 5/1953
SAXON	0-4-0ST	OC	HE	645	1896	New	(2)
BRITON	0-4-0ST	OC	HE	906	1906	New	Scr after 5/1953
NORMAN	0-4-0ST	OC	P	2052	1944	New	Scr 5/1969
-	4wVBT	VCG	S	9398	1950	(a)	(1)
(PLANTAGENET)	4wVBT	VCG	S	9527	1951	New (b)	(4)
102	4wDM		RH	252841	1948	(c)	(5)

(a) ex S, for demonstration, c2/1951.
(b) possibly after demonstration at EMGB, Cambridge Gasworks, 9/1951.
(c) ex Derby Gasworks, 30/11/1958.

(1) returned to S after demonstration, /1951.
(2) scrapped on site by W.J. Redden & Sons, Wellingborough, 12/1960.
(3) retained for preservation; to Nottingham Industrial Museum, 3/1966.
(4) derelict by 6/1959; scrapped on site by W.J. Redden & Sons, Wellingborough, /1965.
(5) to George Cohen, Sons & Co Ltd, Cransley, by 6/12/1970.

EBBW VALE STEEL, IRON & COAL CO LTD
FINEDON PARK IRONSTONE QUARRIES   Q41
R.E.Campbell until 9/11/1915   SP 908714
Keeble & Jellett until 1/10/1914

Quarries, worked from late 1913, on the south-east of Finedon Park, immediately to the west
of Finedon village. A narrow gauge tramway conveyed the ore to a tipping platform to a
standard gauge line which then ran for about ¾ mile west to connect with the Midland
Railway Wellingborough - Kettering line. The narrow gauge line was normally horse worked
but at least one locomotive was used on it for a time. Quarries closed in 1921 and railways
dismantled.

Reference :   "The Ironstone Quarries of the Midlands, Part 4, Wellingborough"; Eric Tonks,
              Runpast Publishing, 1990

Gauge: 4ft 8½in
   No.9   0-6-0ST   OC   P   751 1898   (a)   (1)

(a)   ex Joseph Pugsley, dealer, Lawrence Hill, Bristol, /1911;
       earlier W. Hill & Co, Portland Dockyard (Admiralty) (1896-1909) contract, Dorset.

(1)   to Ebbw Vale Ironworks, c/1921.

Gauge: 2ft 0in
   LITTLE TICH   0-4-0ST   OC   GRE   1897   (a)   (1)
   -                    0-4-0WT   OC   OK   (b)   s/s

(a)   ex Premier Portland Cement Co Ltd, Irthlingborough, on loan.
(b)   origins and identity unknown.

(1)   returned to Premier Portland Cement Co Ltd.

FISONS BASIC SLAG LTD
CORBY IRON & STEEL WORKS   T42
Corby Basic Slag Ltd (registered 4/1935) until 1962
   (Subsidiary of **National Fertilizers Ltd** by 1940; later subsidiary of **Fisons Ltd**)   SP 902898

Company involved in the processing of slag from the steel production at this works. The
narrow gauge tramway was out of use by 10/1963 and was replaced by standard gauge,
worked by Stewarts & Lloyds Ltd.

Gauge: 2ft 0in
   -                    4wDM   Bg/DC   2108 1937 New   s/s
   -                    4wDM   Bg/DC   2137 1938 New   s/s after 5/1964
   -                    4wDM   Bg/DC   2155 1940 New   s/s after 5/1964
   -                    4wDM   Bg/DC   2202 1945 New   s/s after 5/1964

GEISMAR (UK) LTD
NORTHAMPTON WORKS

Registered as a private company 15/12/1980 as a subsidiary of **Soc. L. Geismar SA**, France. The company is the manufacturer and distributer of Geismar railway track maintenance equipment and also offers a hire and maintenance service. A contract for the rebuilding of main line wagons resulted in a locomotive being used from 3/2000 to shunt traffic at these premises in Salthouse Road, Brackmills Industrial Estate, Northampton.

Gauge : 4ft 8½in

JOANNA	4wDH	TH/S	177C	1967		
	reb of S	9401	1950	(a)	(1)	

(a)   ex Willmott Bros (Plant Services) Ltd, Ilkeston, Derbys, hire, 3/2000; earlier Marcroft Engineering, Port Tennant Works, Swansea.

(1)   returned to Willmott Bros (Plant Services) Ltd, Ilkeston, Derbys, 11/12/2000.

GLENDON IRON CO LTD

FINEDON FURNACES
Glendon Iron Co until 23/6/1886
Checkland & Fisher until c1883
Glendon Iron Ore Co until c1872

Furnaces on the east side of the Midland Railway Wellingborough - Kettering line just south of Finedon station. A first furnaces was put into blast in 1866; five furnaces were in operation by 1878 with a fifth added in 1882. These were supplied with ore from quarries to the east and a standard gauge railway about a mile long connected the two. The furnaces closed down in 1891. Site acquired by Islip Iron Co Ltd, and traffic in slag operated (see under Islip Iron Co Ltd). Ironstone quarries acquired by Charles Barlow and re-opened by him (see under Harold Barlow).

Reference :   "The Ironstone Quarries of the Midlands, Part 4, Wellingborough"; Eric Tonks, Runpast Publishing, 1990

Gauge: 4ft 8½in

3	EMILY	0-4-0ST	OC	HCR	163	1875	New	s/s
4	FINEDON	0-4-0ST	OC	HCR	165	1876	New	(1)
	FLORENCE	0-4-0ST	OC	MW	745	1880	New	(1)
	-	0-4-0ST	OC	FE	184	1889	New	(2)

Other locomotives, details unknown, were also used here.

(1)   to Islip Iron Co Ltd, Islip Ironworks.
(2)   to Plevins & Co, Twywell Brickworks, c/1892.

LAMPORT IRONSTONE QUARRIES

Quarries west of Lamport village with a standard gauge railway about ½ mile long to the goods yard at Lamport station on the LNWR Northampton - Market Harborough line. Operations were short lived, from 1882 to 1890.

Reference :   "The Ironstone Quarries of the Midlands, Part 3, Northampton"; Eric Tonks, Runpast Publishing, 1989

Gauge: 4ft 8½in : Worked by unidentified loco(s) - possibly from Finedon Furnaces.

THOS.E. GRAY & CO LTD

ISEBROOK QUARRY, Burton Latimer   R46

Thos.E. Gray Ltd (established 1877) until 5/1922   Standard Gauge SP 887752
Narrow Gauge SP 892755

Workings commenced by this firm of refractory manufacturers in 1925 for silica sand at the former Lloyd's Ironstone Co Ltd's Isham Quarry. A standard gauge line was relaid from the exchange sidings on the east side of the ex-Midland Railway Kettering - Wellingborough line north of Isham & Burton Latimer station and ran east to the quarries. A narrow gauge line was introduced within the quarries. By 1948 the connection to the main line had been cut and thence the standard gauge was used between only the works and the narrow gauge transfer dock. The works closed in early 5/1982 and the site was cleared by 1984.

References : "The Ironstone Quarries of the Midlands, Part 5, Kettering"; Eric Tonks,
Runpast Publishing, 1991
"Industrial Railway Record No.118", September 1989.

Gauge: 4ft 8½in

ANCOATS	4wVBT	HCG	S	5666	1924		
	reb of 0-4-0ST	OC	MW	1091	1888	(a)	(2)
No.2 ISEBROOK	4wVBT	VCG	S	6515	1926	(b)	(3)
KING EDWARD	0-4-0ST	OC	HC	648	1903	(c)	(1)
(MUSKETEER)	4wVBT	VCG	S	9369	1946	(d)	(4)
9365 (BELVEDERE)	4wVBT	VCG	S	9365	1946	(e)	(4)
-	0-4-0DM		HE	2070	1940	(f)	(6)
(YARD No.6953) BUNTY	0-4-0DM		HE	4263	1952	(g)	(7)
No.1	4wDM		RH	275886	1949	(h)	(5)

Note : that LMSR 11202 (0-4-0ST OC Hor /1891) was here on hire 1/5/1937 to 15/5/1937 and LNER 62 (later 8172) (4wVBT S 8323/1930) on hire from LNER, 3/1943.

(a)   ex Blackwell & Son (Engineers) Ltd, Northampton, possibly from trials at United Steel Companies Ltd, Irthlingborough Ironworks; here by 30/7/1929.

(b)   ex S, /1934 (after 5/10/1934); earlier with LMSR for trials (from 29/4/1929); used as works shunter at S from 1/1927; built for GWR, 12, but order cancelled and returned to S, 17/1/1927.

(c)   ex Bold Venture Lime Co Ltd, Chatburn, Lancs, c/1938.

(d)   ex Williams & Williams Ltd, Hooton, Cheshire, per James N. Connell, dealer, Coatbridge, Lanarks, c/1951 (by 7/1951).

(e)   ex TH, Whiston Works, Rotherham, Yorkshire (WR), 25/4/1958; earlier Wm Cory & Son Ltd, Rochester, Kent.

(f)   ex Northampton Corporation.Highways Dept., c2/1972.

(g)   ex Track Supplies & Services Ltd, Wolverton, Bucks, 4/1972; earlier MoDND, Portsmouth, Hampshire.

(h)   ex Track Supplies & Services Ltd, Wolverton, Bucks, 20/2/1982; earlier CEGB, Nechells Power Station, West Midlands.

(1)   to HC, Leeds, for repair, 10/1948; still there on 3/1/1949; repairs not completed; s/s (presumed scrapped).

(2)   withdrawn by 5/1936; to W.J. Redden & Sons, Wellingborough, for scrap, 8/1956.

(3)   withdrawn /1958; to Quainton Railway Society Ltd, Quainton Road, Bucks, 31/5/1972.

(4)   to Northamptonshire Ironstone Railway Trust Ltd, Hunsbury Hill, 27/2/1975.

(5)   returned to Track Supplies & Services Ltd, Wolverton, Bucks, 24/6/1982.

(6)   scrapped on site by Hunt Bros, of Burton Latimer, 15/7/1982.

(7)   scrapped on site by Hunt Bros, of Burton Latimer, 29/7/1982 - 2/8/1982.

Gauge: 2ft 0in

-	4wPM	FH			(a)	(1)
-	4wDM	MR	8594	1940	(b)	(2)
(ISEBROOK)	4wDM	MR	7219	1938	New	Scr /1971
THUNDERBIRD II (ISEBROOK)	4wDM	MR	9411	1948	(c)	(3)
	4wDM	MR	5881	1935	(d)	(3)

(a)   origin and identity unknown
(b)   ex Diesel Loco Hirers Ltd, on hire, 10/1945.
(c)   ex Holloway Bros. (Contractors) Ltd, 4/1965 (earlier at Thurrock Power Station (CEGB) contract, Essex, in 2/1959).
(d)   ex Joseph Arnold & Sons Ltd, Leighton Buzzard, Beds, 13/8/1969.

(1)   to ? , Bytham, Lincs.
(2)   returned to Diesel Loco Hirers Ltd, off hire; later Gunthorpe Gravels (Trent) Ltd, Notts, by 19/8/1951.
(3)   to North Warwickshire Railway Society, Nuneaton, Warwicks, c4/1982 (after 19/9/1981).

HATTON SHAW & CO (IRTHLINGBOROUGH) LTD
THREE CHIMNEYS TANNERY, Irthlingborough   **Q47**
SP 946697

Quarrying was commenced in this area by the Irthlingborough Iron Ore Co Ltd with a ½ mile long standard gauge line to the LNWR Wellingborough - Peterborough line; siding agreement dated 28/8/1890. This company was wound up in 5/1898 and the Irthlingborough Brick & Tile Co Ltd was formed in the same month with permission to use this branch. This company was wound up in 1900. Hatton Shaw & Co (Irthlingborough) Ltd was registered on 30/12/1913 and took over the works, which were located south of Irthlingborough village. Adjacent site acquired by Ebbw Vale Steel, Iron & Coal Co Ltd 1915, and shunting then performed by them until the tannery closed (by 1924).

Gauge: 4ft 8½in

-	4wT	G		(a)	s/s

(a)   rebuilt from steam road wagon.

HEYFORD IRON CO LTD
GAYTON WOOD IRONSTONE QUARRIES   **M48**
Pell & Co until 3/1874   SP 710540
John Hickman until 1858

Quarries, in production by about 1855, located about ¼ mile to the south of Gayton village. Connected by a standard gauge line to the LNWR Roade - Rugby main line north of Blisworth station. Later the S&MJR Blisworth - Fenny Compton line was built parallel to and south of the quarry line. Quarrying extended south of the S&MJR line and a horse worked narrow gauge system was in use in the quarries. Production had ceased by 1900, when the quarries were reopened by R B Sparrow (which see).

Reference :   "The Ironstone Quarries of the Midlands, Part 3, Northampton"; Eric Tonks, Runpast Publishing, 1989

Gauge: 4ft 8½in

JUMBO	0-4-0ST	OC	FW	331	1877	New	(1)

(1)   to Monckton Main Coal Co Ltd, Yorkshire, by 1/1900.

ISLIP IRON CO LTD
FINEDON SIDING SLAG WORKS

Q49

SP 896725

Finedon Furnaces were erected in 1866 on the east side of the Midland Railway Wellingborough - Kettering line south of Finedon station. They were closed in 1891, were taken over by Islip Iron Co Ltd but not reopened. The new owners did however use locomotives for the reclaimation of slag for use as railway ballast. Work ceased in 1925 and the site was taken over by Francis T. Wright Ltd, wagon builders, which see for later history.

Reference : "The Ironstone Quarries of the Midlands, Part 4, Wellingborough"; Eric Tonks, Runpast Publishing, 1990

Gauge: 4ft 8½in

ISLIP No.1	0-4-0ST	OC	HE	138	1875	(a)	(1)
ISLIP No.2	0-4-0ST	OC	HE	201	1878	(a)	(1)

(a)   ex Islip Ironworks (see under Stewarts & Lloyds Minerals Ltd).

(1)   taken over by Francis T. Wright Ltd, with site, /1925.

E.M. JELLETT
EASTON NESTON IRONSTONE QUARRIES

M50

Richard J. Harry until 1918

SP 706508

(Towcester Mineral & Brick Co Ltd title also used)

Quarries about two miles south of Blisworth, on both sides of the Towcester road. Locomotives were used from 1915 on the narrow gauge quarry system, which had been horse worked since it had been installed about 1912. A standard gauge connection to S&MJR Towcester - Olney railway was worked by horse (for earlier history, with locomotives, see under **Towcester Mineral & Brick Co Ltd).** Quarries closed 1920 and track lifted; the company used the title **Blisworth & Towcester Ironstone Estates Ltd** from 1920.

Reference : "The Ironstone Quarries of the Midlands, Part 3, Northampton"; Eric Tonks, Runpast Publishing, 1989

Gauge: 2ft 6in

FERRET II	0-4-0ST	OC	WB	1853	1908	(a)	(1)
RYDER GIBSON	0-4-0ST	OC	WB	2103	1919	New	(2)

(a)   ex A.C. Bealey & Sons Ltd, Radcliffe, Lancs, via E.E. Cornforth, dealer, c12/1914.

(1)   to Holm & Co Ltd, Kingsnorth, Kent, /1925, via Blackwell & Son (Engineers) Ltd, Northampton.

(2)   to Thos.W. Ward Ltd, /1928; later to Hendy Merthyr Colliery Co Ltd, Hendy Merthyr Colliery, West Glamorgan, by 5/1931.

KETTERING BOROUGH COUNCIL
earlier **Kettering Urban District Council**

NORTHFIELD DEPOT, Kettering

R51

SP 862798

Plant depot, in use from about 1929, in Northfield Avenue, on the site of Cunliffe's Northfield Brickworks (which see).

Gauge: 4ft 8½ in

PROGRESS	4wPM	KC	1553	1927	New	(1)

(1)   to George Cohen, Sons & Co Ltd, Cransley, 8/10/1963.

Gauge: 2ft 0in

20	4wPM	FH	1669	1930	(a)	s/s after /1959

(a)   ex New Cransley Reservoir contract; earlier. Finedon Sewage Works.

FINEDON SEWAGE WORKS   Q52
SP 893727

A large sewage disposal plant, on the west side of the BR (ex Midland Railway) main line between Finedon and Burton Latimer, served by a short narrow gauge line, hand worked in its final years. Works built after 1924 and closed by 12/1985.

Gauge: 2ft 0in

20	4wPM	FH	1669	1930	(a)	(1)

(a)   ex Kettering Sewage Works

(1)   to New Cransley Reservoir contract; thence to Northfield Depot.

KETTERING SEWAGE WORKS   R53
SP 872766

A sewage works located in Pytchley Road, south of the BR (ex Midland Railway) Kettering – Burton Latimer main line. Builders records give the locomotive listed below as delivered to this location.

Gauge: 2ft 0in

20	4wPM	FH	1669	1930	New	(1)

(1)   to Finedon Sewage Works.

KETTERING IRON & COAL CO LTD
KETTERING FURNACES & QUARRIES   R54
Kettering Iron Ore Co until 21/4/1876   SP 860800
Subsidiary of **Stewarts & Lloyds Ltd** from 10/1956

Quarrying for ironstone commenced in 1870 in the area to the west of the Midland Railway about a mile north of Kettering station with the 3ft 0in gauge tramway serving a tipping dock by the main line. Two furnaces were built on the site and came into blast in 1878 and a third furnace was added in 1889. Standard gauge sidings and locomotives were used at the furnaces, while the narrow gauge tramway connected the quarries with the ironworks. Over the years quarrying extended for a distance of about four miles to the west of the works, with an extensive system of railways. Furnaces ceased production 4/1959, and were blown out, 24/4/1959; dismantled 5/1959 - 1960. Quarrying ceased on 24/10/1962 and all equipment was dismantled by 7/1963.

Reference :   "The Ironstone Quarries of the Midlands, Part 5, Kettering"; Eric Tonks, Runpast Publishing, 1991

Gauge: 4ft 8½in

KETTERING FURNACES No.1	0-4-0ST	OC	BH	422	1878	New	Scr /1936
KETTERING FURNACES No.5	0-4-0ST	OC	BH	984	1890	New	(2)
9 CARRINGTON *	0-6-0ST	OC	MW	1286	1894	(a)	(1)
10	0-4-0ST	OC	AB	1065	1906		
	reb	AB			1941	(b)	(4)
KETTERING FURNACES No.11	0-6-0ST	OC	AE	1849	1920	New	
	reb	HE			1956		Scr 2/1963
(12) HAROLD	0-6-0ST	IC	HC	1420	1920		
	reb	HC			1943	(c)	(3)
KETTERING FURNACES No.14	0-4-0ST	OC	LG		1931	(d)	Scr 2/1963
KETTERING FURNACES No.15	0-6-0ST	OC	HL	3347	1918		
	reb	AB			1939	(e)	(4)

*name carried from 11/1915 – earlier named CARINGTON.

(a)   ex Holme & King Ltd, contrs, Wigan, Lancs, c/1909; orig. Birmingham Corporation Waterworks, Elan Valley Reservoir (1894-1906) construction, Rhayader, Radnor [Powys], ELAN.

(b)   ex Thos.W. Ward Ltd, c/1912; orig. P. & W. Anderson, contrs, Glasgow.

(c)   ex Wernddu Railway & Colliery Co Ltd, Pontardawe, West Glamorgan, by /1923.

(d)   ex Watts, Hardy & Co Ltd, dismantlers of Lingford Gardiner's works, c7/1932.

(e)   ex WD, Bramley, Hampshire, via Joseph Pugsley & Sons Ltd, dealers, Bristol, c11/1952.

(1)   to Luffenham Iron Ore Co Ltd, Rutland, c/1923.

(2)   to Thos.W. Ward Ltd, for scrap, /1935.

(3)   to HC, for repairs, 10/1953; in bad condition and scrapped at HC, 1/1954.

(4)   to Wellingborough Iron Co Ltd, 5/1960.

Gauge: 3ft 0in

KETTERING FURNACES No.2	0-4-0ST	OC	BH	501	1879	New	Scr 3/1963
KETTERING FURNACES No.3	0-4-0ST	OC	BH	859	1885	New	(2)
KETTERING FURNACES No.4 YUM YUM	0-4-0ST	OC	BH	893	1887	New (a)	(1)
KETTERING FURNACES No.6	0-6-0ST	OC	MW	1123	1889		
(UNION JACK until 6/1934)	reb	RSH			1949	(b)	Scr 4/1963
KETTERING FURNACES No.7	0-6-0ST	OC	MW	1370	1897		
	reb	RSH			1950	New	(3)
KETTERING FURNACES No.8	0-6-0ST	OC	MW	1675	1906	New	(4)
(13)	4w-4wVBT	VCG	S	6412	1926	New	Scr 3/1960

(a)   exhibited at (and probably built for) the Newcastle Exhibition, 1887.

(b)   earlier J.P. Edwards, Chinley – Hathersage (Midland Railway) (1888-1894) contract, Derbys.

(1)   to Luffenham Iron Ore Co Ltd, Rutland, c5/1924; returned 10/1924; to Thos.W. Ward Ltd, for scrap, 4/1927.

(2)   to National Trust, Penrhyn Castle, Caerns (North Wales), for preservation, 21/8/1963, per J.B. Latham.

(3)   scrapped on site, 6/1963

(4)   to Borough of Kettering, Manor House Grounds, for preservation, 26/8/1963.

LLOYDS IRONSTONE CO LTD
ISHAM IRONSTONE QUARRY   R55
Isham Ironstone Co until c1902   SP 890755

Quarries about ½ mile east of Isham & Burton Latimer station on the Midland Railway Kettering - Wellingborough line, with a standard gauge railway connecting with this line. Working probably started about 1900, with the railway initially horse worked. Working ceased about 1910 but the quarry was reopened for ganister quarrying by Thos E Gray & Co Ltd (which see) in 1925.

Reference : "The Ironstone Quarries of the Midlands, Part 5, Kettering"; Eric Tonks,
Runpast Publishing, 1991

Gauge: 4ft 8½in

ISHAM	0-4-0ST	OC	HE	791	1902	(a)	(1)

(a)   locomotive ordered by Lloyds Ironstone Co Ltd for Weldon & Corby Mines; but whether it was the locomotive at Isham is not proven.

(1)   to Corby Works, c/1910.

HENRY MARTIN LTD
NETHER HEYFORD BRICKWORKS   P56
Blisworth & Stowe Brick & Tile Co Ltd until 22/3/1923   SP 652578
form. George King & Son

Brickworks on the south-west side of the LNWR Blisworth - Rugby main line about ½ mile south of Stowe Hill tunnel. Bricks were being made at the old Stowe Ironworks by 1876 and brickmaking machinery was being installed there in 1877. By 1889 the works had three kilns, and there was a 2ft 11in gauge tramway in the quarry on the south side of the works. Brickworks closed 1940 when the site was requisitioned by the War Department for ammunition storage. One locomotive remained stored here until 3/1951 when it was saved for preservation by the Industrial Locomotive Society. Derelict kilns were still extant in 1970 but have since been demolished.

Reference : "The Ironstone Quarries of the Midlands, Part 3, Northampton"; Eric Tonks,
Runpast Publishing, 1989

Gauge: 4ft 8½in

-	4wWT	G	AP	807	1872	(a)	(1)
-	4wWT	G	AP	846	1872	(a)	(2)

(a)   ex Oxford & Aylesbury Tramroad, 23/9/1895.

(1)   to LTE, Neasden Depot, for preservation, 29/3/1951; later to Science Museum, South Kensington, London.
(2)   dismantled and parts used to repair AP 807; remainder scrapped.

METROPOLITAN BRICK CO LTD
BRIXWORTH BRICK & TILE WORKS   M57
A. Hamson & Son Ltd from c1928
A. Hamson (owner) in 1920   SP 733720

A brickworks opened in 1920, with two small circular downdraft kilns, to produce wire-cut bricks. Clay was brought to the works on a cable hauled tramway, powered by a Tangye steam engine, from pits to the east. The premises were taken over in 1932/1933 by

Metropolitan & Yorkshire Brick Co, who installed new plant and developed a new pit to the north of the works, served by a locomotive worked tramway. The company traded as the Brixworth Brick & Tile Co Ltd from c1928 until the works closed about 1939.

A. Hamson & Son Ltd operated Weedon Gravel Pit, Dodford, by 1946 until after 1948; use of a tramway at that site has not been established.

Reference : "Bulletin of Industrial Archeology, in CBA Group 9" No.13, Richard O'Rourke, July 1970.

Gauge: 2ft 0in

-	4wDM	RH 166037	1933	(a)	(1)

A. Hamson & Son Ltd offered for sale ("Contract Journal" 29/1/1941) plant including a 2ft 0in gauge 5hp Lister locomotive. Further details unknown.

(a)   ex RH, Lincoln, 11/6/1934; earlier with R.A. Lister & Co Ltd, Dursley, Gloucs, from new (25/3/1933) until 20/11/1933.

(1)   to Yorkshire Amalgamated Products Ltd, Huttons Ambo Sand Pits, near York, after 25/8/1937, by 14/4/1942.

MIDLAND BRICK CO (WELLINGBORO') LTD
LONG BUCKBY BRICKWORKS   L58
R. Johnson in 1869   SP 623667

This Long Buckby works was operated by the Johnson family from 1831 until 1874, was taken over by Boughtons from c1900 and passed to J.H. Sparrow by 1910. It closed for some years and was then re-opened about 1920 for the production of wire-cut bricks by the Long Buckby Brick Co Ltd (under the ownership of Watson of Coventry and later Bate & Son). During World War II the works was taken over by the WD for the repair of ammunition boxes and after the war was reopened to produce facing bricks.

From about 1900 the Midland Brick Co Ltd operated a large works in Mill Road, Wellingborough. This closed after 1948 (by 1952), and the company had moved to the Long Buckby works after 3/1946, by 1/1947. The Long Buckby works finally closed about 1960 and the site was taken over in 1965 by Daventry Engineering Ltd

Ordnance Survey maps show no evidence of a tramway at the works, but in 1946 plant including a Montania (i.e an OK) type "M" loco and track was offered for sale ("Machinery Market", 1/11/1946).

Gauge: 2ft 0in

-	4wDM	OK 6711	1936	(a)	s/s after 1/1959

(a)   ex Beach's Brickfield Ltd, Rainford End Brickworks, Chelmsford, Essex, by 1/1955.

MINISTRY OF DEFENCE - ARMY DEPARTMENT

WEEDON TECHNICAL STORES DEPOT   P59
No.99 O.S.D., ROYAL ARMY ORDNANCE CORPS by 1920, until after 8/1949
War Department until 1/4/1964   SP 632594 approx

This military depot was the first inland central store and distribution point for ordnance. An Equitation School was later set up nearby. The site, also served by a private branch of the Grand Junction Canal, was on the west side of the ex-LNWR main line south of Weedon station and served from about 1912 by standard gauge sidings connecting with this line. An internal narrow gauge system was used. Rail traffic ceased and track removed 1965.

Gauge: 4ft 8½in

2347	WEEDON	0-4-OST	OC	AB		c1870		
			reb	AB	4793	1910	(a)	(1)
70222	SAPPER	0-4-OST	OC	AB	859	1900	(b)	(2)
	DOUGLAS	0-4-OST	OC	P	820	1900	(c)	(3)
	-	4wPM		H	950	1929	New	s/s
802	(70239)	4wDM		RH	221645	1944	(d)	(4)
803	(72210)	4wDM		RH	224341	1944	(e)	(5)
812	(70227)	4wDM		FH	2016	1937		
			reb of	H	951	1929	(f)	(7)
813		4wDM		RH	411319	1957	(g)	(8)
806	(72213)	4wDM		RH	224344	1944	(h)	(6)

(a)   origin and identity unknown.
(b)   earlier Thos.W. Ward Ltd, Langloan Wagon Repair Works, Coatbridge, Lanarks, until /1942.
(c)   earlier WD Queensferry, Flints [North Wales]; here by /1947
(d)   new to WD [? Cwmavon, West Glamorgan]; to here 5/1947.
(e)   ex Arncott Depot, Bicester, Oxon, after 10/2/1949, by 17/4/1952.
(f)   new to WD Corsham, Wilts, 1/1937; here by 1/1952.
(h)   ex Bicester Workshops, Arncott, Oxon, 5/1961.
(g)   ex Bicester Workshops, Arncott, Oxon, 21/1/1958.

(1)   advertised for sale in "Surplus", 15/2/1921 and again 15/6/1921; s/s
(2)   to Abelson & Co (Engineers) Ltd, Sheldon, Birmingham, 2/1949;
      later Joseph Perrin & Son Ltd, Birkenhead, Cheshire.
(3)   to Abelson & Co (Engineers) Ltd, Sheldon, Birmingham, 2/1949;
      later at Gee, Walker & Slater Ltd, Derby Plant Depot, by 20/4/1952; s/s.
(4)   to Birds Comercial Motors, Long Marston, Worcs, /1965;
      thence to Dowty Group, Ashchurch, Gloucs, c2/1966.
(5)   to Bicester Workshops, Arncott, Oxon, 5/12/1956; retumed here, 24/1/1957;
      to Bicester Workshops, Arncott, again, 2/9/1958.
(6)   to Birds (Swansea) Ltd, Pontymister Depot, Gwent, by 6/1965.
(7)   possibly returned to CAD Corsham, Wilts, before /1956.
(8)   to ROF Bramshall, Staffs, 2/6/1961

YARDLEY CHASE DEPOT   M60

War Department until 1/4/1964   Loco shed SP 833558
Ministry of Supply, ROYAL ORDNANCE FACTORY No.20, until 1961

Explosives storage depot, built by **Sir Robert McAlpine & Sons Ltd** (which see), which extended over a substantial area on the east of the ex-Midland Rly Northampton - Bedford railway near Piddington station. Depot built 1942-1943 and served by an extensive standard gauge railway system. After closure of the BR Northampton - Bedford line on 20/1/1964, the section from the depot to Northampton was retained for MOD traffic. Depot and railway closed 2/1981; the area remains in use for military training and some buildings, including the loco shed, were still extant in 2000.

Gauge: 4ft 8½in

YARDLEY CHASE No.1		0-4-0DM	DC	2169	1942		
863			VF	4861	1942	New	(2)
YARDLEY CHASE No.2		0-4-0DM	DC	2170	1942		
864			VF	4862	1942	New	(3)
YARDLEY CHASE No.3		0-4-0DM	DC	2172	1942		
			VF	4864	1942	New	(1)
865		0-4-0DM	DC	2171	1942		
			VF	4863	1942	(a)	(4)
402	(8202)	0-4-0DH	NBQ	27423	1955	(b)	(5)
404		0-4-0DH	NBQ	27425	1955	(c)	(6)
408		0-4-0DH	NBQ	27429	1955	(d)	(7)
410	(8210)	0-4-0DH	NBQ	27645	1958	(e)	(8)
411		0-4-0DH	NBQ	27646	1959	(f)	(9)
9020		2w-2PMR	Wkm	8084	1958	(g)	(10)
9021		2w-2PMR	Wkm	8085	1958	(h)	(11)
9043		2w-2PMR	Wkm	6965	1955	(i)	(12)
9044		2w-2PMR	Wkm	7438	1956	(j)	(13)
9104		2w-2PMR	Wkm	7397	1957	(k)	(14)
9102		2w-2PMR	DC/Bg	1896	1950	(l)	(15)
9106		2w-2PMR	DC/Bg	2326	1950	(m)	(16)
9116		4wDMR	CE	5427	1968	(n)	(17)
9119		4wDMR	BD	3708	1975	(o)	(18)
9150		4wDMR	BD	3746	1976	(p)	(19)

(a) ex Bicester Workshops, Arncott, Oxon, 13/5/1964
(b) ex Bicester Workshops Arncott, Oxon, 4/4/1968; to AB, Kilmarnock, for overhaul, 18/5/1973; ex Bicester Workshops, Arncott, Oxon, 25/4/1977
(c) ex AB, Kilmarnock, after overhaul, 23/5/1973; earlier CAD Kineton, Warwicks.
(d) ex CAD Kineton, Warwicks, 3/9/1977
(e) ex ROF Ruddington, Notts, 25/7/1968
(f) ex CVD Ludgershall, Wilts, 19/7/1978
(g) ex CAD Kineton, Warwicks, 21/2/1961
(h) ex Bicester Workshops, Arncott, Oxon, 20/4/1961
(i) ex Bicester Workshops, Arncott, Oxon, by 12/1969
(j) ex ROF Bramshall, Staffs, 11/1964
(k) ex PEE Shoeburyness, Essex, 16/4/1979
(l) ex CAD Kineton, Warwicks, 15/9/1975
(m) ex CAD Bramley, Hampshire, 10/4/1968
(n) ex Bicester Workshops, Arncott, Oxon, 24/3/1969
(o) ex CAD Kineton, Warwicks, 18/12/1978
(p) ex Bicester Military Railway, Oxon, 26/1/1977

(1) to ROF Burghfield, Berks, 12/1946.
(2) to Bicester Workshops, Arncott, Oxon, 15/7/1964; returned here, 5/4/1965; to Bicester Workshops, Arncott, Oxon, 28/4/1966
(3) to Bicester Workshops, Arncott, Oxon, 1/6/1965; returned here, 11/2/1966; to West Moors Depot, Dorset, 8/8/1968.
(4) to COD Hilsea, Hampshire, 25/7/1968
(5) to CAD Kineton, Warwicks, 3/8/1977
(6) to Bicester Workshops, Arncott, Oxon, 27/4/1977
(7) to ROF Ruddington, Notts, 17/3/1981
(8) to AB, 3/8/1977
(9) to Bicester Workshops Arncott, Oxon, 19/3/1981

(10) to Bicester Workshops Arncott, Oxon, 30/4/1964
(11) to Bicester Workshops Arncott, Oxon, 5/4/1965
(12) to Kent & East Sussex Railway, Rolvenden, Kent, by 2/1972
(13) to Kent & East Sussex Railway, Rolvenden, Kent, /1969
(14) to MOD Air Force Dept, Caerwent, Gwent, 17/3/1981
(15) to CAD Kineton, Warwicks, 2/2/1977
(16) to CAD Kineton, Warwicks, 25/9/1975
(17) to Bicester Workshops, Arncott, Oxon, 24/8/1979
(18) to CAD Kineton, Warwicks, 18/3/1981
(19) to Bicester Workshops, Arncott, Oxon, 28/3/1979

MIXCONCRETE AGGREGATES LTD
Mackaness Aggregates Ltd until 1965
A.J.Mackaness Ltd until 5/1962.
earlier **A.J. Mackaness** (listed in trade directories as a farmer in 1920 but as a sand and gravel merchant from 1931).

CLIFFORD HILL PITS, Little Houghton   M61
SP 804603

Gravel pits, served by a narrow gauge tramway, on the south side of the River Nene about three miles east of Northampton. Tramway closed and track removed 1974.
Gauge: 2ft 0in

13		4wDM	MR	8810	1943	(a)	(2)
-		4wDM	RH	375362	1955	(b)	(1)
T12		4wDM	MR	21505	1955	(c)	(3)
T4		4wDM	MR	8739	1942	(d)	(3)

(a) ex Delapre Pits, 6/1962; to Delapre Pits, 9/1963; ex St. James End Pits, c/1969 (by 4/1969).
(b) ex Rickmansworth Gravel Co Ltd, Herts, /1968.
(c) ex M.E. Engineering Ltd, dealers, Cricklewood, Middlesex, /1970 (by 6/1970);
     earlier Reading Corporation, Manor Farm Sewage Works, Reading, Berks.
(d) ex Delapre Pits, 9/1963; to Delapre Pits, /1965 (after 8/1965); ex Earls Barton Pits, after 12/1970, by 2/1971.

(1) to Earls Barton Pits, by 4/1969.
(2) s/s, after 12/1970, by 2/1971
(3) to Charlecote Pits, Warwicks, c10/1974.

DELAPRE GRAVEL PITS, Ransome Road, Hardingstone   N62
SP 767593

Gravel pits, served by a narrow gauge tramway, on the Delapre estate about a mile south of Northampton. Pits opened after 1953, closed 1966 and track lifted.
Gauge: 2ft 0in

No.1	4wDM	MR	8739	1942	(a)	(2)
No.2	4wDM	MR	8810	1943	(b)	(1)

(a)   ex Little Billing Pits, /1956 (after 3/1956); to Clifford Hill Pits, 9/1963; returned /1965 (after 8/1965).

(b)   ex Little Billing Pits, /1956 (after 3/1956); to Clifford Hill Pits, 6/1962; returned 9/1963.

(1)   to St.James End Gravel Pits, 4/1966.

(2)   to Earls Barton Sand & Gravel Co Ltd, Earls Barton, 8/1966.

EARLS BARTON GRAVEL PITS   M63

Earls Barton Sand & Gravel Co Ltd from (after 1943, by 1946) until /1965   SP 863621
  - Subsidiary of **Mackaness Aggregates Ltd** from c/1963

Gravel pits at Station Road, Earls Barton, served by a narrow gauge tramway Located south of the River Nene and east of Castle Ashby and Earls Barton station on the ex-LNWR Northampton - Wellingborough line. Tramway closed and track lifted after 1971.

Gauge: 2ft 0in

-		4wPM	L	4414	1932	(a)	(1)
FURY		4wDM	RH	163997	1931	(b)	(1)
-		4wDM	RH	175402	1935	(c)	(2)
-		4wDM	RH	242887	1946	New	(3)
6		4wDM	RH	260724	1948	New	s/s by 3/1971
-		4wDM	RH	331264	1952	New	(5)
4		4wDM	MR	8739	1942	(d)	(7)
5		4wDM	RH	375349	1954	(e)	(6)
-		4wDM	MR	9204	1946	(f)	(5)
-		4wDM	RH	285297	1949	(g)	(5)
2		4wDM	RH	375362	1955	(h)	(6)
-		4wDM	MR	4813	1937	(i)	(8)
T13		4wDM	MR	8969	1945	(j)	(11)
-		4wDM	MR	40S371	1970	New	(9)
-		4wDM	MR	8575	1940	(k)	(10)
T8		4wDM	MR	8731	1941	(l)	(12)
T11		4wDM	MR	9711	1952	(m)	(11)

(a)   ex Wellingborough Gravel & Sand Co, Wellingborough Gravel Pits, after 2/1943, via/per A. Pullen, The Old Dairy, Wingrave, near Aylesbury, Bucks.

(b)   ex Wellingborough Gravel & Sand Co, Wellingborough Gravel Pits, after 2/1943.

(c)   ex Wansford Quarries Ltd, Cambs, after 2/7/1948, by 29/8/1949.

(d)   ex Mixconcrete Aggregates Ltd, Delapre Gravel Pits, Hardingstone, 8/1966; to St.James End Pits, c/1967; ex St.James End Pits, c/1969 (by 4/1969).

(e)   ex Rickmansworth Gravel Co Ltd, Herts, c/1967 (by 8/1968).

(f)   ex St.James End Pits, c/1967 (by 8/1968).

(g)   ex L.W. Vass Ltd, Ampthill, Beds, /1968; earlier Woodside Brick Works (Croydon) Ltd, South Norwood, Surrey, until /1968 (possibly direct from Woodside to Earls Barton).

(h)   ex Clifford Hill Pits, by 4/1969.

(i)   ex Earls Barton Silica Ltd, c/1969 (after 6/1969).

(j)   ex A.J. Keef, Bampton, Oxon, after 11/10/1970, by 12/1970.

(k)   ex Charlecote Pits, Warwicks, c7/1971.

(l)   ex Charlecote Pits, Warwicks, c10/1971.

(m)   ex St.James End Pits, c3/1972.

(1)   to Earls Barton Silica Co Ltd, by 10/1952.

(2)   to ? , for scrap, 4/1964.

(3)   to Billing Aquadrome Narrow Gauge Rly, Northants, /1965, after repairs by Mackaness.

(5) to St.James End Pits, c/1969 (after 13/1/1966, by 4/1969).
(6) to St.James End Pits, after 9/1969.
(7) to Clifford Hill Pits, c1/1971.
(8) to St.James End Pits, c1/1971.
(9) to Charlecote Pits, Warwicks, c7/1971.
(10) to St.James End Pits, c9/1971.
(11) to Northamptonshire Ironstone Railway Trust, Hunsbury Hill, c6/1975.
(12) to Northamptonshire Ironstone Railway Trust, Hunsbury Hill, 9/1975.

LITTLE BILLING SANDPITS   M64

SP 807613 approx

Pits, in production by c1931 and served by a narrow gauge tramway, on the north side of the
River Nene about three miles east of Northampton. Pits closed 1956 and site later used as
Billing Aquadome (which see) with a pleasure railway.

Gauge: 2ft 0in

-	4wPM	MR	6019	1933	New	(1)
-	4wPM	MR	6020	1933	New	(1)
-	4wDM	MR	7031	1936	New	(4)
-	4wDM	MR	7032	1936	New	(2)
-	4wDM	MR	7043	1937	New	(4)
-	4wDM	MR	8739	1942	(a)	(3)
-	4wDM	MR	8810	1943	(b)	(3)

(a) rebuilt loco ex MR, 28/3/1951; earlier Sir Alfred McAlpine & Son Ltd, Hawthorne
     contract, Wilts
(b) rebuilt loco ex MR, 27/2/1951; earlier War Department

(1) returned to MR.
(2) returned to MR; rebuilt as 9539/1951 for Eastwoods Ltd.
(3) to Delapre Pits, Hardingstone, /1956 (after 3/1956).
(4) one to Billing Aquadrome Narrow Gauge Railway., the other to St James' End Gravel
     Pits, Northampton.

ST. JAMES END GRAVEL PITS, Weedon Road, Northampton   N65
F.E.Storton Ltd until 1965.   SP 735604
F.E.Storton from c1931 until 1939

Pits, served by a narrow gauge tramway with locomotives from about 1964, on the north
side of the River Nene about a mile west of Northampton. Tramway replaced by conveyor
belt, c3/1972. F.E. Storton also operated gravel pits at **Dodford** (near Weedon) from c1931.
No evidence has yet been found of the use of tramways at this site.

Gauge : 1ft 11½in

-	4wDM (ex PM)	MR	7035	1936	(a)	s/s
-	4wDM	MR	9204	1946	(b)	s/s /1970
-	4wDM	MR	8810	1943	(c)	(2)
-	4wDM	MR	8739	1942	(d)	(1)
-	4wDM	RH	371545	1954	(e)	(3)
T7	4wDM	RH	331264	1952	(f)	(4)
-	4wDM	RH	285297	1949	(f)	(3)
9	4wDM	RH	375362	1955	(g)	Scr c7/1971
-	4wDM	RH	375349	1954	(g)	s/s c1/1971
-	4wDM	MR	*		(h)	s/s /1970

-	4wDM	MR	9711	1952	(i)	(7)
-	4wDM	MR	8731	1941	(j)	(5)
-	4wDM	MR	4813	1937	(k)	(8)
-	4wDM	MR 40s370	1970		(l)	(6)
-	4wDM	MR	8575	1940	(m)	s/s c3/1972

* believed to have been either MR 7031/1936 or MR 7043/1937.

(a) ex Landbeach Sand & Gravel Co Ltd, Ely Road Sand Pits, Landbeach, Cambs; here by 5/1964 (when spares ordered from MR).

(b) ex E.L. Pitt (Coventry) Ltd, Brackley, c1/1964; to Earls Barton Pits, after 9/1966, by 8/1968; ex Earls Barton Pits, c/1969 (by 4/1969).

(c) ex Delapre Gravel Pits, 4/1966.

(d) ex Earls Barton Pits, c/1968 (by 8/1968).

(e) ex Rickmansworth Gravel Co Ltd, Herts, c/1967 (by 8/1968).

(f) ex Earls Barton Pits, c/1969 (by 4/1969); to Charlecote Works, Warwicks, /1969; returned, c9/1971.

(g) ex Earls Barton Pits, c/1969 (after 9/1969); to Charlecote Works, Warwicks, /1969; returned, c9/1971.

(h) ex Little Billing Sand Pits, c/1969.

(i) ex M.E. Engineering Ltd, dealers, Cricklewood, Middlesex, /1970 (by 6/1970); earlier Greater London Council, Edmonton Sewage Works, Greater London.

(j) ex Charlecote Pits, Warwicks, 10/1970.

(k) ex Earls Barton Pits, c1/1971.

(l) ex Charlecote Pits, Warwicks, 16/5/1971.

(m) ex Earls Barton Pits, c9/1971.

(1) to Earls Barton Pits, after 8/1968, by 4/1969.

(2) to Clifford Hill Pits, after 8/1968, by 4/1969.

(3) s/s after 4/1969, by 4/1970.

(4) scrapped on site by Edward Redden, Little Irchester, c3/1972.

(5) to Charlecote Pits, Warwicks, 5/1971.

(6) returned to Charlecote Pits, Warwicks, c7/1971.

(7) to Earls Barton Pits, c3/1972.

(8) to Charlecote Pits, Warwicks, c3/1972.

WEEDON ROAD WORKSHOPS, Northampton   N66
SP735604

Workshops located at the St James End Gravel Pits, the following loco arriving after removal of the rail system at this location

Gauge: 2ft 0in

T15	4wDM	MR 40S370	1970	(a)	(1)

(a) ex Charlecote Gravel Pits, Warwicks, for repair, after 6/8/1976, by 13/9/1977.

(1) s/s by 7/12/1978.

MIXCONCRETE PLANT LTD
WOLLASTON WORKSHOPS, Grendon Road, near Wellingborough   Q67
SP 90263

Plant depot for this company where at least one locomotive has been stored.

Gauge: 2ft 0in

T2	4wDM	MR	8739	1942	(a)	s/s after 12/1/1984

(a)   ex Mixconcrete Aggregates Ltd, Charlecote Pits, Warwicks, 4/1982.

NASSINGTON BARROWDEN MINING CO LTD
NASSINGTON IRONSTONE QUARRIES   L68
Naylor Benzon Mining Co Ltd (registered 12/1899) until 3/1/1951   TL 05497:

Quarrying commenced in 1939 on an area of about 500 acres to the north of the ex-LNWI Rugby - Peterborough line about a mile west of Nassington station. A standard gauge railwa system connecting with this line served the workings. The BR line west of here closed t traffic on 6/6/1966 and from 1/1969 part of the route was used as access to a new quarr to the south of earlier workings. Production ceased 31/12/1970 and the railway wa dismantled by late 1971.

Reference : "The Ironstone Quarries of the Midlands, Part 6, Corby"; Eric Tonks, Runpast Publishing, 1992

Gauge: 4ft 8½in

	JACKS GREEN	0-6-0ST	IC	HE	1953	1939	New	(3)
	RING HAW	0-6-0ST	IC	HE	1982	1940	New	(4)
	BUCCLEUCH	0-6-0ST	OC	P	1232	1910	(a)	Scr c2/1969
	KING GEORGE V	0-4-0ST	OC	HL	2839	1910	(b)	(1)
No.11		0-4-0ST	OC	AE	1830	1919	(c)	(2)

(a)   ex S & L Minerals Ltd, Harlaxton Mines, 10/1962.
(b)   ex Thos.W. Ward Ltd, Templeborough Works, Sheffield, hire, /1949;
       earlier English Steel Corporation Ltd, Openshaw, Manchester.
(c)   ex Thos.W. Ward Ltd, Templeborough Works, Sheffield, hire, 23/10/1953;
       earlier Birmingham Railway Carriage & Wagon Co Ltd, Smethwick, [West Midlands].

(1)   returned to Thos.W. Ward Ltd, Templeborough Works, Sheffield, by 30/6/1950.
(2)   returned to Thos.W. Ward Ltd, Templeborough Works, Sheffield, off hire, c/1954.
(3)   to British Sugar Corporation Ltd, Peterborough, 1/1/1971 (stored on behalf o Peterborough Locomotive Society).
(4)   to North Norfolk Railway Co Ltd, Sheringham, Norfolk, 19/2/1971.

NENE VALLEY SAND & GRAVEL CO LTD

IRTHLINGBOROUGH WASHED SAND & GRAVEL WORKS   S69
form. Irthlingborough Sand & Gravel Co   SP 961706

Gravel pits, on the east of both the River Nene and the A6 road, one mile east o Irthlingborough. The site was listed in trade directories for 1931 (but not 1928) and closec after 1940. Henry Butcher was to auction 18/9/1945 plant including Simplex 20hp diese locos ("Contract Journal" 29/8/1945).

Gauge: 2ft 0in

-	4wPM	FH		1702	1930	New	s/s
-	4wPM	FH		1703	1930	New	s/s
-	4wPM	FH		1711	1930	New	s/s
-	4wDM	OK				(a)	(1)
-	4wDM	MR		5879	1935	New	(2)
-	4wDM	MR		7137	1936	New	(3)
-	4wDM	MR		7180	1937	(b)	(4)
-	4wDM	RH		175419	1936	New	(5)

(a) origin and identity unknown.
(b) ex Sander's Lodge Pit, Rushden

(1) to Smith & Son (Raunds) Ltd, Raunds Manor Brickworks, c/1935.
(2) to P.F. Rose, dealer, Cowgate, Peterborough, Cambs, by 5/1943; later Coton Gravel Co Ltd, Warwicks.
(3) to P.F. Rose, dealer, Cowgate, Peterborough, Cambs, by 5/1943; later Baillie Brind & Co Ltd, Ryton, Warwicks.
(4) returned to Sander's Lodge Pit, Rushden.
(5) to P.F. Rose, dealer, Cowgate, Peterborough, Cambs, by 5/1943; resold to Newark (Peterborough) Sand & Gravel Co Ltd, by 25/6/1943.

SANDER'S LODGE PIT, Rushden
Q70

SP 938682 approx

Gravel pits, on the south side of the River Nene about a mile north-west of Rushden, served by a narrow gauge tramway. Tramway lifted; pits closed and flooded.

Gauge: 2ft 0in

-	4wDM	MR	7180	1937	New (a)	(1)

(a) to Irthlingborough Pits; returned.

(1) to P.F. Rose, dealer, Cowgate, Peterborough, Cambs, by 5/1943

NEW CRANSLEY IRON & STEEL CO LTD

CRANSLEY IRONWORKS
R71

Cransley Iron Co Ltd (registerd 1874) until 4/12/1889
SP 850775

Ironworks located on the south of the Midland Railway Cransley branch (opened 19/2/1877) to the west of the Kettering - Northampton (A43) road. The first two furnaces were built in 1875 and the first put into blast in 1877; a third furnace was added in 1882. Ironworks closed 1/11/1957 and mostly dismantled 1959. Two locos remained in their shed and with the site were purchased by George Cohen, Sons & Co Ltd (which see), c1960.

Reference : "The Ironstone Quarries of the Midlands, Part 5, Kettering"; Eric Tonks, Runpast Publishing, 1991

Gauge: 4ft 8½in

-	0-6-0ST	IC	HE	176	1876	New	s/s
NEW CRANSLEY No.1	0-4-0ST	OC	BH	1045	1894	New	Scr 1/1958
NEW CRANSLEY No.2	0-6-0ST	OC	P	500	1891	New	Scr /1934
NEW CRANSLEY No.3	0-4-0ST	OC	CF	1194	1900	New	
		reb	HIW		1952	(a)	(1)

NEW CRANSLEY No.4

(PEACOCK)	0-4-0ST	OC	WB	2517	1934	New	Scr 9/1958

ELLISON (PEACOCK until c6/1947;

DAVID in 3/1936)	0-4-0ST	OC	P	832	1900	(b)	(1)

A locomotive named HERON is said to have been here prior to BH 1045, was derelict in 1895 and later scrapped. This locomotive has not yet been identified.

(a)   to Loddington Ironstone Co Ltd, on loan 9/11/1952; returned 6/1953.
(b)   ex Gibbs & Canning Ltd, Glascote Works, near Tamworth, Warwicks, 9/1952.

(1)   to George Cohen, Sons & Co Ltd, with site, /1962.

CRANSLEY IRONSTONE QUARRIES   R72
Cransley Iron Co Ltd until 4/12/1889   SP 838777
Cransley Iron Co until 1874
Plevins & Co

Quarries, opened 1873, two miles south west of Kettering. By 1877 a narrow gauge tramway connected these workings to Cransley Ironworks (which see). These workings had closed by 1897 but from about 1885 other quarries had opened at White Hill Lodge, about ¾ mile to the north. These were also served by a narrow gauge line to the terminus of the Midland Railway Cransley branch and to the Ironworks. This narrow gauge line was dismantled about 1891 and replaced by a standard gauge extension of the Midland Railway line to Loddington Quarries (which see).

Reference : "The Ironstone Quarries of the Midlands, Part 5, Kettering"; Eric Tonks,
                        Runpast Publishing, 1991

Gauge: 2ft 6in

LITTLE EGRET	0-4-0ST	OC	HE	175	1877	New	(1)

(1)   regauged to 3ft 0in; later Enoch Tempest, Clough Bottom Reservoir (Bury & District Joint Water Board) (1891-1896) contract, Waterfoot, Lancs.

THRAPSTON LIMESTONE QUARRIES   S73
earlier Excelsior Limestone Co Ltd   SP 997777
orig. Amalgamated Stone & Lime Co Ltd

Quarries, on the east side of the LMSR (ex Midland Railway) Kettering - Huntingdon railway and south of the town centre, closed 1939; became MoS Rubber Reclamation Depot, also later closed.

Gauge: 1ft 11½in

-	4wDM	MR	5886	1935	New (a)	(1)
CP 551	4wPM	HC	P254c1925	(b)	(2)
CP 552	4wPM	KC		(c)	(2)

(a)   ex MR, on hire, 14/10/1935 (purchased 11/9/1936).
(b)   ex Shardlow, contr, Leeds.
(c)   origin and identity unknown.

(1)   to MR, 8/11/1937; later took identity MR 9337, 20/7/1948..
(2)   scrapped by W.J. Redden & Sons, c/1955.

NINE CHURCHES IRON ORE CO
STOWE IRONSTONE QUARRIES   P74
(for early history see **Castle Dykes Iron Ore Co Ltd**)   SP 647578

Quarries located about a mile south west of Stowe Hill tunnel on the LNWR main line south of Weedon. This company was formed in 1875 and reopened and operated the quarries until about 1877, using a standard gauge line to the Stowe Furnaces alongside the LNWR. Quarries closed c/1877.

Reference :   "The Ironstone Quarries of the Midlands, Part 3, Northampton"; Eric Tonks,
               Runpast Publishing, 1989

Gauge: 4ft 8½in

"COFFEE POT"	0-4-0VBT	VCG	Chaplin	1056	1869	(a)	(1)
CARLISLE	0-6-0ST	IC	MW	428	1873	(b)	(2)

(a)   believed acquired from Castle Dykes Iron Ore Co, with site, /1875.
(b)   ex John Bayliss, Settle & Carlisle Railway contract No.4 (Crowdundle - Petteril Bridge, Carlisle), Cumberland, CARLISLE, /1875.

(1)   to Henry Mobbs, Vulcan Ironworks, Northampton, by /1878.
(2)   to MW (?), 8/1877; later Monk & Edwards, contrs.

NORTH LINCOLNSHIRE IRON CO LTD
EASTON-ON-THE-HILL IRONSTONE QUARRY, near Stamford   L75
Marquess of Exeter, 1902 to 11/1/1911   TL 005048
Wingerworth Iron Co, 1873 - 1881

Quarry about ½ mile north-west of Easton-on-the-Hill village, 2 miles south-west of Stamford. Production took place from 1873 using a rope and horse worked tramway to an exchange point with the Midland Rly Manton - Stamford railway near Tinwell Crossing. There were several phases of workings here and the tramway was lifted and later relaid in 1903. The North Lincolnshire Iron Co Ltd was the final operator of the workings, from 13/1/1913, and the only one to use a locomotive. Quarry closed c1919 and track lifted; the locomotive remained on site for several years before removal.

Reference :   "The Ironstone Quarries of the Midlands, Part 6, Corby"; Eric Tonks,
               Runpast Publishing, 1992

Gauge: 3ft 0in

UTHIE	0-4-0ST	OC	HC	1106	1915	New	(1)

(1)   to Bloxham & Whiston Ironstone Co Ltd, Harringworth Quarries, /1931.

COUNTY BOROUGH OF NORTHAMPTON
earlier **Northampton Corporation**

HIGHWAYS DEPARTMENT, WEST BRIDGE DEPOT, Northampton   N76
                                                               SP 745602

Engineers yard on the west side of the ex-LNWR lines south of Northampton Castle station; served by standard gauge sidings (private siding agreement 5/12/1906) connecting with these lines. There was no standard gauge locomotive on the premises from 1954 to 8/1956; shunting was carried out by road tractor during this period. By 1961 the rail connection from BR also served an adjacent oil depot. Rail traffic ceased by 1970 and track later lifted.

A narrow gauge line served an incinerator at this site; this line was closed and dismantled in the 1950s. Some or all of the narrow gauge locomotives listed at Great Billing Sewage Works visited here for repair or storage from time to time; not all transfers have been recorded.

Gauge: 4ft 8½in

-	0-4-0ST	OC	MW	915	1883		
		reb	MW		1896	(a)	Scr /1930
-	0-4-0ST	OC	AB	1658	1920	(b)	(1)
(HEATHER)	0-4-0DM		HE	2070	1940	(c)	(2)

LMSR 11212 (0-4-0ST OC Hor /1894) was on hire here in 1934.

(a)   ex Robert Finnegan, contr, Northampton, c/1914 (earlier 3ft 0in gauge, until 1888, and used on Finnegan's Cromer – Mundesley (1903-1906) railway contract, Norfolk).

(b)   ex J. Wardell & Co, contrs, Ellesmere Port, Cheshire, 1/8/1925; earlier Ardrossan Dry Dock & Shipbuilding Co Ltd, Ayrshire

(c)   ex Penmaenmawr & Welsh Granite Co Ltd, Caerns [North Wales]. per J.N. Connell Ltd, dealers Coatbridge, Lanarks, 8/1956.

(1)   scrapped /1954 (after 7/1954)
(2)   to Thos.E. Gray Ltd, Burton Latimer, c2/1972.

Gauge: 2ft 0in

-	4wPM	L	14005	1940	New	(1)
-	4wPM	L	14006	1940	New	(1)
-	4wPM	L	20696	1942	New	(1)

An unidentified 0-6-0T of German build, purchased from Robert Finnegan, cont, may also have been used here; details uncertain.

(1)   to Great Billing Works, by 3/1957.

GREAT BILLING SEWAGE PURIFICATION WORKS   M77

SP 816618

Sewage disposal works, which used a narrow gauge system, on the east side of the minor road about ½ mile south of Great Billing village. The works was first laid out in 1875 and extended in 1895 over 554 acres of farmland. Further extensions including settlement tanks were undertaken during 1930-1933. The works was further reconstructed and extended between 1951 and 1957 (main contractors Kottler Heron Ltd for the Power House, Wm Moss & Sons Ltd of Loughborough for the sludge and settling tanks and W.H. Allen Sons & Co Ltd of Bedford supplying pumps and power plant). The rail system was in use here by the mid-1900s but was replaced and dismantled c1974.

Gauge: 2ft 0in

-	4wPM	MH	109	1931	New (a)	s/s
-	4wPM	L	8913	1937	New (a)	s/s
-	4wPM	L	14005	1940	(b)	(1)
-	4wPM	L	20696	1942	(b)	(2)
-	4wPM	L	14006	1940	(b)	(3)

(a)   delivered to Northampton Corporation, location not stated, but may have worked here.
(b)   ex West Bridge Depot, Northampton, by 3/1957.

(1)   to Church Farm, Newbold Verdon, Leics, 12/11/1966, per C. Pealling, Kingswinford, Worcs.

(2)	sold or scrapped c/1966 (after 10/9/1966)
(3)	to Northamptonshire Ironstone Railway Trust (stored at Richmond Terrace Pumping Station, Northampton), 2/3/1974 and to Hunsbury Hill, 9/1975.

NORTHAMPTON RAIL & GRAIN TERMINAL LTD
NORTHAMPTON WAREHOUSE, Hardingstone Road, Far Cotton **N78**
Farthingstone Silos Ltd until c5/1982 SP 763597

This company of grain dealers set up, from 1978, a storage depot on the site of CEGB, Northampton Power Station, served by standard gauge sidings connecting with the remaining section of the Northampton - Wellingborough railway. Rail traffic ceased by 1988 and track later lifted. Operation of the depot later passed to Amacroft Ltd.

Gauge : 4ft 8½in

(No.4)	HOTWHEELS	0-6-0DM	AB	422	1958	(a)	(2)
(126)	SPEEDY	0-4-0DM	AB	361	1942	(b)	(3)
(127)	SMOKY	0-4-0DM	AB	363	1942	(b)	(1)

(a)	ex CEGB, Earley Power Station, Reading, Berks, 11/4/1978.
(b)	ex MoDAD, Bicester, Oxon, 20/12/1978.

(1)	to Ampthill Scrap Metal Processing Co Ltd, Beds, 22/3/1985; then to Rushden Historical Transport Society, Rushden, 12/12/1987
(2)	to South Yorkshire Railway Preservation Society, Attercliffe, South Yorkshire, 2/1988; then to Meadowhall, South Yorkshire, 15/9/1988.
(3)	to South Yorkshire Railway Preservation Society, Attercliffe, South Yorkshire, 2/1988; then to Meadowhall, South Yorkshire, 10/1988.

JAMES PAIN LTD
CORBY BRICKWORKS & IRONSTONE PITS **T79**
James Pain until 9/1905 Brickworks SP 895882, Quarries SP 897884

Quarry, active from 1886, located ¼ mile south-east of Weldon & Corby station. Later an extensive brickworks (operated under the name of **Weldon & Corby Patent Brick Co Ltd**) was built also and both were connected by a standard gauge railway to the station goods yard. This line was horse worked before the purchase of a locomotive. Quarries closed in 1912 and railway lifted.

Reference : "The Ironstone Quarries of the Midlands, Part 6, Corby"; Eric Tonks,
Runpast Publishing, 1992

Gauge: 4ft 8½in

| | MARY BEATRICE | 0-4-0ST | OC | FW | 314 | 1876 | | |
| | | reb | P | | | 1892 | (a) | s/s |

(a)	ex P, 12/1892 (ex Peckett works, 20/12/1892); earlier Wm. Williams & Co, Morriston, West Glamorgan. (which see as Upper Forest & Worcester Steel & Tinplate Works Ltd).

PARK GATE IRON & STEEL CO LTD
CHARWELTON IRONSTONE QUARRIES
L80

Park Gate Iron Co Ltd until 14/6/1919

SP 526568

Quarries about 2 miles north-west of Charwelton station on the GCR Rugby - Aylesbury main line. A standard gauge railway served the workings and connected them with the goods yard at Charwelton station. Production commenced about 5/1917 and continued, with breaks, until it finally ceased on 18/11/1961. Locos left in shed until scrapped by 1964.

Reference : "The Ironstone Quarries of the Midlands, Part 2, Oxfordshire"; Eric Tonks, Runpast Publishing, 1988

Gauge: 4ft 8½in

	CHARWELTON	0-6-0ST	IC	MW	1955	1917	New	(2)
	HOLMES	0-4-0ST	OC	MW	345	1871	(a)	(1)
	HELLIDON	0-6-0ST	IC	HE	2415	1941	New	(3)
	CHERWELL	0-6-0ST	OC	WB	2654	1942	New	(4)
	(BYFIELD)	0-6-0ST	IC	HC	347	1892	(b)	(5)
No.8		0-4-0ST	OC	YE	784	1905	(c)	Scr 11-12/1963
No.5		0-4-0ST	OC	WB	2659	1942	(d)	Scr 11-12/1963

(a) ex Park Gate Ironworks, Rotherham, Yorkshire (WR), c/1930.
(b) ex Byfield Ironstone Co Ltd, c2/1951.
(c) ex Park Gate Ironworks, Rotherham, Yorkshire (WR), 24/2/1952.
(d) ex Park Gate Ironworks, Rotherham, Yorkshire (WR), 1/1957.

(1) to Pitsford Ironstone Co, Pitsford Ironstone Quarries, c/1935.
(2) to Sproxton Quarries, Leics, 3/1942.
(3) to Oxfordshire Ironstone Co Ltd, 8/1/1943.
(4) to Byfield Quarries, c10/1945; ex Byfield Quarries, 12/1947;
     to Byfield Quarries, 1/1948.
(5) to Byfield Quarries, 12/1956.

PARKINSON INDUSTRIALISED BUILDING LTD
WELLINGBOROUGH WORKS
Q81

SP 899694

Manufacturing works on the site of Wellingborough Ironworks. A narrow gauge system, using much new equipment, was built by early 1966 to serve the site. Works closed and derelict by 1996.

Gauge: 3ft 0in

S.L.P. 3531	4wDM	RH	466588	1961	(a)	(1)
S.L.P. 3532	4wDM	RH	466589	1961	(a)	(1)

(a) ex Sir Lindsay Parkinson & Co Ltd, c8/1965 (new to their Oldbury Power Station (CEGB) contract, Thornbury, Gloucs).

(1) sold or scrapped c/1968 (after 3/1966).

PARTINGTON STEEL & IRON CO LTD
WAKERLEY IRONSTONE QUARRIES

T82

Wakerley Ironstone Co until c1919

SP 947991

Bell Bros Ltd until 20/11/1914

Quarries to the south west of Wakerley village connected by a narrow gauge tramway to an exchange siding on the LNWR Seaton - Peterborough railway. The working by Bell Bros was short lived from 1913 to 2/1914 and Wakerley Ironstone Co commenced work from 10/1915. Quarries closed 1921 and track lifted; one locomotive remained until c1929..

Reference : "The Ironstone Quarries of the Midlands, Part 6, Corby"; Eric Tonks, Runpast Publishing, 1992

Gauge: 2ft 6in

-	0-4-0ST	OC	WB	1554	1898	(a)	(1)
-	0-4-0ST	OC	WB	2089	1919	New	(2)

(a)   ex D. Thomas & Son, Llandough Limeworks, Penarth, South Glamorgan, LLANDOUGH, c1/1916.

(1)   possibly to Southhill Ironstone Mines Ltd, Wellingborough, c/1920; otherwise s/s.

(2)   scrapped on site by Thos W. Ward Ltd, c10/1929.

EXORS OF P. PHIPPS

P. Phipps until prior to 7/1897
Hunsbury Hill Iron Co until 23/2/1889
Hunsbury Hill Coal & Iron Co Ltd until 1883;
Northampton Coal, Iron & Wagon Co Ltd (registered 1872) until 1876

HUNSBURY HILL QUARRIES

N83

SP 735585

Quarries, about a mile south-west of the centre of Northampton, in production from about 1873, in association with Hunsbury Hill Iron Works (which see). Workings were on both sides of, and above, Hunsbury Hill tunnel on the LNWR Northampton - Roade railway. A narrow gauge line, horse worked until 1912, connected the quarries and ironworks. Production ceased in 1921 and the equipment was stored for many years. Richard Thomas & Co Ltd purchased the workings in 9/1935 but did not resume production. Locomotives and rolling stock were transferred away for further use or scrap by about 1941. The area has since seen railways re-laid as a preservation project by the Northamptonshire Ironstone Railway Trust Ltd (which see).

Reference : "The Ironstone Quarries of the Midlands, Part 3, Northampton"; Eric Tonks, Runpast Publishing, 1989

Gauge: 3ft 8in

HARDINGSTONE	0-6-0ST	OC	WB	1955	1912	New	Scr /1940
WOOTTON	0-6-0ST	OC	WB	1956	1912	New	(1)
NORTHAMPTON	0-6-0ST	OC	WB	1957	1912	New	Scr /1940

(1)   to Richard Thomas & Co Ltd, Finedon Quarries, /1937.

HUNSBURY HILL IRON WORKS

SP 732592

Ironworks built 1873 on the south side of the LNWR Northampton - Blisworth railway, with standard gauge sidings connecting with that line. Served by a narrow gauge tramway from Hunsbury Hill Quarries, which see. Two furnaces were built in 1873 and put into blast in 10 and 11/1874. Furnaces out of use from 10/1915 until 6/1917; finally closed on 28/1/1921 and were demolished in 1937. Together with the quarries, the ironworks was taken over by Richard Thomas & Co Ltd in 9/1935 but neither was re-opened.

Gauge: 4ft 8½in

ORYZA	0-4-0ST	OC	SS	2329	1873	New (a)	s/s
BILLY	0-4-0ST	OC	HE	133	1875	New (a)	(1)
PATIENCE	0-4-0ST	OC	HE	239	1881	New	(2)
CARDIFF	0-6-0ST	IC	HE	370	1885	(b)	Scr /1941
BURY	0-6-0ST	IC	HE	456	1888	(c)	Scr /1937
HUNSBURY	0-6-0ST	IC	HE	899	1906	New	Scr /1937
WHISTON	0-4-0ST	OC	AB	1333	1914	(d)	(3)

(a)   supplied per Rice & Co, Founders, Northampton, as agents.

(b)   ex Thos W Ward, dealer, Manchester, after 30/9/1897 by 14/10/1897;
      earlier Exors of T.A. Walker, Manchester Ship Canal contract, Lancs.

(c)   ex Thos W Ward, dealer, Manchester, 9/1897 (by 17/9/1897);
      earlier Exors of T.A. Walker, Manchester Ship Canal contract, Lancs.

(d)   ex Whiston Ironstone Co Ltd, Whiston Pits, /1921.

(1)   to HE, 7/1897; to Thomas Firth & Sons Ltd, Sheffield, 5/1898.

(2)   to Thos W.Ward Ltd, after 5/11/1901 by 3/10/1907.

(3)   to Richard Thomas & Co Ltd, Finedon Quarries, c/1940.

PLEVINS & CO
TWYWELL BRICKWORKS

(for the earlier history see **Twywell Iron Ore Co Ltd**)

SP 952776

Brickworks about ½ mile south west of Twywell station on the Midland Railway Kettering - Thrapston railway, connected to that line by a standard gauge railway. Works taken over by Plevins & Co about 1890 after the closure of the Woodford Quarries; later closed and track lifted by World War I, although some remains were still extant in 1960.

Reference :   "The Ironstone Quarries of the Midlands, Part 5, Kettering"; Eric Tonks,
              Runpast Publishing, 1991

Gauge: 4ft 8½in

-	0-4-0ST	OC	FE	184	1889	(a)	(1)

Also another locomotive (details unknown), possibly ex Twywell Iron Ore Co Ltd.

(a)   ex Glendon Iron Co Ltd, Finedon Furnaces, c/1892.

(1)   to Wellingborough Iron Co Ltd, Wellingborough Ironworks.

RAILCAR SERVICES LTD
WELLINGBOROUGH WORKS

Q86

Wagon Repairs Ltd until 1982

SP 903695

Wagon repair shops situated in Neilson Road, Finedon Road Industrial Estate. This location was on the west side of the ex- Midland Railway Wellingborough - Kettering line, to the north of Wellingborough Ironworks. Served by standard gauge sidings connecting with the main line. Works closed 12/1983.

Gauge : 4ft 8½in

	-	4wDM	FH	3044	1945	New (a)	(1)
	-	4wDM	BgE	2071	1931	(b)	(2)
L 10		4wDM	RH	224345	1945	(c)	(3)
L 8		4wDM	RH	393303	1955	(d)	s/s c/1984
L 4	CHATSWORTH	4wDM	RH	235517	1945	(e)	(3)
45	4	4wDM	FH	3909	1959	(f)	(4)

(a) to Port Tennant Works, West Glamorgan; returned.
(b) ex Gloucester Works, 9/1959.
(c) ex E.L. Pitt & Co (Coventry) Ltd, Brackley, /1960 (by 9/1960); earlier WD, Longmoor, Hampshire, 807.
(d) ex Branston Works, Staffs, 2/1968.
(e) ex Chatsworth Works, Sheepbridge, Derbys, 17/2/1981.
(f) ex Long Eaton Works, Derbys, 6/1982.

(1) to FH for repairs, /1960; then to Port Tennant Works, West Glamorgan, c7/1961
(2) returned to Gloucester Works, c/1961 (after 9/1960).
(3) scrapped on site, 12/1983.
(4) to Stoke Works, Stoke-on-Trent, Staffs, after 21/10/1983, by 20/2/1984.

RAUNDS IRON & LIMESTONE QUARRIES CO LTD
RAUNDS QUARRY

S87

TL 000728

Quarries on the east side of Raunds village operating from 12/1880 until 1882, connected by a standard gauge line about a mile long to Raunds station on the Midland Rly Thrapston - Cambridge railway. Installation sold to East Northamptonshire Ironstone Co Ltd on 5/4/1882 but not operated by them. Track later lifted although some still in place in the 1920s.

Gauge: 4ft 8½in

RAUNDS	0-4-0ST	OC	HC	219	1881	New	(1)

(1) probably to T. Walters, Addington Quarries, c/1883.

RUTLAND RECYCLING LTD
CORBY TUBEWORKS SITE

T88

SP 910901

The company recycled scrap tubes from the nearby British Steel works and had a plant within the tubeworks site. Scrap from the shearer was loaded into internal user HEA hopper wagons for storage prior to being transferred by magnetic crane into lorries for onward shipment.

Ownership of the locos reverted to British Steel plc, Tubes & Pipes, c1/10/1997, whilst the plant was subsequently operated by Allen Rowland & Co Ltd.

Gauge : 4ft 8½in

BSC 2	0-6-0DH		GECT	5395	1974	(a)	(1)
3 (BSC 3)	0-6-0DH		GECT	5365	1972	(a)	(1)

(a)   ex British Steel plc, Corby Works, 3/1995.

(1)   returned to British Steel plc, Tubes & Pipes, Corby Works, c1/10/1997.

SHANKS & McEWAN (ENGLAND) LTD
SLAG CONTRACTORS, CORBY STEELWORKS
form. Shanks & McEwan Ltd

T89
SP 915899

This firm of contractors was involved in the reconstruction of Corby Works during 1933 - 1937 (which see in the Contractors section). Following on from this contract, it processed the slag from the steelworks and used its own locomotives to handle traffic within the works. The locomotives listed below include those thought to have been used on this later operation (which ceased about 11/1982), plus those stored here on completion of the earlier contract work.

Gauge: 4ft 8½in

LAUCHOPE	0-6-0ST	IC	HE	619	1894	(a)	Scr 5/1951
DON	0-6-0ST	IC	MW	1293	1895	(a)	Scr 5/1951
53	0-4-0ST	OC	AB	1027	1904	(a)	(1)
7	0-4-0ST	OC	AB	306	1888	(a)	s/s after 6/1956
No.83 GLENGARNOCK	0-4-0ST	OC	Glengarnock		1911	(a)	Scr 5/1951
DESPATCH	0-4-0CT	OC	HL	2669	1907	(b)	s/s
-	0-4-0ST	OC	AB	43	1866		
	reb		AB		1896	(c)	Scr 5/1951
10	0-4-0ST	OC	B	318	1885		
	reb		AB	9331	1912	(d)	Scr /1956
No.10 ROSEHALL	0-4-0ST	OC	AE	1435	1901	(e)	Scr /1957
GLENDON	0-4-0ST	OC	HC	1285	1917	(f)	Scr c/1959
IAN D.McLEAN (SIFTA)	0-4-0ST	OC	HE	1677	1937	(g)	Scr after 3/1965
C57 T.S.WILSON	0-4-0ST	OC	P	2026	1942	(h)	Scr after 3/1965
C58	0-4-0DH		NBQ	27658	1957	New (i)	(2)
21.90.01 (C59A)	0-4-0DH		AB	499	1965	New	(4)
21.90.02	0-4-0DH		RH	504565	1965	New (j)	(5)
21.90.03 J.D.THOMSON	0-6-0DH		EEV	3990	1970	New	(3)

(a)   ex Corby Works reconstruction contract; to Islip contract, /1942; returned, /1943.

(b)   ex Carnbroe Plant Depot, Lanarks, after 7/1936, by 8/1943 (use at this site not confirmed).

(c)   ex Clydesdale Steelworks (Stewarts & Lloyds Ltd) contract, Mossend, Lanarks, after 5/1945, by 7/1949.

(d)   ex Carnbroe Plant Depot, Lanarks, after 8/1943, by 12/1949.

(e)   ex Robert Addie & Sons Collieries Ltd, Rosehall Collieries, Lanarkshire, 1/1944.

(f)   ex Stewarts & Lloyds Minerals Ltd, Glendon East Quarries, 12/1953.

(g)   ex Palmer, Mann & Co Ltd, Sandbach, Cheshire, 6/1956.

(h)   ex Eagre Construction Co Ltd, Manvers Main contract, Yorkshire (WR), by 2/1957.

(i)   to here after demonstrations at various sites.

(j)   ex RH, Lincoln, new, on hire, 10/3/1965; purchased 30/7/1965.

(1) mostly scrapped by 2/1950, frame only in 2/1951 and later scrapped.
(2) to Sobermai NV, Maldegen, Belgium, /1971.
(3) to Resco (Railways) Ltd, Woolwich, London, after 31/10/1980, by 13/5/1981.
(4) to Rutland Railway Museum, Cottesmore, Leics, 10/8/1983
(5) to Rutland Railway Museum, Cottesmore, Leics, 9/8/1983

SMITH & SON (RAUNDS) LTD
RAUNDS MANOR BRICKWORKS
formerly **Manor Brickworks Co**
E. Smith & Son by c1894

S90
SP 003725

Brickworks located to the east of Raunds town centre and south of the standard gauge line to Raunds Quarries. Originally opened with three drying sheds and a large updraft kiln with a capacity of 80,000 bricks. Later new downdraft kilns were built, two circular (capacity 29,000 bricks each), in 1935 and 1947, and one rectangular (35,000 bricks), in 1947. A 2ft gauge tramway was used to convey clay in Hudson side tip wagons from clay pits to the east and south east of the works. Works and tramway closed c1969.

Reference : "Bulletin of Industrial Archaeology, in CBA Group 9" No.13, Richard O'Rourke, July 1970.

Gauge: 2ft 0in

-	4wDM	OK			(a)	(1)
-	4wPM	L	7280	1936	New	(2)
-	4wPM	L	36743	1951	New	
	reb to 4wDM			1962		(4)
-	4wDM	RH	193984	1939	(b)	(3)

(a) ex Irthlingborough Sand & Gravel Co, Irthlingborough, c/1935.
(b) ex F. Watkins (Boilers) Ltd, Coleford, Gloucs, c/1959; earlier ICI, Shevington, Lancs.

(1) to Hawell (?), dealer, Birmingham, c/1936.
(2) to R.P. Morris, Longfield, Kent, for preservation, 22/4/1967.
(3) to Festiniog Railway Co Ltd, Merioneth (North Wales), 7/4/1974.
(4) to J. Woolmer, Woodford, near Thrapston, for preservation, by 31/12/1973.

SOUTHHILL IRONSTONE MINES LTD
SOUTH HILL FARM QUARRIES

Q91
Quarry SP 913690

Reference : "The Ironstone Quarries of the Midlands, Part 4, Wellingborough"; Eric Tonks, Runpast Publishing, 1990

Ironstone quarries to the north of South Hill farm were worked by **J Clarke** of Rushden from c1918 - 1924 with a tramway connected to the closed Finedon Hill line of the Stanton Ironworks Co Ltd

Gauge : 2ft 6in

-	0-4-0ST	OC	WB	1554	1898	(a)	s/s

(a) ex Partington Steel & Iron Co Ltd, Wakerley Quarries c/1920 (identity of loco unconfirmed)

R.B. SPARROW

GAYTON WOOD IRONSTONE QUARRIES, near Blisworth   M92

SP 710540

Quarries about ¾ mile west of Blisworth station on the LNWR main line. Workings north of the Blisworth - Gayton road, in the area formerly worked by the Heyford Iron Co, were reopened by R.B. Sparrow in 1900 and were served by a narrow gauge tramway. This in turn connected with a horse worked standard gauge tramway to the LNWR. Quarries closed 1921; equipment auctioned 10/6/1925.

Part of site was subsequently worked by Richard Thomas & Baldwin Ltd, which see for later history.

Reference : "The Ironstone Quarries of the Midlands, Part 3, Northampton"; Eric Tonks, Runpast Publishing, 1989

Gauge: c.2ft 10in

GAYTON	0-4-0ST	OC	?	(a)	s/s c/1918
	4wPM		Groom & Tattershall	(a)	s/s

(a)   origins and identities unknown.

STANTON IRONWORKS CO LTD

ROTHWELL HILL (DESBOROUGH) IRONSTONE QUARRIES   R93

SP 809821

Quarries, about a mile north of Rothwell, with workings extending both sides of the Desborough - Rothwell road. A locomotive worked narrow gauge system served the quarries and ran north via rope worked inclines to an exchange siding with the ex-Midland Rly main line south of Desborough station. Quarrying commenced in 1897 and the workings closed 1926 with track lifted c1931. Later workings in the area by Stewarts & Lloyds Minerals Ltd were served by road vehicles and an aerial ropeway to the Corby quarries system.

Reference : "The Ironstone Quarries of the Midlands, Part 6, Corby"; Eric Tonks, Runpast Publishing, 1992

Gauge: 3ft 0in

HELEN	0-4-0ST	OC	HC	419	1894	(a)	Scr c/1933
HARSTON	0-4-0ST	OC	WB	1587	1900	(b)	(1)
KITTY	0-4-0ST	OC	HC	596	1901	(c)	(2)
STANTON No.19	0-4-0ST	OC	MW	1038	1887	(d)	(3)

(a)   ex Newcastle & Gateshead Water Co, HEUGH, c/1898.
(b)   ex Harston Quarries, Leics, c/1905.
(c)   ex Orton Quarries, /1920.
(d)   ex Earls Barton Iron Ore Co Ltd, c/1921.

(1)   to Wartnaby Quarries, Leics, 3/1928.
(2)   to Harston Quarries, Leics, 10/1931, via Holwell Works.
(3)   to Harston Quarries, Leics, c/1922.

ORTON IRONSTONE QUARRIES, near Lamport   L94

SP 779781

Quarries about two miles south-west of Rothwell, south of Harrington Lodge and just north of the Loddington Quarry workings. Output commenced in 1902 and was conveyed by a narrow gauge line which ran west for about a mile to an exchange point on the LNWR Northampton - Market Harborough line at Draughton Crossing. Quarries closed 1920 and track lifted; unworked ground in the lease was later incorporated into the Loddington workings..

Reference :"The Ironstone Quarries of the Midlands, Part 5, Kettering"; Eric Tonks, Runpast Publishing, 1991

Gauge: 3ft 0in

JUBILEE	0-4-0IST	OC	WB	840	1887	(a)	s/s /1920
LIZZIE	0-4-0ST	OC	MW	1038	1887	(b)	(1)
KITTY	0-4-0ST	OC	HC	596	1901	(c)	(2)

(a)   earlier John Shelbourne & Co, Rainham, Essex, until 4/1908 at least.
(b)   earlier W. Cunliffe, 11/1897; previously H.M.Nowell & Co, contrs.
(c)   ex HC, 5/1913; earlier Newcastle & Gateshead Water Co.

(1)   to Earls Barton Iron Ore Co Ltd, Earls Barton Quarries, c/1920.
(2)   to Rothwell Hill Quarries, /1920.

STEEL & IRON CO LTD
STOWE IRONWORKS, Nether Heyford, near Weedon   P95
William McClure until 1888   SP 652578

Ironworks on the south-west side of the LNWR main line about ½ mile south of Stowe Hill tunnel (and on the opposite side of the line to Heyford Ironworks and the Grand Junction Canal). Associated with the Stowe Nine Churches Quarries (which see). Ironworks were put in blast briefly in 1866 but then closed until reconstructed by William McClure in 1873, when a second blast furnace was added. Closed 1892, but limestone traffic worked until 1900. By 1890 **King & Smith** were brickmakers here – this enterprise became **George King & Son** from 1894 until 1906 and then the **Blisworth & Stowe Siding Brick & Tile Co Ltd**. Track lifted 1920, apart from that serving the brickworks – for the history of the latter, see under Henry Martin Ltd.

Reference : "The Ironstone Quarries of the Midlands, Part 3, Northampton"; Eric Tonks, Runpast Publishing, 1989

Gauge: 4ft 8½in

IRON DUKE	0-4-0ST	OC	MW	537	1875	New	(1)

(1)   to Lever Bros Ltd, Port Sunlight, Cheshire, c/1894.

F.J. STEWARD & SON,
Trading as BRIGSTOCK GRAVEL & SAND CO
Stanion Rd, Brigstock, near Corby   T96
                                                                  SP 934859

Gravel pits, to the north-west of Brigstock village and the A6116 road. F.J. Steward was listed as a farmer in trade directories from 1906 until 1928. In October 1939 plant including a 10hp Planet petrol loco was to be sold at auction ("Machinery Market" 6/10/1939)

Gauge: 1ft 11½in

-	4wPM	FH	1856	1934	New (a)	(1)

(a)   rebuild of KC 1548; earlier with W.E. Cornish Ltd, Bush Mill Park (LNER), Middlesex.

(1)   sold to ?

STEWARTS & LLOYDS MINERALS LTD

CHURCH MINE, near Islip   S97

SP 970785

Extensive ironstone workings in the Islip area included several underground operations. Willow Close and Woodfield mines, near Slipton, opened in 1902 and the Church Mine, immediately north of the Kettering - Thrapston railway line, in 1910. 2ft 6in gauge railways were used underground, tipping at the mine entrances into the 3ft 0in gauge system of Islip Quarries and Ironworks. Horses were used underground but from 1933 were supplemented by diesel locomotives, primarily in Church Mine. This mine closed 22/8/1947 and the locomotives were stored until finally disposed of.

Reference : "The Ironstone Quarries of the Midlands, Part 5, Kettering"; Eric Tonks, Runpast Publishing, 1991

Gauge: 2ft 6in

1	4wDM	RH	166051	1933	New		Scr /1953
-	4wDM	RH	166042	1934	New		(1)
-	4wDM	RH	168841	1933	New		(3)
-	4wDM	RH	186340	1937	(a)		(4)
-	4wDM	RH	186337	1937	(b)		(2)

(a)   ex Corby (Northants) & District Water Co, Eye Brook Reservoir, re-gauged from 2ft 0in, after 25/3/1939, by 9/7/1940.

(b)   ex Corby (Northants) & District Water Co, Eye Brook Reservoir, re-gauged from 2ft 0in, after 12/6/1940, by 22/11/1940.

(1)   s/s after 10/2/1947.

(2)   possibly to Buckminster Quarry, c7/1949, for conversion to 2ft 8½in gauge; to South Witham Quarries, Lincs, after 4/9/1946, by 7/6/1950.

(3)   to Bowne & Shaw Ltd, Wirksworth Quarry, Derbys (presumably converted to 3ft 0in gauge), after 29/5/1947, by 23/8/1949.

(4)   to Bowne & Shaw Ltd, Wirksworth Quarry, Derbys (presumably converted to 3ft 0in gauge), after 8/7/1947, by 16/8/1949.

DESBOROUGH IRONSTONE QUARRIES   R98

Staveley Minerals Ltd   SP 806837
   (subsidiary of **Staveley Iron & Chemical Co Ltd**) until 1/1/1966;
Sheepbridge Co Ltd until 7/3/1961;
Sheepbridge Coal & Iron Co Ltd until 27/7/1948

Extensive quarries were operated north and north-east of Desborough station on the Midland Railway Market Harborough - Kettering railway. Workings commenced in 1882 and were served by a tramway, probably narrow gauge and horse worked. The Sheepbridge Co took over the workings in 1907, extended them and introduced a locomotive worked standard gauge railway system, connecting with the Midland Rly south of Desborough station. Locomotives were frequently exchanged with Sheepbridge works, with a normal allocation here of three locomotives. Quarries closed 10/1966 and track lifted by 1968.

Reference : "The Ironstone Quarries of the Midlands, Part 6, Corby"; Eric Tonks, Runpast Publishing, 1992

Gauge: 4ft 8½in

1	0-4-0ST	OC	HC	275	1885	(a)		(9)
3	0-6-0ST	OC	BH		1883			
		reb	Sb	1915 & 1935		(b)		Scr 2/1962

5		0-6-0ST	OC	AE	1395	1898	(c)	(1)
7	SHEEPBRIDGE No.22	0-6-0ST	OC	HC	899	1909	New (d)	
	(DESBOROUGH)	reb		Woodwards		1956		Scr c11/1966
	SHEEPBRIDGE No.23	0-6-0ST	OC	HC	1022	1913	(e)	(2)
9		0-6-0ST	OC	HC	1023	1913	(f)	(3)
	BODNANT	0-6-0ST	OC	HC	396	1892	(g)	(4)
13		0-6-0ST	OC	AE	1727	1916	(h)	(5)
(15)		0-6-0ST	OC	HC	431	1895		
		reb		Sb		1944	(i)	(10)
16		0-6-0ST	OC	AE	1825	1919	(j)	(6)
(No.17)	(SHEEPBRIDGE No.27)	0-6-0T	OC	HC	1695	1938	(k)	Scr 5/1966
18		0-6-0ST	OC	YE	2413	1943	New	(7)
	STAVELEY	0-6-0ST	OC	WB	2629	1941	(l)	(8)
	HARTINGTON	0-6-0ST	OC	AE	1869	1921	(m)	s/s c5/1968

*   Sb = Sheepbridge Ironworks, Derbyshire.

BR 41518 (0-4-0ST IC Derby /1897) was on loan here, 4/1956; returned to BR 5/1956.

(a)   ex Sb*, /1907.

(b)   ex Sb, 7/5/1935; to Sb, 22/1/1937; ex Sb, 14/9/1942.

(c)   ex Sb, by 6/1923; returned by 9/1927; ex Glapwell Coll., Derbys, 7/1/1932; to Sb, 28/3/1936; ex Glapwell Coll., 23/5/1940.

(d)   to Sb;   ex Sb, 28/10/1952;   to Woodwards Ltd, Birdingbury, c7/1955;   returned 6/1956.

(e)   ex Sb, 10/1952.

(f)   ex Sb, 26/10/1927.

(g)   ex Sb, 17/7/1929; to Sb, 19/6/1935; ex Sb, 27/3/1936 to Sb, 30/11/1940; ex Sb, 15/5/1941.

(h)   ex Sb, 1/1927.

(i)   ex Sb, 20/3/1951; to E.E. Kimbell & Co, Engineers, Boughton, Northampton, for repair, c10/1955; returned 9/1956.

(j)   ex Sb, 17/1/1937; to Sb, 8/1940; ex Sb, 25/11/1940; to Sb, 26/7/1942; ex Sb, 6/8/1943.

(k)   ex Sb, 6/7/1942; to Sb, 16/8/1943; ex Sb, 12/1946; to Sb, 21/3/1951; ex Sb, 8/1951; to Sb, 10/1952; ex Sb, 1/1954.

(l)   ex Staveley Iron & Chemical Co Ltd, Pilton Ironstone Quarries, Rutland, 12/1955.

(m)   ex Lamport Ironstone Mines, 5/1965.

(1)   to Sb, 21/9/1942.

(2)   to Sb, 20/1/1954.

(3)   to Sb, 22/7/1929.

(4)   to Sb, 9/11/1943.

(5)   to Sb, 11/1932.

(6)   to Sb, 7/11/1946.

(7)   to Sb, 3/8/1951.

(8)   to Pilton Ironstone Quarries, 9/10/1956.

(9)   scrapped on site by Thos W. Ward Ltd, c/1930.

(10) to Railway Preservation Society, Chasewater, Staffs, 2/12/1967.

GLENDON NORTH IRONSTONE QUARRIES

Stanton Ironworks Co Ltd until 1/1/1950
James Pain Ltd until /1928
James Pain until 9/1905

SP 852823

Quarries on the west side of the Midland Railway lines at Glendon North Junction. Worked
from 1873 but extended and locomotive worked standard gauge railways, connecting with
the Midland Railway line, introduced from 1903. From 1911 the quarry railway extended
west for about 1½ miles to workings near Glen Hill Farm. Workings ceased in 1920 until the
quarries were reopened by the Stanton Co from 1928 until 1931 and again from 1941 until
final closure in 2/1957. One locomotive remained until 12/1961 and most of the track was
lifted in 1967.

Reference :   "The Ironstone Quarries of the Midlands, Part 6, Corby"; Eric Tonks,
Runpast Publishing, 1992

Gauge: 4ft 8½ in

	GLENDON	0-6-0ST	OC	FW	326	1876		
		reb	P			1906	(a)	s/s c/1928
	FORWARD	0-6-0ST	IC	P	1235	1910	New	(1)
	ROTHWELL	0-4-0ST	OC	P	1258	1912	New	(2)
	IRONSTONE	0-4-0ST	OC	P	1050	1907	(b)	(3)
No.84	(SWORDFISH to /56)	0-6-0ST	OC	AB	2138	1941	New (c)	(6)
No.81	HOLWELL No.14	0-6-0ST	OC	HL	3138	1915	(d)	(4)
35		0-6-0ST	IC	MW	1317	1895	(e)	(5)

(a)   ex P, 27/8/1906; earlier Coalpit Heath Coal Co Ltd, Gloucs.
(b)   ex Market Overton Quarries, Rutland, /1928.
(c)   to Glendon East Quarries, 18/4/1957; returned by 11/1957.
(d)   ex Glendon East Quarries, /1955.
(e)   ex Corby Quarries, 8/1956.

(1)   to Wellingborough Iron Co Ltd, 11/1934.
(2)   to Glendon East Quarries.
(3)   to Eaton Quarries, Leics, 7/1930.
(4)   to Glendon East Quarries, c3/1956.
(5)   to Glendon East Quarries, 8/1956; returned to Corby c9/1956.
(6)   to Glendon East Quarries, 12/1961.

HARRINGWORTH IRONSTONE QUARRIES

Stewarts & Lloyds Ltd until 1/1/1950
Lloyds Ironstone Co Ltd until 1/10/1932
Bloxham & Whiston Ironstone Co Ltd until 1/1/1932

T100

SP 913967

Quarry, working from 1923, about a mile south-east of Harringworth village. This was
served by a narrow gauge tramway which ran for about ¾ mile east to an exchange point
with standard gauge sidings on the east of the Midland Rly Corby - Manton line north of
Harringworth station. The narrow gauge line was replaced by standard gauge in 1933 and
locomotives were supplied by Corby (which see), changing as required. On 15/4/1952 a
connection about 2 miles in length to the Corby Quarries system was opened and
Harringworth shed was disused thereafter.

Reference :   "The Ironstone Quarries of the Midlands, Part 6, Corby"; Eric Tonks,
Runpast Publishing, 1992

Gauge: 4ft 8½in

Locomotives were supplied from the Corby fleet and exact details and transfer dates are not known. It is worthy of note that CARDIGAN (K 5473) and CARNARVON (K 5474) were delivered new to traffic here before transfer to Corby, and that S 7299 came here from Corby in 1/1932, returning to Corby in 1934.

Gauge: 3ft 0in

SLIPTON No.1	0-4-0ST	OC	HE	139	1875	(a)	(1)
SLIPTON No.2	0-4-0ST	OC	HE	209	1878	(a)	(1)
NANNIE	0-4-2ST	OC	HC	1087	1914		
	reb		HIW		1920	(b)	(2)
UTHIE	0-4-0ST	OC	HC	1106	1915	(c)	(1)

a) ex Islip Iron Co Ltd, c/1924.
b) ex Earls Barton Iron Ore Co Ltd, Earls Barton Quarries, /1924.
c) ex North Lincolnshire Iron Co Ltd, Easton on the Hill Quarries, /1931.

1) to Islip Iron Co Ltd, c/1932.
2) to Islip Iron Co Ltd, /1932.

ISLIP IRONWORKS   S101
Stewarts & Lloyds Ltd until 1/1/1950   SP 969782
Islip Iron Co Ltd until /1932
Islip Iron Co until 8/8/1903;
Nevins & Co until 2/1875

Quarrying of ironstone in the Islip area began about 1867, shortly after the construction of the Midland Railway Kettering - Thrapston railway (opened 21/2/1866) through the area. Islip Ironworks was built on the north side of the Midland Railway. The first two blast furnaces were built in 1871 and put into blast in 1874; two more furnaces were added in 1879. The works was served by standard gauge railways connecting with the Midland Railway, and by narrow gauge lines bringing ironstone from the extensive system of quarries and mines, mainly to the north of the works. After 1933 quarrying was increased to supply the then-new Corby Steelworks while the ironworks continued production of foundry iron until Stewarts & Lloyds obtained control of Stanton Ironworks, Derbys, in 1939. The ironworks furnaces were blown out on 6/10/1942 and had been dismantled by 1951; the railways remained to handle ironstone traffic until 10/1952 after which track had been lifted and plant scrapped by the end of 1953.

Reference : "The Ironstone Quarries of the Midlands, Part 6, Corby"; Eric Tonks, Runpast Publishing, 1992

Gauge: 4ft 8½in

ISLIP No.1	0-4-0ST	OC	HE	138	1875	New	(1)
ISLIP No.2	0-4-0ST	OC	HE	201	1878	New	(1)
ISLIP No.3	0-4-0ST	OC	HCR	165	1876	(a)	Scr
ISLIP No.4	0-4-0ST	OC	HC	427	1894	(b)	(2)
ISLIP No.5	0-4-0ST	OC	MW	745	1880	(a)	(3)
MARGOT	0-6-0ST	OC	P	1456	1918	(c)	(4)
BETTY	0-6-0ST	OC	P	1549	1919	(d)	(5)
LONDONDERRY	0-6-0ST	OC	P	806	1900	(e)	(6)

a) ex Glendon Iron Co Ltd, Finedon Furnaces.
b) ex Woolpit Brick & Tile Co Ltd, Suffolk, by /1909.

(c)   ex Bloxham & Whiston Ironstone Co Ltd, Milton Pits, Oxon, /1929.

(d)   ex Bloxham & Whiston Ironstone Co Ltd, Milton Pits, Oxon, /1931.

(e)   ex George Cohen, Sons & Co Ltd, Stanningley, Yorkshire (WR), /1933; earlier. S Pearson & Son Ltd, Silent Valley Reservoir contract, N.Ireland.

(1)   to Islip Iron Co Ltd, Finedon Siding Slag Works.

(2)   to Wellingborough Iron Co Ltd, /1949; returned /1951; scrapped 4/1954.

(3)   to Wellingborough Iron Co Ltd, /1947.

(4)   to Corby Works, 12/5/1950.

(5)   to Buckminster Mines, Lincs, 12/1952.

(6)   to Bilston Works, Staffs, /1948.

ISLIP IRONSTONE QUARRIES   S102

Stewarts & Lloyds Ltd until 1/1/1950   SP 969782
Islip Iron Co Ltd until /1932
Islip Iron Co until 8/8/1903
Plevins & Co until 2/1875

An extensive narrow gauge system served, from 1867, the many ironstone quarry and mine workings from which the ore was conveyed to Islip Ironworks (which see) and standard gauge exchange sidings. Locomotives were introduced from 1875. Production continued until 10/1952, after which track was lifted.

Reference : "The Ironstone Quarries of the Midlands, Part 6, Corby"; Eric Tonks, Runpast Publishing, 1992

Gauge: 3ft 0in

	SLIPTON No.1	0-4-0ST	OC	HE	139	1875	New	(1)
	SLIPTON No.2	0-4-0ST	OC	HE	209	1878	New	(1)
	SLIPTON No.3							
	(GERTRUDE)	0-4-0IST	OC	WB	1024	1888	New	Scr c8/1949
4	(SLIPTON NO.4)	0-4-0ST	OC	WB	1563	1899	New	Scr 7/1953
5	(SLIPTON NO.5)	0-4-0T	OC	WB	1946	1911	New	Scr 8/1953
6	(SLIPTON NO.6)	0-4-0T	OC	DK		1918	New	Scr by 6/1953
	SLIPTON No.7	0-4-0T	OC	KE	509	1920	New	Scr by 6/1953
	SLIPTON No.8	0-4-0T	OC	KE	510	1920	New	Scr by 6/1953
9	(NANNIE)	0-4-2ST	OC	HC	1087	1914		
		reb		HIW		1920	(a)	Scr 6/1952
10	UTHIE	0-4-0ST	OC	HC	1106	1915	(b)	
		reb		HC		1936		Scr by 6/1953
11	DIKE	0-4-0ST	OC	HC	1452	1921	(c)	Scr by 6/1953
12	STOCKS	0-4-0ST	OC	HE	1436	1922	(c)	Scr 7/1953

(a)   ex Harringworth Quarries, /1932.

(b)   ex Harringworth Quarries, c/1932.

(c)   ex Whitley Bros, contrs, of Wrexham, Flints [North Wales], after 5/1936, by /1940. Previously used on Shotwick-Frodsham road construction contract, Cheshire.

(1)   to Harringworth Quarries, c/1924; returned c/1932; scrapped c/1936.

LODDINGTON IRONSTONE QUARRIES

R103

SP 811770

Staveley Minerals Ltd until 1/1/1966
(subsidiary of **Staveley Iron & Chemical Co Ltd**)
Eastwell & Loddington Ironstone Co Ltd until 7/3/1961
Loddington Ironstone Co Ltd until 23/10/1959

Extensive quarry workings in an arc to the west of Loddington village. Production commenced about 1893 and the workings were served by a narrow gauge tramway which ran to a tipping dock at the terminus of the extended Midland Railway Cransley branch. This extension opened to traffic in 1/1893 and ultimately the narrow gauge ran northwards for about 2 miles from the tipping point. From 1891 to 1897 the White Hill Lodge Quarries were served by a short standard gauge branch from the Midland Railway. The metre gauge system closed 20/8/1958 and was replaced by an extension to the standard gauge tramway. The BR Cransley branch closed to traffic on 6/7/1963 as did the quarries. Track and plant were retained in reserve for some years but the locomotives were removed in 1966 and the track finally lifted from 6/1971.

Reference : "The Ironstone Quarries of the Midlands, Part 5, Kettering"; Eric Tonks, Runpast Publishing, 1991

Gauge: Metre

J.D.ELLIS	0-4-0ST	OC	SS	2298	1873	(a)		Scr 1/1959
LODDINGTON	0-4-0ST	OC	SS	2299	1873	(a)		Scr c/1935
DREADNOUGHT	0-4-0ST	OC	MW	1757	1910	(b)		(1)
THE BARONET	0-4-0ST	OC	Oliver	102	1889	(c)		(2)
WILLIAM ELLIS	0-6-0ST	OC	AE	2054	1930	New		(5)
HANDYMAN	0-4-0ST	OC	HC	573	1900	(e)		(4)
CAMBRAI	0-6-0T	OC	Corpet	493	1888	(d)		(3)

(a) ex Bolckow, Vaughan & Co Ltd, Cleveland Works, Middlesbrough, Yorkshire (NR).
(b) ex Waltham Iron Ore Co Ltd, Leics, c/1920.
(c) ex Cranford Ironstone Co Ltd, c/1923.
(d) ex Chemin de Fer du Cambresis, France, CLARY, via Thos.W.Ward Ltd, /1936.
(e) ex Cranford Ironstone Co Ltd, Cranford, c/1935.

(1) returned to Waltham Iron Ore Co Ltd, by /1935.
(2) to Waltham Iron Ore Co Ltd, c/1924.
(3) to Waltham Iron Ore Co Ltd, 4/3/1956.
(4) returned to Cranford, c/1935.
(5) scrapped on site by George Cohen, Sons & Co Ltd, 5/1966.

The frame of BANSHEE, ex Staveley Iron & Chemical Co Ltd, Scaldwell, was noted here in 1951.

Gauge: 4ft 8½in (White Hill Lodge Quarry)

-	0-4-0ST	OC	N	601	1891	(a)		(1)

(a) ex Duston Iron Ore Co Ltd, Northampton, hire, 11/1894 (identity assumed).

(1) returned to Duston Iron Ore Co Ltd, Northampton, 10/1896.

Gauge: 4ft 8½in

LODDINGTON No.2 (BYFIELD No.2								
until c12/1956)	0-6-0ST	OC	WB	2655	1942	(a)		(2)
NEW CRANSLEY No.3	0-4-0ST	OC	CF	1194	1900	(b)		(1)
(No.3)	0-6-0ST	OC	HL	3883	1936	(c)		(3)
(7)	0-6-0ST	OC	HL	3884	1936	(d)		(3)

(a)   ex Oxfordshire Ironstone Co Ltd, Banbury, Oxon, 1/1947.
(b)   ex New Cransley Iron Co Ltd, on loan, 11/1952.
(c)   ex Appleby-Frodingham Steel Co Ltd, Frodingham, Lincs, 15/6/1957.
(d)   ex Appleby-Frodingham Steel Co Ltd, Frodingham, Lincs, 17/6/1957.

(1)   returned to New Cransley Iron Co Ltd, off loan, /1953.
(2)   to Cranford Quarries, 28/4/1966.
(3)   scrapped on site by George Cohen, Sons & Co Ltd, 9/1966.

WELLINGBOROUGH IRONSTONE QUARRIES   Q104
Wellingborough Iron Co Ltd until 1/1/1950   SP 905695
Rixon's Iron & Brick Co Ltd until 12/2/1889
Rixon & Co until 18/6/1883

Quarries south of Finedon were in use from 1874 and were served by a horse worked narrow gauge tramway. Construction of Wellingborough Ironworks commenced in 1883 and when this operation was taken over by the Wellingborough Iron Co Ltd in 1889 a new metre gauge line was built from the ironworks to the Finedon Quarries. This line tunnelled under the Midland Railway Wellingborough - Kettering railway north of Wellingborough station and ran east to the quarries. There were also underground workings at Thingdon Mines which were served by 2ft 4in gauge lines which transhipped ore to the metre gauge tramway. Mines, quarries and ironworks closed on 22/9/1932 and were taken over and rebuilt as a subsidiary of the Stanton Ironworks Co Ltd. The modernised operation reopened and diesel locomotives were introduced in the underground workings (see under Wellingborough Iron Co Ltd). The ironworks closed on 29/10/1962 and was demolished by mid-1964; the ore transfer came under the control of Stewarts & Lloyds (Minerals) Ltd. Production of ore ceased 14/10/1966 and the track was lifted by 2/1967.

Reference :   "The Ironstone Quarries of the Midlands, Part 4, Wellingborough"; Eric Tonks,
              Runpast Publishing, 1990

Gauge: 3ft 3in/metre

No.1		0-4-0ST	OC	HE	348	1884	New	(1)
No.3		0-4-0ST	OC	HE	405	1887	New	(2)
No.4		0-4-0ST	OC	HE	473	1888	New	Scr 10/1959
No.1		0-4-0ST	OC	HE	562	1892	New	Scr c/1933
No.3		0-4-0ST	OC	HE	603	1894	New	Scr c/1933
No.10		0-4-0ST	OC	WB	1942	1918	New	Scr c/1934
No.85		0-6-0ST	OC	P	1870	1934	New	(3)
No.86		0-6-0ST	OC	P	1871	1934	New	(4)
No.87	"9"	0-6-0ST	OC	P	2029	1942	New	(5)

(1)   to HE, /1892; rebuilt to 3ft 6in gauge; resold to Thomas Oliver, Dore & Chinley (Midland Railway) contract, Derbys, 26/8/1892; subsequently used by Oliver at Green Withens Reservoir (1892-1898) contract, Rishworth, Yorkshire (WR), VIOLET; apparently for sale by J. Wardell, dealer, London, in 1902; subsequently to John H. Hope, Penmon Park Marble Quarries, Anglesey, [North Wales], by /1904.
(2)   to HE, /1892; rebuilt to 3ft 6in gauge and sold to Thomas Oliver, Green Withens Reservoir (1892-1898) contract, Rishworth, Yorkshire (WR), IRIS, /1893; subsequently to Lagos Railway, Nigeria, 11/1897.
(3)   to Alan Bloom, Bressingham Hall, Diss, Norfolk, 12/1966.
(4)   to John R. Billows Ltd, plant contractors, Pytchley Road Industrial Estate, Kettering, 6/1967, for use on a pleasure railway.
(5)   to F.G. Cann & Son, haulage contractors, The Poplars, Thrapston Road, Finedon, 8/1967.

WELLINGBOROUGH IRONWORKS SITE   Q105

Locomotive stabled at the old Ironworks site for some time to shunt standard gauge wagons carrying ore transhipped from the narrow gauge system.

Gauge : 4ft 8½in

50	CARMARTHEN	0-6-0ST	IC	K	5478	1936	(a)	(1)

(a)   ex Glendon East Quarries, 1/1964.

(1)   returned to Glendon East Quarries, 5/10/1964.

RICHARD THOMAS & BALDWINS LTD
BLISWORTH IRONSTONE QUARRIES   M106
Richard Thomas & Co Ltd until 3/1/1945   SP 713536

Quarrying, which included reopening of earlier workings, took place over a substantial area to the west of Blisworth village, as far as Gayton Wood House. The area was leased in 9/1935 but production did not commence until 11/1942. A standard gauge railway served the quarries and ran north to exchange sidings with the ex-SMJR line about ¾ mile west of Blisworth station. Quarries closed 3/1944 and equipment (including the locomotive) transferred elsewhere. The workings were reopened in 1954 and remained in production until 30/9/1967. Track was lifted and much of the area restored to agriculture; however one locomotive (AB 2365) remained in the shed until 1970.

Reference :   "The Ironstone Quarries of the Midlands, Part 3, Northampton"; Eric Tonks,
                    Runpast Publishing, 1989

Gauge: 4ft 8½in

	-	4wPM		Hardy		1930	(a)	s/s /1943
	BLISWORTH No.1	0-4-0ST	OC	AB	2143	1942	New	(1)
	HENRY CORT	0-4-0ST	OC	P	933	1903		
			reb	EV		1920 & 1937	(b)	(2)
	BLISWORTH No.1	0-4-0ST	OC	AB	2365	1955	New	(4)
	ETTRICK	0-4-0ST	OC	HL	3721	1928	(c)	(3)
49		0-6-0ST	IC	HE	2082	1940	(d)	Scr 3/1968
25	SIEMENS	0-4-0ST	OC	EV	3	1909	(e)	Scr 4/1968

(a)   ex Air Ministry, Henlow, Beds, No.134, after /1939, by /1943.
(b)   ex Ebbw Vale Steelworks, Gwent, /1954.
(c)   ex Abelson & Co (Engineers) Ltd, Sheldon, Birmingham, 5/1957.
(d)   ex Ebbw Vale Steelworks, Gwent, 8/1962.
(e)   ex Irthlingborough Mines, 7/4/1966.

(1)   to South Durham Steel & Iron Co Ltd, Storefield Mines, 9/1944.
(2)   to Irthlingborough Mines, 10/7/1957.
(3)   to Burton Transport Preservation Society, Marchington, near Tutbury, Staffs, 5/1969; later scrapped.
(4)   to CEGB, Goldington Power Station, Beds, 29/5/1970.

Richard Thomas & Co Ltd until 3/1/1945

Ebbw Vale Steel, Iron & Coal Co Ltd until 9/11/1935

SP 940697

From 1914 ironstone was mined in extensive underground workings to the west and north of Irthlingborough. For a short time a surface narrow gauge line ran to a quarry on the north of the Irthlingborough - Wellingborough road. Narrow gauge lines served the underground workings, with overhed wire electrification on the main run and battery locomotives used at the working faces. This system emerged at an adit south of the Irthingborough - Wellingborough road and ran to feed calcining kilns. The output from these was conveyed by a standard gauge system south to exchange sidings on the LNWR Wellingborough - Thrapston railway about 1 mile south-west of Irthlingborough station. In 1937 the main mine tramway was extended north and east to re-appear at surface in order to convey the output from the new Buccleugh Quarry, north of Finedon village. By 1962 this exit from the mine had been closed to traffic and new safety regulations meant that the overhead wire system was removed and the locomotives converted to battery operation. Workings closed 30/9/1965 and track and plant was then soon removed from the mines and disposed of, by 3/1967.

Reference :   "The Ironstone Quarries of the Midlands, Part 4, Wellingborough"; Eric Tonks, Runpast Publishing, 1990

Gauge: 4ft 8½ in

	MARY ANN	4-4-0T	OC	?			(a)	Scr c/1920
	SUNSHINE	0-4-0ST	OC	?			(a)	s/s after 8/1936
28	No.9	0-6-0ST	OC	P	751	1898	(b)	Scr 8/1957
	STEPHENSON	0-6-0ST	IC	RS	2837	1896	(c)	Scr 4/1960
		0-4-0ST	OC	AB	1466	1916	(d)	Scr c8/1965
	HENRY CORT	0-4-0ST	OC	P	933	1903		
		reb	EV		1920 & 1937		(e)	(2)
25	SIEMENS	0-4-0ST	OC	EV	3	1909	(f)	(1)

(a)   ex Ebbw Vale Ironworks, Gwent, c/1915.

(b)   ex Ebbw Vale Ironworks, Gwent, c/1925, after repair.

(c)   ex Graig Fawr Collieries, Gwent, c/1935.

(d)   ex Panteg Steelworks, Gwent, 4/1956.

(e)   ex Blisworth Mines, 10/7/1957.

(f)   ex Ebbw Vale Works, Gwent, 2/1962.

(1)   to Blisworth Quarries, 7/4/1966.

(2)   to Foxfield Light Railway Society, Dilhorne, Staffs, 4/2/1967.

Gauge: 3ft 0in (Overland line)

29		0-4-0ST	OC	HC	505	1898	(a)	s/s

(a)   ex J.F. Wake, dealer, Darlington, Co.Durham, /1918; earlier John Best, contractor; orig. Newcastle & Gateshead Water Co.

Gauge: 3ft 0in (Mining system)

1	4wWE	GEU	6100	1916	New	Scr /1966
2	4wWE	GEU	6099	1916	New	(1)
3	4wWE	GB	1545	1938	New	
	reb to 4wBE RTB			1/1964		(2)
4	4wWE	GB	1566	1938	New	
	reb to 4wBE RTB			12/1964		(2)

5		4wWE	GB	1567	1938	New	
		reb to 4wBE	RTB		3/1962		(2)
6	(9)	4wWE	GB	1746	1941	New	
		reb to 4wBE	RTB		7/1964		(2)
1		4wBE	BEV	78	1919	New	Scr /1966
2		4wBE	BEV	79	1919	New	Scr /1966
3		4wBE	BEV	156	1919	New	Scr /1966
4		4wBE	BEV	157	1920	New	Scr /1966
5		4wBE	BEV	252	1920	New	Scr c10/1966
6		4wBE	BEV	253	1920	New	Scr c12/1966
7		4wBE	BEV	254	1920	New	Scr c10/1966
8		4wBE	BEV	255	1920	New	Scr c10/1966
9		4wBE	BEV	374	1922	New	Scr c12/1966
10		4wBE	BEV	375	1922	New	Scr c10/1966
11		4wBE	BEV	376	1922	New	Scr /1966
12		4wBE	BEV	377	1922	New	Scr c12/1966
13		4wBE	BEV	378	1922	New	Scr /1966
14		4wBE	BEV	379	1922	New	Scr /1966
15		4wBE	RTB		c1938	New	Scr /1966
16		4wBE	RTB		c1938	New	Scr c12/1966
69		4wBE	GB	1569	1938	New	(2)
18	(70 until /1963)	4wBE	GB	1570	1938	New	(2)
20	(71 until /1963)	4wBE	GB	1571	1938	New	(2)
23	(72 until /1963)	4wBE	GB	1572	1938	New	(2)
24	(73 until /1963)	4wBE	GB	1573	1938	New	(2)
74		4wBE	GB	1574	1938	New	(2)
61		4wBE	GB	2061	1947	New	(2)
62		4wBE	GB	2062	1947	New	(2)
22	(63 until /1963)	4wBE	GB	2063	1947	New	(2)
78		4wBE	GB	2078	1947	New	(2)
79		4wBE	GB	2079	1947	New	(2)
80		4wBE	GB	2080	1947	New	(2)
21	(91 until /1963)	4wBE	GB	2291	1950	New	(2)
92		4wBE	GB	2292	1950	New	(2)
93		4wBE	GB	2293	1950	New	(2)
19	(94 until /1963)	4wBE	GB	2294	1950	New	(2)
95		4wBE	GB	2295	1950	New	(2)
17	(96 until /1963)	4wBE	GB	2296	1950	New	(2)
	LOCO No.1	4wDM	RH	187074	1938	(a)	(2)
	-	4wDM	RH	187076	1938	(a)	(2)
3		4wDM	RH	418803	1957	(b)	(2)
4		4wDM	RH	353491	1953	(b)	(2)
5		4wDM	RH	338439	1953	(b)	(2)
6		4wDM	RH	375694	1954	(b)	(2)
7		4wDM	RH	418764	1957	(b)	(2)
8		4wDM	RH	427802	1958	(b)	(2)
24		4wDMF	RH	433388	1959	(d)	(2)
	-	4wDMF	RH	451900	1961	(c)	(2)

(a)   ex Finedon Quarries, c/1945.
(b)   ex Dorman, Long (Steel) Ltd, Lingdale Mines, Yorkshire (NR), /1962.
(c)   ex Dorman, Long (Steel) Ltd, Kilton Mines, Yorkshire (NR), /1963.
(d)   ex Dorman, Long (Steel) Ltd, Lingdale Mines, Yorkshire (NR), c1/1964.

(1)   to W.J. Redden & Sons Ltd, Wellingborough, for scrap, 3/1966.
(2)   to W.T. Sheppard & Sons Ltd, Isebrook Works, Wellingborough, for scrap, 3/1967.

Gauge: 2ft 6in (purchased for spares only - not used here).

-	4wDM	RH	375693	1954	(a)	(1)
-	4wDM	RH	338438	1953	(b)	(1)
-	4wDM	RH	418765	1957	(b)	(1)
-	4wDM	RH	375329	1954	(b)	(1)
-	4wDM	RH	353486	1953	(b)	(1)

(a)   ex Dorman, Long (Steel) Ltd, North Skelton Mines, Yorkshire (NR), /1964. (Purchased for spares only).
(b)   ex Dorman, Long (Steel) Ltd, Kilton Mines, Yorkshire (NR), /1964. (Purchased for spares only; all in poor condition, and some incomplete).

(1)   to W.T.Sheppard & Sons Ltd, Isebrook Works, Wellingborough, for scrap, 3/1967.

FINEDON IRONSTONE QUARRIES   Q108

From 9/1937 Richard Thomas & Co Ltd reopened quarry workings to the north of Finedon village (for earlier history see under Harold Barlow). A temporary 3ft 8in gauge line was used in the preliminary stages of work. A standard gauge system served the quarries and initially allowed the ore to be transferred to narrow gauge wagons which were moved on the underground system to Irthlingborough (which see). Some ore was moved this way until about 1945 but from 1941 the standard gauge was extended to run about 1 mile south-west to Wellingborough sidings on the ex-Midland Railway line. Quarrying ceased on 23/5/1946 but the track remained in situ until about 1966. About 1951 a locomotive (51217) was hired from BR to help move calcined ore from the quarry area using this line; later BR 51235 was hired in the spring of 1954. (Both were 0-4-0ST OC Hor)

Reference :   "The Ironstone Quarries of the Midlands, Part 4, Wellingborough"; Eric Tonks,
                        Runpast Publishing, 1990

Gauge: 3ft 8in

WOOTON	0-6-0ST	OC	WB	1956	1912	(a)	s/s by 9/1944

(a)   ex Exors of P. Phipps, Hunsbury Hill Quarries, /1937.

After its initial use, this locomotive stood on an isolated piece of track for many years.

Gauge: 4ft 8½in

WHISTON	0-4-0ST	OC	AB	1333	1914	(a)	(1)
NEPTUNE	0-4-0ST	OC	AB	1361	1913	(b)	(2)
No.6	0-4-0ST	OC	HCR	180	1876		
	reb	HC			1920	(c)	(3)
FINEDON	0-4-0ST	OC	AB	2129	1941	New	(4)

(a)   ex Exors of P. Phipps, Hunsbury Hill Quarries, c/1940.
(b)   ex George Cohen, Sons & Co Ltd, 2/7/1939, earlier New Westbury Iron Co Ltd, Wilts.
(c)   ex Wellingborough Iron Co Ltd, Wellingborough Ironworks, on loan, /1941.

(1)   to Llandore Steelworks, West Glamorgan, 4/1951.
(2)   to Elba Steelworks, Gowerton, West Glamorgan, 8/1950.
(3)   to Wellingborough Iron Co Ltd, Wellingborough Ironworks, /1941.
(4)   to W. Gilbertson & Co Ltd, Pontardawe, West Glamorgan, 20/2/1946.

Gauge: 3ft 0in

| | | 4wDM | RH | 187074 1938 | New | (1) |
| | | 4wDM | RH | 187076 1938 | New | (1) |

(1) to Irthlingborough Mines, c/1945.

THRAPSTON WASHED SAND & BALLAST CO
(owners Thos Roberts (Westminster) Ltd)
THRAPSTON GRAVEL PITS   S109
SP 996791

Gravel workings, served by a narrow gauge tramway, located between the River Nene and the BR (ex Midland Railway) line north of Thrapston town centre. Quarries closed by 1963 and railway lifted after 1968.

Gauge: 2ft 0in

		4wPM	MR	5055 1930	New	(1)
		4wPM	MR	5062 1930	New	Scr after 9/1960
		4wPM	MR	5235 1930	New	(2)
		4wPM	MR	5236 1930	New	(3)
		4wDM	MR	7120 1936	New	Scr c/1968
		4wDM	MR	7125 1936	New	(4)

(1) to Bletchley Concrete Aggregates Co, Fenny Stratford, Bucks.
(2) to MR, 20/8/1936, and then to A.E. Farr Ltd, contrs. Twyford, Bucks.
(3) to MR and transferred to Petrol Locomotive Hirers, 15/6/1936; re-gauged to 3ft 0in and then to Dinmor Quarries Ltd, Anglesey (North Wales), 30/10/1936.
(4) to W.J. Keen & Sons, Bishops Stortford Sand Pits, Herts, 6/2/1957.

TOWCESTER MINERAL & BRICK CO LTD
(registered 4/11/1889)
EASTON NESTON IRONSTONE QUARRIES & BRICKWORKS   M110
Easton Estate & Mining Co Ltd until 2/6/1883   SP 706508
Towcester Co Ltd (registered 1874) until 17/7/1878

Quarries about midway between Blisworth and Towcester, on the east of the present A43 road. A narrow gauge tramway in the quarries conveyed ore to a tipping dock on a standard gauge line. This ran west from the quarry, across the road to serve a brickworks on the west side and then continued for about a mile to Towcester Ironworks on the east side of the S&MJR Blisworth - Towcester railway. Quarrying commenced in 1873, with the ironworks in production from 1875. Quarry and furnaces closed in 1882. From 1889 the brickworks was taken over by Towcester Mineral & Brick Co Ltd and limited ironstone quarrying resumed. At this time the original line was replaced by a much shorter connection to the S&MJR Towcester - Ravenstone Wood Junction line (which had opened 18/4/1891). Works closed by 1901; later reopened, for details of which see under E.M.Jellett.

Reference : "The Ironstone Quarries of the Midlands, Part 3, Northampton"; Eric Tonks, Runpast Publishing, 1989

Gauge: 4ft 8½in

| FORWARD | 0-6-0ST | IC | HE | 119 1874 | New | (1) |
| | | 0-4-0ST | OC | HC | 427 1894 | New | (2) |

(1) to Stanton Ironworks Co Ltd, Derbys.
(2) to Woolpit Brick & Tile Co Ltd, Suffolk, c/1902.

TWYWELL IRON ORE CO LTD
WOODFORD IRONSTONE QUARRIES
Woodford Iron Ore Co until 1882

In 1866, with the opening of the Midland Railway Kettering - Thrapston line, a standard gauge railway was laid from Twywell station yard and ran for about a mile south-west to serve the Woodford Quarries. A narrow gauge line was used within the quarries. Quarries closed 1890 and track lifted.

Reference : "The Ironstone Quarries of the Midlands, Part 5, Kettering"; Eric Tonks, Runpast Publishing, 1991

Gauge: 4ft 8½in

-	0-4-0ST				(a)	(1)
-	0-4-0ST	OC	HE	238 1880	New	(2)

(a)   origin and identity unknown.

(1)   offered for sale, 28/1/1880; s/s, possibly to Plevins & Co, Twywell Brickworks.
(2)   to ? , Chesterfield, Derbys; later to T.Mitchell & Sons, dealers, Bolton, Lancs, by 1/1900; to Thomas Robinson & Son, Rochdale, Lancs, 2/5/1903.

Gauge: 2ft 6in

-	0-4-0ST	OC	HE	307 1883	New	(1)

(1)   to E.P. Davis, Gretton Quarries, c/1890 (by 3/1898).

UNITED STEEL COMPANIES LTD
IRTHLINGBOROUGH IRONWORKS
Thos. Butlin & Co Ltd until 4/1920
Butlin Bevan & Co Ltd until 27/6/1889

Ironworks on the east side of the Midland Railway main line south of Wellingborough station. The first two furnaces were built in 1866 and in blast by 1869; two more were added in 1879 and 1882. The works was served by standard gauge sidings which connected both with the Midland Railway and also with the LNWR Wellingborough - Peterborough line ½ mile to the south-east. Associated ironstone quarries were worked to the east. The ironworks was acquired by United Steel Companies Ltd in 4/1920. Furnaces closed 1925, but foundry continued working until taken over by Morris Motors Ltd, 1947, which see for later history.

Reference : "The Ironstone Quarries of the Midlands, Part 4, Wellingborough"; Eric Tonks, Runpast Publishing, 1990

Gauge: 4ft 8½in

	PORTLAND	2-4-0ST	OC				
		reb by IWB from 2-4-0			c1867	(a)	s/s
	DAVID	0-4-0ST	OC	HCR	119 1872	New	(3)
No.2	SAUL	0-4-0ST	OC	HCR	158 1875	New	(4)
	-	0-4-0ST	OC	D&S	58c1875	New	(1)
	-	0-4-0ST	OC	D&S		(b)	(2)
No.1	JOAB	0-4-0ST	OC	HCR	180 1876	New	(5)
(1	EDGAR) 624/9	0-4-0ST	OC	HC	428 1894	New	(9)
U.S.C. No.2 (f. 2 HUGH)		0-4-0ST	OC	HC	527 1899	New	(7)
	ANCOATS	4wVBT	HCG S		5666 1924		
		reb of 0-4-0ST	OC	MW	1091 1888	(c)	(6)

		0-4-0VBT	HCG	S	6005CH	1925	(d)	s/s after 4/1944
3	THOMAS	0-4-0ST	OC	HC	763	1907	New	s/s
No.18	624/16	0-4-0ST	OC	HL	3423	1920	(e)	(8)

Note that some sources suggest that 0-4-0ST OC locos HCR 86/1867 and HC 252/1884, both owned by Butlin Bevan & Co, saw use here – see entries Q21 (Irchester Ironstone Quarries) and S22 (Great Adington Ironstone Quarries) for details of the locos.

(a)   ex I.W. Boulton, dealer, Ashton-under-Lyne, Lancs, 2/1872; identity uncertain, possibly ex Norfolk Railway, one of RS 396-398 of 1843

(b)   origins and identity not known

(c)   ex Blackwell & Son (Engineers) Ltd, Northampton, c/1924, possibly after trials at Irchester Ironstone Co Ltd, Irchester Quarries, prior to the rebuild of HC 527 as S 6005CH in /1925.

(d)   rebuilt from HC 527/1899.

(e)   ex Steel Peech & Tozer Works, Rotherham, Yorkshire (WR), c/1933.

(1)   to HC, c/1876; hire loco from 9/1877; to T.D. Ridley, Dovercourt, Essex, 4/11/1879.

(2)   to HC, c/1876; hire loco from 1/1877; to John Rhodes, Pontefract, Yorkshire (WR), RHINOCEROS, 1/1882.

(3)   to HC; later to Wrexham, Mold & Connah's Quay Junction Railway Co, 9 DEE, 10/1881 (or 9/11/1881).

(4)   to HC, c/1909; thence to Wellingborough Iron Co Ltd, Wellingborough Ironworks.

(5)   to Wellingborough Iron Co Ltd, Wellingborough Ironworks, by c/1909.

(6)   later at Thos E. Gray & Co Ltd, Isebrook Quarry, Burton Latimer, by 30/7/1929

(7)   rebuilt to S 6005/1925.

(8)   taken over by Morris Motors Ltd, with site, /1947.

Note that "Machinery Market" 11/12/1908 advertised for sale two standard gauge 4 coupled saddletank locos, 13 x 20in cyls, 3ft 6in driving wheels, also a small contractor's loco - Thos. Butlin & Co, Wellingborough. The dimensions of the first two correspond with those of HCR 158 and 180 in the list above.

THOMAS WALTERS
ADDINGTON IRONSTONE QUARRIES

S113

SP 972753

Quarries, worked from before 1871 to 1885, situated about ¼ mile east of Addington village. (The 1871 census records Thomas Walters of Addington Hall as farmer and ironmaster employing 100 men and boys.) A standard gauge railway about ½ mile long connected the workings to exchange sidings on the LNWR Wellingborough - Thrapston line ¼ mile north of Ringstead & Addington station. Track lifted about 1885.

Reference :   "The Ironstone Quarries of the Midlands, Part 4, Wellingborough"; Eric Tonks, Runpast Publishing, 1990

Gauge : 4ft 8½in

RAUNDS	0-4-0ST	OC	HC	219	1881	(a)	(1)

The information regarding the locomotive here is subject to confirmation

(a)   ex Raunds Iron & Limestone Quarries Co Ltd, c/1883.

(1)   to Stanton Ironworks Co Ltd, Teversal Colliery, Notts.

WAR DEPARTMENT
BARBY DEPOT

This Royal Army Ordnance Corps Depot was opened in 1943 and operated by No.1 Railway (Home) Group, Royal Engineers. Situated 4 miles south of Rugby, just in Northamptonshire, on the west side of the LNER (ex GCR) Rugby - Woodford Halse railway, it was served by standard gauge sidings with a locomotive shed and servicing facilities alongside the main line. Many of the steam locomotives listed below may have been here for storage rather than use. The depot was closed in 1955 and the sidings lifted; the main line connection closed on 29/9/1955. The loco shed was still standing in 1996, but the site has since been restored to agriculture, with the M45 motorway passing alongside the northern perimeter.

Reference : "British Railway Journal" No.59, Wild Swan Publications, 1998.

Gauge: 4ft 8½ in

	75035	0-6-0ST	IC	HE	2884	1943	New	(1)
	75036	0-6-0ST	IC	HE	2885	1943	New	(2)
	75052	0-6-0ST	IC	HC	1753	1943	(a)	(3)
	75095	0-6-0ST	IC	HC	1758	1944	New	(4)
	75142	0-6-0ST	IC	HE	3193	1944	New	(5)
	75151	0-6-0ST	IC	WB	2739	1944	(b)	(6)
	75155	0-6-0ST	IC	WB	2743	1944	New	(7)
	75166	0-6-0ST	IC	WB	2754	1944	New	(8)
	75197	0-6-0ST	IC	RSHN	7147	1944	New	(7)
	75198	0-6-0ST	IC	RSHN	7148	1944	New	(7)
	75199	0-6-0ST	IC	RSHN	7149	1944	New	(7)
	75254	0-6-0ST	IC	WB	2777	1945	(c)	(9)
	75282	0-6-0ST	IC	VF	5272	1945	(d)	(10)
	71450	0-6-0ST	IC	HE	3214	1945	New	(11)
	71489	0-6-0ST	IC	HC	1765	1944	New	(7)
	71494	0-6-0ST	IC	HC	1770	1944	New	(12)
	70042	0-4-0DM		AB	357	1941	(e)	(13)
827	(70047)	0-4-0DM		AB	362	1942	(f)	(14)
879	(70273)	0-6-0DE	Derby			1945	(g)	(15)

(a)   ex Ministry of Fuel & Power, Silverwood Colliery, Yorkshire (WR), after 4/1946.
(b)   ex Long Marston Depot, Warwicks, after 9/1944, by 2/1946.
(c)   ex Bicester Depot, Oxon, after 8/1949, by 1/1950.
(d)   ex Longmoor Military Railway, Hampshire, 6/1945.
(e)   ex Bicester Depot, Oxon, 9/1946.
(f)   earlier West Moors Depot, Dorset; here by 1/1952.
(g)   ex Longmoor Military Railway, Hampshire, after 8/1945, by /1946; returned to Longmoor, by 31/12/1946; to here again by 1/1952.

(1)   to Kineton Depot, Warwicks, after 5/1946, by 1/1947.
(2)   to Sudbury Depot, Staffs, after 6/1945, by 6/1948.
(3)   to Kineton Depot, Warwicks, 8/1947.
(4)   to Kineton Depot, Warwicks, by 8/1946; returned by 1/1948; to Appleby-Frodingham Steel Co Ltd, Scunthorpe, Lincs, 8/1950.
(5)   to Lockerley Depot, Wilts, 8/2/1945.
(6)   to Honeybourne Depot, Worcs, by 5/1947.
(7)   to Southampton Docks for shipment, 11/11/1944.
(8)   to Ministry of Fuel & Power, Pilsley, Derbys, by 7/1946.
(9)   to Bramley Depot, Hampshire, by 8/1955.
(10)   to Shoeburyness Depot, Essex, 21/7/1945.

(11) to Shoeburyness Depot, Essex, 16/7/1945.
(12) to Ministry of Fuel & Power, Giltbrook, Notts, by 1/1946.
(13) later at Suez, by 1/1952.
(14) to Suez, 2/1952; ex Bicester Depot, Oxon, after 3/1955; to Bicester 7/9/1959.
(15) to BAOR, Willich, Germany, c/1952; later Danish State Railways, 6, /1959.

WELLINGBOROUGH GRAVEL & SAND CO
DODDINGTON ROAD GRAVEL PITS, Wellingborough

Q115
? SP 898666

Pits in production by 1939 and closed after 1943, by 1946. A tramway may have run from a loading dock in Doddington Road to the workings, but this is not confirmed.

Gauge: 2ft 0in

-	4wPM	L		4414	1932	New	(1)
-	4wDM	RH	163997	1931		(a)	(1)

Both these locos were advertised for sale ("Contract Journal" 17/2/1943) by A. Pullen, The Old Dairy, Wingrave, near Aylesbury.

(a)   ex Manchester Corporation Waterworks Department, Haweswater Scheme, Westmorland, /1934 (after 30/8/1934).

(1)   to Earls Barton Sand & Gravel Co Ltd, Earls Barton Gravel Pits, after 2/1943

WELLINGBOROUGH IRON CO LTD
(Registered 24/9/1888; Subsidiary of **Stanton Ironworks Co Ltd** from 1933)

WELLINGBOROUGH IRONWORKS

Q116

Rixon's Iron & Brick Co Ltd (registered 18/6/1883) until 30/6/1887   SP 903694

Ironworks on the west side of the Midland Railway main line north of Wellingborough station, served by standard gauge sidings connecting with this line, and also by a narrow gauge line to Wellingborough Quarries (which see under Stewarts & Lloyds Minerals Ltd). The works was built from 1883 with a first blast furnace in use from 1885, a second from 1886 and a third from 1898. From 1870 until about 1927 a brickworks (at SP 904693) was in production, with a tramway from a nearby clay pit in use by 1900. The ironworks closed 22/9/1932 and was then rebuilt in association with Stanton Ironworks Co. It reopened about 1933 (one furnace in blast in 1934) and continued in production until final closure on 29/10/1962. The works was dismantled and much track lifted although some facilities were retained for ore transfer from the narrow gauge until the closure of that system.

Reference :   "The Ironstone Quarries of the Midlands, Part 4, Wellingborough"; Eric Tonks, Runpast Publishing, 1990

Gauge: 4ft 8½in

2	0-4-0ST	OC	HE	359	1885	New	Scr /1930
No.5	0-4-0ST	OC	HE	61	1871	(a)	s/s by /1930
WELLINGBORO' No.6	0-4-0ST	OC	HCR	180	1876		
	reb		HC		1920	(b)	Scr 4/1961
No.7	0-4-0ST	OC	HCR	158	1875		
	reb		HC		1909	(c)	Scr /1933
No.8	0-4-0ST	OC	FE	184	1889	(d)	Scr

No.9		0-4-0ST	OC	HC	1285	1917	New	(1)
2		0-4-0ST	OC	HC	576	1900	(e)	(2)
	(FORWARD)	0-6-0ST	IC	P	1235	1910	(f)	Scr /1963
	WELLINGBORO' No.3	0-4-0ST	OC	HL	3813	1935	New	(6)
	WELLINGBORO' No.5	0-4-0ST	OC	AB	2063	1939	(g)	Scr c7/1964
7		0-4-0ST	OC	AB	2135	1941	New	(7)
8		0-4-0ST	OC	AB	2136	1941	New	(8)
	HOLWELL No.19	0-4-0ST	OC	AB	1826	1924	(h)	Scr 3/1963
61A		0-4-0ST	OC	AB	1479	1917	(i)	(3)
5	ISLIP	0-4-0ST	OC	MW	745	1880	(j)	Scr 8/1955
	ISLIP No.4	0-4-0ST	OC	HC	427	1894	(k)	(4)
36	ISHAM	0-4-0ST	OC	HE	791	1902	(l)	Scr 12/1955
5	IRONWORKS No.1	0-6-0ST	OC	AB	1241	1911	(m)	(5)
	THE BROKE	0-4-0ST	OC	AB	1592	1918	(n)	Scr 4/1963
	FOCH	0-4-0ST	OC	AB	1645	1919	(o)	Scr /1963
(No.10)		0-4-0ST	OC	AB	1065	1906		
		reb		AB		1941	(p)	Scr 2/1963
(No.15)		0-6-0ST	OC	HL	3347	1918	(p)	Scr 2/1963

(a) ex R.T. Relf, contr, WREN.
(b) ex Thos. Butlin & Co Ltd, Irthlingborough Ironworks; to Richard Thomas & Co Ltd, Finedon Quarries, /1941; returned, /1941.
(c) ex HC, after rebuild, /1910; earlier Thos Butlin & Co Ltd, Wellingborough.
(d) ex Plevins & Co, Twywell Brickworks.
(e) ex George Cohen, Sons & Co Ltd, /1928; earlier Thomas Salt & Co Ltd, Burton on Trent, Staffs.
(f) ex Stanton Ironworks Co Ltd, Glendon North Quarries, 11/1934.
(g) ex Stanton Ironworks Co Ltd, Stanton Ironworks, Derbys.
(h) ex Stanton Ironworks Co Ltd, Holwell Ironworks, Melton Mowbray, Leics, /1943.
(i) ex Stewarts & Lloyds Ltd, Corby Works, c5/1946.
(j) ex Stewarts & Lloyds Ltd, Islip Ironworks, /1947.
(k) ex Stewarts & Lloyds Ltd, Islip Ironworks, /1949.
(l) ex Stewarts & Lloyds Ltd, Corby Works, 12/1952.
(m) ex Stewarts & Lloyds Ltd, Corby Works, /1953.
(n) ex Stewarts & Lloyds Ltd, Bilston Works, Staffs, 3/9/1954.
(o) ex Stewarts & Lloyds Ltd, Bilston Works, Staffs, 16/3/1955.
(p) ex Kettering Iron & Coal Co Ltd, Kettering, 5/1960.

(1) to Stanton Ironworks Co Ltd, Holwell Ironworks, Melton Mowbray, Leics, /1935.
(2) to Stanton Ironworks Co Ltd, Teversal Colliery, Notts.
(3) to Stewarts & Lloyds Ltd, Corby Works, /1948.
(4) to Stewarts & Lloyds Minerals Ltd, Islip Ironworks, /1951 (by 29/3/1951).
(5) to Stewarts & Lloyds Ltd, Corby Works, c12/1954.
(6) to Stewarts & Lloyds Ltd, Corby Works, c8/1963.
(7) to Stewarts & Lloyds Ltd, Corby Works, c2/1964.
(8) scrapped on site by W.J. Redden, Wellingborough, w/e 2/2/1963

THINGDON IRONSTONE MINES, Finedon   Q117
SP 919709

Ironstone mines in the area south-east of Finedon village, served by a narrow gauge system, which in turn transhipped to the Wellingborough quarries railway. Workings commenced in 1911 and the tramway was horse worked until the introduction of diesel locomotives in

1934. Production ceased about 1944 and railway dismantled. The area was subsequently worked opencast by an extension of the 3ft 3in system.

Reference : "The Ironstone Quarries of the Midlands, Part 4, Wellingborough"; Eric Tonks, Runpast Publishing, 1990

Gauge: 2ft 4in

No.1	4wDM	RH	168831	1933	(a)	(1)
No.2	4wDM	RH	172888	1934	New	(2)
No.3	4wDM	RH	174140	1935	New	(3)
No.4	4wDM	RH	177608	1936	New	(4)
No.5	4wDM	RH	200494	1940	New	(5)

(a) ex Stanton Ironworks Co Ltd, Holwell Mines, Leics, 12/1933 (by 27/12/1933).

(1) to Gunthorpe Gravels (Trent) Ltd, Asfordby, Leics, after 11/10/1945, by 17/3/1950.

(2) to Stanton Ironworks Co Ltd, Nuthall Sandpits, Notts, 6/1947.

(3) to Stanton Ironworks Co Ltd, South Witham Quarries, Lincs, 6/1947.

(4) converted to compressor unit after 12/12/1944 and later sent to South Witham Quarries, Lincs.

(5) to Bowne & Shaw Ltd, Wirksworth, Derbys, 6/1947.

WHISTON IRONSTONE CO LTD
WHISTON IRONSTONE QUARRIES, near Castle Ashby   M118
Bloxham & Whiston Ironstone Co Ltd until 25/3/1919   SP 846606
Whiston Ironstone Co until 27/12/1917
J.W. Pain until c1915.

Ironstone workings to the south of the LNWR Northampton - Wellingborough line about a mile west of Castle Ashby & Earls Barton station. Opened in 1914 and served by a standard gauge line about a mile in length from the LNWR line. Quarries closed 1921 and track lifted.

Reference : "The Ironstone Quarries of the Midlands, Part 3, Northampton"; Eric Tonks, Runpast Publishing, 1989

Gauge: 4ft 8½ in

WHISTON	0-4-0ST	OC	AB	1333	1914	New	(1)

(1) to Exors of P. Phipps, Hunsbury Hill Ironworks, Northampton, /1921.

THOMAS WHITEHOUSE
NORTHAMPTON GASWORKS   N119

Whitehouse was a local coal merchant who had a contract to cart coal from canal wharves to Northampton Gas Works and, from 1845, also from the LNWR station (later Bridge Street). When the private sidings were installed at the gasworks in 1871, he experimented with locomotive haulage there using the locomotive listed below, but then reverted to horse traction until 1876. After this date the gas company provided its own locomotives.

Reference : "The Industrial Locomotive No.94" (p.123), Industrial Locomotive Society, 1999.

Gauge : 4ft 8½ in

JACKAL	0-4-0ST	IC	Harrison & Clayton	1870	New	(1)

(1) to S. Pearson & Son, Southport Main Drainage (1876-1878) contract, Lancs

FRANCIS T. WRIGHT LTD
FINEDON RAILWAY WAGON WORKS

This Nottingham-based company (registered 2/1920) took over, in 1925, the site of Finedon Furnaces, on the east side of the Midland Railway south of Finedon station, for use as a wagon repair works. The works was served by standard gauge sidings connecting with the main line. For earlier history see Islip Iron Co Ltd. Works closed c1960 and track lifted.

Reference : "The Ironstone Quarries of the Midlands, Part 4, Wellingborough"; Eric Tonks, Runpast Publishing, 1990

Gauge: 4ft 8½ in

ISLIP No.1	0-4-0ST	OC	HE	138	1875	(a)	Scr c/1930
ISLIP No.2	0-4-0ST	OC	HE	201	1878	(a)	(1)
-	4wVBT	G	AtW	109	1928	(b)	Scr 10/1950
-	4wDM		RH	294265	1950	New	(2)

(a) ex Islip Iron Co Ltd, Finedon Siding, with site, /1925.
(b) ex Alpha Cement Ltd, Oxon, via George Cohen, Sons & Co Ltd, c/1937.

(1) advertised for sale ("Machinery Market" 3/9/1943) as 'needing new boiler'. Scr /1951.
(2) to William Rigley & Sons (Nottingham) Ltd, Bulwell Wagon Works, Notts, c/1960 (after 2/1959).

CONTRACTORS LOCOMOTIVES

JOHN AIRD & SON
TOWCESTER CONTRACT   LC1

Construction of the Northampton & Banbury Junction Railway from Bradden to Cockley Brake Jct. The line was first authorised on 27/8/1863; the Blisworth to Towcester section (4 miles) built by C.N. Foster (which see), had opened 4/1866 for freight and on 1/5/1866 for passengers. This further section, to Cockley Brake (10 miles) was apparently first let to W. Shrimpton, and from Board of Trade returns it appears that Towcester-Bradden (3 miles) had been built prior to Shrimpton failing. The Bradden to Cockley Brake section was re-authorised by Act of 14/7/1870 and the contract was let to John Aird & Sons in 1870. The line was opened to Helmdon for goods traffic by 31/8/1871 and throughout on 1/6/1872. The Northampton & Banbury Junction Railway passed to the Stratford-upon-Avon & Midland Junction Railway in 1910.

Gauge : 4ft 8½ in

-	0-6-0	IC	(Longridge	1846?)	(a)	(1)

a)   ex I.W. Boulton, of Ashton-under-Lyne, Cheshire, hire, (apparently delivered direct from LNWR Wolverton), c/1871.

1)   returned to I.W. Boulton, Ashton-under-Lyne, Cheshire.

BALDRY & YERBURGH
TOWCESTER CONTRACT   MC2

Contract let in 1887 for the completion of the construction of the 10½ mile long Towcester to Ravenstone Wood (Olney) railway. This line had been authorised as the Easton Neston Mineral & Towcester, Roade & Olney Junction Railway on 15/8/1879. Construction was protracted and an Act of 1882 changed the company name to the Stratford-upon-Avon, Towcester & Midland Junction Railway

Work had been initially commenced by Watson Smith & Watson (which see). A "first sod" ceremony took place on 15/12/1887 and work was in hand by 1/1888. The line was finally opened to freight on 13/4/1891, and to passengers 1/12/1892.

Reference : "Stratford & Midland Junction Railway", J.M. Dunn, Oakwood Press,1952

Gauge : 4ft 8½ in

HESKETH	0-4-0ST	OC	MW	634	1877	(a)	(1)
GAVIN	0-6-0ST	OC	BH	471	1881	(a)	(2)
-	0-4-0ST	OC	MW	900	1884	(b)	(3)

Additionally, it is possible that Baldry & Yerburgh purchased an ex-LNWR loco at the Pitsea contract sale in 6/1888 for use on this contract. If so, it could connect with a loco, variously described as LLIW or LNWR, which was repaired by Markham at around this time.

a)   earlier Watson, Smith & Watson, with contract, /1887.
b)   ex Kirk & Parry, Cheadle Railway contract, Staffs, No.8, c/1890 (after 6/1888).

1)   repaired by Mkm, 3-6/1890;
later (thence?) to Annesley-Staveley (MS&LR) (1890-1892) contract, Notts.
2)   probably later Annesley-Staveley (MS&LR) (1890-1892) contract, Notts, No.10.
3)   (? possibly to Annesley-Staveley (MS&LR) (1890-1892) contract, Notts);
later Staveley Coal & Iron Co Ltd, Staveley Works, Derbys.

JOHN BROGDEN & JOHN STEPHENSON
LONDON & BIRMINGHAM RAILWAY CONTRACTS   LC3

Contracts for the construction of the London & Birmingham Rly, Blisworth-Northampton-Peterborough section, 1844-1846. The contracts were let in three sections on 11/1/1844:
- C.1   Blisworth to Wellingboro to John Stephenson
- C.2   Wellingboro to Oundle to John Stephenson
- C.3   Oundle to Peterborough to John Brogden

and each contract included one year's maintenance after public opening. The line from Blisworth to Northampton was double track and opened to passengers 13/5/1845; to Peterborough for passengers on 2/6/1845; opened throughout for freight traffic 15/12/1845.

The Northampton to Peterborough section, built as single track, was soon widened to double track under a further contract by John Stephenson, and completed 9/1846.

References : "The Nene Valley Railway", John Rhodes, Turntable, 1976/1983

"Peterborough' First Railway", Waszak & Ginns, Nene Valley Railway, 1995

Gauge : 4ft 8½in

John Stephenson requested the London & Birmingham Railway in 12/1844 to loan/hire to him "a couple" of locos and this was agreed (the identites of the locos have not been established, and they may not connect to the following information). The first loco was put onto the line at Thrapston on 19/2/1845 (or 19/3/1845 per another source) and hauled from Weedon through Northampton by 16 horses. On 10/3/1845 a complaint was registered about the ballast engines crossing a turnpike road without gates. On 24/3/1845 a crowd observed a ballast train steam through the new station at Cotton End, Northampton, and on 21/4/1845 a ballast train derailed near Duston Bridge. On 3/5/1945 the directors had an inspection train over the line. In 5/1846, during the widening works, a luggage train collided head-on with a "ballast" (contractor's ?) train, wrecking both locos.

From these details it is clear that this is an early example of railway contractors using locomotives which they have hired. Unfortunately, none of the locomotives has yet been identified.

CONDUIT CONSTRUCTION CO LTD
WELLINGBOROUGH CONTRACT   QC4

SP 906686 approx

Construction by this Salford based firm of four miles of drainage tunnels from Morris Motors Ltd, Wellingborough, to Finedon in 1964.

Gauge : 2ft 0in

-	4wDM	MR	4813	1937	(a)	(1)
-	4wDM	MR	21287	1959	(b)	(2)

(a)   ex W.J. Redden & Sons Ltd, Wellingborough, c/1964; earlier Bedford Corporation Water Board, Manton Lane Water Works, Bedford..

(b)   ex Diesel Loco Hirers Ltd

(1)   to W.J. Redden & Sons Ltd, dealers, Wellingborough, after 7/1964; later to Earls Barton Silica Co Ltd, /1969 (after 6/1969).

(2)   returned to Diesel Loco Hirers Ltd, by 8/1965.

CORBY (NORTHANTS) & DISTRICT WATER CO
EYE BROOK RESERVOIR, Caldecot
Subsidiary of **Stewarts & Lloyds Ltd**

TC5

SP 855943

Locomotives used during the construction of this reservoir situated about three miles north-west of Corby. Work commenced in 5/1937 and was completed about 1940. Locomotives used in the construction work were advertised for sale in "Contract Journal" 2/8/1939 and 2/7/1941.

Gauge : 2ft 0in

-		0-4-0T	OC	AE	2072	1933	(a)	(4)
-		0-4-0T	OC	AE	2073	1933	(a)	(5)
-		0-4-0WT	OC	AB	1855	1931	(a)	(5)
-		0-4-0WT	OC	AB	1995	1931	(a)	(6)
No.1		4wDM		RH	186337	1937	New	(2)
No.2		4wDM		RH	186340	1937	New	(1)
	(ROMFORD)	4wDM		JF	21408	1936	(b)	(3)

(a)   ex Durham County Water Board, Burnhope Reservoir construction, Co.Durham, c/1937.

(b)   ex South Essex Waterworks Co, Abberton Reservoir, near Colchester, Essex.

(1)   to Stewarts & Lloyds Ltd, Church Mine, near Islip, after 25/3/1939, by 9/7/1940.

(2)   to Stewarts & Lloyds Ltd, Church Mine, near Islip, after 12/6/1940, by 22/11/1940.

(3)   to George Cohen, Sons & Co Ltd, dealers, c/1940.

(4)   to Joseph Pugsley & Sons Ltd, dealers, Bristol, c11/1941;
       thence to Roads Reconstruction (1934) Ltd, Vallis Vale Quarry, Frome, Somerset.

(5)   to Joseph Pugsley & Sons Ltd, dealers, Bristol, c11/1941;
       thence to Roads Reconstruction (1934) Ltd, Grovesend Quarry, Tytherington, Glos.

(6)   to F.W. Dobson & Co Ltd, Raisby Hill Lime Works, Coxhoe, Co.Durham, c/1941 (after 2/7/1941)

CRAMPTON & SONS
TOWCESTER CONTRACT
T.R. Crampton until 8/1866

LC6

This firm (headed by Thomas Russell Crampton) built the East & West Junction Railway from Green's Norton Jct (Towcester) to Stratford-on-Avon (Warwicks). This totalled 33 miles of which 17 were within Northants. Construction was authorised by Act of 23/6/1864, and the "first sod" ceremony took place at Towcester on 3/8/1864. Work was in hand by 1865, but the contractor, who by now was involved with Peto, Betts & Crampton, was declared bankrupt in 7/1867, no work having been done since 8/1866 following the bank crash of 5/1866. Crampton & Sons, having been discharged from bankruptcy, resumed work late in 1870 and the 6½ mile section from Fenny Compton to Kineton (all in Warwickshire) opened on 1/6/1871. The remaining two sections opened on 1/7/1873 and equipment, including locos, was auctioned by Fuller Horsey, on behalf of Crampton & Sons, on 23/2/1874.

Gauge : 4ft 8½in

No.1	SHAKESPEARE	0-6-0ST	IC	MW	177	1865	New	(1)
	CRAMPTON #	0-6-0ST	IC	MW	178	1866	New	(2)
	FENNY COMPTON	0-4-0ST	OC	N	1633	1871	New	(3)
	BYFIELD	0-4-0ST	OC	N	1703	1872	New	(4)

Also a 4wheel-coupled saddle tank OC 10/12x20in loco by Hawthorne/s & Co (RWH, BH or H(L) ? in Cramptons' sale 23/2/1874

renamed KINETON by 1/6/1871.

(1)　to Brassey & Ballard, St. Albans (Midland Railway) (1865-1868) contract, Herts.

(2)　to E&WJR, 1, 1/6/1871 (used 1874-1877 at Crampton's Gravel Pits, near Woodford).

(3)　later Benton & Woodiwiss, Ashburys Junction to Romiley (MS&LR/Midland Railway) (1871-1875) contract, Cheshire, after 15/4/1873, by 9/1/1875.

(4)　to Wm Richards, Golynos Colliery, Abersychan, Gwent, after 15/4/1873, by 26/4/1876.

CHARLES DEACON, JNR

Charles Deacon until 1876

WELLINGBOROUGH CONTRACT   RC7

Finedon to Glendon North Junction widening contract (14 miles) for the Midland Railway, let 11/1875 and completed 19/10/1879.

Gauge : 4ft 8½in

SOLOMON	0-6-0ST	IC	MW	641	1877	New	(1)
-	0-4-0ST	OC	HCR	193	1877	New	(2)
-	0-4-0ST	OC	DS	58			
		reb	HC	195	1877	(a)	(3)

"The Engineer" 6/6/1879 advertised - R. Boyce to auction 17-19/6/1879 re Chas. Deacon, Midland Railway Rushden to Bedford widening at Wellingborough and Kettering stations, plant including two nearly new locos - MW 1877 six-wheel 12in and the other by Hudswell & Co, Leeds, 1877, 12in.

(a)　hired by HCR sometime during period /1877 to 11/1879 to C. Deacon; no location shown, but possibly this contract (no alternative location yet known). Perhaps on loan pending delivery of HCR 193.

(1)　later Joseph Firbank, Lewes-East Grinstead (LBSCR) (1876-1883) contract, Sussex, SHARPTHORN.

(2)　for sale here 6/1879; no further trace

(3)　if here, then returned to HCR, Leeds, by /1879

RICHARD DUNKLEY

NORTHAMPTON-MARKET HARBOROUGH CONTRACT   LC8

The contract for the construction of new line from Northampton to Market Harborough for the LNWR was awarded to Dunkley, of Blisworth, in the latter months of 1856. Work was in hand by 4/1857, and the line was opened 16/2/1859. The contract included a period of subsequent maintenance, which was terminated on 1/1/1861.

Reference : "The Northampton & Harborough Line", John Gough, R&CHS, 1984

Gauge : 4ft 8½in

On 3/8/1858, a Board of Trade inspection was carried out "using the contractor's engine". This loco has not yet been identified.

NORTHAMPTON-LAMPORT WIDENING CONTRACT LC9

Contract awarded by the LNWR to Dunkley after a decision on 13/4/1860 to put work in hand; the Board of Trade inspection was on 16/4/1862 and the line presumably opened soon afterwards.

Gauge : 4ft 8½in

A LNWR Southern Division Minute of 20/2/1861 refers to "one of the small Bury engines" hired to Mr Dunkley for ballasting second line at £1 per day, "Mr Dunkley finding his own driver". This loco has not yet been identified.

EAGRE CONSTRUCTION CO LTD
BLISWORTH CONTRACT LC10

Contract for the lifting of track on the former S&MJR railway from Blisworth (Ironstone sidings) to Woodford West Junction. The line closed on 3/2/1964 and track lifting was completed at Woodford by 6/1965. Work also included the lifting of sidings at Woodford Halse, in progress in 9/1965. Other contracts undertaken by this company included the laying of new sidings at Cransley, near Kettering, for George Cohen Sons & Co Ltd in 1962 and the lifting of the ex LNWR line from Banbury to Verney Junction (Bucks) in 1967. It is possible that the locomotive listed here was also used on these jobs.

Gauge : 4ft 8½in

-	0-6-0DM	JF	22885	1940	(a)	(1)

(a) earlier Thos.W. Ward Ltd, Colombia Works, Grays, Essex, until after 7/2/1961; orig Air Ministry, Halton Camp, Bucks; here by 24/5/1965.

(1) possibly to other contracts; scrapped by 10/1968.

C.N. FOSTER
BLISWORTH CONTRACT MC11

Contract for construction of the Blisworth to Towcester section of the Northampton & Banbury Junction Railway. The line was authorised on 28/7/1863; and this 4-mile section opened in 4/1866 for freight and on 1/5/1866 for passengers.

The contract for construction of (at least) the Towcester to Cockley Brake section was originally awarded to W. Shrimpton, who had completed some work before failing due to the 10/5/1866 Overend, Gurney bank crash. Shrimpton is known to have had locomotives elsewhere but, as yet, none have been traced to his work on this Northampton & Banbury Junction Railway contract.

Construction of the line from Bradden to Cockley Brake Junction was subsequently undertaken by John Aird & Son (which see). The Northampton & Banbury Junction Railway passed to the Stratford-upon-Avon & Midland Junction Railway in 1910.

Foster, sometimes mis-reported as Charles Fowler, of Whitefriars, London, was summoned in the Court of Exchequer in 11/1866 for having forcibly removed a locomotive, but which had been seized by the Sheriff and chained to the track. Forster claimed this locomotive was his property. It has not yet been positively identified. It may have been the property of the N&BJR, as this company was similarly charged with having forcibly removed "some trucks". The writ of fieri facias under which the Sheriff had made the seizures is variously reported in contemporary sources as being either against the contractor, or against the company.

A similar incident, or a different version of the same incident, appears in the Riley & Simpson book, which suggests the loco was an IWB loco ex LNWR 1125. However, the names of the leading characters are all different.

Apart from the loco VULCAN listed below, the Northampton & Banbury Junction Railway had two locomotives in use prior to the opening of the railway. When the line first opened, the Northampton & Banbury Junction Railway was in severe financial difficulties, and it seems likely that the contractor/s operated the trains on behalf of the company, which could explain why Foster had had his loco (VULCAN maybe ?) seized by the Sheriff. One at least of the "N&BJR" locos (IWB No.11) was apparently used (possibly by Foster) during completion of construction, and the second loco (OWL) may well have been similarly used. Pending clarification, we include these locos in this list.

References :
"Stratford & Midland Junction Railway", J.M.Dunn, Oakwood, 1952
"Northampton & Banbury Junction Railway", S.C.Jenkins, Oakwood, 1980
"Locomotive Building in Northampton", The Industrial Locomotive, No.94, p.123

Gauge : 4ft 8½in

	VULCAN	0-6-0ST	IC	HE	4	1865	New	
	VULCAN	0-6-0ST	IC	HE	4	1865	New	(1)
1125	IWB No.11	2-2-2	IC	SR	193	1842	(a)	(2)
	OWL						(b)	(3)

(a)   ex I.W.Boulton, dealer, Ashton-under-Lyne, Cheshire, c3/1866
(b)   here c/1886, source not known. Was a "decrepit antique" per Jenkins book.

(1)   possibly hired to N&BJR for train operation, c/1866; later Leather, Smith & Co, Portsmouth Dockyard (Admiralty) (1867-1877/8) contract, Hampshire, No.10, (? c/1870)
(2)   used by N&BJR for train operation; returned to I.W. Boulton, Ashton-under-Lyne, Cheshire, by 7/1866
(3)   used by N&BJR for train operation - no further trace

GRANT LYON EAGRE LTD
CORBY CONTRACT   TC12

Track maintenance contract at Corby Tube Works for British Steel Corporation, 1993
Gauge : 4ft 8½in

No.3	4wDM	Robel	54.12-56-RTI	1966	(a)	(1)

(a)   ex Scunthorpe Plant Depot, South Humberside; here by 6/8/1993.

(1)   returned to Scunthorpe Plant Depot, South Humberside.

KETTERING URBAN DISTRICT COUNCIL
NEW CRANSLEY CONTRACT   RC13

Work at New Cransley Reservoir.
Gauge : 1ft 11½in

20	4wPM	FH	1669	1930	(a)	(1)

(a)   ex Finedon Sewage Works

(1)   to Northfield depot, Kettering.

KOTTLER & HERON LTD
NORTHAMPTON

NC14

Details of the use of the loco not known. Possibly used in the contract for the reconstruction of Great Billing sewage works.

Gauge : 2ft 0in

-	4wDM	MR	7391	1939	(a)	(1)

(a) earlier Sir Lindsay Parkinson & Co Ltd, East Bridgeford (RAF Station) (1939-1940) contract, Notts; here by 17/2/1947.

(1) advertised as for hire by Kottler & Heron Ltd, in Contract Journal 15/10/1947; later Slindon Gravels Ltd, Slindon, Sussex, by 2/2/1955.

JOHN LAING & SON LTD
CRICK CONTRACT

LC15

Construction of the M1 motorway at Crick, c1957 – 1958.

Gauge : 2ft 0in ?

-	4wDM	RH	(a)	s/s

(a) identity and origin unknown.

LONDON & BIRMINGHAM RAILWAY CONTRACTS

LC16

An extensive length of the London Euston-Tring-Rugby-Birmingham railway was built 1834-1838 through the county of Northamptonshire. Locomotives were definitely used by contractors during these works. Many of the locos appear to have been L&B locos on hire, for both construction and subsequent maintenance works. Although at least 10 such locos have been traced, their details are very scanty. It is not, therefore, possible to publish any definitive information at this stage, but contributions of relevant data would be very welcome.

LUCAS & AIRD
KETTERING - MANTON CONTRACT

TC17

Construction of the Glendon Jct to Manton (Rutland) section of the Midland Railway. This was a length of 15 miles, of which 11 lay in Northamptonshire. The contract was let in 7-8/1875, work was in hand by 2/1876, and the line opened for various classes of traffic from 1/12/1879 to 1/6/1880.

Gauge : 4ft 8½in

OAKLEY	0-6-0ST	IC	MW	597	1876	New	(1)
-	0-6-0ST	IC	MW	617	1876	New	(2)

(1) to J Firbank, South Croydon - Oxted (SER) (1880-1884) contract, Surrey, OXTED.
(2) later Eckersley, Godfrey & Liddelow, New Southgate widening (GNR) (1889-1890) contract, London, OAKLEIGH.

SIR ROBERT McALPINE & SONS LTD

HOLLOWELL CONTRACT   MC18

Construction of Hollowell Reservoir, about six miles north west of Northampton, 1936-1938.

Gauge : 4ft 8½in

No.9	0-6-0ST	IC	HC	492	1898	(a)	(5)
No.15	0-4-0ST	OC	HC	529	1899	(b)	(1)
No.33	0-6-0ST	IC	HC	1029	1913	(c)	(2)
No.44	0-6-0ST	IC	HC	1529	1924	(d)	(4)
No.53	0-6-0ST	IC	MW	1560	1902	(e)	(6)
No.56	0-6-0ST	IC	HC	1494	1923	(f)	(4)
No.57	0-6-0ST	IC	HC	1538	1924	(g)	(3)

(a)   ex Hayes Depot, Middlesex, 11/5/1936
(b)   earlier at Great Stanney Depot, Cheshire, /1935; here by /1936
(c)   ex Cheddar Reservoir (Bristol Waterworks Co) contract, Somerset, /1936
(d)   ex East Moors (GK&B) contract, Cardiff, 16/4/1936.
(e)   earlier at Southampton Docks (SR) contract, Hampshire, /1935; to here 1/8/1936
(f)   ex Hayes Depot, Middlesex, 14/5/1936
(g)   ex Hayes Depot, Middlesex, 15/6/1936

(1)   to Hayes Depot, Middlesex, 28/5/1936
(2)   to Hayes Depot, Middlesex, /1937
(3)   to Scunthorpe (Appleby Frodingham Steel Co Ltd) contract, Lincs, 26/11/1937
(4)   to Scunthorpe (Appleby Frodingham Steel Co Ltd) contract, Lincs, 30/11/1937
(5)   to Scunthorpe (Appleby Frodingham Steel Co Ltd) contract, Lincs, 7/3/1938
(6)   to Scunthorpe (Appleby Frodingham Steel Co Ltd) contract, Lincs, 7/7/1938

Gauge : 2ft 0in

-	4wDM	MR	7127	1936	(a)	(1)
-	4wDM	MR	7130	1936	(a)	(2)

(a)   ex MR, 18/11/1937; orig Diesel Loco Hirers Ltd.

(1)   later at Hayes Plant Depot, Middlesex, by 13/1/1951;
        then to George W. Bungey Ltd, Heston Airport Depot, Middlesex, by 9/1962 and s/s.
(2)   later Ham River Grit Co, Ham Pits, Surrey, 109, by /1951;
        later with Concrete Aggregates, Darenth Pits, Dartford, Kent.

NORTHAMPTON CONTRACT   NC19

'
Construction of Hardingstone Power Station for Northampton Electric Light & Power Co Ltd, 1935 - 1936.

Gauge : 4ft 8½in

No.54	0-6-0ST	IC	HC	1601	1927	(a)	(1)

(a)   ex Hayes Depot, Middlesex, 13/2/1935

(1)   to Ebbw Vale Steelworks (Richard Thomas & Co Ltd) contract, Gwent, 6/5/1936

YARDLEY CHASE CONTRACT   MC20

Construction of ROF Yardley Chase for the Ministry of Supply, 1942-1943

Gauge : 4ft 8½in

ROF 6 No.11	0-4-0DM		JF	22988 1942	New (a)	(1)
No.32	0-6-0ST	IC	HC	1028 1913	(b)	(2)
No.45	0-6-0ST	IC	HC	1586 1927	(c)	(3)
No.56	0-6-0ST	IC	HC	1494 1923	(d)	(4)

A second JF diesel loco may have been here on loan from JF for construction work; possibly then to ROF Pontrilas, Herefords.

(a)   ex JF, loan, for construction work, 20/10/1942
(b)   ex hire to Electrical & Musical Industries Ltd, Hayes, Middlesex, 4/1/1943
(c)   ex Cheltenham - Gloucester widening (GWR/LMSR) contract, 30/4/1942
(d)   ex hire to Bedfordshire, Cambridgeshire & Huntingdonshire Electricity Co, Little Barford Power Station, Beds, 10/6/1942

(1)   to ROF Risley, Lancs, (possibly via JF), 1/3/1943.
(2)   to Hayes Depot, Middlesex, 24/4/1943
(3)   to Hayes Depot, Middlesex, 8/4/1943
(4)   to Hayes Depot, Middlesex, 13/10/1942

KETTERING PLANT DEPOT   RC21
SP 865769

Locos repaired and stored at this depot (still in existence in 2001) between use on contracts.

Gauge : 4ft 8½in

PN A6444	0-6-0DM	HE	2697 1944	(a)	(1)

(a)   ex Hayes Depot, Middlesex, by 20/4/1971

(1)   to Flying Scotsman Enterprises, Market Overton, Rutland, 5/1974.

Gauge : 750mm

-	4wBE	CE	B4057A 1994	New
-	4wBE	CE	B4057B 1994	New

Gauge : 900mm ?

-	4wDH	HE	9342 1995	New	(1)
-	4wDH	HE	9343 1995	New	(1)
-	4wDH	HE	9344 1995	New	(1)
-	4wDH	HE	9345 1995	New	(1)

Note : The above four locos were rebuilt respectively from 4wBE/WE locos HE 9446/ HAB 770, HE 9436/HAB 768, HE 9437/HAB 769, and HE 9448, all of 1990. The locomotives were the property of HE and were used by McAlpine-Wayss-Freytag J V, Jubilee Line contract No.107, London

(1)   returned to Hunslet-Barclay Ltd, Kilmarnock, Strathclyde, c4/1996 (by 9/9/1996).

Gauge : 2ft 0in

-	4wBE	PWR	B0367.01 1993	New	s/s
-	4wBE	PWR	A0296V.01 1993	(a)	s/s

	A34818	0-4-0BE	WR	2065	1941	(b)	(1)
	A26120	0-4-0BE	WR	6309	1961	(c)	(1)
	A2613-	0-4-0BE	WR	6310	1961	(d)	(1)
5	A066925	4wBE	WR	J7206	1969	New	(1)
3	A056915	4wBE	WR	J7208	1969	(c)	(1)
	-	4wBE	WR	J7271	1969	(e)	(1)
2	A056917	4wBE	WR	J7272	1969	(c)	(1)
6	A056920	4wBE	WR	J7273	1969	(e)	(1)
1	A066923	4wBE	WR	J7274	1969	(f)	(1)
	A116917	4wBE	WR	J7275	1969	(f)	(1)
4	A037001	4wBE	WR	K7282	1970	(f)	(1)

(a)   ex J.F. Donelan & Co Ltd, 23/2/1994.

(b)   orig Plessey Co Ltd, LPTB Aircraft Factory, Chiswick, London.

(c)   new to Lowdham Plant Depot, Notts.

(d)   new to Hayes Plant Depot, Middlesex.

(e)   new to Hinckley Point Power Station contract, Somerset.

(f)   new to Hunterston Power Station contract, Ayrshire.

(1)   Four of these locos were sold to an unknown purchaser in Canada, the remainder to Air Operated Equipment, Bromacq Industrial estate, Witney, Oxon; WR 2065, 6309 and 6310 by 2/6/1975, the remainder by 17/5/1980.

Gauge : 1ft 3in

P W 3	REDGAUNTLET	4wPM	Jacot	1963	(a)	(1)

(a)   ex Romney, Hythe & Dymchurch Railway, Kent, for repairs, by 8/4/1974.

(1)   returned to Romney, Hythe & Dymchurch Railway, Kent, by 3/8/1975 (then to Alan Keef Ltd, Bampton, Oxon, by 19/3/1977).

MEAKIN & DEAN LTD
ROADE CONTRACT   MC22

Construction of the Roade - Northampton line (5 miles) for the LNWR. The line was authorised as part of the widening of the LNWR main line in 1876; the contract was let 22/11/1876 but a report of 4/1878 stated that preliminary earthworks were in hand. The line was opened to freight traffic on 1/8/1881, and to passengers on 3/4/1882. Widening works between Roade and Bletchley were concurrently undertaken by Thomas Nelson, who see.

Gauge : 4ft 8½in

-	0-4-0ST	OC	FW	353	1878	New	s/s
-	0-6-0ST	OC	FW	371	(1878 ?)	(a)	(1)

(a)   loco not confirmed as owned by Meakin & Dean, or on this contract (see footnote (1)).

(1)   the 10/1887 dispersal sale of the Meakin & Dean Alnwick-Cornhill (NER) (1883-1887) contract, Northumberland, included 7 locos one at least being by "Fox & Co". This could have been FW 353, or possibly FW 371 because a loco of this type is apparently credited to the Broomhill Coal Co, near Alnwick, who are reputed to have obtained it c/1887. The evidence is entirely inconclusive, but if the loco was FW 371, then prior use on the Roade contract does seem possible.

MITCHELL CONSTRUCTION CO LTD
DAVENTRY CONTRACT LC23

Construction of a drainage culvert in 1970. The work ran from SP 579623 to SP 578626; a tramway was used to convey concrete in three Hudson Raletruck wagons (with removable tubs) to sites along the line.

Gauge : 2ft 0in

-		4wDM	MR	22031	1959	(a)	(1)
-		4wDM	MR	22032	1959	(a)	(1)

(a)   ex previous Mitchell contract (location uncertain).

(1)   to Alan Keef Ltd, Cote Farm, Bampton, Oxon, c10/1971;
      thence to A. Waddington & Son Ltd, Farningham Sewer contract, Kent, /1972.

WILLIAM MOSS
SEATON CONTRACT LC24

Construction of the Seaton to Wansford railway (9 miles, of which 5 were in Northamptonshire) for the LNWR. Authorised 21/7/1873; tenders required by 6/5/1875. Opened to freight 21/7/1879, and to passengers 1/11/1879.

Gauge : 4ft 8½in

NASSINGTON	0-6-0ST	IC	MW	636	1876	New	(1)
STAFFORD	0-4-0ST	OC	MW	651	1877	New	(2)
SEATON	0-6-0ST	IC	MW	662	1877	New	(3)
WANSFORD	0-6-0ST	IC	MW	683	1878	New	(4)
KINGS CLIFFE	0-6-0ST	IC	MW	687	1878	New	(4)
(SAM ?)	0-6-0ST	IC	MW	(106	1864 ?) (a)		(1)
(16 MERSEY ?)	0-6-0					(b)	(5)
	0-4-2	IC	Wolverton	1854			
	reb			1868	(c)		(5)

The dispersal sales on the line 29/6-1/7/1880 included a 4wc 8in MW, FIVE 6wc 12in MW and "6 & 4wc locos 17in". Subsequently, Moss was selling at Stafford in 9/1880 THREE 6wc MW 12in nearly new, one 6wc 18in Main Line loco, one 6wd 4wc 18in Main Line loco. Suggesting the 8in and two 12in MWs had sold in the first sale.

(a)   if MW 106 then presumably ex another Moss contract; loco with Moss by c/1872 and possibly from new (one MW source has new to James Bray & Co, Methley Branch (WYR) contract, but may not have gone there in fact).

(b)   ex an earlier contract; identity unconfirmed – the loco given was purchased by Wm Moss ex LNWR, 1132, 1/1870; earlier St.Helens Railway, Lancs.

(c)   ex LNWR, 1171, 12/1877

(1)   to Exe Valley Railway (GWR) (1879-1884) contract, Devon.

(2)   later Geo Furness, Hundred of Hoo Railway (1880-1882) construction, Higham, Kent.

(3)   later Falkiner & Tancred, Didcot, Newbury & Southampton Railway contract (1879-1884), Berks, NEWBURY, by 7/1881.

(4)   possibly to Exe Valley Railway (GWR) (1879-1884) contract, Devon.

(5)   for sale at contract auction 29/6-1/7/1880, and apparently these locos for sale by Moss, Stafford, 9/1880. No further trace.

ADDITIONAL DATA –

Moss also had a contract for the doubling of the LNWR line from Lamport to Market Harborough; contract let 11/1875 and line opened 4/8/1879. No confirmed locos.

A collision took place on 18/10/1877 between Billing Road station and Northampton involving a "loaded ballast train belonging to Mr Moss of Stafford" and a Midland Railway passenger train, in which the engine and tender of the ballast train were badly damaged. The ballast train *may* have been in connection with either the Lamport or Seaton contracts. LNWR Minutes of 12/12/1877 state that Moss was to give up his old engine and tender (destroyed) to purchase an LNWR duplicate engine of a similar class (which may well have been LNWR 1171 in the list above).

An 0-4-2 IC BCK /1848 (LNWR S.Divn. 206; 806 (5/1862); 1148 (2/1863) and 1858 (12/1871)) had been sold by the LNWR to Wm Moss in 4/1873 and could be the loco in the collision.

NAYLOR BROS
DAVENTRY CONTRACT   LC25

Construction, by this Denby Dale (Yorkshire (WR)) based contractor, of the 3¾ mile Weedon - Daventry line for LNWR. The line was promoted as the Weedon & Daventry Rly, incorporated 31/7/1868, but it was reported in 1869 that "progress of the line was not as rapid as wished" and when a new Bill was promulgated in 1885 it was reported that the line had actually been started with contractors plant on the site. The identity of this early contractor is not known, nor whether the plant included locomotives although "ballast trucks" are mentioned. Naylor Bros re-started the works in 1886 and the line opened on 1/3/1888. (The 14 mile continuation from Daventry to Marton Jct was built by Walter Scott & Co and opened 1/8/1895).

Gauge : 4ft 8½in

DAVENTRY	0-6-0ST	IC	MW	973	1886	New	(1)
WEEDON	0-6-0ST	IC	MW	976	1886	New	(2)
DODFORD	0-4-0ST	OC	MW	977	1886	New	(3)

(1) later Abram Kellett & Sons Ltd, St.Andrews Dock Extension (1894-1897) contract, Hull, Yorkshire (ER).

(2) later Davies Bros, Wrexham-Ellesmere Railway (1892-1895) contract, Denbighs/Flints [North Wales] (MW 977 named DOROTHY).

THOMAS NELSON & CO
T.B. Nelson until 7/1878
ROADE CONTRACTS   MC26

Widening of the Bletchley - Roade line, and works at Wolverton Station for the LNWR. Contract let 22/11/1876; T.B. Nelson died on 2/7/1878 during the work, and the contract was completed by his father, with possibly an intervening period when executors were in control. The contract included a diversion and new station at Wolverton, for which T. Nelson & Co required carpenters as late as 7/1882. Final completion date not known, but the widened lines were opened to freight 1/8/1881, and to passengers 31/7/1882. The new line between Roade and Northampton was undertaken by Meakin & Dean, which see.

Gauge : 4ft 8½in

7	CARLISLE	0-6-0	IC	K	1421	1867	(a)	(1)

earlier at York - Selby - Doncaster (NER) line contract (1866-1871), Yorkshire (ER).

(1) later Aston - Lawley Street widening (LNWR) (1888-1890) contract, Birmingham.

THOMAS OLIVER

IRCHESTER CONTRACTS   QC27

Thomas Oliver was involved in at least two consecutive or concurrent contracts for the Midland Railway and it is very probable that the locomotives transferred between these as required. The letting dates of the contracts have not been established, but contemporary reports suggest dates from late 1880. The works involved a new line from Souldrop (near Sharnbrook) to Irchester South including a new Sharnbrook tunnel, opened 4/5/1884. Also widening lines which were opened to freight as follows: Wellingborough South to Finedon Road down goods line 12/3/1882, Wellingborough South to Wellingborough Junction up goods line 19/3/1882, Wellingborough South to Irchester South up and down goods lines 3/12/1883, and Sharnbrook Junction to Irchester South up and down goods lines 4/5/1884. The line from Sharnbrook south to Oakley etc was let to Walter Scott in early 1890s.

Gauge : 4ft 8½in

NENE	0-6-0ST	IC	HE	242	1881	New	(1)
ANNIE	0-4-0ST	OC	HE	17	1866	(a)	(1)
NELLIE	0-4-0ST	OC	HE	29	1868	(a)	(1)
WILLIE	0-6-0ST	IC	HE	65	1871	(a)	(1)
FRED	0-4-0ST	OC	HE	137	1875	(a)	(1)
FRANK	0-6-0ST	IC	HE	161	1876	(a)	(1)
FLORENCE	0-6-0ST	OC	BH	466	1878	(b)	(1)

(a) ex Chichester-Midhurst (LBSCR) (1879-1881) contract, Sussex.
(b) ex Walter Scott, Rugby-Northampton (LNWR) (1877-1882) contract.

(1) to Lawrence Hill, Bristol (GWR) (1884-1887) contract.

THOMAS OLIVER & SON
WOODFORD CONTRACT   LC28

Construction of the Rugby (Warwicks) to Woodford & Hinton railway (16 miles, of which 4 were in Warwicks) for the MS&LR. This was Contract No.4 of the MS&LR London Extension and was originally to end at Charwelton but was extended to Woodford & Hinton by mutual agreement. Contracts let 10/1894 and the line was opened to freight on 26/7/1898, and to passengers on 15/3/1899. Dow states that plant used on this contract included 20 steam locomotives.

Reference : "Great Central, Vol.2", George Dow, Locomotive Publishing Co, 1962.

Gauge : 4ft 8½in

ANNIE	0-4-0ST	OC	HE	17	1866	(a)	(1)
NELLIE	0-4-0ST	OC	HE	29	1868	(a)	s/s after 7/1898
WILLIE	0-6-0ST	IC	HE	65	1871	(a)	(4)
FRED	0-4-0ST	OC	HE	137	1875	(a)	(10)
FRANK	0-6-0ST	IC	HE	161	1876	(a)	(7)
FLORENCE	0-6-0ST	OC	BH	466	1878	(a)	s/s after 28/2/1900
NENE	0-6-0ST	IC	HE	242	1881	(a)	(8)
GIBBON	0-6-0ST	IC	HE	545	1891	(a)	(12)

LENN	0-6-0ST	IC	HE	549	1891	(a)	(6)
BROUGHTON	0-6-0T	IC	MW	1062	1888	(a)	(15)
BARRY	0-6-0ST	IC	HE	363	1885	(b)	(2)
BLACKPOOL	0-6-0ST	IC	HE	369	1885	(b)	(11)
MERSEY	0-6-0ST	IC	HE	434	1887	(b)	(9)
IRWELL	0-6-0ST	IC	HE	435	1887	(b)	(13)
ARPLEY	0-4-0ST	OC	HE	442	1888	(b)	(5)
ST GEORGES	0-6-0ST	IC	MW	1003	1887	(b)	(16)
SUTTON	0-4-0ST	OC	MW	1016	1887	(b)	s/s
RUBY	0-4-0ST	OC	HE	104	1874	(c)	(3)
15	0-6-0ST	IC	MW	1145	1890	(d)	(14)
14	0-6-0ST	IC	MW	1153	1890	(e)	(16)

(a) earlier Dore - Hathersage (Midland Railway) (1888-1894) contract, Derbys.

(b) ex Manchester Ship Canal Co (prev T.A. Walker), MSC construction (1887-1894) contract, Lancs, probably c/1894-5

(c) ex HE, Leeds, 4/11/1891 (to Thos Oliver at unspecified location);
earlier Mountsorrel Granite Co Ltd, Mountsorrel, Leics.

(d) ex Logan & Hemingway, Beighton-Chesterfield (MS&LR) (1890-1892) contract, Derbys.

(e) ex Logan & Hemingway, Beighton-Chesterfield (MS&LR) (1890-1892) contract, Derbys, or Annesley - East Leake (MS&LR) (1894-1898) contract, Notts.

(1) to Stoats Nest-Earlswood (Quarry Line) (LBSCR) (1896-1899) contract, Surrey, by 8/1897.

(2) to Stoats Nest-Earlswood (Quarry Line) (LBSCR) (1896-1899) contract, Surrey, by 1/1898

(3) to Stoats Nest-Earlswood (Quarry Line) (LBSCR) (1896-1899) contract, Surrey, by 7/1898.

(4) to Beighton-Treeton (Midland Railway) (1898-1900) widening contract, Yorkshire (WR), after 4/1898, by 5/1899.

(5) to Beighton-Treeton (Midland Railway) (1898-1900) widening contract, Yorkshire (WR), after 6/1898, by 8/1898.

(6) to Beighton-Treeton (Midland Railway) (1898-1900) widening contract, Yorkshire (WR), after 3/1899, by 6/6/1899.

(7) to Thackley (Midland Railway) (1898-1902) widening contract, Yorkshire (WR), after 9/1898, by 5/1899.

(8) to Thackley (Midland Railway) (1898-1902) widening contract, Yorkshire (WR), after 11/1898, by 4/1899

(9) to Thackley widening (Midland Railway) (1898-1902) widening contract, Yorkshire (WR), after 11/1898, by 12/1899.

(10) to Alfreton - Clay Cross (Midland Railway) (1899-1902) widening contract, Derbys, after 9/1899, by 12/1899

(11) to Alfreton - Clay Cross (Midland Railway) (1899-1902) widening contract, Derbys, after 8/1899, by 10/1899.

(12) to Alfreton - Clay Cross (Midland Railway) (1899-1902) widening contract, Derbys, after 10/1899, by 11/1899.

(13) to Garswood Hall Colliery Co Ltd, Garswood Hall Colliery, Lancs, c/1898.

(14) later Neasden - Northolt (GCR) (1901-1905) contract, Middx.

(15) later Redhill widening (LBSCR) (1909) contract, Surrey.

(16) later Swansea District Lines (GWR) (1907-1915) contract, West Glamorgan

WALTER SCOTT

In addition to the contracts listed below, Walter Scott (& Co) had other significant contracts in the area on which locomotives were very probably used, but no details are yet known. Such jobs include:-

Sharnbrook-Oakley (MR) (1891-1893) widening contract.
Irchester-Higham Ferrers (MR) (1891-1894) construction.
Cransley-Loddington (MR) (by 1892-1893) [with confused and conflicting details].
Daventry-Leamington (LNWR) (1892-1895) [mostly in Warwickshire]
Ashendon-Aynho (GWR) (1906-1910 [with locos; listed under Oxfordshire]

NORTHAMPTON CONTRACT   LC29

Construction of the Rugby - Northampton line for the LNWR. The line was authorised as part of the widening of the LNWR main line in 1876 and the contract had been awarded to Scott by 7/1877. The line opened to traffic on 3/4/1882.

Gauge : 4ft 8½in

No.7	ANNIE MARY	0-6-0ST	OC	BH	415	1878	New	(1)
	FANNY	0-4-0ST	OC	BH	423	1878	New	(2)
No.9	BENTINCK	0-6-0ST	OC	BH	466	1878	New	(3)
No.8	TYNE	0-6-0ST	OC	BH	467	1878	New	(4)
	RUBY	0-6-0ST	IC	MW	678	1877	(a)	(5)
No.11	CYPRUS	0-6-0ST	IC	MW	596	1876	(b)	(5)
		0-4-0ST	OC	J&T Young		1863	(c)	(6)

(a) ex MW, Leeds, on hire, 2/8/1878; purchased 18/9/1878; earlier on hire to W.T. Mousley, Sutton-St.Ives (GER) (1876-1878) contract, Hunts, RUBY

(b) ex MW, Leeds, 29/5/1879; earlier Lucas & Aird, Albert Dock contract, London.

(c) not confirmed here, but if here then may have been earlier Taylor & Co, Annbank Colliery, Ayr; and may perhaps have been used by Walter Scott on Ayr New Wet Dock (1874-1878) contract.

(1) to Exors of James Diggle, Westleigh Collieries, Lancs, after 11/1881 (by 1/11/1882).

(2) to John Waddell & Sons, Downham & Stoke Ferry railway (1881-1882) contract, Norfolk (arrived c8/4/1882; may have spent a short period with Waddell on Reepham-County School (East Norfolk Rly) (1880-1882) contract first.

(3) to Thomas Oliver, Irchester (Midland Railway) (1880-1884) contracts, FLORENCE.

(4) later Thomas Docwra & Son, West Moseley Reservoirs enlargement (1897/8-1903) contracts, Surrey

(5) later on Woodford- Quainton Road (MS&LR) (1894-1898) contract.

(6) for sale at Crick, 3/1882; s/s

Seven locos were advertised for sale 9-10/3/1882 at Crick and Kilsby - 6 & 4 wheels coupled by BH, MW and J & T Young with 8, 12, & 14in cyls.

WALTER SCOTT & CO

BRACKLEY CONTRACT   LC30

Construction of the Woodford & Hinton - Quainton Road railway (25 miles) for the MS&LR (later GCR), 1894 - 1898. Contract No.5 was Charwelton to Brackley, and Contract No.6 was Brackley to Quainton Road. Then Contract No.5 was altered to begin south of Woodford station, with curves to E&WJR as well as temporary connections to the LNWR Banbury branch and LNWR Bletchley-Oxford line. The contracts were let in 10/1894 and the line was opened to freight on 26/7/1898, and to passengers on 15/3/1899. There was a main plant depot at Brackley together with a second site and a brickworks near Helmdon. Dow states that plant used on this contract included 18 steam locomotives.

References : "Great Central, Vol.2", George Dow, Locomotive Publishing Co, 1962.
"The Last Main Line", R.D.Abbott, Leicester Museums, 1961
"Contractors Locomotives GCR", N. Cossons, Leicester Museums, 1963.

Gauge : 4ft 8½in

	J R WRIGHT	0-6-0ST	IC	MW	1228	1895	New	(1)
	THE AUDITOR	0-6-0ST	OC	BH	1105	1895	New	(2)
	BRACKLEY	0-6-0ST	IC	HE	164	1876	(a)	(3)
	BRADFORD	0-6-0ST	IC	MW	899	1884	(b)	(4)
	TRAFALGAR	0-6-0ST	IC	MW	911	1884	(c)	(5)
	PELLON	0-6-0ST	IC	MW	1112	1889	(d)	(6)
	TYERSALL	0-6-0ST	IC	MW	1068	1888	(d)	(7)
	C H STANTON	0-6-0ST	OC	BH	758	1885	(e)	s/s
	NEWCASTLE	0-6-0ST	OC	HC	237	1883	(e)	(8)
	CICETER	0-6-0ST	IC	MW	583	1876	(f)	(9)
	COREA	0-6-0ST	IC	MW	971	1885	(f)	(9)
	CYPRUS	0-6-0ST	IC	MW	596	1876	(g)	(10)
	RUBY	0-6-0ST	IC	MW	678	1877	(g)	(11)
	GROSVENOR	0-6-0ST	IC	HE	288	1884	(h)	(12)
No.16	LULI	0-4-0ST	OC	MW	892	1884	(i)	(13)
	CUMBRIA	0-6-0ST	OC	MW	202	1878	(j)	(14)
	WALTER SCOTT	0-6-0ST	IC	MW	1237	1892	(k)	(15)
	BUTTERFLY	0-4-0ST	OC	MW	942	1885	(l)	(16)

(a) photographed at Brackley; probably here by 1/1898, when HE supplied spares to W. Scott & Co for this loco at unrecorded location, but quoting name BRACKLEY, which fits this GC contract;
possibly ex Chapeltown-Barnsley (Midland Railway) (1894-1897) contract; earlier Dransfield & Smith, Chapeltown branch (Midland Railway) (1891-1894) contract, LIZZIE

(b) ex Monk & Newell, Crewe-Sandbach (LNWR) (1893-1895) contract, Cheshire
earlier Chas Baker & Sons, Pudsey & Low Moor-Dudley Hill (GNR) (1891-1895) contract, Yorkshire (WR); (for sale here from 3/1893)

(c) ex Chas Baker & Sons, Pudsey & Low Moor-Dudley Hill (GNR) (1891-1895) contract, Yorkshire (WR); possibly via MW, Leeds, where loco was repaired 3/1895

(d) ex Chas Baker & Sons, Pudsey & Low Moor-Dudley Hill (GNR) (1891-1895) contract, Yorkshire (WR); (for sale here from 3/1893)

(e) earlier Maldon-Woodham Ferrers-Southminster-Wickford-Southend (GER) (1886-1889) contract, Essex

(f) earlier John Wilson & Sons, Sheffield City Goods Station (LNWR) (1892?-1895) contract, Sheffield (MW 971 named JANET).

(g) earlier Rugby - Northampton (LNWR) (1877-1882) contract.

(h) with Walter Scott & Co, presumably at this Brackley Contract, by 5/1895
possibly earlier John Mowlem & Co, Grays-Upminster (LTSR) (1889-1892) contract, Essex; earlier John Mowlem & Co, Bournemouth (LSWR) (1884-1886) contract, Dorset.

(i) earlier McGregor & Smith, Stairfoot-Houghton Main Colliery (MS&LR) (c1890-1892) contract, Yorkshire (WR), until after 22/9/1892

(j) here by 6/1898; loco owned by Walter Scott since c/1886 when re-gauged at HE, Leeds, from 5ft 3in gauge; earlier McCrea & Macfarland, Limavady & Dungiven Rly construction (1880-1883) contract, Co.Londonderry, Ireland

(k) ex Corby - Stoke (GNR) (c1891-c1893) widening contract, Lincs.

(l) ex MW, earlier Chas Braddock, St Michaels-Halewood (CLC) widening (1895-1896) contract, Liverpool

(1)   later Admiralty, Royal Naval Cordite Factory, Holton Heath, Dorset, by 11/1917.
(2)   to New Mills-Hazel Grove (Midland Railway) (1898-1902) contract, Derbys.
(3)   to Woodford Junction-Banbury (MS&LR) (1897-1899) contract, by 11/1898
(4)   later (to ?) MW, for rebuild, by 3/1899;
      later Seaham - Hartlepool (NER) (1899-1905) contract, Co Durham.
(5)   later rebuilt by MW, /1901; later Walter Scott & Middleton Ltd, Chalk Farm-Willesden
      (LNWR) (1913-1917) widening contract, London.
(6)   to Pauling & Co Ltd, Westbury (GWR) (1897-1900) contract, Wiltshire, /1897 (by
      6/1897).
(7)   to Pauling & Co Ltd, Westbury (GWR) (1897-1900) contract, Wiltshire (possibly after
      1/1898)
(8)   later C.D. Phillips, dealer, Gloucester, 3446g, for sale 4/1901-5/1902;
      thence possibly to A.Y. Dinas Silica Brick & Lime Co, Kidwelly, Carms, after 5/1902.
(9)   later Cheltenham - Stratford on Avon (GWR) (1902-1908) contract, Glos/Warwicks.
(10) possibly to Pembrey Burrows (Admiralty) (1914-1916) contract, Carms;
      later Redbourne Hill Ironworks (1916-1920) contract, Scunthorpe, Lincs.
(11) new boiler supplied by MW 10/1902 hence probably at Leeds /1902;
      later Cheltenham-Stratford on Avon (GWR) (1902-1908) contract, Glos/Warwicks.
(12) to Pauling & Co Ltd, Westbury (GWR) (1897-1900) contract, Wiltshire, after 10/1897,
      by 1/1898.
(13) later Cheltenham-Stratford on Avon (GWR) (1902-1908) contract, Glos/Warwicks.
(14) to Darfield-Wath (Midland Railway) (1898-1900) widening contract, Yorkshire (WR),
      after 13/9/1898 by 24/1/1899
(15) later Felin Fran-Pontardawe (GWR) (1914-1921) contract, West Glamorgan.
(16) later Smith, Patterson & Co Ltd, Pioneer Foundry, Blaydon, Co.Durham

Gauge : 3ft 0in (used in the construction of the approaches to Brackley station)

LANCASHIRE WITCH	0-4-0ST	OC	MW	614	1876	(a)	(1)

(a)   ex Blackton and Hury Reservoirs (Stockton and Middlesbrough Water Board) (1884-
      1896) contract, Cotherstone, Yorkshire (NR), /1896.

(1)   later Walter Scott & Middleton Ltd, Bamford & Howden Railway (Derwent Valley Water
      Board) (1901-1903) contract, Derbys, by 5/1901.

WOODFORD CONTRACT   LC31

The contract for the construction of the Woodford Junction - Banbury branch for the MS&LR
was awarded at the end of 7/1897, and a first sod ceremony took place on 6/10/1897.
Work started almost immediately. The line opened to freight on 1/6/1900, to passengers on
13/8/1900.

Gauge : 4ft 8½in

BRACKLEY	0-6-0ST	IC	HE	164	1876	(a)	(1)
FASHODA	0-6-0ST	IC	MW	1432	1899	New	(2)
BANBURY	0-6-0ST	IC	MW	1444	1899	New	(2)

(a)   ex Woodford-Quainton Road (MSLR) (1894-1898) contract, by 11/1898

(1)   to HE, 4/1899, for rebuilding; then to Seaham-Hartlepool (NER) (1899-1905) contract,
      Co.Durham, by 11/1899.

(2)   later Walter Scott & Middleton Ltd, Ashenden-Aynho (GWR) (1906-1910) contract,
      Oxon.

SHANKS & McEWAN LTD

CORBY WORKS CONTRACT   TC32

Construction of extensions at Corby Works for Stewarts & Lloyds Ltd, 1933 - 1937. On completion of this construction contract the company undertook long term operation of the slag reduction plant at the works. For details of this latter operation, see the entry in the Industrial locations section.

Gauge : 4ft 8½in

	FULWOOD	0-6-0ST	IC	HE	529	1891	(a)	(2)
	LAUCHOPE	0-6-0ST	IC	HE	619	1894	(b)	(5)
55	PETERHEAD	0-6-0ST	IC	MW	1378	1898	(c)	(1)
12		0-6-0ST	IC	MW	1301	1895	(d)	(4)
38	ROSEHALL	0-6-0ST	IC	HC	531	1899	(e)	(4)
53		0-4-0ST	OC	AB	1027	1904	(e)	(5)
	DON	0-6-0ST	IC	MW	1293	1895	(e)	(5)
37	WOODHALL	0-6-0ST	IC	MW	1668	1905	(f)	(3)
No.83	GLENGARNOCK	0-4-0ST	OC	Glengarnock	1911		(g)	(5)
7		0-4-0ST	OC	AB	306	1888	(h)	(5)

(a)   ex Bromsgrove-Stoke Works (LMSR) contract, Worcs, after 9/1932, by 12/1933.
(b)   ex Bromsgrove-Stoke Works (LMSR) contract, Worcs, by 12/1933.
(c)   ex Bromsgrove-Stoke Works (LMSR) contract, Worcs, after 9/1932, by 1/1934.
(d)   earlier Shieldhall Dock (Clyde Navigation Trust) (1924-1931) contract, Glasgow; to here by c/1934.
(e)   earlier Farnsfield-Ollerton (LNER/LMSR) (1929-1932) contract, Notts; here by /1935.
(f)   earlier Ambergate (LMSR) (1930-1932) widening contract, Derbys; here by /1936.
(g)   ex Carnbroe Plant Depot, Coatbridge, Lanarks, by 7/1936.
(h)   ex Ardeer Plant Depot, Ayrshire, /1936.

(1)   to Carnbroe Plant Depot, Lanarks, by 6/1935;
        later Airdriehill Quarry, Airdrie, Lanarks, after 7/1936.
(2)   to Carnbroe Plant Depot, Lanarks, after 6/1935, by 6/1935.
(3)   to Carnbroe Plant Depot, Lanarks, after 6/1935, by 7/1936.
(4)   scrapped on site by 7/1949.
(5)   to Slag Reduction Plant on completion of construction contract.

Gauge : 2ft 0in

-		4wPM	MR	2103	1921	(a)	s/s

(a)   ex NER, Croft Junction Permanent Way Yard, Darlington, Co Durham

ISLIP CONTRACT   SC33

Clearance work at the closed Islip Ironworks for Stewarts & Lloyds Ltd, 1942 - 1943

Gauge : 4ft 8½in

No.83	GLENGARNOCK	0-4-0ST	OC	Glengarnock	1911		(a)	(1)
	LAUCHOPE	0-6-0ST	IC	HE	619	1894	(a)	(1)

(a)   ex Corby Slag Reduction Plant, /1942.

(1)   returned to Corby Plant, /1943

JOHN STRACHAN
WELHAM CONTRACT, Ashley   LC34

Contract for the construction of a small fan of sidings known as Welham Marshalling Yard, located near Welham Junction and Ashley & Weston Station on the LNWR Market Harborough - Peterborough railway. Contract let in 1903; yard opened 1/7/1904.

Gauge : 2ft 6in

J. STRACHAN No.9   0-4-0ST   OC   WB   1655 1901   (a)   (1)

(a)   ex Welshpool & Llanfair Railway contract, Montgomeryshire, after 6/1903 by 9/1903.

(1)   later Exors of John Strachan, assets dispersal sales at Red Wharf Bay Station, Anglesey, North Wales, after 5/1908 by 28/7/1909; thence to WB, Stafford, 5/1913, for alteration to 2ft 61/2in gauge; thence to Jees Hartshill Granite & Brick Co Ltd, Nuneaton, Warwickshire, by 11/1913.

TRACKWORK LTD
CRICK CONTRACT   LC35

Construction of sidings by this South Yorkshire based contractor for the Daventry International Rail Freight Terminal (SP 566726), which opened on 27/5/1997.

Gauge : 4ft 8½in

-       4wDM   RH 398616 1956   (a)   (1)

(a)   ex Long Sandall Plant Depot, South Yorkshire; here by c8/1996.

(1)   to ?

WARING BROTHERS
KETTERING & THRAPSTON RAILWAY CONTRACT   RC36

The Kettering & Thrapstone (sic) Railway was authorised 29/7/1862, and the extension from Thrapston to Huntingdon, together with a renaming of the company as Kettering, Thrapston & Huntingdon Railway, was authorised 28/7/1863. Waring Bros were described as being the "main contractors" for the line (presumably the entire route); work apparently started in the latter half of 1862. Work was still in hand when, on 22/4/1865, a man was run over by a "ballast train". The line opened throughout on 21/2/1866 for freight, 1/3/1866 for passengers, being worked from the outset by the Midland Railway.

Reference : "Kettering to Huntingdon Line", J. Rhodes, Oakwood Press, 1984

Gauge : 4ft 8½in

An LNWR Minute of 15/12/1864 confirms the sale of LNWR loco 1142 to Waring Bros, contractors for the Kettering, Thrapstone etc Co, for £500. This would appear to be a 2-4-0T (IC ?) loco with 14x20in cylinders, 5ft 0in wheels, built by Carrett, Marshall & Co, Leeds, in 1851 for the Kendal & Windermere Rly, where it carried the name GRASMERE. In due course it passed to the LNWR becoming LNW 532, and renumbered LNW 1142 in 5/1862. However, Kendal & Windermere Rly locos present many queries, and Carrett, Marshall order No.257 related to a 14in cylinder loco and this was apparently invoiced on 23/7/1856. For notes refer to The Industrial Locomotive No.49, p.23. No positive evidence has yet been found to confirm the use of this loco by Waring Bros at Kettering, though it seems very likely. Waring Bros had several other ex-main line locos during this era, probably used elsewhere.

WATSON, SMITH & WATSON
TOWCESTER CONTRACTS

The Towcester to Ravenstone Wood (Olney) railway had been promoted by the East & West Junction Rly and authorised as the Easton Neston Mineral & Towcester, Roade & Olney Junction Railway on 15/8/1879. Construction was protracted and an Act of 1882 changed the company name to the Stratford-upon-Avon, Towcester & Midland Junction Railway and a further Act of 1883 authorised this company to improve the East & West Junction Railway. The contract was initially let to Watson, Smith & Watson (possibly in early 1884), who appear to have concentrated on the upgrading of the E&WJR, which reopened to passengers 2/3/1885 (per Railway Times), or 22/3/1885 (per Dunn), and thus made only little progress on the line to Olney before they failed mid-1885, and work ceased. The contract was subsequently re-let to Baldry & Yerburgh, which see.

Gauge : 4ft 8½in

HESKETH	0-4-0ST	OC	MW	634	1877	(a)	(1)
BRUCE	0-4-0ST	OC	HE			(a)	(2)
GAVIN	0-6-0ST	OC	BH	471	1881	(b)	(1)

(a) ex Marlborough-Andover (SM&AR) (1879-1884) contract, Wiltshire, c/1884

(b) possibly ex Marlborough-Andover (SM&AR) (1879-1884) contract, Wiltshire; here by /1886

(1) to Baldry & Yerburgh, with contract, /1887

(2) described as 13x18in cylinders, 3ft 0in wheels. For sale here, /1886-/1887; no further trace.

DEALERS & REPAIRERS

ALLCHIN, LINNELL & CO LTD
WESTON STREET ENGINEERING WORKS, Northampton   **ND1**

Frank Allchin, Linnell & Co until 27/8/1889

The company was a general engineering merchant, dealing in stationary engines, belting, jacks, etc, and are known to have advertised locomotives (not necessarily located at these premises).

Gauge : 4ft 8½in

A six-wheels four-coupled standard gauge contractor's Saddle Tank loco, with 10x14in cylinders, was for sale in 3/1889 ("Colliery Guardian" 1/3/1889; "Contract Journal" 6/3/1889, "The Engineer" 15/3/1889 - only the latter quoting the gauge). This loco has not yet been identified.

What appears to be the same loco was subsequently advertised in Machinery Market 7/1889 with further details. Described as a Contractors Saddle Tank, six wheels four coupled, standard gauge, 4ft 6in wheels, 10x14in cylinders, by Brotherhood, £300.

The wheel diameter is rather large, as known Brotherhood 2-4-0ST locos have 3ft 6in (or possibly 4ft 0in) wheels. A possible identification appears to be the Brotherhood loco at Duston Iron Ore Co, whose loco is supposedly a 0-4-0ST but this could possibly be a misunderstanding of a phrase such as "four coupled".

BLACKWELL & SON (ENGINEERS) LTD
COTTON END WORKS, Northampton   **ND2**

earlier **Blackwell & Son**   SP 758593

A firm of general engineers and boilermakers, established 1899 by George Blackwell and his son Joseph. Both had had many years previous experience having previously worked for Wm Allchin Ltd, Globe Works, Northampton, where George was foreman. The company carried out repairs to heavy road engines, stationary engines and other plant, and had ceased trading by 1948.

Gauge : 4ft 8½in

ANCOATS	0-4-0ST	OC	MW	1091	1888	(a)	
	reb to 4wVBT	HCG	Blackwell		1922		
	reb to 4wVBT		S	5666	1924		(1)
MOLTKE	0-6-0ST	IC	MW	848	1882	(b)	
	reb to 0-6-0VBT	HCG	S	5667	1924		(2)
JUBILEE	0-6-0ST		OC	P	1254	1913	(c)	(3)
PROGRESS	0-6-0ST		OC	P	1402	1915	(c)	(4)
MARWIN	0-4-0ST	OC					(5)
	reb	AB			1902	(d)	

(a)   ex Stanley Bros Ltd, Stockingford Colliery, Warwicks; rebuilt as 4wVBT HCG and to The Arlesey Brick Co (Beart's) Ltd, Arlesey Works, Beds, for trials c/1922-/1924; returned.
(b)   ex The Arlesey Brick Co (Beart's) Ltd, Arlesey Works, Beds, for rebuilding, /1924.
(c)   ex Cochrane & Co Ltd, Desborough Ironstone Quarries, /1926.
(d)   ex British Gas Purifying Materials Co Ltd, Desborough Works, for repair, 10/1943.

(1) to Irchester Ironstone Co Ltd, Irchester Quarries, trials, /1924; believed thence to United Steel Companies Ltd, Irthlingborough Ironworks, trials, c/1924; and thence to Thos.E. Gray Ltd, Burton Latimer, c/1924.

(2) to The Arlesey Brick Co (Beart's) Ltd, Arlesey Works, Beds, c/1924

(3) to Furnace Hill & Renishaw Park Collieries Ltd, Renishaw Park Colliery, Derbys.

(4) to Irchester Ironstone Co Ltd, Irchester Quarries, c/1927.

(5) returned to British Gas Purifying Materials Co Ltd, Desborough Works, 16/5/1944.

Gauge : 4ft 0in

BRIXWORTH No.1	0-4-0ST	OC	HCR	212	1879	(a)	(1)
BRIXWORTH No.2	0-4-0ST	OC	HC	227	1881	(a)	(2)

(a) ex Brixworth Ironstone Co Ltd, Brixworth Ironstone Quarries, /1938

(1) dismantled and parts used to rebuild HC 227, remainder s/s.

(2) returned to Brixworth Ironstone Co Ltd, Brixworth Quarries, after rebuilding, c/1938

Gauge : 3ft 0in

HANDYMAN	0-4-0ST	OC	HC	573	1900	(a)	(1)

(a) ex Cranford Ironstone Co Ltd, Cranford Quarries, for repair and alteration to 3ft 0in gauge, /1936.

(1) to Staveley Coal & Iron Co Ltd, Lamport Quarries, /1936.

Gauge : 2ft 6in

FERRET II	0-4-0ST	OC	WB	1853	1908	(a)	(1)

(a) ex E.M. Jellett, Easton Neston Ironstone Quarries.

(1) to Holm & Co Ltd, Kingsnorth, Kent, /1925 (possibly directly from Easton Neston).

R. FENWICK & CO LTD
St. JAMES' WORKS, Brackley   LD3
E.L. Pitt & Co (Coventry) Ltd until 1/3/1965   SP 586364

A yard adjacent to Brackley Town (ex-LNWR) station where locomotives were stored prior to disposal. Locos were offered for sale and hired to contractors, in some cases for track lifting from closed BR lines.

Gauge : 4ft 8½in

	BEATTY	0-4-0ST	OC	HC	1696	1939	(a)	(1)
	VICTORIA	0-4-0ST	OC	P	2028	1942	(b)	(2)
WD 144		0-6-0ST	IC	WB	2746	1944	(c)	(3)
WD 807		4wDM		RH	224345	1945	(d)	(4)
	ALLENBY	0-4-0ST	OC	P	1978	1940	(e)	Scr 7/1961
107		0-4-0ST	OC	P	2002	1941	(f)	(5)
110		0-4-0ST	OC	P	2020	1942	(f)	(5)
RISLEY MED YARD No.109		0-4-0ST	OC	HC	1726	1941	(f)	(8)
-		0-4-0ST	OC	P	2048	1944	(g)	(6)
116		0-4-0DM		JF	22892	1940	(h)	(7)

WD 9110	2w-2PMR	Wkm	2878	1940	(i)	(8)
WD 883	0-6-0DE	AW	D58	1936	(j)	(9)
-	0-4-0DM	JF	3900001	1946	(k)	(8)
-	0-4-0PM	JF	17209	1927	(k)	(8)
-	0-4-0DM	JF	22917	1940	(l)	(10)
WD 8324	0-4-0DM	JF	22906	1940	(m)	(10)

(a) ex Royal Arsenal, Woolwich, London, after mid/1957, by 1/1958.
(b) ex ROF, Fazakerley, Liverpool; here by 20/7/1958.
(c) ex WD, Bicester, Oxon for repairs, c11/1958.
(d) ex WD, Longmoor, Hampshire, 8/1959 (by 9/8/1959)
(e) ex Royal Arsenal, Woolwich, London, 8/1959 (by 30/8/1959).
(f) ex ROF, Risley, Lancs, c8/1961 (by 4/11/1961).
(g) ex ROF, Risley, Lancs, /1961 (by 14/12/1961).
(h) ex ROF, Risley, Lancs, c2/1962 (by 22/2/1962).
(i) ex WD, Longmoor, Hampshire, by 22/2/1962.
(j) ex WD, Bicester, Oxon, 8/1963.
(k) ex T.B. & S. Batchelor & Co Ltd, Newport, Gwent, here by 22/4/1963.
(l) ex English China Clays Ltd, Marsh Mills, Devon, /1964 (by 3/8/1964).
(m) ex WD, Bicester, Oxon, by 14/6/1964.

(1) to Oxfordshire Ironstone Co Ltd, Banbury, Oxon, 1/1958.
(2) to Whitehaven Harbour Commissioners, Whitehaven Docks, Cumberland, 3/1959.
(3) returned to WD, Bicester, Oxon, after 5/1959, by 1/1961.
(4) to Wagon Repairs Ltd, Wellingborough Works, 9/1960.
(5) to Skinningrove Iron Co Ltd, Skinningrove Ironworks, Carlin How, Yorkshire (NR), 1/1962.
(6) scrapped after 18/8/1962, by 22/4/1963
(7) to Pittrail Ltd, Aldridge Plant Depot, West Midlands, after 4/10/1964, by 9/3/1965.
(8) s/s after 1/3/1965.
(9) to CEGB, Hams Hall Power Station, Warwicks, 2/1966 and scrapped there 12/1967.
(10) advertised in "Machinery Market" 18/8/1966 as being dismantled for spares; scrapped /1966.

Gauge : 2ft 0in

-	4wDM		OK	8650	c1939	(a)	(1)
MESOZOIC	0-6-0ST	OC	P	1327	1913	(b)	(3)
-	4wDM		MR	9204	1946	(c)	(2)
-	4wDM		RH	211590	1941	(d)	(4)

(a) ex M.E. Engineering Ltd, dealers, Cricklewood, London, 7/1958.
(b) ex Rugby Portland Cement Ltd, Southam Works, Warwicks, 7/1961.
(c) ex Cosgrove Sand & Gravel Co Ltd, Cosgrove, by 7/1963.
(d) origins unknown; originally MoS

(1) to M.E. Engineering Ltd, dealers, Cricklewood, London, 5/1958; thence to Earls Barton Silica Co Ltd, 7/1958.
(2) to F.E. Storton, St James' End Gravel Pits, Northampton, c1/1964
(3) to G.J. Mullis, Coley Farm Pits, Wychbold, near Droitwich, Worcs, 3/1969.
(4) to M.E. Engineering Ltd, dealers, Cricklewood, London; rebuilt with parts from another loco and exported to Malaya (with incorrect works plates fitted).

Gauge : 1ft 6in

-	4wDM		RH 213839 1942	(a)	(1)
WOOLWICH	0-4-0T	OC	AE 1748 1916	(b)	(2)

(a) earlier Royal Arsenal, Woolwich, London; here by 17/4/1958.

(b) ex Royal Arsenal, Woolwich, London, 8/1959.

(1) offered for sale ("Machinery Market", 17/4/1958 and 9/4/1959); later M.E. Engineering Ltd, dealers, Cricklewood, London, by 5/1963; then to Bicton Woodland Railway, Devon.

(2) to M.E. Engineering Ltd, Cricklewood, London, by 4/1962; thence to Bicton Woodland Railway, Devon.

HARRISON & CLAYTON
GRAND JUNCTION WORKS, Cotton End, Northampton   ND4
H. Harrison & Son until 1869
Henry Harrison from c1861 until c1864

Henry Harrison was a millwright and engineer from Yorkshire who established an engineering business on the banks of the Grand Junction Canal in Hardingstone. The enterprise commenced after 1854 and was in existence by 1861. It was listed in trade directories as Harrison & Clayton in 1870 and 1871 but appears to have closed by 1877 since it is not listed in directories for that or later years. The company built a small number of locomotives and is said to have repaired locomotives for the Blisworth & Towcester (N&BJR) railway. After losing the court case reported in the Northampton Mercury of 15/7/1871 it is thought that the partnership with Philip Clayton was dissolved. By 1874 Henry Harrison had established a business as an engineer and millwright in Bletchley Road, Fenny Stratford, Bucks, which closed after 1877, by 1883.

Reference : "The Industrial Locomotive No.94", Industrial Locomotive Society, 1999.

Gauge : 4ft 8½in

JACKALL	0-4-0ST	IC	Harrison & Clayton 1870 New	(1)

(1) built for Thomas Whitehouse, Northampton (which see in Industrial section).

"The Engineer", 27/11/1874 - For sale small 4hp vertical boiler loco, 2ft 6in gauge, only worked a few weeks, suit as hoisting engine, H. Harrison, Fenny Stratford.

HENRY MOBBS
VULCAN IRONWORKS, Northampton   ND5
SP 756602

A works located in Guildhall Road, in the centre of Northampton, with no rail connection. A loco may have been repired here or acquired for resale.

Gauge : 4ft 8½in

"COFFEE POT"	0-4-0VBT	VCG	Chaplin1056 1869	(a)	(1)

(a) ex Nine Churches Iron Ore Co Ltd, Stowe Quarries, by /1878.

(1) possibly to Blisworth & Stowe Brick & Tile Co Ltd, Gayton Brickworks.

EDWARD REDDEN LTD
LITTLE IRCHESTER SCRAP YARD   QD6
SP 903664

Company in existence from 1965, using a yard where locos were cut up for scrap occasionally. At least one loco was resold from this site :

Gauge : 2ft 0in

-	4wDM	MR	8969	1945	(a)	(1)

(a)   ex Bedford Corporation Water Board, Manton Lane Waterworks, Bedford, by 12/1967.

(1)   to Alan Keef Ltd, Cote Farm, Bampton, Oxon, /1969.

W.J. REDDEN & SONS LTD
HIGHFIELD WORKS, Leys Road, Wellingborough   QD7

A company of scrap iron and metal merchants and demolition contractors registered in 6/1953. The company purchased several locomotives for scrap; most of these were disposed of at the vendors' sites, but one locomotive is known to have been retained for some time :

Gauge : 2ft 0in

-	4wPM	MR	4813	1938	(a)	(1)

(a)   ex Bedford Corporation Water Board, Manton Lane Works, Bedford, c/1962; to Conduit Construction Co Ltd, Wellingborough contract, /1964; repurchased, 7/1964.

(1)   to Earls Barton Silica Sand Co Ltd, Earls Barton, /1969.

RICE & CO
EAGLE FOUNDRY, Bridge Street, Northampton   ND8
SP 754598

Locomotives possibly purchased on behalf of Hunsbury Ironworks and used there from new.

Gauge : 4ft 8½in

ORYZA	0-4-0ST	OC	SS	2329	1873	New	(1)
BILLY	0-4-0ST	OC	HE	133	1875	New	(1)

(1)   to Northampton Coal, Iron & Wagon Co Ltd, Hunsbury Ironworks, Northampton.

W.T. SHEPPARD & SONS LTD
ISEBROOK WORKS, Finedon Road, Wellingborough   QD9
SP 908697

A firm of scrap metal dealers which purchased a number of locomotives from Irthingborough mines on the closure of the latter. The locos have remained on site awaiting disposal since their purchase.

Gauge : 3ft 0in (Mining system)

3	4wWE	GB		1545	1938	
	Reb to 4wBE	RTB		Jan/1964	(a)	(7)
4	4wWE	GB		1566	1938	
	Reb to 4wBE	RTB		Dec/1964	(a)	(5)

5		4wWE	GB	1567	1938		
		Reb to 4wBE	RTB	Mar/1962		(a)	(4)
6	46	4wWE	GB	1746	1941		
		Reb to 4wBE	RTB	Jul/1964		(a)	(4)
-		4wBE	GB	1569	1938	(a)	
-		4wBE	GB	1570	1938	(a)	(6)
24		4wBE	GB	1573	1938	(a)	(7)
-		4wBE	GB	1574	1938	(a)	(7)
61		4wBE	GB	2061	1946	(a)	(7)
22		4wBE	GB	2063	1946	(a)	(7)
-		4wBE	GB	2079	1947	(a)	(7)
-		4wBE	GB	2080	1947	(a)	(7)
21		4wBE	GB	2292	1950	(a)	(7)
19		4wBE	GB	2294	1950	(a)	(7)
-		4wBE	GB	2295	1950	(a)	(7)
-		4wDMF	RH	433388	1959	(a)	(2)
5		4wDMF	RH	338439	1953	(a)	(3)
-		4wDMF	RH	353491	1953	(a)	(6)
-		4wDMF	RH	375694	1954	(a)	(6)
3		4wDMF	RH	418764	1957	(a)	(1)
3		4wDMF	RH	418803	1957	(a)	(2)

(a) ex RTB, Irthlingborough Mines, 3/1967.

(1) to Alan Odell, private site, near Northampton.

(2) to Higham Ferrers Locomotives, near Wellingborough, 26/6/1999.

(3) to Northamptonshire Ironstone Trust, Hunsbury Hill, Northampton, 2/7/1999.

(4) to European Metal Recycling, Kingsbury, Warwicks, for scrap, 28/10/1999.

(5) to European Metal Recycling, Kingsbury, Warwicks, for scrap, 29/10/1999.

(6) to Higham Ferrers Locomotives, private site near Wellingborough, 12/11/1999.

(7) one loco to Lavendon Narrow Gauge Railway, Bucks, the remainder to European Metal Recycling, Kingsbury, Warwicks, for scrap, by 1/2000.

Gauge : 2ft 6in

-	4wDMF	RH	338438	1953	(a)	(1)
-	4wDM	RH	375693	1954	(a)	(1)

(a) ex RTB, Irthlingborough Mines, 3/1967.

(1) to Higham Ferrers Locomotives, private site near Wellingborough, 25/11/2000.

WINSON ENGINEERING LTD
Unit 3, Faraday Close, Drayton Fields, Daventry   **LD10**
SP 560640

Workshops for the overhaul and renovation of equipment including locomotives.

Gauge : 4ft 8½in

-	0-4-0T	OC	HE	1684	1931	(a)	(1)
-	0-6-0T	OC	HC	1731	1942	(b)	

(a) ex Swanage Railway Society, Swanage, Dorset, 11/1994 (by 22/11/1994).

(b) ex Penrhyndeudraeth Works, near Porthmadog, Gwynedd, [North Wales] after 23/7/1998, by 20/8/1998.

(1) to Great Central Railway, Loughborough, Leics, c12/1996 (by 27/12/1996).

Gauge : 2ft 0in

-	4wDHF	HE	8518	1977			#
		AB	632	1977	(a)	#	

parts of main frames in use as a wheel press

(a) ex Welsh Highland Light Railway (1964) Ltd, Porthmadog, Gwynedd [North Wales], by 22/11/1994

UNCORRELATED DATA :

"The Engineer", 27/11/1879 - For sale, nearly new four-wheel coupled tank loco, standard gauge, 5ft 6in wheelbase - C.S. Warden, Albert St, Kettering. A possible candidate for this loco could be the HCR loco listed herein under contractor Chas.Deacon Jnr, Wellingborough contract.

I.W.Boulton, dealer, of Ashton under Lyne, Cheshire, is recorded as having sent his locomotive RATTLESNAKE "to Northampton" sometime in the 1875-1883 period. The reason for this transfer, and the identity of the hirer, has not been established. Additionally, Boulton is said to have purchased a loco ORWELL 0-4-0ST OC HH from the LNWR at Northampton, where it had been used as a shunting loco.

"Colliery Guardian", 31/1/1896 - For sale, six-wheel coupled tank loco by Peckett, standard gauge, 13in, recently rebuilt, £475 - Mallard, Gordon St, Northampton.
This loco has not yet been identified, but the only 13in Peckett class was the XL series, of which only a few were built and all appear to be accounted for (see Industrial Railway Record No.74). One suggested possibility is that it may have been a Fox Walker (or other) loco that had lost its identity, and gained a Peckett plate, during the "recent" rebuild mentioned in the advertisement. One perhaps possible link could be to a loco later advertised ("Contract Journal" 12/4/1893) not far away. S.& W.Pattinson, contractors, Ruskington, near Sleaford, Lincolnshire had for sale a 13in 6wc Peckett "just thoroughly overhauled" - also advertised in The Engineer more specifically as "just overhauled by Peckett".

"Colliery Guardian", 27/7/1900 - For sale, 11in 6wc standard gauge loco, £200
"Contract Journal", 19/9/1900 - For sale, standard gauge 0-6-0ST
  – (both) Armstrongs, Northampton".

"Contractors Chronicle", 11/4/1921 - For sale at Fuller, Horsey auction 26/4/1921 at West Bridge yard, Northampton: contractors plant including 2ft gauge steam locomotive. (The advertisement does not mention the identity of the vendor).

"Contract Journal", 25/7/1934 - For sale, plant including one 6hp Lister petrol loco, eight wagons and track, 2ft 0in gauge - J.R. Hardman Ltd, Houghton Rd, Northampton.

PRESERVATION LOCATIONS

C.W. BARTHOLOMEW
BLAKESLEY HALL RAILWAY   LP1

Mr C.W. Bartholomew constructed a miniature railway from Blakesley Hall to Blakesley station, on the East & West Junction Railway, in 1903. At the station a platform and waiting room were constructed and an exchange siding was added later to allow coal and other freight to be transferred to the miniature railway for delivery to the Hall. The railway operated regularly from 1903. After the death of Mr Bartholomew in 1919 his widow kept the line in operation until 1939 when it was dismantled. The remaining equipment was sold in 1943.

Gauge : 1ft 3in

	BLACOLVESLEY	4-4-4PM	S/O	BL	1909	New	(1)
2	CAGNEY	4-4-0	OC	McGarigle	1902	(a)	(2)
		4-4-0	OC	McGarigle	1902	(a)	(3)
	PETROLEA	4-4-4PM	S/O	Bartholomew		New	Scr c/1940

(a)   new to Cagney Bros, New York, USA

(1)   to Miss Elliott, Wombwell, Yorkshire (WR), c/1939; then to William Younger, Ponteland, Co Durham, c/1943

(2)   to W.S. & J.W.H. Key, Strumpshaw Hall Steam Museum, Norfolk, via Romney, Hythe & Dymchurch Railway, Kent, 1/1971.

(3)   possibly to Ettrick Bay Miniature Railway, Stathclyde, /1936.

BILLING AQUADROME LTD
BILLING AQUADROME, Billing, near Northampton   MP2
SP 808615

Narrow gauge pleasure line at this location.

Gauge : 2ft 0in

	-	4wDM		RH	242887	1946	(a)	(1)
	-	4wDM		MR	+		(b)	s/s
S1380		4wDM	S/O	RH			(c)	(2)
S87741	OLIVER	4wDM	S/O	MR	9869	1953	(d)	(3)
	-	4wDH		AK	15	1984	(e)	(4)
(006)		4wDH	S/O	AK	14	1984	(f)	

+   one (or both) of MR 7031/1936 and MR 7043/1937.

(a)   ex Earls Barton Sand & Gravel Co Ltd, /1965.
(b)   ex Mixconcrete Ltd, with site.
(c)   ex Leisure Track Ltd, Stratford-upon-Avon, Warwicks, /1980 (by 27/4/1980).
(d)   ex Leisure Track Ltd, Cotswold Wildlife Park, Burford, Oxon, c6/1980 (after 12/1979, by 17/8/1980).
(e)   ex Alan Keef Ltd, Lea Line, Hereford & Worcs, hire, c6/1987
(f)   ex Alan Keef Ltd, Bampton, Oxon, c9/1987 (by 9/9/1987).

(1)   to R. French, 'The White Hart' (Public House), Hackleton, after 17/5/1980, by 17/8/1980; stored at a farm at Billing and returned here by 29/4/1984; to farm c/1986 and s/s c6/1986.

(2)   to Alan Keef Ltd, Cote Farm, Bampton, Oxon, by 12/4/1984, after 3/10/1982

(3) to R French, 'The White Hart' (Public House), Hackleton, c/1986 (after 9/12/1984, by 9/9/1987); then to Burgh Hall Bygone Village, Fleggburgh, Norfolk, 6/2/1988, via Yaxham Light Railways, Yaxham, Norfolk, 30/1/1988.

(4) returned from hire to Alan Keef Ltd, Lea Line, Hereford & Worcs, c6/1987.

JOHN R. BILLOWES LTD
Pytchley Road Industrial Estate, Kettering   RP3

SP 872765

Preserved motive power kept at this location for a time.

Gauge : 4ft 8½in

A16W		2w-2PMR	Wkm	6887	1954	(a)	(1)
-		2w-2PMR	Wkm	7688	1957	(a)	(2)
-		2w-2PMR	Wkm	8264	1959	(a)	(2)

(a) ex BR.

(1) to Northamptonshire Ironstone Railway Trust Ltd, Northampton, 6/6/1975.

(2) scrapped by 31/12/1969.

Gauge : Metre

No.86		0-6-0ST	OC	P	1871	1934	(a)	(1)

(a) ex Stewarts & Lloyds Minerals Ltd, Wellingborough Quarries, 6/1967.

(1) to Northamptonshire Ironstone Railway Trust Ltd, Northampton, 10/6/1975.

F.G. CANN & SON
Thrapston Road, Finedon   QP4

SP 936738

Locomotive preserved here; restored to working order and steamed here on one occasion only.

Gauge : Metre

No.87		0-6-0ST	OC	P	2029	1942	(a)	(1)

(a) ex Stewarts & Lloyds Minerals Ltd, Wellingborough Quarries, 8/1967.

(1) to Northamptonshire Ironstone Railway Trust Ltd, Northampton, 6/6/1975.

CORBY DISTRICT COUNCIL

EAST CARLTON COUNTRYSIDE PARK AND STEEL HERITAGE CENTRE
near Corby   TP5

SP 834893

Locomotive preserved as a static exhibit at this park.

Gauge : 4ft 8½in

-		0-6-0ST	OC	HL	3827	1934	(a)

(a) ex The Vic Berry Company Ltd, Western Boulevard, Leicester, 7/9/1990 after asbestos removal and repainting; formerly at West Glebe Park, Corby.

WEST GLEBE PARK, Cottingham Road, Corby

TP6

Corby Urban District Council until 1/4/1974.

SP 88689C

Locomotive preserved as a static exhibit at this park.

Gauge : 4ft 8½in

14	0-6-0ST	OC	HL	3827	1934	(a)	(1)

(a) ex British Steel Corporation, Tubes Division, Corby Works, 9/1971.

(1) to The Vic Berry Company Ltd, Western Boulevard, Leicester, 11/1/1989 for asbesto removal and repainting; thence to East Carlton Countryside Park.

CORBY & DISTRICT MODEL RAILWAY CLUB
WEST GLEBE PARK, Corby

TP7

SP 89289

Locomotive preserved as a static exhibit at this park.

Gauge : 4ft 8½in

(No.24)	0-6-0ST	IC	HE	2411	1941	(a)	(1)

(a) ex British Steel Corporation, Tubes Division, Corby Works, c19/10/1973.

(1) to Market Overton Industrial Railway Association, Cottesmore, Rutland, 28/8/1980.

DAVENTRY DISTRICT COUNCIL
NEW STREET RECREATION GROUND, Daventry

LP8

Daventry Borough Council until 1/4/1974

SP 57462

Locomotive preserved as a static exhibit at this park.

Gauge : 4ft 8½in

001 (CHERWELL)	0-6-0ST	OC	WB	2654	1942	(a)	

(a) ex Byfield Ironstone Co Ltd, Byfield, 11/8/1966.

HIGHAM FERRERS LOCOMOTIVES
Private Sites

XP9

Locomotives under restoration at private locations near Rushden and near Wellingborough.

Gauge : metre

ND 3647	4wDM	MR	22144	1962	(a)	

(a) ex Irchester Narrow Gauge Railway Trust, Irchester Country Park, 3/4/1991.

Gauge : 3ft 0in

-	4wDMF	RH	433388	1959	(a)
3	4wDMF	RH	418803	1957	(a)
-	4wBE	GB	1570	1938	(b)
-	4wDMF	RH	353491	1953	(b)
-	4wDMF	RH	375694	1954	(b)

(a) ex W.T. Sheppard & Sons Ltd, Isebrook Works, Wellingborough, 26/6/1999.

(b) ex W.T. Sheppard & Sons Ltd, Isebrook Works, Wellingborough, 12/11/1999.

Gauge : 2ft 6in

-		4wDMF	RH	338438	1953	(a)
-		4wDM	RH	375693	1954	(a)

(a)   ex W.T. Sheppard & Sons Ltd, Isebrook Works, Wellingborough, 25/11/2000.

IRCHESTER NARROW GAUGE RAILWAY TRUST
prev **Northamptonshire Locomotive Group.**

IRCHESTER COUNTRY PARK, near Wellingborough   QP10
SP 904659

Preservation group with a museum / workshop building and demonstration running line incorporated as an attraction at this Country Park. Activities were moved here in 1988 from a site at Irchester Station.

Gauge : metre.

4	CAMBRAI		0-6-0T	OC	Corpet	493	1888	(a)	
No.85	1	(BANSHEE)	0-6-0ST	OC	P	1870	1934	(a)	
No.86	2		0-6-0ST	OC	P	1871	1934	(b)	
No.87	3		0-6-0ST	OC	P	2029	1942	(c)	
9	THE ROCK		0-4-0DM		HE	2419	1941	(a)	
	ND 3647		4wDM		MR	22144	1962	(a)	(1)
10	ND 3645	MILFORD	4wDM		RH	211679	1941	(a)	
11	(ED 10)		4wDM		RH	411322	1958	(d)	

(a)   ex Irchester Station Goods Shed, 27/4/1988.
(b)   ex Northamptonshire Ironstone Railway Trust, Hunsbury Hill, Northampton, 25/2/1990.
(c)   ex Northamptonshire Ironstone Railway Trust, Hunsbury Hill, Northampton, 20/3/1993.
(d)   regauged from 3ft 0in at this location, by 5/5/1991.

(1)   to Higham Ferrers Locomotives, private site for repair, 3/4/1991.

Gauge : 3ft 0in

12 EDWARD CHARLES HAMPTON	0-6-0DM	RH	281290	1949	(a)		
(ED 10)	4wDM	RH	411322	1958	(a)	(1)	

(a)   ex Irchester Station Goods Shed, 8/6/1988.

(1)   regauged to metre, by 5/5/1991.

Gauge : 2ft 0in

LR 3084	4wDM	MR	3797	1926	
	reb of MR	1363	1918	(a)	

(a)   ex M.P. Burgoyne, Willington, Beds, 19/8/1989.

IRCHESTER STATION GOODS SHED

Site used for storage and restoration of stock for this group from 1982. In 1988 activitie were transferred to a more spacious depot at Irchester Country Park.

Gauge : metre

No.85	(BANSHEE)	0-6-0ST	OC	P	1870	1934	(a)	(1)
	THE ROCK	0-4-0DM		HE	2419	1941	(b)	(1)
	CAMBRAI	0-6-0T	OC	Corpet	493	1888	(c)	(1)
	ND 3645	4wDM		RH	211679	1941	(d)	(1)
	ND 3647	4wDM		MR	22144	1962	(d)	(1)

(a)   ex Pitsford Quarry site, 30/1/1982.
(b)   ex Alan Keef Ltd, Bampton, Oxon., 20/2/1982.
(c)   ex Alan Keef Ltd, Bampton, Oxon., 4/6/1983.
(d)   ex Ministry of Defence, Navy Dept, RNAD, Milford Haven, Dyfed, 31/1/1986.

(1)   to Irchester Country Park, 27/4/1988

Gauge : 3ft 0in

-	0-6-0DM	RH	281290	1949	(a)	(1)
(ED 10)	4wDM	RH	411322	1958	(b)	(1)

(a)   ex Blue Circle Industries Ltd, Kilvington Works, Notts, 15/12/1984.
(b)   ex J. Hampton, Church Farm, Fenstanton, Cambs, 28/9/1987.

(1)   to Irchester Country Park, 8/6/1988.

PITSFORD QUARRY

Initial site used for storage of stock by the Northamptonshire Locomotive Group. Operations moved to Irchester Station site, 1982.

Gauge : Metre

8315/85 BANSHEE	0-6-0ST	OC	P	1870	1934	(a)	(1)

(a)   ex Northamptonshire Ironstone Railway Trust, Hunsbury Hill, 5/1979.

(1)   to Irchester Station, 30/1/1982.

IRCHESTER PARISH COUNCIL
WOLLASTON ROAD RECREATION GROUND, Irchester

Locomotive placed on static display at this site for some years.

Gauge : 4ft 8½in

(No.9)	0-4-0ST	OC	AB	2323	1952	(a)	(1)

(a)   ex South Durham Steel & Iron Co Ltd, Irchester Ironstone Quarries, 8/1969.

(1)   to Wicksteed Park, Kettering, 6/6/1979.

KETTERING BOROUGH COUNCIL
MANOR HOUSE GARDENS, Sheep Street, Kettering

QP14

SP 867783

Locomotive placed on static display at this site for some years.

Gauge : 3ft 0in

KETTERING FURNACES No.8	0-6-0ST	OC	MW	1675	1906	(a)	(1)

(a)   ex Kettering Iron & Coal Co Ltd, 26/8/1963.

(1)   to Welland Valley Vintage Traction Club, Market Harborough, 12/1/1974.

KNIGHTS OF OLD LTD
OLD DEPOT, Cherry Hill Estate, Walgrave Road, Old
Member of the **Taff Shipping Group**

MP15

SP 793734

Locomotives stored at this depot for a private owner pending transfer to a preservation site.

Gauge : 4ft 8½in

03084	0-6-0DM	Don		1959	(a)	(2)
03158	0-6-0DM	Sdn		1960	(a)	(2)
03027	0-6-0DM	Sdn		1958	(b)	(2)
D2334	0-6-0DM	RSHD	8193	1961		
		DC	2715	1961	(b)	(1)

(a)   ex British Rail, March Depot, Cambs, 1/1992

(b)   ex South Yorkshire Railway Preservation Society, Meadowhall, Sheffield, 1/10/1993

(1)   to North Staffordshire Railway Co, Cheddleton, Staffs, 10/7/1994

(2)   to Peak Rail, Darley Dale, Derbys, 3/1/1997.

N. LeCOUNT
Hardwick

LP16

Locomotive stored for preservation and restoration at this private site.

Gauge : 4ft 8½in

-	0-4-0ST	OC	WB	2565	1936	(a)	(1)

(a)   ex G. Davies, Stephens Green Farm, near Pembroke, Dyfed, after 13/8/1993, by 26/8/1993; prev CEGB, Hardingstone Road Power Station, Northampton.

(1)   to Northamptonshire Ironstone Railway Trust, Hunsbury Hill, Northampton, 2/11/1997

NORTHAMPTON & LAMPORT RAILWAY PRESERVATION SOCIETY

NORTHAMPTON STEAM RAILWAY   MP17
PITSFORD & BRAMPTON STATION, Chapel Brampton, Northampton.

Northampton Steam Railway Preservation Society until 1/1/1992   SP 735667
Welland Valley Rail Revival Group until 1983

Preservation group active from 1981. Pitsford Station has been used as a base for the storage and restoration of stock. A Light Railway Order was made in early 1994 to permit operation of passenger services over the first 1.2km of line, with the intention of extending further to Lamport Crossing, which would give a total operating line of 9.6km.

Gauge : 4ft 8½in

3862		2-8-0	OC	Sdn		1942	(a)	
7283	YVONNE	0-4-0VBT	OC	Cockerill	2945	1920	(b)	(3)
45	COLWYN	0-6-0ST	IC	K	5470	1933	(c)
		0-4-0ST	OC	P	2104+	1950	(d)
NS 8812		0-6-0ST	IC	HE	3155	1944	(e)	(1)
D67	45118						
	THE ROYAL ARTILLERYMAN	1Co-Co1.DE		Crewe		1962	(f)
D5185	(25035)						
	CASTELL DINAS BRAN	Bo-Bo.DE		Dar		1963	(g)
(D5370)	27024 ABB968028	Bo-Bo.DE		BRCW	DEL213	1962	(h)	(2)
D5401	27056	Bo-Bo.DE		BRCW	DEL244	1962	(i)
(D5310)	26010	Bo-Bo.DE		BRCW	DEL55	1960	(o)
4002	S13004S	4w-4w.RER		Elh		1949	(j)	(5)
	51367	2-2w-2w-2DMR	PS			1960	(p)
(No.1)	MERRY TOM	4wDM		RH	275886	1949	(k)
764	SIR GILES ISHAM	0-4-0DM		RH	319286	1953	(l)
	REDLAND	0-4-0DH		TH	146C	1964	
		Reb of 0-4-0DM		JF	4210018	1950	(m)
(Tkh-7)	5374 VANGUARD	0-6-0T	OC	Chr	5374	1959	(n)
	SIR ALFRED WOOD	0-6-0DM		RH	319294	1953	(q)	(4)
Tkh 17646		0-6-0T	OC	Chr	3112	1952	(r)
	55003	2-2w-2w-2DMR	GRC			1958	(s)
975023	(55001)	2-2w-2w-2DMR	GRC			1958	(t)
	WESTMINSTER	0-6-0ST	OC	P	1378	1914	(u)
	97651	0-6-0DE		RH	431758	1959	(v)
	51402	2-2w-2w-2DMR	PS			1960	(w)
	51359	2-2w-2w-2DMR	PS			1960	(x)
21		0-4-0DH		JF	4210094	1954	(y)
	51400	2-2w-2w-2DMR	PS			1960	(z)

+   Built in 1948, but carries plates dated 1950.

(a)   ex Woodham Bros, Barry Dock, South Glamorgan, 11/4/1989.
(b)   ex Charles Focquet & Cie, Belgium, 11/12/1987.
(c)   ex North Norfolk Railway, Sheringham, Norfolk, 6/7/1985.
(d)   ex Buckinghamshire Railway Centre, Quainton Road, Bucks, 23/3/1989.
(e)   ex Van Raak, scrap dealer, Tilburg, Holland, per P.E. Waters & Associates, Bromley, Kent, 22/11/1988.
(f)   ex BR, March Depot, Cambs, 16/9/1990.
(g)   ex BR, Crewe, via Vic Berry Ltd, Leicester, 14/7/1988.
(h)   ex BR, Eastfield, Glasgow, 5/2/1991.

(i)   ex BR, via Vic Berry Ltd, Leicester, 12/3/1988.

(j)   ex South Eastern Steam Centre, Ashford MPD, Kent, 3/11/1984.

(k)   ex Track Supplies & Services Ltd, Wolverton, Bucks, 6/9/1984.

(l)   ex Track Supplies & Services Ltd, Wolverton, Bucks, 8/10/1983.

(m)   ex Redland Roadstone Ltd, Barrow-on-Soar Rail Loading Terminal, Leics, 25/2/1989.

(n)   ex Huta Ostroweic Steelworks, Poland, 1/8/1992.

(o)   ex MC Metals, Glasgow, 24/1/1995; prev BR

(p)   ex BR, c10/1994 (by 9/4/1995).

(q)   ex Nene Valley Railway, Wansford, Cambs, 10/6/1994.

(r)   ex Saturn Cement Works, Poland, c11/1996.

(s)   ex Chinnor & Princes Risborough Railway Association, Oxon, 26/3/1997.

(t)   ex BR, Longsight, Greater Manchester, 4/1998.

(u)   ex P. Davies, Tistead Station, Hants, 27/10/1998.

(v)   ex BR, Cardiff, 10/11/1998.

(w)   ex LNWR Ltd, Crewe Carriage Works, Crewe, Cheshire, 25/8/1999.

(x)   ex BR, Bletchley, Bucks, c10/1999.

(y)   ex North Yorkshire Moors Railway, New Bridge, North Yorkshire, 28/2/2000 (reb by JF from 0-4-0DM, 8/1966).

(z)   ex Angel Trains, Bletchley, Bucks, 1/2/2001.

(1)   to Steamport, Southport, Merseyside, 13/10/1989.

(2)   to Caledonian Railway (Brechin) Ltd, Brechin, Tayside, c29/4/1992.

(3)   to Northamptonshire Ironstone Railway Trust Ltd, Northampton, 26/4/1995.

(4)   to Northamptonshire Ironstone Railway Trust Ltd, Northampton, 29/3/1996.

(5)   to Northamptonshire Ironstone Railway Trust Ltd, Northampton, 4/6/1999.

Visiting Locomotives (Gauge : 4ft 8½in).

DORA	0-4-0ST	OC	AE	1973	1927	(a)	(6)
47298	0-6-0T	IC	HE	1463	1924	(b)	(1)
LAMPORT No.3	0-6-0ST	OC	WB	2670		(c)	(2)
THE LADY ARMAGHDALE	0-6-0T	IC	HE	686	1898	(d)	(3)
D9555	0-6-0DH	Sdn			1965	(e)	(4)
D7629	Bo-Bo.DE		BP	8039	1965	(f)	(5)

(a)   ex Rutland Railway Museum, Cottesmore, Rutland, via Rugby Group plc, Barrington Cement Works, Cambs, 10/6/1994; returned to Rutland Railway Museum, c8/1994 (by 24/8/1994); to here again 22/9/1999.

(b)   ex Llangollen Railway, Denbighs, 27/3/1996.

(c)   ex The Battlefield Line, Shackerstone, Leics, 10/1996.

(d)   ex Severn Valley Railway, Shropshire, 5/1997.

(e)   ex Rutland Railway Museum, Cottesmore, Rutland, 5/1998.

(f)   ex GWR, Toddington, Glos, 10/4/1999.

(1)   returned to Llangollen Railway, Denbighs, 4/1996.

(2)   returned to The Battlefield Line, Shackerstone, Leics, c/1996.

(3)   returned to Severn Valley Railway, Shropshire, /1997.

(4)   returned to Rutland Railway Museum, 27/10/1998.

(5)   to GCR, Loughborough, Leics, 26/6/2000.

(6)   returned to Rutland Railway Museum, 18/1/2000.

NORTHAMPTONSHIRE IRONSTONE RAILWAY TRUST LTD.
HUNSBURY HILL INDUSTRIAL MUSEUM, Northampton.   NP18

SP 735584

Museum of railway items relating to the Northamptonshire Ironstone industry. Established as part of the Hunsbury Hill Country Park, on the southern edge of Northampton. Stock is kept in a museum / workshop building and there is also an operating line some 400 yards in length.

Gauge : 4ft 8½in

No.	Name	Type		Builder	Works No.	Year		
No.16	89-19	0-4-0DM		HE	2087	1940	(a)	
9365	BELVEDERE 89-17	4wVBT	VCG	S	9365	1946	(b)	
	MUSKETEER	4wVBT	VCG	S	9369	1946	(b)	
No.14	BRILL 89-31	0-4-0ST	OC	MW	1795	1912	(c)	(9)
	(HYLTON) (ELY)	4wDH		FH	3967	1961	(d)	
1	(EXPRESS) MABEL	4wDM		RH	235511	1945	(e)	(1)
		4wDM		RH	299100	1950	(f)	(2)
46	MUFFIN							
(39	SPITFIRE 89-32)	4wDM		RH	242868	1946	(g)	
	TRYM 89-94	0-4-0ST	OC	HE	287	1883	(h)	
	SIR VINCENT	4wWT	G	AP	8800	1917	(i)	(6)
	THE BLUE CIRCLE	2-2-0WT	G	AP	9449	1926	(j)	(7)
	89-20	4wDM		RH	386875	1955	(k)	(4)
	A16W	2w-2PMR		Wkm	6887	1954	(l)	(3)
7283	YVONNE	0-4-0VBT	OC	Cockerill	2945	1920	(m)	(8)
	MAT	4wDM		RH	321734	1952	(n)	(5)
No.53	SIR ALFRED WOOD	0-6-0DM		RH	319294	1953	(o)	
	LOIS	0-4-0DH		JF	4220033	1965	(p)	
	SHIRE LODGE	0-4-0DM		RH	327974	1954	(q)	
(RS 154)	AMOCO	0-4-0DM		RH	395305	1956	(r)	
	-	0-4-0ST	OC	WB	2565	1936	(s)	
		0-4-0DM		JF	4220001	1959	(t)	
4002	S13004S	4w-4w.RER		Elh		1949	(u)	
44	CONWAY	0-6-0ST	IC	K	5469	1933	(v)	

(a)   ex Anglian Building Products Ltd, Lenwade, Norfolk, 10/7/1974;
      stored at Blackwood Hodge & Co Ltd, Northampton, until 8/1976.
(b)   ex Thos.E.Gray Ltd, Burton Latimer, 27/2/1975.
(c)   ex Quainton Railway Society, Bucks, 26/9/1977.
(d)   ex Track Supplies & Services Ltd, Wolverton, Bucks, 3/12/1983;
      prev Wiggins Teape Ltd, Ely Paper Works, Cardiff, South Glamorgan.
(e)   ex Alan Keef Ltd, Bampton, Oxon, 18/9/1978;
      prev. South Eastern Steam Centre, Ashford, Kent.
(f)   ex Lancashire Tar Distillers Ltd, Cadishead Works, Irlam, Manchester, 7/1981.
(g)   ex Isle of Wight Steam Railway, 6/11/1988.
(h)   ex Buckinghamshire Railway Centre, Quainton Road, Bucks, 4/11/1989.
(i)   ex Rushden Historical Transport Society, The Old Station, Rushden, 5/1/1992.
(j)   ex Bluebell Railway, Horsted Keynes, East Sussex, 9/9/1993.
(k)   ex K.G. Lawrence Group, Wellingborough Foundries, 26/11/1983.
(l)   ex John R. Billows Ltd, Kettering, 6/6/1975
(m)   ex Northampton & Lamport Railway Preservation Society, Pitsford, 26/4/1995.
(n)   ex East Kent Light Railway Society, Shepherdswell, Kent, 14/7/1995.
(o)   ex Northampton & Lamport Railway Preservation Society, Lamport, 29/3/1996.
(p)   ex Nene Valley Railway, Wansford, Cambs, 27/9/1996.
(q)   ex Great Eastern Traction, Hardingham, Norfolk, 28/6/1997.
(r)   ex Foxfield Light Railway, Dilhorne, Staffs, 2/9/1997

(s)   ex N. Le Count, Hardwick, 2/11/1997.
(t)   ex AEM (Avon) Ltd, Chittening Trading Estate, Avonmouth, Bristol, 9/12/1998.
(u)   ex Northampton & Lamport Railway Preservation Society, Pitsford, 4/6/1999.
(v)   ex Mr Drage, New Buildings Farm, Heydon, near Royston, Cambs, 21/6/2000.

(1)   dismantled on site and chassis used as engineless service vehicle; remains to J.Scholes, Ripppingale, Lincs, 30/10/1998.
(2)   scrapped on site by S.M. McGregor & Co, Bicester, Oxon, w/e 26/6/1992.
(3)   regauged to metre, /1977.
(4)   to Somerset & Avon Railway Co Ltd, Radstock, Avon, 6/3/1994
(5)   dismantled and frame in use as a wagon.
(6)   to Nene Valley Railway, Wansford, Cambs, 1/7/1997.
(7)   to Buckinghamshire Railway Centre, Quainton Road, Bucks, 24/10/1997.
(8)   to The Battlefield Line, Shackerstone, Leics, 8/1997.
(9)   to Buckinghamshire Railway Centre, Quainton Road, Bucks, 19/10/1998.

Visiting Locomotives (Gauge : 4ft 8½in).

THOMAS	0-6-0T	OC	HC	1800	1947	(a)	(1)
-	0-6-0T	IC	NBH	25464	1939	(b)	(2)

(a)   ex Nene Valley Railway, Wansford, Cambs, 2/6/1994.
(b)   ex Buckinghamshire Railway Centre, Quainton Road, Bucks, by 4/10/1998.

(1)   returned to Nene Valley Railway, 8/6/1994.
(2)   returned to Buckinghamshire Railway Centre, Quainton Road, Bucks, c/1998.

Gauge : Metre

No.87	8315/87	89-12	0-6-0ST	OC	P	2029	1942	(a)	(3)
No.86	8315/86		0-6-0ST	OC	P	1871	1934	(b)	(2)
(No.85)	8315/85	BANSHEE	0-6-0ST	OC	P	1870	1934	(c)	(1)
(A16W)			2w-2PMR		Wkm	6887	1954	(d)	(4)

(a)   ex F.G. Cann & Son, Finedon, 6/6/1975.
(b)   ex John R. Billows Ltd, Kettering, 10/6/1975.
(c)   ex Yorkshire Dales Railway, Embsay, Yorkshire (WR), 20/8/1977.
(d)   converted from 4ft 8½in gauge, /1977.

(1)   to Northampton Locomotive Group, Pitsford Quarry, 5/1979.
(2)   to Irchester Narrow Gauge Railway Trust, Irchester Country Park, 25/2/1990.
(3)   to Irchester Narrow Gauge Railway Trust, Irchester Country Park, 20/3/1993.
(4)   to C. Cross, Upwell, Cambs, 19/1/1993.

Gauge : 3ft 0in

5	4wDMF	RH	338439	1953	(a)

(a)   ex W.T. Sheppard & Sons Ltd, Isebrook Works, Wellingborough, 2/7/1999.

Gauge : 2ft 0in

89-18	4wPM		L	14006	1940	(a)	(7)
(T11)	4wDM		MR	9711	1952	(b)	(6)
(T13)	4wDM		MR	8969	1945	(b)	(2)
(T8)	4wDM		MR	8731	1941	(c)	(3)
(22)	4wDM		MR	8756	1942	(d)	(4)
85049	4wDM		RH	393325	1956	(e)	(1)
-	4wDM	S/O	RH	217967	1942	(f)	(5)

(a)   ex County Borough of Northampton, Little Billing Sewage Works, 2/3/1974; stored at Richmond Terrace Pumping Station, Northampton, until 9/1975.
(b)   ex Mixconcrete Aggregates Ltd, Earls Barton, c6/1975.
(c)   ex Mixconcrete Aggregates Ltd, Earls Barton, 9/1975.
(d)   ex Joseph Arnold & Sons Ltd, Leighton Buzzard, Beds, 17/2/1979.
(e)   ex BR (ER), Central Materials Depot, Chesterton Junction, Cambridge, 2/8/1986.
(f)   ex Knebworth House, Herts, after 10/4/1988, by 8/5/1988.

(1)   to private site by 17/6/1990, after 29/5/1989; then to Vobster Light Railway, Mells, Somerset, 13/1/1992.
(2)   frame only to Leighton Buzzard Narrow Gauge Railway, Beds, 7/2/1993.
(3)   frame only to Leighton Buzzard Narrow Gauge Railway, Beds, 2/1/1994.
(4)   to H. Frampton-Jones, private site, Surrey, 22/7/1992.
(5)   returned to Knebworth House, Herts, by 4/6/1988.
(6)   to FMB Engineering Ltd, Hants, 12/3/1995.
(7)   to J. Woolmer, Woodford, 25/1/1996.

ALAN ODELL
near Northampton   XP19

Locomotive purchased for preservation and moved to this private site.

Gauge : 3ft 0in

	-	4wDMF		RH	418764	1957	(a)

(a)   ex W.T. Sheppard & Sons Ltd, Isebrook Works, Wellingborough, /1999.

OVERSTONE SOLARIUM LIGHT RAILWAY
OVERSTONE SOLARIUM, Sywell, near Northampton   MP20
                                                                 SP 819654

Pleasure lines laid in this park. The standard gauge was a short demonstration line only and was lifted after 10/1970, while the passenger carrying narrow gauge line was closed and was lifted c7/1992.

Gauge : 4ft 8½in

CRANFORD No.2	0-6-0ST	OC	WB	2668	1942	(a)	(1)

(a)   ex Staveley Minerals Ltd, Cranford Ironstone Quarries, Northants, 28/1/1970.

(1)   to Somerset & Dorset Railway Circle, Radstock, Somerset, c8/1971.

Gauge : 1ft 11½in

No.1	0-4-0ST	OC	HE	1429	1922	(a)	(1)
No.2	4wDM		MR	8993	1946	(a)	(1)
	4wDM	S/O	MR	8727	1941	(b)	(2)

(a)   ex Woburn Park Railway, Beds, c1/1969.
(b)   ex Joseph Arnold & Sons Ltd, Leighton Buzzard, Beds, 7/1970.

(1)   to Pleasure-Rail Ltd, Knebworth, Herts, c10/1970.
(2)   to A. Johnston, Wedmore, Somerset, c11/1992 (by 15/11/1992).

RUSHDEN HISTORICAL TRANSPORT SOCIETY
THE OLD STATION, Rectory Rd, Rushden

The former Rushden Station has been restored as a museum and clubhouse. The aim is to operate a rail service over part of the former BR (ex- Midland Railway) Higham Ferrers branch.

Gauge : 4ft 8½ in.

-	0-4-0DM		AB	363	1942	(a)	
-	0-4-0ST	OC	AB	2323	1952	(b)	
SIR VINCENT	4wWT	G	AP	8800	1917	(c)	(1)
EDMUNDSONS	0-4-0ST	OC	AB	2168	1943	(d)	
2	4wDH		S	10159	1963	(e)	

(a)   ex Ampthill Scrap Metal Processing Co Ltd, Ampthill, Beds, 13/12/1987

(b)   ex Wicksteed Park, Kettering, 16/8/1992.

(c)   ex Hollycombe Woodland Steam Museum, Hollycombe, near Liphook, Hants, 11/3/1989.

(d)   ex Great Eastern Railway Trust (1989) Ltd, County School Station, North Elmham, Norfolk, 17/4/1998; to Birmingham Railway Museum, Tyseley, West Midlands, for repairs, after 29/5/2000, by 12/8/2000; returned 5/10/2000.

(e)   ex Castle Cement (Pitstone) Ltd, Pitstone Cement Works, Bucks, 15/5/1998.

(1)   to Northamptonshire Ironstone Railway Trust, Hunsbury Hill, Northampton, 5/1/1992.

Gauge : 2ft 0in

2 81 A 26	4wDM		MR	7333	1938	(a)	(1)

(a)   ex S.W. Tomlinson, Rushden, c5/1988 (by 6/8/1988).

(1)   to J. Lloyd, Castleton, North Yorkshire, 3/1998.

S.W. TOMLINSON
50, Blackfriars, Rushden

Locomotive stored at this private site for a time.

Gauge : 2ft 0in

2 81 A 26	4wDM		MR	7333	1938	(a)	(1)

(a)   ex Moseley Industrial Tramway Museum, Stockport, Cheshire, between 21/9/1986 and 5/1988.

(1)   to Rushden Historical Transport Society, Rushden, c5/1988 (by 6/8/1988).

WICKSTEED PARK
LAKESIDE RAILWAY, WICKSTEED LEISURE PARK, Kettering

Standard gauge locomotive on static display here (SP 879773) for some years in addition to a long established passenger carrying 2ft 0in gauge pleasure line (SP 883770) - the Lakeside Railway.

Gauge : 4ft 8½in

| | 0-4-0ST | OC | AB | 2323 | 1952 | (a) | (1) |

(a)   ex Irchester Parish Council, Irchester, 6/6/1979.

(1)   to Rushden Historical Transport Society, Rushden, 16/8/1992.

Gauge : 2ft 0in

LADY OF THE LAKE	0-4-0DM#S/O	Bg	2042	1931	New
KING ARTHUR	0-4-0DM#S/O	Bg	2043	1931	New
CHEYENNE	4wDM	S/O	MR	22224	1966	New

\# formerly 0-4-0PM

J. WOOLMER
Woodford, near Thrapston   SP24

Locomotive and equipment used for building work &/or garden restoration and preserved at this private site.

Gauge : 2ft 0in

| - | 4wDM (ex PM) | L | 36743 | 1951 | (a) |
| - | 4wPM | L | 14006 | 1940 | (b) |

(a)   ex Smith & Son (Raunds) Ltd, Raunds Manor Brickworks, by 31/12/1973.
(b)   ex Northamptonshire Ironstone Railway Trust, Hunsbury Hill, Northampton, 25/1/1996.

NON-LOCOMOTIVE WORKED SYSTEMS

ACALOR PROTECTIVE MATERIALS LTD
AIRMANSHIP HALL, Silverstone Airfield
LH1

SP 666408

This company commenced operations here in 1948. A 2ft 0in gauge line, 70 yards in length, was laid, set in concrete, through a booth used for shot blasting. About 1980 a second line, of 2ft 6in gauge and about 150 yards in length, was laid the full length of the works through a second shot blasting booth. Wagons on both lines were hauled by a fork-lift truck. Both lines ceased operating in 1990 and all wagons sold for scrap, although remains of the tracks were still present in 1997.

ANGLIAN WATER AUTHORITY, OUNDLE DIVISION
RAVENSTHORPE WATER TREATMENT WORKS, Ravensthorpe
MH2

SP 682703

A 2ft 0in gauge, hand operated, line about 200 yards long was used in conjunction with the cleaning of the filter beds. Stock comprised six skips and two flat wagons.

ASHBY SMELTING CO
DEANSHANGER OXIDE WORKS
LH3

SP 765397

The company was established in 1935 to use the premises of E.& H. Roberts Ltd, agricultural engineers, for the production of iron oxide pigments and red lead. Soon afterwards a narrow gauge tramway was laid from the company's wharf on the Buckingham Arm of the Grand Union Canal into the works. It is likely that this was disused sometime before the Buckingham branch canal was abandoned in 1961. A small section of tramway was still in situ in the middle of the works when production ceased in 1999 under the ownership of Elementis. The site has subsequently been cleared for housing development.

FREDK. BARLOW (?)
ROTHWELL BRICKWORKS
RH4

possibly **Wm. H. Liner & Sons** until 1894   SP 808800
possibly **T. Liner** by 1869

Brickworks on the Orton Road, in production by 1884, probably operated by the Liner family. Possibly taken over by Fredk. Barlow from 1894. The works originally had a large Scotch Kiln; a continuous kiln was built about the turn of the century, was extended in 1911, and had been converted to oil firing by 1945. A short cable worked tramway operated from 1927 and ran from clay pits to the west of the works to an elevated clay shed. The works was one of the last remaining in Northamptonshire at the time of its closure about 1963.

Reference : "Bulletin of Industrial Archaeology in CBA Group 9" No.13, Richard O'Rourke, July 1970.

G.E. BEVAN & CO LTD
DALLINGTON QUARRIES
NH5

Quarry SP 745615 approx

Little is known of this ironstone quarry other than it had a tramway worked by horses and may have been connected to a siding off the Northampton to Market Harborough railway. The quarry was in operation from c1859 to 1863; the siding had been removed by 1872.

Reference : "The Ironstone Quarries of the Midlands, Part 3, Northampton", Eric S Tonks, Runpast Publishing, 1989, p153

S.H. BLACKWELL & S.W. SMITH
MANOR FARM IRONSTONE QUARRIES
QH6
Quarry SP 908676

Quarrying commenced here c1852, on a site to east of the river Ise and later occupied by Irthlingborough Ironworks. A tramway, possibly horse worked and thought to be the first Ironstone tramway, ran southeast to a point adjacent to the LNWR Wellingborough to Irthlingborough railway.

Reference : "The Ironstone Quarries of the Midlands, Part 4, Wellingborough", Eric S Tonks, Runpast Publishing, 1988, p.15

S.H. BLACKWELL & CO
HARDINGSTONE QUARRIES
LH7
Quarry SP 770572

Ironstone workings known as Warren Quarries, in existence by 1882, were worked by Samuel Holden Blackwell, an Ironmaster of Dudley, Worcs. A tramway about a mile long ran from the pits to the LNWR Northampton to Peterborough railway; little is known of its operation but the line may have been standard gauge and cable operated

Reference : "The Ironstone Quarries of the Midlands, Part 3, Northampton", Eric S Tonks, Runpast Publishing, 1989, p122

WILLIAM BLUNDELL
BRIXWORTH BRICKWORKS
MH8
William Holt 1849 - 1863
SP 750685

A small village brick and tile works, in the parish of Pitsford, operated by William Blundell from 1883, expanded by 1927 but closed about 1936. The works included four circualr downdraft kilns and a tramway ran to the works from a quarry at the north end of the site.

Reference : "Bulletin of Industrial Archaeology in CBA Group 9" No.13, Richard O'Rourke, July 1970.

JOSEPH BONSER
HOLLOWELL BRICKWORKS
MH9
SP 693719

Brickworks opened by 1883 and under the ownership of Joseph Bonser by 1894. A cable worked tramway ran from the pits to the works, where wire cut bricks were produced in two updraft kilns, each with a capacity of 50,000 bricks. In 1935 the works was commissioned to produce puddling clay, together with one million bricks, for the construction of the nearby Hollowell Reservoir. This was the last major order for the works and wartime conditions resulted in its closure in 1940.

Reference : "Bulletin of Industrial Archaeology in CBA Group 9" No.13, Richard O'Rourke, July 1970.

JOSEPH BROWN
WHARF LANE BRICKWORKS, Higham Ferrers
QH10
Joseph & George Brown before 1885
SP 952687 & SP 952683

Two large brickworks opened by Joseph & George Brown, brick & tile makers. By 1885 Joseph Brown was owner after the death of George. The works at Wharf Lane (SP 952687) had, by 1900, a Decauville tramway which ran towards the town. Works closed by 1927.

Reference : "Bulletin of Industrial Archaeology in CBA Group 9" No.13, Richard O'Rourke, July 1970.

BUTLIN BEVAN & CO
CRANFORD IRONSTONE QUARRIES
RH11
Quarry SP 908769 approx

An ironstone quarry located to the north of the A604 Kettering to Cranford road. A tramway was in existence by c1884 which ran from the quarry via a tunnel under the A604 to a loading dock adjacent to the Midland Railway Kettering to Thrapston line. Little is known of this system.

Reference : "The Ironstone Quarries of the Midlands, Part 5, Kettering", Eric S Tonks, Runpast Publishing, 1988, p.30

DEAN & CHAPTER IRONSTONE QUARRIES
RH12
The Dean & Chapter of Peterborough Cathedral until 1870
Quarry SP 908680

These quarries were an extension of Manor Farm quarries and began production c1867. A tramway, possibly of 3ft 8¼in gauge, which may have been loco worked, ran from the quarries to a wharf on the river Nene. In April 1871 SAMSON, an 0-4-0ST built by Hudswell Clarke & Rodgers, was delivered to T. Butlin, Wellingborough and may have been tried here.

Reference : "The Ironstone Quarries of the Midlands, Part 4, Wellingborough", Eric S Tonks, Runpast Publishing, 1988, p.19

DITCHFORD IRONSTONE QUARRIES
QH13
Thrapston Iron Ore Co Ltd until 1879
Quarries SP 933687 approx
Thomas Whitehouse until 1875

Quarries to the north of the LNWR Wellingborough to Peterborough railway east of Ditchford station with a tramway, possibly narrow gauge, to an end on connection at a siding off the LNWR line. The quarries closed in 1885.

Reference : "The Ironstone Quarries of the Midlands, Part 4, Wellingborough", Eric S Tonks, Runpast Publishing, 1988, p.163

BUTLIN BEVAN & CO LTD
RINGSTEAD IRONSTONE QUARRIES
SH14
Butlin Bevan & Co until 27/6/1889
Quarry SP 973742

Quarries opened in 11/1871, with a horse worked narrow gauge tramway from the quarry to a tipping dock adjacent to standard gauge sidings at Ringstead & Addington Halt. The quarries closed in 1891.

Reference : "The Ironstone Quarries of the Midlands, Part 4, Wellingborough", Eric S Tonks, Runpast Publishing, 1988, p.204

THOMAS BUTLIN & CO
EAST END IRONWORKS & QUARRIES, Wellingborough
QH15
Ironworks SP 895682: Quarries SP 900683

East End Ironworks was the first ironworks to be built in Northamptonshire, the first furnace being put in blast in 6/1853. Ironstone workings extended to the north and east of the works from where ironstone was brought to the works by horse and cart; these workings were taken over by Butlin Bevan & Co on 16/12/1861. Further quarries opened c1862 in an area between Finedon Road and Mill Road. These had standard gauge tramways, probably horse worked, connected to the Midland Railway Wellingborough to Kettering line opposite Wellingborough locomotive shed. The site was later occupied by the Midland Brick Co

(Wellingborough) Ltd (which see). East End Ironworks had no rail connection to the Midland Railway and closed c1876.

Reference : "Bulletin of Industrial Archaeology in CBA Group 9" No.11, G.H. Starmer, January 1970.

THOMAS BUTLIN & CO LTD

BARTON SEAGRAVE IRONSTONE QUARRIES   RH16
Butlin Bevan & Co until 27/6/1889   Quarry SP889757 approx

Quarries opened in 1883 to the south of the Midland Railway Kettering to Thrapston railway and adjacent to Polwell lane. A narrow gauge tramway, probably hand or horse worked, ran from the quarry to a tipping dock adjacent to the standard gauge siding connecting to the Midland Railway line. The quarries closed c1891

Reference : "The Ironstone Quarries of the Midlands, Part 5, Kettering", Eric S Tonks, Runpast Publishing, 1988, p.13

CHELVESTON QUARRIES   SH17
Hunsbury Hill Iron Co from 1881 until c1889   Quarries SP 978697 & 976708

There were two quarries for ironstone and limestone in the Chelveston area, each with its own tramway of about 1ft 6in gauge. The southern quarry lay about half a mile east of Chelveston Lodge and had a tramway which ran westwards to a tipping dock adjacent to the Stanwick to Higham Ferrers road. The northern quarry was about half a mile from Chelveston Lodge on this same road, and its tramway ran westwards to a tipping dock on the Stanwick to Irthlingborough road; there were limekilns near to the quarry. Both tramways were horse worked with ore being carted to Irthlingborough station.

Reference : "The Ironstone Quarries of the Midlands, Part 4, Wellingborough", Eric S Tonks, Runpast Publishing, 1988, p.200

CHOWNS
STOKE BRUERNE BRICKWORKS   MH18
orig George Savage   SP 745495

Brickworks opened prior to 1849 by George Savage. By 1883 it was an extensive works with a canal basin inside the works and four downdraft kilns around it. After World War II the site was taken over by Chowns (builders) of Northampton. Clay was obtained from pits north of the works served by two tramways, one owned by the tenant and the other by the Grand Junction Canal Co. The clay was carried in side-tipping wagons on Jubilee track, hand worked from the pits to the receiving shed and then cable hauled to the top of the shed for tipping into a hopper above the Pug Mill. The works closed c1949.

Reference : "Bulletin of Industrial Archaeology in CBA Group 9" No.13, Richard O'Rourke, July 1970.

CO-OPERATIVE WHOLESALE SOCIETY
RUSH MILLS FELLMONGERING DEPOT, Bedford Road, Northampton   NH19
Parker Grey & Co Ltd until 1948   SP 777593

The business was conducted in the buildings remaining from the destruction of Rush Mills by fire in 1924. These were on an island formed by the River Nene and the watercourses from the watermill. A 2ft gauge tramway ran to the mills from a store at the lorry unloading point, crossing the former tail-race from the mill on a planked bridge. Skins were carried on flat wagons, manually propelled one at a time. Six flat wagons were in use in 1966. The business closed in the 1970s and the site was subsequently cleared.

EBBW VALE STEEL IRON & COAL CO LTD
DENFORD IRONSTONE QUARRIES　　　　　　　　　　　　　　　**QH20**
R.E. Campbell until 9/11/1915　　　　　　　　　　　　　Quarry SP977761
G. Keeble & E.M. Jellett until 1/10/1914

These quarries commenced production in 1913 and were served by a horse worked narrow gauge tramway, possibly 2ft gauge, which ran from the quarries to an elevated tipping dock adjacent to Keeble's siding on the LNWR Northampton to Peterborough railway. The quarry closed c1918 and track was removed.

Reference : "The Ironstone Quarries of the Midlands, Part 4, Wellingborough", Eric S Tonks,
　　　　　　　Runpast Publishing, 1988, p.213

ALFRED HICKMAN LTD
ASTROP QUARRIES, near Kings Sutton　　　　　　　　　　　**LH21**
　　　　　　　　　　　　　　　　　　　　　　　　　　　Quarry SP 502383
Construction commenced in August 1896. The quarries were served by a 2ft 1in gauge double track tramway operated by an endless steel cable powered by a steam engine. The pits closed in March 1924 and the tramway was dismantled.

Reference : The Ironstone Quarries of the Midlands, Part 2 Oxfordshire, Eric Tonks,
　　　　　　　Runpast Publishing, 1988

IRTHLINGBOROUGH BRICK & TILE CO LTD
IRTHLINGBOROUGH BRICKWORKS　　　　　　　　　　　　　**QH22**
A. Dunmore from c1894　　　　　　　　　　　　　　　　SP 946697

A brickworks served by the standard gauge tramway of the former Irthlingborough Iron Ore Co Ltd. The works was in two halves, one very extensive plant had three continuous kilns whilst the other works had three circular downdraft kilns. Narrow gauge tramways were used within the clay pit. The works closed c1908 and was later taken over in 1913 by Hatton Shaw & Co (Irthlingborough) Ltd (which see)

IRTHLINGBOROUGH IRON ORE CO LTD
(Registered 25/2/1890)
IRTHLINGBOROUGH IRONSTONE QUARRIES　　　　　　　　**QH23**
　　　　　　　　　　　　　　　　　　　　　　　　Quarries SP 943699
These quarries were connected to the LNWR Wellingborough to Peterborough railway by a half mile long standard gauge tramway. The method of operation of the tramway is unknown, possibly loco worked although none are known to have been owned by the company.
The company was wound up in 5/1898 and a new company of the same name formed which was dissolved on 9/12/1902. In 5/1898 the Irthlingborough Brick & Tile Co Ltd was formed and took over the abandoned area as the site of a brickworks which closed c1908.

Reference : "The Ironstone Quarries of the Midlands, Part 4, Wellingborough", Eric S Tonks,
　　　　　　　Runpast Publishing, 1988, p.198

KETTERING BRICK & TILE CO (1905) LTD
LONDON ROAD WORKS, Kettering
Kettering Brick & Tile Co Ltd until 1905

RH24
SP 874778

This was a large works, opened c1877, with a 100ft diameter Hoffman kiln and two smaller rectangular kilns. It is shown on the 1900 OS map as having two short narrow gauge tramways connecting the works and adjacent clay pits. On the liquidation of the original company in 1904, tenders were invited for plant including "3 hauling gears with endless chain, tram roads etc with 40 iron trucks and 10 wooden ditto." The works closed in 1927.

MABBUT & SON
STATION ROAD SAWMILLS, Brixworth

MH25
SP 738719

After the closure of Brixworth station goods yard in 1964, the good shed was used for creosoting timber which was brought by lorry from the firm's sawmills nearer to the village. The timber was off-loaded onto bogie wagons running on narrow (about 2ft) gauge tracks through to creosoting plant. It is believed that this ceased during the 1980s and the system was removed before the demolition of the goods shed.

HENRY MARTIN
NORTHAMPTON BRICKWORKS

NH26
SP747616

A brickworks, opened c1895, on the east side of the LNWR Northampton to Rugby railway. By 1927 the it had two circular downdraft kilns and the 25in OS map for 1938 shows it connected to the clay pit by a parallel double track tramway (possibly cable worked). The works had closed by 1940.

METROPOLITAN BRICK & TILE CO (IRTHLINGBOROUGH) LTD
IRTHLINGBOROUGH BRICKWORKS

QH27
SP 940696

Works, opened 1899, with a Sercombes Patent Improved Barrel Kiln (rectangular with eight chambers and a 120ft tall chimney) and also a rectangular kiln with 18 chambers. A tramway, operated by an endless haulage system powered by a stationary steam engine, connected the clay pits to the works. Up to 270,000 bricks per month were despatched by rail by 1905. The works closed c1910 and the site was taken over in 1918 by the Ebbw Vale Steel Iron & Coal Co when iron ore mines were developed in the area.

Reference : "Bulletin of Industrial Archaeology in CBA Group 9" No.13, Richard O'Rourke, July 1970.

MIDLAND BRICK CO (WELLINGBOROUGH) LTD
WELLINGBOROUGH IRONSTONE QUARRIES

QH28
SP 902686

This quarry, a redevelopment of the area between Eastfield road and the Midland Railway, had earlier been worked by Butlins in the 1880s. A 2ft gauge, hand worked, line ran from the quarry to a tipping dock by a Midland Railway siding. The quarry was later worked from 1940 by the Wellingborough Iron Co Ltd using a Ruston 21RB dragline and road transport.

Reference : "The Ironstone Quarries of the Midlands, Part 4, Wellingborough", Eric S Tonks, Runpast Publishing, 1988, p.73

WALTER NEILSON
THINGDON QUARRIES & MINES
QH29

Western quarries SP 913712 approx: Eastern quarries SP 921713 approx

Walter Neilson commenced quarrying iron ore in 1882 in an area between Finedon road and Harrowdon road. A tramway of 2ft 4in gauge was constructed to the quarries, the upper section being worked by horses and the lower section a double track cable operated tramway powered by a steam engine. The line was two miles long and terminated at sidings by the Midland Railway, these being known later as **Neilson's Sidings**. Quarrying continued south of Harrowdon road until 1892 when a tramway was laid to limestone quarries and iron ore mines east of Finedon. In 1911 the Wellingborough Iron Co Ltd took over the mines (which see) and continued to use Neilson's tramway until 1929, when the output was diverted to Wellingborough's metre gauge line. Neilson's tramway was taken up in 1933-34

Reference : "The Ironstone Quarries of the Midlands, Part 4, Wellingborough", Eric S Tonks, Runpast Publishing, 1988, p.83

NELL BRIDGE IRON ORE CO
NELL BRIDGE QUARRIES, Kings Sutton
LH30

Kings Sutton Ironstone Co from 1870 until 1873   Quarry SP 500349

A narrow gauge tramway about ½ mile in length ran downhill from the quarry to a tipping dock adjacent to a GWR siding. The line was probably worked by gravity for loaded traffic with horses being used to return the empty wagons to the quarry.

Reference : The Ironstone Quarries of the Midlands, Part 2 Oxfordshire, Eric S Tonks, Runpast Publishing, 1988

NEWBRIDGE IRON ORE CO

NEWBRIDGE IRONSTONE QUARRIES
RH31

Thomas Walters until 1873

South Quarry SP 963776
North Quarry SP 955782

Quarries, in existence by 1867, to the north and south of the Midland Railway Kettering to Thrapston line. Both used tramways with tipping docks adjacent to that line; the quarries to the south used a tramway of 4ft gauge and those to the north a line believed to be narrow gauge, possibly 2ft. Both tramways were worked by horses.

Reference : "The Ironstone Quarries of the Midlands, Part 5, Kettering", Eric S Tonks, Runpast Publishing, 1988, p.86

RINGSTEAD QUARRIES
RH32

Quarry SP 968757

An ironstone quarry in existence by 1873, adjacent to Rectory Farm, with a narrow gauge tramway, possibly horse worked, to the LNWR Northampton to Peterborough railway. The exact route is uncertain; the quarry closed c1881

Reference : "The Ironstone Quarries of the Midlands, Part 4, Wellingborough", Eric S Tonks, Runpast Publishing, 1988, p.210

EXORS OF PICKERING PHIPPS
BLISWORTH QUARRIES (1)   MH33
G.E. Bevan & Co Ltd until 1903   Ironstone quarry SP 732535
Blisworth Iron Stone Mining Co Ltd from 1859 until 1861   Limestone quarry SP 735530
John Hickman until 1855

These quarries, opened in 1852 by John Hickman, and located to the south of the Courteenhall road, together with later quarries to the north, worked by the Blisworth Iron Stone Mining Co Ltd, were connected to the Grand Junction Canal by a 3ft 7in gauge tramway. This was horse worked from the quarries as far as the head of a cable worked incline which ran down to the canal, where the contents of loaded wagons were tipped into barges. The quarries closed 1/1/1921. A limestone quarry, opened in 1821 by **John Roper**, had a horse worked tramway using wooden side tipping wagons which ran to the same wharf but had no physical connection to the ironstone line, this quarry was acquired by the Exors of Pickering Phipps on 29/9/1902 and closed c1912

Reference : "The Ironstone Quarries of the Midlands, Part 3, Northampton", Eric S Tonks,
Runpast Publishing, 1989, p.14

BLISWORTH QUARRIES (2)   MH34
G.E. Bevan & Co Ltd until 1901   North quarry SP 718540
South quarry SP 716536

Quarrying at the northern most site probably commenced c1873; the 6in OS map for 1883 shows a tramway which ran from the pits to a wharf on the Grand Junction Canal. Nothing is known of its operation but there was probably a cable worked incline down the hillside to the canal; the system had closed by c1900. The quarries to the south at Fox Covert opened c1899 and a tramway to the canal used wooden end tipping wagons gravity run to a loading stage on the canal, where ironstone was tipped into barges. Horses returned the empty wagons to the pits, which closed c1914

Reference : "The Ironstone Quarries of the Midlands, Part 3, Northampton", Eric S Tonks,
Runpast Publishing, 1989, p.28

RIXON'S IRON & BRICK CO LTD
DITCHFORD IRONSTONE QUARRIES   QH35
Rixon & Co until 18/6/1883   Quarry SP 932692

Rixon's quarry had a horse worked tramway, possibly of 3ft 3in gauge, which ran from the quarry to a tipping dock adjacent to the LNWR line east of Ditchford station. The exact course of the tramway is unknown, it had closed by 1886, although the quarries were later reopened by the Wellingborough Iron Co Ltd

Reference : "The Ironstone Quarries of the Midlands, Part 4, Wellingborough", Eric S Tonks,
Runpast Publishing, 1988, p.163

RUSHDEN BRICK & TILE CO
WELLINGBOROUGH ROAD BRICKWORKS, Rushden   QH36
SP 942675

A large brickworks, with a sizeable continuous kiln, in operation from 1894 to 1927. Served by a tramway from a clay pit to the south of the works and another tramway served a sand pit to the east of the works. Extensive sidings, apparently standard gauge, existed around the works but without known connection to the Wellingborough - Higham Ferrers branch.

Reference : "Bulletin of Industrial Archaeology in CBA Group 9" No.13, Richard O'Rourke,
July 1970.

SHEEPBRIDGE COAL & IRON CO LTD
BRIXWORTH QUARRIES
MH37

Quarry SP 742715

Ironstone quarries with a 2ft gauge tramway. A double track cable worked incline, installed in 1883, ran to a tipping dock adjacent to standard gauge sidings at Brixworth station. Production commenced on 9/1/1884; the quarries closed in 6/1896

Reference : "The Ironstone Quarries of the Midlands, Part 3, Northampton", Eric S Tonks, Runpast Publishing, 1989, p.169

SMITH & GRACE SCREW BOSS PULLEY CO LTD
NENESIDE WORKS, Thrapston
SH38

Quarry SP 995783

A 15inch gauge tramway ran the length of the moulding shop with wagon turntables to short branches at right angles to the main run. The tramway was little used by the 1980s although a few four-wheel flat wagons were standing on it. The works closed in the 1990s and have since been demolished and the site used for housing.

STANTON IRONWORKS CO LTD AND THOMAS BUTLIN & CO LTD
STANTONGATE IRONSTONE QUARRIES
QH39

Quarry SP 884692

A narrow gauge tramway, possibly horse worked, ran from quarries both east and west of the Wellingborough to Kettering road near to Vicarage Farm. The line crossed the road via a level crossing to a tipping dock at the terminus of the standard gauge branch which connected with the Midland Railway north of Finedon Road bridge. Traffic commenced in 1875, the quarries closed c1895 and the tramway had been lifted by 1899

Reference : "The Ironstone Quarries of the Midlands, Part 4 Wellingborough", Eric S Tonks, Runpast Publishing, 1988, p.71

STANTON IRONWORKS CO LTD
DESBOROUGH IRONSTONE QUARRIES
RH40

Desborough Iron Ore Co (John Hickman) until 1873   South quarry SP 809836 approx
North quarry SP 812838 approx

Quarries, opened c1859 by John Hickman, located to the south of the Midland Railway Kettering to Market Harborough Railway near the Pipewell Road bridge. Later operations by Stanton Ironworks Co Ltd used narrow gauge tramways (possibly of 3ft 0in gauge) between these quarries and a loading stage adjacent to the Midland Railway main line. In 1883 quarrying began north of Rushton Road and a tramway was laid to these quarries via a tunnel under the Midland Railway line. The tramway was probably horse worked in the quarries with cable operation to the tipping dock and had closed by 1899.

Reference : "The Ironstone Quarries of the Midlands, Part 6, Corby", Eric S Tonks, Runpast Publishing, 1992, p.10

FINEDON HILL IRONSTONE QUARRIES & MINES
RH41

SP 914701 & SP 918696

Quarries, opened by 1875, north east of South Hill Farm. By 1884 workings had reached Sidegate Lane and a tramway of 2ft 6in gauge, horse worked at this time, ran from the quarry to an elevated tipping dock adjacent to the Midland Railway at Finedon Road bridge.

By 1899 quarries north of Sidegate Lane were opened up and a cable worked tramway installed, powered by a steam engine located near the Midland Railway

Reference : "The Ironstone Quarries of the Midlands, Part 4 Wellingborough", Eric S Tonks, Runpast Publishing, 1988, p.75

GEORGE THOMPSON
IRTHLINGBOROUGH BRICKWORKS

QH42
SP 951714

Brickworks, owned by George Thompson from 1885 to 1900, on the east side of the Little Addington road. The 25in OS map for 1900 shows a quarry on the west side of the road with a tramway running to a run-round loop alongside the road. The line, probably horse worked, had closed by 1927.

THRAPSTON IRON ORE CO LTD
THRAPSTON QUARRIES
Thomas Whitehouse until 1875

SH43
Quarry SP 999775

Quarries, opened in 1873, with a standard gauge line, probably horse worked, running from the quarry to a siding at Thrapston Midland Railway station. The quarries closed in 5/1881 but were acquired by the Glendon Iron Co in 1881 for the extraction of limestone. This continued until 1900, after which the track was lifted. In 1933 the site was reopened for quarrying limestone by the Amalgamated Stone & Lime Co Ltd (which see). Thrapston Iron Ore Co Ltd was officially wound up on 15/6/1883

Reference : "The Ironstone Quarries of the Midlands, Part 4, Wellingborough", Eric S Tonks, Runpast Publishing, 1988, p.215

TOWCESTER MINERAL & BRICK CO LTD
SHOWSLEY (SEWARDSLEY) QUARRIES

LH44
Quarry SP 720502

Shallow opencast ironstone quarries with a narrow gauge tramway, worked by two horses, to a standard gauge siding (opened 27/9/1909) on the S&MJR Towcester to Olney railway. The quarries closed c1918

Reference : "The Ironstone Quarries of the Midlands, Part 3, Northampton", Eric S Tonks, Runpast Publishing, 1989, p.60

TRENERY & SONS LTD
Timber Yard, Bridge Street, Northampton

NH45
SP 753596

This timber yard had an 18inch gauge hand-worked tramway within the yard and sheds. The line was out of use in 1965 with wagons still present.

T.W. WARD
DITCHFORD IRONSTONE QUARRY

QH46
Quarry SP 928686

The quarry commenced production in 1913 with a narrow gauge tramway, probably horse worked, which ran from the quarry across Ditchford Lane to a standard gauge siding installed in 1912 by Ditchford station. The quarry closed by 1918 and siding removed on 27/10/1918

Reference : "The Ironstone Quarries of the Midlands, Part 4, Wellingborough", Eric S Tonks, Runpast Publishing, 1988, p.160

WELLINGBOROUGH BRICK & TILE CO
WELLINGBOROUGH BRICKWORKS

QH47

SP 884675

Brickworks opened in 1835 and owned by the Wellingborough Brick & Tile Co by 1877. By 1887 it included a large Hoffman kiln and a small circular downdraft kiln (the latter closed and demolished by 1901). A tramway ran east from clay pits to the works. Works closed about the time of World War I.

Reference : "Bulletin of Industrial Archaeology in CBA Group 9" No.13, Richard O'Rourke, July 1970.

HENRY W. WELDON
GAYTON QUARRIES

MH48

Quarry SP 706540

Little is known of the operation of these quarries, the 6in OS map for 1883 shows a tramway running from the pits to Wheldon's siding on the SMJ Blisworth to Towcester railway. The quarries appear to have started production about 1863 and had closed by 1885

Reference : "The Ironstone Quarries of the Midlands, Part 3, Northampton", Eric S Tonks, Runpast Publishing, 1989, p.39

WESTERN FAVELL BRICK & TILE CO
BUTTOCKS BOOTH BRICKWORKS, Northampton
(subsidiary of **A. Glenn & Son**)

MH49

SP 783644

An early brickworks here was in existence by 1835 and disused by 1883. It lay dormant until after World War I, when it was re-opened by A. Glenn & Son, trading as Western Favell Brick & Tile Co. A tramway served the claypit and works; after closure of the works about 1941 the wagons passed to the Chowns works at Stoke Bruerne.

Reference : "Bulletin of Industrial Archaeology in CBA Group 9" No.13, Richard O'Rourke, July 1970.

Unknown Owner
STOKE BRUERNE LIME KILN

MH50

SP 743502

A tramway of about 2ft gauge ran in a straight line from a lime kiln (demolished many years ago) to the canal. A turn-out just east of the towpath gave access to a short line running parallel to the canal.

Unknown Owner
WELDON STONE QUARRIES

TH51

SP 933892

The stone quarries at Weldon date from the 13th century and by about 1890 they were served by an extensive narrow gauge tramway system with branches serving the quarries and at least one incline down to underground workings. Horses hauled flat wagons carrying large blocks of stone from the workings to a stock yard served by a large wooden gantry crane. Work seems to have ended during the early part of the 20th century but the evidence remained until the 1970s when the British Steel iron ore workings at Barn Close cleared the area.

APPENDIX

RAILWAY CRANES

Many works employed rail cranes both for lifting and for moving wagons on the internal rail system. Known details are given here.

CRANE TYPES :

Wheel arrangement in the usual notation followed by -

DC	Diesel crane (transmission unknown)
DEC	Diesel electric crane
DMC	Diesel mechanical crane
HA	Hand operated
SC	Steam crane.

BUILDERS :

JB	Joseph Booth & Bros, Union Crane Works, Rodley, Leeds.
C	Coles Cranes, Crown Works, Sunderland, Co.Durham.
G	Grafton Cranes Ltd, Vulcan Works, Bedford.
HJC	Henry J Coles Ltd, London Crane Works, Derby.
I	Isles Ltd, Stanningley, Yorks (WR)
PR	Priestman Bros Ltd, Hull.
T&H	Taylor & Hubbard Ltd, Kent St, Leicester.
TS	Thomas Smith & Sons (Rodley), The Old Foundry, Rodley, Leeds.

BUCKINGHAMSHIRE

BLETCHLEY CONCRETE AGGREGATES CO, Stoney Stratford

Gauge : 4ft 8½in

4wSC	TS	12247	1936	New	s/s	5 ton capacity
4wSC	TS	14129	1941	New	s/s	5 ton capacity
4wDMC	TS	24650	1959	New	s/s	3 ton capacity

FOLLEY BROS LTD, Marlow

Gauge : ?

4wDMC	TS	12254	1936	New	s/s	5 ton capacity
4wDMC	TS	20217	1952	New	s/s	5 ton capacity

GRAND JUNCTION CANAL CO, Bletchley

Gauge : 5ft 6in

4wSC	G	1814	1919	New	s/s	3 ton capacity

G.F.X. HARTIGAN LTD, Newport Pagnell

Gauge : ?

4wSC	TS	11803	1934	New	s/s	5 ton capacity
4wSC	TS	16585	1945	New	s/s	7 ton capacity

JOHN HAWTREY & CO LTD, Chalfont Common, Chalfont St Peter

Builders merchants (?) located (at SU 000888) near to Gerrards Cross station on the ex-GW&GCR Joint main line.

Gauge : 4ft 8½in

4wSC	TS	16458	1945	New	(1)	5 ton capacity
4wDMC	TS	23827	1956	New	s/s	7 ton capacity

(1) to Harbour & General Works Ltd, Morecambe, Lancs; later Whitehaven Harbour Commissioners

MARLOW SAND & GRAVEL CO LTD

Gauge : 4ft 8½in

4wSC	TS	19794	1951	New	s/s	5 ton capacity

TRACK SUPPLIES & SERVICES LTD, Wolverton

Gauge : 4ft 8½in

63063	4wDM	Grafton	1540	1951	(a)	(1)

(a) ex MoDAD, Bramley, Hants.

(1) to East Somerset Railway, Cranmore, Somerset, by 8/1984.

BUCKINGHAMSHIRE RAILWAY CENTRE, Quainton Road

Gauge : 7ft 1in

562	4wDC	Grafton	2357	1931	(a)

(a) ex A.Hingley & Son (Timber) Ltd, Duffield Sawmills, Derbyshire, /1991.

Gauge : 4ft 8½in

Met&GC No.1	4wHA	CS	3282	1914	(a)	5 ton capacity
ADM27	4wHA	CS	7601	1944	(b)	10 ton capacity

(a) ex LT, Harrow, c5/1970.
(b) ex BR, Rugby, c12/1982.

SIR W.H. McALPINE, Fawley Hill

Gauge : 4ft 8½in

ADM33	4wHA	CS	7557	1942	(a)		6½ ton capacity
9066	4wSC	TS	10758	1944	(b)	(1)	5 ton capacity
9067	4wSC	TS		1946			
	reb to 4wDC				(b)		5 ton capacity

(a) ex BR, Workington, Cumbria, by 9/1981
(b) ex Sir Robert McAlpine & Sons Ltd, Hayes Plant Depot, Middx, c/1972.

(1) to Market Overton, Rutland, c/1973.

BEDFORDSHIRE

W H ALLEN, SONS & CO, Bedford
Gauge : 4ft 8½in

4wSC	G	1712	1917	New	(1)	5 ton capacity
4wSC	G	1679	1918	New	s/s	10 ton capacity

(1)   to British Celanese Ltd, Spondon, Derbys, /1938

JOSEPH ARNOLD & SONS LTD, Leighton Buzzard
Gauge : uncertain

4wSC	G	530	1898	(a)	(1)

(a)   ex London County Council

(1)   to Government Rolling Mills, /1916.

ASTELL BROS LTD, St Leonards Saw Mill, Bedford
Gauge : 4ft 8½in

4wSC	G	2049	1925	New	s/s	5 ton capacity

BEDFORD CORPORATION
Gauge : 4ft 8½in

4wSC	G	1815	1919	New	s/s	3 ton capacity

BEDFORD & DISTRICT GAS CO
Gauge : 4ft 8½in

4wSC	G	1831	1919	(a)	s/s	2 ton capacity
4wSC	G	2011	1924	New	s/s c/1974	5 ton capy.
4wDMC (ex SC)	G	2556	1940	New	s/s c/1974	5 ton capy.

(a)   New via R.H. Neal, No.82.

BLUE CIRCLE INDUSTRIES, Dunstable Works
Gauge : 4ft 8½in

4wSC	TS	21032	1952	New	s/s	5 ton capacity

GEORGE GARSIDE (SAND) LTD, Leighton Buzzard
Gauge : 4ft 8½in

4wSC	HJC	360	1905	(a)	s/s	3 ton capacity

(a)   ex London County Council

GRAFTON CRANES LTD, Bedford
Gauge : 4ft 8½in

	4wSC	G	1249	1909	New	s/s	5 ton capacity
	4wDC	G	2944	1955	New	s/s	5 ton capacity
	4wDC	G	3000	1960	New	s/s	5 ton capacity

C.A.E.C. HOWARD LTD, Bedford
Gauge : 4ft 8½in

	4wSC	G	700	1901	New	s/s	5 ton capacity

LAPORTE INDUSTRIES LTD, Luton
Gauge : 4ft 8½in

	4wSC	T&H		1899	(a)	s/s	

(a)   ex Arnold Ltd, Doncaster, /1922

HAYWARD TYLER & CO, Luton
Gauge : 4ft 8½in

	4wSC	TS	18539	1949	New	s/s	5 ton capacity

VAUXHALL MOTORS LTD, Luton
Gauge : 4ft 8½in

	4wSC	JB	5871	1952	(a)	s/s	5 ton capacity
	4wSC	JB	5872	1954	(b)	Scr c/1957 5 ton capy.	
	4wDEC	C				s/s	10 ton capacity

(a)   ex Joseph Booth, orig JB 5662/1950
(b)   ex Joseph Booth, orig JB 5663/1950

GREAT WHIPSNADE RAILWAY, Whipsnade Zoo
Gauge : 4ft 8½in

	4wDC	TS	10613	1936		(1)	5 ton capacity

(1)   scrapped on site c4/2000..

NORTHAMPTONSHIRE

BILLING GRAVEL CO LTD
Gauge : 4ft 8½in

	4wSC	T&H	1014	1922	(a)	s/s	3 ton capacity

(a)   ex Kinnear, Moodie

BLETCHLEY CONCRETE AGGREGATES, Thrapston

Gauge : 4ft 8½in

4wSC	TS	12440	1936	New	s/s	5 ton capacity

BRITISH LEYLAND UK LTD, Wellingborough

Gauge : 4ft 8½in

4wSC	G	799	1903	New	s/s	5 ton capacity

BRITISH STEEL CORPORATION, Corby Works

Gauge : 4ft 8½in

No.1	4wSC					s/s	
No.7	4wSC	TS				s/s	
No.15	4wSC	TS				s/s	
No.23	4wSC					s/s	
	4wSC	T&H	900	1919	(a)	s/s	3 ton capacity
	4wSC	TS	? 6516	c1910		(2)	5 ton capacity
	4wSC	TS				s/s	
	4wSC	JB	5805	1930	New	s/s	5 ton capacity
	4wSC	JB	6086	1953	New	s/s	5 ton capacity
	4wSC	TS	21058	1953	New	(1)	5 ton capacity
	4wDEC	TS	25317	1961	New		
	4w-4wDEC	TS	26213	1965	New	(3)	30 ton capacity

(a)   ex Yarrow & Co, Glasgow, /1934.

(1)   to Shackerstone Railway Society, Leics, /1975.

(2)   to Rutland Railway Museum, Cottesmore, Rutland, 16/1/1981.

(3)   to Hudsons of Dudley, Brierley Hill, West Midlands, /1992 (after 6/1992).

CEGB, Northampton Power Station

Gauge : 4ft 8½in

4wSC	PR	A1204	1920	New	s/s	5 ton capacity

COOK & SONS, Northampton

Gauge : 4ft 8½in ?

4wSC	TS	10628	1926	New	s/s	3 ton capacity

EAST MIDLANDS GAS BOARD, Northampton Works

Gauge : 4ft 8½in

4wSC	T&H	734	1915	New	s/s	3 ton capacity
4wSC	G	1883	1919	New	s/s	3 ton capacity
4wSC	G	2588	1941	New	s/s	5 ton capacity
4wSC	G	2736	1945	New	s/s	5 ton capacity

HIGGS & HILL LTD, Contractors, Wellingborough

Gauge : 4ft 8½in

	4wSC	I	4125		(1)	1½ ton capacity

(1)   to Mid Hants Railway, Ropley, Hampshire, 16/10/1976

JOHNSON & CO LTD, Kettering

Gauge : ?

	4wSC	T&H	B51	1900	New	s/s	1½ ton capacity
	4wSC	T&H	B54	1900	New	s/s	1½ ton capacity

KETTERING IRON & COAL CO LTD, Kettering Furnaces

Gauge : 4ft 8½in

	4wSC	G	937	1905	New	s/s	5 ton capacity
	4wSC	JB	2097	1907	(a)	s/s	

(a)   ex Riley, boilermakers, Stockton-on-Tees, /1912

SIR ROBERT McALPINE & SONS LTD, Kettering Plant Depot

Gauge : 4ft 8½in

	4w-4wSC	TS	16905	1946	New	s/s c/1980	10 ton capy.
	4w-4wSC	TS	19766	1952	New	s/s c/1980	10 ton capy.
	4wDC	TS	21417	1955	New	s/s c/1980	5 ton capy.
	4wDC	TS	21418	1955	New	s/s c/1980	5 ton capy.
	4wDC	TS	21419	1955	New	s/s c/1980	5 ton capy.
	4wDC	TS	21420	1955	New	s/s c/1980	5 ton capy.

BOROUGH OF NORTHAMPTON, Fish Street, Northampton

Gauge : 4ft 8½in

	4wSC	TS	7942	1911	New	s/s	3 ton capacity.

SHANKS & McEWAN LTD, Slag Contractor, Corby Steelworks

Gauge : 4ft 8½in

No.1	4wSC		s/s
No.27	4wSC		s/s

THRAPSTON WASHED SAND & BALLAST CO LTD, Thrapston Quarries

Gauge : ?

	4wSC	TS	11796	1953	New	s/s
	4wDMC	TS	24462	1957	New	s/s

IRCHESTER NARROW GAUGE RAILWAY TRUST, Irchester Country Park

Gauge : ?

4wHA		(a)	

(a)   ex MoDND, Milford Haven, Dyfed.

NORTHAMPTONSHIRE IRONSTONE RAILWAY TRUST, Hunsbury Hill

Gauge : 4ft 8½in

4wSC	G	2930	(a)	10 ton capacity

(a)   ex Redpath Dorman Long Ltd, Britannia Works, Cleveland, by 6/1972.

RUSHDEN HISTORICAL TRANSPORT SOCIETY, Rushden

Gauge : 4ft 8½in

4wSC	G	2733	1949	(a)	7 ton capacity

(a)   ex Southport Railway Centre, Lancs, /1989; orig NCB, Bold Colliery, Lancs.

INDEXES

Index of Locomotives

Index of Locomotive Names

Index of Locations and Owners

LOCOMOTIVE INDEX

NOTES : Information normally relates to the locomotive as built.

Column 1	Works Number (or original company running number for locomotives built in main line workshops without a works number).
Column 2	Date ex-works where known - this may be a later year than the year of building or the year recorded on the worksplate.
Column 3	Gauge.
Column 4	Wheel arrangement.

	Steam Locomotives :	**Diesel Locomotives :**
Column 5	Cylinder position	Horse power
Column 6	Cylinder size	Engine type #
Column 7	Driving wheel diameter	Weight in working order
Column 8	Either weight in working order and/or Manufacturers type designation	Page references
Column 9	Page references	

Manufacturers of petrol and diesel engines :

Ailsa	- Ailsa Craig Ltd, Salfords, Redhill, Surrey
Beardmore	- William Beardmore & Co Ltd, Parkhead, Glasgow
Blackstone	- Blackstone & Co Ltd, Rutland Engineering Works, Stamford, Lincs
Caterpillar	- Caterpillar Tractor Co Ltd
Cummins	- Cummins Engine Co Ltd, Shotts, Lanarkshire
Dorman	- W.H.Dorman & Co Ltd, Tixall Rd, Stafford
EE	- English Electric Co Ltd
Ferguson	- Harry Ferguson Ltd, Coventry
Ford	- Ford Motor Co Ltd, Dearborn, Michigan, USA
Fowler	- John Fowler & Co (Leeds) Ltd, Hunslet, Leeds
Gardner	- L. Gardner & Sons Ltd, Barton Hall Engine Works, Patricroft, Manchester
JAP	- J.A.Prestwich Industries Ltd, Northumberland Park, Tottenham, London
Leyland	- Leyland Motors Ltd, Leyland, Lancashire
Lister	- R.A. Lister & Co Ltd, Dursley, Gloucestershire
MAN	- Maschinenfabrik Augsurg-Nürnburg AG, Germany
McLaren	- J. & H. McLaren Ltd, Midland Engineering Works, Leeds
National	- National Gas & Oil Engine Co Ltd,Ashton-under-Lyne, Lancashire
Paxman	- Davey, Paxman & Co Ltd, Colchester,Essex
Perkins	Perkins Engine Co Ltd, Peterborough, Northants
Petters	- Petters Ltd, Staines, Middx
R-R	- Rolls-Royce Ltd, Oil Engine Division, Shrewsbury
Ruston	- Ruston & Hornsby Ltd, Lincoln
Saurer	- Armstrong Saurer Ltd, Newcastle upon Tyne

43	1866	4ft 8½in	0-4-0ST	OC	10 x 17	3ft0in	264
306	27.7.1888	4ft 8½in	0-4-0ST	OC	12 x 20	3ft2in	264,304
678	22.9.1890	4ft 8½in	0-4-0ST	OC	14 x 22	3ft7in	210
699	22.7.1891	4ft 8½in	0-4-0ST	OC	11 x 18	3ft0in	103,192
762	21.10.1895	4ft 8½in	0-4-0ST	OC	14 x 22	3ft5in	209
776	23.11.1896	4ft 8½in	0-4-0ST	OC	13 x 20	3ft2in	103,125,192
811	29.12.1897	4ft 8½in	0-4-0ST	OC	14 x 22	3ft5in	209
859	28.2.1900	4ft 8½in	0-4-0ST	OC	14 x 22	3ft5in	248
919	14.3.1902	4ft 8½in	0-4-0ST	OC	10 x 18	3ft0in	145
984	26.11.1903	2ft 6in	0-4-0T	OC	7 x 10	2ft0in	183,191
1027	28.10.1904	4ft 8½in	0-4-0ST	OC	12 x 20	3ft6in	264,304
1034	22.12.1904	4ft 8½in	0-4-0ST	OC	13½x20	3ft8in	209
1047	16.6.1905	4ft 8½in	0-4-0ST	OC	14 x 22	3ft5in	221,224,230
1065	3.9.1906	4ft 8½in	0-4-0ST	OC	14 x 22	3ft5in	245,284
1241	4.3.1911	4ft 8½in	0-6-0ST	OC	14 x 22	3ft5in	210,284
1242	3.4.1911	4ft 8½in	0-6-0ST	OC	14 x 22	3ft5in	210
1268	10.6.1912	4ft 8½in	0-6-0ST	OC	14 x 22	3ft5in	210
1318	28.10.1913	4ft 8½in	0-4-0ST	OC	16 x 24	3ft7in	210
1333	3.8.1914	4ft 8½in	0-4-0ST	OC	14 x 22	3ft5in	262,278,285
1361	23.12.1913	4ft 8½in	0-4-0ST	OC	14 x 22	3ft5in	278
1363	19.1.1914	4ft 8½in	0-4-0ST	OC	16 x 24	3ft7in	221,232
1398	7.9.1915	4ft 8½in	0-4-0ST	OC	10 x 18	3ft0in	114,155
1457	29.12.1915	4ft 8½in	0-6-0ST	OC	14 x 22	3ft5in	210
1466	28.7.1916	4ft 8½in	0-4-0ST	OC	14 x 22	3ft5in	276
1477	12.10.1916	4ft 8½in	0-4-0F	OC	15 x 20	3ft0in	103,137
1479	19.6.1917	4ft 8½in	0-4-0ST	OC	14 x 22	3ft5in	210,284
1492	27.12.1916	4ft 8½in	0-4-0F	OC	15 x 20	3ft0in	137,233
1493	27.12.1916	4ft 8½in	0-4-0F	OC	15 x 20	3ft0in	103,137
1497	11.12.1916	4ft 8½in	0-6-0ST	OC	14 x 22	3ft5in	221,224,233
1592	5.6.1918	4ft 8½in	0-4-0ST	OC	14 x 22	3ft5in	284
1609	30.9.1918	4ft 8½in	0-4-0ST	OC	16 x 24	3ft7in	221,232
1641	1.8.1919	2ft 0in	0-6-0T	OC	7 x 14	2ft2½in	186
1645	8.12.1919	4ft 8½in	0-4-0ST	OC	14 x 22	3ft5in	284
1658	15.4.1920	4ft 8½in	0-4-0ST	OC	10 x 18	3ft0in	258
1711	20.4.1921	4ft 8½in	0-4-0ST	OC	12 x 20	3ft2in	56,232
1826	4.4.1924	4ft 8½in	0-4-0ST	OC	16 x 24	3ft7in	284
1828	16.4.1924	4ft 8½in	0-4-0ST	OC	12 x 20	3ft2in	125
1855	30.3.1931	2ft 0in	0-4-0WT	OC	7 x 11	1ft10in	289
1865	15.3.1926	4ft 8½in	0-4-0ST	OC	12 x 20	3ft2in	103,192
1995	30.11.1931	2ft 0in	0-4-0WT	OC	7 x 11	1ft11½in	289
2015	29.8.1935	4ft 8½in	0-4-0ST	OC	12 x 20	3ft2in	61,103,125,192
2063	3.2.1939	4ft 8½in	0-4-0ST	OC	16 x 24	3ft7in	284
2069	17.7.1939	4ft 8½in	0-4-0ST	OC	14 x 22	3ft5in	128,129
2088	28.5.1940	4ft 8½in	0-4-0ST	OC	14 x 22	3ft5in	129
2101	24.6.1940	4ft 8½in	0-4-0ST	OC	16 x 24	3ft7in	221,224,231
2129	17.11.1941	4ft 8½in	0-4-0ST	OC	14 x 22	3ft5in	278
2135	27.1.1941	4ft 8½in	0-4-0ST	OC	16 x 24	3ft7in	211,284
2136	3.9.1941	4ft 8½in	0-4-0ST	OC	16 x 24	3ft7in	284
2138	29.12.1941	4ft 8½in	0-6-0ST	OC	14 x 22	3ft5in	92,103,220,270
2143	28.8.1942	4ft 8½in	0-4-0ST	OC	14 x 22	3ft5in	224,233,275
2168	14.12.1943	4ft 8½in	0-4-0ST	OC	16 x 24	3ft7in	129,325

2207	.1946	2ft 6in	0-4-0T	OC	7 x 10	2ft0in		185
2243	14.7.1948	4ft 8½in	0-4-0F	OC	15 x 18	3ft0in		103,137
2323	25.2.1952	4ft 8½in	0-4-0ST	OC	16 x 24	3ft7in		222,318,325,326
2324	3.3.1952	4ft 8½in	0-4-0ST	OC	16 x 24	3ft7in		222,233
2352	1.7.1954	4ft 8½in	0-4-0ST	OC	14 x 22	3ft5in		128
2353	6.9.1954	4ft 8½in	0-4-0ST	OC	14 x 22	3ft5in		129
2354	23.9.1954	4ft 8½in	0-4-0ST	OC	14 x 22	3ft5in		128
2365	15.2.1955	4ft 8½in	0-4-0ST	OC	14 x 22	3ft5in		129,275

342	13.9.1940	4ft 8½in	0-4-0DM	153hp		Gardner 6L3	233
357	29.9.1941	4ft 8½in	0-4-0DM	153hp		Gardner 6L3	282
361	11.2.1942	4ft 8½in	0-4-0DM	153hp		Gardner 6L3	259
362	26.2.1942	4ft 8½in	0-4-0DM	153hp		Gardner 6L3	259,282
363	2.4.1942	4ft 8½in	0-4-0DM	153hp		Gardner 6L3	175,325
367	1.10.1945	4ft 8½in	6wDE	350hp		Paxman 8cyl [CP 101]	211
369	11.5.1945	4ft 8½in	0-4-0DM	153hp		Gardner 6L3	156
370	22.6.1945	4ft 8½in	0-4-0DM	153hp		Gardner 6L3	156
413	14.6.1957	4ft 8½in	0-4-0DM	204hp		Gardner 8L3	129,175
422	1.4.1958	4ft 8½in	0-6-0DM	204hp		Gardner 8L3	259
476	10.3.1961	4ft 8½in	0-4-0DH	120hp		R-R C4NFL	214
499	29.7.1965	4ft 8½in	0-4-0DH	240hp		Cummins NH250	264
632	21.3.1978	2ft 0in	4wDH	90hp	Perkins 6354 [HE 8518]		312

AVONSIDE ENGINE CO LTD, Bristol   AE

1395	.1898	4ft 8½in	0-6-0ST	OC	14 x 20	3ft3in		269
1435	1901	4ft 8½in	0-4-0ST	OC	14 x 20	3ft3in	SS	264
1694	1915	4ft 8½in	0-6-0ST	OC	14½x20	3ft3in	B4	219
1727	1916	4ft 8½in	0-6-0ST	OC	14½x20	3ft3in	B4	269
1738	1916	1ft 11½in	0-4-0T	OC	8½x12	2ft0in	2815	184,189
1748	1916	1ft6in	0-4-0T	OC	8½x12	2ft1in	2814	310
1787	1917	4ft 8½in	0-6-0ST	OC	14½x20	3ft3in	B4	221
1822	19.3.1919	4ft 8½in	0-4-0ST	OC	14 x 20	3ft4in	SS3	232
1825	31.5.1919	4ft 8½in	0-6-0ST	OC	15 x 22	3ft3in		269
1830	15.7.1919	4ft 8½in	0-4-0ST	OC	14 x 20	3ft4in	SS3	254
1832	14.10.1919	4ft 8½in	0-6-0ST	OC	15 x 20	3ft6in	B4	233
1849	12.4.1920	4ft 8½in	0-6-0ST	OC	14½x20	3ft3in	B4	245
1865	4.5.1922	4ft 8½in	0-4-0ST	OC	14½x20	3ft3in	SS4	101
1869	15.6.1921	4ft 8½in	0-6-0ST	OC	14½x20	3ft3in	B5	223,269
1875	5.2.1921	4ft 8½in	0-4-0ST	OC	12 x 18	2ft11in	Std	158
1917	31.12.1923	4ft 8½in	0-6-0ST	OC	15 x 20	3ft6in	B5	101,228
1918	31.12.1923	4ft 8½in	0-6-0ST	OC	15 x 20	3ft6in	B5	218
1919	19.3.1924	4ft 8½in	0-6-0ST	OC	14½x20	3ft6in	B5	218,227
1972	23.2.1927	4ft 8½in	0-6-0ST	OC	15 x 20	3ft6in	B5	218
1973	12.1.1927	4ft 8½in	0-4-0ST	OC	14½x20	3ft3in	SS4	321
2054	21.2.1930	Metre	0-6-0ST	OC	12 x 18	2ft8½in		273
2068	22.5.1933	4ft 8½in	0-6-0ST	OC	15 x 20	3ft6in		100,103,223
2072	30.6.1933	2ft 0in	0-4-0T	OC	7½x 12	2ft0in		289
2073	6.7.1933	2ft 0in	0-4-0T	OC	7½x 12	2ft0in		289

ALAN KEEF LTD, Bampton, Oxon / Lea Line, Hereford & Worcs   AK

	c4.1982	1ft 8in	4-6-4DH		[reb of HC D570]	185
14	31.7.1984	2ft 0in	4wDH	S/O	Lister TS31	314

15	20.12.1984	2ft 0in	4wDH	20hp	Petter P600/2			314
28	19.6.1989	2ft 0in	4wDM	40hp	Deutz F3L912			189
38	14.12.1991	600mm	0-4-0T	OC	7 x 10 1ft7in			189
# 59R	26.6.1999	2ft 0in	4wDH	112hp	Dorman			187

\# - rebuild of SMH 101T019

AVELING & PORTER LTD, INVICTA WORKS, Rochester, Kent   AP

807	24.1.1872	4ft 8½in	4wWT	G	7¾x10		6hp	69,246
846	22.6.1872	4ft 8½in	4wWT	G	7¾x10		6hp	69,246
3567	26.7.1895	4ft 8½in	4wWT	G	7&13x13		10hp	103,192
3730	22.6.1896	4ft 8½in	4wWT	G	7½&11½x12	10hp		162
5935	25.1.1906	4ft 8½in	4wWT	G	9&14x14		8hp	62,64,143,176
6158	20.12.1906	4ft 8½in	4wWT	G	16¼&10x14			101
8800	12.1.1917	4ft 8½in	4wWT	G	8&13x14			103,106,322,325
9449	4.2.1926	4ft 8½in	2-2-0WT	G	11 x 12		10hp	103,322
11087	27.4.1927	4ft 8½in	4wWT	G				158,162

ATKINSON WALKER WAGONS LTD, FRENCHWOOD WORKS, Preston, Lancs   AtW

109	1928	4ft 8½in	4wVBT	G	7 x 10	3ft0in	Type A	286

23 AUGUST WORKS, Bucharest, Romania   AUG

24376	.1981	2ft 0in	0-6-0DH	184

SIR W G ARMSTRONG, WHITWORTH & CO LTD, SCOTSWOOD WORKS, Newcastle-upon-Tyne   AW

D58	9.1936	4ft 8½in	0-6-0DE	375hp	309

BARCLAYS & CO, RIVER BANK ENGINE WORKS, Kilmarnock   B

255	1878	2ft 6in	0-6-0ST	OC	9 x ?	2ft6in	235
318	1885	4ft 8½in	0-4-0ST	OC	13 x 20		264

BRUSH BAGNALL TRACTION   BBT
Built jointly by **Brush Traction Ltd**, Loughborough & **W G Bagnall Ltd**, Stafford

3094	11.1955	4ft 8½in	0-6-0DE	300hp	Mirlees TL6	211
3095	3.1956	4ft 8½in	0-6-0DE	300hp	Mirlees TL6	211

BAGULEY DREWRY LTD, Burton-on-Trent, Staffs   BD

3708	30.6.1975	4ft 8½in	4wDMR	75hp	Perkins P4	249
3746	3.2.1977	4ft 8½in	4wDMR	75hp	Perkins P4	249

BRUSH ELECTRICAL ENGINEERING CO LTD, Loughborough — BE

308	.1904	3ft 6in	0-4-0Tram OC	7½ x 12		73

BRITISH ELECTRIC VEHICLES LTD, Southport — BEV

78	17.3.1919	3ft 0in	4wBE	2hp	No.1 Type	277
79	31.3.1919	3ft 0in	4wBE	2hp	No.1 Type	277
156	17.11.1919	3ft 0in	4wBE	2hp	No.1 Type	277
157	28.2.1920	3ft 0in	4wBE	2hp	No.1 Type	277
252	19.5.1920	3ft 0in	4wBE	2hp	No.1 Type	277
253	28.5.1920	3ft 0in	4wBE	2hp	No.1 Type	277
254	30.8.1920	3ft 0in	4wBE	2hp	No.1 Type	277
255	23.8.1920	3ft 0in	4wBE	2hp	No.1 Type	277
374	27.1.1922	3ft 0in	4wBE	2hp	No.1 Type	277
375	28.1.1922	3ft 0in	4wBE	4.8hp	No.1 Type	277
376	31.1.1922	3ft 0in	4wBE	4.8hp	No.1 Type	277
377	31.1.1922	3ft 0in	4wBE	2hp	No.1 Type	277
378	31.1.1922	3ft 0in	4wBE	2hp	No.1 Type	277
379	31.1.1922	3ft 0in	4wBE	2hp	No.1 Type	277

BAGULEY CARS LTD, Burton-on-Trent, Staffs — BgC

608	4.4.1918	600mm	0-4-0PM	10hp	Baguley 2cyl	206
760	14.11.1918	2ft 0in	0-4-0PM	10hp	Baguley	100,119,185

BAGULEY (ENGINEERS) LTD, Burton-on-Trent, Staffs — BgE

2007	28.11.1921	2ft 0in	0-4-0T	OC	4 x 8	1ft3½in	186
2042	4.1931	2ft 0in	0-4-0DM	S/O	25hp	Perkins	326
2043	4.1931	2ft 0in	0-4-0DM	S/O	25hp	Perkins	326
2071	10.1931	4ft 8½in	4wDM		25hp	Ford	263

E. E. BAGULEY LTD, Burton-on-Trent, Staffs — Bg

2108	10.1937	2ft 0in	4wDM	16hp	Ailsa Craig 2cyl	239
2137	30.7.1938	2ft 0in	4wDM	16hp	Ailsa Craig 2cyl	23
2155	1940	2ft 0in	4wDM	16hp	Ailsa Craig 2cyl	23
2202	1945	2ft 0in	4wDM	16hp	Ailsa Craig 2cyl	23
3002	1937	2ft 0in	4wPM	10hp	Ford	189
3027	10.12.1939	4ft 8½in	0-4-0DM	85hp	Gardner 4L3	101
3538	16.11.1959	4ft 8½in	4wDMR	35hp	Perkins P4	101
3539	19.11.1959	2ft 0in	4wDHR	35hp	Perkins P4	187

BLACK, HAWTHORN & CO LTD, Gateshead — BH

415	27.5.1878	4ft 8½in	0-6-0ST	OC	14 x 20	3ft6in	301
422	13.5.1878	4ft 8½in	0-4-0ST	OC	12 x 19	3ft2in	245

423	1.6.1878	4ft 8½in	0-4-0ST	OC	12 x 19	3ft2in		301
466	12.12.1878	4ft 8½in	0-6-0ST	OC	12 x 19	3ft2in		299,301
467	25.6.1878	4ft 8½in	0-6-0ST	OC	13 x 19	3ft2in		301
471	1.7.1878	4ft 8½in	0-6-0ST	OC	13 x 19	3ft2in		287,306
501	8.2.1879	3ft 0in	0-4-0ST	OC	8 x 14	2ft6in		245
758	27.8.1883	4ft 8½in	0-6-0ST	OC	12 x 19	3ft2in		302
859	26.8.1885	3ft 0in	0-4-0ST	OC	8 x 14	2ft6in		245
893	1.3.1887	3ft 0in	0-4-0ST	OC	6 x 10	2ft0in		245
984	31.1.1890	4ft 8½in	0-4-0ST	OC	14 x 19	3ft2in		245
1045	11.9.1891	4ft 8½in	0-4-0ST	OC	14 x 19	3ft2in		255
1046	7.11.1892	3ft 0in	0-4-0ST	OC	8 x 14	2ft6in		226
1099	21.7.1894	4ft 8½in	0-4-0ST	OC	10 x 17	2ft11in		52
1105	21.5.1895	4ft 8½in	0-6-0ST	OC	14 x 20	3ft7in		302

Note that the dates quoted for this builder are order dates rather than delivery dates.

W.J. BASSETT LOWKE LTD, Northampton BL

	.1909	1ft 3in	4-4-4PM	314

BLACKWELL & SON, Northampton Blackwell

	.1922	4ft 8½in	4wVBT	HCG	141

BALDWIN LOCOMOTIVE WORKS, Philadelphia, U S A BLW

44656	1916	2ft 0in	4-6-0T	OC	186

BEYER, PEACOCK & CO LTD, GORTON FOUNDRY, Manchester BP

1414	3.6.1874	4ft 8½in	2-4-0WT	OC	16½x20	5ft7in	102
8039	9.1965	4ft 8½in	Bo-Bo.DE	1250hp	Sulzer 6LDA28	76T	321

BIRMINGHAM RAILWAY CARRIAGE & WAGON CO LTD, Smethwick
BRCW

[LT 53028]	1937	4ft 8½in	2w-2-2-2wRER				104
DEL55	1.1959	4ft 8½in	Bo-Bo.DE	1160hp	Sulzer 6LDA28	72½T	320
DEL213	1.1962	4ft 8½in	Bo-Bo.DE	1160hp	Sulzer 6LDA28	72½T	320
DEL244	7.1962	4ft 8½in	Bo-Bo.DE	1160hp	Sulzer 6LDA28	72½T	320

ROWLAND BROTHERHOOD, Chippenham, Wilts R.Bro

	c1866	4ft 8½in	0-4-0ST	OC	236

BRIGHTON WORKS, Sussex (LBSCR / SR / BR) Bton

[LBSCR 57]	1.1876	4ft 8½in	0-6-0T	IC	12 x 20	4ft0in	28T	65
[LBSCR 52]	2.1876	4ft 8½in	0-6-0T	IC	12 x 20	4ft0in	28T	85
[LBSCR 49]	12.1876	4ft 8½in	0-6-0T	IC	12 x 20	4ft0in	28T	85
[LBSCR 39]	5.1878	4ft 8½in	0-6-0T	IC	12 x 20	4ft0in	28T	85
[LBSCR 36]	6.1878	4ft 8½in	0-6-0T	IC	12 x 20	4ft0in	28T	85
[BR 34016]	1945	4ft 8½in	4-6-2	3C	16¾x24	6ft2in		102

BURY, CURTIS & KENNEDY, Liverpool   Bury

	1848	4ft 8½in	0-4-2	IC		298

NEI MINING EQUIPMENT LTD, CLAYTON EQUIPMENT, Hatton, Derbys   CE
Originally **CLARKE CHAPMAN LTD.**
Note that, to save space, batches of locomotives are indexed as single entries. For example, 5792A-D refers to locomotives 5792A, 5792B, 5792C and 5792D.

5370	1968	1ft 6in	4wBE		2½T	97
5427	14.6.1968	4ft 8½in	4wDMR	38hp Perkins 3152	3T	249
5806	10.1970	1ft 6in	4wBE	7hp	1¾T	173
5827	1970	1ft 6in	4wBE	7hp	1¾T	77
5858	1.1971	1ft 6in	4wBE	7hp	1¾T	77
5940B	6.1972	2ft0in	4wBE	7hp	1¾T	173
5942A-C	6.1972	1ft 6in	4wBE	7hp	1¾T	173
5961A-D	.1972	2ft 0in	4wBE	7hp	1¾T	88
5965A-C	1.1973	1ft 6in	4wBE	7hp	1¾T	78
B0107A-B	2.1973	2ft 0in	4wBE	7hp	1¾T	88
B0113A-B	4.1973	2ft 0in	4wBE	7hp	1¾T	88
B0156	1973	2ft 0in	4wBE	14hp	3½T	173
B0176A	2.1974	2ft 0in	4wBE	14hp	3T	173
B0182A-C	1974	2ft 0in	4wBE	14hp	3T	96,173
B0402A/C	1974	2ft 0in	4wBE	21hp	4T	173
B0943	1976	2ft 0in	4wBE	14hp	3½T	169
B1534A	6.1977	2ft 0in	4wBE	25hp	5½T	173
B1559	1977	2ft 0in	4wBE	14hp	3½T	96
B1563Q	.1978	2ft 6in	4wDH	78hp Dtz F6L912	7¼T	172
B1808	1978	1ft 6in	4wBE	14hp	3½T	172
B3070A-D #	1983	2ft 0in	4wBE	21hp	3½T	89
B3204A	1985	3ft 0in	4wBEF	17½hp	4T CRT3½ Pony	172
B3214A	1985	2ft 0in	4wBE	14hp (reb of CE B1808)	3½T	69,96
B3214B	1985	2ft 0in	4wBE	14hp (reb of CE B1559)	3½T	89,96,172
B3329B	1986	2ft 0in	4wBE	25hp	5½T	173
B3686B	7.1990	2ft 0in	4wBE	25hp	5½T	173
B3825	1992	2ft 0in	4wBE	14hp (reb of CE B3214A)	3½T	172
B4056A-F	2.1995	2ft 6in	4wBE	50hp	9T	172
B4057A	13.12.1994	750mm	4wBE	25hp	5½T	295
B4057B	13.12.1994	750mm	4wBE	25hp	5½T	295

ex-works dates - B3070A 24.6.1983, B3070B 25.7.1983 and B3070C & D 12.8.1983.

CHAPMAN & FURNEAUX LTD, Gateshead   CF
(Successors to **Black, Hawthorn & Co Ltd**)

1194	1900	4ft 8½in	0-4-0ST	OC	14 x 19	3ft2in	231,255,273
1195	1900	4ft 8½in	0-4-0ST	OC	14 x 19	3ft2in	221

ALEXANDER CHAPLIN & CO LTD, CRANSTONHILL WORKS, Glasgow Chaplin

1056	28.7.1869	4ft 8½in	0-4-0VBT	VC	6 x 13	[12hp]	206,229, 257,310
2368	22.12.1885	4ft 8½in	0-4-0VBT	VC	7 x 12	2ft1½in [15hp]	238

FABRYKA LOKOMOTYW "F DZIERZYNSKIEGO", Chrzanow, Poland — Chr

3112	1952	4ft 8½in	0-6-0T	OC	320
3459	1957	2ft 0in	0-6-0WTT	OC	189
5374	1959	4ft 8½in	0-6-0T	OC	320

CLAY CROSS CO LTD, Clay Cross, Derbys — Clay Cross

	c1927	4ft 0in	4wPE	225

SOCIETE JOHN COCKERILL, Seraing, Belgium — Cockerill

2945	1920	4ft 8½in	0-4-0VBT	OC	320,322

CORPET, LOUVET & CIE, La Courneuve, Seine, France — Corpet

493	1888	Metre	0-6-0T	OC	273,318

CROMPTON PARKINSON LTD, Chelmsford, Essex — CP

101	1945	4ft 8½in	6wDE	[AB 367]	211

CREWE WORKS, Cheshire (LNWR / LMSR / BR) — Crewe

186	6.1851	4ft 8½in	2-4-0	IC	15 x 20	5ft0in		55
204	3.1851	4ft 8½in	2-4-0	IC	15 x 20	5ft0in		55
217	8.1852	4ft 8½in	2-4-0	IC	15 x 20	5ft0in		55
228	11.1852	4ft 8½in	2-4-0	IC	15 x 20	5ft0in		55
1944	10.1875	4ft 8½in	0-6-0ST	IC	17 x 24	4ft5½in		55
2107	4.1877	4ft 8½in	0-6-0ST	IC	17 x 24	4ft5½in		55
2200	8.1878	4ft 8½in	0-6-0ST	IC	17 x 24	4ft5½in		55
2308	12.1879	4ft 8½in	0-6-0ST	IC	17 x 24	4ft5½in		55
2342	4.1880	4ft 8½in	0-6-0ST	IC	17 x 24	4ft5½in		55
3437	11.1894	4ft 8½in	0-4-2CST	IC	14 x 20	4ft0in	33T	55
3438	11.1894	4ft 8½in	0-4-2CST	IC	14 x 20	4ft0in	33T	55
[BR 46447]	3.1950	4ft 8½in	2-6-0	OC	16 x 24	5ft0in		102
[BR 41298]	10.1951	4ft 8½in	2-6-2T	OC	16½x24	5ft0in		102
[BR 41312]	5.1952	4ft 8½in	2-6-2T	OC	16½x24	5ft0in		106
[BR 41313]	5.1952	4ft 8½in	2-6-2T	OC	16½x24	5ft0in		102
[BR D67]	5.1962	4ft 8½in	1Co-Co1.DE					320

DICK & STEVENSON, AIRDRIE ENGINE WORKS, Airdrie — D&S

58	c1875	4ft 8½in	0-4-0ST	OC	280,290

DARLINGTON WORKS, Co Durham (NER / LNER / BR) — Dar

[BR D5185]	5.1963	4ft 8½in	Bo-Bo.DE	1250hp	Sulzer 6LDA28B		320

DREWRY CAR CO LTD, London (Suppliers only) DC

2047	1933	4ft 8½in	0-4-0DM	[EE 874]	156
2108	10.1937	2ft 0in	4wDM	[Bg 2108]	239
2137	30.7.1938	2ft 0in	4wDM	[Bg 2137]	239
2155	1940	2ft 0in	4wDM	[Bg 2155]	239
2161	1941	4ft 8½in	0-4-0DM	[EE 1192]	103
2169	22.1.1943	4ft 8½in	0-4-0DM	[VF 4861]	249
2170	22.1.1943	4ft 8½in	0-4-0DM	[VF 4862]	249
2171	1942	4ft 8½in	0-4-0DM	[VF 4863]	249
2172	22.2.1943	4ft 8½in	0-4-0DM	[VF 4864]	249
2202	1945	2ft 0in	4wDM	[Bg 2202]	239
2565	6.1956	4ft 8½in	0-6-0DM	[VF D291]	231
2566	1955	4ft 8½in	0-4-0DM	[VF D293]	194
2679	9.1960	4ft 8½in	0-6-0DM	[RSHD 8157]	103
2705	4.1961	4ft 8½in	0-6-0DM	[RSHD 8183]	54
2715	7.1961	4ft 8½in	0-6-0DM	[RSHD 8193]	319

DREWRY CAR CO LTD / E.E. BAGULEY LTD DC/Bg

1896	1950	4ft 8½in	2w-2PMR	249
2326	1950	4ft 8½in	2w-2PMR	249

SOCIETE DECAUVILLE AINE, Corbeil, France Decauville

1126	1950	2ft 0in	0-4-0T	OC	189

DERBY WORKS (Midland Rly / LMSR / BR) Derby

[MR 1708]	1880	4ft 8½in	0-6-0T	IC	17 x 24	4ft7in	106,182
[WD 273]	1945	4ft 8½in	0-6-0DE	350hp	EE 6KT		282
[BR 73080]	1955	4ft 8½in	4-6-0	OC	19 x 28	6ft2in	106
[BR D3796]	11.1959	4ft 8½in	0-6-0DE	350hp	EE 6KT		70
[BR D5207]	22.6.1963	4ft 8½in	Bo-Bo.DE	1250hp	Sulzer 6LDA-28B		103

DERBY CARRIAGE & WAGON WORKS (BR) DerbyC&W

[BR 51886]	9.1960	4ft 8½in	2-2w-2w-2DMR	104
[BR 51899]	12.1960	4ft 8½in	2-2w-2w-2DMR	104

DESBOROUGH CO-OPERATIVE SOCIETY LTD Desborough

4ft 8½in	4wPM	207

DeWINTON & CO, UNION FOUNDRY, Caernarvon DeW

1877	2ft 0in	0-4-0VBT	VC	6 x12	1ft8in	100,186

DIEPHOLZER MASCHINENFABRIK (Fr SCHOTTLER Gmbh), Diepholz, Germany Diema

568	28.51930	2ft 0in	4wDM		LR10	60
1600	24.8.1953	2ft 0in	4wDM	16hp	DS16	194

DICK, KERR & CO LTD, BRITANNIA ENGINEERING WORKS, Kilmarnock
DK

	1918	3ft 0in	0-4-0T	OC	8 x 14 2ft5in	272

DONCASTER WORKS, (BR)
Don

[BR D2084]	3.1959	4ft 8½in	0-6-0DM	204hp	Gardner 8L3	31T	319
[LTE L44]	1973	4ft 8½in	4w-4w.BE/RE				106

MOTORENFABRIK DEUTZ AG, Köln, Germany
Dtz

10248	27.8.1931	2ft 0in	4wDM	PME117F	189

EDGE HILL WORKSHOPS, Liverpool & Manchester Railway
Edge Hill

	c1845	4ft 8½in	2-4-0ST	IC	13 x 20 3ft6in	174

ENGLISH ELECTRIC CO LTD, DICK, KERR WORKS, Preston
EE

687	1925	4ft 8½in	4wBE			115
750	1929	2ft 11in	4wWE	40hp		147
751	1929	2ft 11in	4wWE	40hp		147
776	1930	2ft 11in	4wWE	40hp		62,150
791	1930	2ft 11in	4wWE	40hp		147
792	1930	2ft 11in	4wWE	40hp		147
803	1931	2ft 0in	2w-2-2-2wRE			107
874	1933	4ft 8½in	0-4-0DM		[DC 2047]	156
899	1935	4ft 8½in	4wWE	40hp		143
904	1935	2ft 11in	6wWE			143
1086	1937	2ft 11in	6wWE			143
1192	1941	4ft 8½in	0-4-0DM	153hp	Gardner 6L3 [DC 2161]	103

ENGLISH ELECTRIC CO LTD, VULCAN WORKS, Newton-le-Willows
EEV

D911	1964	4ft 8½in	0-6-0DH	455hp	Dorman 8QAT	217
D913	4.12.1964	4ft 8½in	0-6-0DH	447hp	Paxman 8RPHXL	211
D914	11.12.1964	4ft 8½in	0-6-0DH	447hp	Paxman 8RPHXL	211
D915	23.12.1964	4ft 8½in	0-6-0DH	447hp	Paxman 8RPHXL	211
D916	7.1.1965	4ft 8½in	0-6-0DH	447hp	Paxman 8RPHXL	211
D1048	1.6.1965	4ft 8½in	0-6-0DH	447hp	Paxman 8RPHXL	211
D1049	14.6.1965	4ft 8½in	0-6-0DH	447hp	Paxman 8RPHXL	211
D1050	17.6.1965	4ft 8½in	0-6-0DH	447hp	Paxman 8RPHXL	211
D1051	30.6.1965	4ft 8½in	0-6-0DH	447hp	Paxman 8RPHXL	211
D1052	6.7.1965	4ft 8½in	0-6-0DH	447hp	Paxman 8RPHXL	211
D1053	13.7.1965	4ft 8½in	0-6-0DH	447hp	Paxman 8RPHXL	211
D1122	1966	4ft 8½in	0-4-0DH	305hp	Cummins NHRS6B1	125
3970	23.12.1969	4ft 8½in	0-6-0DH	447hp	Paxman 8RPHXL	211
3971	31.12.1969	4ft 8½in	0-6-0DH	447hp	Paxman 8RPHXL	211
3990	1970	4ft 8½in	0-6-0DH	344hp	Dorman 6QT	264
5354	8.4.1971	4ft 8½in	0-6-0DH	447hp	Paxman 8RPHXL	211

5355	30.4.1971	4ft 8½in	0-6-0DH	447hp	Paxman 8RPHXL			211
5356	12.5.1971	4ft 8½in	0-6-0DH	447hp	Paxman 8RPHXL			211
5357	13.5.1971	4ft 8½in	0-6-0DH	447hp	Paxman 8RPHXL			211
5358	3.6.1971	4ft 8½in	0-6-0DH	447hp	Paxman 8RPHXL			211

EASTLEIGH WORKS, Hants (BR)   Elh

[BR S13004S]	1949	4ft 8½in	4w-4w.RER					320,322

EBBW VALE STEEL, IRON & COAL CO LTD, Ebbw Vale, Mon.   EV

3	1909	4ft 8½in	0-4-0ST	OC				275,276

FALCON ENGINE & CAR WORKS LTD, Loughborough   FE

	c1882	2ft 6in	0-4-0ST	OC				135
184	1889	4ft 8½in	0-4-0ST	OC				240,262,283

F.C. HIBBERD & CO LTD, Park Royal, London   FH

1568	10.1927	2ft 0in	4wPM	10hp				187
1657	3.1930	2ft 0in	4wPM	20SX	Meadows 4EC	1¾T		71
1668	4.1930	2ft 0in	4wPM	10hp	Meadows 4EC			157
1669	5.1930	2ft 0in	4wPM	10hp	Meadows			244,292
1676	4.1930	2ft 0in	4wPM	6hp				157
1702	8.1930	2ft 0in	4wPM	20hp	Meadows 4EH	2½T		255
1703	8.1930	2ft 0in	4wPM	20hp	Meadows 4EH	2½T		255
1711	10.1930	2ft 0in	4wPM	20hp	Meadows 4EH	2½T		255
1767	7.1931	2ft 0in	4wPM	20SX	Dorman 2JOR	2½T		194
1776	22.10.1931	2ft 0in	4wPM	20SX	Dorman 2JOR	3½T		189
1823	30.6.1933	2ft 0in	4wDM	10/14hp	Lister	2½T		146
1835	5.10.1933	2ft 0in	4wPM	20SX	Dorman 2JO	2½T		72
1851	2.1934	2ft 0in	4wPM	20SX	Dorman 2JO	2½T		116
1853	13.3.1934	4ft 8½in	4wDM	30D	National 3D	6T		160
1856	4.1934	1ft 11½in	4wPM	10R	Meadows 4EC	1¾T		267
1893	10.1934	2ft 0in	4wDM	20SXRD	National 2D	2½T		116
1911	2.1935	1ft 10½in	4wDM	20SXD	National 2D	2½T		151,179
1913	4.1935	2ft 11in	4wDM	20SXD	National 2D	4T		
								65,141,147,149
1914	4.1935	2ft 11in	4wDM	20SXD	National 2D	4T		
								65,141,147,148,149
1917	5.1935	2ft 0in	4wDM	20SXD	National 2D	2½T		117
1922	11.5.1935	2ft 0in	4wPM	20SX	Dorman 2JO	2½T		117
1960	11.1935	2ft 0in	4wPM	20SXR	Dorman 2JO	2½T		116
1977	7.1936	4ft 8½in	4wDM	55H	Paxman 5RQ	13T		160
2016	1.1937	4ft 8½in	4wDM	40H	Paxman 4RQ	9T		224
2051	6.1937	2ft 0in	4wDM	25hp	Paxman 2RQT	2½T		146
2102	27.5.1938	4ft 8½in	4wDM	70H	Paxman 6RQT	18T		57,103
2151	3.1940	4ft 8½in	0-4-0DM	135D	Paxman 6RWT	24T		180
2161	30.11.1938	2ft 0in	4wDM	25SXR	Paxman 2QRT	2½T		117
2196	2.1940	2ft 6in	4wDMR		Vixen CUB 4-seat railcar	2¾T		108
2288	7.1940	2ft 0in	4wDM	20SXD	National 2D	2½T		117

2514	4.1941	1ft 11½in	4wDM	20D	National 2D	2¾T			186
2586	9.1941	1ft 11½in	4wDM	20SX	Paxman 2QRT	2½T			107,187
2631	2.1943	1ft 11½in	4wDM	20SXD	National	2½T			187
3044	8.1945	4ft 8½in	4wDM			10T			263
3264	25.11.1947	4ft 8½in	4wDM	20hp	National 2D				57
3271	21.2.1949	4ft 8½in	0-4-0DM		Paxman 6RW	24T			103
3477	6.12.1950	4ft 8½in	4wDM	48hp	Dorman 3DLIII	11T			207
3582	29.9.1954	2ft 0in	4wDM		Perkins L4	4LD	5½T		187
3765	22.2.1956	4ft 8½in	4wDM	57hp	Dorman 3DL		11T		103
3894	16.1.1959	4ft 8½in	4wDM	132hp	Dorman 6KUD	6KD	24T		101
3909	20.6.1959	4ft 8½in	4wDM	117hp	Dorman 6DLIII	6SC	23T		263
3967	8.1961	4ft 8½in	4wDH		Ford 590E		16T	94,322
3990	11.1.1963	3ft 6½in	4wDM	174hp	Leyland UE902	LTC	25T		125

Note that entries such as "20SXDR" in the horse-power column are Hibberd type codes which indicate the power rating. Exceptionally, FH 2051, of type 20SX, was of 25hp.

FLETCHER, JENNINGS & CO, LOWCA ENGINE WORKS, Whitehaven   FJ

48	12.9.1865	4ft 8½in	0-4-0WT	OC	10 x 20	Patent	166

B.J. FORDER & SONS, Stewartby, Bedfordshire   Forder

	c1920	2ft 11in	6wWT	VCG	148

STAHLBAHNWERKE FREUDENSTEIN & CO, Berlin, Germany   Freud

73	1901	2ft 0in	0-4-0WT	OC	186

FOX, WALKER & CO LTD, ATLAS ENGINE WORKS, Bristol   FW

314	1876	4ft 8½in	0-4-0ST	OC	10 x 14	3ft6½in	HPE	259
326	22.12.1876	4ft 8½in	0-6-0ST	OC	14 x 20	3ft7in	B1	270
328	30.4.1877	4ft 8½in	0-6-0ST	OC	13 x 20	3ft6in	B1	143
331	14.6.1877	4ft 8½in	0-4-0ST	OC	12 x 18	3ft0½in	W	242
353	1878	4ft 8½in	0-4-0ST	OC	12 x 18		W1	296
371	1878	4ft 8½in	0-6-0ST	OC	13 x 20	3ft6in	B1	296
383	1878	4ft 8½in	0-6-0ST	OC	14 x 20	3ft6in	B1	176

RICHARD GARRETT ENGINEERING WORKS LTD, Leiston, Suffolk   Garrett

32792	1915	4ft 8½in	4wT	G	176

GREENWOOD & BATLEY LTD, Armley, Leeds   GB

1210	#28.11.1930	4ft 8½in	4wBE	2x15hp		130
1371	#15.11.1934	4ft 8½in	4wBE	2x25hp	15T	214
1372	#15.11.1934	4ft 8½in	4wBE	2x25hp	15T	214
1426	(a) 1935	2ft/2ft6in	4wBE	2x6hp	3T	81
1427	(a) 1935	2ft/2ft6in	4wBE	2x6hp	3T	81
1428	(a) 1935	2ft/2ft6in	4wBE	2x6hp	3T	81

1429	(a) 1935	2ft/2ft6in	4wBE	2x6hp	3T	81
1430	(a) 1935	2ft/2ft6in	4wBE	2x6hp	3T	81
1545	#24.5.1938	3ft 0in	4wWE	2x40hp	8T	276,311
1566	#30.7.1938	3ft 0in	4wWE	2x40hp	7T	276,311
1567	#27.8.1938	3ft 0in	4wWE	2x40hp	7T	277,311
1569	(b) 1938	3ft 0in	4wBE	4½hp	3T	277,311
1570	(b) 1938	3ft 0in	4wBE	4½hp	3T	277,311,316
1571	(b) 1938	3ft 0in	4wBE	4½hp	3T	277
1572	(b) 1938	3ft 0in	4wBE	4½hp	3T	277
1573	(b) 1938	3ft 0in	4wBE	4½hp	3T	277,311
1574	(b) 1938	3ft 0in	4wBE	4½hp	3T	277,311
1611	#25.5.1939	2ft 0in	4wBE	2x20hp	8T	96
1612	#25.5.1939	2ft 0in	4wBE	2x20hp	8T	96
1613	#25.5.1939	2ft 0in	4wBE	2x20hp	8T	96
1746	#27.8.1941	3ft 0in	4wWE	2x40hp	8T	277,311
2061	7.7.1947	3ft 0in	4wBE	4½hp	3T	277,311
2062	7.7.1947	3ft 0in	4wBE	4½hp	3T	277
2063	7.7.1947	3ft 0in	4wBE	4½hp	3T	277,311
2078	23.6.1947	3ft 0in	4wBE	4½hp	3T	277
2079	23.6.1947	3ft 0in	4wBE	4½hp	3T	277,311
2080	23.6.1947	3ft 0in	4wBE	4½hp	3T	277,311
2291	14.6.1950	3ft 0in	4wBE	4½hp	3T	277
2292	14.6.1950	3ft 0in	4wBE	4½hp	3T	277,311
2293	14.6.1950	3ft 0in	4wBE	4½hp	3T	277
2294	27.6.1950	3ft 0in	4wBE	4½hp	3T	277,311
2295	27.6.1950	3ft 0in	4wBE	4½hp	3T	277,311
2296	27.6.1950	3ft 0in	4wBE	4½hp	3T	277
2779	20.3.1957	2ft 0in	4wBE	11hp	5T	82
2780	20.3.1957	2ft 0in	4wBE	11hp	5T	82
2781	20.3.1957	2ft 0in	4wBE	11hp	5T	82
2873	13.2.1958	2ft 0in	4wBE	2 x 7hp	4T	82
420274/1	6.1970	3ft 0in	4wBE	2 x 11hp	5/6T	81
420274/2	6.1970	3ft 0in	4wBE	2 x 11hp	5/6T	81
420365/1	8.1974	4ft 8½in	4wWE	2x75hp	20T	214
420365/2	8.1974	4ft 8½in	4wWE	2x75hp	20T	214

\# Quoted delivery dates. (a) Delivery due between 7.12.1935 and 4.1.1936.
(b) Delivery for this batch was quoted to begin by 6.7.1938 and be completed by 14.9.1938

GEORGE ENGLAND & CO, HATCHAM IRONWORKS, London   GE

	1850	4ft 8½in	2-2-2WT	IC	9 x 12 4ft6in	159
	5.1857	4ft 8½in	0-4-0WT	OC	9 x 12 3ft0in	159,168

GEC TRACTION LTD, Newton-le-Willows, Lancs   GECT

5365	27.10.1972	4ft 8½in	0-6-0DH	447hp	Paxman 8RPHXL	211,234,264
5366	31.10.1972	4ft 8½in	0-6-0DH	447hp	Paxman 8RPHXL	211
5367	30.11.1972	4ft 8½in	0-6-0DH	447hp	Paxman 8RPHXL	211
5387	1.7.1974	4ft 8½in	0-6-0DH	447hp	Paxman 8RPHXL	211
5388	1.7.1974	4ft 8½in	0-6-0DH	447hp	Paxman 8RPHXL	211
5394	3.3.1975	4ft 8½in	0-6-0DH	447hp	Paxman 8RPHXL	211

5395	22.6.1975	4ft 8½in	0-6-0DH	447hp	Paxman 8RPHXL		211,234,264
5407	2.7.1976	4ft 8½in	0-6-0DH	447hp	Paxman 8RPHXL		211
5408	15.7.1976	4ft 8½in	0-6-0DH	447hp	Paxman 8RPHXL		211

GENERAL ELECTRIC CO, Erie, Pennsylvania, USA — GEU

| 6099 | 1916 | 3ft 0in | 4wWE | | 276 |
| 6100 | 1916 | 3ft 0in | 4wWE | | 276 |

GLASGOW RAILWAY ENGINEERING CO LTD — GRE

| | 1897 | 2ft 0in | 0-4-0ST | OC | | 208,236,239 |

GLENGARNOCK IRON & STEEL WORKS, Ayrshire — Glengarnock

| | 1911 | 4ft 8½in | 0-4-0ST | OC | 14½x22 3ft6in | 264,304 |

GLOUCESTER RAILWAY CARRIAGE & WAGON CO LTD, Gloucester — GRC

[LT 54233]	1939	4ft 8½in	2w-2-2-2wRER			104
[BR 55001]	5.1958	4ft 8½in	2-2w-2w-2DMR	2 x AEC 150hp		320
[BR 55003]	5.1958	4ft 8½in	2-2w-2w-2DMR	2 x AEC 150hp		320

GROOM & TATTERSHALL LTD, Towcester, Northants — Groom & Tattershall

| | | 2ft 10in | 4wPM | | 266 |

GULLIVER'S LAND THEME PARK, Milton Keynes — Gulliver

| | | 1ft 3in | 2-4-0+6wDE | S/O | 100 |

JAMES & FREDK HOWARD LTD, BRITANNIA IRONWORKS, Bedford — H

	12.1895	4ft 8½in	2-2-0WT	IC	8 x 12	12T	135
937	6.6.1928	2ft 6in	4wPM	25hp	Dorman 4JU	3T	62,65,148,149
950	28.3.1929	4ft 8½in	4wPM	40hp	Dorman 4JUL	7T	248
957	1926	4ft 8½in	4wPM	31.2hp	Dorman 4JUD	7T	127,135
966	20.1.1930	2ft 6in	4wPM	31.6hp	Dorman 4JUD	3T	151
967	13.2.1930	2ft 6in	4wPM	31hp	Dorman 4JUD	3T	151
968	7.2.1930	2ft 6in	4wPM	31.5hp	Dorman 4JUD	3T	151
969	20.1.1930	2ft 0in	4wPM	31hp	Dorman 4JUD	3T	63,151,176
975	19.4.1932	2ft 0in	4wPM	26.8hp	Dorman 4JU	3T	153
978	23.10.1930	2ft 0in	4wPM	20hp	Morris IM	2T	146
981	22.7.1931	2ft 0in	4wDM	20hp	Blackstone BHV2	4T	151,176
982	22.7.1931	1ft 10½in	4wDM	20hp	Blackstone BHV2	4T	151,176
987	19.4.1932	2ft 0in	4wDM	20hp	Blackstone BHV2	4T	153

Surviving Howard records indicate that the identities of 937 and 969 were exchanged whilst at the various works of the London Brick Co Ltd.

HARDY RAILMOTOR CO LTD, Slough   Hardy

1930	4ft 8½in	4wPM		114,275

HARRISON & CLAYTON, Northampton   Harrison & Clayton

c1871	4ft 8½in	0-4-0ST	7 x 22		285,310

HUDSWELL, CLARKE & RODGERS, RAILWAY FOUNDRY, Leeds   HCR

#	No.	Date	Gauge	Wheels		Cylinders	Wheel		Refs
#	26	11.4.1864	4ft 8½in	0-4-0ST	OC	8½ x 13	2ft6in		75
	86	15.6.1867	4ft 8½in	0-4-0ST	OC	10 x 16	2ft9in		226,280
	104	12.4.1871	3ft 8¼in	0-4-0ST	OC	7 x 12	2ft0in	7T	226
	119	28.3.1872	4ft 8½in	0-4-0ST	OC	13 x 20	3ft6in	17T	280
	145	13.5.1874	3ft 8¼in	0-4-0ST	OC	8 x 15	2ft6in	8T	226
	156	15.1.1875	3ft 8¼in	0-4-0ST	OC	8 x 15	2ft6in	8T	226
	158	19.3.1875	4ft 8½in	0-4-0ST	OC	13 x 20	3ft6½in	17T	280,283
	163	20.5.1875	4ft 8½in	0-4-0ST	OC	10 x 16	2ft9in	11T	240
	165	18.2.1876	4ft 8½in	0-4-0ST	OC	13 x 20	3ft6in	18T	240,271
	173	2.12.1875	4ft 8½in	0-6-0ST	OC	11 x 17	3ft0in	13T	135
	180	3.11.1876	4ft 8½in	0-4-0ST	OC	13 x 20	3ft3in	18T	278,280,283
	185	8.9.1876	3ft 8¼in	0-4-0ST	OC	7 x 12	2ft0in	7T	226
	186	28.9.1876	3ft 8¼in	0-4-0ST	OC	7 x 12	2ft0in	7T	226
	193	10.8.1877	4ft 8½in	0-4-0ST	OC	10 x 16	2ft9in		290
	195	4.11.1879	4ft 8½in	0-4-0ST	OC	8 x 16	2ft4in		290
	212	16.4.1879	4ft 0in	0-4-0ST	OC	7 x 12	2ft0in	7T	225,308

\# builder Hudswell & Clarke (H&C)

HUDSWELL, CLARKE & CO LTD, RAILWAY FOUNDRY, Leeds   HC

No.	Date	Gauge	Wheels		Cylinders	Wheel		Refs
219	5.2.1881	4ft 8½in	0-4-0ST	OC	14 x 20	3ft6½in	18T	263,281
227	18.11.1881	4ft 0in	0-4-0ST	OC	7 x 12	2ft0in	7T	205,225,308
237	28.3.1883	4ft 8½in	0-6-0ST	OC	13 x 20	3ft3in	20T	302
252	30.1.1884	4ft 8½in	0-4-0ST	OC	13 x 20	3ft6in	17½T	227,280
275	2.3.1885	4ft 8½in	0-4-0ST	OC	12 x 18	3ft0in	16½T	268
309	4.10.1888	4ft 8½in	0-4-0ST	OC	10 x 16	2ft9in	12T	122
347	20.1.1892	4ft 8½in	0-6-0ST	IC	13 x 20	3ft3in	20T	227,260
396	8.8.1892	4ft 8½in	0-6-0ST	OC	14 x 20	3ft6in	23T	269
419	18.4.1894	3ft 0in	0-4-0ST	OC	8 x 12	2ft0in		266
427	3.12.1894	4ft 8½in	0-4-0ST	OC	13 x 18	3ft0in	16T	271,279,284
428	28.2.1894	4ft 8½in	0-4-0ST	OC	13 x 18	3ft0in	16T	207,286
431	4.4.1895	4ft 8½in	0-6-0ST	OC	14 x 20	3ft6in	23T	269
440	27.3.1896	4ft 8½in	0-6-0ST	IC	13 x 20	3ft3in	20T	80
444	5.8.1895	4ft 8½in	0-4-0ST	OC	10 x 16	2ft9in	13T	78
492	29.8.1898	4ft 8½in	0-6-0ST	IC	12 x 18	3ft0in	19T	294
505	27.10.1899	3ft 0in	0-4-0ST	OC	9 x 15	2ft3in	9¾T	276
527	31.7.1899	4ft 8½in	0-4-0ST	OC	13 x 18	3ft0in	17¼T	280
529	25.9.1899	4ft 8½in	0-4-0ST	OC	9 x 15	2ft9in	10¾T	294
531	11.9.1899	4ft 8½in	0-6-0ST	IC	12 x 18	3ft0in	17¾T	304
535	9.4.1900	4ft 8½in	0-4-0ST	OC	10 x 16	2ft9in	12½T	221
573	16.10.1900	3ft 0in	0-4-0ST	OC	10 x 16	2ft9½in	12T	218,223,

576	14.12.1900	4ft 8½in	0-4-0ST	OC	14 x 20	3ft7in	21T	284
596	27.9.1901	3ft 0in	0-4-0ST	OC	9 x 15	2ft6in	10¼T	266,267
599	6.10.1902	4ft 8½in	0-4-0ST	OC	10 x 16	2ft9½in	13T	79
607	12.2.1903	4ft 8½in	0-6-0ST	IC	13 x 20	3ft3½in	19¾T	209
637	26.1.1903	4ft 8½in	0-4-0ST	OC	10 x 16	2ft9½in	19¾T	79
648	16.3.1903	4ft 8½in	0-4-0ST	OC	11 x 16	2ft9½in	17T	241
650	30.3.1903	4ft 8½in	0-4-0ST	OC	10 x 16	2ft9½in	12¾T	79
654	10.8.1903	4ft 8½in	0-6-0ST	IC	13 x 20	3ft3½in	20T	79
671	23.3.1904	4ft 8½in	0-6-0ST	IC	13 x 20	3ft3½in	19T	164
680	26.9.1903	4ft 8½in	0-6-0T	IC	15½x20	3ft4in	26T	106
745	22.12.1905	4ft 8½in	0-6-0T	IC	15½x20	3ft4in	25¼T	210
763	30.3.1907	4ft 8½in	0-4-0ST	OC	14 x 20	3ft3½in	21T	281
899	30.11.1909	4ft 8½in	0-6-0ST	OC	15 x 22	3ft7in	25½T	269
1022	29.3.1913	4ft 8½in	0-6-0ST	OC	15 x 22	3ft7in	25¾T	269
1023	7.10.1913	4ft 8½in	0-6-0ST	OC	15 x 22	3ft7in	25¾T	269
1026	14.4.1913	4ft 8½in	0-6-0ST	IC	15 x 20	3ft7in	26T	101
1028	14.5.1913	4ft 8½in	0-6-0ST	IC	12 x 18	3ft1in	18¼T	295
1029	30.5.1913	4ft 8½in	0-6-0ST	IC	12 x 18	3ft1in	18¼T	294
1087	25.9.1914	3ft 0in	0-4-2ST	OC	9½x 15	2ft6½in	11¼T	237,271,272
1106	14.4.1915	3ft 0in	0-4-0ST	OC	9 x 15	2ft6½in	10¼T	257,271,272
1167	31.1.1918	2ft 0in	0-4-0WT	OC	5 x 8	1ft8in		204
1168	8.2.1918	2ft 0in	0-4-0WT	OC	5 x 8	1ft8in		204
1196	4.5.1916	4ft 8½in	0-6-0ST	OC	14 x 20	3ft7in	23¼T	219
1285	31.8.1917	4ft 8½in	0-4-0ST	OC	13 x 18	3ft1in	17¾T	219,264,284
1308	15.1.1918	4ft 8½in	0-6-0ST	OC	15 x 22	3ft7in	26T	210,214,220
1334	30.4.1918	4ft 8½in	0-6-0T	OC	16 x 24	3ft9in	32¾T	103
1377	31.5.1919	600mm	0-6-0WT	OC	6½x 12	1ft11in	5¾T	138
1378	31.5.1919	600mm	0-6-0WT	OC	6½x 12	1ft11in	5¾T	138
1383	1.7.1919	4ft 8½in	0-6-0ST	OC	15 x 22	3ft7in	26T	210
1420	14.10.1920	4ft 8½in	0-6-0ST	IC	14 x 20	3ft3½in	23¼T	245
1452	2.3.1921	3ft 0in	0-4-0ST	OC	9 x 15	2ft6½in	10¼T	272
1494	18.9.1923	4ft 8½in	0-6-0ST	IC	12 x 18	3ft1in	18T	129
1529	2.6.1924	4ft 8½in	0-6-0ST	IC	13 x 20	3ft3½in	20T	294
1538	16.7.1924	4ft 8½in	0-6-0ST	IC	13 x 20	3ft3½in	20T	294
1544	6.10.1924	4ft 8½in	0-6-0ST	OC	15 x 22	3ft7in	26T	108
1579	12.1.1927	4ft 8½in	0-6-0ST	OC	15 x 22	3ft4in	27T	218
1586	30.8.1927	4ft 8½in	0-6-0ST	IC	13 x 20	3ft3½in	19¾T	295
1595	9.1.1936	4ft 8½in	0-6-0T	IC	15½x20	3ft4½in		210
1601	23.7.1927	4ft 8½in	0-6-0ST	IC	12 x 18	3ft1½in	18T	294
1631	10.5.1929	4ft 8½in	0-6-0ST	OC	15 x 22	3ft4in	27T	228
1695	29.9.1938	4ft 8½in	0-6-0T	OC	16 x 24	3ft9in		269
1696	21.9.1939	4ft 8½in	0-4-0ST	OC	14 x 22	3ft3½in	22¼T	232,308
1726	26.10.1941	4ft 8½in	0-4-0ST	OC	14 x 22	3ft3½in	22¼T	308
1727	11.12.1941	4ft 8½in	0-4-0ST	OC	14 x 22	3ft3½in	22¼T	156,176
1731	2.11.1942	4ft 8½in	0-6-0T	OC	17 x 24	3ft9in	34½T	312
1742	16.4.1946	4ft 8½in	0-4-0ST	OC	12 x 18	3ft1in	17½T	103
1753	30.11.1943	4ft 8½in	0-6-0ST	IC	18 x 26	4ft3in	48T	282
1758	1.2.1944	4ft 8½in	0-6-0ST	IC	18 x 26	4ft3in	48T	282
1765	26.6.1944	4ft 8½in	0-6-0ST	IC	18 x 26	4ft3in	48T	282
1770	22.9.1944	4ft 8½in	0-6-0ST	IC	18 x 26	4ft3in	48T	282
1800	30.6.1947	4ft 8½in	0-6-0T	OC	16 x 24	3ft9in		323
1818	2.8.1950	4ft 8½in	0-4-0ST	OC	14 x 22	3ft3½in	22T	232
1864	5.12.1950	4ft 8½in	0-6-0T	OC	16 x 24	3ft9in		101

	No.	Date	Gauge	Type		Cylinder	Wheel	Weight	Ref
	1868	30.6.1953	4ft 8½in	0-4-0ST	OC	14 x 22	3ft3½in	23½T	232
	1869	30.6.1953	4ft 8½in	0-4-0ST	OC	14 x 22	3ft3½in	23½T	232
	P254	c1925	1ft 11½in	4wPM					256
	D570	21.3.1932	1ft 8in	4-6-4TDM	S/O	20hp	Dorman 2cyl		185
	D582	30.5.1933	1ft 8in	4-6-2DM	S/O	26hp	Dorman Ricardo 2RBL		185
	DM1117	24.3.1958	2ft 0in	0-6-0DMF		100hp	Gardner 6LW		189

Hudswell Clarke 'Class Names' : Countess of Warwick – 671, 1494, 1529, 1538, 1586, 1601. Philadelphia – 680, 745. Swansea – 763. Thornhill – 1022, 1308, 1383. San Justo – 1087. Donegal – 1106, 1452. Fords – 1196. Hero – 1285, 1742. Devonport – 1334, 1695. Ganges – 1377, 1378. Sweden – 1595. Appleby – 1631. Irlam – 1696, 1726, 1727, 1818. Cornist - 1731. 'LMS Class 3' (actually HE Austerity design) – 1753, 1758, 1765, 1770.

HUNSLET ENGINE CO LTD, Hunslet, Leeds — HE

	No.	Date	Gauge	Type		Cylinder	Wheel	Ref
	1	18.7.1865	4ft 8½in	0-6-0ST	IC	14 x 18	3ft4in	166
	4	13.12.1865	4ft 8½in	0-6-0ST	IC	12 x 18	3ft1in	292
	5	9.1.1866	4ft 8½in	0-6-0ST	IC	12 x 18	3ft1in	166
	17	22.12.1866	4ft 8½in	0-4-0ST	OC	10 x 15	2ft9in	299
	29	2.11.1868	4ft 8½in	0-4-0ST	OC	10 x 15	2ft9in	299
	45	1.11.1870	4ft 8½in	0-6-0ST	IC	12 x 18	3ft1in	76
	57	26.4.1871	4ft 8½in	0-6-0ST	IC	12 x 18	3ft1in	169
	61	7.9.1871	4ft 8½in	0-4-0ST	OC	12 x 18	3ft1in	283
	63	7.7.1871	4ft 8½in	0-6-0ST	IC	13 x 18	3ft1in	78
	65	26.9.1871	4ft 8½in	0-6-0ST	IC	12 x 18	3ft1in	299
	72	28.2.1872	4ft 8½in	0-6-0ST	IC	12 x 18	3ft1in	76
	104	9.10.1874	4ft 8½in	0-4-0ST	OC	10 x 15	2ft9in	300
	119	16.2.1874	4ft 8½in	0-6-0ST	IC	12 x 18	3ft1in	279
	133	9.2.1875	4ft 8½in	0-4-0ST	OC	12 x 18	3ft1in	262,311
	137	1.7.1875	4ft 8½in	0-4-0ST	OC	10 x 15	2ft9in	299
	138	22.3.1875	4ft 8½in	0-4-0ST	OC	10 x 15	2ft9in	243,271,286
	139	20.4.1875	3ft 0in	0-4-0ST	OC	8 x 14	2ft4in	271,272
	161	27.3.1876	4ft 8½in	0-6-0ST	IC	12 x 18	3ft1in	299
#	164	31.5.1876	4ft 8½in	0-6-0ST	IC	12 x 18	3ft1in	302,303
	175	20.2.1877	2ft 6in	0-4-0ST	OC	5 x 8	1ft6in	256
	176	9.1.1877	4ft 8½in	0-6-0ST	IC	13 x 18	3ft1in	255
	183	21.2.1877	4ft 8½in	0-4-0ST	OC	8 x 14	2ft8½in	238
	199	10.3.1879	4ft 8½in	0-4-0ST	OC	12 x 18	3ft1in	79
	201	4.7.1878	4ft 8½in	0-4-0ST	OC	10 x 15	2ft9in	243,271,286
#	202	20.3.1878	5ft 3in	0-6-0ST	OC	10 x 15	2ft6in	302
	209	23.9.1878	3ft 0in	0-4-0ST	OC	8 x 14	2ft4in	271,272
	224	24.4.1879	4ft 8½in	0-6-0ST	IC	13 x 18	3ft1in	76
	238	7.6.1880	4ft 8½in	0-4-0ST	OC	10 x 15	2ft9in	280
	239	15.2.1881	4ft 8½in	0-4-0ST	OC	10 x 15	2ft9in	262
	242	12.1.1881	4ft 8½in	0-6-0ST	IC	12 x 18	3ft1in	299
	256	7.2.1881	4ft 8½in	0-6-0ST	IC	12 x 18	3ft1in	85
	287	2.11.1883	4ft 8½in	0-4-0ST	OC	10 x 15	2ft9in	76,103,192,322
	288	30.4.1884	4ft 8½in	0-6-0ST	IC	12 x 18	3ft1in	85,302
	298	18.10.1882	3ft 11in	0-4-0ST	OC	9 x 14	2ft8½in	205,225
	307	12.3.1883	2ft 6in	0-4-0ST	OC	7 x 10	1ft8in	235,280
	344	20.1.1885	4ft 8½in	0-4-0ST	OC	13 x 18	3ft1in	210,214
	348	30.7.1884	3ft 3in	0-4-0ST	OC	9 x 14	2ft4½in	274

359	26.2.1885	4ft 8½in	0-4-0ST	OC	12 x 18	3ft1in		283
363	10.2.1885	4ft 8½in	0-6-0ST	IC	13 x 18	3ft1in		300
369	2.4.1885	4ft 8½in	0-6-0ST	IC	13 x 18	3ft1in		300
370	14.4.1885	4ft 8½in	0-6-0ST	IC	13 x 18	3ft1in		262
386	22.10.1885	4ft 8½in	0-4-0ST	OC	9 x 14	2ft8½in		76
392	3.3.1886	4ft 8½in	0-6-0ST	IC	13 x 18	3ft1in		52
405	14.1.1887	3ft 3in	0-4-0ST	OC	9 x 14	2ft4½in		274
421	7.7.1887	4ft 8½in	0-6-0ST	IC	14 x 18	3ft1in		219
425	11.11.1887	4ft 8½in	0-4-0ST	OC	10 x 15	2ft 9in		52
434	29.11.1887	4ft 8½in	0-6-0ST	IC	13 x 18	3ft1in		300
435	29.11.1887	4ft 8½in	0-6-0ST	IC	13 x 18	3ft1in		300
442	4.1.1888	4ft 8½in	0-4-0ST	OC	10 x 15	2ft9in		219,300
454	18.5.1888	4ft 8½in	0-6-0ST	IC	12 x 18	3ft1in		79
456	5.6.1888	4ft 8½in	0-6-0ST	IC	13 x 18	3ft1in		262
464	3.8.1888	4ft 8½in	0-6-0ST	IC	13 x 18	3ft1in		85
473	5.12.1888	3ft 3in	0-4-0ST	OC	10 x 16	2ft6½in		274
493	12.11.1889	1ft10¾in	0-4-0ST	OC	7 x 10	1ft8in		189
525	19.11.1890	4ft 8½in	0-4-0ST	OC	10 x 15	2ft9in		165
529	31.1.1891	4ft 8½in	0-6-0ST	IC	13 x 18	3ft1in		304
542	21.8.1891	1ft10¾in	0-4-0ST	OC	7 x 10	1ft8in		189
545	26.6.1891	4ft 8½in	0-6-0ST	IC	12 x 18	3ft1in		189,299
549	20.10.1891	4ft 8½in	0-6-0ST	IC	13 x 18	3ft1in		300
562	22.4.1892	3ft 3in	0-4-0ST	OC	10 x 16	2ft6½in		274
569	16.2.1893	4ft 8½in	0-4-0ST	OC	13 x 18	3ft1in		210,214
573	13.1.1893	4ft 8½in	0-6-0ST	OC	11 x 15	2ft6in		114,165
588	18.5.1893	4ft 8½in	0-4-0ST	OC	12 x 18	3ft1in		114
603	2.2.1894	3ft 3in	0-4-0ST	OC	10 x 16	2ft6½in		274
606	7.5.1894	1ft10¾in	0-4-0ST	OC	7 x 10	1ft8in		189
619	20.12.1894	4ft 8½in	0-6-0ST	IC	13 x 18	3ft1in		264,304
645	12.10.1896	4ft 8½in	0-4-0ST	OC	12 x 18	3ft1in		238
686	19.12.1898	4ft 8½in	0-6-0T	IC	15½x20	3ft4in		321
707	29.12.1899	2ft 0in	0-4-0ST	OC	7 x 10	1ft8in		189
779	29.5.1902	1ft 10¾in	0-4-0ST	OC	7 x 10	1ft8in		108
780	16.6.1902	2ft 0in	0-4-0ST	OC	7 x 10	1ft8in		186
791	14.10.1902	4ft 8½in	0-4-0ST	OC	13 x 18	3ft1in		210,246,284
808	24.4.1903	3ft 0in	0-4-0ST	OC	7 x 10	1ft8in		141
823	30.10.1903	1ft10¾in	0-4-0ST	OC	7 x 10	1ft8in		189
899	25.4.1906	4ft 8½in	0-6-0ST	IC	13 x 18	3ft2½in		262
906	24.7.1906	4ft 8½in	0-4-0ST	OC	12 x 18	3ft1in		238
1429	1.8.1922	1ft10¾in	0-4-0ST	OC	7 x 10	1ft8in		195,324
1436	24.10.1922	3ft 0in	0-4-0ST	OC	9 x 14	2ft6in		272
1446	16.7.1929	4ft 8½in	0-6-0ST	OC	15 x 22	3ft7in		210
1463	29.10.1924	4ft 8½in	0-6-0T	IC	18 x 2	4ft7in		321
1644	4.11.1929	4ft 8½in	0-4-0ST	OC	14 x 20	3ft4in		56
1677	1.4.1937	4ft 8½in	0-4-0ST	OC	15 x 20	3ft6in		264
1684	24.8.1931	4ft 8½in	0-4-0T	OC	12 x 18	3ft4in		312
1685	13.7.1931	4ft 8½in	0-6-0ST	OC	14 x 20	3ft4in		80
1686	13.7.1931	4ft 8½in	0-6-0ST	OC	14 x 20	3ft4in		80
1688	20.7.1931	4ft 8½in	0-6-0ST	OC	14 x 20	3ft4in		80
1690	27.7.1931	4ft 8½in	0-6-0ST	OC	14 x 20	3ft4in		80,103,182
1953	2.10.1939	4ft 8½in	0-6-0ST	IC	16 x 22	3ft9in		254
1964	.1939	2ft 0in	4wDM	20hp		Ailsa Craig CF2	3½T	71
1975	17.11.1939	2ft 0in	4wDM	20hp		Ailsa Craig CF2	3½T	207
1982	27.2.1940	4ft 8½in	0-6-0ST	IC	16 x 22	3ft9in		254

2067	11.6.1940	4ft 8½in	0-4-0DM	153hp	Gardner 6L3	20T	103
2068	8.7.1940	4ft 8½in	0-4-0DM	153hp	Gardner 6L3	20T	130,231
2070	8.10.1940	4ft 8½in	0-4-0DM	70/77hp	Gardner 6L2	12¼T	241,258
2082	24.10.1940	4ft 8½in	0-6-0ST	IC	16 x 22 3ft9in		275
2087	30.7.1940	4ft 8½in	0-4-0DM	40/44hp	Fowler 4B	9¼T	322
2176	17.8.1940	600mm	4wDM	25hp	McLaren LMR2	4¼T	186,194
2268	22.4.1941	2ft 6in	0-4-0DM	50hp	Gardner 4L2	8½T	95
2269	19.6.1941	2ft 6in	0-4-0DM	50hp	Gardner 4L2	8½T	95
2401	2.6.1942	2ft 6in	0-4-0DM	50hp	Gardner 4L2	8½T	95
2403	21.7.1942	2ft 6in	0-4-0DM	50hp	Gardner 4L2	8½T	95
2411	27.11.1941	4ft 8½in	0-6-0ST	IC	18 x 26 4ft0½in		210,316
2415	25.2.1942	4ft 8½in	0-6-0ST	IC	18 x 26 4ft0½in		260
2417	17.4.1942	4ft 8½in	0-6-0ST	IC	18 x 26 4ft0½in		215,220,233
2419	14.1.1942	Metre	0-4-0DM	50hp	Gardner 4L2	9T	317,318
2459	29.7.1941	600mm	4wDM	20hp	Ailsa Craig RF2	3T	207
2477	5.9.1941	600mm	4wDM	20hp	Ailsa Craig RF2	3T	95
2536	12.12.1941	600mm	4wDM	20hp	Ailsa Craig RF2	3T	187
2665	9.2.1942	2ft 0in	4wDM	25hp	McLaren LMR W2	4½T	89
2666	9.2.1942	2ft 0in	4wDM	25hp	McLaren LMR W2	4½T	89
2697	20.6.1944	4ft 8½in	0-6-0DM	186/204hp	Gardner 8L3		295
2884	23.11.1943	4ft 8½in	0-6-0ST	IC	18 x 26 4ft3in	48T	282
2885	29.11.1943	4ft 8½in	0-6-0ST	IC	18 x 26 4ft3in	48T	282
3155	11.3.1944	4ft 8½in	0-6-0ST	IC	18 x 26 4ft3in	48T	320
3193	10.11.1944	4ft 8½in	0-6-0ST	IC	18 x 26 4ft3in	48T	282
3214	18.5.1945	4ft 8½in	0-6-0ST	IC	18 x 26 4ft3in	48T	282
3646	23.3.1948	2ft 0in	4wDM	25hp	McLaren LMR W2		186
3782	29.9.1953	4ft 8½in	0-6-0ST	IC	16 x 22 3ft9in		103
3815	8.10.1954	2ft 6in	2-6-2T	OC	10¾x15 2ft4in		185
3850	31.3.1958	4ft 8½in	0-6-0ST	IC	18 x 26 4ft3in	48T	103
3889	18.3.1964	4ft 8½in	0-6-0ST	IC	18 x 26 4ft3in	48T	103
3890	27.3.1964	4ft 8½in	0-6-0ST	IC	18 x 26 4ft3in	48T	103
4187	28.10.1948	600mm	4wDM	20hp	Ailsa-Craig RFS2		82
4263	31.3.1952	4ft 8½in	0-4-0DM	93/102hp	Gardner 4L3		94,241
4264	30.5.1952	4ft 8½in	0-4-0DM	93/102hp	Gardner 4L3		84
4351	30.4.1952	2ft 0in	4wDM	21hp	Ailsa-Craig RFS2		187
4679	28.2.1955	4ft 8½in	0-4-0DM	153hp	Gardner 6L3		233
4758	22.12.1954	2ft0in	4wDM	22hp	Ailsa-Craig RFS2		193
6008	29.5.1963	2ft 0in	4wDM	24hp	Perkins 3.152		186
6013	17.5.1961	2ft 0in	4wDM	21hp	Ailsa-Craig RF2		99
6619	30.6.1966	2ft 0in	0-4-0DM	66hp	Gardner 4LW		187
6691	12.8.1968	4ft 8½in	0-6-0DH	260hp	Gardner 8L3B		233
7016	30.6.1971	4ft 8½in	0-6-0DH	400hp	R-R C8TFL		104
8518	21.3.1978	2ft 0in	4wDH	90hp	Perkins 6354 [AB 632]		313
9342	.1995	900mm	4wDH	128kw	Deutz F8L 413FW		295
9343	.1995	900mm	4wDH	128kw	Deutz F8L 413FW		295
9344	.1995	900mm	4wDH	128kw	Deutz F8L 413FW		295
9345	.1995	900mm	4wDH	128kw	Deutz F8L 413FW		295

\# HE 164 was altered to 13 x 18in cyls by HE in 1886.
HE 202 was altered to 4ft 8½in gauge by HE in 1886.

HAIGH FOUNDRY CO LTD, Wigan   HF

42		1840	4ft 8½in	2-4-0			166

R & W HAWTHORN, LESLIE & CO LTD, FORTH BANK WORKS, Newcastle-upon-Tyne HL

2081	25.1.1888	4ft 8½in	0-6-0ST	OC	14 x 20	3ft6in	210
2412	3.1899	4ft 8½in	0-4-0ST	OC	14 x 20	3ft6in	221,224
2469	6.7.1900	4ft 8½in	0-6-0ST	OC	14 x 20	3ft6in	210
2669	21.6.1907	4ft 8½in	0-4-0CT	OC	12 x 15	2ft10in	264
2839	31.12.1910	4ft 8½in	0-4-0ST	OC	14 x 22	3ft6in	254
3138	23.8.1915	4ft 8½in	0-6-0ST	OC	14 x 22	3ft6in	92,219,270
3347	8.8.1918	4ft 8½in	0-6-0ST	OC	14 x 22	3ft6in	245,284
3375	30.7.1919	4ft 8½in	0-6-0ST	OC	16 x 24	3ft10in	210
3423	18.9.1920	4ft 8½in	0-4-0ST	OC	14 x 22	3ft6in	207,281
3717	17.8.1928	4ft 8½in	0-4-0ST	OC	15 x 22	3ft5in	103
3721	14.4.1928	4ft 8½in	0-4-0ST	OC	14 x 22	3ft6in	275
3780	16.3.1932	4ft 8½in	0-4-0ST	OC	16 x 24	3ft10in	222,233
3813	16.12.1935	4ft 8½in	0-4-0ST	OC	16 x 24	3ft8in	211,284
3820	27.4.1934	4ft 8½in	0-4-0WE	80hp	2ft9in		214
3824	22.2.1934	4ft 8½in	0-6-0ST	OC	16 x 24	3ft8in	210
3825	27.2.1934	4ft 8½in	0-6-0ST	OC	16 x 24	3ft8in	210
3826	17.3.1934	4ft 8½in	0-6-0ST	OC	16 x 24	3ft8in	210
3827	24.3.1934	4ft 8½in	0-6-0ST	OC	16 x 24	3ft8in	210,315,316
3829	30.4.1934	4ft 8½in	0-4-0F	OC	17 x 26	2ft11in	230
3836	16.10.1934	4ft 8½in	0-6-0ST	OC	16 x 24	3ft8in	210
3837	16.10.1934	4ft 8½in	0-6-0ST	OC	16 x 24	3ft8in	210
3883	8.9.1936	4ft 8½in	0-6-0ST	OC	15 x 22	3ft5in	273
3884	16.9.1936	4ft 8½in	0-6-0ST	OC	15 x 22	3ft5in	273
3888	2.6.1936	4ft 8½in	0-6-0ST	OC	16 x 24	3ft8in	210
3889	15.6.1936	4ft 8½in	0-6-0ST	OC	16 x 24	3ft8in	210
3892	8.10.1936	4ft 8½in	0-4-0ST	OC	16 x 24	3ft8in	221,232
3896	2.11.1936	4ft 8½in	0-6-0ST	OC	16 x 24	3ft8in	210
3897	9.11.1936	4ft 8½in	0-6-0ST	OC	16 x 24	3ft8in	210
3931	6.12.1937	4ft 8½in	0-6-0ST	OC	16 x 24	3ft8in	210
3946	20.12.1937	4ft 8½in	0-4-0ST	OC	14 x 22	3ft6in	221,233

HORWICH WORKS, Lancs (L&YR / LMSR / BR) Hor

1097	5.1910	4ft 8½in	0-4-0ST	OC	13 x 18	3ft0in [LMSR 11243]	192
[BR 76017]	6.1953	4ft 8½in	2-6-0	OC	17½x26	5ft3in	103,106
[BR D3599]	10.1958	4ft 8½in	0-6-0DE	350hp	4ft6in	EE 6KT	70

ROBERT HUDSON LTD, GILDERSOME FOUNDRY, Leeds HU

38384	1930	2ft 0in	4wPM	187

ISO SPEEDIC CO LTD, Warwick Iso

T15	17.7.1972	1ft 6in	2w-2BE	T1A	173
T40	13.7.1973	1ft 6in	2w-2BE	T1B	173
T41	9.10.1973	1ft 6in	2w-2BE	T1B	173
T46	1974	1ft 6in	2w-2BE	T1B	173
T49	1974	1ft 6in	2w-2BE	T1B	173
T57	1974	1ft 6in	2w-2BE	T2A	173
T66	1974	1ft 6in	2w-2BE	T2A	173

17209	7.1927	4ft 8½in	0-4-0PM	30hp		309
19024	9.1930	4ft 8½in	0-4-0DM	65/70hp	MAN	231
20067	10.1933	4ft 8½in	0-4-0DM	45hp	Ruston	103
21086	11.1.1936	4ft 8½in	0-4-0DM	52hp	Ruston 3VQB	223
21322	24.6.1936	4ft 8½in	0-4-0DM	80hp	Fowler 6A	125
21408	30.10.1936	2ft 0in	4wDM	40hp	Fowler 4B	289
21455	24.9.1936	4ft 8½in	0-4-0DM	80hp	Fowler 6A	125
21941	26.6.1937	4ft 8½in	0-4-0DM	80hp	Fowler 6A	125
22000	29.7.1937	4ft 8½in	0-4-0DM	40hp	Fowler 4B	156
22604	31.5.1939	4ft 8½in	0-4-0DM	150hp	Fowler 4C	114
22885	31.10.1940	4ft 8½in	0-6-0DM	200hp	Fowler 6C	52,291
# 22887	29.12.1939	4ft 8½in	0-4-0DM	150hp	Fowler 4C	125
22888	22.1.1940	4ft 8½in	0-4-0DM	150hp	Fowler 4C	64
22890	20.9.1939	4ft 8½in	0-4-0DM	150hp	Fowler 4C	231
22892	5.3.1940	4ft 8½in	0-4-0DM	150hp	Fowler 4C	308
22895	30.3.1940	4ft 8½in	0-4-0DM	80hp	Fowler 6A	64
22906	3.9.1940	4ft 8½in	0-4-0DM	80hp	Fowler 6A	309
22917	5.8.1940	4ft 8½in	0-4-0DM	150hp	Fowler 4C	309
22950	18.12.1941	4ft 8½in	0-4-0DM	150hp	Fowler 4C	156
22960	10.6.1941	4ft 8½in	0-4-0DM	150hp	Fowler 4C	114,155
22961	10.7.1941	4ft 8½in	0-4-0DM	150hp	Fowler 4C	155
22966	28.10.1941	4ft 8½in	0-4-0DM	150hp	Fowler 4C	52,114
22968	8.1.1942	4ft 8½in	0-4-0DM	150hp	Fowler 4C	231
22970	31.1.1942	4ft 8½in	0-4-0DM	150hp	Fowler 4C	52
22974	15.4.1942	4ft 8½in	0-4-0DM	150hp	Fowler 4C	176
22977	28.5.1942	4ft 8½in	0-4-0DM	150hp	Fowler 4C	156
22981	28.7.1942	4ft 8½in	0-4-0DM	150hp	Fowler 4C	156
22984	31.8.1942	4ft 8½in	0-4-0DM	150hp	Fowler 4C	176
22988	20.10.1942	4ft 8½in	0-4-0DM	150hp	Fowler 4C	295
22994	25.8.1942	4ft 8½in	0-4-0DM	150hp	Fowler 4C	52,114,155
23001	22.6.1943	4ft 8½in	0-4-0DM	150hp	Fowler 4C	155
23003	29.7.1943	4ft 8½in	0-4-0DM	150hp	Fowler 4C	160
23009	3.10.1944	4ft 8½in	0-4-0DM	150hp	Fowler 4C	231
23010	1.1.1945	4ft 8½in	0-4-0DM	150hp	Fowler 4C	231
3900001	6.5.1946	4ft 8½in	0-4-0DM	40hp	Fowler 4B	309
3930044	17.7.1950	3ft 0in	4wDM	40hp	Marshall	120
4110008	28.9.1950	4ft 8½in	0-4-0DM	80hp	McLaren MR3	125
4160004	24.9.1951	2ft 6in	0-6-0DM	100hp	McLaren M4	184
4160005	26.9.1951	2ft 6in	0-6-0DM	100hp	McLaren M4	184
4200022	2.3.1948	4ft 8½in	0-4-0DM	150hp	Fowler 4C	163,231
4200042	14.3.1949	4ft 8½in	0-4-0DM	150hp	Fowler 4C	128,232
4200043	8.6.1949	4ft 8½in	0-4-0DM	150hp	Fowler 4C	209
4210012	24.7.1950	4ft 8½in	0-4-0DM	150hp	McLaren M6	163,231
4210094	2.9.1954	4ft 8½in	0-4-0DM	150hp	McLaren M6 #	130
4210143	28.8.1958	4ft 8½in	0-4-0DM	150hp	McLaren M6	231
4220001	26.2.1959	4ft 8½in	0-4-0DM	176hp	Leyland EN900 28T	322
4220031	10.11.1964	4ft 8½in	0-4-0DH	203hp	Leyland EN900 28T	108
4220033	2.3.1965	4ft 8½in	0-4-0DH	203hp	Leyland EN900 28T	322
4220037	29.6.1966	4ft 8½in	0-4-0DH	203hp	Leyland EN900	120,125
4230001	8.1959	4ft 8½in	0-4-0DH	185hp	Leyland	125
4240017	28.1.1966	4ft 8½in	0-6-0DH	275hp	Leyland	125

22887 was rebuilt by JF as 0-4-0DH 203hp Leyland UE902/41/1, ex-works 3.10.1963
4210094 was rebuilt by JF to 0-4-0DH in 8/1966

JONES, TURNER & EVANS, VIADUCT FOUNDRY, Newton-le-Willows   JTE

	1838	4ft 8½in	0-4-2	IC	74,166

ARN. JUNG LOKOMOTIVEFABRIK GmbH, Jungenthal, Germany   Jung

939	2.5.1906	2ft 0in	0-4-0WT	OC	40hp	6T		189
3872	30.4.1931	2ft 0in	0-6-0WT	OC	30hp	6½T		189
4465	24.4.1929	600mm	4wDM				MS131	132
5215	28.5.1931	600mm	4wDM				MS131	132

KITSON & CO LTD, AIREDALE FOUNDRY, Leeds   K

1421	7.5.1867	4ft 8½in	0-6-0	IC	16 x 24	4ft6in	297
1829	17.2.1872	4ft 8½in	0-6-0ST	IC	13 x 20	3ft6in	78
1841	22.3.1876	4ft 8½in	0-4-0ST	OC	12 x 18	3ft0½in	208,236
5469	27.3.1933	4ft 8½in	0-6-0ST	IC	16 x 22	3ft6in	210,214,322
5470	27.3.1933	4ft 8½in	0-6-0ST	IC	16 x 22	3ft6in	210,214,224,320
5473	27.11.1933	4ft 8½in	0-6-0ST	IC	16 x 22	3ft6in	210,214
5474	27.11.1933	4ft 8½in	0-6-0ST	IC	16 x 22	3ft6in	210,215
5476	26.10.1936	4ft 8½in	0-6-0ST	IC	16 x 22	3ft6in	210,215
5477	26.10.1936	4ft 8½in	0-6-0ST	IC	16 x 22	3ft6in	210,215,220, 224,233
5478	26.10.1936	4ft 8½in	0-6-0ST	IC	16 x 22	3ft6in	210,215,220, 222,233,275

Locos 5469, 5473, 5474, 5476 – 5478 above were built to MW design.

KENT CONSTRUCTION & ENGINEERING CO LTD, Ashford, Kent   KC

1553	6.1927	4ft 8½in	4wPM	40hp Dorman 4JO	231,244

KILMARNOCK ENGINEERING CO LTD, BRITANNIA WORKS   KE

509	1920	3ft 0in	0-4-0T	OC	8 x 14	2ft5in	272
510	1920	3ft 0in	0-4-0T	OC	8 x 14	2ft5in	272

LOCOMOTIVFABRIK KRAUSS & CO, Munich   Krauss

1861	1886	3ft 6in	0-4-0Tram	OC	8 x 12	2ft6in	73
1862	1886	3ft 6in	0-4-0Tram	OC	8 x 12	2ft6in	73
1863	1887	3ft 6in	0-4-0Tram	OC	8 x 12	2ft6in	73
1864	1887	3ft 6in	0-4-0Tram	OC	8 x 12	2ft6in	73

KERR, STUART & CO LTD, CALIFORNIA WORKS, Stoke-on-Trent   KS

1049	31.10.1908	2ft 6in	0-4-2ST	OC	9 x 15	2ft6in	Brazil	184
1252	15.12.1914	2ft 0in	0-4-0ST	OC	6 x 9	1ft8in	Wren	53
2397	14.1.1918	2ft 0in	0-4-2ST	OC	7 x 12	2ft0in	Tattoo	204
2420	21.6.1915	2ft 0in	0-4-0ST	OC	6 x 9	1ft8in	Wren	90,205
2467	17.7.1916	2ft 0in	0-4-0ST	OC	6 x 9	1ft8in	Wren	208
2473	2.10.1916	2ft 0in	0-4-0ST	OC	6 x 9	1ft8in	Wren	90
2474	2.10.1916	2ft 0in	0-4-0ST	OC	6 x 9	1ft8in	Wren	90
2477	9.12.1916	2ft 0in	0-4-0ST	OC	6 x 9	1ft8in	Wren	90
3024	17.10.1916	3ft 0in	0-4-2ST	OC	9 x 15	2ft6in	Brazil	183
3084	19.11.1917	3ft 0in	0-6-0T	OC	8½ x 11	1ft11½	Haig	126
3103	14.2.1918	2ft 0in	0-4-0ST	OC	6 x 9	1ft8in	Wren	208
3105	27.4.1918	2ft 0in	0-4-0ST	OC	6 x 9	1ft8in	Wren	137
3118	27.11.1918	2ft 0in	0-6-0T	OC	8½ x 11	1ft11½	Haig	204
4002	20.12.1918	2ft 0in	0-4-0ST	OC	6 x 9	1ft8in	Wren	115
4003	20.12.1918	2ft 0in	0-4-0ST	OC	6 x 9	1ft8in	Wren	115
4004	20.12.1918	2ft 0in	0-4-0ST	OC	6 x 9	1ft8in	Wren	115
4005	31.12.1918	2ft 0in	0-4-0ST	OC	6 x 9	1ft8in	Wren	115
4023	24.6.1919	2ft 0in	0-4-0ST	OC	6 x 9	1ft8in	Wren	90
4034	1.5.1920	2ft 6in	0-6-2T	OC	10 x 15	2ft3in	Barreto	102,184
4256	8.3.1922	2ft 0in	0-4-0ST	OC	6 x 9	1ft8in	Wren	186
4260	27.3.1922	2ft 0in	0-4-0ST	OC	6 x 9	1ft8in	Wren	186
4262	27.3.1922	2ft 0in	0-4-0ST	OC	6 x 9	1ft8in	Wren	90,205
4267	21.7.1922	2ft 0in	0-4-0ST	OC	6 x 9	1ft8in	Wren	90
4428	6.5.1929	4ft 8½in	4wDM	90hp	McLaren Benz 6cyl			103,145
4450	29.4.1930	4ft 8½in	0-6-0PT	IC	17½x24	4ft7½in		102

R. & A. LISTER & CO LTD, Dursley, Gloucestershire   L

3834	24.4.1931	2ft 0in	4wPM	6hp	JAP	Type R	58
4088	21.9.1931	2ft 0in	4wPM	6hp	JAP	Type R	186
4228	12.12.1931	2ft 0in	4wPM	6hp	JAP	Type R	99,187
4414	2.4.1932	2ft 0in	4wPM	6hp	JAP	Type R	238,251,283
4460	11.6.1932	2ft 0in	4wPM	6hp	JAP	Type R	58,179
7280	8.1.1936	2ft 0in	4wPM	6hp	JAP	Type R	265
8913	7.4.1937	2ft 0in	4wPM	6hp	JAP	Type R	258
10063	1938	2ft 0in	4wPM	9.8hp	JAP	Type RT	238
11221	4.7.1939	2ft 0in	4wDM	9.8hp	JAP	Type RT	186
14005	4.11.1940	2ft 0in	4wPM	6hp	JAP	Type R	258
14006	4.11.1940	2ft 0in	4wPM	6hp	JAP	Type R	258,323,326
20696	4.12.1942	2ft 0in	4wPM	6hp	JAP	Type R	258
26288	8.12.1944	2ft 0in	4wPM	6hp	JAP	Type R	99
36743	9.3.1951	2ft 0in	4wPM	6hp	JAP	Type R	265,326
37170	14.6.1951	2ft 0in	4wPM	6hp	JAP	Type R	187
37911	23.7.1952	2ft 0in	4wDM	6hp	JAP	Type R	193

LONDON BRICK CO LTD   LBC

	2ft 11in	4wWE		65,141,147

LEIGHTON BUZZARD NARROW GAUGE RAILWAY SOCIETY   LBNGRS

1	1989	2ft 0in	4wDM	187

STEPHEN LEWIN, DORSET FOUNDRY, Poole, Dorset

Lewin

	1876	4ft 8½in	0-4-0WT	G	7½ x 12	238

LINGFORD, GARDINER

LG

	1931	4ft 8½in	0-4-0ST	OC	245

LOGAN MACHINERY & MINING

LMM

1001-5	4wBE	106

LOCOMOTIVE ENTERPRISES (1975) LTD, Gateshead

Loco Ent

1	1975	4ft 8½in	0-4-0	VC	106
2	1979	4ft 8½in	0-2-2	OC	106

P. McGARIGLE, Niagara Falls, nar Buffalo, New York, U.S.A

McGarigle

	.1902	1ft3in	4-4-0	OC	314
	.1902	1ft3in	4-4-0	OC	314

THE MERCURY TRUCK & TRACTOR CO, Gloucester

Mercury

5337	1927	4ft 8½in	4wPM	55

MUIR-HILL (ENGINEERS) LTD, Trafford Park, Manchester

MH

8	9.11.1926	2ft 0in	4wPM	70
22	16.2.1927	2ft 0in	4wPM	58
30	6.7.1928	4ft 8½in	4wPM	57
109	23.7.1931	2ft 0in	4wPM	258

MARKHAM & CO LTD, Chesterfield, Derbyshire

Mkm

101 #	1889	Metre	0-4-0ST	OC	8 x 10	2ft0in	218
102 #	1889	Metre	0-4-0ST	OC	8 x 10	2ft0in	218,273
103	1891	4ft 8½in	0-4-0ST	OC	13 x 20	3ft6in	237

locomotives built by Oliver & Co Ltd, predecessors to Markham & Co.

R.P. MORRIS, Longfield, Kent

R.P.Morris

	1967	2ft 0in	4-2-0PMR	187

MOTOR RAIL LTD, SIMPLEX WORKS, Bedford

MR

270	1916	600mm	4wPM	20hp	Dorman 2JO		71
341	27.4.1917	600mm	4wPM	20hp	Dorman 2JO	2½T	117
374	25.5.1917	600mm	4wPM	20hp	Dorman 2JO		131
468	26.3.1918	600mm	4wPM	40hp	Dorman 4JO	2½T	138
478	28.3.1918	600mm	4wPM	40hp	Dorman 4JO		138
574	20.2.1918	600mm	4wPM	40hp	Dorman 4JO		138
849	20.4.1918	600mm	4wPM	20hp	Dorman 2JO	2½T	138
916	10.6.1918	600mm	4wPM	20hp	Dorman 2JO		117

974	29.7.1918	600mm	4wPM	20hp	Dorman 2JO		131
999	26.8.1918	600mm	4wPM	20hp	Dorman 2JO		117
1013	9.9.1918	600mm	4wPM	20hp	Dorman 2JO	2½T	66,151,179
1044	31.8.1918	600mm	4wPM	20hp	Dorman 2JO		131
1080	12.11.1918	600mm	4wPM	20hp	Dorman 2JO		71
1107	3.12.1918	600mm	4wPM	20hp	Dorman 2JO		131
1169	8.10.1918	600mm	4wPM	20hp	Dorman 2JO		116
1283	15.7.1918	600mm	4wPM	40hp	Dorman 4JO		138
1299	29.7.1918	600mm	4wPM	40hp	Dorman 4JO		138
1363	25.11.1918	600mm	4wPM	40hp	Dorman 4JO		120,182,317
1377	17.12.1918	600mm	4wPM	40hp	Dorman 4JO		187
1383	17.12.1918	600mm	4wPM	40hp	Dorman 4JO		138
1670	31.5.1918	600mm	4wPM	20hp	Dorman 2JO	2½T	142
1704	2.7.1918	600mm	4wPM	20hp	Dorman 2JO		116
1757	26.8.1918	600mm	4wPM	20hp	Dorman 2JO		116,138
1796	30.9.1918	600mm	4wPM	20hp	Dorman 2JO		71
1797	30.9.1918	600mm	4wPM	20hp	Dorman 2JO		71
1856	1.8.1919	2ft 0in	4wPM	20hp	Dorman 2JO	2½T	131,138,168
1896	10.9.1919	2ft 11in	4wPM	20hp	Dorman 2JO	2½T	179
1901	20.10.1919	3ft 0in	4wPM	20hp	Dorman 2JO	2½T	120
1933	25.11.1919	2ft 0in	4wPM	20hp	Dorman 2JO	2½T	59
2003	18.5.1920	3ft 0in	4wPM	20hp	Dorman 2JO	3½T	128
2004	8.6.1920	3ft 0in	4wPM	20hp	Dorman 2JO	4T	120
2020	23.12.1921	3ft 0in	4wPM	20hp	Dorman 2JO	2½T	120,127
2029	13.9.1920	4ft 8½in	4wPM	40hp	Dorman 4JO	8T	208
2075	13.4.1922	2ft 6in	4wPM	40hp	Dorman 4JO	4T	148
2079	15.5.1922	2ft 6in	4wPM	40hp	Dorman 4JO	4T	148,179
2103	8.4.1921	2ft 0in	4wPM	20hp	Dorman 2JO	2½T	304
2113	27.3.1922	600mm	4wPM	20hp	Dorman 2JO	2½T	119
2132	29.5.1922	4ft 8½in	4wPM	40hp	Dorman 4JO	8T	135
2213	12.3.1924	600mm	4wPM	20hp	Dorman 2JO	2½T	138
3660	24.6.1924	600mm	4wPM	20hp	Dorman 2JO	2½T	151,176
3664	20.2.1925	2ft 0in	4wPM	40hp	Dorman 4JO	6T	153,154
3674	3.5.1924	600mm	4wPM	40hp	Dorman 4JO	6T	138
3675	1.10.1924	600mm	4wPM	40hp	Dorman 4JO	6T	138
3738	5.5.1925	2ft 11in	4wPM	20hp	Dorman 2JO	4T	62,148,149,179
3786	14.8.1925	4ft 8½in	4wPM	40hp	Dorman 4JO	8T	125
3789	24.2.1926	600mm	4wPM	20hp	Dorman 2JO	2½T	131
3792	19.4.1926	2ft 11in	4wPM	20hp	Dorman 2JO	2½T	179
3795	13.7.1926	600mm	4wPM	20hp	Dorman 2JO	2½T	131
3797	16.6.1926	2ft 6in	4wPM	40hp	Dorman 4JO	6T	120,182,317
3822	c11.1925	4ft 8½in	4wPM	50hp	Thorneycroft BB4	10T	64
3828	22.3.1926	600mm	4wPM	20hp	Dorman 2JO	2½T	131
3832	18.6.1926	3ft 1¼in	4wPM	20hp	Dorman 2JO	2½T	65,149
3838	25.9.1926	3ft 1¼in	4wPM	20hp	Dorman 2JO	2½T	65,66,149,176
3841	13.11.1926	2ft 0in	4wPM	20hp	Dorman 2JO	2½T	132
3848	.1934	2ft 0in	4wPM	40hp	Dorman 4JO	6T	138
3850	2.6.1927	2ft 0in	4wPM	20hp	Dorman 2JO	2½T	132
3854	.1927	2ft 0in	4wPM	20hp	Dorman 2JO	2½T	124,154
3856	25.7.1934	2ft 6in	4wPM	40hp	Dorman 4JO	6T	153
3857	25.7.1934	2ft 0in	4wPM	20hp	Dorman 2JO	2½T	67
3861	.1928	600mm	4wPM	20hp	Dorman 2JO	2½T	153,154

3862	14.2.1929	600mm	4wPM	20hp	Dorman 2JO	2½T	116
3868	30.6.1929	2ft 0in	4wPM	20hp	Dorman 2JO	2½T	63,142,
							151,176
3965	30.8.1939	3ft 0in	4wDM	40hp	Fowler 4RB	6T	120,182
3982	1936	2ft 0in	4wDM	20hp	Dorman 2JO	2½T	116
3990	21.11.1934	2ft 0in	4wPM	20hp	Dorman 2JO	2½T	66,151
3996	20.10.1933	2ft 0in	4wPM	20hp	Dorman 2JO	2½T	116
4019	25.1.1926	2ft 0in	4wPM	20hp	Dorman 2JO	2½T	132
4027	31.3.1926	2ft 0in	4wPM	20hp	Dorman 2JO	2½T	127
4073	12.4.1927	2ft 0in	4wPM	20hp	Dorman 2JO	2½T	63,151
4155	8.4.1926	2ft 11in	4wPM	20hp	Dorman 2JO	4¾T	148,179
4568	21.3.1929	2ft 0in	4wPM	20hp	Dorman 2JO	2½T	132
4570	15.4.1929	2ft 0in	4wPM	20hp	Dorman 2JO	2½T	132,186
4578	22.5.1930	2ft 0in	4wPM	20hp	Dorman 2JO	2½T	116
4599	23.2.1932	2ft 0in	4wPM	20hp	Dorman 2JO	2½T	53,116
4701	21.11.1934	2ft 0in	4wPM	20hp	Dorman 2JO	2½T	117
4703	21.11.1934	2ft 0in	4wPM	20hp	Dorman 2JO	2½T	68
4705	4.3.1935	2ft 0in	4wPM	20hp	Dorman 2JO	2½T	117
4707	18.1.1936	2ft 0in	4wPM	20hp	Dorman 2JO	2½T	117
4708	18.1.1936	2ft 0in	4wPM	20hp	Dorman 2JO	2½T	117
4709	5.2.1936	2ft 0in	4wPM	20hp	Dorman 2JO	2½T	117
4803	3.12.1934	2ft 0in	.4wPM	20hp	Dorman 2JO	2½T	117
4805	3.12.1934	2ft 0in	4wPM	20hp	Dorman 2JO	2½T	117,186
4806	12.11.1936	2ft 0in	4wPM	20/26hp	Dorman 2JO	3½T	60
4807	22.9.1936	2ft 0in	4wPM	20/26hp	Dorman 2JO	2½T	60,136
4808	2.12.1936	2ft 0in	4wPM	20/26hp	Dorman 2JO	2½T	132
4809	9.12.1936	2ft 0in	4wPM	20/26hp	Dorman 2JO	2½T	132
4813	2.9.1938	2ft 0in	4wPM	20/26hp	Dorman 2JO	2½T	122,124,
							238,251,253,288,311
5002	20.4.1929	600mm	4wPM	20hp	Dorman 2JO	2½T	132
5006	16.5.1929	600mm	4wPM	20hp	Dorman 2JO	2½T	124
5008	16.5.1929	600mm	4wPM	20hp	Dorman 2JO	2½T	132
5011	22.5.1929	600mm	4wPM	20hp	Dorman 2JO	2½T	132
5018	31.8.1929	2ft 0in	4wPM	20hp	Dorman 2JO	2½T	54,92
5026	15.8.1929	2ft 0in	4wPM	20hp	Dorman 2JO	4T	62,148,149
5055	4.3.1930	2ft 0in	4wPM	20hp	Dorman 2JO	2½T	279
5062	4.4.1930	2ft 0in	4wPM	20hp	Dorman 2JO	2½T	279
5073	3.5.1930	2ft 0in	4wPM	20hp	Dorman 2JO	2½T	116
5235	13.11.1930	2ft 0in	4wPM	20/35hp	Dorman 4MRX	4T	279
5236	13.11.1930	2ft 0in	4wPM	20/35hp	Dorman 4MRX	4T	279
5252	24.12.1930	2ft 0in	4wPM	20/35hp	Dorman 4MRX	2½T	153,154
5265	4.2.1931	2ft 0in	4wPM	20/35hp	Dorman 4MRX	2½T	58
5345	20.8.1931	2ft 0in	4wPM	20/35hp	Dorman 4MRX	2½T	153,154
5346	20.8.1931	2ft 0in	4wPM	20/35hp	Dorman 4MRX	2½T	153,154
5363	2.1.1932	2ft 0in	4wPM	20/35hp	Dorman 4MRX	2½T	71
5368	2.6.1932	2ft 0in	4wPM	20/35hp	Dorman 4MRX	2½T	153,154
5410	10.3.1933	2ft 0in	4wPM	20/35hp	Dorman 4MRX	4T	153
5412	19.10.1933	2ft 0in	4wPM	20/35hp	Dorman 4MRX	4T	72
5601	25.9.1930	2ft 0in	4wDM	20hp	Dorman 2RB	4T	63,142,151
5603	26.2.1931	2ft 0in	4wDM	20hp	Dorman 2RB	4T	146,186
5606	23.2.1931	2ft 0in	4wDM	20hp	Dorman 2RB	4T	62,63,149,184
5607	2.3.1931	2ft 11in	4wDM	20hp	Dorman 2RB	4T	62,149
5608	3.7.1931	2ft 0in	4wDM	20hp	Dorman 2RB	4T	186
5612	20.8.1931	2ft 0in	4wDM	20hp	Dorman 2RB	4T	186

5613	1.9.1931	2ft 0in	4wDM	20hp	Dorman 2RB	4T		186
5634	6.3.1933	2ft 0in	4wDM	20/36hp	Dorman 2RB	2½T		59
5635	29.3.1933	2ft 0in	4wDM	20/36hp	Dorman 2RB	2½T		59
5636	18.2.1933	2ft 0in	4wDM	20/36hp	Dorman 2RB	2½T		59
5637	18.2.1933	2ft 0in	4wDM	20/36hp	Dorman 2RB	2½T		59
5662	24.3.1934	2ft 0in	4wDM	25/36hp	Dorman 2RB	3T		60
5667	25.7.1934	1ft11½in	4wDM	25/36hp	Dorman 2RB	4T		63,145,151
5668	27.7.1934	1ft11½in	4wDM	25/36hp	Dorman 2RB	4T		63,143,145,151
5716	9.3.1937	2ft 0in	4wDM	25/36hp	Dorman 2RB	4T		136
5722	6.5.1939	2ft 11in	4wDM	25/36hp	Dorman 2RB	4T		65,144,150
5723	6.5.1939	2ft 11in	4wDM	25/36hp	Dorman 2RB	4T		65,144
5724	24.5.1939	2ft 11in	4wDM	25/36hp	Dorman 2RB	4T		65,144,150
5725	24.5.1939	2ft 11in	4wDM	25/36hp	Dorman 2RB	4T		65,144,150
5752	17.10.1939	4ft 8½in	4wDM	65/85hp	Dorman 4DL	20T		125
5852	18.10.1933	2ft 0in	4wDM	20/28hp	Dorman 2HW	2½T		132
5854	20.1.1934	2ft 0in	4wDM	20/28hp	Dorman 2HW	3½T		116
5859	29.5.1934	2ft 0in	4wDM	20/28hp	Dorman 2HW	3½T		117
5863	31.5.1934	2ft 0in	4wDM	20/28hp	Dorman 2HW	3½T		117
5864	16.8.1934	2ft 0in	4wDM	20/28hp	Dorman 2HW	3½T		132
5867	3.9.1934	2ft 0in	4wDM	20/28hp	Dorman 2HW	3½T		68,96
5870	16.1.1935	2ft 0in	4wDM	20/28hp	Dorman 2HW	2½T		93,132
5873	16.1.1935	2ft 0in	4wDM	20/28hp	Dorman 2HW	2½T		59,186
5879	10.4.1935	2ft 0in	4wDM	20/28hp	Dorman 2HW	3½T		255
5880	12.4.1935	2ft 0in	4wDM	20/28hp	Dorman 2HW	2½T		66,67,151
5881	16.5.1935	2ft 0in	4wDM	20/28hp	Dorman 2HW	3½T		117,242
5886	14.10.1935	2ft 0in	4wDM	20/28hp	Dorman 2HW	3½T		256
5913	13.5.1935	2ft 0in	4wDM	32/42hp	Dorman 2RBL	5T		136
5931	25.7.1935	2ft 0in	4wDM	32/42hp	Dorman 2RBL	6T		136
5932	2.10.1935	2ft 0in	4wDM	32/42hp	Dorman 2RBL	6T		61
5933	30.3.1936	2ft 0in	4wDM	32/42hp	Dorman 2RBL	6T		61
5945	6.2.1937	2ft 6in	4wDM	32/42hp	Dorman 2RBL	5T		136,154
5946	5.3.1937	2ft 6in	4wDM	32/42hp	Dorman 2RBL	5T		154
5947	13.3.1937	2ft 6in	4wDM	32/42hp	Dorman 2RBL	5T		154
6012	6.12.1930	2ft 0in	4wPM	12/20hp	Dorman 4MVR	2T		186
6019	19.1.1933	2ft 0in	4wPM	12/20hp	Dorman 4MVR	2T		252
6020	21.1.1933	2ft 0in	4wPM	12/20hp	Dorman 4MVR	2T		252
7016	.1936	2ft 0in	4wPM	20/26hp	Dorman 2JO	2½T		60
7031	11.9.1936	2ft 0in	4wPM	20/26hp	Dorman 2JO	2½T		252,314
7032	2.10.1936	2ft 0in	4wPM	20/26hp	Dorman 2JO	2½T		252
7035	15.12.1936	2ft 0in	4wPM	20/26hp	Dorman 2JO	2½T		252
7036	16.12.1936	2ft 0in	4wPM	20/26hp	Dorman 2JO	2½T		132,186
7037	16.12.1936	2ft 0in	4wPM	20/26hp	Dorman 2JO	2½T		117
7043	4.2.1937	2ft 0in	4wPM	20/26hp	Dorman 2JO	2½T		314
7046	23.3.1937	2ft 0in	4wPM	20/26hp	Dorman 2JO	2½T		60,130
7105	21.1.1936	2ft 0in	4wDM	20/28hp	Dorman 2HW	2½T		132,186
7108	28.1.1936	2ft 0in	4wDM	20/28hp	Dorman 2HW	2½T		132,186
7115	27.2.1936	2ft 0in	4wDM	20/28hp	Dorman 2HW	2½T		93,132
7120	3.1936	2ft 0in	4wDM	20/28hp	Dorman 2HW	3½T		279
7125	24.3.1936	2ft 0in	4wDM	20/28hp	Dorman 2HW	3½T		279
7126	30.4.1936	2ft 0in	4wDM	20/28hp	Dorman 2HW	3½T		117
7127	18.5.1936	2ft 0in	4wDM	20/28hp	Dorman 2HW	3½T		294
7128	21.5.1936	2ft 0in	4wDM	20/28hp	Dorman 2HW	3½T		117,184
7129	14.5.1936	2ft 0in	4wDM	20/28hp	Dorman 2HW	2½T		146,186
7130	14.5.1936	2ft 0in	4wDM	20/28hp	Dorman 2HW	2½T		294

7137	11.9.1936	2ft 0in	4wDM	20/28hp Dorman 2HW	3½T	255
7140	12.11.1936	2ft 0in	4wDM	20/28hp Dorman 2HW	3½T	132
7141	14.7.1936	2ft 6in	4wDM	20/28hp Dorman 2HW	3½T	153,154
7142	14.7.1936	2ft 6in	4wDM	20/28hp Dorman 2HW	3½T	153,154
7145	19.11.1936	2ft 0in	4wDM	20/28hp Dorman 2HW	2½T	93,132
7148	8.12.1936	2ft 0in	4wDM	20/28hp Dorman 2HW	2½T	132
7149	8.12.1936	2ft 0in	4wDM	20/28hp Dorman 2HW	2½T	132
7152	31.12.1936	2ft 0in	4wDM	20/28hp Dorman 2HW	2½T	93
7153	1.1.1937	2ft 0in	4wDM	20/28hp Dorman 2HW	2½T	117
7154	22.1.1937	2ft 0in	4wDM	20/28hp Dorman 2HW	2½T	93,132
7176	6.5.1937	2ft 0in	4wDM	20/28hp Dorman 2HW	3½T	68,72,96
7180	4.6.1937	2ft 0in	4wDM	20/28hp Dorman 2HW	3½T	255
7188	1.7.1937	2ft 0in	4wDM	20/28hp Dorman 2HW	2½T	117
7195	30.9.1937	2ft 0in	4wDM	20/28hp Dorman 2HW	2½T	93,132
7201	20.10.1937	2ft 0in	4wDM	20/28hp Dorman 2HW	2½T	117
7214	28.2.1938	2ft 0in	4wDM	20/28hp Dorman 2HW	2½T	117,186
7215	9.3.1938	2ft 0in	4wDM	20/28hp Dorman 2HW	3½T	53,117
7219	16.3.1938	2ft 0in	4wDM	20/28hp Dorman 2HW	2½T	242
7302	30.4.1938	2ft 6in	4wDM	20/28hp Dorman 2DWD	3½T	153,154
7303	4.5.1938	2ft 6in	4wDM	20/28hp Dorman 2DWD	3½T	153,154
7333	6.12.1938	2ft 0in	4wDM	20/28hp Dorman 2DWD	2½T	325
7371	13.2.1939	2ft 0in	4wDM	20/28hp Dorman 2DWD	2½T	132
7372	13.2.1939	2ft 0in	4wDM	20/28hp Dorman 2DWD	2½T	132
7374	22.2.1939	2ft 0in	4wDM	20/28hp Dorman 2DWD	2½T	132
7391	11.3.1939	2ft 0in	4wDM	20/28hp Dorman 2DWD	2½T	293
7403	17.8.1939	2ft 0in	4wDM	20/28hp Dorman 2DWD	2½T	117
7414	31.7.1939	2ft 0in	4wDM	20/28hp Dorman 2DWD	2½T	93,132
7457	16.12.1939	2ft 0in	4wDM	20/28hp Dorman 2DWD	2½T	60
7474	c2.1940	2ft 0in	4wDM	20/28hp Dorman 2DWD	2½T	142,151
7492	4.10.1940	2ft 0in	4wDM	20/28hp Dorman 2DWD	3½T	93,132
7710	9.6.1939	2ft 0in	4wDM	32/42hp Dorman 2DL	5T	117,139
7932	29.10.1941	2ft 0in	4wDM	32/42hp Dorman 2DL	5T	93,132,139
7933	31.10.1941	2ft 0in	4wDM	32/42hp Dorman 2DL	5T	117,139,186
7956	17.7.1945	2ft 0in	4wDM	32/42hp Dorman 2DL	5T	186
7998	15.5.1947	2ft 11in	4wDM	32/42hp Dorman 2DL	5T	65
7999	21.5.1947	2ft 11in	4wDM	32/42hp Dorman 2DL	5T	65
8540	25.7.1940	600mm	4wDM	20/28hp Dorman 2DWD	2½T	117
8575	28.10.1940	600mm	4wDM	20/28hp Dorman 2DWD	2½T	251,253
8587	14.1.1941	600mm	4wDM	20/28hp Dorman 2DWD	2½T	132
8588	14.1.1941	600mm	4wDM	20/28hp Dorman 2DWD	2½T	59,123
8592	6.12.1940	2ft 0in	4wDM	20/28hp Dorman 2DWD	2½T	59,123
8594	10.12.1940	2ft 0in	4wDM	20/28hp Dorman 2DWD	2½T	242
8596	12.12.1940	2ft 0in	4wDM	20/28hp Dorman 2DWD	2½T	123
8597	12.12.1940	2ft 0in	4wDM	20/28hp Dorman 2DWD	2½T	117
8598	4.12.1940	2ft 0in	4wDM	20/28hp Dorman 2DWD	2½T	60
8677	15.5.1942	2ft 0in	4wDM	20/28hp Dorman 2DWD	2½T	123
8682	17.10.1941	2ft 0in	4wDM	20/28hp Dorman 2DWD	2½T	138
8683	14.11.1941	2ft 0in	4wDM	20/28hp Dorman 2DWD	2½T	117
8695	26.12.1941	2ft 0in	4wDM	20/28hp Dorman 2DWD	2½T	117,182,186
8700	22.12.1941	2ft 0in	4wDM	20/28hp Dorman 2DWD	2½T	117
8704	13.1.1942	2ft 0in	4wDM	20/28hp Dorman 2DWD	2½T	60
8713	25.3.1941	2ft 0in	4wDM	20/28hp Dorman 2DWD	2½T	93,132
8717	21.3.1941	2ft 0in	4wDM	20/28hp Dorman 2DWD	2½T	108
8720	21.3.1941	2ft 0in	4wDM	20/28hp Dorman 2DWD	2½T	117

8723	3.4.1941	2ft 0in	4wDM	20/28hp	Dorman 2DWD	2½T	117
8724	3.4.1941	2ft 0in	4wDM	20/28hp	Dorman 2DWD	2½T	117
8725	4.4.1941	2ft 0in	4wDM	20/28hp	Dorman 2DWD	2½T	93,132
8727	22.5.1941	2ft 0in	4wDM	20/28hp	Dorman 2DWD	2½T	117,324
8731	7.6.1941	2ft 0in	4wDM	20/28hp	Dorman 2DWD	2½T	187,238, 251,253,323
8732	7.6.1941	2ft 0in	4wDM	20/28hp	Dorman 2DWD	2½T	117
8739	26.1.1942	2ft 0in	4wDM	20/28hp	Dorman 2DWD	2½T	250-254
8748	17.2.1942	2ft 0in	4wDM	20/28hp	Dorman 2DWD	2½T	117
8756	24.2.1942	2ft 0in	4wDM	20/28hp	Dorman 2DWD	2½T	117,323
8790	26.3.1943	2ft 0in	4wDM	20/28hp	Dorman 2DWD	2½T	68,96
8810	17.3.1943	600mm	4wDM	20/28hp	Dorman 2DWD	2½T	250,252
8917	19.9.1944	600mm	4wDM	20/28hp	Dorman 2DWD	2½T	93,132
8927	9.11.1944	600mm	4wDM	20/28hp	Dorman 2DWD	2½T	142,151
8936	4.12.1944	600mm	4wDM	20/28hp	Dorman 2DWD	2½T	143
8969	18.9.1945	2ft 0in	4wDM	20/28hp	Dorman 2DWD	2½T	122,189, 251,311,323
8993	18.3.1946	2ft 0in	4wDM	20/28hp	Dorman 2DWD	2½T	195,324
8994	3.4.1946	2ft 0in	4wDM	20/28hp	Dorman 2DWD	2½T	117
8995	18.3.1946	2ft 0in	4wDM	20/28hp	Dorman 2DWD	2½T	108
8998	20.3.1946	2ft 0in	4wDM	20/28hp	Dorman 2DWD	2½T	102
9010	19.12.1949	2ft 11in	4wDM	45/63hp	Dorman 3DL	9T	148
9204	3.6.1946	2ft 0in	4wDM	20/28hp	Dorman 2DWD	2½T	234,251, 252,309
9235	17.10.1946	2ft 0in	4wDM	20/28hp	Dorman 2DWD	3½T	146
9263	16.5.1947	2ft 0in	4wDM	20/28hp	Dorman 2DWD	3½T	68
9409	7.12.1948	2ft 0in	4wDM	20/28hp	Dorman 2DWD	3½T	53,117
9411	13.12.1948	2ft 0in	4wDM	20/28hp	Dorman 2DWD	3½T	242
9415	27.4.1949	2ft 0in	4wDM	20/28hp	Dorman 2DWD	3½T	117
9418	14.6.1949	2ft 0in	4wDM	20/28hp	Dorman 2DWD	3½T	117
9547	28.11.1950	600mm	4wDM	20/28hp	Dorman 2DWD	2½T	117,138
9655	16.10.1951	2ft 0in	4wDM	20/28hp	Dorman 2DWD	2½T	191,194
9711	11.11.1952	2ft 0in	4wDM	20/28hp	Dorman 2DWD	2½T	251.253,323
9778	18.2.1953	2ft 0in	4wDM	20/28hp	Dorman 2DWD	2½T	178
9869	18.9.1953	2ft 0in	4wDM	20/28hp	Dorman 2DWD	2½T	96,314
9921	21.9.1959	4ft 8½in	4wDM	50hp	Dorman 3LB	7T	177,178
9922	16.4.1959	4ft 8½in	4wDM	50hp	Dorman 3LB	7T	64,231
9978	19.5.1954	2ft 0in	4wDM	20/28hp	Dorman 2DWD	2½T	96
10031	9.7.1948	2ft 0in	4wDM	32/42hp	Dorman 2DL	6T	136
10118	31.5.1949	3ft 0in	4wDM	32/42hp	Dorman 2DL	5T	120
10125	4.5.1949	2ft 11in	4wDM	32/42hp	Dorman 2DL	7T	62
10126	19.7.1949	2ft 11in	4wDM	32/42hp	Dorman 2DL	7T	62
10127	22.9.1949	2ft 11in	4wDM	32/42hp	Dorman 2DL	7T	62
10128	28.12.1949	2ft 11in	4wDM	32/42hp	Dorman 2DL	7T	62
10158	15.11.1949	2ft 11in	4wDM	32/42hp	Dorman 2DL	5T	65
10159	6.1.1950	2ft 11in	4wDM	32/42hp	Dorman 2DL	5T	62,65,120
10160	7.2.1950	2ft 11in	4wDM	32/42hp	Dorman 2DL	5T	65,95,141
10161	14.2.1950	2ft 11in	4wDM	32/42hp	Dorman 2DL	5T	65,141,148,193
10272	27.11.1951	2ft 0in	4wDM	32/42hp	Dorman 2DL	6T	93,132,138
10409	14.1.1954	2ft 0in	4wDM	32/42hp	Dorman 2DL	6T	117,139,186
10430	18.8.1954	2ft 11in	4wDM	32/42hp	Dorman 2DL	7T	62
10455	11.5.1955	2ft 11in	4wDM	32/42hp	Dorman 2DL	5T	65,141,150
11001	2.3.1956	2ft 0in	4wDM	50hp	Dorman 3LA	6T	142,193
11002	25.9.1957	2ft 0in	4wDM	50hp	Dorman 3LA	6T	146

11003	8.11.1956	2ft 0in	4wDM	50hp	Dorman 3LA	5T	186
11206	15.6.1962	2ft 11in	4wDM	50hp	Dorman 3LB	7T	120
11264	13.7.1964	2ft 0in	4wDM	60hp	Dorman 3LB	6T	146
11297	14.6.1965	600mm	4wDM	60hp	Dorman 3LB	7T	186
11298	14.6.1965	600mm	4wDM	60hp	Dorman 3LB	7T	186
11311	4.3.1966	2ft 0in	4wDM	60hp	Dorman 3LB	7T	146
11312	7.3.1966	2ft 0in	4wDM	60hp	Dorman 3LB	7T	142
20054	4.10.1949	2ft 6in	4wDM	20/28hp	Dorman 2DWD	2½T	144,151,
20055	4.10.1949	2ft 6in	4wDM	20/28hp	Dorman 2DWD	2½T	144
20080	10.2.1953	2ft 6in	4wDM	20/28hp	Dorman 2DWD	2½T	142
20081	21.5.1953	2ft 6in	4wDM	20/28hp	Dorman 2DWD	2½T	144
20558	7.4.1955	600mm	4wDM	20/28hp	Dorman 2DWD	2½T	117
21282	4.9.1960	2ft 0in	4wDM	20/28hp	Dorman 2DWD	2½T	146
21283	28.4.1965	600mm	4wDM	20/28hp	Dorman 2DWD	2½T	68,96
21286	11.6.1959	600mm	4wDM	20/28hp	Dorman 2DWD	2½T	122
21287	11.6.1959	600mm	4wDM	20/28hp	Dorman 2DWD	2½T	288
21505	7.6.1955	600mm	4wDM	20/28hp	Dorman 2DWD	2½T	250
21615	13.9.1957	600mm	4wDM	20/28hp	Dorman 2DWD	2½T	187
22031	26.6.1959	600mm	4wDM	40hp	Dorman 2LB	4½T	297
22032	26.6.1959	600mm	4wDM	40hp	Dorman 2LB	4½T	297
22070	6.5.1960	600mm	4wDM	30hp	Dorman 2DWD	3½T	146
22119	24.4.1961	600mm	4wDM	30hp	Dorman 2LB	2½T	96
22144	29.5.1962	Metre	4wDM	30hp	Dorman 2LA	3½T	316-318
22224	26.2.1966	2ft 0in	4wDM	40hp	Dorman 2LB	3½T	326
40S273	16.8.1966	2ft 0in	4wDM	40hp	Dorman 2LB	2½T	108
40S343	1966	2ft 0in	4wDM	40hp	Dorman 2LB		195
40S370	15.1.1970	2ft 0in	4wDM	40hp	Perkins 3.152		253
40S371	15.1.1970	2ft 0in	4wDM	40hp	Perkins 3.152		251
60S317	31.3.1966	2ft 0in	4wDM	60hp	Dorman 3LB	7T	186
60S318	21.7.1966	2ft 0in	4wDM	60hp	Dorman 3LB	7T	189
60S393	.1970	3ft 0in	4wDM	72hp			81
121U117/							
121U123	27.2.1974	2ft 0in	4wDH	44hp	Deutz F4L812	5½T	146,189

MANNING, WARDLE & CO LTD, BOYNE ENGINE WORKS, Leeds   MW

40	30.12.1861	4ft 8½in	0-4-0ST	OC	9½ x 14	2ft9in	E	231
45	30.4.1862	4ft 8½in	0-6-0ST	IC	12 x 17	3ft1$^{3}/_{8}$in	Old I	89
56	3.11.1862	4ft 8½in	0-6-0ST	IC	12 x 17	3ft1$^{3}/_{8}$in	Old I	75,167
81	30.6.1863	4ft 8½in	0-6-0ST	IC	11 x 17	3ft1$^{3}/_{8}$in	Old I	76
106	8.4.1864	4ft 8½in	0-6-0ST	IC	11 x 17	3ft1$^{3}/_{8}$in	Old I	297
129	20.6.1864	4ft 8½in	0-6-0ST	IC	11 x 17	3ft1$^{3}/_{8}$in	Old I	76
155	28.7.1865	4ft 8½in	0-6-0ST	IC	11 x 17	3ft1$^{3}/_{8}$in	Old I	166
165	22.6.1865	4ft 8½in	0-6-0ST	IC	11 x 17	3ft1$^{3}/_{8}$in	Old I	166
174	25.8.1865	4ft 8½in	0-6-0ST	IC	11 x 17	3ft1$^{3}/_{8}$in	Old I	85,166
177	13.11.1865	4ft 8½in	0-6-0ST	IC	11 x 17	3ft1$^{3}/_{8}$in	Old I	166
178	8.2.1866	4ft 8½in	0-6-0ST	IC	11 x 17	3ft1$^{3}/_{8}$in	Old I	289
180	30.1.1866	4ft 8½in	0-6-0ST	IC	12 x 17	3ft1$^{3}/_{8}$in	K	166
196	16.11.1866	4ft 8½in	0-6-0ST	IC	12 x 17	3ft1$^{3}/_{8}$in	K	166

No.	Date	Gauge	Wheels		Cylinder	Wheel dia	Class	Pages
204	24.4.1866	4ft 8½in	0-6-0ST	IC	11 x 17	3ft1³/₈in	Old I	166
205	9.7.1866	4ft 8½in	0-6-0ST	IC	11 x 17	3ft1³/₈in	Old I	64,79,166
212	10.7.1866	4ft 8½in	0-6-0ST	IC	12 x 17	3ft1³/₈in	K	52
315	6.9.1870	4ft 8½in	0-6-0ST	IC	12 x 17	3ft1³/₈in	K	167
325	3.11.1870	4ft 8½in	0-6-0ST	IC	12 x 17	3ft1³/₈in	K	167
334	3.1.1871	4ft 8½in	0-4-0ST	OC	12 x 18	3ft0in	H	85
345	3.5.1871	4ft 8½in	0-4-0ST	OC	12 x 18	3ft0in	H	228,260
368	8.4.1871	4ft 8½in	0-6-0ST	IC	12 x 17	3ft1³/₈in	K	167
428	10.7.1873	4ft 8½in	0-6-0ST	IC	12 x 17	3ft1³/₈in	K	257
537	25.3.1875	4ft 8½in	0-4-0ST	OC	12 x 18	3ft0in	H	267
583	7.8.1876	4ft 8½in	0-6-0ST	IC	13 x 18	3ft0in	M	302
590	16.11.1876	4ft 8½in	0-4-0ST	OC	12 x 18	3ft0in	H	210
593	20.12.1877	4ft 8½in	0-4-0ST	OC	12 x 18	3ft0in	H	208
596	20.4.1876	4ft 8½in	0-6-0ST	IC	12 x 17	3ft1³/₈in	K	301,302
597	1.5.1876	4ft 8½in	0-6-0ST	IC	12 x 17	3ft1³/₈in	K	293
614	30.6.1876	3ft 0in	0-4-0ST	OC	7 x 12	2ft6in	C	303
616	28.7.1876	4ft 8½in	0-6-0ST	IC	12 x 17	3ft1³/₈in	K	69
617	26.7.1876	4ft 8½in	0-6-0ST	IC	12 x 17	3ft1³/₈in	K	293
620	22.8.1876	4ft 8½in	0-6-0ST	IC	12 x 17	3ft1³/₈in	K	78
634	2.2.1877	4ft 8½in	0-4-0ST	OC	10 x 16	2ft9in	F	287,306
636	11.12.1876	4ft 8½in	0-6-0ST	IC	12 x 17	3ft1³/₈in	K	297
641	20.3.1877	4ft 8½in	0-6-0ST	IC	12 x 17	3ft1³/₈in	K	290
651	14.3.1878	4ft 8½in	0-4-0ST	OC	9 x 14	2ft9in	E	297
655	27.6.1877	4ft 8½in	0-6-0ST	IC	13 x 18	3ft0in	M	76
662	25.6.1877	4ft 8½in	0-6-0ST	IC	12 x 17	3ft1³/₈in	K	297
678	2.11.1877	4ft 8½in	0-6-0ST	IC	12 x 17	3ft1³/₈in	K	301,302
683	22.1.1878	4ft 8½in	0-6-0ST	IC	12 x 17	3ft1³/₈in	K	85,297
687	25.3.1878	4ft 8½in	0-6-0ST	IC	12 x 17	3ft1³/₈in	K	297
688	24.6.1878	4ft 8½in	0-6-0ST	IC	12 x 17	3ft1³/₈in	K	236
692	8.7.1878	4ft 8½in	0-4-0ST	OC	10 x 16	2ft9in	F	85
713	23.1.1879	4ft 8½in	0-4-0ST	OC	9½ x 14	2ft9in	E	85
720	23.12.1880	4ft 8½in	0-4-0ST	OC	9 x 14	2ft9in	E	234
722	28.5.1879	4ft 8½in	0-4-0T	OC	10 x 16	2ft9in	F alt	85
738	11.4.1881	4ft 8½in	0-6-0ST	IC	12 x 17	3ft1³/₈in	K	140
745	19.5.1880	4ft 8½in	0-4-0ST	OC	12 x 18	3ft0in	H	240,271,284
818	24.3.1882	4ft 8½in	0-6-0ST	IC	12 x 17	3ft1³/₈in	K	79
848	12.12.1882	4ft 8½in	0-6-0ST	IC	12 x 17	3ft1³/₈in	K	141,176,307
887	24.6.1884	4ft 8½in	0-4-0ST	OC	8 x 14	2ft8in	D	165
890	1.5.1883	4ft 8½in	0-6-0ST	IC	12 x 17	3ft1³/₈in	K	85
892	2.7.1884	4ft 8½in	0-4-0ST	OC	8 x 14	2ft8in	D	302
893	2.12.1894	4ft 8½in	0-4-0ST	OC	8 x 14	2ft8in	D	78
899	31.5.1884	4ft 8½in	0-6-0ST	IC	13 x 18	3ft0in	M	302
900	6.3.1884	4ft 8½in	0-4-0ST	OC	9 x 14	2ft9in	E	287
901	19.1.1885	4ft 8½in	0-4-0ST	OC	9 x 14	2ft9in	E	76
911	10.9.1884	4ft 8½in	0-6-0ST	IC	12 x 17	3ft1³/₈in	K	302
915	26.11.1883	3ft 0in	0-4-0ST	OC	8½x 14	2ft8in		258
932	2.2.1885	4ft 8½in	0-4-0ST	OC	10 x 16	2ft9in	F	85
942	9.4.1885	4ft 8½in	0-4-0ST	OC	8 x 14	2ft8in	D	302
952	3.2.1886	4ft 8½in	0-4-0ST	OC	12 x 18	3ft0in	H	236
971	26.6.1885	4ft 8½in	0-6-0ST	IC	12 x 17	3ft1³/₈in	K	302
973	26.5.1886	4ft 8½in	0-6-0ST	IC	12 x 17	3ft1³/₈in	K	297
976	6.8.1886	4ft 8½in	0-6-0ST	IC	12 x 17	3ft1³/₈in	K	297
977	19.4.1886	4ft 8½in	0-4-0ST	OC	8 x 14	2ft8in	D	297
990	25.1.1887	4ft 8½in	0-4-0ST	OC	9 x 14	2ft9in	E	169

996	29.10.1886	4ft 8½in	0-6-0ST	IC	12 x 17	3ft0in	K	169
1003	19.5.1887	4ft 8½in	0-6-0ST	IC	12 x 17	3ft0in	K	300
1005	15.6.1887	4ft 8½in	0-6-0T	IC	13 x 18	3ft0in	Spl M	85
1016	2.11.1887	4ft 8½in	0-4-0ST	OC	9½ x 14	2ft9in	E	300
1023	15.6.1887	4ft 8½in	0-4-0ST	OC	12 x 18	3ft0in	H	237
1038	19.8.1887	3ft 0in	0-4-0ST	OC	9 x 14	2ft9in	E	237,266,267
1062	28.3.1888	4ft 8½in	0-6-0T	IC	13 x 18	3ft0in	Spl M	300
1065	24.5.1888	4ft 8½in	0-6-0T	IC	13 x 18	3ft0in	Spl M	79
1068	21.6.1888	4ft 8½in	0-6-0ST	IC	12 x 17	3ft0in	K	85,302
1070	26.10.1888	4ft 8½in	0-6-0ST	IC	12 x 17	3ft0in	K	85
1071	19.12.1888	4ft 8½in	0-6-0ST	IC	12 x 17	3ft0in	K	85
1081	19.12.1888	4ft 8½in	0-4-0ST	OC	10 x 16	2ft9in	F	85
1091	19.12.1888	4ft 8½in	0-4-0ST	OC	12 x 18	3ft0in	H	141,221,241, 281,307
1100	2.11.1888	4ft 8½in	0-6-0T	IC	13 x 18	3ft0in	Spl M	52
1112	24.1.1889	4ft 8½in	0-6-0ST	IC	12 x 17	3ft0in	K	85,302
1123	8.5.1889	3ft 0in	0-6-0ST	OC	11½x17	2ft9in	Spl	245
1141	29.10.1889	4ft 8½in	0-4-0ST	OC	12 x 18	3ft0in	H	85
1145	27.6.1890	4ft 8½in	0-6-0ST	IC	12 x 17	3ft0in	K	300
1146	2.7.1890	4ft 8½in	0-6-0ST	IC	12 x 17	3ft0in	K	85
1153	7.4.1890	4ft 8½in	0-6-0ST	IC	12 x 18	3ft0in	L	300
1210	22.12.1890	4ft 8½in	0-6-0ST	IC	12 x 18	3ft0in	L	218,227
1211	2.3.1891	4ft 8½in	0-6-0ST	IC	12 x 18	3ft0in	L	85
1214	28.3.1891	4ft 8½in	0-6-0ST	IC	12 x 18	3ft0in	L	85
1228	25.3.1895	4ft 8½in	0-6-0ST	IC	12 x 18	3ft0in	L	302
1232	24.8.1891	4ft 8½in	0-6-0ST	IC	12 x 17	3ft0in	K	85
1235	16.10.1891	4ft 8½in	0-6-0ST	IC	12 x 17	3ft0in	K	227
1237	20.6.1892	4ft 8½in	0-6-0ST	IC	12 x 17	3ft0in	K	302
1245	17.9.1894	4ft 8½in	0-6-0ST	IC	13 x 18	3ft0in	M	125
1249	5.12.1894	4ft 8½in	0-6-0ST	IC	12 x 17	3ft0in	K	69
1276	1.3.1894	3ft 0in	0-6-0ST	OC	9 x 14	2ft6in	E	223,226
1286	28.6.1894	4ft 8½in	0-6-0ST	OC	15 x 20	3ft1in	Spl	245
1293	31.5.1895	4ft 8½in	0-6-0ST	IC	12 x 17	3ft0in	K	264,304
1301	13.5.1895	4ft 8½in	0-6-0ST	IC	12 x 18	3ft0in	L	304
1316	29.10.1895	4ft 8½in	0-6-0ST	IC	15 x 22	3ft6in	Spl	210,214,220
1317	30.10.1895	4ft 8½in	0-6-0ST	IC	15 x 22	3ft6in	Spl	210,214,220
1359	31.12.1896	4ft 8½in	0-6-0ST	IC	15 x 22	3ft9in	O	228
1370	28.5.1897	3ft 0in	0-6-0ST	OC	11½x17	2ft9in	Spl	215
1378	25.4.1898	4ft 8½in	0-6-0ST	IC	13 x 18	3ft0in	M	79,304
1381	17.4.1897	4ft 8½in	0-4-0ST	OC	9 x 14	2ft9in	E	121,135
1415	7.2.1899	4ft 8½in	0-6-0ST	IC	12 x 17	3ft0in	K	69
1432	1.5.1899	4ft 8½in	0-6-0ST	IC	12 x 18	3ft0in	L	303
1444	12.5.1899	4ft 8½in	0-6-0ST	IC	13 x 18	3ft0in	M	303
1518	7.3.1901	4ft 8½in	0-4-0ST	OC	12 x 18	3ft0in	H	79
1523	29.7.1901	4ft 8½in	0-4-0ST	OC	12 x 18	3ft0in	H	155
1535	7.2.1902	4ft 8½in	0-6-0ST	IC	12 x 17	3ft0in	K	85
1539	17.2.1902	4ft 8½in	0-6-0ST	IC	12 x 17	3ft0in	K	85
1541	7.2.1902	4ft 8½in	0-6-0ST	IC	12 x 18	3ft0in	L	85
1542	17.2.1902	4ft 8½in	0-6-0ST	IC	12 x 18	3ft0in	L	85
1555	28.2.1902	4ft 8½in	0-6-0ST	IC	14 x20	3ft6in	Q	85
1556	7.3.1902	4ft 8½in	0-6-0ST	IC	14 x20	3ft6in	Q	85
1560	16.5.1902	4ft 8½in	0-6-0ST	IC	12 x 18	3ft0in	L	294
1598	18.6.1903	4ft 8½in	0-6-0ST	IC	12 x 18	3ft0in	L	64
1599	8.10.1903	4ft 8½in	0-6-0ST	IC	12 x 18	3ft0in	L	64

1668	13.11.1905	4ft 8½in	0-6-0ST	IC	12 x 18	3ft0in	L	304
1675	31.1.1906	3ft 0in	0-6-0ST	OC	11½x17	2ft9in	-	245,319
1733	25.5.1908	4ft 8½in	0-6-0ST	IC	13 x 18	3ft0in	M	80
1757	18.2.1910	Metre	0-4-0ST	OC	11 x 17	2ft9in	Spl	273
1762	20.10.1910	4ft 8½in	0-6-0ST	IC	16 x 22	3ft6in	-	210,214
1795	24.6.1912	4ft 8½in	0-4-0ST	OC	14 x 20	3ft6in	P	103,221,322
1843	19.4.1915	4ft 8½in	0-4-0ST	OC	14 x 20	3ft6in	P	164
1877	23.3.1915	2ft 6in	0-6-2T	OC	12 x 16	2ft6in	-	102,184
1955	20.12.1917	4ft 8½in	0-6-0ST	IC	15 x 22	3ft9in	O	260
1972	25.1.1919	4ft 8½in	0-6-0ST	IC	12 x 18	3ft0in	L	158
1995	10.11.1920	4ft 8½in	0-6-0ST	IC	12 x 18	3ft0in	L	158
2009	1.11.1921	4ft 8½in	0-6-0ST	IC	16 x 22	3ft6in	-	210,214
2010	1.11.1921	4ft 8½in	0-6-0ST	IC	16 x 22	3ft6in	-	210,214,217

Note : 'alt' = altered, 'Spl' = Special

NEILSON & CO LTD, SPRINGBURN WORKS, Glasgow   N

601	1861	4ft 8½in	0-4-0ST	OC	10 x 18	5ft9in		236,273
1633	25.9.1871	4ft 8½in	0-4-0ST	OC	12 x 20	3ft7in		289
1703	c1.1872	4ft 8½in	0-4-0ST	OC	12 x 20	3ft7in		289

NORTH BRITISH LOCOMOTIVE CO LTD, Glasgow   NB
HYDE PARK WORKS, Glasgow   NBH

22600	1921	4ft 8½in	0-6-2T	IC	19 x 26	5ft8in	106
24564	1939	4ft 8½in	0-6-0T	IC	18 x 26	4ft3in	103,323
27079	1950	4ft 8½in	0-4-0DH	200hp	Paxman 6RPHL/I		211
27291	1953	3ft 6in	4-8-4	OC	24 x 28	5ft0in	107

QUEENS PARK WORKS, Glasgow   NBQ

24042	12.1930	4ft 8½in	0-6-0PT	IC	17½x24	4ft7½in	106
24048	12.1930	4ft 8½in	0-6-0PT	IC	17½x24	4ft7½in	106
27407	1954	4ft 8½in	0-6-0DH	275hp	Paxman 6RPH		211
27408	1954	4ft 8½in	0-6-0DH	275hp	Paxman 6RPH		211
27409	1954	4ft 8½in	0-6-0DH	275hp	Paxman 6RPH		211
27422	1955	4ft 8½in	0-4-0DH	275hp	National M4AAU5		94
27423	1955	4ft 8½in	0-4-0DH	275hp	National M4AAU5		249
27424	1955	4ft 8½in	0-4-0DH	275hp	National M4AAU5		94
27425	1955	4ft 8½in	0-4-0DH	275hp	National M4AAU5		249
27429	1955	4ft 8½in	0-4-0DH	275hp	National M4AAU5		249
27544	1959	4ft 8½in	4wDH	180hp	MAN W6V		130,175,231
27645	1958	4ft 8½in	0-4-0DH	275hp	National M4AAU5		249
27646	1959	4ft 8½in	0-4-0DH	275hp	National M4AAU5		249
27658	1957	4ft 8½in	0-4-0DH	330hp	MAN W6V		264
27717	1956	4ft 8½in	0-6-0DH	520hp	MAN W6V		217
27871	1960	4ft 8½in	0-6-0DH	440hp	MAN W8V		211
28051	1962	4ft 8½in	0-6-0DH	500hp	Paxman 12RPH Mk.II		211
28052	1962	4ft 8½in	0-6-0DH	500hp	Paxman 12RPH Mk.II		211

NEASDEN WORKS, London (Metropolitan Railway)   Neasden

3	1896	4ft 8½in	0-4-4T	IC	17 x 26	5ft6in	61,102,192

NORTHAMPTON ELECTRIC LIGHT & POWER CO, Northampton — NELP

	1919	4ft 8½in	4wBE	230

NYDQUIST & HOLM AB, Trollhattan, Sweden — Nohab

1164	1919	4ft 8½in	2-6-0	OC	103

OLIVER & CO LTD, Chesterfield - (see Markham & Co Ltd) — Oliver

ORENSTEIN & KOPPEL AG, Berlin & Nordhausen, Germany — OK

686	10.1.1901	2ft 3in	0-4-0T	OC	20hp			91
2343	4.1907	2ft 0in	0-6-0T	OC	150hp			186
3558	10.4.1909	2ft 3in	0-4-0T	OC	30hp			229
5834	10.2.1913	2ft 0in	0-4-0WT	OC	20hp			186
6335	6.1913	2ft 0in	0-4-0WT	OC	50hp			189
6641	10.1913	2ft 0in	0-4-0WT	OC	30hp			189
9998	5.1922	2ft 0in	0-6-0WT	OC	50hp			189
12740	8.1936	2ft 0in	0-6-0WT	OC	50hp			186

[Note that the ex-works dates for the i/c locos below are those of despatch in kit form from the Nordhausen factory. Final assembly was undertaken by William Jones at Greenwich, under the 'Montania' brand name, and so the dates to traffic were considerably later.]

3040	27.7.1928	610mm	4wDM				RL2	144
3685	12.7.1929	610mm	4wDM	11hp	OK 1-cyl	3T	RL1a	194
4105	12.6.1930	605mm	4wDM	11hp	OK 1-cyl	3T	RL1a	157
4112	22.5.1930	605mm	4wDM				RL2	144,151,176
4547	c1931	762mm	4wPM					159,163
4621	22.10.1931	605mm	4wPM	11hp	OK 1-cyl	3T	RL1a	159,163
4626	29.10.1931	605mm	4wDM	11hp	OK 1-cyl	3T	RL1a	151
4805	3.2.1933	605mm	4wDM	11hp	OK 1-cyl	3T	RL1b	99
5122	23.10.1933	605mm	4wDM	11hp	OK 1-cyl	3T	RL1b	151
5123	23.10.1933	605mm	4wDM	11hp	OK 1-cyl	3T	RL1b	142,176
5124	18.11.1933	605mm	4wDM	11hp	OK 1-cyl	3T	RL1b	144,151,176
5125	18.11.1933	605mm	4wDM	11hp	OK 1-cyl	3T	RL1b	142
5480	25.7.1934	605mm	4wDM	11hp	OK 1-cyl	3T	RL1b	142,151,176
5484	10.8.1934	605mm	4wDM	11hp	OK 1-cyl	3T	RL1b	143,151
5668	14.11.1934	605mm	4wDM	11hp	OK 1-cyl	3T	RL1b	144,151,176
5926	10.4.1935	762mm	4wDM	11hp	OK 1-cyl	3T	RL1b	189
6135	18.6.1935	605mm	4wDM	11hp	OK 1-cyl	3T	RL1b	73
6504	11.1.1936	605mm	4wDM	11hp	OK 1-cyl	3T	RL1b	191,194
6703	14.3.1936	605mm	4wDM	11hp	OK 1-cyl	3T	RL1b	121,193
6705	27.3.1936	605mm	4wDM	11hp	OK 1-cyl	3T	RL1b	99
6711	27.5.1936	605mm	4wDM	11hp	OK 1-cyl	3T	RL1b	247
7055	22.9.1936	605mm	4wDM	22hp	OK 2-cyl	3T	MD2	151
7371	9.1.1937	605mm	4wDM	14hp	OK 1-cyl	3T	RL1c	99
7595	10.3.1937	605mm	4wDM	11hp	OK 1-cyl	2¼T	MD1	238
7600	23.3.1937	605mm	4wDM	14hp	OK 1-cyl	3T	RL1c	99,187
7728	3.8.1937	605mm	4wDM	14hp	OK 1-cyl	3T	RL1c	184
8650	c1939	605mm	4wDM	11hp	OK 1-cyl	2¼T	MD1	238,309
8986	11.5.1938	605mm	4wDM	22hp	OK 2-cyl	3T	MD2	73,92,186

10253	4.2.1939	605mm	4wDM	14hp	OK 1-cyl	3T	RL1c	73
10283	22.2.1939	605mm	4wDM	14hp	OK 1-cyl	3T	RL1c	73

PECKETT & SON LTD, ATLAS ENGINE WORKS, Bristol P

464	21.9.1888	4ft 8½in	0-6-0ST	IC	16 x 22	3ft10in	X	227
485	4.9.1889	4ft 8½in	0-4-0ST	OC	14 x 20	3ft2in	W4	209
500	9.12.1891	4ft 8½in	0-6-0ST	OC	14 x 20	3ft7in	B1	255
634	24.2.1897	4ft 8½in	0-4-0ST	OC	12 x 18	3ft0in	R1	170
679	19.7.1898	4ft 8½in	0-6-0ST	IC	16 x 22	3ft10in	X	210
717	9.5.1898	4ft 8½in	0-6-0ST	OC	14 x 20	3ft7in	B1	227
751	18.11.1898	4ft 8½in	0-6-0ST	OC	14 x 20	3ft7in	B1	239,276
806	28.12.1899	4ft 8½in	0-6-0ST	OC	14 x 20	3ft7in	B1	271
819	4.9.1900	4ft 8½in	0-4-0ST	OC	10 x 14	2ft6in	M4	219
820	14.9.1900	4ft 8½in	0-4-0ST	OC	10 x 14	2ft6in	M4	219,248
832	21.5.1900	4ft 8½in	0-4-0ST	OC	14 x 20	3ft2in	W4	231,256
906	25.4.1902	4ft 8½in	0-4-0ST	OC	14 x 20	3ft2in	W4	145
933	12.1.1903	4ft 8½in	0-4-0ST	OC	14 x 20	3ft2in	W4	275,276
947	20.4.1903	4ft 8½in	0-4-0ST	OC	10 x 14	2ft6in	M4	158
996	16.3.1904	4ft 8½in	0-4-0ST	OC	10 x 14	2ft6in	M4	219,227
1008	6.10.1903	2ft 0in	0-6-0ST	OC	7 x 10	1ft86in	7 inch	189
1043	30.9.1905	4ft 8½in	0-4-0ST	OC	10 x 14	2ft6in	M4	230
1050	28.2.1907	4ft 8½in	0-4-0ST	OC	12 x 18	3ft0in	R1	270
1232	17.10.1910	4ft 8½in	0-6-0ST	OC	14 x 20	3ft7in	B2	219,254
1235	11.8.1910	4ft 8½in	0-6-0ST	IC	16 x 22	3ft10in	X2	270,284
1254	23.4.1913	4ft 8½in	0-6-0ST	OC	14 x 20	3ft7in	B2	230,307
1258	18.12.1912	4ft 8½in	0-4-0ST	OC	12 x 18	3ft0in	R2	219,221, 232,270
1289	5.12.1912	4ft 8½in	0-4-0ST	OC	15 x 21	3ft7in	E	221,224
1315	19.5.1913	3ft 0in	0-6-0ST	OC	11 x 16			223
1316	16.5.1913	3ft 0in	0-6-0ST	OC	11 x 16			223
1318	17.3.1913	4ft 8½in	0-4-0ST	OC	12 x 18	3ft0in	R2	56
1327	16.5.1913	2ft 0in	0-6-0ST	OC	7 x 10	1ft8in		309
1378	6.11.1914	4ft 8½in	0-6-0ST	OC	14 x 20	3ft7in	B2	125,320
1391	1.1.1915	4ft 8½in	0-6-0ST	OC	12 x 18	3ft0in	R2	125
1402	12.5.1915	4ft 8½in	0-6-0ST	OC	14 x 20	3ft7in	B2	221,230, 232,270
1438	10.7.1916	4ft 8½in	0-4-0ST	OC	14 x 20	3ft2in	W5	230
1456	19.9.1918	4ft 8½in	0-6-0ST	OC	14 x 20	3ft7in	B2	210,271
1509	8.1.1919	4ft 8½in	0-4-0ST	OC	14 x 20	3ft2½in	W5	155
1521	19.8.1918	4ft 8½in	0-4-0ST	OC	12 x 18	3ft6in	R2	155,160
1549	27.11.1919	4ft 8½in	0-6-0ST	OC	14 x 20	3ft7in	B2	271
1649	10.1.1924	4ft 8½in	0-4-0ST	OC	12 x 18	3ft0in	R2	207
1756	20.2.1928	4ft 8½in	0-4-0ST	OC	12 x 18	3ft6in	R2	103
1870	3.9.1934	Metre	0-6-0ST	OC	10 x 18	3ft0in	M7	274,317, 318,323
1871	7.9.1934	Metre	0-6-0ST	OC	10 x 18	3ft0in	M7	274,315, 317,323
1874	17.2.1935	4ft 8½in	0-4-0ST	OC	10 x 15	2ft9in	M5	164
1894	21.9.1936	4ft 8½in	0-4-0ST	OC	14 x 22	3ft2½in	W6	232
1900	31.12.1935	4ft 8½in	0-4-0T	OC	8 x 12	2ft0in	8x12	103
1923	14.4.1937	4ft 8½in	0-6-0ST	OC	14 x 22	3ft7in	B3	56
1937	10.1.1938	4ft 8½in	0-4-0ST	OC	14 x 22	3ft2½in	W6	232

1978	27.7.1939	4ft 8½in	0-4-0ST	OC	14 x 22	3ft2½in	W7	308
1981	16.12.1940	4ft 8½in	0-6-0ST	OC	14 x 22	3ft7in	B3	232
2002	2.4.1941	4ft 8½in	0-4-0ST	OC	14 x 22	3ft2½in	W7	308
2020	12.1.1942	4ft 8½in	0-4-0ST	OC	14 x 22	3ft2½in	W7	308
2026	22.6.1942	4ft 8½in	0-4-0ST	OC	14 x 22	3ft2½in	W7	264
2028	5.8.1942	4ft 8½in	0-4-0ST	OC	14 x 22	3ft2½in	W7	308
2029	28.10.1942	Metre	0-6-0ST	OC	12 x 20	3ft0½in	Spl R4	274,315, 317,323
2048	14.2.1944	4ft 8½in	0-4-0ST	OC	12 x 20	3ft0½in	R4	308
2052	30.10.1944	4ft 8½in	0-4-0ST	OC	12 x 20	3ft0½in	R4	238
2087	16.6.1948	4ft 8½in	0-4-0ST	OC	16 x 24	3ft10in	Spl OY1	103
2104	28.4.1950	4ft 8½in	0-4-0ST	OC	12 x 20	3ft0½in	R4	103,320
2105	9.4.1951	4ft 8½in	0-4-0ST	OC	12 x 20	3ft0½in	R4	103
2129	5.2.1952	4ft 8½in	0-4-0ST	OC	12 x 20	3ft0½in	R4	103

PRESSED STEEL LTD, Linwood, Paisley   PS

[BR 51359]	7.1960	4ft 8½in	2-2w-2w-2DMR 2xBUT 150hp		320
[BR 51367]	9.1960	4ft 8½in	2-2w-2w-2DMR 2xBUT 150hp		320
[BR 51400]	7.1960	4ft 8½in	2-2w-2w-2DMR 2xBUT 150hp		320
[BR 51402]	7.1960	4ft 8½in	2-2w-2w-2DMR 2xBUT 150hp		320

PIKROSE & CO LTD, Audenshaw, Greater Manchester   PWR

A0296V.01	.1992	2ft 0in	4wBE	7hp	WR7	2 ton	295
B0367.01	1993	2ft 0in	4wBE	20hp	WR20	4 ton	295

RANSOMES & RAPIER LTD, RIVERSIDE WORKS, Ipswich   R&R

67	1935	2ft 0in	4wDM	20hp	60

RUSTON & HORNSBY LTD, Lincoln   RH

163997	1.9.1931	2ft 0in	4wDM	10HP	Lister 10/2	2½T	238,251,283
164346	30.12.1932	2ft 0in	4wDM	10HP	Lister 10/2	2½T	186
166037	11.6.1933	2ft 0in	4wDM	10HP	Lister 10/2	2½T	247
166042	7.3.1934	2ft 6in	4wDM	10HP	Lister 10/2	2½T	268
166051	3.4.1933	2ft 6in	4wDM	10HP	Lister 10/2	2½T	268
168831	1.11.1933	2ft 4in	4wDM	16HP	Lister 18/2	2¾T	285
168841	10.1.1934	2ft 6in	4wDM	22/28HP	Lister 3JP	4T	268
170200	7.6.1934	3ft 0in	4wDM	16HP	Lister 18/2	2¾T	95
172334	30.5.1935	2ft 6in	4wDM	10HP	Lister 10/2	2½T	159,163
172336	5.6.1935	2ft 6in	4wDM	10HP	Lister 10/2	2½T	159,163
172337	7.6.1935	2ft 6in	4wDM	10HP	Lister 10/2	2½T	159,163
172342	19.8.1935	2ft 6in	4wDM	10HP	Lister 10/2	2½T	159,163
172888	1.8.1934	2ft 4in	4wDM	22/28HP	Lister 3JP	2¾T	285
172892	7.12.1934	2ft 0in	4wDM	22/28HP	Lister 3JP	2¾T	187
172900	6.10.1934	2ft 0in	4wDM	18/21HP	Lister 18/2	2¾T	170
172901	11.1.1935	2ft 0in	4wDM	18/21HP	Lister 18/2	2¾T	187
172902	7.12.1934	2ft 0in	4wDM	16/20HP	Lister 18/2	2¾T	137

172904	12.2.1935	2ft 0in	4wDM	16/20HP Lister 18/2	2¾T	143,144,151
172906	16.11.1934	2ft 0in	4wDM	18/21HP Lister 18/2	2¾T	170
173397	10.1.1935	2ft 0in	4wDM	18/21HP Lister 18/2	2¾T	81
173399	10.1.1935	2ft 0in	4wDM	18/21HP Lister 18/2	2¾T	81
173401	29.1.1935	2ft 0in	4wDM	18/21HP Lister 18/2	2¾T	170
173402	29.1.1935	2ft 0in	4wDM	18/21HP Lister 18/2	2¾T	170
174139	11.2.1935	2ft 0in	4wDM	27/32HP Lister 3JP	4T	96
174140	18.2.1935	2ft 4in	4wDM	27/32HP Lister 3JP	4T	285
174538	14.3.1935	2ft 0in	4wDM	18/21HP Lister 18/2	2¾T	170
174545	28.3.1935	2ft 0in	4wDM	18/21HP Lister 18/2	2¾T	137
174546	12.4.1935	2ft 0in	4wDM	18/21HP Lister 18/2	2¾T	170
175122	16.5.1935	2ft 0in	4wDM	18/21HP Lister 18/2	2¾T	81,170
175123	16.5.1935	2ft 0in	4wDM	18/21HP Lister 18/2	2¾T	81,170
175128	7.6.1935	2ft 0in	4wDM	18/21HP Lister 18/2	2¾T	170
175129	27.5.1935	2ft 0in	4wDM	18/21HP Lister 18/2	2¾T	81
175402	31.1.1936	2ft 0in	4wDM	18/21HP Lister 18/2	2¾T	251
175419	25.2.1936	2ft 0in	4wDM	18/21HP Lister 18/2	2¾T	255
175828	21.9.1935	2ft 11in	4wDM	36/42HP Lister 4JP	5½T	62,148,149
177608	15.8.1936	2ft 4in	4wDM	27/32HP Lister 3JP	4T	285
179880	17.9.1936	2ft 0in	4wDM	27/32HP Lister 3JP	4T	181
181822	19.11.1936	2ft 0in	4wDM	20HP Lister 18/2	2¾T	81,170
182134	30.11.1936	2ft 0in	4wDM	20HP Lister 18/2	2¾T	81,170
182137	25.11.1936	2ft 0in	4wDM	20HP Lister 18/2	2¾T	96
182146	23.1.1937	3ft 0in	4wDM	33/40HP Ruston 3VRO	4T	95
182155	15.1.1937	2ft 0in	4wDM	20HP Lister 18/2	2¾T	74
183427	8.3.1937	2ft 6in	4wDM	12HP Lister 10/2	2½T	159
183430	26.2.1937	2ft 0in	4wDM	20HP Lister 18/2	2¾T	162
183748	24.4.1937	2ft 0in	4wDM	25/30HP Ruston 3VSO	4T	81
183750	3.6.1937	2ft 0in	4wDM	25/30HP Ruston 3VSO	4T	81
183759	21.4.1937	2ft 0in	4wDM	16/20HP Ruston 2VSO	2¼T	170
183761	4.5.1937	2ft 0in	4wDM	16/20HP Ruston 2VSO	3¼T	170
183768	21.5.1937	2ft 0in	4wDM	16/20HP Ruston 2VSO	2¼T	81
183769	29.5.1937	2ft 0in	4wDM	16/20HP Ruston 2VSO	2¼T	170
183771	25.11.1937	2ft 0in	4wDM	25/30HP Ruston 3VSO	4T	81,170,195
183773	21.7.1937	2ft 0in	4wDM	30HP Lister 3JP	4T	96,99
186304	19.6.1937	3ft 0in	4wDM	33/40HP Ruston 3VRO	4T	95
186318	31.5.1937	2ft 0in	4wDM	16/20HP Ruston 2VSO	3¼T	181
186337	22.7.1937	2ft 0in	4wDM	33/40HP Ruston 3VRO	5¾T	268,289
186340	11.10.1937	2ft 0in	4wDM	33/40HP Ruston 3VRO	5¾T	268,289
187067	16.10.1937	2ft 0in	4wDM	25/30HP Ruston 3VSO	3¼T	82
187058	27.8.1937	3ft 0in	4wDM	33/40HP Ruston 3VRO	3½T	95
187074	24.1.1938	3ft 0in	4wDM	44/48HP Ruston 4VRO	6T	277,279
187076	5.5.1938	3ft 0in	4wDM	44/48HP Ruston 4VRO	6T	277,279
187093	25.11.1937	2ft 0in	4wDM	25/30HP Ruston 3VSO	3¼T	82
187102	9.11.1937	2ft 0in	4wDM	16/20HP Ruston 2VSO	2¾T	74
187110	25.11.1937	2ft 0in	4wDM	25/30HP Ruston 3VSO	3¼T	82
187111	8.12.1937	2ft 0in	4wDM	25/30HP Ruston 3VSO	3¼T	82
187112	23.12.1937	2ft 0in	4wDM	25/30HP Ruston 3VSO	3¼T	81
187113	17.12.1937	2ft 0in	4wDM	25/30HP Ruston 3VSO	4T	82
187117	17.12.1937	2ft 0in	4wDM	25/30HP Ruston 3VSO	4T	170
189938	20.12.1937	2ft 0in	4wDM	25/30HP Ruston 3VSO	4T	170
189939	21.12.1937	2ft 0in	4wDM	25/30HP Ruston 3VSO	4T	81,170
189943	12.1.1938	2ft 0in	4wDM	25/30HP Ruston 3VSO	4T	81
189945	14.1.1938	2ft 0in	4wDM	25/30HP Ruston 3VSO	3¼T	82

189946	20.1.1938	2ft 0in	4wDM	25/30HP Ruston 3VSO	4T	82
189948	22.1.1938	2ft 0in	4wDM	25/30HP Ruston 3VSO	4T	81
189949	21.1.1938	2ft 0in	4wDM	25/30HP Ruston 3VSO	4T	81,170
189952	18.1.1938	2ft 0in	4wDM	25/30HP Ruston 3VSO	4T	81
189980	8.2.1938	2ft 0in	4wDM	25/30HP Ruston 3VSO	3¼T	82
189981	8.2.1938	2ft 0in	4wDM	25/30HP Ruston 3VSO	3¼T	82
189984	19.2.1938	2ft 0in	4wDM	25/30HP Ruston 3VSO	3¼T	82
189988	24.2.1938	2ft 0in	4wDM	25/30HP Ruston 3VSO	3¼T	82
191661	7.4.1938	2ft 0in	4wDM	16/20HP Ruston 2VSO	2¾T	52
193974	23.12.1938	2ft 0in	4wDM	16/20HP Ruston 2VSO	3T	187
193975	31.12.1938	2ft 0in	4wDM	16/20HP Ruston 2VSO	2¾T	60,205
193984	10.5.1939	2ft 0in	4wDM	11/13HP Ruston 2VTO	2½T	265
193987	23.5.1939	2ft 0in	4wDM	44/48HP Ruston 4VRO	7½T	96
194771	28.1.1939	2ft 0in	4wDM	33/40HP Ruston 3VRO	5½T	96
198270	12.9.1939	2ft 0in	4wDM	25/30HP Ruston 3VSO	4T	81,170
200494	12.1940	2ft 4in	4wDM	25/30HP Ruston 3VSO	4T	285
200516	8.6.1940	2ft 0in	4wDM	44/48HP Ruston 4VRO	7½T	186
200779	21.7.1941	2ft 0in	4wDM	25/30HP Ruston 3VSO	4T	81
200780	21.7.1941	2ft 0in	4wDM	25/30HP Ruston 3VSO	4T	81
200781	23.8.1941	2ft 0in	4wDM	25/30HP Ruston 3VSO	4T	81
200782	23.8.1941	2ft 0in	4wDM	25/30HP Ruston 3VSO	4T	81
200785	4.11.1941	2ft 0in	4wDM	25/30HP Ruston 3VSO	4T	81
200786	4.11.1941	2ft 0in	4wDM	25/30HP Ruston 3VSO	4T	81
200796	11.12.1940	4ft 8½in	4wDM	44/48HP Ruston 4VRO	7½T	94
200802	18.4.1941	2ft 0in	4wDM	44/48HP Ruston 4VRO	7½T	96
202029	5.3.1941	2ft 0in	4wDM	33/40HP Ruston 3VRO	4½T	82
202030	5.3.1941	2ft 0in	4wDM	33/40HP Ruston 3VRO	4½T	82
202032	12.7.1941	2ft 0in	4wDM	33/40HP Ruston 3VRO	4½T	82
202033	12.7.1941	2ft 0in	4wDM	33/40HP Ruston 3VRO	4½T	82
202034	29.7.1941	2ft 0in	4wDM	33/40HP Ruston 3VRO	4½T	82
202969	12.1940	2ft 0in	4wDM	20DL Ruston 2VSO	2¾T	82,96
203020	26.6.1941	2ft 0in	4wDM	44/48HP Ruston 4VRO	7½T	96
203026	31.3.1942	2ft 0in	4wDM	44/48HP Ruston 4VRO	7½T	186
207103	29.4.1941	4ft 8½in	4wDM	44/48HP Ruston 4VRO	7½T	127
209430	1942	2ft 0in	4wDM	13DL Ruston 2VTO	2½T	187
210482	8.1.1942	4ft 8½in	4wDM	48DS Ruston 4VRO	7½T	61,92
211590	17.4.1941	2ft 0in	4wDM	20DL Ruston 2VSO	2¾T	309
211606	31.5.1941	2ft 0in	4wDM	20DL Ruston 2VSO	2¾T	202
211609	31.5.1941	2ft 0in	4wDM	20DL Ruston 2VSO	2¾T	108
211648	19.2.1942	2ft 0in	4wDM	20DL Ruston 2VSO	2¾T	59
211679	5.1.1942	Metre	4wDM	30DL Ruston 3VSO	4½T	317,318
213839	24.4.1942	1ft 7in	4wDM	20DL Ruston 2VSO	2¾T	310
217967	30.10.1942	2ft 0in	4wDM	20DL Ruston 2VSO	2¾T	96,108,323
217999	7.12.1942	2ft 0in	4wDM	20DL Ruston 2VSO	2¾T	186
218016	11.3.1943	2ft 0in	4wDM	20DL Ruston 2VSO	2¾T	187
218046	8.1.1943	4ft 8½in	4wDM	48DS Ruston 4VRO	7½T	231
221625	17.8.1943	2ft 6in	4wDM	48DL Ruston 4VRO	7T	184
221644	11.1.1943	4ft 8½in	4wDM	48DS Ruston 4VRO	7½T	94
221645	14.1.1944	4ft 8½in	4wDM	48DS Ruston 4VRO	7½T	248
223692	8.1.1944	2ft 0in	4wDM	20DL Ruston 2VSO	2¾T	187
223700	31.1.1944	2ft 0in	4wDM	20DL Ruston 2VSO	2¾T	189
223738	14.3.1944	2ft 0in	4wDM	20DL Ruston 2VSO	2¾T	59
223749	6.4.1944	2ft 0in	4wDM	20DL Ruston 2VSO	2¾T	95,195
224341	2.10.1944	4ft 8½in	4wDM	48DS Ruston 4VRO	7½T	94,248

224344	18.12.1944	4ft 8½in	4wDM	48DS	Ruston 4VRO	7½T	248
224345	19.1.1945	4ft 8½in	4wDM	48DS	Ruston 4VRO	7½T	263
226278	4.7.1944	2ft 0in	4wDM	20DL	Ruston 2VSO	2¾T	95
229631	11.10.1944	2ft 0in	4wDM	20DL	Ruston 2VSH	2¾T	95
229640	25.11.1944	2ft 0in	4wDM	20DL	Ruston 2VSH	2¾T	59
235511	24.8.1945	4ft 8½in	4wDM	48DS	Ruston 4VRO	7½T	322
235517	11.10.1945	4ft 8½in	4wDM	48DS	Ruston 4VRO	7½T	263
237923	14.5.1946	4ft 8½in	4wDM	48DS	Ruston 4VRO	7½T	233
239381	12.2.1946	2ft 0in	4wDM	40DL	Ruston 3VRH	4½T	96,195
242868	1.11.1946	4ft 8½in	4wDM	88DS	Ruston 4VPH	17T	322
242887	8.4.1946	2ft 0in	4wDM	20DL	Ruston 2VSH	2¾T	251,314
242903	16.5.1946	2ft 0in	4wDM	48DL	Ruston 4YC	5½T	88
244574	23.4.1947	3ft 0in	4wDM	20DL	Ruston 2VSH	2¾T	95
244575	23.4.1947	3ft 0in	4wDM	20DL	Ruston 2VSH	2¾T	95
252798	22.4.1947	3ft 0in	4wDM	30DL	Ruston 3VSH	3½T	95
252841	16.9.1948	4ft 8½in	4wDM	88DS	Ruston 4VPH	17T	238
260724	20.10.1948	2ft 0in	4wDM	20DL	Ruston 2VSH	2¾T	251
260744	6.1.1949	2ft 0in	4wDM	20DL	Ruston 2VSO	2¾T	181
263000	7.3.1949	4ft 8½in	4wDM	88DS	Ruston 4VPH	17T	94
275886	7.11.1949	4ft 8½in	4wDM	88DS	Ruston 4VPH	17T	94,241,320
277273	31.3.1949	2ft 0in	4wDM	30DL	Ruston 3VSH	3¼T	107,181
281290	17.11.1949	3ft 0in	0-6-0DM	100DL	Ruston 6VRH	14T	317,318
283507	21.7.1949	2ft 0in	4wDM	30DL	Ruston 3VSH	3¼T	187
285297	11.10.1949	2ft 0in	4wDM	20DL	Ruston 2VSH	2¾T	181,251,252
294265	23.6.1950	4ft 8½in	4wDM	48DS	Ruston 4VRH	7½T	286
294266	30.3.1951	4ft 8½in	4wDM	48DS	Ruston 4VRH	7½T	101
297066	29.11.1950	2ft 6in	4wDM	30DL	Ruston 3VSH	4T	180
299100	6.10.1950	4ft 8½in	4wDM	88DS	Ruston 4VPH	17T	322
310081	24.8.1951	4ft 8½in	0-4-0DM	165DS	Ruston 6VPH	28T	56
312433	9.11.1951	4ft 8½in	4wDM	88DS	Ruston 4VPH	20T	68
319286	25.3.1953	4ft 8½in	0-4-0DM	165DS	Ruston 6VPH	28T	94,320
319294	14.9.1953	4ft 8½in	0-6-0DM	165DS	Ruston 6VPH	28T	320,322
321734	21.6.1952	4ft 8½in	4wDM	88DS	Ruston 4VPH	17T	322
327931	10.7.1952	2ft 0in	4wDM	20DLU	Ruston 2VSH	3¼T	169
327974	15.10.1954	4ft 8½in	0-4-0DM	165DS	Ruston 6VPH	28T	322
331251	12.7.1952	2ft 0in	4wDM	20DLU	Ruston 2VSH	3¼T	169
331264	12.7.1952	2ft 0in	4wDM	20DL	Ruston 2VSH	2¾T	251,252
331267	11.11.1952	2ft 0in	4wDM	20DLU	Ruston 2VSH	3¼T	169
338419	15.2.1954	4ft 8½in	4wDM	88DS	Ruston 4VPH	20T	164,179
338433	3.2.1953	2ft 0in	4wDM	LAT	Ruston 3VSH	3½T	181
338438	7.5.1953	2ft 6in	4wDM	LBU	Ruston 3VSH	3½T	278,311,317
338439	12.6.1953	3ft 0in	4wDM	LBU	Ruston 3VSH	3½T	277,311,323
339209	8.12.1952	2ft 0in	4wDM	30DLU	Ruston 3VSH	4½T	169
339210	23.12.1952	2ft 0in	4wDM	30DLU	Ruston 3VSH	4½T	169
346001	23.12.1952	2ft 0in	4wDM	20DLU	Ruston 2VSH	3¼T	169
346007	23.12.1952	2ft 0in	4wDM	20DLU	Ruston 2VSH	3¼T	169
347731	17.2.1953	2ft 0in	4wDM	30DLU	Ruston 3VSH	4½T	169
353486	15.10.1953	2ft 6in	4wDM	LBU	Ruston 3VSH	3½T	278
353491	29.1.1954	3ft 0in	4wDM	LBU	Ruston 3VSH	3½T	277,311,316
354043	21.4.1953	2ft 0in	4wDM	40DL	Ruston 3VRH	4½T	96
371545	19.10.1954	2ft 0in	4wDM	LAT	Ruston 2VSH	3½T	252
371971	30.11.1954	4ft 8½in	4wDM	48DS	Ruston 4VRH	7½T	207
373359	1.11.1954	2ft 0in	4wDM	20DL	Ruston 2VSH	2¾T	194
375316	26.4.1954	2ft 0in	4wDM	40DL	Ruston 3VRH	4½T	186

375329	25.6.1954	2ft 6in	4wDM	48DLU	Ruston 4VRH	7T		278
375349	10.11.1954	2ft 0in	4wDM	LAT	Ruston 2VSH	3½T	251,252
375362	1.2.1955	2ft 0in	4wDM	LAT	Ruston 2VSH	3½T	250,251,252
375693	25.8.1954	2ft 6in	4wDM	LBU	Ruston 3VSH	3½T	278,311,317
375694	1.7.1954	3ft 0in	4wDM	LBU	Ruston 3VSH	3½T	277,311,316
386871	4.3.1955	4ft 8½in	4wDM	48DS	Ruston 4VRH	7½T		231
386875	17.10.1955	4ft 8½in	4wDM	48DS	Ruston 4VRH	7½T		207,322
393303	20.1.1955	4ft 8½in	4wDM	48DS	Ruston 4VRH	7½T		263
393325	15.2.1956	2ft 0in	4wDM	LBT	Ruston 3VSH	3¾T		323
394012	24.2.1956	4ft 8½in	4wDM	88DS	Ruston 4VPH	20T		163,179
395305	26.11.1956	4ft 8½in	0-4-0DM	165DS	Ruston 6VPH	28T		322
398616	1.10.1956	4ft 8½in	4wDM	88DS	Ruston 4VPH	17T		305
408430	29.5.1957	2ft 0in	4wDM	LAT	Ruston 2VSH	3½T		186
411319	21.6.1957	4ft 8½in	4wDM	48DSG	Ruston 4VRH	7½T		248
411322	28.2.1958	3ft 0in	4wDM	48DS	Ruston 4VRH	7½T		317,318
418764	4.10.1957	3ft 0in	4wDM	LBU	Ruston 3VSH	3¾T	277,311,324
418765	3.10.1957	2ft 6in	4wDM	LBU	Ruston 3VSH	3¾T		278
418803	31.12.1957	3ft 0in	4wDM	48DL	Ruston 4VRH	7T	277,311,316
421437	12.5.1958	4ft 8½in	0-4-0DE	165DE	Ruston 6VPH	25T		120,125
425477	9.2.1959	4ft 8½in	0-4-0DE	165DE	Ruston 6VPH		25T125,175,183
425798	4.11.1958	2ft 0in	4wDMF	48DLG	Ruston 4VRH	7T		186
427802	28.7.1958	3ft 0in	4wDM	LBU	Ruston 3VSH	3¾T		277
431758	3.7.1959	4ft 8½in	0-4-0DE	165DE	Ruston 6VPH	30T		320
432652	20.2.1959	2ft 0in	4wDM	LBT	Ruston 2YDA	4½T		96
433388	19.10.1959	3ft 0in	4wDMF	48DLG	Ruston 4VRH	7T	277,311,316
435403	28.7.1961	2ft 6in	0-4-0DMF	LHG	Ruston 4YE	10T		184
441951	28.1.1960	2ft 0in	4wDM	LBT	Ruston 2YDA	3½T		193
444207	28.3.1961	2ft 0in	4wDM	48DL	Ruston 4VRH	7T		186
448157	3.11.1962	4ft 8½in	0-6-0DH	LVSH	Rn-Px 12YGA	44T		217
448158	28.2.1963	4ft 8½in	0-6-0DH	LVSH	Rn-Px 12YGA	44T		180
451900	6.7.1961	3ft 0in	4wDMF	48DLG	Ruston 4VRH	7T		277
462374	23.3.1961	2ft 0in	4Wdm	LBU	Ruston 2YDA	4½T		82
462375	23.3.1961	2ft 0in	4Wdm	LBU	Ruston 2YDA	4½T		82
463153	21.7.1961	4ft 8½in	4wDM	88DS	Ruston 4VPH	20T		103
466588	24.10.1961	3ft 0in	4wDM	LBT	Ruston 2YDA	3½T		260
466589	24.10.1961	3ft 0in	4wDM	LBT	Ruston 2YDA	3½T		260
468048	20.11.1963	4ft 8½in	0-4-0DH	LSSH	Paxman 6RPH	45T		217
504565	10.3.1965	4ft 8½in	0-4-0DH	LSSH	Paxman 6RPH	32T		264
7002/0467/2	17.8.1966	2ft0in	4wDM	LBT	Ruston 2YDA	3½T		82

NOTE that the details in the 'Horse power' column are the Ruston Classes, which normally indicate the horsepower. Details for the later 'lettered' classes are :
LAT - 20hp   LBT/LBU - 31½hp   LHG - 75hp   LSSH - 287hp
LVSH - 400hp

ROBEL & CO MASCHINENFABRIK, Munich   Robel

54-12-56-RTI	1966	4ft 8½in	4wDM

ROLLS-ROYCE LTD, SENTINEL WORKS, Shrewsbury   RR

10204	21.1.1965	4ft 8½in	0-4-0DH	311hp	R-R C8SFL	31T	215,220,224
10205	9.6.1965	4ft 8½in	0-4-0DH	311hp	R-R C8SFL	40T	211

10206	9.6.1965	4ft 8½in	0-4-0DH	311hp	R-R C8SFL	40T	211
10208	7.7.1965	4ft 8½in	0-4-0DH	311hp	R-R C8SFL	40T	211
10212	5.10.1966	4ft 8½in	0-6-0DH	445hp	R-R DV8N	52T	217
10230	18.2.1965	4ft 8½in	4wDH	230hp	R-R C6SFL	34T	56
10264	29.12.1966	4ft 8½in	4wDH	230hp	R-R C6SFL	34T	56
10265	12.10.1967	4ft 8½in	6wDH	608hp	R-R DV8TCA	56T	215
10270	26.9.1967	4ft 8½in	0-6-0DH	325hp	R-R C8SFL	48T	215
10271	12.10.1967	4ft 8½in	0-6-0DH	325hp	R-R C8SFL	48T	215
10272	28.11.1967	4ft 8½in	0-6-0DH	325hp	R-R C8SFL	48T	215
10273	19.12.1968	4ft 8½in	6wDH	445hp	R-R DV8N	52T	211,215,220
10274	9.1.1969	4ft 8½in	6wDH	445hp	R-R DV8N	52T	215
10275	24.9.1969	4ft 8½in	6wDH	445hp	R-R DV8N	52T	212,215

ROBERT STEPHENSON & CO LTD, Newcastle-upon-Tyne — RS

1959	4.7.1870	4ft 8½in	4-4-0ST	IC	13 x 18	3ft6in	231
2837	5.1896	4ft 8½in	0-6-0ST	IC	14 x 20	3ft6in	276

ROBERT STEPHENSON & HAWTHORNS LTD — RSH

DARLINGTON WORKS — RSHD

7025	25.7.1941	4ft 8½in	0-6-0ST	OC	16 x 24 3ft8in	210
8157	11.10.1960	4ft 8½in	0-6-0DM	204hp	Gardner 8L3 [DC 2679]	103
8183	26.4.1961	4ft 8½in	0-6-0DM	204hp	Gardner 8L3 [DC 2705]	54
8193	25.7.1961	4ft 8½in	0-6-0DM	204hp	Gardner 8L3 [DC 2715]	319
8368	1962	4ft 8½in	0-4-0DH	262hp	Dorman 6QA [WB 3213]	129

NEWCASTLE-UPON-TYNE WORKS — RSHN

6944	11.1.1940	4ft 8½in	0-6-0ST	OC	16 x 24 3ft8in	210
6967	26.4.1939	4ft 8½in	0-4-0DM	150hp	Crossley 5C	177,233
6968	5.6.1939	4ft 8½in	0-4-0DM	150hp	Crossley 5C	177,233
6979	6.2.1940	4ft 8½in	0-4-0DM	150hp	Fowler 4C	114
6989	21.9.1940	4ft 8½in	0-4-0DM	150hp	Fowler 4C	155
6990	18.10.1940	4ft 8½in	0-4-0DM	150hp	Fowler 4C	54,93,114
6991	26.12.1940	4ft 8½in	0-4-0DM	150hp	Fowler 4C	114
7003	11.4.1940	4ft 8½in	0-6-0ST	IC	16 x 22 3ft6in	211,215
7004	30.4.1940	4ft 8½in	0-6-0ST	IC	16 x 22 3ft6in	211,215,233
7005	16.5.1940	4ft 8½in	0-4-0WE	80hp	2ft9in	214
7030	12.5.1941	4ft 8½in	0-6-0ST	IC	16 x 22 3ft6in	211,215
7031	22.5.1941	4ft 8½in	0-6-0ST	IC	16 x 22 3ft6in	211,215
7032	25.6.1941	4ft 8½in	0-6-0ST	IC	16 x 22 3ft6in	211,215,220
7147	27.7.1944	4ft 8½in	0-6-0ST	IC	18 x 26 4ft3in	282
7148	3.8.1944	4ft 8½in	0-6-0ST	IC	18 x 26 4ft3in	282
7149	14.8.1944	4ft 8½in	0-6-0ST	IC	18 x 26 4ft3in	282
7386	18.5.1948	4ft 8½in	0-4-0ST	OC	14 x 22 3ft6in	128
7413	1.7.1948	4ft 8½in	0-6-0ST	OC	14 x 22 3ft6in	158
7617	28.1.1952	4ft 8½in	0-6-0PT	IC	17½x24 4ft7½in	72
7667	29.8.1950	4ft 8½in	0-6-0ST	IC	18 x 26 4ft0½in	106,215
7668	11.9.1950	4ft 8½in	0-6-0ST	IC	18 x 26 4ft0½in	215
7669	6.10.1950	4ft 8½in	0-6-0ST	IC	18 x 26 4ft0½in	215
7670	23.10.1950	4ft 8½in	0-6-0ST	IC	18 x 26 4ft0½in	215
7671	10.11.1950	4ft 8½in	0-6-0ST	IC	18 x 26 4ft0½in	102,215
7672	1.12.1950	4ft 8½in	0-6-0ST	IC	18 x 26 4ft0½in	215

7673	16.1.1951	4ft 8½in	0-6-0ST	IC	18 x 26	4ft0½in			·215
7761	22.6.1954	4ft 8½in	0-6-0ST	IC	18 x 26	4ft0½in			215
8050	10.1958	4ft 8½in	0-6-0ST	IC	18 x 26	4ft0½in			215

RICHARD THOMAS & BALDWINS LTD, Irthlingborough   RTB

| | c1938 | 3ft 0in | 4wBE | | | | | | 277 |
| | c1938 | 3ft 0in | 4wBE | | | | | | 277 |

SENTINEL (SHREWSBURY) LTD, BATTLEFIELD WORKS, Shrewsbury   S

5666	.1924	4ft 8½in	4wVBT	HCG				221,241,281,307
5667	2.1924	4ft 8½in	0-6-0VBT	HCG	6¾x 9	3ft1½in		141,176,307
6005CH	1925	4ft 8½in	0-4-0VBT	HCG	6¾x 9	3ft0in		281
6020	c1926	4ft 8½in	4wVBT	VCG	6¾x 9	2ft6in	100hp	125
6412	1926	3ft 0in	4w-4wVBT	VCG	6¾x 9			245
6515	1926	4ft 8½in	4wVBT	VCG	6¾x 9	2ft6in	100hp	103,241
6711CH	1926	4ft 8½in	0-6-0VBT	VCG	6¾x 9			64,176
6754CH	1927	2ft 11in	4wVBT	HCG	6¾x 9	1ft8in	80hp	141,148,149
6994	1927	4ft 8½in	4wVBT	VCG	6¾x 9	2ft6in		92
7109	1927	4ft 8½in	4wVBT	VCG	6¾x 9	3ft2in	200hp	101
7243	1928	2ft 11in	4wVBT	HCG	6¾x 9	1ft8in	80hp	148
7299	1928	4ft 8½in	4wVBT	VCG	6¾x 9	2ft6in	100hp	210
7699	1929	2ft 11in	4wVBT	HCG	6¾x 9	1ft8in	80hp	141,148,149
7700	1929	2ft 11in	4wVBT	HCG	6¾x 9	1ft8in	80hp	148
7701	1929	2ft 6in	4wVBT	HCG	6¾x 9	1ft8in	80hp	184
8837	1933	4ft 8½in	4wVBT	VCG	6¾x 9	2ft6in	100hp	106
9149	1934	2ft 6in	4wVBT	HCG	6¾x 9	1ft8in	80hp	153,154
9221	1935	2ft 11in	4wVBT	HCG	6¾x 9	1ft8in	80hp	148,149
9259	1936	2ft 11in	4wVBT	HCG	6¾x 9	1ft8in	80hp	148
9284	1937	4ft 8½in	4wVBT	VCG	6¾x 9	2ft6in	100hp	64,141
9322	1937	4ft 8½in	4wVBT	VCG	6¾x 9	2ft6in	100hp	62,64,143
9365	1946	4ft 8½in	4wVBT	VCG	6¾x 9	2ft6in	100hp	241,322
9366	1945	4ft 8½in	4wVBT	VCG	6¾x 9	2ft6in	100hp	103
9369	1946	4ft 8½in	4wVBT	VCG	6¾x 9	2ft6in	100hp	241,322
9376	1947	4ft 8½in	4wVBT	VCG	6¾x 9	2ft6in	100hp	103
9398	1.1.1950	4ft 8½in	4wVBT	VCG	6¾x 9	2ft6in	100hp	238
9418	1950	4ft 8½in	2w-2-2-2w-4-4R					
				12CG	6 x 7	2ft9½in	370hp	103
9527	12.9.1951	4ft 8½in	4wVBT	VCG	6¾x 9	2ft6in	100hp	238
9537	30.5.1952	4ft 8½in	4wVBT	VCG	6¾x 9	2ft6in	100hp	103
9547	13.11.1952	4ft 8½in	4wVBT	VCG	6¾x 9	2ft6in	200hp	56
9556	30.3.1953	4ft 8½in	4wVBT	VCG	6¾x 9	2ft6in	100hp	158
9559	24.7.1953	4ft 8½in	4wVBT	VCG	6¾x 9	2ft6in	100hp	158
9564	1.7.1954	4ft 8½in	4wVBT	VCG	6¾x 9	2ft6in	100hp	158
9565	23.7.1954	4ft 8½in	4wVBT	VCG	6¾x 9	2ft6in	100hp	158
9615	26.7.1956	4ft 8½in	4wVBT	VCG	6¾x 9	3ft2in	200hp	232
9627	11.7.1957	4ft 8½in	4wVBT	VCG	6¾x 9	2ft6in	100hp	158

NOTE : Diesel locomotive with works numbers from 10001 were built by Rolls Royce using the 'Sentinel' title.

| 10055 | 26.7.1961 | 4ft 8½in | 0-6-0DH | 325hp | R-R C8SFL | 48T | 217 |
| 10090 | 30.11.1961 | 4ft 8½in | 0-4-0DH | 311hp | R-R C8SFL | 32T | 211 |

10142	18.12.1962	4ft 8½in	0-4-0DH	311hp	R-R C8SFL	32T	220,222,224
10159	24.4.1963	4ft 8½in	4wDH	230hp	R-R C6SFL	34T	56,325

BERLINER MASCHINENBAU AG, Berlin   Sch

9124	1927	2ft 0in	0-4-0WT	OC

SWINDON WORKS, Wilts (GWR / BR)   Sdn

[GWR 5541]	1928	4ft 8½in	2-6-2T	OC	17 x 24	4ft7½in	61T	106
[GWR 6024]	1930	4ft 8½in	4-6-0	4C	16¼x28	6ft6in	89T	102
[GWR 6106]	1931	4ft 8½in	2-6-2T	OC	18 x 30	5ft8in	78½T	106
[GWR 7200]	1934	4ft 8½in	2-8-2T	OC	19 x 30	4ft7½in	92T	102
[GWR 5080]	1939	4ft 8½in	4-6-0	4C	16 x 26	6ft8½in	80T	106
[GWR 3862]	1942	4ft 8½in	2-8-0	OC	18½x30	4ft7½in	76T	320
[BR 6989]	1948	4ft 8½in	4-6-0	OC	18½x30	6ft0in	76T	102
[BR D2018]	14.4.1958	4ft 8½in	0-6-0DM	204hp	Gardner 8L3	31T	231
[BR D2027]	16.9.1958	4ft 8½in	0-6-0DM	204hp	Gardner 8L3	31T	319
[BR D2120]	10.1959	4ft 8½in	0-6-0DM	204hp	Gardner 8L3	31T	101
[BR D2158]	22.8.1960	4ft 8½in	0-6-0DM	204hp	Gardner 8L3	31T	319
[BR D2176]	15.12.1961	4ft 8½in	0-6-0DM	204hp	Gardner 8L3	31T	231
[BR D9503]	7.1964	4ft 8½in	0-6-0DH	650hp	Paxman 6YJX	50T	215
[BR D9507]	8.1964	4ft 8½in	0-6-0DH	650hp	Paxman 6YJX	50T	212,215
[BR D9510]	9.1964	4ft 8½in	0-6-0DH	650hp	Paxman 6YJX	50T	211,215
[BR D9512]	9.1964	4ft 8½in	0-6-0DH	650hp	Paxman 6YJX	50T	212,215
[BR D9515]	10.1964	4ft 8½in	0-6-0DH	650hp	Paxman 6YJX	50T	212,215
[BR D9516]	10.1964	4ft 8½in	0-6-0DH	650hp	Paxman 6YJX	50T	212,215
[BR D9520]	11.1964	4ft 8½in	0-6-0DH	650hp	Paxman 6YJX	50T	211,215,220
[BR D9523]	12.1964	4ft 8½in	0-6-0DH	650hp	Paxman 6YJX	50T	212,215,220
[BR D9526]	1.1965	4ft 8½in	0-6-0DH	650hp	Paxman 6YJX	50T	125
[BR D9529]	1.1965	4ft 8½in	0-6-0DH	650hp	Paxman 6YJX	50T	212,215
[BR D9532]	2.1965	4ft 8½in	0-6-0DH	650hp	Paxman 6YJX	50T	212,215
[BR D9533]	2.1965	4ft 8½in	0-6-0DH	650hp	Paxman 6YJX	50T	212,215
[BR D9537]	3.1965	4ft 8½in	0-6-0DH	650hp	Paxman 6YJX	50T	215
[BR D9538]	3.1965	4ft 8½in	0-6-0DH	650hp	Paxman 6YJX	50T	212,215
[BR D9539]	4.1965	4ft 8½in	0-6-0DH	650hp	Paxman 6YJX	50T	212,215
[BR D9541]	4.1965	4ft 8½in	0-6-0DH	650hp	Paxman 6YJX	50T	215
[BR D9542]	5.1965	4ft 8½in	0-6-0DH	650hp	Paxman 6YJX	50T	212,215
[BR D9544]	5.1965	4ft 8½in	0-6-0DH	650hp	Paxman 6YJX	50T	215
[BR D9547]	7.1965	4ft 8½in	0-6-0DH	650hp	Paxman 6YJX	50T	212,215
[BR D9548]	7.1965	4ft 8½in	0-6-0DH	650hp	Paxman 6YJX	50T	212,215
[BR D9549]	8.1965	4ft 8½in	0-6-0DH	650hp	Paxman 6YJX	50T	211,212,215
[BR D9551]	9.1965	4ft 8½in	0-6-0DH	650hp	Paxman 6YJX	50T	211,215
[BR D9552]	9.1965	4ft 8½in	0-6-0DH	650hp	Paxman 6YJX	50T	215
[BR D9553]	9.1965	4ft 8½in	0-6-0DH	650hp	Paxman 6YJX	50T	212,215
[BR D9554]	10.1965	4ft 8½in	0-6-0DH	650hp	Paxman 6YJX	50T	212,215
[BR D9555]	10.1965	4ft 8½in	0-6-0DH	650hp	Paxman 6YJX	50T	321

SLAUGHTER, GRUNING & CO, Bristol   SG

438	1861	4ft 8½in	4-4-0T	OC	16½x 22	5ft3in	37T

SIMPLEX MECHANICAL HANDLING LTD, Bedford — SMH

103GA078	8.4.1978	4ft 8½in	4wDM	20hp	Petter PJ2	55,70
101T018	31.10.1979	2ft 6in	4wDH	112hp	Dorman	187

SHARP, ROBERTS &CO, ATLAS WORKS, Manchester — SR

193	11.1842	4ft 8½in	2-2-2	IC	14¼x20 5ft6in	292

SHARP BROTHERS, ATLAS WORKS, Manchester — SB

663	1850	4ft 8½in	0-4-0tank IC		55

SHARP, STEWART & CO LTD, ATLAS WORKS, Manchester/#Glasgow — SS

	2298	1873	Metre	0-4-0ST	OC	12 x 18 3ft6in	273
	2299	1873	Metre	0-4-0ST	OC	12 x 18 3ft6in	273
	2329	1873	4ft 8½in	0-4-0ST	OC	9½x 15 2ft6in	262,311
#	4150	1896	3ft 6in	4-8-0	OC	17 x 23 3ft6¾in	183

ST ROLLOX WORKS, Glasgow (Caledonian Rly) — St.Rollox

[CR 628]	1902	4ft 8½in	0-4-0ST	OC	14 x 20 3ft8in	27½T	210

STRATFORD WORKS, London (Great Eastern Railway) — Str

[GER 541]	10.1888	4ft 8½in	0-6-0	IC	17½x 24 4ft11in	37T	67
[GER 835]	7.1889	4ft 8½in	0-6-0	IC	17½x 24 4ft11in	37T	67

THOMAS GREEN & SONS LTD, Smithfield Ironworks, Leeds — TG

43	29.7.1887	3ft 6in	0-4-0Tram OC	9 x 14		73
51	14.10.1887	3ft 6in	0-4-0Tram OC	9 x 14		73

THOMAS HILL (ROTHERHAM) LTD, VANGUARD WORKS, Kilnhurst — TH

	124C	12.3.1963	4ft 8½in	0-6-0DH	340hp	R-R C8SFL	55½T	
#				[rebuild of S 9655?]				217
	146C	24.11.1964	4ft 8½in	0-4-0DH	179hp	R-R C6NFL	28T	
				[rebuild of JF 4210018]				320
	177C	13.1.1967	4ft 8½in	4wDH	173hp	R-R SF65C	25T	240
	188C	19.10.1967	4ft 8½in	4wDH	173hp	R-R SF65C		
				[rebuild of S 9597]				104

Six 0-6-0F 'Receiver' locos (S 9650–9655) built in 1957 for Dorman, Long (Steel) Ltd, Lackenby, Middlesbrough, were obtained by TH for rebuilding to 0-6-0DH. 124C is definitely one of 9650/9651/9654/9655 and possibly 9655.

TRACK SUPPLIES & SERVICES LTD, Wolverton, Bucks — Track Supplies

1984	1ft 6in	4wBE	97

VULCAN FOUNDRY LTD, Newton-le-Willows, Lancs   VF

4861	1.1943	4ft 8½in	0-4-0DM	153hp	Gdnr 6L3	[DC 2169]	249
4862	1.1943	4ft 8½in	0-4-0DM	153hp	Gdnr 6L3	[DC 2170]	249
4863	1942	4ft 8½in	0-4-0DM	153hp	Gdnr 6L3	[DC 2171]	249
4864	1942	4ft 8½in	0-4-0DM	153hp	Gdnr 6L3	[DC 2172]	249
5272	1945	4ft 8½in	0-6-0ST	IC	18 x 26 4ft3in	48T	282
D291	15.6.1956	4ft 8½in	0-6-0DM	204hp	Gdnr 8L3	[DC2565]	231
D293	1955	4ft 8½in	0-4-0DM	153hp	Gdnr 6L3	[DC2566]	194

VULCAN IRON WORKS, Wilkes-Barre, Pennsylvania, USA   VIW

4433	2.1943	4ft 8½in	0-6-0T	OC	16½x24 4ft6in	106

VULCAN; STETTINER MASCHINENBAU AG, Stettin, Germany   VW

3852	1925	600mm	0-8-0	OC	184

W G BAGNALL LTD, CASTLE ENGINE WORKS, Stafford   WB

16	12.1876	4ft 8½in	0-4-0ST	IC	7½x11		69
120	12.1877	4ft 8½in	0-4-0IST	IC	8 x 12	2ft6in	69
840	3.1887	3ft 0in	0-4-0ST	OC	8 x 12	2ft0in	267
1024	10.1888	3ft 0in	0-4-0T	OC	8 x 14	2ft0in	272
1116	5.1889	3ft 0in	0-4-0ST	OC	9 x13½	2ft3in	87
1493	12.1896	4ft 8½in	0-4-0ST	OC	10 x 15	2ft9in	52
1554	17.12.1898	2ft 6in	0-4-0ST	OC	6 x 9	1ft7in	261,265
1563	27.5.1899	3ft 0in	0-4-0ST	OC	9 x 14	2ft6½in	272
1587	3.2.1900	3ft 0in	0-4-0ST	OC	9 x 14	2ft3½in	266
1643	28.9.1901	1ft 11½in	0-4-0ST	OC	6 x 9	1ft7in	205
1655	17.9.1901	2ft 6in	0-4-0ST	OC	7 x12	1ft9½in	305
1662	12.9.1902	1ft 11½in	0-4-0ST	OC	6 x 9	1ft6in	205
1668	30.4.1903	2ft 0in	0-4-0ST	OC	6 x 9	1ft6in	208
1739	1.4.1907	4ft 8½in	0-4-0ST	OC	14 x 20	3ft6½in	221,224,233
1785	11.10.1905	2ft 6in	0-6-0T	OC	10 x 15	2ft6in	235
1802	21.12.1907	1ft 11½in	0-4-0ST	OC	6 x 9	1ft7in	205
1853	13.4.1908	2ft 6in	0-4-0ST	OC	7 x12	1ft9½in	243,308
1861	21.9.1907	2ft 6in	0-6-0T	OC	10 x 15	2ft6in	235
1942	24.5.1918	3ft 3in	0-4-0ST	OC	8 x 12	2ft0½in	274
1946	15.11.1911	3ft 0in	0-4-0T	OC	9 x 14	2ft7in	272
1955	27.9.1912	3ft 8in	0-6-0ST	OC	13 x 18	2ft9¼in	261
1956	1.11.1912	3ft 8in	0-6-0ST	OC	13 x 18	2ft9¼in	261,278
1957	31.12.1912	3ft 8in	0-6-0ST	OC	13 x 18	2ft9¼in	261
2042	17.12.1917	2ft 0in	0-4-0ST	OC	6 x 9	1ft7in	115
2044	17.12.1917	2ft 0in	0-4-0ST	OC	6 x 9	1ft7in	204
2077	1.10.1918	2ft 0in	0-4-0ST	OC	6 x 9	1ft7in	204
2089	15.4.1919	2ft 6in	0-4-0ST	OC	6 x 9	1ft7in	261
2090	16.4.1919	2ft 0in	0-4-0ST	OC	6 x 9	1ft7in	228
2091	28.8.1919	2ft 0in	0-4-0ST	OC	6 x 9	1ft7in	189
2103	28.7.1919	2ft 6in	0-4-0ST	OC	7 x12	1ft9½in	243

2133	10.7.1924	2ft 0in	0-4-0ST	OC	7 x12	1ft9½in		189
2153	21.11.1921	3ft 6in	0-4-0ST	OC	10 x 15	2ft9¾in		73
2167	24.12.1921	4ft 8½in	0-6-0ST	OC	13 x 18	2ft9¼in		91
2169	23.2.1922	4ft 8½in	0-6-0ST	OC	13 x 18	2ft9¼in		75
2192	20.9.1922	2ft 6in	0-6-2T	OC	13 x 18	2ft9¼in		102,184
2469	8.3.1932	4ft 8½in	0-4-0ST	OC	12 x 18	3ft0¼in		103,192
2517	15.10.1934	4ft 8½in	0-4-0ST	OC	14 x 20	3ft6½in		256
2565	18.11.1936	4ft 8½in	0-4-0ST	OC	13 x 18	3ft0½in		230,319,322
2586	31.3.1938	4ft 8½in	0-4-0ST	OC	14 x 22	3ft6½in		64
2629	27.2.1941	4ft 8½in	0-6-0ST	OC	15 x 22	3ft4½in		269
2649	12.1941	4ft 8½in	0-4-0ST	OC	14½x22	3ft6½in		156
2650	.1942	4ft 8½in	0-4-0ST	OC	14½x22	3ft6½in		156
2654	11.2.1942	4ft 8½in	0-6-0ST	OC	15 x 22	3ft4½in		227,260,316
2655	18.2.1942	4ft 8½in	0-6-0ST	OC	15 x 22	3ft4½in		227,273
2659	4.4.1942	4ft 8½in	0-4-0ST	OC	12 x 18	2ft9in		260
2665	19.5.1942	4ft 8½in	0-4-0ST	OC	14½x22	3ft6½in		129
2668	31.5.1942	4ft 8½in	0-6-0ST	OC	15 x 22	3ft4½in		218,324
2669	31.7.1942	4ft 8½in	0-6-0ST	OC	15 x 22	3ft4½in		223
2670	31.7.1942	4ft 8½in	0-6-0ST	OC	15 x 22	3ft4½in		223,321
2677	28.10.1943	4ft 8½in	0-4-0ST	OC	14½x22	3ft6½in		156,176
2739	5.1944	4ft 8½in	0-6-0ST	IC	18 x 26	4ft3in	Austerity	282
2743	6.1944	4ft 8½in	0-6-0ST	IC	18 x 26	4ft3in	Austerity	282
2746	7.1944	4ft 8½in	0-6-0ST	IC	18 x 26	4ft3in	Austerity	308
2754	9.1944	4ft 8½in	0-6-0ST	IC	18 x 26	4ft3in	Austerity	282
2777	4.5.1945	4ft 8½in	0-6-0ST	IC	18 x 26	4ft3in	Austerity	282
3160	30.11.1962	4ft 8½in	0-6-0DM	370hp	Dorman 6QT			56
3213	1962	4ft 8½in	0-4-0DH	262hp	Dorman 6QA		[RSHD 8368]	129

D. WICKHAM & CO LTD, Ware, Hertfordshire — Wkm

2559	29.3.1939	2ft 0in	2w-2PMR	1323cc	JAP	R1293	193
2878	15.5.1940	4ft 8½in	2w-2PMR		Ford V8	R1360	309
3033	25.10.1941	2ft 0in	2w-2PMR	1323cc	JAP	R1389	193
6887	28.10.1954	4ft 8½in	2w-2PMR	600cc	JAP	4B	315,322,323
6963	10.1.1955	4ft 8½in	2w-2PMR	30hp	Ford V8	40 MkIV	104
6965	6.1.1955	4ft 8½in	2w-2PMR	10hp	Ford	27A MkIII	249
7397	16.1.1957	4ft 8½in	2w-2PMR	30hp	Perkins P4	40 MkIIA	249
7438	18.5.1956	4ft 8½in	2w-2PMR	10hp	Ford	27A MkIII	249
7688	22.3.1957	4ft 8½in	2w-2PMR	1323cc	JAP	17A	315
8084	22.10.1958	4ft 8½in	2w-2PMR	10hp	Ford	27 MkIII	249
8085	22.10.1958	4ft 8½in	2w-2PMR	10hp	Ford	27 MkIII	249
8197	20.11.1958	4ft 8½in	2w-2PMR	10hp	Ford	27 MkIII	104
8198	20.11.1958	4ft 8½in	2w-2PMR	10hp	Ford	27 MkIII	231
8263	27.2.1959	4ft 8½in	2w-2PMR	1323cc	JAP	17A	104,192
8264	27.2.1959	4ft 8½in	2w-2PMR	1323cc	JAP	17A	315

WINGROVE & ROGERS LTD, Kirkby, Liverpool — WR

1393	13.11.1939	2ft 6in	4wBE	W117	184
1616	24.1.1941	2ft 6in	4wBE	W117	184
1800	23.1.1941	2ft 6in	4wBE	W117	184

1801	23.1.1941	2ft 6in	4wBE		W117			184
2065	15.9.1941	2ft 0in	0-4-0BE	4.8hp	W217			296
4320		1ft 6in	0-4-0BE					77
6309	7.2.1961	2ft 0in	0-4-0BE	4.8hp	W217			296
6310	27.2.1961	2ft 0in	0-4-0BE	4.8hp	W217			296
6600	25.7.1962	1ft 6in	0-4-0BE	4hp	W217	1½T		75,77
C6711	27.3.1963	1ft 6in	0-4-0BE	4hp	W217			75,77
D6892	25.3.1964	2ft 0in	4wBE		W527	5T		82
D6893	25.3.1964	2ft 0in	4wBE		W527	5T		82
D6894	25.3.1964	2ft 0in	4wBE		W527	5T		82
D6895	15.6.1964	2ft 0in	4wBE		W527	5T		82
D6896	15.6.1964	2ft 0in	4wBE		W527	5T		82
D6897	30.6.1964	2ft 0in	4wBE		W527	5T		82
E6946	13.9.1965	2ft 0in	0-4-0BE	4hp	W217	1½T		88
F7026	31.3.1965	2ft 0in	0-4-0BE	4hp	W217	1½T		88
J7206	30.5.1969	2ft 0in	4wBE		W227			296
J7208	7.5.1969	2ft 0in	4wBE		W227			296
J7271	13.5.1969	2ft 0in	4wBE		W227			296
J7272	19.5.1969	2ft 0in	4wBE		W227			296
J7273	30.5.1969	2ft 0in	4wBE		W227			296
J7274	30.5.1969	2ft 0in	4wBE		W227			296
J7275	31.10.1969	2ft 0in	4wBE		W227			296
K7282	27.2.1970	2ft 0in	4wBE		W227			296
M7556	16.3.1972	2ft 0in	4wBE		W227			96
N7611	20.12.1972	1ft 6in	0-4-0BE	5hp	WR5L	1½T		77
N7612	31.1.1973	1ft 6in	0-4-0BE	5hp	WR5L	1½T		77
N7613	31.1.1973	1ft 6in	0-4-0BE	5hp	WR5L	1½T		77
N7614	15.2.1973	1ft 6in	0-4-0BE	5hp	WR5L	1½T		77
L800	1983	1ft 6in	2w-2BE	3hp	WR3			173
L801	1983	1ft 6in	2w-2BE	3hp	WR3			173
544901	5.9.1986	1ft 6in	2w-2BE	3hp	WR3			173
546001	1987	1ft 6in	2w-2BE	3hp	WR3			173
546602	1987	1ft 6in	2w-2BE	3hp	WR3			173

WELLMAN SMITH OWEN ENGINEERING CORPORATION LTD
Darlaston, Staffordshire   WSO

4622	1947	4ft 8½in	4wWE		214

YORKSHIRE ENGINE CO LTD, MEADOW HALL WORKS, Sheffield   YE

327	4.1882	4ft 8½in	0-6-0ST	OC	14 x 20	3ft3in	Cx	210
784	1905	4ft 8½in	0-4-0ST	OC	14 x 20	3ft3in	Ex	260
2413	27.10.1943	4ft 8½in	0-6-0ST	OC	16 x 22	3ft8in		269
2498	1.1.1952	4ft 8½in	0-6-0ST	OC	16 x 24	3ft8in	Type 1	103
2595	1.6.1956	4ft 8½in	0-6-0DE	400hp	2xR-R C6SFL	Janus		217
2854	1.5.1961	4ft 8½in	0-4-0DE	220hp	R-R C6SFL			56
2875	27.3.1961	4ft 8½in	0-8-0DH	600hp	2x R-R C8SFL	Taurus		217
2894	13.8.1962	4ft 8½in	0-8-0DH	600hp	2x R-R C8SFL	Indus		212,215

-        1863 4ft 8½in   0-4-0ST   OC

INDEX OF LOCOMOTIVE NAMES

CHARWELTON	260	(THE) DOLL	186
CHATSWORTH	263	DOLLY	78
CHEARSLEY	79	DOLOBRAN	210,214
CHERWELL	227,260,316	DOM	92
CHESHAM	77	DON	264,304
CHEVALLIER	102,184	DONALD	78
CHEYENNE	326	DORA	321
CHORLEY	180	DOUGAL	185
CICETER	302	DOUGLAS	219,223,248
CIDER APPLE	132	DOUTELLE	93,132
CLARABELL	193	DOVER	236
CLAYTON No.9	172	DREADNOUGHT	273
CLOISTER	189	DUCHESS	195
CLYDESDALE	209,210	DUDLEY HILL	85
COBDEN	166	DUNRAGIT	85
COCKSPUR	221,224	DUSTON	237
COFFEE POT	229,257,310		
COLLINGWOOD	194	**E**	
COLWYN	210,214,320	EARL TEMPLE	69
CONQUEROR	102,184	EARLESTOWN	55
CONWAY	210,214,322	ECCLES	125
COREA	302	EDGAR	280
COURTYBELLA	158	EDITH	125
COVENTRY No.1	103	EDMUNDSONS	129,325
CRAMPTON	289	EL ALAMEIN	132
CRANFORD No.2	218	ELF	186
CRANFORD	218	ELIDIR	189
CRAVEN	158	ELIZABETH	101
CREEPY	186	ELLISON	256
CRIGGION	210,215	ELOUISE	189
CROCODILE	238	ELY	85,94,322
CUMBRIA	302	EMILY	240
CUNARDER	80,103,182	ENTERPRISE	221,224,233
CURZON	219	ETTRICK	275
CYPRUS	301,302	EXCELSIOR	184
		EXPRESS	322
D			
DAISY	221	**F**	
DAMREDUB	186	FABIAN	234
DANE	238	FALCON	186
DARLINGTON	219	FANNY	301
DAVENTRY	298	FARMERS FRIEND	135
DAVID	256,280	FASHODA	303
DEFIANT	106	FEANOR	186
DELILAH	226	FENNY COMPTON	289
DENHAM	85	FERRET II	243,308
DENMARK	85	FESTOON	132,186
DESPATCH	264	FILEY	235
DEVIL	205	FILTON	204
DEVON LOCH	93,132	FINEDON	240,278
DEVONSHIRE	169	FINGOLFIN	187
DIKE	272	FIREFLY	101
DODFORD	298	FLORENCE	208,240,299

FLUSH ROYAL	93,132
FLYING FLEA	101
FLYING SCOTSMAN	185,195
FOCH	284
FORWARD	270,279,284
FRANK	299
FRED	299
FREDERICK	166
FULWOOD	304
FURY	238,251

G

GAVIN	287,306
GAYTON	266
GEDDINGTON	220
GENERAL WADE HAYES	129
GERRARDS CROSS	85
GERTRUDE	272
GIBBON	299
GIBRALTAR	103
GIPSY LASS	166
GLENDON	219,264,270
GLENGARNOCK	264,304
GOLLUM	186
GORDON	219
GOTHENBURG	106
GRACE	211,232
GRAHAMS	125
GREENWICH	165
GROOMBRIDGE	76
GROSVENOR	85,302

H

H. LOVATT	169
HAD-A-CAB	186
HADDENHAM	79
HAIG	137
HALTON	52
HANDYMAN	218,223,226,273,308
HARBORO'	76
HARD RIDDEN	132
HARDINGSTONE	261
HARDWICKE	114
HAROLD	78,245
HARRY B	187
HARSTON	266
HARTINGTON	223,269
HAYDN TAYLOR	186
HEATHER	258
HECTOR	184
HELEN	78,266
HELLIDON	260
HENLOW	115

HENRY APPLEBY	76
HENRY CORT	275,276
HESKETH	167,287,306
HOLMES	228,260
HOLWELL No.14	219,270
HOLWELL No.19	284
HOLWELL No.30	222,233
HOLY WAR	108
HORATIO	108
HORNBY	85
HORNPIPE	103
HORSA	129
HOTWHEELS	259
HOUGHTON	125
HUDDERSFIELD	69
HUGH	280
HUNSBURY	262
HYLTON	322

I

IAN D. McLEAN	264
INCE	52
IRENE	228
IRISH MAIL	189
IRON DUKE	267
IRONSTONE	209,210,270
IRONWORKS No.1	210,284
IRONWORKS No.2	210
IRWELL	300
ISEBROOK	103,241,242
ISHAM	210,246,284
ISLIP No.1	243,271,286
ISLIP No.2	243,271,286
ISLIP No.3	271
ISLIP No.4	271,284
ISLIP No.5	271
ISLIP	284
ISOBEL	158
IWB No.11	292

J

J.D.ELLIS	273
J.D.THOMSON	264
J.R.WRIGHT	302
J.STRACHAN No.9	305
JACKAL	285
JACKALL	310
JACKS GREEN	254
JAMES	219,227
JANE	78
JANICE	107
JANSON	210,214
JEAN	220,232

MONARCH	56	PENN		85
MONTALBAN	189	PETER PAN		186
MUFFIN	322	PETERHEAD		79,304
MURIEL	210	PETERSTONE		237
MUSKETEER	241,322	PETROLEA		314
MY LOVE	131	PEVERIL		174
		PHOENIX		210
N		PHORPRES		64
NAIROBI	75	PHYLLIS		232
NAKLO	189	PILTON		233
NANNIE	237,271	PITSFORD		101,228
NASSINGTON	297	PIXIE		186,219,228
NEEDHAM	194	PLANTAGENET		238
NELLIE	299	POPPY		186
NENE	299	PORTLAND		280
NEPTUNE	278	PRESTON		64,79
NEW CRANSLEY No.1	255	PROGRESS	221, 230, 232,244,307	
NEW CRANSLEY No.2	255	PUNCH HULL	103,125,192	
NEW CRANSLEY No.3	255	PUNCH		85
NEW CRANSLEY No.3	273			
NEW CRANSLEY No.4	256	**Q**		
NEW CRANSLEY	231	QWAG		207
NEW STAR	186			
NEWCASTLE	302	**R**		
NORMAN	79,238	R.A.F. STANBRIDGE		186
NORSEMAN	56,232	RAUNDS		263,281
NORTHAMPTON	167,261	RED RUM		132,187
NORTHFIELD	227	REDLAND		103,320
NORTHOLT	85	REDLANDS		186
NUTTALL	80,170	RELKO		93,132
NUTTY LBC L1	184	RETRIAL		93,132
		RHIWNANT		210
O		RHONDDA		210,214,220
OAKLEY	293	RHOS		210,214,220
OLDE	194	RHYL		210,214
OLIVER	314	RICHARD TREVITHICK		128
OLNEY	75	RICKMANSWORTH		76
ORYZA	262,311	RING HAW		254
OSRAM	103	RISHRA		186
OWL	292	RISLEY MED YARD No.109		308
		RIVER		85
P		ROBERT		100,103,223
P.C. ALLEN	186	ROBIN HOOD		185
PALACIOS	85	ROCA		85
PAM	186	ROCKET		106,235
PARANA	85	ROF 6 No.11		295
PATIENCE	262	ROMFORD		289
PATRICIA	125	ROSEHALL		264,304
PAUL COOPER	194	ROTHWELL	219,221,232,270	
PEACOCK	256	RUBY		300,301,302
PELLON	85,302	RUTH		143
PEN GREEN	209	RYDER GIBSON		243
PENLEE	186			

S		STAMFORD	218
SAM	78,297	STANLEY	85
SAMSON	226	STANTON No.19	266
SAPPER	248	STATTER	208,236
SARAH	187	STAVELEY	269
SAUL	280	STEADY AIM	131
SAXON	238	STEPHENSON	276
SCALDWELL	223	STOCKS	272
SCOTCHMAN	235	STONEYWAY	166
SCRATCH II	132	SUNSHINE	276
SEATON	297	SUPERIOR	102,184
SENTINEL No.1	56	SURREY	85
SENTINEL No.3	56	SUSAN	103
SENTINEL	176,210	SUTTON	300
SEWELL	125	SWANSCOMBE	103,192
SEZELA	184,186,189	SWANSEA	79
SHAKESPEARE	166,289	SWORDFISH	92,103, 220, 270
SHANNON	159	SYDENHAM	103,192
SHEEPSBRIDGE No.22	269		
SHEEPSBRIDGE No.23	269	**T**	
SHEEPSBRIDGE No.27	269	T.S.WILSON	264
SHIRE LODGE	322	T.W. LEWIS	186
SIEMENS	275,276	TALBOT	114,165
SIFTA	264	TAY	125
SIR ALFRED WOOD	322	THAMES	85
SIR BERKELEY	218,227	THE AUDITOR	302
SIR GILES ISHAM	320	THE BARONET	218,273
SIR JOSEPH	219	THE BLUE CIRCLE	103,322
SIR THOMAS ROYDEN	129	THE BROKE	284
SIR THOMAS	103	THE BUGGY	94
SIR TOM	108	THE LADY ARMAGHDALE	321
SIR VINCENT	103,106,322,325	THE ROCK	318,317
SIR WILLIAM	101	THE ROYAL ARTILLARYMAN	320
SIRAPITE	101	THOMAS	281,323
SLIPTON No.1	271,272	THORIN OAKENSHIELD	186
SLIPTON No.2	271,272	THUNDERBIRD II	242
SLIPTON No.3	272	TITCHIE	55,70
SLIPTON No.4	272	TOGO	235
SLIPTON No.5	272	TOM BOMBADIL	186
SLIPTON No.6	272	TOM PARRY	61,103,125,192
SLIPTON No.7	272	TRAFALGAR	302
SLIPTON No.8	272	TRANMERE	79
SLOUGH ESTATES No.3	108	TREASURER	210
SMOKY	259	TRENT	187
SOLOMAN	226,290	TRIO	74,166
SOMERS TOWN	210	TRYM	76,103,192,322
SOUTHERN	80	TURVEY	167
SOUTHPORT	52	TYERSALL	85,302
SPEEDY	259	TYNE	301
SPITFIRE	322		
SPRATTON	205		
ST GEORGES	300		
STAFFORD	235,297		

U	
UNION JACK	245
UTHIE	257,271,272
UTRILLO	132

V	
VANGUARD	320
VICTOR	184
VICTORIA	170,308
VIGILANT	209
VULCAN	292

W	
WAINWRIGHT	106
WALLASEY	80
WALRUS	103
WALTER SCOTT	302
WANSFORD	297
WEEDON	248,298
WELLINGBORO' No.3	211
WELLINGBORO' No.3	284
WELLINGBORO' No.5	284
WELLINGBORO' No.6	283
WELLINGTON	76
WENDY	189
WESTMINSTER	85,125,320
WHISTON	262,278,285
WHITMORE	89

WIGHTWICK HALL	102
WILFRED	209
WILLIAM ELLIS	273
WILLIAM	218
WILLIE	299
WINNIE	116
WOLVERTON	70,102
WOODCOCK	226
WOODHALL	304
WOOLWICH	310
WOOTON	278
WOOTTON	261
WOTO	189
WOTTON No.1	69
WOTTON No.2	69
WOTTON	69
WREN	208
WREXHAM	76
WYCOMBE	85

Y	
YARDLEY CHASE No.1	249
YARDLEY CHASE No.2	249
YARDLEY CHASE No.3	249
YAXLEY	166
YIMKIN	186
YVONNE	320,322

INDEX TO LOCATIONS AND OWNERS

Thompson, George	336	Ward & Son	201
Thrapston Gravel Pits	279	Ward, T.W.	336
Thrapston Iron Ore Co	329,336	Waring Brothers	305
Thrapston Lime Quarries	256	Warren Woods	202
Thrapston Quarries	336	Waste Recovery Syndicate	123
Thrapston Washed Sand & Ballast		Water Eaton Brickworks	58
	279,343	Watling Steet Gravel Pits	54
Three Chimneys Tannery	242	Watson	247
Three Counties Hospital	201	Watson, Aubrey	90
Three Counties Lime Works	196	Watson, Smith & Watson	306
Three Stars (Luton)	180	Way & Son, David	72
Thyssen (GB)	89	Weedon Gravel Pit	247
Tomlinson, S.W.	325	Weedon Road Workshops	253
Totternhoe Lime & Stone Co	162	Weedon Technical Stores Depot	247
Totternhoe Lime Stone & Cement Co	162	Weldon & Corby Patent Brick Co	259
Totternhoe Limeworks	162	Weldon Stone Quarries	337
Totternhoe Quarries	157	Weldon, Henry W.	337
Towcester Co	279	Welham Contract	305
Towcester Contract	287,289,306	Well End Pits	59
Towcester Mineral & Brick Co		Welland Valley Rail Revival Group	320
	243,279,336	Wellingborough Brick & Tile Co	337
Track Supplies & Services	94,339	Wellingborough Brickworks	337
Trackwork	305	Wellingborough Contract	288,290
Tredwell, Thomas	90	Wellingborough Gravel & Sand Co	283
Trenery & Sons	336	Wellingborough Iron Co	274,283
Tunnel Cement (Pitstone)	56	Wellingborough Ironstone Quarries	
Tunnel Portland Cement Co	56		274,332
Turvey Station	194	Wellingborough Ironworks	275,283
Twenty One Acres Quarry	116	Wellingborough Plant Depot	172
Twywell Brickworks	262	Wellingborough Road Brickworks	334
Twywell Iron Ore Co	262,280	Wellingborough Works	260,263
Twywell Ironstone Quarries	229	West Bridge Depot	257
		West Glebe Park	316
		Westcott Rocket Works	68
United Steel Companies	280	Western Favell Brick & Tile Co	337
Upper Sundon Rubbish Tip	136	Westhorpe Farm	72
Uxbridge Contract	85	Westhorpe Pits	68
Uxbridge Sand & Ballast Co	71	Weston Street Engineering Works	307
		Westoning Brickworks	198
Vandyke Sand Lime Brick	202	Wharf Lane Brickworks	328
Vass, L.W.	180	Whipsnade & Umfolozi Railway	183
Vauxhall Motors	163,341	Whipsnade Wild Animal Park	183
Vulcan Ironworks	310	Whipsnade Zoo	183
Vulcan Works	198	Whiston Ironstone Co	285
		Whiston Ironstone Quarries	285
Waddesden Manor	111	Whitehouse, Thomas	285,329,336
Wagon Repairs	263	Whiting Works	198
Wakerley Ironstone Co	261	Whiting, C.R.	234
Wakerley Ironstone Quarries	261	Wicksteed Park	325
Walters, Thomas	281,333	Wilkinson, T.	91
Walton Engine Works	69	Wilstead Contract	165
War Department		Wilstead Sawmills	193
	72,112,156,202,247,282	Wimpey & Co, George	91

INDUSTRIAL RAILWAY SOCIETY

The Industrial Railway Society, which was formed in 1949 as the Industrial Locomotive Information Section of the Birmingham Locomotive Club, caters for enthusiasts interested in privately owned locomotives and railways. Members receive the INDUSTRIAL RAILWAY RECORD, a profusely illustrated magazine; a bi-monthly bulletin containing topical news and amendments to the Society's handbook series; access to a well stocked library; visits to and rail tours of industrial railway systems; a book sales service, many Society publications being available at discounted prices; loco information service from the Society's team of records officers; photograph sales service; and access to archives held at the National Railway Museum, York. Further details are available by sending two first class stamps to : -

Mr B. Mettam, 27 Glenfield Crescent, Newbold, Chesterfield, S41 8SF.

Subscriptions to the INDUSTRIAL RAILWAY RECORD are available to non-members of the Society. Enquiries regarding subscriptions and back numbers should be addressed to :

Mr R.V. Mulligan, Owls Barn, The Chestnuts, Aylesbeare, Exeter, Devon, EX5 2BY.

[Fig 1] S9547 1952 4wVBT G SENTINEL   [Frank Jones]
Tunnel Portland Cement Co Ltd, Pitstone.

{Fig 2] P1923 1937 0-6-0ST OC MONARCH   [Frank Jones]
Tunnel Portland Cement Co Ltd, Pitstone.

[Fig 3] RR10264 1966 4wDH   [Kevin Lane]
Tunnel Portland Cement Co Ltd, Pitstone. 9-1977

[Fig 4] WB 3160 1959 0-6-0DM   [Robin Waywell]
Castle Cement (Pitstone) Ltd, Pitstone. 6-4-1989

[Fig 5] S9322 1937 4wVBT G [Frank Jones]
London Brick Co Ltd, Bletchley Brickworks, Newton Longville.

[Fig 6] AP5935 1905 4wWT G [IRS: K J Cooper collection]
London Brick Co Ltd Calvert Brickworks. 27-3-1951

[Fig 7] WB2586 1938 0-4-0ST OC   [IRS: K J Cooper collection]
London Brick Co Ltd, Calvert Brickworks. 27-3-1951

[Fig 8] JF 22895 1940 0-4-0DM   [Kevin Lane]
London Brick Co Ltd, Calvert Brickworks. 5-1975

[Fig 9 MW1141 1889 0-4-0ST OC PARANA   [Frank Jones]
used by Pauling & Co Ltd, on their High Wycombe Contract.

[Fig 10] MW1214 1891 0-6-0ST IC ABER   [Frank Jones]
used by Pauling & Co Ltd on their High Wycombe Contract.

[Fig 11] KS4267, 2474, 2473, & 4023   [Frank Jones]
Aubrey Watson Ltd, Denham Contract.

[Fig 12] KS3105 1918 0-4-0ST OC HAIG   [Robin Waywell collection]
Leighton Buzzard Brick Co Ltd, Potsgrove Quarries. 6-1949

[Fig 13] MR7214 1938 4wDM [Kevin Lane]
Joseph Arnold & Sons Ltd, Double Arches Pit. 22-1-1976

[Fig 14] MR7371 1939 4wDM [Kevin Lane]
George Garside (Sand) Ltd, Churchways Pit. 23-11-1978

[Fig 15] JF3930044 1950 4wDM [Kevin Lane]
Associated Portland Cement Manufacturers Ltd, Sundon Cement Works. 11-1974

[Fig 16] MW1381 1897 0-4-0ST OC [J E Simpson: J K Williams collection]
Bedford Corporation, Public Works Department, Goldington Depot.

[Fig 17] HC 1727 1941 0-4-0ST OC   [S A Leleux]
formerly of ROF Elstow seen in Cox & Danks yard at Bedford. 4-1961

[Fig 18] H957 1926 4wDM   [S A Leleux]
Britannia Iron & Steel Works Ltd, Bedford. 29-3-1961

[Fig 19] P1391 1915 0-6-0ST OC EDITH,   [J M Jarvis]
Associated Portland Cement Manufacturers Ltd, Dunstable Cement Works. 27-8-1938

[Fig 20] AB776 1896 PUNCH HULL   [Jack Faithfull, Railway Correspondence and Travel Society]
& AB2015 1935 TOM PARRY 0-4-0ST OC
Associated Portland Cement Manufacturers Ltd, Dunstable Cement Works, 19-6-1954

[Fig 21] RH421437 1958 0-4-0DE   [Kevin Lane]
Associated Portland Cement Manufacturers Ltd, Dunstable Cement Works. 10-1975

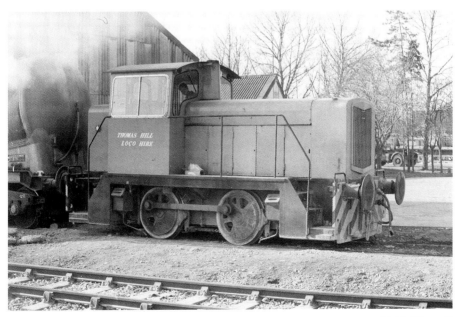

[Fig 22] EEV D1122 1966 0-4-0DH   [Robin Waywell]
Blue Circle Industries Plc, Dunstable Cement works. 19-2-1988

[Fig 23] AB2352 1954 0-4-0ST OC   [Frank Jones]
Central Electricity Authority Goldington Power Station.

[Fig 24] AB2354 1954 0-4-0ST OC   [Frank Jones]
Central Electricity Authority, Goldington Power Station.

[Fig 25] AB2168 1943 0-4-0ST OC EDMUNDSONS [Jack Faithfull Railway Correspondence
Central Electricity Generating Board, Little Barford Power Station. 27-7-1957 and Travel Society]

[Fig 26] AB2069 1939 0-4-0ST OC LITTLE BARFORD [Jack Faithfull Railway Correspondence
Central Electricity Generating Board, Little Barford Power Station. 27-7-1957 and Travel Society]

[Fig 27] AB1477 1916 0-4-0F OC   [IRS: John Hill collection]
Laporte Chemicals Ltd. 14-8-1963

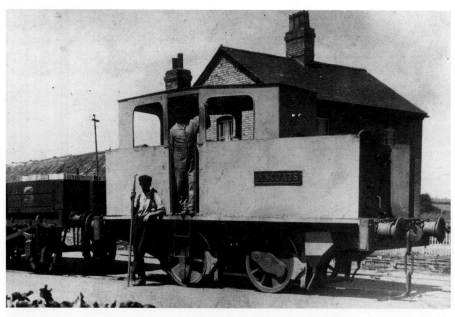

[Fig 28] Blackwell built 1922 4wVBT ANCOATS Reb of MW 1091 1888   [Frank Jones]
Arlesey Brick Co (Bearts) Ltd. c1922-1924

[Fig 29] 4wWe LBC 'Hoffman Tram' [S A Leleux]
London Brick Co Ltd Arlesey Brickworks. 21-4-1958

[Fig 30] KS4428 1930 4wDM [S A Leleux]
Redlands (Flettons) Ltd, Kempston Hardwick, Brickworks. 13-9-1967

[Fig 31] FW328 1877 0-6-0ST OC AVON   [J M Jarvis]
Bedford Brick Co Ltd, Bedford Brickworks. 18-4-1936

[Fig 32] EE899 1935 4wWE RUTH   [J E Simpson, J K Williams collection]
Bedford Brick Co Ltd, Coronation Brickworks. 1935

[Fig 33] B J Forder 6wWT G   [Robin Waywell collection]
B J Forder & Son, Pillinge Brickworks. c1920

[Fig 34] S9221 1935 4wWT G   [Jack Faithfull: Railway Correspondence and Travel Society]
London Brick Co Ltd, Stewartby Brickworks. 28-3-1953

[Fig 35] Unidentified 2ft 11in gauge Motor Rail, fresh from overhaul   [Robin Waywell collection]
in the engineering workshops, poses in the yard at London Brick Co Ltd, Stewartby Brickworks.

[Fig 36] 2ft-6in gauge cable hauled tramway of the Marston Valley   [Kevin Lane]
Brick Co Ltd adjacent to the B557 road near the village of Brogborough. 4-1976

[Fig 37] AP11087 1927 4wWT G   [J E Simpson: J K Williams collection]
Rugby Portland Cement Co Ltd, Totternhoe Quarries.

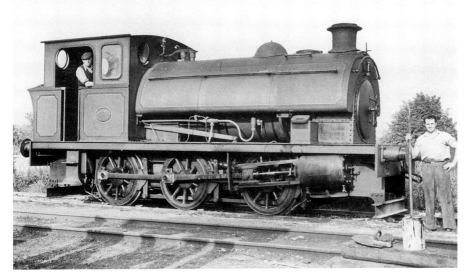

[Fig 38] RSHN 7413 1948 0-6-0ST OC   [Elias Henderson collection]
Rugby Portland Cement Co Ltd, Totternhoe Quarries. c1949

[Fig 39] MW1972 1919 0-6-0ST IC   [Jack Faithfull, Railway Correspondence
Rugby Portland Cement Co Ltd, Totternhoe Quarries. 19-6-1954   and Travel Society]

[Fig 40] AE1875 1921 0-4-0ST OC   [Jack Faithfull, Railway Correspondence
Rugby Portland Cement Co Ltd, Totternhoe Quarries. 19-6-1954   and Travel Society]

[Fig 41] S9564 1953 4wVBT G   [IRS: John Hill, collection]
Rugby Portland Cement Co Ltd, Totternhoe Quarries. 14-8-1963

[Fig 42] Rugby Portland Cement Co Ltd, Totternhoe Quarries,   [S A Leleux]
view showing the rope hauled incline between the quarries & the exchange sidings 27-6-1961

[Fig 43] MW1843 1915 0-4-0ST OC KITCHENER   [Harold Clements:Brian Cross collection]
Vauxhall Motors Ltd, Luton Works. 29-12-1953

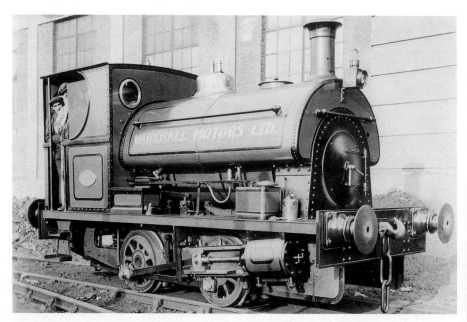

[Fig 44] P1874 1935 0-4-0ST OC   [Harold Clements: Brian Cross collection]
Vauxhall Motors Ltd, Luton Works. 1-11-1948

[Fig 45] RH338419 1954 4wDM   [Harold Clements, Brian Cross collection]
Vauxhall Motors Ltd, Luton Works.

[Fig 46] KS2420 1915 0-4-0ST OC   [L Hanson]
Billing Gravel Co Ltd, Great Billing, Northants. 1935

[Fig 47] HL2469 1900 0-6-0ST OC BEAUMONT   [IRS: K J Cooper collection]
Stewarts & Lloyds Ltd Corby Works. 1-7-1951

[Fig 48] HL3837 1934 0-6-0ST OC   [Kevin Lane]
Stewarts & Lloyds Ltd Corby Works.

[Fig 49] HE1446 1929 0-6-0ST OC   [Kevin Lane]
Stewarts & Lloyds Ltd Corby Works.

[Fig 50] AB762 1895 0-4-0ST OC   [Kevin Lane]
Stewarts & Lloyds Ltd Corby Works.

[Fig 51] HC1595 1936 0-6-0T IC   [Kevin Lane]
Stewarts & Lloyds Ltd Corby Works.

[Fig 52] EEV1048 1965 0-6-0DH   [Kevin Lane]
British Steel Corporation, Corby Works. 9-1977

[Fig 53] NBQ28051 1962 0-6-0DH   [Kevin Lane]
British Steel Corporation, Corby Works. 23-8-1979

[Fig 54] HC1308 1918 0-6-0ST OC RHOS   [IRS: K J Cooper collection]
Stewarts & Lloyds Minerals Ltd, Corby Quarries.

[Fig 55] MW1316 1895 0-6-0ST IC CALETTWR   [IRS: K J Cooper collection]
Stewarts & Lloyds Minerals Ltd, Corby Quarries.

[Fig 56] RSHN7761 1954 0-6-0ST IC   [IRS: K J Cooper collection]
Stewarts & Lloyds Minerals Ltd, Corby Quarries.

[Fig 57] EEV D911 1964 0-6-0DH   [Robin Waywell collection]
on trial at Stewarts & Lloyds Minerals Ltd, Oakley Quarries, Corby. c11-1964

[Fig 58] YE2894 1962 0-8-0 DH   [IRS: Brian Webb, collection]
Stewart & Lloyds Minerals Ltd, Corby. 20-5-1964

[Fig 59] RR10272 1967 0-6-0DH   [R K Hateley]
Stewarts & Lloyds Minerals Ltd, Pen Green, Corby. 23-7-1968

[Fig 60] RR10265 1967 0-6-0DH   [R K Hateley]
the prototype Steelman loco Stewarts & Lloyds Minerals Ltd, Pen Green, Corby. 23-7-1968

[Fig 61] 64 (ex D9549) built Sdn 1965   [Kevin Lane]
passes the Tarmac Plant with empties in 8 -1979, Stewart & Lloyds Minerals Ltd, Corby Quarries.

[Fig 62] Loco's 58, 32, 62   [Kevin Lane]
inside Gretton Brook Loco Shed, 23-8-1979, Stewarts & Lloyds Minerals Ltd Corby Quarries.

[Fig 63] HC1579 1926 0-6-0ST OC   [S A Leleux]
Stewarts & Lloyds Minerals Ltd, Cranford Ironstone Quarries. 24-3-1960

[Fig 64] HE2417 1941 0-6-0ST IC   [IRS: K J Cooper collection]
Stewarts & Lloyds Minerals Ltd, Glendon East Quarries.

[Fig 65] MW1795 1912 0-4-0ST OC   [J A Peden]
South Durham Steel & Iron Co Ltd, Irchester Quarries. 22-4-1965

[Fig 66] AB2324 1952 0-4-0ST   [IRS: K J Cooper collection]
OC South Durham Steel & Iron Co Ltd, Irchester Quarries. 22-7-1966

[Fig 67] HC573 1900 0-4-0ST OC   [IRS: K J Cooper collection]
Staveley Iron & Chemical Co Ltd, Lamport Quarries. 7-1949

[Fig 68] P1315 1913 0-6-0ST OC LAMPORT   [IRS: K J Cooper collection]
Staveley Iron & Chemical Co Ltd, Lamport Quarries. 7-1949

[Fig 69] P1289 1912 0-4-0ST OC COCKSPUR   [IRS: K J Cooper collection]
South Durham Steel & Iron Co Ltd, Storfield Quarries. 6-5-1961

[Fig 70] AE1917 1923 0-6-0ST OC PITSFORD   [S A Leleux]
Byfield Ironstone Co Ltd Pitsford Quarries. 30-6-1958

[Fig 71] HL3829 1934 0-4-0F OC   [Ray Hobbs]
Central Electricity Generating Board, Hardingstone Power Station, Northampton. 2-9-1967

[Fig 72] Chaplin 2368 1885 0-4-0VBT   [IRS: Brian Webb collection]
East Midlands Gas Board, Northampton Gas Works. 25-9-1962

[Fig 73] S9527 1951 4wVBT PLANTAGENET   [Robin Waywell collection]
East Midlands Gas Board Northampton Gas Works. 4-1958

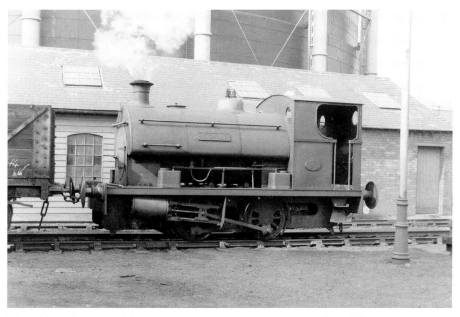

[Fig 74] P2052 1944 0-4-0ST OC   [IRS: Brian Webb collection]
East Midlands Gas Board Northampton Gas Works. 25-9-1962

[Fig 75] Bg/DC 4wDM   [S A Leleux]
Fisons Basic Slag Ltd, Corby Iron & Steel Works.13-6-1964

[Fig 76] KC1553 1927 4wPM   [S A Leleux]
Kettering Borough Council, Northfield Depot, Kettering. 30-4-1962

[Fig 77] S6515 1926 4wVBT G   [J A Peden]
Thos E Gray & Co Ltd, Isebrook Quarry, Burton Latimer. 7-6-1958

[Fig 78] S9365 1946 4wVBT G BELVEDERE   [S A Leleux]
Thos E Gray & Co Ltd, Isebrook Quarry, Burton Latimer. 27-9-1962

[Fig 79] MW1370 1897 0-6-0ST OC   [S A Leleux]
Kettering Iron & Coal Co Ltd, Kettering Furnaces. 7-9-1962

[Fig 80] Lingford Gardiner of 1931 0-4-0ST OC   [S A Leleux]
Kettering Iron & Coal Co Ltd, Kettering Furnaces. 5-7-1960

[Fig 81] CF1194 1900 0-4-0ST OC   [IRS: Bernard Mettam collection]
New Cransley Iron & Steel Co Ltd, Cransley Ironworks. 22-4-1956

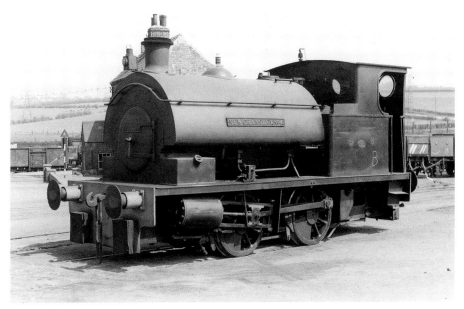

[Fig 82] WB2517 1934 0-4-0ST OC   [IRS: Bernard Mettam collection]
New Cransley Iron & Steel Co Ltd, Cransley Ironworks. 22-4-1956

[Fig 83] AP807 1872 4wWT G   [IRS: K J Cooper collection]
Henry Martin Ltd, Nether Heyford Brickworks. 27-3-1951

[Fig 84] YE784 1905 0-4-0ST OC   [IRS: Bernard Mettam collection]
Park Gate Iron & Steel Co Ltd Charwelton Quarries. 5-5-1956

[Fig 85] HE2070 1940 0-4-0DM [S A Leleux]
County Borough of Northampton, West Bridge Depot, Northampton. 28-5-1966

[Fig 86] RH224345 1945 4wDM [S A Leleux]
Wagon Repairs Ltd, Wellingborough. 13-6-1962

[Fig 87] GECT5365 1972 0-6-0DH   [Robin Waywell]
Rutland Recycling Ltd, Corby Tubeworks Site. 8-2-1997

[Fig 88] AB306 1888 0-4-0ST OC   [IRS: Bernard Mettam collection][
Shanks & McEwan Ltd, Corby Steelworks. 22-4-1956

[Fig 89] HE1677 1937 0-4-0ST OC IAN D McLEAN   [S A Leleux]
Shanks & McEwan Ltd, Corby Steelworks. 13-6-1964

[Fig 90] NB 27658 1957 0-4-0DH   [S A Leleux]
Shanks & McEwan Ltd, Corby Steelworks. 13-6-1964

[Fig 91] HC1452 1921 0-4-0ST OC   [IRS: K J Cooper collection]
Stewarts & Lloyds Ltd, Islip Ironstone Quarries. 7-1949

[Fig 92] HL3883 1936 0-6-0ST OC   [S A Leleux]
Staveley Minerals Ltd, Loddington Quarries. 4-7-1960

[Fig 93] HL3721 1928 0-4-0ST OC ETTRICK   [S A Leleux]
Richard Thomas & Baldwins Ltd, Blisworth Quarries. 6-1957

[Fig 94] P1870 1934 0-6-0ST OC   [IRS: K J Cooper collection]
Stewarts & Lloyds Minerals Ltd, Wellingborough Quarries. 6-1962

[Fig 95] AB2136 1941 0-4-0ST OC   [S A Leleux]
Wellingborough Iron Co Ltd, Wellingborough Ironworks. 15-7-1957

[Fig 96] P1235 1910 0-6-0ST OC FORWARD   [S A Leleux]
Wellingborough Iron Co Ltd, Wellingborough Ironworks. 13-6-1962